MUNK'S ROLL

VOL. VII

LIVES OF THE FELLOWS OF THE ROYAL COLLEGE OF PHYSICIANS OF LONDON

continued to 1983

Edited by

GORDON WOLSTENHOLME

Kt, OBE, LLD, DTech, FRCP, FIBiol
Harveian Librarian

assisted by
Valérie Luniewska BA

IRL PRESS
Oxford · Washington DC

1984

Royal College of Physicians of London
11 St. Andrew's Place
London, N.W.1
1984

British Library Cataloguing in Publication Data
Munk's Roll
Vol. 7 : 1976-1983
1. Royal College of Physicians of London
—Directories
I. Wolstenholme, G.E.W.
610'.6'0421 R773.R7

ISBN 0 904147 68 1

The engraving of the College arms on
the title-page was made by
Reynolds Stone

Printed by Information Printing Ltd., Eynsham

FOREWORD

The appearance of the seventh volume of Munk's *Roll* so soon after the sixth reflects the increased number of Fellows rather than an increase in the mortality rate. This volume brings us to the end of 1983 so that the compilers have now reduced the back-log to manageable proportions. This has meant a lot of hard work and we are grateful to the Harveian Librarian and Mrs. Valérie Luniewska for their efforts. We are also grateful to those who have responded to our requests for biographies; it is so much nicer to have personal recollections of Fellows who have died.

R HOFFENBERG

President

PREFACE

The publication of this volume extends the range of Munk's *Roll* to 465 years of the College's history. Volume VII carries biographies of 415 Fellows who died between 1 January 1976 and 31 December 1983 and one further biography, that of Lieutenant Colonel FP Mackie, which was somehow omitted from Volume IV.

We have continued from Volume VI the inclusion of photographs. This new volume contains 348 photographs which were available in the College collection and which were suitable for reproduction.

We are deeply grateful to the many authors of the biographies who have put so much time and care, as well as affection, into their preparation. We hope that in due course they will be equally well served.

We have made a greater effort than before to expand the scope of the biographies beyond the confines of the customary obituaries. Where no biography could be obtained, and information in the College was sparse, we have had to rely heavily on published obituaries and are most grateful to the editors of the *BMJ*, *Lancet*, and other journals and papers, for the use of such material.

We are also largely dependent on information provided by Fellows during their lifetime; an up to date CV is of great value to the biographer, and we wish the collection of photographs could be complete. In addition, we should like to build up 'dossiers' for every Fellow, holding all possible information of career, circumstances of training, practice, research and publications, to be maintained indefinitely on file in the hope that this material will prove of value to the future historian.

The great tradition of publishing the lives of Fellows in Munk's *Roll* can only be kept up if Fellows, Members and libraries, demonstrate their interest and support by the purchase of Volume VII and, perhaps for the sake of completion, other volumes in the series.

We are grateful to the committee of the History of Medicine Programme of the Wellcome Trust for the grant of £1000 towards the cost of publication of this volume.

The editors express their indebtedness and gratitude to Elaine Coast and Eva Gooding of IRL Press, who have so companionably and patiently seen this book through to publication.

June 1984

Sir Gordon Wolstenholme
Valérie Luniewska

ABBREVIATIONS

AAMC	Australian Army Medical Corps
Aberd	Aberdeen
ADMS	Assistant Director of Medical Services
AER	Army Emergency Reserve
AFC	Air Force Cross
AIF	Australian Imperial Force
AKC	Associate of King's College
AMA	American Medical Association
ASTMS	Association of Scientific Technical and Managerial Staff
BA	Bachelor of Arts
BAO	Baccalaureus Artis Obstetricae (Bachelor of Obstetric Art)
BAOR	British Army of the Rhine
BCh	Baccalaureus Chirurgiae (Bachelor of Surgery)
BChir	Baccalaureus Chirurgiae (Bachelor of Surgery)
BEF	British Expeditionary Force
BM	Bachelor of Medicine
BMA	British Medical Association
BRCS	British Red Cross Society
BS	Bachelor of Surgery
BSc	Bachelor of Science
BSc Med	Bachelor of Science in Medicine
Belf	Belfast
Birm	Birmingham
Br Col	British Columbia
Bt	Baronet
CAMC	Canadian Army Medical Corps
CB	Companion of the Order of the Bath
CBE	Commander of the Order of the British Empire
CC	Companion of the Order of Canada
CD	Canadian Forces Decoration
CH	Companion of Honour
CIE	Companion of the Order of the Indian Empire
CM	Chirurgiae Magister (Master of Surgery)
CMG	Companion of the Order of St. Michael and St. George
CSI	Companion of the Order of the Star of India
CVCP	Committee of Vice-Chancellors and Principals
CVO	Companion of the Royal Victorian Order
Cantab	Cambridge
Capt	Captain
ChB	Chirurgiae Baccalaureus (Bachelor of Surgery)
ChM	Chirurgiae Magister (Master of Surgery)
Co	County
Col	Colonel
DADMS	Deputy Assistant Director of Medical Services
DC	District of Columbia
DCH	Diploma in Child Health
DCL	Doctor of Civil Law
DChO	Diploma in Ophthalmic Surgery
DD	Doctor of Divinity
DDMS	Deputy Director of Medical Services
DDS	Doctor of Dental Surgery
DFC	Distinguished Flying Cross
DGMS	Director General of Medical Services
DHMSA	Diploma of the History of Medicine
DIH	Diploma in Industrial Health
DJMK	Datoship Paducka Mahkuta Kelantan

DKSM	Diploma of the Kitchener School of Medicine
DL	Deputy Lieutenant
DLitt	Doctor of Letters
DM	Doctor of Medicine
DMR	Diploma in Medical Radiology
DMRD	Diploma in Medical Radio-diagnosis
DMRE	Diploma in Medical Radiology and Electrology
DMS	Director of Medical Services
DO Dubl	Diploma of Ophthalmology Dublin
DPH	Diploma in Public Health
DPM	Diploma in Psychological Medicine
DSM	Distinguished Service Medal
DSO	Distinguished Service Order
DSc	Doctor of Science
DTM	Diploma in Tropical Medicine
DTM&H	Diploma in Tropical Medicine and Hygiene
Dip Bact	Diploma in Bacteriology
Dubl	Dublin, Trinity College
Durh	Durham
EMS	Emergency Medical Service
Edin	Edinburgh
Eng	(following Diploma) Royal College of Physicians of London, and Surgeons of England
FAAP	Fellow of the American Academy of Pediatrics
FACP	Fellow of the American College of Physicians
FACS	Fellow of the American College of Surgeons
FAMSI	Fellow of the Academy of Medical Sciences of India
FANZPsych	Fellow of the Australian and New Zealand College of Psychiatrists
FCGP	Fellow of the College (later Royal College) of General Practitioners
FCOG	Fellow of the British (later Royal) College of Obstetricians and Gynaecologists
FCP Philad	Fellow of the College of Physicians of Philadelphia
FCPS Pak	Fellow of the College of Physicians and Surgeons of Pakistan
FCPath	Fellow of the College (later Royal) of Pathologists
FCRA	Fellow of the College of Radiologists of Australia
FEIS	Fellow of the Educational Institute of Scotland
FFCM	Fellow of the Faculty of Community Medicine
FFOM	Fellow of the Faculty of Occupational Medicine
FFR	Fellow of the Faculty of Radiologists
FICS	Fellow of the International College of Surgeons
FPAS	Fellow of the Pakistan Academy of Sciences
FPS	Fellow of the Pharmaceutical Society
FRACP	Fellow of the Royal Australasian College of Physicians
FRACS	Fellow of the Royal Australasian College of Surgeons
FRCGP	Fellow of the Royal College of General Practitioners
FRCOG	Fellow of the Royal College of Obstetricians and Gynaecologists
FRCP	Fellow of the Royal College of Physicians of London
FRCPath	Fellow of the Royal College of Pathologists
FRCPC	Fellow of the Royal College of Physicians of Canada
FRCPE	Fellow of the Royal College of Physicians of Edinburgh
FRCPI	Fellow of the Royal College of Physicians of Ireland
FRCPsych	Fellow of the Royal College of Psychiatrists
FRCR	Fellow of the Royal College of Radiologists
FRCS	Fellow of the Royal College of Surgeons of England
FRCSE	Fellow of the Royal College of Surgeons of Edinburgh
FRCSI	Fellow of the Royal College of Surgeons of Ireland

FRFPS	Fellow of the Royal Faculty (later College) of Physicians and Surgeons of Glasgow
FRIBA	Fellow of the Royal Institute of British Architects
FRIC	Fellow of the Royal Institute of Chemistry
FRS	Fellow of the Royal Society
FRSC	Fellow of the Royal Society of Canada
FRSE	Fellow of the Royal Society of Edinburgh
FRSS	Fellow of the Royal Statistical Society
FRSSAfr	Fellow of the Royal Society of South Africa
FSA	Fellow of the Society of Antiquaries
FSc(Med)	Fellow in Medical Sciences
GCVO	Knight Grand Cross of the Royal Victorian Order
GLC	Greater London Council
GM	George Medal
GOC	General Officer Commanding
Glasg	Glasgow
HAC (RHA)	Honourable Artillery Company (Royal Horse Artillery)
HMS	His/Her Majesty's Ship
Heidelb	Heidelberg
Hon	Honorary; Honourable
HP	House Physician
HS	House Surgeon
IATA	International Air Transport Association
IBP	International Biological Programme
IMS	Indian Medical Service
Irel	(following Diploma) Royal College of Physicians and Surgeons in Ireland
JP	Justice of the Peace
KBE	Knight Commander of the Order of the British Empire
KC	King's Counsel
KCB	Knight Commander of the Bath
KCMG	Knight Commander of St. Michael and St. George
KCSI	Knight Commander of the Star of India
KCVO	Knight Commander of the Royal Victorian Order
KG	Knight of the Order of the Garter
KCSG	Papal Knight of the Order of St. Gregory
KSG	Papal Knight of the Order of St. Gregory
Kt	Knight
LCC	London County Council
LFPS	Licentiate of the Faculty (later Royal Faculty) of Physicians and Surgeons of Glasgow
LM	Licentiate in Midwifery
LMCC	Licentiate of the Medical Council of Canada
LMS	Licentiate in Medicine and Surgery
LMSSA	Licentiate in Medicine and Surgery, Society of Apothecaries
LRCP	Licentiate of the Royal College of Physicians of London
LRCPE	Licentiate of the Royal College of Physicians of Edinburgh
LRCPI	Licentiate of the Royal College of Physicians of Ireland
LRCSE	Licentiate of the Royal College of Surgeons of Edinburgh
LRCSI	Licentiate of the Royal College of Surgeons in Ireland
LRFPS	Licentiate of the Royal Faculty (later College) of Physicians and Surgeons of Glasgow
LSA	Licentiate of the Society of Apothecaries
Liverp	Liverpool
LLD	Doctor of Laws
Lond	London
Lt-Cdr	Lieutenant-Commander
Lt-Col	Lieutenant-Colonel

Lt-Gen	Lieutenant-General
Luck	Lucknow
MA	Master of Arts
MB	Bachelor of Medicine
MBE	Member of the Order of the British Empire
MC	Military Cross
MCh	Magister Chirurgiae (Master of Surgery)
MCCM(NZ)	Member of the New Zealand College of Community Medicine
MCPSA	Member of the College of Physicians, South Africa MCPSA
MD	Medicine Doctor (Doctor of Medicine)
MD (Psychol Med)	Doctor of Medicine in Psychological Medicine
MD (State Med)	Doctor of Medicine in State Medicine
MEF	Middle East Forces
MICE	Member of the Institution of Civil Engineers
MMSA	Master of Midwifery of the Society of Apothecaries
MP	Member of Parliament
MPS	Member of the Pharmaceutical Society
MRCP	Member of the Royal College of Physicians of London
MRCPE	Member of the Royal College of Physicians of Edinburgh
MRCPI	Member of the Royal College of Physicians of Ireland
MRCS	Member of the Royal College of Surgeons of England
MRIA	Member of the Royal Irish Academy
MS	Master of Surgery
MSc	Master of Science
Manch	Manchester
Melb	Melbourne
Minn	Minnesota
NAPT	National Association for the Prevention of Tuberculosis
NAS	National Academy of Sciences (US)
New Bruns	New Brunswick
NRC	National Research Council (US)
NUI	National University of Ireland
NZ	New Zealand
OBE	Officer of the Order of the British Empire
OC	Officier of the Order of Canada
OM	Order of Merit
OTC	Officers' Training Corps
Oxon	Oxford
PC	Privy Councillor
PJG	Pingat Jasa Gemilang
PRCP	President of the Royal College of Physicians of London
PhD	Doctor of Philosophy
Punj	Punjab
Queen's	Queen's University, Kingston, Ontario, Canada
RAAF	Royal Australian Air Force
RAAMC	Royal Australian Army Medical Corps
RACP	Royal Australasian College of Physicians
RAF	Royal Air Force
RAFVR	Royal Air Force Volunteer Reserve
RAMC	Royal Army Medical Corps
RAMC (SR)	Royal Army Medical Corps (Special Reserve)
RAMC (T)	Royal Army Medical Corps (Territorial)
RCAMC	Royal Canadian Army Medical Corps
RCVNR	Royal Canadian Volunteer Naval Reserve
RRC	Royal Red Cross
RSCI	Royal College of Surgeons in Ireland
RFA	Royal Field Artillery
RMO	Regimental Medical Officer; Resident Medical Officer

RN	Royal Navy
RNVR	Royal Naval Volunteer Reserve
RSA	Royal Society of Arts
RSM	Royal Society of Medicine
RUI	Royal University of Ireland
Revd	Reverend
Roch	Rochester
S.Afr	South Africa
St.And	St. Andrews
Sask	Saskatchewan
ScD	Scientiae Doctor (Doctor of Science)
Sgt	Sergeant
Sheff	Sheffield
Sqdn Ldr	Squadron Leader
TA	Territorial Army
TC	Trinity Cross of Republic of Trinidad and Tobago
TD	Territorial Decoration
UC Dubl	University College, Dublin
VAD	Voluntary Aid Detachment
VD	Colonial Auxiliary Forces Officers' Decoration (Volunteer Decoration, later VRD)
VJ (Day)	Victory over Japan (1939–1945)
VRD	Volunteer Reserve Decoration
WAust	Western Australia
WHO	World Health Organization
West Ont	Western Ontario
Wits	Witwatersrand

Abbreviations of journal titles follow the system used in *World Medical Periodicals* and *World List of Scientific Periodicals*.

An asterisk (*) against FRCP means that the Fellow was elected under the special bye-law which provides for the election to the Fellowship of "Persons holding a medical qualification, but not Members of the College, who have distinguished themselves in the practice of medicine, or in the pursuit of Medical or General Science or Literature ...". A dagger (†) is used where the list of honorary degrees is too lengthy to include in entirety in the heading. A list is available in the library.

CORRIGENDA

p.LXXX THOMSON, Sir Arthur: This photograph has been included in error; it is not that of Sir Arthur Peregrine Thomson (p.575).

p.637 SAMUEL GEE LECTURES: The 1983 lecture was given by Dr Charles Richard Astley Clarke and not Sir Cyril Astley Clarke KBE.

MUNK'S ROLL

OF THE

ROYAL COLLEGE OF PHYSICIANS OF LONDON

VOLUME VII

ABRAHAMS, Derek Gordon *b.*29 Aug 1918 *d.*16 July 1981
MB BChir Cantab (1945) MRCP (1947) MD (1950
MRACP (1967) FRACP (1971) FRCP (1979

Derek Abrahams was born at St Neots, Huntingdonshire, a member of a distinguished and somewhat complicated family. His father was Lionel Abrahams, a solicitor, and his mother Gertrude Ann was the daughter of an orchardist, James William Funk. She was killed in an accident when he was still very young; his father died at an early age. Three uncles achieved eminence: Sir Adolphe, the London physician and rheumatologist, Sir Solly, a chief justice in the Colonial Service and Harold, the Olympic gold medallist whose fame was rekindled by the film 'Chariots of Fire'. Derek was educated at Bedford School and Caius College, Cambridge, and completed his medical studies at St. George's Hospital in 1943. The start to his medical career was somewhat less than illustrious; he had enjoyed the 'good life' and later regretted that his medical ambitions had only developed several years after graduation. I first met him during his term as senior registrar at the National Heart Hospital, 1949 – 1952. He was an excellent clinician and teacher but not always adequately supported by his superiors. In 1949 he published a paper 'The Q-T Interval in Acute Rheumatic Carditis', the conclusions of which were not supported by subsequent investigations. His immediate superior, Paul Wood, rather ungraciously stated 'What can you expect, Abrahams is so short-sighted that he probably could not measure the Q-T interval accurately'.

In 1952 he was awarded a travelling fellowship in medicine to the United States of America and in the following year was appointed lecturer in medicine at the London Hospital. There seemed no prospect of further advancement and he therefore moved in 1956 to Ibadan in Nigeria as senior lecturer in medicine, University College, and was later given a personal chair in medicine.

In 1963 he moved again, this time to Australia as associate professor in medicine at the newly established University of New South Wales. His ability was quickly recognized, but because of his rather inflexible and uncompromising adherence to self-imposed standards and principles, he clashed with the head of the department of medicine, Ralph Blacket, and resigned from his university post. His last decade was spent as consultant physician in the northern suburbs of Sydney, with attachments to Royal North Shore Hospital, Mona Vale District Hospital and Manly District Hospital. His opinions were eagerly sought by many general practitioners and patients. Until his final illness he retained a keen interest in teaching, and his ward rounds were always popular with undergraduates and graduates alike.

Derek was a very determined and courageous man. When his malignant lung lesion was diagnosed and deemed inoperable he underwent radiotherapy. He used to go for treatment in the morning and did his medical work later in the day, testimony to his iron self-discipline. After his death a colleague was heard to say 'What a great pity, Derek was mellowing to such a degree that he might have become a marvellous old man for reminiscences'. GEB

[RACP, *College Newsletter,* Aug 1981, **13**, 5; Photo]

ADAMSON, Douglas George *b.*5 Feb 1915 *d.*9 April 1979
MB ChB St And (1938) MRCP (1948) MD (1952)
FRCP (1965) MRCPE (1969) FRCPE (1971)

Douglas Adamson was the younger son of James Kinnear Adamson, schoolmaster, and Georgina Key. He was educated at Morgan Academy, Dundee, and at St Andrews University, where his all round ability was shown from an early age. He was captain of his school and sports champion. At university he was capped for rugby and in his final examinations passed with distinction in medicine. He had already acquired skills in mountaineering and angling, as well as a deep love of nature and a special interest in ornithology.

After serving as a house surgeon at Sunderland Royal Infirmary, followed by a brief spell in general practice, he enlisted in the RAMC, serving throughout the second world war, mostly in the Middle East and Burma. For his distinguished service in anti-malarial control, particularly in the advance from Imphal to Mandalay, he was twice mentioned in despatches.

In 1946 he returned to Dundee as lecturer (and later senior lecturer) in medicine under his former mentor, Adam Patrick. In 1953 he became a part-time consultant physician based at Dundee Royal Infirmary. Eventually, as senior physician and chairman of the division of medicine of the Dundee General Hospitals, he exerted strong influence in upholding standards of integrity, compassion and professional competence, especially at the difficult time of the commissioning of the new teaching hospital at Ninewells in 1973. He was a popular and busy consultant, a first class administrator and a very good clinical instructor. His research interests were restricted by his busy clinical practice but he published papers on blood disorders, endocrine and metabolic disease and tropical disorders. He also made an important contribution to medical research in his community as a founder member of Tenovus Tayside, a fund raising organization which has successfully sponsored a number of important research projects in the Tayside area. He played a full part in community life in Dundee and was a well known member of the Royal and Ancient Golf Club in St. Andrews. He was still at the height of his professional career when he was overtaken by serious illness, but with courage and dignity remained at work for two years, till the day when he died of cardiac arrest at the age of 64.

In 1950 he married Catherine Nicholson Miller and they had one daughter and two sons; the elder son also entered the medical profession. KGL/GW

[*Brit. med. J.*, 1979, **1**, 1288; *Lancet*, 1979, **1**, 937; Photo]

ADRIAN, Lord **(Edgar Douglas)** 1st Baron Adrian of Cambridge
*b.*30 Nov 1889 *d.*4 Aug 1977
OM (1942) BA Cantab (1910) MB BChir (1915) MRCP (1916)
MA MD (1919) FRS (1923) FRCP (1924) PRS (1950–55)
Nobel laureate, Medicine (1932)†

ED Adrian came of Huguenot stock on his father's side. His father, ADA Adrian, was legal adviser to the Local Government Board, his maternal grandfather taught mathematics at the RMC Sandhurst. Adrian's visits to seaside towns were restricted by his father's expert knowledge of the deficiencies of their sewage systems! He was educated at Westminster School and Trinity College Cambridge, where he obtained 30% more marks in Pt I of the Tripos than anyone had had in living memory. He obtained a first in Pt II of the Tripos in the following year and in 1913 became a fellow of Trinity College. In the next year he left Cambridge and qualified from St Bartholomew's Hospital in 1915. In spite of efforts to get to France, he was kept at the Connaught Military Hospital at Aldershot, where he was influenced by Adolphe Abrahams and Francis Walshe. He worked chiefly on nerve injuries, on 'shell shock' and on various forms of hysteria, using electrical stimuli and vigorous suggestion, and he had some success with 'neurasthenia' treated by evoking suppressed experience.

His pre-war work with Keith Lucas on nerve conduction had made him well aware of the difficulties of interpretation which arise when dealing with whole nerve trunks containing hundreds of nerve fibres. He was therefore looking for ways of recording the activity of single fibres, and with advice from A Forbes and later from HS Gasser, he built a valve amplifier and recorded the output with a capillary electrometer. In his first experiment with this apparatus, he found that he could record afferent discharges from muscle spindles in a sciatic-gastrocnemius preparation from the frog, and he settled down to recording single units either by cutting down the muscle, or by dissecting fibres from the nerve trunk. In his first book, *The Basis of Sensation* (1926), he established that sensory discharge consists of all or none impulses whose frequency increases with the strength of the stimulus. His second book, *The Mechanism of Nervous Action* (1932), expanded the work on sensory channels and established the corresponding activity of motor nerves in reflex and voluntary motor action. This work, and the Adrian-Bronk needle developed for it, provided the starting point for clinical electromyography. In the same year, 1932, he shared the Nobel prize with Sir Charles Sherrington for their researches into neuromuscular coordination.

Adrian then became interested in the synchronization of neuronal discharge, and with BHC Matthews and later with Yamagiwa analysed the Berger rhythm and began the search for its neuronal basis. This led directly to clinical electroencephalography. He also began recording directly from the cerebral cortex in the cat, monkey, pig, sheep and Shetland pony. He pointed out that there are very large differences in the amount of cortex devoted to somatic representation in different ungulates depending on the use made of the part, the snout, the nostril or the fore-leg, in the investigation of the environment. He also was the first to observe the second somatic sensory area, a finding which has led to the recognition of a multiplicity of somatic, auditory and visual areas. Work with Moruzzi began our understanding of what goes on in the motor area.

He made notable additions to knowledge of touch, pain and retinal activity and also investigated afferent fibres in the vagus from the lung, from the carotid sinus, from the vestibular apparatus and from the olfactory bulb, as well as the efferent activity of the autonomic nervous system. On each subject he wrote not merely the first but the classical paper. His third and last book, *The Physical Background of Perception* (1947), deals with peripheral and central sensory events, and the neuronal basis of recognition, learning and memory.

He was Fullerton research professor of the Royal Society from 1929 to 1937, when he became professor of physiology at Cambridge. He was a modest but brilliant lecturer and his demonstrations were long remembered. In 1951 he became master of Trinity and retired in 1965. Two of these years he had to spend as vice-chancellor of the University of Cambridge and he was chancellor, the first medical man to be so honoured since at least the 15th century, from 1967 to 1975. He was made a hereditary peer in 1955. He was a member of some 48 learned societies and was given 29 honorary degrees.

Although difficult to approach in the laboratory, he could be extraordinarily helpful. In 1936, he excused himself from a visit from me with a six page letter in long hand, containing all the details of technique necessary for dissecting out single mammalian nerve fibres! After he was raised to the peerage he continued to ride a very old bicycle around Cambridge, doing the shopping after his wife's mountaineering accident.

In 1934 he married Hester Pinsent, later DBE; they had two daughters and a son, RH Adrian FRS, who succeeded to the title.

DW

[*Biog. Mem. roy. Soc.*, 1979, **25**, pp. 1-73; *Brit. med. J.*, 1977, **2**, 463; *Lancet*, **2**, 414-15; *Times* 6 Aug 1977; Nobel Foundation: *Nobel lectures...physiology or medicine, 1922-1941* (Amsterdam 1965) pp. 273-7, 293-304; Photo]

AITKEN, Janet Kerr *b.* – 1886 *d.*21 Apr 1982
CBE (1950) MRCS LRCP (1922) MB BS Lond (1922) MD (1924) MRCP (1926) FRCP (1943)

Janet Aitken was born in Buenos Aires, Argentina, of Scottish parents, being the second of five sisters. Her grandfather was the engineer concerned with the building of the ill-fated Tay Bridge. When she was four years old the family returned to Lancashire, England.

Janet could have succeeded in almost any walk of life, certainly in music – which was her first love – and in medicine or administration. In fact, in these three things she succeeded admirably. She was educated at St Leonard's School, St Andrews, where she became head of her house. She studied piano, taking her LRAM, and also singing, being a pupil of Madame Fillunger who was a friend of Robert Schumann. The Manchester School of Music awarded her the gold medal for singing in 1912, which almost decided her future career. When the first world war broke out, however, she trained as a masseuse and passed the examinations for the Incorporated Society of Masseurs, which led to an interest in anatomy and physiology and a decision to study medicine. She entered the London School of Medicine for Women in 1917 and qualified in 1922, proceeding MD in 1924, and obtaining the MRCP in 1926. She began her medical career at the Elizabeth Garrett Anderson Hospital as house physician, was clinical assistant during time spent in general practice in Kensington, and was appointed consultant physician in 1929. In that same year she was appointed physician in charge of the Kensington Supervisory Rheumatic Clinic for Children, and juvenile rheumatism remained always of special interest to her. From 1930 to 1934 she was vice-dean of the Royal Free Hospital School of Medicine, a member of the Central Health Services Council and of four hospital management committees. She was appointed CBE in 1950.

She was elected FRCP in 1943, and was the second woman to serve on the Council. She was the first woman to serve on the General Medical Council. For six years she was the women's member of council of the BMA. From her earliest days she did a great deal for women in medicine, being president of the Medical Women's Federation from 1942 to 1944. Her outstanding service was to the Medical Women's International Association, founded in 1919 and the oldest existing international medical organization. She was honorary secretary from 1950 and her home became the office of the association. She was appointed president in 1958 and undertook a world tour, visiting many of the countries represented in the association.

Janet was a tall, handsome and dignified woman with a lovely sparkle, whose entry into a room could not be ignored. She was dark, with brown wavy hair and dark eyes. She was a very warm person, infinitely generous with her money, and her possessions, her time and her concern. No one ever went to her for help, advice or interest and came away empty-handed. Her beautiful speaking voice had a Scottish lilt which became more pronounced when she was excited. And she was such fun; her twinkling brown eyes, wit, humour – always kindly, but sometimes critical and sharp – were unforgettable. She enjoyed everything she did, and did it well; playing as hard as she worked. She performed as a solo singer at the Queen's Hall Proms and enchanted her colleagues by singing in the Royal Free productions of Gilbert and Sullivan.

During the second world war she remained in London in charge of the casualty clearing unit at the Elizabeth Garrett Anderson Hospital, and her presence, well dressed and elegant, had a magical effect on hospital and patient morale. She would talk to the residents calmly and naturally as the bombs fell.

In addition to her work and her music, she loved books and dachshunds, and revelled in the beautiful Donegal island home of her friends, Helen Mayo and Andy Sharpe. Although she never married she had a large and devoted family, among whom she was a leader, and she delighted in all her nephews and nieces. In her last years she was devotedly cared for by her companion and friend, Althea Jackson, and her niece Lilias Grey-Turner. She aged remarkably little in appearance; her hair was barely streaked with grey and her eyes were as bright as ever. Even when confined to a chair, and later bed-ridden, she loved to see her friends and hear of their doings. She was quick to enjoy the company of young people, to whom she transmitted much of her wisdom, with unfailing wit and humour.

ALW/GW

[*Brit. med. J.*, 1982, **284**, 1482; *Times*, 23 April 1982; Photo]

ALLISON, Richard Sydney *b.*15 May 1899 *d.*27 April 1978
VRD (1943) MB BCh BAO Belfast (1921) MD (1924) MRCP (1924) FRCP (1938) DPM (1944) FRCPI (1972) Hon DSc Belfast (1975)

Sydney Allison was born in Belfast where his father, William Lowcock Allison, was a professional photographer, and his mother was Eliza Russell, née Patterson. He was educated at the Royal Belfast Academical Institution, and entered Queen's University, Belfast, qualifying with honours in 1921. As a medical student he spent a year in the Royal Navy as a surgeon probationer in a destroyer. The great 'flu epidemic wiped out many of the crew and made a profound impression upon him. Before becoming a houseman at the Royal Victoria Hospital he spent a year at sea with the Shaw Saville Company in the Far East. In 1923 he became a house physician in the West London Hospital, Hammersmith, and after obtaining his MD and the London membership was appointed registrar. From 1925 to 1930 he was assistant physician at the Ruthin Castle in North Wales. Here he developed an interest in diseases of the gastrointestinal tract, and carried out his first epidemiological study of multiple sclerosis. In 1930 he was appointed to the staff of the Royal Victoria Hospital, Belfast, and became a visiting physician to Claremont Street Hospital in 1939.

He was always interested in the sea and the Navy, becoming a surgeon lieutenant RNVR in 1925. During the second world war he spent his time as a medical specialist, chiefly at Plymouth and Barrow Gurney, and was promoted to surgeon captain RNVR. In 1943 he was awarded the Volunteer Reserve Decoration, the year in which his book *Sea Diseases; the story of a great natural experiment in preventive medicine in the Royal Navy* was published. This book gives a vivid picture of life below deck through the centuries. He also continued his interest in teaching, and could regularly command an audience of undergraduate and postgraduate students at 11 am on Sunday mornings, which was one of his teaching sessions prewar.

After the war, as honorary secretary of medical staff of the Royal Victoria Hospital, Belfast, he was concerned with the establishment of the departments of neurology and neurosurgery, with his friend Mr Cecil Calvert. He then became a full time neurologist and gave up his general medical beds. This allowed him to devote much more of his time to his two chief interests, multiple sclerosis and organic mental states. He became probably the leading world authority on how to conduct epidemiological work in multiple sclerosis. His studies in North Wales, Northern Ireland and the Orkney and Shetland Islands and Faroes, are well known both to neurologists and epidemiologists. In 1957 he was invited to supervise two studies in North America to test the theory that latitude had a part to play in the disease. He was then made a visiting professor to the Medical College of South Carolina and the University of Dalhousie, Nova Scotia. These studies were the subject of the Florence Tong Lecture in 1959, and of his presidential address to the section of neurology of the Royal Society of Medicine in 1962. His interest in organic mental states began during the war, and in the post-war years he spent hours of his leisure time studying cases of carbon monoxide poisoning during the recovery phase. This work culminated in the publication of *The Senile Brain* in 1962, which is a clinical study of organic mental states due to different causes. The subject of his Croonian Lecture was 'Perseveration, as a sign of diffuse and focal brain damage', given in 1966.

He had numerous publications to his credit. In 1938, with Cecil Calvert, he edited the eighth edition of Whitla's *Dictionary of Treatment* and the ninth edition, with Howard Crozier, in 1957. On retirement he was invited to become honorary archivist at the Royal Victoria Hospital, which allowed him to maintain his interest in medical and Naval history. In 1969 he published *The Very Faculties*, a short history of the development of ophthalmological and otorhinolaryngological services in Belfast, and in 1972 *The Seeds of Time*, being a short history of the Belfast General and Royal Hospital 1850–1903. This was followed in 1974 by the publication of the history of *HMS Caroline*, a survivor of the Battle of Jutland and training ship of the Ulster Division of the Royal Naval Reserves. His last book *The Surgeon-Probationers* was published in 1979.

Among his many honours were presidencies of the Association of Physicians of Great Britain and Ireland (1967), Association of British Neurologists (1966), Ulster Medical Society (1969) and Ulster Neuropsychiatric Society (1952).

A few weeks before he died Sydney had returned from a three-month appointment to the department of neurosurgery, University of Rhodesia, Salisbury, where he was asked to revise their record system. Just before his final illness, he had written to ask permission to examine all cases of aphasia admitted to hospital, as there were two ideas he wanted to investigate.

His name is perpetuated in Belfast in the form of the annual Allison Lecture and prize. Sydney Allison was warmhearted and generous, a mildly obsessional and dedicated physician. In his younger days he played tennis and after his retirement spent happy hours watching cricket. In 1925 he married Elizabeth Newett Barnett Steen, the daughter of James Barnett Steen, director of a linen firm, and Annie Newett; both of Belfast. He had two daughters and a son.

JHDM/GW

[*Brit. med. J.*, 1978, **1**, 1427, 1631; *Lancet,* 1978, **1**, 1108-9; *Times*, 13 May 1978; Photo]

ALLOTT, Eric Newmarch *b.*28 May 1899 *d.*31 Dec 1980
BA Oxon (1920) BSc (1923) MA (1924) BM BCh (1925)
MRCP (1929) FRCP (1936) FRIC (now FRSC) (1950) DM (1951)

Eric Newmarch Allott, the elder son of Henry Newmarch Allott, a civil engineer, and Helen, daughter of William Smith, a timber merchant, was born at Stretford, Lancashire. A foundation scholar at Manchester Grammar School, he went to Balliol College, Oxford, in 1916 as a Brackenbury scholar but served as lieutenant in the Royal Flying Corps (later Royal Air Force) and returned to Oxford in 1919. While a demonstrator in organic chemistry at Oxford he began his medical studies, partly at Oxford and partly (for anatomy) at the University of Heidelberg. He completed his clinical studies at St Bartholomew's Hospital, London, qualifying in 1925.

After a period as house physician to the medical professorial unit at Bart's, he was awarded a Beit memorial fellowship which took him to Emmanuel College, Cambridge, to work under Professor (later Sir Frederick) Gowland Hopkins. Following a brief appointment in 1928 as assistant physiologist at Sheffield Royal Hospital, he became in 1929 chief assistant to the medical professorial unit at Bart's.

In 1931 he was appointed by the London County Council (LCC) as group pathologist and director of the Group Laboratory at Lewisham Hospital, London, a position which he held until his retirement in 1963. During the first nine years he expanded the pathology service from a single laboratory with two technicians, serving seven hospitals in south-east London, until, in 1940, his staff consisted of two assistant pathologists and twelve technicians, providing a specialized pathology service for the seventy-odd LCC hospitals. He was transfusion officer at Lewisham Hospital and started the blood donor service which led to the creation of the Lewisham Transfusion Centre. By 1947 the Central Pathological Laboratory had four specialist pathologists and four senior registrars.

Allott became a member of the Biochemical Society in 1925, serving on the committee from 1948 to 1952, and was elected directly to the fellowship of the Royal Institute of Chemistry (now Royal Society of Chemistry) in 1950, serving on the council from 1962 to 1965. He was a founder member of the Association of Clinical Pathologists, serving as president in 1955 and chairman of council from 1957 to 1961. He was a member of the editorial board of the *Journal of Clinical Pathology* until his death; latterly in an advisory capacity. Like several other pathologists with clinical backgrounds he was not initially in favour of the formation of the College of Pathology and would have preferred a Faculty of Pathologists within the Royal College of Physicians. When the importance of the College in the training and teaching of pathologists became evident he accepted founder fellowship and served on the council from 1963 to 1966. From his retirement in 1963 until 1968 he was adviser in chemical pathology to the Ministry of Health and played an important part in setting up the Guy's Hospital poisons unit at New Cross Hospital in 1955, and was chairman of the Steering Committee for the unit until his death. His attachment to the medical professorial unit at Bart's was undoubtedly responsible for his strong clinical approach to the problems of pathology; he was frequently asked by his colleagues to visit the wards and to express an opinion in relation to metabolic disorders, especially of abnormalities of electrolyte balance.

As Beit memorial research fellow from 1925 to 1927, under the direction of Gowland Hopkins, he studied in detail some earlier inconsistent observations of Hopkins on the influence of glutathione on the oxidation of linseed oil and linoleic acid. Later he investigated the rates of disappearance of α, β and γ-glucose after injection into the circulation of rats. He played an important role in fostering scientific clinical medicine at a time when the scientific basis of medicine had not progressed to the creation of clinical research units. At a time when few specialized chemical pathological laboratories were available for estimating 'electrolytes', other than plasma chloride and bicarbonate, and probably stimulated by McCance's work on experimental salt deficiency, he studied plasma levels and urinary excretion of sodium and potassium and published a series of important papers in this field. The most important of these described the low plasma potassium concentrations associated with familial periodic paralysis. He also investigated the effect of various therapeutic regimes on the low sodium and high potassium concentrations in the plasma in Addison's disease. He later demonstrated retention of sodium and potassium without renal disease in five patients with brain damage. His presidential address to the section of experimental medicine of the Royal Society of Medicine, in 1945, was an excellent survey, up to date for the time, of electrolyte changes in nephritis, diabetic ketosis, alkalosis and Addison's disease. In 1951, the mineralocorticoid deoxycorticosterone (doca) and the glucocorticoid cortisone had been synthesised, and Allott showed that cortisone was more effective than the adrenal extract Eucortone, doca and/or glucose saline in the treatment of crises in hypopituitarism. He contributed sections on 'Haemolytic Disease of the Newborn' and on 'Laboratory Aids to Diagnosis and Treatment' in the 1951 edition of *Modern Trends in Paediatrics*. Subsequent publications were concerned with hypernatraemia and hyperchloraemia in bulbar poliomyelitis and in the 'stiff man syndrome'; in the latter condition plasma inorganic phosphate paradoxically increased when glucose or insulin was administered.

He began his studies of the clinical importance of the Rh factor in 1941. In 1946, when routine testing of women for the Rh factor was not widely available because of slender resources, he wrote with CA Holman an LCC memorandum on the Rh factor for the use of the LCC staff. Three years later, again with Holman, he published a careful study of 200 Rh negative women, demonstrating the importance of screening during pregnancy to permit early diagnosis and then early induction of labour or exchange transfusion.

His presidential address, 'The Challenge of the Future', to the Association of Clinical Pathologists in 1955 forecast many trends, including the organization of the laboratory, the problems of quality control, and the setting up of specialist laboratories (such as reference laboratories and supra-regional assay services).

Allott was a man of singular modesty and great kindness, readily accessible to his colleagues, particularly his juniors, taking a continuing interest in the careers of the many who had spent a period of training in his laboratory. As well as gardening, philately, and the study of languages, he was interested in railways and had put this to practical, if brief, use when he worked as a volunteer signalman and railway guard during the general strike of 1926.

In 1930 he married Edith Mary Kydd, who supported him throughout his long and distinguished career until her death in 1974. He subsequently lived, contentedly, near his daughter and her family at Oxford. CHG/NFM

[*Brit. med. J.*, 1981, **282**, 394, 746; *Lancet*, 1981, **1**, 286, 510; *Times*, 8 Jan 1981; Photo]

AMOROSO, Emmanuel Ciprian *b.*16 Sept 1901 *d.*30 Oct 1982
CBE (1969) TC (1977) MB BCh BAO Dubl (1929) FRCS (1960) MD NUI (1964) FRCOG (1965) FRCP* (1966) FRCPath (1973) FRS (1957)†

EC Amoroso, who died at the age of 81, enjoyed a life marked with honour and crowded with friends. He graduated in medicine in 1929 from the National University of Ireland. By the end of his professional career, he had the unique distinction of being a fellow of four of the Royal Colleges: Surgeons in 1960, Obstetricians and Gynaecologists in 1965, Physicians in 1966, and Pathologists in 1973. He had been elected FRS in 1957, so far the only native-born West Indian to achieve that particular distinction.

The Trinidad into which 'Amo' was born was vastly different from what it is today. It was then a colony with a population of fewer than a quarter of a million, a small number privileged and rich, but most poor; a people of mixed and different blood; a polyglot world where Amo presumably began to acquire his remarkable linguistic gifts.

Amo was not born among the rich. Nor did he win one of the only four scholarships that were then available to native Trinidadians who wanted to study at a British university. In his early twenties, he managed to make his own way to Ireland where, after a short time, he was able to enter University College, Dublin – now the National University. A first-class mind, powered by a determination to succeed in the professional, sophisticated and competitive world to which he was attracted, did the rest. Prizeman throughout his years at the University, and then armed with a medical degree, he spent a year on a travelling scholarship in Germany before becoming, in 1933, a temporary demonstrator in histology and embryology at University College London. Two years later he was appointed to a permanent post in the same disciplines at the Royal Veterinary College. After twelve years, he was elected to the chair of physiology, an office which he retained until his retirement in 1968, when he was made professor emeritus.

But it was retirement only in a statutory sense. Nothing could stop Amo from keeping abreast of, and working in, what had become his chosen field of study – reproductive physiology.

His first published paper (1931) was on the epithelium of the pancreas. It followed classical anatomical lines. Then came others on diverse topics. Twenty years passed before he began to focus on the problem of placentation, with which his name will be best remembered. Here his gift of synthesis found full play. He threw new light on the evolutionary adaptation of the placenta for viviparous reproduction, his conclusions being based not just on his own researches and experience as a microanatomist and general biologist, but on his familiarity with the literature in several disciplines. His work always bore the mark of critical scholarship. He saw scientific problems 'in the round', and it was a manifestation of his nature that he never sought to impress by the dotting of i's and the crossing of t's, or by adding some trivial, even if interesting, new observation to generalisations that were already established. So it was that in his candidature for the fellowship of the Royal College of Physicians he listed as the first of his important publications, not some conventional monograph on a piece of personal research, but a review of 'ovarian activity during gestation, ovum transport and implantation', which he had contributed to a two-volume (now three-volume) work on the ovary.

Amo had an exceptional memory, and a gift for expression to which he gave full and pleasurable rein whether in a letter, or in the way he addressed an audience, or in his lectures to students, which were always delivered in the rotund classical manner that had been current in his student days. His way of saying things often sounded unduly flowery, but if he had said them differently, if he had stumbled over his words, if his sentences had not been properly phrased, it would not have been Amo. Amo was not one for the solitary life. His style was idiosyncratic, and no one would have guessed from his social graces, or in the way he smoked a cigar, that he had been a successful amateur boxer in his twenties.

In 1964, as chairman of the British Society of Endocrinology, he had to preside over the Second International Congress of Endocrinology in London. Amo was in his element. There was a flourish to all he did. The late George Corner, the foremost of the overseas guests at the conferences, tells in his memoirs how impressed and surprised he was when he found that he was to be furnished with a chauffeur-driven Rolls Royce during his stay in London. Only Amo, brought up in a country ruled over by a resplendent, plumed Governor, who presumably was driven about in a colourful carriage, could have thought of that.

The Zoological Society of London, of which he became a fellow in 1947, benefited greatly from Amo's broad experience, his diverse interests, and his deep humanity.

When, in 1963, Sir Arthur Lewis resigned the vice-chancellorship of the new University of the West Indies, Amo was suggested as a possible successor. He seemed uninterested. If approached formally, he clearly must have declined, although later he became the representative for Trinidad and Tobago on a Commonwealth scientific committee. Amo preferred to stay in England, intellectually alert to the end, and always enjoying the glamour of life in the country that had once been the centre of the Empire, the centre to which he had been beckoned from a small colony sixty years before.

Z

[*Brit. med. J.*, 1982, **285**, 1569; *Lancet,* 1982, **2**, 1230; *Times,* 4 Nov 1982; Photo]

AMULREE, *Lord* **(Basil William Sholto Mackenzie)**
2nd Baron Amulree *b.*25 July 1900 *d.*15 Dec 1983
KBE (1977) MRCS LRCP (1925) MB BChir Cantab (1927)
MRCP (1928) MA MD (1936) FRCP (1946)

Sholto Mackenzie was the son of a lawyer who became Lord Amulree as a member of Ramsay Macdonald's first Labour Government. Sholto was himself Liberal Whip in the Lords from 1955 to 1977, but did not play a leading role in politics, rather following his uncle Sir James Mackenzie into medicine. He turned to pathology on qualification and worked mainly in that field at UCH and the Royal Northern Hospital until he joined the medical staff of the Ministry of Health in 1936. After three years working on the provision of cancer treatment facilities, on which he wrote a published report, he was deflected by the chances of war to the Ministry's concern with the care of the 'chronic sick' in public assistance institutions. He was also made the Ministry's medical specialist on the safety of water supplies, but the possibility of better care for the elderly caught his attention and held it for the rest of his career.

Marjorie Warren had done her pioneer work at the North Middlesex Hospital in the late 1930s. Trevor Howell, Lionel Cosin, EW Brook, Joseph Sheldon and O Olbrich had all shown the possibilities, and Sholto had been their trusted ally in the Ministry. For someone who was a physician rather than an administrator the transition to a clinical post in the new specialty was to be expected, but the actual opportunity was important. UCH, having acquired St Pancras Hospital and a large number of static beds for chronically ill older people from their district, could not continue in the blinkered fashion of most teaching hospitals of the time. They had the sense to offer Sholto the opportunity of organizing a geriatric service. He accepted the challenge and created something quite new for a London teaching hospital; only Oxford among the teaching hospitals acted similarly, with Lionel Cosin's unit at Cowley Road.

Sholto's first departure was to carry the service into the community. He saw that the rehabilitation of the elderly had to be attuned to what their home situations would allow them to do. Their problems were – and are – more social than technically medical. Narrow statutory demarcations of health, or welfare authorities' boundaries of responsibility, are equally unsuitable. The question is not merely 'What disease afflicts this patient?' but 'What help does this person need and who can give it?'. The answer is always multiple, and Sholto and senior registrar disciples demonstrated that. It was the theme of his book *Adding Life to Years*. He did not waste time debating the doctrinal justification of his specialty; he just showed that it worked. It was not by chance that the first chair of geriatrics in London was set up in his old unit nor that the first professor had been his first senior registrar.

Sholto will not be remembered, as his uncle is, for outstanding clinical or research activity. He saw the best way to cope with one of the major problems of developed societies today – care of the elderly – and he made it work. The succeeding generation should not forget that he had to climb his mountain before they could even locate theirs. Nor was his influence narrowly medical. He was president of the Society for the Study of Medical Ethics, the London County Division of the BRCS, the Association of Occupational Therapists, the British Geriatric Society and, most remarkable of all, the Association of Welfare Officers. He was chairman of the council of the London Medical Group. One of his less known, but more important, activities was the chairmanship of the Attendance Allowance Board from its inception, opening an important new contribution to care of the handicapped. The KBE awarded to him in 1977 recognized a lifetime of public service.

Sholto was a friendly, but modest, almost diffident man, yet he was tenacious and transparently without personal ambition. He had a severe stammer and learned to control it, and he met his other problems with the same resolution. He was unmarried but had a wide circle of friends. There may have been other more flamboyant figures in the fields he cultivated, but none of them raised a better crop. GEG

[*Brit. med. J.*, 1984, **288**, 156, 649; *Times*, 16 Dec 1983; Photo]

ANDERSON, Edward William *b*.7 Aug 1901 *d*.3 Sept 1981
MB ChB Edin (1923) DPM (1925) MD (1927) MRCP (1930)
FRCP (1946) Hon MSc Manch (1953) FRCPsych (1972)

Edward Anderson was born in Edinburgh to Edward Ross Anderson and Elizabeth Leith (née Dow). He was educated at Daniel Stewart College, and in 1923 graduated in medicine at the University of Edinburgh. Following this he came south to undertake postgraduate study in London.

While in London, Anderson gained a wide range of psychiatric experience, firstly as an assistant medical officer with the Metropolitan Asylums Board of the London County Council, and in 1929 at the Maudsley Hospital. In 1935 he became medical director of the Cassel Hospital for Functional Nervous Disorders and then, in 1937, having been granted a Rockefeller fellowship, studied under Karl Kleist in Frankfurt-am-Main. It was here that he gained his very considerable knowledge of German psychiatry and of phenomenological psychopathology, a subject which was to interest him throughout the rest of his professional life, and of which he was to become probably the foremost exponent in the United Kingdom.

Following his return from Germany in 1938, Anderson became consultant psychiatrist to Devon County Council and honorary consultant at Torbay Hospital. From 1940 to 1945 he served as neuropsychiatric specialist in the RNVR, being promoted in 1943 to the rank of surgeon commander. In 1947 he returned to the Maudsley Hospital as consultant physician and lecturer at the Institute of Psychiatry. He also taught psychiatry at the Royal Postgraduate Medical School in Hammersmith. In 1949 he was appointed professor of psychiatry at the Victoria University of Manchester, becoming the first holder of the chair. He relinquished this post in 1965, a year prior to the normal age of retirement, in order to become a medical visitor in the Office of the Lord Chancellor, while remaining professor emeritus at the University of Manchester.

Other appointments which Anderson held during the course of his career included the presidency of the psychiatric section of the Royal Society of Medicine 1961–1962; of the psychiatric section of the Manchester Medical Society, 1964; and later the same year visiting professor and honorary fellow at the University of Capetown. He was also at one or other time examiner in psychological medicine for the University of London, for the membership examination of the Royal College of Physicians and for the Conjoint Board.

A modest, somewhat self-effacing man, Edward Anderson shunned the limelight, seemingly finding himself more at ease with a small group of his peers or postgraduate students than on the rostrum of a lecture theatre or on some other relatively public occasion. Many of the postgraduates whom he taught benefited greatly by his erudition and later achieved considerable eminence in their chosen specialty. With undergraduates he was less successful, in that being overawed by the profundity of his knowledge, their interest in psychiatry was not aroused. Wisely, therefore, he tended to delegate much of their teaching to other members of the staff of his department. He was, however, the author of a very successful textbook, *Psychiatry*, in the Concise Medical Textbook series, which has run into several editions and is widely read by medical students and others both at home and abroad. Although his overall contribution to medical literature was not extensive, some of the papers he wrote must be considered classics of their kind. These included an investigation of collective hallucinations in sailors whose ship was sunk in wartime, a study of depressive illnesses in later life, and perhaps most memorable of all, a masterly pathographical study of the Swedish playwright, Strindberg.

Although Anderson, on account of his retiring nature, was less well known to psychiatrists outside the Maudsley and the Manchester area than perhaps he should have been, he undoubtedly left his mark on the development of British psychiatry, to its lasting benefit.

In 1934 he married Margaret Mottram Hutton who survived him, having borne him two sons and a daughter. WHT

[*Brit. med. J.*, 1981, **283**, 799; *Lancet*, 1981, **2**, 647; *Times*, 7 Sept 1981; *J. Ment. Sci.*, 1936, **82**, 559; *J. Roy. Nav. Med. Serv.*, 1942, **28**, 361; *Psychol. Med.*, 1971, **1**, 104; Photo]

ANNING, Stephen Towers *b*.31 Mar 1908 *d*.9 Nov 1983
TD MRCS LRCP (1932) BChir Cantab (1933) MB (1938)
MRCP (1948) FRCP (1958)

Stephen Anning was born in Leeds and came from a medical family, his father and two uncles being general practitioners in Leeds; his brother and two cousins were also doctors. He was educated at Leeds Grammar School and from there went to Clare College, Cambridge, returning to Leeds for his clinical experience. He qualified in 1932 and, after house appointments at the Leeds Infirmary, he served as a ship's surgeon with the Blue Funnel Line before joining a general practice in Leeds.

He enlisted in the Territorials and was in camp when war was declared. He served as a medical officer in the Middle East and became a graded specialist, and later an OC medical division with the rank of lieutenant colonel. He served in North Africa, Persia (as it then was), and later in Greece and Italy. He became very fond of the latter country and frequently visited it after the war, renewing war time friendships with Italian families there. While in the Middle East he successfully completed an MD thesis on *Desert Sores*. After the war ended he remained on the Territorial reserve of officers and in 1953 was commissioned in the Army Emergency Reserve, being appointed OC medical division of No 27 General Hospital which (on paper) had 1800 beds. In 1955 he was given command of this hospital with the rank of full colonel, which he held until 1959. He was awarded the Territorial Decoration.

He returned to general practice for a short time, but decided to specialize; this entailed his taking the MRCP which he obtained in 1948, becoming an FRCP ten years later. He was encouraged to take up dermatology by John Ingram, and joined the skin department of

Leeds General Infirmary as dermatological tutor in 1946. Ingram's choice of Anning was influenced partly by his MD thesis on *Desert Sores*, but probably more so by the contribution which his experience in general and social medicine, gained from his time in general practice, would bring to a department where the importance of these factors in skin patients was constantly being stressed. He was appointed assistant physician in 1950 and full physician in 1960. He was head of the department from 1969 until he retired in 1973.

When he joined the skin department he took over the leg ulcer clinic and his experience there led him eventually to write a very useful book on the subject. It was no coincidence that the first chapter dealt with the history of such ulcers, as he had always been interested in medical history. He wrote numerous articles and several books on the subject, including two volumes on the history of the Leeds General Infirmary (*The General Infirmary at Leeds*, Edin. 1963 – 1966), a history of medicine in Leeds, and a history of the Leeds School of Medicine published, with K Walls, in time for the 150th anniversary of the School. On this occasion his historical writing was recognized by Leeds University who awarded him the honorary degree of master of philosophy. His historical work was also appreciated beyond Leeds, and the Society of Apothecaries appointed him as one of their small group of honorary lecturers in the history of medicine. He also became the first librarian of the Willan library at the Royal College of Physicians, and was on the College library committee for three years.

Besides his clinical work, Stephen Anning contributed a great deal to the Leeds General Infirmary in other ways. He was on the board of governors, and for many years the very conscientious secretary of the medical faculty. He was on the combined planning committee of the Infirmary and University to consider the erection of an integrated medical centre in Leeds. For some years he was a non-professorial member of the University senate. He had his year of office as president of the Leeds and West Riding Medico-chirurgical Society, and also of the Leeds and West Riding Medico-legal Society. He was an active member of the Thoresby society, the main historical society in Leeds, and on the committee of the Leeds library, the oldest private library in the country, founded in 1768, about the same time as the Leeds Infirmary.

Stephen Anning was a very sociable and hospitable man with a happy family life and a large circle of friends, many of whom had been patients when he was in general practice. He was a great reader and was interested in antique furniture and china, and also in motor cars. Above all, he was a sympathetic and understanding physician. He was survived by his wife, son and daughter. FFH

[*Brit. med. J.*, 1984, **288**, 80; *Lancet*, 1983, **2**, 1434; Photo]

APLEY, John *b.*3 Sept 1908 *d.*6 Oct 1980
CBE (1968) MB BS Lond (1932) MD (1938) MRCP (1942)
FRCP (1959) JP (1966 – 73)†

John Apley was born in London, son of Samuel, a merchant, and of Marion Hilda (née Tannis) also from a mercantile family. From local schools he won a state scholarship in 1927 to University College and University College Hospital, London. There he was awarded the first Bucknill Exhibition (1928 – 1929). Soon after qualifying, in 1932, he entered general practice in Eastcote Lane, Pinner, Middlesex. While in this practice he acted as honorary clinical assistant to Eric Pritchard at the Westminster Children's Hospital and he also set up a children's clinic in his practice – a pioneer endeavour in the area at the time, and an indication of his leaning to paediatrics.

The outbreak of war took him into the RAF Volunteer Reserve, where he became a medical specialist with the rank of squadron leader. His service duties were entirely in England, largely in Wiltshire, and during this time he became interested in stress in relation to peptic ulcer among airmen. He also made contacts in Bath and Bristol which persuaded him to go into paediatrics after the war in the West Country rather than return to general practice.

After demobilization in 1945 he became registrar at the Royal Hospital for Sick Children, Bristol, and while in this post he became part time consultant in paediatrics to the Royal United Hospital, Bath, from 1946. In 1948 he was co-author, with JM Naish, of his first book *The Clinical Apprentice*, now in its fifth edition.

From 1948 to 1949 he was fellow in pediatrics at the Children's Medical Center, Boston, Massachusetts, USA. Soon after his return he was promoted to be consultant in Bristol and Shaw lecturer in diseases of children in the University of Bristol (1950).

He remained in the combined post of NHS consultant at Bath and Bristol and University lecturer until his retirement in 1973, except for a term as visiting professor of pediatrics at Louisville, Kentucky in 1963, and a year in Saigon, 1967 – 1968, as leader of the British Paediatric Team. During his time there the Tet offensive by the North Vietnamese over-ran his hospital and he kept it going with the greatest difficulty, having to collect supplies himself – accompanied sometimes by his wife. For this magnificent work he was created CBE in 1968 and also given the Dawson Williams Memorial prize.

John was a great raconteur and a most successful lecturer, chatty and persuasive rather than declamatory and dogmatic, spicing his message with sparks of humour. His writing began with short articles in 1944, but he tended later to deeper thinking about the philosophy of paediatrics – psychosomatic disorders, ecology, chronology and violence in the family – before becoming author of a standard text on paediatrics (1973), the editor of *Modern Trends in Paediatrics*, and then a still larger library of texts on major branches of paediatric practice.

First and foremost he remained a clinician and a generalist. Even so, he was for 15 years the paediatric cardiologist for the South West (recognized by his colleagues if not by his contract), drawing patients from a distance but also visiting Exeter, Taunton and Plymouth to follow his patients and advise local paediatricians. 'Apley's sign' of cardiac pulsation palpable below the xiphoid, indicating a hypertrophied right ventricle (except in the newborn or in acute asthma), is still taught in the South West region.

He was concerned that a view was taken of the whole child, that sound clinical methods were used first, and the minimum of appropriate tests undertaken later to reach a diagnosis. He soon realized that such diagnosis did not always mean organic disease, and his international reputation was based on his original painstaking study which appeared in 1959 as his book *The Child with Abdominal Pains*, soon widely renamed familiarly as 'Little Bellyachers'. In similar vein he was co-author with Ronnie (RC) MacKeith of a book *The Child and his Symptoms* (1962). Both books have been translated into Spanish, German, Swedish and Portuguese.

John had great gifts as a teacher, supremely so at the bedside, and he was a master of the epigram. He could also draw the best out of a candidate, as he would do when he was an examiner at Bristol and in the Diploma of Child Health, where he ended as chairman of the examiners (1969 – 1973).

His performance as lecturer led to repeated appearances on television, and this in turn to his doing two stints as chairman of the South West Region Advisory Council for the BBC. With approaching retirement, and even more after he had retired, he took increasingly to writing, travelling and lecturing. He wrote regular features for 'Personal View' in the *BMJ*, countless reviews of books, and wrote or shared in the authorship of almost 100 articles in medical journals. His own textbook on *Paediatrics* appeared in 1973, and from 1977 onwards he was editor-in-chief for Butterworth's *Postgraduate Paediatrics* series which numbered 16 volumes by 1980, excluding second editions. He also edited two volumes of *Modern Trends in Paediatrics*. All bear the mark of his great love for the English language and his consummate skill in its use.

He became a member of the British Paediatric Association in 1952, was on its Council from 1958 to 1961, and was elected an honorary member in 1975.

He became president of the paediatric section of the Royal Society of Medicine, and was also president of the Clinical Society of Bath, the Bristol Medico-Chirurgical Society and the Bristol Medico-Legal Society. He was founder member, and secretary for years, of the South West Paediatric Club, of which he later became the president, and he was also a founder member, and secretary for fifteen years, of the Paediatric Visiting Club, promoting friendships amongst paediatricians throughout Europe.

Outside medicine, he was a musical performer both on oboe and clarinet, a first class chess player and a golfer. He was keen on ski-ing. He was prominent in the Bath Preservation Trust, and at his death was chairman of the local Conservation Society.

In 1947 he married Marina Griselda Nora Palmer, always known as Poo, and she helped him maintain a standard of hospitality which could always cope with unexpected visitors, as well as gracious entertaining of their many friends. There were no children.

SDVW

[*Brit. med. J.*, 1980, **281**, 1075, 1124, 1150; *Lancet*, 1980, **2**, 869, 928; *Times*, 10 Oct 1980, *Daily Telegraph*, 10 Oct 1980; Photo]

ARTHUR, Leonard John Henry *b.*20 Apr 1926 *d.*25 Dec 1983
MB BChir Cantab (1951) DObst RCOG (1954) MRCP (1957) FRCP (1983)

Leonard Arthur was born in Peckham, London, the son of the Reverend John Arthur MC, and his wife Amy. Educated at Aldenham School, Elstree and Magdalene College, Cambridge, he qualified from the Middlesex Hospital in 1951. His house jobs were followed by two years National Service with the RAMC attached to the Durham Light Infantry serving in Korea, after which he decided on a career in general practice. However, 'leafing through the advertisements in the BMJ, I eschewed family practice temporarily and hitched my wagon to Dr Jolly's staff as paediatric registrar in Plymouth. By this time I had MRCP ... Having no particular place to go, I wrote to West India and the University of Ibadan and they appointed me as senior registrar without more ado ...'. After nearly three years in Ibadan, he completed his training in Bristol before his appointment as consultant paediatrician in Derby.

His early meandering career allowed him to develop his interest in family medicine, gastroenterology and growth and nutrition, although he was first and foremost a general paediatrician. Always keen to maintain the academic tradition in Derby established by his predecessor Douglas Hubble (*q.v.*), and colleague Bernard Laurance, Leonard produced a steady flow of papers and encouraged his juniors to do likewise. His article *Non-accidental injury – what we do in Derby* published in 1975, set the scene for changes in national policy in this field. He resisted successfully his colleagues' attempts to increase admissions to the neonatal unit, insisting that unless sick, a baby should always be nursed next to the mother, thus pre-empting the current trend out of neonatal units to the wards by nearly a decade.

Although hospital based, Leonard saw himself as a community paediatrician before the word was invented, forging personal links with psychologists, social workers, teachers, parent groups, police and others, to built a truly comprehensive team. It was this approach combined with his honesty, compassion and integrity which enabled him to break new ground in child abuse management.

Leonard was a keen teacher, especially on ward rounds and case presentations, where his critical approach would often unnerve the unprepared. He would follow his juniors' careers with great interest and they were generally devoted to him. When he introduced a screening programme for congenital hip dislocation to the postnatal wards, a prize of a bottle of champagne went to the first successful hunter. The success of an early morning journal club was secured when Leonard arrived with fresh, hot, crusty bread under his arm – a tradition which continues still. A midsummer lunchtime biochemistry meeting, marred by a lack of the usual refreshments, was resurrected when he nipped out to return with a box of choc-ices from the corner shop. He enjoyed getting down to meetings of the Royal Society of Medicine, when he succeeded in catching the train, and was secretary to the section of paediatrics in 1972–1973. It should be recorded that in 1973 he first refused fellowship of the Royal College of Physicians, on conscientious grounds – he eventually accepted it in 1983 'to please his friends', which it did.

Leonard was a champion of the weak or poor and showed considerable tenacity in furthering their cause both publicly and in many small ways in his work, from a portable telephone for his child inpatients, to wholemeal bread for their meals. It was in his dealings with parents that Leonard was particularly skilled – he would wrap a badly handicapped baby carefully, give it to the mother to hold, then unwrap it gradually and explain the abnormality. His compassionate approach allowed him to develop close relationships with the parents of the many mentally, physically and socially deprived children he cared for over the years.

It was therefore ironic that in 1981, Leonard Arthur should be charged with the attempted murder of a Down's baby. The response of his medical colleagues in Derby to his suspension from work was immediate and unanimous, and resulted in his continuing to work while awaiting the three weeks trial after which he was acquitted of all charges. The community, and especially the many parents of handicapped children for whom he had cared, lent their vociferous support in the long months preceding the trial. Inevitably the ordeal took a terrible toll, shattering his self-confidence, but he bore no grudge against those who had accused him. He regretted he was unable to give evidence at his trial; his views on management of severely handicapped babies were carefully considered and had previously been published. Although no change in the law followed as he had perhaps hoped, the public debate of the issues eased the task of his fellow paediatricians.

A little over a year after his trial, he developed an inoperable brain tumour. Typically, he put off his radiotherapy for a couple of days to attend the annual meeting of the British Paediatric Association, and then continued to work during the course of his treatment. When the inevitable progression prevented him physically from working, he would still turn up for clinical meetings on sticks, crutches or Zimmer frame, woolly hat pulled over his irradiated head, and polythene bag containing journals and dictaphone in his good hand. Using the latter, he continued to reel off letters in his patients' interests to the end, and also produced a whimsical tale of how bureaucracy was by-passed to replace the curtains in his hospital room (*Lancet,* 1983, **2**, p.843).

Trying to write his obituary, he produced the following brief account of his eighteen years in Derby. 'Finally I had a conventional career since 1965 if not before. I have adopted Derby and Derby has adopted me, and it has been a happy association. I remember saying some years ago that my bones would whiten in Derbyshire. There was a slight upset two years ago when I was tried for murder. It lasted about three weeks and I was well defended. My contact with the lawyers converted me to enormous respect for them, a profession I had only hitherto touched at a distance. Not only did I learn to respect them, I also realized for the first time that they were truly concerned about the right and wrong of their cases'.

Leonard was married to Janet, daughter of Lord Brain, and they had six children. He loved his home and the village where he was a valued member of their successful radio quiz team, and bell ringer. One year he held a party in the church hall for the old and poor who had not been invited to the Christmas cocktail party. It was his village friends who buried him in their church at a delightful funeral service. His dedication to the people of Derbyshire and their love for him was acknowledged by the huge congregation which overflowed Derby Cathedral at his memorial service. KLD

[*Brit. med. J.,* 1984, **288**, 334; *Lancet,* 1984, **1**, 115 & 236; *Times,* 5 Jan 1984; *Guardian,* 6 Nov 1981; Photo]

ATKINS, *Sir* **Hedley (John Barnard)** *b.*30 Dec 1905 *d.*26 Nov 1983
KBE (1967) KStJ (1970) MRCS LRCP (1932) BM BCh Oxon (1932)
FRCS (1934) MCh (1936) DM (1937) FRCP* (1972)
Hon FACS (1957) Hon FRACS (1961) Hon FCPS(SA) (1968)
Hon DSc East Anglia (1968) Hon FRCSG (1973)

Hedley Atkins was the only son of a distinguished Guy's general practitioner, Sir John Atkins KCMG KCVO FRCS. Hedley, by which name he was always known, was educated at Rugby, Trinity College Oxford and Guy's. He was a man of commanding presence and excellent physique, playing rugby football for his school, Middlesex, Harlequins and Guy's. He seldom missed attending Guy's matches for the rest of his life. He was a keen sailor and latterly a dedicated gardener.

Having obtained first class honours in his physiology degree at Oxford, he went to Guy's with an entrance scholarship where he won the treasurer's gold medal in clinical surgery, qualifying in 1932. All his resident appointments were at Guy's and he became an FRCS in 1934, gaining the Hallett prize, and Master of Chirurgery at Oxford in 1935. Two years later, in 1937, at the early age of 31 he was appointed to the staff of Guy's as assistant surgeon and spent all his professional life in that institution.

In 1942 he went to North Africa with the RAMC and subsequently served in Italy and the UK, was mentioned in despatches and was demobilized with the rank of lieutenant colonel. Hedley returned to Guy's after the war determined to bring a scientist's approach to what was then very much the art of surgery. He was appointed director of the department of surgery and pursued his own special interest in breast diseases. He was a pioneer in using controlled trials to evaluate different modes of treatment of breast cancer, and meticulous in his observance of ethical principles, which was no easy task in such an emotive subject. Distinguished visitors from both home and abroad were regularly invited to take the Saturday morning rounds at Guy's, and he also hosted outstanding courses of lectures on modern methods of measurement in science, which were published in three volumes as *Tools of Biological Research*.

Hedley's contribution to the field of breast cancer was twofold; first an appreciation of the importance of controlled clinical trials and second, a study of the hormonal factors influencing the prognosis. This work has a fitting memorial in the Hedley Atkins breast unit at New Cross hospital.

At the Royal College of Surgeons Hedley joined the court of examiners in 1949, was elected to council in 1952, vice-president 1964–1966, and was president from 1966 to 1969. His natural gifts made him the ideal choice for such a position and these were probably the happiest and proudest years of his life. He was Bradshaw lecturer in 1965, Hunterian orator in 1971 and joined the court of patrons in 1972. Hedley was a fluent speaker and enjoyed the opportunity which the College's monthly dinners gave him to address informally the fellows and their guests. He had an excellent command of the English language due to his grounding in the classics and his lifelong habit of reading. He seldom used notes when lecturing.

His opinions were sought by many bodies and he served on the General Medical Council, the General Dental Council, and on the clinical research board of the Medical Research Council. He presided over the Surgical Research Society in 1960. At this period many honours were conferred on him and he became an honorary fellow of most of the colleges of surgeons.

He enjoyed visiting surgical centres abroad and was Sims travelling commonwealth professor in 1961, and acted as visiting professor in a number of American universities. He gave many eponymous lectures and was visiting examiner at the universities of Cambridge, Durham, London, Birmingham and the West Indies. As an author he contributed widely to surgical and medical journals, mainly on breast disease, and his most recent publication in 1977 was autobiographical, *Memoirs of a Surgeon*.

In 1953 the Royal College of Surgeons of England acquired Down House, the former home of Charles Darwin in the village of Downe in Kent, and adjoining the College's Buckston Browne Research Farm. The ground floor of the house became a museum dedicated to Darwin, and Hedley and his wife moved into the upper floors which became their home. He was the honorary, and indeed enthusiastic, curator of the museum and tended it with reverent care. His love of gardening was given full rein on retirement and many generations of surgeons have enjoyed his gracious hospitality in Down House and its gardens.

Hedley married in 1933 Gladys Gwendoline Jones, the daughter of a civil engineer, and his family life gave him great happiness. One of his sons is a physician in Canada. Hedley will be remembered as a kind, scholarly surgeon who enjoyed helping the younger members of his profession. SFT

[*Brit. med. J.*, 1983, **287**, 1803; *Lancet,* 1983, **2**, 1375; *Times,* 2 Dec 1983; Photo]

BANERJEA, Joges Chandra *b.* – 1901 *d.*24 Aug 1979
MB Calcutta (1925) MRCS LRCP (1930) MRCP (1930)
FRCP (1961)

A distinguished West Bengal physician, with special interests in cardiology and respiratory diseases, Joges Chandra Banerjea had, in a long life, a profound influence on medical practice and medical education in India. He was born in Bankura in 1901, the son of an eminent lawyer. He made a brilliant start to his career in medicine in Calcutta, winning gold medals and other distinctions in many examinations. He was awarded the Coates medal by the University of Calcutta for outstanding contributions to medical research at an early stage of his career.

After qualifying MB from Calcutta University with distinctions, in 1925, he went to England to take his MRCS LRCP and later his MRCP. On return to India he joined the Medical College and Hospital of Calcutta and ultimately became professor and director of medicine from 1955 until retirement in 1966. He was an active member of the Senate of Calcutta University for many years. He was awarded 'Padmabhusan' by the President of India in 1965 (a very distinguished national award) for his life-long dedication to medical research 'for the benefit of mankind'. When he was elected FRCP in 1961 he was believed to be the first physician in West Bengal to be so honoured. Later he was the first West Bengal doctor, possibly the first in India, to become a fellow emeritus of the American College of Chest Physicians.

He was a president of the Indian Medical Association, the Association of Physicians of India, the Cardiological Society of India, the Diabetic Association of India, the Society of Experimental Medical Sciences of India and the Calcutta Medical Club. He was editor of the *Indian Heart Journal* for many years, and published more than 150 papers on his own work in many medical journals in India and abroad.

Banerjea was a most kindhearted person. After his death it was learnt that he had helped a number of distressed students who were unable to continue their studies through lack of money. He was a generous contributor to religious organizations, and gave a considerable sum to the Cardiological Society of India to enable them to offer a prize in the name of his deceased beloved wife: the 'Uma Rani Banerjea Memorial Oration Award'. GW/VL

[Sources: RCP records and personal communications from his family; Photo]

BARKLEY, Harry *b*.27 June 1918 *d*.15 Oct 1978
BSc Liverp (1940) ARIC (1942) MB BS Lond (1950)
MRCS LRCP (1950) MRCP (1955) FRCPath (1968) FRCP (1974)

Harry Barkley was the youngest of five sons of Edward Barkley, master mariner, and Mabel Banks. He was educated at Oldershaw Grammar School, Wallasey, Cheshire, and Liverpool University, where he joined the department of biochemistry. He then moved to Glaxo, working on the development of penicillin during the second world war and serving as a part-time leading fireman in the industrial branch of the National Fire Service. He continued to work for Glaxo until 1949, studying medicine as a part-time student, and qualified in 1950 from St Mary's Hospital.

While at St. Mary's, he married Brenda Edith Ryman, who became professor of biochemistry at Charing Cross and subsequently mistress of Girton. They had two children, both of whom entered the medical profession.

After house officer posts at Fulham Hospital, Harry returned to St Mary's, joining the department of pathology under Wilfred Newcomb, and in 1956 he became senior lecturer in histopathology. In 1960 he moved to the Hertford Group of hospitals as consultant histopathologist, returning to London in 1963 as consultant histopathologist at the Bolingbroke, before joining St James's Hospital, Balham, in 1971.

As a pathologist he was devoted to the service of the patient. In committees he spoke little, but what he said was to the point, and he earned great respect for his common sense and tolerance. In the latter part of his career he became outstandingly successful in the interpretation of very small endoscopic biopsies.

As a young man Harry was a versatile athlete. His hobbies included photography and golf, and he had a keen appreciation of music, but his family was his abiding interest. GW/VL

[*Brit. med. J.*, 1978, **2**, 1650; Photo]

BARTTER, Frederic Crosby *b*.10 Sept 1914 *d*.5 May 1983
BA Harvard (1935) MD (1940) FRCP*

The son of a Kentish Anglican missionary priest, Fred Bartter was born in the Phillipines but this in no way detracted from his devotion to North America. For he was, as a *magna cum laude* graduate of Harvard Medical School and as an intern and clinical fellow of the Massachusett's General Hospital, a thorough-going New Englander. A major prop of the US Public Health Service since 1942, Fred became chief of the endocrinology branch of the National Heart and Lung Institute (National Institutes of Health, Bethesda, Maryland) in 1951. He became clinical director of the whole Institute in 1970 and chief of the refurbished hypertension-endocrine branch of the Institute in 1972. His retirement in 1979 came as a shock to his postgraduate alumni because he always seemed so young. He remained very active in academic medicine and it was highly appropriate that he died, suddenly, while contributing to a scientific conference.

Throughout his professional life, Fred Bartter was beset by two conflicting interests. On the one hand he had an intense interest in bone and the behaviour of the parathyroid, and on the other was his interest in sodium metabolism and the control of the plasma volume. The bone dimension was a heavy one if only because Fuller Albright, his mentor at the Harvard Medical School, had, on his death, bequeathed to Fred all his slides pertaining to his studies on bone problems. Fred took this bequest very seriously, possibly more so than Fuller Albright actually intended, because Fred Bartter had a mammoth sense of loyalty which edged into the religious. The need to uphold the Albright cause in bone metabolism consumed an enormous amount of his time. He became a doyen of the field and he made many interesting original contributions to it. He was in much demand as a reviewer and referee but he himself never actually made that contribution which could be regarded as thoroughly original.

By contrast, his activities in the field of sodium metabolism were peppered with new ideas and new data. This was truly his own area and his close friendship with Alexander Leaf and other members of the 'salt and water' club must have been seminal. When the relevant active principle in the so-called 'amorphous fraction' of adrenocortical extracts was identified as aldosterone by Simpson and Tait in London, England, and when the corresponding clinical syndrome had been so vividly described by Conn from Ann Arbor, Michigan, Fred was galvanized to discover the controlling mechanism for aldosterone secretion. Being a clinician he was fully aware that there were conditions, such as cirrhosis of the liver and the nephrotic syndrome, where hyperaldosteronism was likely to be the dominant factor in explaining the intense sodium retention that intermittently characterizes these conditions, yet he was also aware that, in these conditions, there was no increase in the rate of secretion of cortisol. At that time the pituitary was the 'conductor' of the endocrine orchestra so that without an identified pituitary trophic hormone to control aldosterone secretion, it was difficult to identify what the major controlling mechanism was. Naturally various physiologists took up the challenge, in particular James O Davies who also worked at the National Institutes of Health, Bethesda, Maryland. Fred stuck resolutely to his clinical limb and was able to demonstrate, largely by a series of elegant studies in man, that aldosterone secretion was dominated by changes of plasma volume rather than changes of plasma sodium concentration which had been the favoured candidate amongst the physiologists. This contribution, made against heavy odds intellectually, stands out as Fred Bartter's academic zenith. He went on to identify a dwarfed negro boy as having bilateral adrenal hyperplasia due to a massive overstimulation of the renin-angiotensin system, whose importance in the control of aldosterone secretion became increasingly evident at that time, the early 1960s. The concept of over-production of renin from a *primarily* hyperplasic juxta-glomerula apparatus is now entrenched in the appellation 'Bartter's syndrome'. For the past twenty years this concept has been a major stimulus to clinical and experimental research on the renin-aldosterone system. Fred could hardly have wished for a better epitaph. He loved the cut and thrust of academic argument. He was, nonetheless, a real pillar when it came to the validity of scientific data. He would spare nothing to get at the truth. This was so strong as to have the flavour of an almost Christian fervour. Many of this patients will remember, with perhaps a somewhat wry smile, how painstaking and rigorous Bartter's metabolic requirements were. But it is a tribute to his endearing personality and his ability to make his 'subjects' feel their need to contribute to medical science that Fred managed to complete so many longterm and exacting studies so successfully. He was an intensely religious man and it is this quality when applied to the contentious field of scientific endeavour which shines above all. It is a corollary of these qualities that as a person he was exceptionally generous both with his time and his intellect. He had no sense of envy and little sense of the importance of his own time. He had an impish sense of humour, designed to kindly deflate the pompous, to which he gave expression in his love of mushrooms. To identify thoroughly the bad and thoroughly extol the good were perhaps qualities which led him to become an expert mycologist. Janey, his wife, provided enormous and loving support to Fred's self-imposed difficult and lifelong academic assignment. JDHS

[Photo]

BATTEN, Lindsey Willett *b*.16 Nov 1889 *d*.3 Oct 1981
MRCS LRCP (1914) MB BChir Cantab (1921) MRCP (1923)
MRCGP (1952) FRCP (1964) FRCGP (1973)

Lindsey Batten was educated at Blundell's College and Sidney Sussex College, Cambridge. He was born in London, the son of Rayner D Batten MD and his wife Katherine, daughter of Eustace Condor, a congregational minister. He received his medical training at St Bartholomew's Hospital, qualifying in 1914, and held the posts of house physician, medical receiving officer, and clinical assistant in the children's department. He then served as a captain in the RAMC from 1915 to 1919. On demobilization he returned to Bart's and to paediatrics, becoming chief assistant in the department for diseases of children, and was also appointed assistant physician to the East London Hospital for Children. These experiences contributed to his enduring concern for children and their parents, and helped to inspire the successful books *The Single-handed Mother* (1939) and *Health for the Young* (1942).

Lindsey rejected a consultant's career in favour of general practice and became one of its most powerful advocates, at a time when its survival was seriously in question. His advocacy was effective, for he had a skill with language, a love of literature, and a capacity to quote from English, Latin or Greek, uncommon in doctors even in his day. His 1960 James Mackenzie lecture was so successful that the whole audience in the Great Hall at BMA House rose spontaneously from their seats to applaud, as they had never done for any of his predecessors. His knowledge and skill was recognized in 1964 by his election to the fellowship of the College, an award not often given at that time to general practitioners. He became a founder member of the Royal College of General Practitioners and was a member of council from 1955 until his retirement in 1959. He was the first chairman of the library committee and provost of his faculty; he was elected a fellow in 1973.

Continual personal care of the patient was something Lindsey stressed. He was against the idea of group practice: 'single, individual, personal responsibility for patients seems to me to lie at the very heart of practice, as I have known it and understood it. We doctors can, with great advantage, interchange opinions; but the patient, and responsibility for him, we cannot share. If we attempt it, he must be the loser'. These are uncompromising words. He added: 'Between personal, continuing care and even the milder forms of collective responsibility, there is a fundamental, inescapable conflict'.

In 1919 he married Ellen Mary (Mollie), daughter of George Lindsay Turnbull, a general practitioner. They had two sons and three daughters. Lindsey had a great love of music and was a prominent member of the Hampstead Choral Society. On retirement, he went to live at Crockham Hill, Kent, where he and his wife cultivated a large garden with a zest remarkable for their years. Molly was a painter, and Lindsey continued to write and read widely. He also organized small groups of singers at his home, and there were madrigals and motets to compensate for leaving the Hampstead Choral Society which he had helped to run. He was a man of great charm and true culture.

JPH

[*Brit. med. J.*, 1981, **283**, 1181; *Lancet,* 1981, **2**, 999; *Times,* 12 Oct 1981; Photo]

BEATTY, Cyril Carlyle *b.*26 Feb 1888 *d.*6 Apr 1980
MC (1916) MRCS LRCP (1911) MB BS Lond (1920) MRCP (1922) FRCP (1940)

Cyril Beatty was born at Stockton-on-Tees and educated at Barnard Castle and the University of London. He was the son of William John Beatty, also a medical practitioner, and his wife, Alice Letitia Fitzgerald, the daughter of John Scott, a clerk in holy orders. His clinical training was undertaken at the London Hospital where, after qualifying in 1911, he held appointments as house physician, house surgeon, emergency officer, and medical registrar. His studies had been interrupted by the outbreak of the first world war when he joined the RAMC, serving until 1917 and winning the Military Cross. On demobilization, he became clinical assistant at the Hospital for Sick Children, Great Ormond Street. He was later appointed physician to the Royal Northern Hospital, the Evelina Hospital for Children, Chalfont and Gerrard's Cross Hospital, and Wood Green and Southgate Hospital.

Cyril Beatty had very definite ideas on the National Health Service and, on its inauguration, resigned from the staff of the Royal Northern. He married Constance Hermine, daughter of Arthur Vandeleur Despard, in 1919, and they had three sons, two of whom became medical practitioners. This made five generations of doctors in the Beatty family. Cyril listed his hobbies as 'living in the country and philately'. After his retirement he was troubled with increasing deafness. He was a very able physician, courteous to patients and staff, and gifted with charm and a quiet wit. His only fault was that he was too shy and retiring. IGR/GW

[Photo]

BEDFORD, Davis Evan *b*.21 Aug 1898 *d*.24 Jan 1978
CBE (1963) MRCS LRCP (1921) MB BS Lond (1921) MD (1925) FRCP (1931) Hon MD Cairo (1944)

Evan Bedford was born in Boston, Lincolnshire, the son of William and Lilian Bedford. He was educated at Epsom College and the Middlesex Hospital Medical School. He interrupted his medical studies in 1918 to serve as surgeon sub-lieutenant RNVR, and at the end of the war returned to his medical school to qualfy in 1921. At the Middlesex Hospital, he was in turn house physician, casualty medical officer, medical registrar and resident anaesthetist. His appointment as medical officer in charge of the cardiac wards at the Ministry of Pensions Hospital at Orpington, was to fashion his future career as a cardiologist. It was here that he first came under the influence of John (later Sir John) Parkinson, already a recognized authority on heart disease, to mark the beginning of an association which later was to make the names of Parkinson and Bedford one of the best known combinations in the contemporary literature of cardiology.

Evan Bedford spent 1926 in Paris with Charles Laubry, and in Lyons with Louis Gallavardin, the greatest cardiological savants of the day. He was recalled from France to become Paterson Research Scholar at the London Hospital, where he was reunited with Parkinson. Together they studied cardiac infarction, and went on to publish a series of papers on the electrocardiograms in that condition, which soon became internationally acclaimed classics.

In 1926, Bedford was appointed assistant physician to the Middlesex Hospital and in 1933, physician to outpatients at the National Heart Hospital. He served in the Royal Army Medical Corps throughout the second world war, during which he was appointed consulting physician to the Middle East Forces. Brigadier Bedford became known as an efficient if demanding officer among the medical divisions, from Aleppo on the Turkish frontier to the hospitals behind the Eighth Army in Cyprus, Malta, and Khartoum. In December 1943, he was summoned by Lord Moran to attend Winston Churchill, who had developed pneumonia complicated by atrial fibrillation when staying at General Eisenhower's villa at Carthage. 'His presence' Moran wrote at the time, 'will keep the people at home quiet...'. It also provided the Prime Minister with the idea that M&B 693, one of the vehicles of his recovery, should be renamed Moran and Bedford.

The war over, Bedford returned to his hospital duties at the Middlesex and National Heart Hospitals, and to a private practice which soon became the largest and most distinguished in his specialty. In the meantime, cardiac catheterization, angiocardiography, and surgery had ushered in new dimensions to the diagnosis and treatment of valvular and congenital heart disease. The new cardiology brought with it the vocabulary of surgical anatomy with which Bedford was already fluent from his apprenticeship in the postmortem room. He felt a special kinship in the early days of cardiac surgery with Holmes Sellors and Brock, and spent many hours in the operating theatre, spellbound by the sight of the living tissues whose structure had intrigued him for so long. Post-operative discussion about an unusual mitral valve or septal defect would be illuminated by extempore quotations from Rokitansky's *Die Defecte der Scheidewande des Herzens,* Lower's *Tractatus de Corde* or his special favourites, the Irish Victorians, Adams, Stokes and Corrigan.

Bedford was now in his prime, and was acknowledged as an international authority on the new cardiology. National and foreign professional bodies honoured him; he was elected president of the British Cardiac Society and of the European Society of Cardiology, chairman of council of the British Heart Foundation, and vice-president of the International Society of Cardiology. He was consultant in cardiology to the Royal Air Force, the Army, and other public bodies, and editor of the *British Heart Journal.* His fame was recognized abroad by honorary membership of numerous foreign cardiological societies, including French, Swiss, Belgian, Italian, Egyptian, Brazilian, Indian, and Australian. At home, he delivered all the relevant, distinguished named lectures, including the Harveian Oration, Bradshaw, Lumleian, Strickland Goodall, St Cyres, and Carey Coombs lectures. He was appointed CBE in 1963.

In his early days, Bedford was a capable athlete, excelling at cricket, hockey, golf, and billiards. He generated an aura of admiration and affection in a succession of house physicians and registrars, which endured, even thrived on affectations of irascibility and intolerance to noise, hospital administrators, traffic congestion in the streets around the Middlesex, and ever-increasing neurotic ill health in his outpatients.

Bedford's interest in collecting rare books on the heart and circulation began when he was a registrar, evolving through his professional life into a unique and internationally acclaimed library now housed in the Harveian Library of the Royal College of Physicians. He spent the last few years of his life cataloguing his collection, and bibliographers who predicted the outcome to be of a high standard have been proved right. With the publication of the *Catalogue of the Evan Bedford Library of Cardiology,* Bedford considered his contribution to his craft complete. He withdrew unobtrusively from society and died in 1978, appropriately the 400th anniversary of the birth of William Harvey.

In 1935, he married Audrey Selina, daughter of Milton Ely, for many years chairman of the Board of Governors of the National Heart Hospital. They had two sons. WS

[*Brit. med. J.*, 1978, **1**, 308, 515; *Lancet*, 1978, **1**, 288; *Times*, 28 Jan 1978; *Brit. Heart J.*, 1978, **40**; Photo]

BEDSON, Henry Samuel *b*.29 Sept 1929 *d*:6 Sept 1978
MB BS Lond (1952) MRCP (1958) MD (1964) FRCP (1978)

Henry Bedson was the second son of Sir Sam Bedson FRS, of Hove, who had been professor of bacteriology at the London Hospital. His paternal grandfather, Peter Philips Bedson, was professor of chemistry at Newcastle. Bedson's mother was Dorothea Annie Hoffert PhD, who worked on aeroplane dopes and subsequently did research on oils and fats at the Lister Institute. His maternal grandfather was Henry Hoffert, a senior inspector of schools. Bedson was educated at Brighton, Hove and Sussex Grammar School, and entered the London Medical College where he was awarded the Charrington prize for anatomical dissection, and received honorary certificates of distinction in the 2nd MB examination, and the clinical surgery prize examinations. He qualified in 1952.

Bedson became house physician to Bomford and Heson, and house surgeon to Perry and Tresidder. In 1953 he became house officer in morbid anatomy and in clinical pathology, and in 1954 junior registrar in pathology. He joined the RAMC in 1955 and served in Hong Kong until July 1957. During this period he became a junior specialist in pathology, working in a small military hospital; he was also part-time demonstrator in morbid anatomy at the University of Hong Kong. 1957 saw him back again at the London Hospital as first assistant to the medical professorial unit. He received his MRCP in the following year and was elected FRCP in 1978.

In 1958 he embarked on his virological career and was appointed John W Garrett research fellow in the department of bacteriology at the University of Liverpool. In 1959 he became assistant lecturer, and after one year was appointed a full lecturer. In 1964 he moved to the department of virology, University of Birmingham, being appointed senior lecturer and honorary NHS consultant in bacteriology and virology. He became reader in virology in 1969, and in 1976 professor and head of the reconstituted department of medical microbiology. He was in that post at the time of his death.

Bedson developed an interest in poxviruses while he was in AW Downie's department in Liverpool. At that time smallpox was still an important disease in many parts of the world and, together with KR Dumbell, Bedson examined the effects of temperature on the growth of poxviruses. This led to the introduction of discriminating but robust tests for distinguishing various poxviruses, particularly between *variola major* and *minor*. There followed an analysis of the phenotypic characters of variola by the use of recombinant viruses in the rabbit. For this work Bedson was awarded the MD degree in 1964.

At Birmingham Bedson continued his work with poxviruses, driving his investigation to a far deeper level and obtaining biochemical explanations for the properties of some poxviruses. As the WHO eradication programme became effective the problems to be solved changed too. By 1977 natural smallpox appeared extinct, but newly discovered viruses had been isolated from rodents which are indistinguishable from *variola major* in the laboratory. Bedson's final work was the investigation of these strains, and it forms a most important contribution to the smallpox eradication scheme and the science of virology. Bedson was a member of the International Commission for the assessment of smallpox eradication in Pakistan and Afghanistan in 1976, and of the WHO informal group on monkeypox and related viruses.

His special interest led indirectly to the tragic end of his life. A fatal case of smallpox occurred in a person who worked in another part of the same building in Birmingham. Journalists launched a relentless effort to fix the blame on him and his staff for a breach of technique, and union officials stirred up public fears by confusing the issues with those then arising from genetic manipulation. Harassed as the chosen 'villain' of the tragedy, Henry Bedson's normally stable personality broke down and he took his own life. It could be said that he was a victim of his own dedicated conscientiousness, and of his extreme sense of responsibility.

Henry Bedson was a medical academic with the highest standards. He had a fine analytical mind and was a useful editorial board member of the *Journal of General Virology*. He took his teaching very seriously and his work was always thoroughly organized. He was a quiet man with a taste for trout fishing (at which he excelled) and cricket.

In 1961 Bedson married Ann Patricia, daughter of Eric James Ducker of Bramhope, near Otley, Yorkshire. They had three children; a son and two daughters. PW/GW

[*Brit. med. J.*, 1978, **2**, 840, 904; *Lancet*, 1978, **2**, 641, 799; *Times*, 1 Sept 1978]

BELL, Julia *b.*28 Jan 1879 *d.*26 Apr 1979
MA Dubl (1901) MRCS LRCP (1920) MRCP (1926) FRCP (1938)

Julia Bell died peacefully shortly after her 100th birthday. She was one of the pioneers of human genetics and worked at University College, London, throughout her professional life.

She was educated at Nottingham Girls' High School and Girton College, Cambridge, where she read mathematics. At that time a Cambridge degree was not open to women, and on the basis of postgraduate research at Cambridge on solar parallax she was awarded an MA by Trinity College, Dublin. From 1908 to 1914 she worked as Karl Pearson's statistical assistant at University College, London. Pearson had become aware of a lack of medical expertise in the Galton Laboratory and persuaded her to take a medical degree. She studied medicine at the London School of Medicine for Women, at the Royal Free Hospital, and qualified with the conjoint diploma in 1920. In 1926 she was made Galton research fellow under the Medical Research Council. She was elected FRCP in 1938, and won the Weldon medal and prize of Oxford University in 1941 for her contribution to biometric science.

Applied statistics and medicine formed the basis of the work for which she became famous: the collections of human pedigrees published under the general title of *Treasury of Human Inheritance*. This was the first systematic attempt to document the distribution of human disease within families, and so anxious was Karl Pearson that these pedigrees should be most scrupulously recorded that in his 1912 preface he promised that the *Treasury*... would contain 'no reference to theoretical opinions'. In Julia Bell he found a fellow perfectionist with regard to the data, but by the 1920s a few mild opinions were obviously becoming acceptable. Subsequently, Julia Bell wrote analytical articles which are among the classical papers on the subject. Perhaps the most notable are her 1940 paper on consanguinity rates and her 1937 paper, with JBS Haldane, on the linkage between the genes for colour-blindness and haemophilia. This was the first demonstration 'that the principles of linkage which have been worked out for other animals also hold good for man'. At the age of 80 she contributed an original article to the *BMJ* on rubella in pregnancy.

She was on the staff of the Galton Laboratory until her official retirement after the age of 86. Although never Galton professor of human genetics herself, she outlived the first three, Pearson, Fisher and Penrose, and in her 90s was still sufficiently concerned with the Laboratory to remonstrate with the Galton professor when she felt it to be necessary. She was a supporter of the Women's Suffrage Movement, but never a militant. She was something rarer; one of the first generation of women to engage in professional scientific research and to do it supremely well. She never married, but enjoyed the affection of nephews, nieces and many friends. EBR/GW

[*Brit. med. J.*, 1979, **1**, 1289; *Lancet*, 1979, **1**, 1152; *Nature*, 1979, **281**, 163; *Times*, 19 Nov 1979; *Daily Telegraph*, 2 May 1979; Photo]

BENNET, *Maj. Gen.* **John** *b*.12 Feb 1893 *d*.4 Mar 1976
MB ChB Edin (1916) DPM (1926) MD (1935) MRCP (1937)
DTM&H (1938) FRCP (1948)

John Bennet was born at Ratho, Midlothian, in 1893 and was educated at George Heriot's School. He received his medical education at Edinburgh University, graduating with honours in 1916.

In the same year he was mobilized into the RAMC and was immediately posted to Salonika as regimental medical officer to the 1/3 City of London Yeomanry. With this cavalry unit he subsequently went to Egypt, and took part in Allenby's advance through Palestine into Syria. Following the cessation of hostilities he remained in the Middle East, and from there applied for and was granted a regular commission.

In the years between the two world wars his career was typical of that of medical officers primarily interested in clinical medicine, as opposed to administration. He was at first employed in the Military Hospital, Aleppo and then spent two years in India. Returning to the United Kingdom in 1924 he was stationed at the Royal Herbert Hospital, Woolwich, where he studied psychiatry, taking the DPM, and where he also married a QARNC sister, Margaret Turner. After a few months in China he returned to the Royal Army Medical College and the Queen Alexandra Military Hospital, Millbank, where he qualified with distinction as a medical specialist (the equivalent of a modern registrar). Then followed six years in India during which he was successively medical specialist to the military hospitals at Lucknow, Raniket and Meerut, where he gained considerable clinical experience which proved its worth when he returned to Millbank and obtained the MD (Edinburgh), MRCP (London) and DTM&H.

In 1938 he returned to the East, this time as physician to the large military hospital in Singapore, and three years later became consultant physician to the Malayan Command with the rank of colonel. In 1942 when Singapore was overrun by the Japanese he was made prisoner, and spent three years in captivity, mostly in Taiwan, before eventually being released by the allied forces in Manchuria. For his services to his fellow prisoners he was mentioned in despatches.

After a short period for recuperation, during which he commanded a military hospital in his native Scotland, he was appointed director of medicine and consultant physician to the Army, at first as a brigadier and later as major general. At this time he was also elected FRCP.

He retired from the Army in 1951 at the age of 58. He returned to Scotland and for eight years was medical superintendent of the East Fife Hospital Group of hospitals. There he was actively concerned with the development of the Victoria Hospital, Kirkcaldy, and in the inauguration of a wide variety of new services in the hospitals under his control. He retired finally at the age of 65 and died in Edinburgh in 1976 aged 83 years. He was survived by his wife and two sons.

Bennet was small in stature and always looked younger than his years. He was a quiet, reserved, rather self-effacing man, but this gentleness of disposition rose rather from quiet self-confidence than from any weakness of character, as certain administrative authorities found to their discomfiture. He was a shrewd physician with a wide knowledge of tropical medicine and this, with his personal qualities, earned him wide respect and affection within the Service. He bore good times and bad with equal composure. WO'B

[*Brit. med. J.*, 1976, **1**, 1022; Photo]

BERRIDGE, Francis Richard *b.*21 Dec 1910 *d.*19 Apr 1978
BA Cantab (1931) MRCS LRCP (1934) BChir (1936)
DMR Lond (1936) MB (1937) MA (1938) FFR (1951) MRCP (1961)
FRCP (1968) Hon FFRI (1974)

Francis Berridge was born in London, the second son of Richard

Berridge (1870–1941), landowner, of Ballynahinch Castle, Co. Galway, where he spent much of his youth. His mother was Mary Eulalia, daughter of Robert Whitman Lesley, an engineer, lawyer and business man of Haverford, Penn., USA. His paternal grandfather, Richard Berridge (1808–1887) of Ballynahinch Castle, donated £46 000 to the Lister Foundation of Preventive Medicine in Chelsea and Elstree.

He was educated at Downside School, and his deafness started at about that time. From 1928 to 1931, he was at Trinity College Cambridge. He then entered St George's Hospital Medical School, London, with the Anne Selina Fernee Exhibition in anatomy and physiology. He qualified with the conjoint diploma in 1934. From January 1935 to June 1936, he studied in the radiological department of St George's Hospital with the post of clinical assistant. During the last year of this appointment he also studied at the Royal Cancer Hospital, London. In 1936, he obtained the diploma in medical radiology of the University of London, being awarded a mark of distinction. From June 1936 to September 1938, he was resident radiologist at Oldchurch Hospital, Romford, working with GR Mather Cordiner. It was there that he gained remarkable experience in the radiology of the gastro-intestinal tract.

The regius professor of physics in Cambridge, John A Ryle, invited him to join his team in October 1938, as assistant in research in radiology. When war came in 1939, Berridge volunteered for all the medical services of the armed forces, but was medically unfit. During the war he worked as specialist-radiologist in the Emergency Medical Service at Addenbrooke's Hospital and White Lodge Emergency Hospital, Newmarket; which later became Newmarket General Hospital. His association with these hospitals continued until he retired. Despite difficulties he started a high standard of radiology. After the war, he worked with RA McCance and Elsie M Widdowson in an MRC Unit in Germany; his chapter on 'Radiological observations on the alimentary tract' in the MRC Special Report (No. 275) on *Studies of Undernutrition, Wuppertal,* 1946–1949, is a classic.

In 1948 he was appointed associate lecturer in radiology in the University of Cambridge, and in 1951 was elected FFR. From 1956 to 1961 he was honorary medical editor of the *British Journal of Radiology*. In 1963 he was awarded the Barclay medal of the British Institute of Radiology. He was particularly gratified by his election in 1974 as honorary fellow, Faculty of Radiologists, Royal College of Surgeons in Ireland.

Francis Berridge was a diagnostic radiologist of great clinical ability and distinction. He was very interested in teaching, and his patients loved him. He was modest and sensitive, and kind and gentle. The planning of the X-ray department at the new Addenbrooke's Hospital, Hills Road, Cambridge showed his considerable administrative and organizing ability.

Outside his work he was equally enthusiastic. His hobbies were ski mountaineering, sailing, fishing and shooting. After he retired, he went to live at Wells-next-the-Sea in Norfolk, and worked part-time as radiologist at Cromer and District Hospital.

He was fortunate in his happy home life. He married Margaret Virginia Daw, who was a radiographer, on 6 July 1940; her father was Samuel Wilfred Peter Daw, an ENT surgeon. They had one son and three daughters. JSM(2)

[*Brit. med. J.*, 1978, **1**, 1558; *Lancet*, 1978, **1**, 1372; *Clinical Radiology*, **30**, No 3, 360; Photo]

BEST, Charles Herbert *b*.27 Feb 1899 *d*.30 Mar 1978
CC (1967) CH (1971) CBE (1944) BA Toronto (1921) MA (1922)
MD (1925) DSc Lond (1928) FRCP Canada (1931)
FRS Canada (1931) FRS (1938) FRCPE (1953) FRCP* (1961)†

Charles Herbert Best became one of the most distinguished of Canadian international figures and one of the most widely and favourably known of Canadian scientists. He was revered by diabetics throughout the world and spent much of his life working for their good.

Born of Canadian parents at West Pembroke, Maine, he spent the early part of his life in that region of the United States, near the New Brunswick border. His father, Herbert Huestis Best, also a physician, started his medical training at Dalhousie University in Nova Scotia and finished it in New York; after graduation, he took a locum tenens in Maine, thinking it would be a temporary position, but he stayed and did exemplary medical practice in that area for the next 45 years. His wife, Charles Best's mother, Luella Fisher, came also from King's County, Nova Scotia. These Nova Scotian roots went far back to William Best and John Burbidge who in 1749 travelled from the Isle of Wight with Cornwallis to help found Halifax, Nova Scotia. They joined in building St Paul's Church in Halifax, the first Protestant church in Canada, and assisted in the laying out of the public gardens as well as sitting in the first legislative assembly in 1758.

When Charles Best was sixteen he went to Toronto, Canada, to prepare for his university entrance examinations. Soon after entering University he volunteered for military service and went overseas with the Canadian Army as a sergeant in the 70th Horse Artillery.

After the war, he took up his studies again at the University of Toronto, transferring from a general Arts course to the more specialized course in physiology and biochemistry. In the fifth and final year of that course he studied advanced biochemical procedures and physiological techniques and was appointed a fellow in physiology in 1920. During that year he met Fredrick Grant Banting and became interested in his ideas concerning the pancreas and diabetes. On May 17, 1921, one day after his final examinations were finished, he started to work with Banting on the experiments which culminated in the discovery of insulin. By November of that year they had 75 positive results, providing good evidence for an internal secretion of the pancreas, and on January 11, 1922, the first insulin was given successfully to a 14 year old diabetic at the Toronto General Hospital. During that year a series of papers was published by the Toronto group, which showed that the metabolic disorders of animals made diabetic by removal of the pancreas could be alleviated by their pancreatic extracts.

The improvement in insulin production developed by JB Collip was incorporated, but the large scale production of insulin required for clinical use brought many problems. Charles Best was made director of the insulin division of Connaught Laboratories, while at the same time continuing his course in medicine. With the cooperation of scientists from the Eli Lilly Company and others, methods for insulin production and purification were developed on a scale satisfactory for clinical use.

In 1925, following graduation in medicine, Charles Best went to Europe for postgraduate work. He spent a good part of that time in London in the laboratory of Sir Henry Dale, where he studied the actions of choline and histamine as well as the actions of insulin. He became interested in the disappearance of histamine under the action of a heat-labile agent, which at the time was called histaminase. Subsequently it was shown by others that histamine catabolism proceeded along several pathways and could result from the action of more than one enzyme.

Completing his degree work in London, he returned to Toronto and became head of the department of physiological hygiene in 1927. In 1929 he succeeded JJR MacLeod as professor and head of the department of physiology in the University of Toronto. In 1941, after the tragic death of Sir Frederick Banting, Best became head of the Banting and Best Department of Medical Research, giving up his position in physiological hygiene.

In their experiments, Banting and Best produced diabetes in animals by removal of the pancreas. They found that the administration of insulin could keep such animals alive, but subsequently it was discovered that when such animals were kept alive for long periods of time, signs of liver damage developed unless raw pancreas was added to the diet. It was reported by Hershey and Soskin that some component of crude lecithin could substitute for beef pancreas. This procedure took a long time and hence investigation was slow. A means of producing fatty livers in rats by using a high-fat low-protein diet was developed by Best, Hershey and Huntsman and the studies were accelerated. They found that the effect of crude lecithin was not due to impurities, and soon identified choline as the active constituent. There followed extensive work on the investigation of dietary choline and other lipotropic agents.

Charles Best recognized the need for a purer and more active anticoagulant, and organized a team to find sources and methods of purification of heparin (an anticoagulant discovered earlier by McLean and Howell). Heparin was successfully purified by his colleagues Arthur Charles and DA Scott and many experiments on the effects of this purified heparin on thrombosis were carried out in association with TS Perrett, LB Jaques, Gordon Murray and others.

With the availability of a purified potent anticoagulant, it became possible to do various procedures such as exchange transfusions, and to attempt the use of artificial kidneys and artificial hearts. Later it became important in the development of cardiovascular surgery.

When the second world war broke out, interest centred first on the effects of injury and blood loss, and one of the projects initiated was the preparation of dried human serum. A blood donor system was developed which ultimately provided over two million contributions of blood serum for the prevention and treatment of shock secondary to injury. With the cooperation of the Canadian Red Cross Society the blood donor project was extended across the country.

Once the blood serum project was established, Best joined the Royal Canadian Navy as director of the Royal Canadian Naval Medical Research Unit, achieving the rank of surgeon captain. Here he directed his energies and those of his colleagues to problems related to the war effort, including shock secondary to injury, motion sickness, protective clothing, immersion foot, nutrition, life-saving equipment, and auditory and visual problems. In connection with the latter, red lighting in naval units was important. The stimulus for the work on this problem and some of the basic information was provided by AV Hill. Best's associate in the investigation was DY Solandt. This red lighting preserved night vision, a factor of importance in actions at night. It was subsequently used by all branches of the service and by the United States and Great Britain as well.

After Charles Best had taken over the responsibilities of the Banting and Best Department of Medical Research, following Banting's death, CC Lucas of that department and Phillip Greey of the department of bacteriology, set up a pilot plant for the production of penicillin. This was transferred later to the Connaught Laboratories, where large scale production was continued.

When the war was over, Best returned to studies on insulin, heparin and choline. The choline studies were reviewed in his Croonian Lecture of 1955. The pathological changes resulting from choline deficiency and the effects of choline deficiency in early life were investigated in association with WS Hartroft.

Studies on pituitary factors were carried out with James Campbell, and on metaglucagon diabetes with John Logothetopoulos. Reports on these and other studies are included in a volume *The Selected Papers of Charles H Best,* published in 1963 by the University of Toronto Press. The 61 papers it contains give a good indication of the variety of his interests.

In 1953, the Charles H Best Institute, built in his honour, was opened by Sir Henry Dale. This Institute housed the department of physiology and part of the Banting and Best Department of Medical Research. Later, when the Medical Sciences Building was built at the University of Toronto, the department of physiology moved to the new building and the remainder of the Banting and Best Department of Medical Research moved into the Best Institute.

In collaboration with NB Taylor, Best wrote several textbooks of physiology, the best known being *The Physiological Basis of Medical*

Practice, a most successful and popular text, first published in 1937. The other texts were *The Living Body,* an intermediate textbook and *The Human Body*, an introductory textbook of physiology. He was the author of many scientific papers and addresses and was a member of numerous commissions, committees and councils. He was a member of diabetic associations, medical and physiological societies in many different countries and was honorary president of the Canadian Diabetic Association, the British Diabetic Association, the American Diabetes Association and the International Diabetes Federation. Throughout his life he was interested in people, and especially in diabetics, and worked to promote their welfare. He received awards from all over the world and many civilian and military honours were bestowed on him by national and regional governments, cities and societies. In 1955 he was elected to the Pontifical Academy of Sciences, the first Canadian to receive this honour.

In 1924 Charles Best married Margaret Hooper Mahon, daughter of Alexander Wylie Mahon, BD, and Flora Cameron Macleod Mahon. Margaret was a strength and inspiration for him throughout his life. He had two sons, Charles Alexander Best, who died shortly before his own death, and Henry Bruce Macleod Best, who became president of Laurentian University at Sudbury, Ontario.

Charles Best – Charley, as he was known to his many friends – will be remembered as the co-discoverer of insulin and as an inspiring champion of diabetics around the world. He was a very popular speaker, greatly in demand, and did not spare himself in their cause. As a scientist he made major contributions, but he generously helped others, especially young scientists, to make their contributions too, encouraging them and inspiring them in their work. It was an honour and a great privilege to have known and worked with him.

REH

[*Brit. med. J.,* 1978, **1**, 927; *Lancet,* 1978, **1**, 835; *Canad. med. Ass. J.,* **118**, 1167-8; *Biogr. Mem. roy. Soc.,* 1982, **28**, 1-25; Photo]

BETT, David Charles Gore *b*.8 May 1921 *d*.5 Feb 1977
VRD (1966) BM BCh Oxon (1945) MRCP (1954) FRCP (1976)

David Bett was born at Palmerston North in New Zealand. Both his parents were second generation New Zealanders and each was one of eight children. David himself, however, was an only child. His father, Douglas Home Bett, was a surgeon who practised in New Zealand. His mother, Olive, was the daughter of Richard Gore. When David was aged about 14 his father retired from practice and came with the family to live in Jersey, in the Channel Islands. David was sent to school in Sherborne, Dorset, and in 1939 he entered Exeter College, Oxford. At this time the war caught up on him and the family, but they managed to escape from Jersey before the German invasion. From Oxford he went to Westminster Hospital for his clinical training and after qualification became casualty officer at Westminster Hospital. In 1946 he took a three year short service commission in the RNVR and this was later extended to six years. Most of his naval service was spent on naval airfields but he was also involved in stopping illegal immigrants from Europe entering Israel. He reached the rank of lieutenant commander.

It was not until after he left the Navy that he decided to specialize in dermatology. He obtained the MRCP in 1954 and then went to Edgware General Hospital as a houseman to refresh his mind and bring him up to date with hospital medicine. He was better qualified than most of the registrars at the time. Later he became registrar at St John's Hospital for Diseases of the Skin and senior registrar to Charing Cross Hospital. He was the first person to undertake a regular dermabrasion session at St John's.

As a consultant in the NHS he practised at Bromley and Farnborough (Kent), Sidcup and St Stephen's Hospital, Fulham. With the reorganization of the health service St Stephen's became part of the Kensington and Chelsea and Westminster Area Health Authority (Teaching) and so he became a member of the Westminster teaching staff. His busy practice left little time for research, but he published a few papers in medical journals, including one on dermabrasion and one on sugar consumption in acne and seborrhoeic dermatitis.

As an individual David was self-effacing, tending to underestimate his ability. He was conscientious and friendly and very well liked by his patients and colleagues.

David's chief interest outside medicine was the theatre. He took part in amateur dramatics before his marriage, and he also tried his hand at writing plays and short stories. He hoped that on his retirement he would be able to move back to the Channel Islands and take up writing more seriously. Unfortunately this was not to be. His other interest was the great outdoors, and the family had regular camping holidays in France. It was within a few minutes of returning home from a ski-ing holiday that he had his fatal coronary.

Whilst at Edgware General Hospital he met and married Rosemary Hall, an occupational therapist. Rosemary's father was Norman Ball, who practised as a general practitioner in Greenwich until his death in a car accident in 1936. There were many other doctors on both sides of her family and she is a cousin of Sir Edward Pochin FRCP. They had two sons and a daughter. PDS

[*Lancet,* 1977, **1**, 612; Photo]

BHAGAT, Maneck *b.*16 May 1917 *d.*17 June 1982
BSc Bombay (1935) MB BS (1940) MD (1943) MRCP (1945) FRCP (1970)

The untimely death of Maneck Bhagat, at the age of 65, when he was still active in his professional work, left a void in the field of paediatrics in Bombay.

He was born into a middle class Parsi family in 1917. During an unremarkable school career he revealed traits of character which were to stand him in good stead all his life. Although not financially obliged to do so, he insisted on paying his own way through medical college by teaching music.

He had a passionate love for western classical music, which, at one time, he wanted to make his life's work. This was no mere hobby – he displayed real talent at the piano, which earned him the fellowship of Trinity College London at the early age of 17; and later the BMus degree of the same institution.

During the second world war, when a visiting pianist was unable to come for a concert, Maneck was asked if he would prepare the Grieg piano concerto in the short space of two weeks. He readily accepted the challenge, studying the music while travelling to hospital every day by tramcar. He gave an accomplished performance, without using the score. He performed frequently over All India Radio, gave concerts, and taught music even when active in paediatric practice. His efforts at teaching music were amply rewarded when a charming pupil became his wife, and gave him the support and understanding so essential to his career.

Bhagat's medical education was at the KEM Hospital, where he graduated, and later obtained his doctorate. He was one of the few doctors to obtain the MRCP (London) on the single occasion that the examination was held in Poona during the war (1945).

He was influenced to adopt paediatrics as a career by Dr. Coelho, who had virtually founded the specialty in Bombay. Appointed paediatrician to the Wadia Hospital and later to the teaching staff of his *alma mater*, he set up the department of paediatrics at the KEM Hospital. His diligence led to his election as president of the Association of Paediatricians of India in 1960, and fellowship of the Royal College of Physicians in 1970. Visiting professorships followed, and when he retired, he was appointed emeritus professor of paediatrics at the GS Medical College and KEM Hospital. His colleagues instituted a gold medal in his name, to be awarded to the best candidate who passed the MD degree in paediatrics.

Maneck Bhagat was a man of determination, discipline, and integrity; traits all too rare in the *laissez-faire* environment of flexible morals that obtain today. His outspoken attitude was sometimes misunderstood. He never pandered to cheap popularity at the expense of compromising his convictions.

In his private practice he displayed a rare compassion for his patients. Many a time, even early in his practice, rather than take his fee, he would unobtrusively pay the mother, so that his baby-patient could obtain better nourishment.

Another facet of Bhagat's personality was a subtle sense of humour. He would make the most outrageously funny remarks with a perfect poker face, which often left his not-too-bright listeners guessing.

Photography was another of his interests. He delighted in making his own slides, and produced an excellent movie film on the examination of the new born baby.

Maneck Bhagat will be remembered as an accomplished musician, paediatrician, and a man of discipline and integrity. **JSM(3)**

[Photo]

BHATIA, *Maj. Gen.* **Sohan Lal** *b.*5 Aug 1891 *d.*16 July 1981
CIE (1945) MB BChir Cantab (1917) MC (1918) MA (1919)
MD (1923) MRCP (1927) FRSE (1932) FRCP (1936)
Hon FAMSI (1961)

Sohan Lal Bhatia was born at Amritsar, India, the eldest son of Rai Bajadur Hiralal Bhatia, who was an eminent surgeon at Lahore. He was educated at the Central Model School, Lahore, and the Government College (Punjab University), coming to England in 1910 to enter Peterhouse College, Cambridge, where he began his medical studies. He pursued his clinical studies at St Thomas's Hospital, London, but these were interrupted by the advent of the first world war, when Sohan Lal volunteered as a surgical dresser on the hospital ship *Guildford Castle*. On graduation in 1917, he returned to India to join the Indian Medical Service. In May 1918 he was posted to the 105th Maharatta Light Infantry (Egyptian Expeditionary Force), serving in Palestine and Syria. He was awarded the MC in 1918 for personal courage and outstanding service.

During his studies at Cambridge, Sohan Lal came into contact with AV Hill, who encouraged him to specialise in physiology, and after the war he was transferred to the civil department of the IMS, being appointed professor of physiology and hygiene at Grant Medical College, Bombay, which was then reckoned to be the best medical college east of Suez. He was appointed dean of the College in 1924, being the first Indian to occupy this post, and in 1937 he became principal of the College and superintendent of the JJ Group of hospitals. He held these posts until 1941, serving the College for a total of 21 years. During his administration, he increased the number of hospital beds, strengthened the teaching departments and improved conditions for student welfare. He was an able administrator and an excellent teacher.

At the outbreak of the second world war his proved excellence in administration, and his personal contacts with Indian Universities, made him the obvious choice for the post of deputy director-general of the IMS, which he held from 1941 to 1945. While serving on the Bhor Committee he played a key role in the formation of the All India Institute of Medical Sciences, and was a member of the Scientific Mission which visited the USA, Canada and the United Kingdom. From 1945 to 1947 he served as inspector-general of civil hospitals and prisons in Assam, re-establishing the hospitals destroyed during the war, and helping to convert the medical school at Dibrugarh to a medical college. From 1947 to 1950 he held the post of surgeon-general to the Government of Madras.

Although he retired from the IMS, with the rank of major-general, in 1950, Sohan Lal never retired from work. In the same year, the Government of Hyderabad appointed him inspector-general of medical and health services and secretary of the medical department, where his administrative experience proved invaluable. In 1953 he chaired the pharmaceutical enquiry committee, Government of India, whose detailed report made several important recommendations for the manufacture and control of drugs in India. In 1954, the Karnataka State Government appointed him to report on improvements which could be made to the medical and health services in the State, and in medical education, and from 1962 to 1974 he served as chairman of the newly-established State Board of Medical Research.

He was a founder member of the Medical Council of India; a fellow and former president of the Indian Academy of Sciences; a member and former president of the physiology section of the Indian Science Congress, a member of the Indian Medical Association and a member of the Physiological Society of Great Britain. He attended a conference of the World Medical Association in Rome as a member of the Indian delegation; was elected a fellow of the College in 1936, and awarded the CIE in 1945 for his service in World War II.

Sohan Lal established postgraduate awards and medals in physiology in several universities and medical colleges, both in India and the United Kingdom, including Cambridge and St Thomas's Hospital. He provided gold medal awards in surgery for postgraduates at the All India Institute of Medical Sciences, New Delhi, in memory of his father. And, as a believer in the interdependence of mind and body, he encouraged students to participate in sport, and awarded shields for excellence.

His charismatic personality combined the best in Eastern and Western cultures. He believed in the synthesis of science and religion for the welfare of mankind, and wrote up his theory in his book *Science and the Humanities* (Bombay, 1962), with a foreword by AV Hill, FRS. The habit of study, and his concern for humanity, made his retirement productive and he developed a special interest in the history of medicine. He spent several years collecting material for his book *A History of Medicine with special reference to the Orient*, which was published by the Medical Council of India in 1977. His other publications include *Greek Medicine in Asia and other essays* (1970) and *Medical Science in Ancient India* (1972). He was a fine educationist and scientist, contributing much to medicine and serving his country well. His wife, Sharyu, who survived him, was also a doctor.

SB/GW/VL

[Photo]

BIGGART, *Sir* **John (Henry)** *b.*17 Nov 1905 *d.*21 May 1979
KBE (1967) CBE (1948) MB BCh BAO Belf (1928) MD (1931)
DSc (1937) MRCP (1952) FRCP (1957) FRCPath (1964)
Hon MD Dublin (1957) Hon FRCGP (1971) Hon LLD Belf (1971)
Hon DSc NUI (1973)

John Henry was born in Templepatrick, Co. Antrim, the elder son of John Henry Biggart, the headmaster of the local national school, in which his mother was also a teacher. From both parents he inherited a great love of learning, and during his school days at the Royal Belfast Academical Institution he was an outstanding student, excellent both in the classics and the sciences. His final choice of a career must have been a difficult one, but he was possessed of great humanity and compassion and no doubt these were the qualities which directed him towards the study of medicine. However, his love of the classics and of English literature remained with him and gave him great pleasure in his moments of leisure in an otherwise extraordinarily busy life.

He entered Queen's Medical School in 1923, with an exhibition and the Sullivan scholarship. He had a brilliant undergraduate career, winning most of the prizes, medals and scholarships. He also participated in all student activities, including sport, being a keen rugby enthusiast, and eventually became president of the Students' Union. After graduating with honours and completing his houseman's year in the Royal Victoria Hospital, Belfast, his career in pathology began. He was appointed assistant lecturer in 1929 in the department of pathology, Queen's University, under A Murray Drennan, and in 1931 his thesis on the eosinophil cell earned him the degree of MD with gold medal. Then followed the award of a Commonwealth Fund fellowship and two years of postgraduate study in the Johns Hopkins Hospital, Baltimore, where his interest in neuropathology developed. On his return from America he was appointed to a lectureship in neuropathology in Edinburgh, under his former chief, Professor Drennan. At this time neuropathology as a discipline had made little progress from the beginning of the century, and John Henry, as he was known to all, applied himself to its study, having access to a wealth of material as research pathologist to the Scottish Asylums' Board. One of his main interests was the hypothalamus and in particular diabetes insipidus, and he made observations at that time which were often speculative, but which have since been confirmed with the more advanced techniques now available. He kept in close touch with general pathology in the University and Royal Infirmary, and indeed always regarded himself as primarily concerned with general pathology, but with a special interest in neuropathology. He was most anxious that the one should not be studied in isolation from the other. He developed many new histopathological techniques, which still remain in use in the study of cell morphology in the brain. At this stage his main achievement was the publication of his book, *Pathology of the Nervous System*, which he modestly described as a student's introduction to the subject, but which has long been valued by neurologists, neuropathologists and pathologists, not only in Britain but throughout the world.

In 1937, at the early age of 31, he was appointed professor of pathology in his old medical school, Queen's University, little thinking that he would become one of its longest serving and most distinguished members of staff. As a teacher he was without equal, to his students his lectures were memorable occasions; pathology became a living subject, always relating disease to the sick patient, to the disturbance of function and to the interpretation of clinical findings. John Henry firmly believed that pathology was the basic clinical science and constituted the true and fundamental approach to clinical medicine. As taught by him it certainly fulfilled this function. He became a father figure to his students, and his birthday was celebrated by them annually with a revue which, though often bawdy, was always humorous, and culminated in a short address from him delivered in biblical or Oslerian style. His students were spellbound as he expounded on his favourite themes, one of which was to impress on them the privilege of their vocation as undergraduates in medicine, the supreme importance of a sympathetic doctor-patient relationship, and the necessity of cultivating not only the science but also the art of medicine.

As a young professor, it soon became evident to the university authorities and to those responsible for the development of the health services in Northern Ireland that not only was John Henry a brilliant pathologist, teacher and research worker, but he was a man of vision, with a unique gift for administration coupled with sound judgement and creative drive. His services were sought by all university and public bodies and it was not long before he became the dominant figure in every aspect of medicine in Ulster. He was appointed dean of the Faculty of Medicine, a post he held from 1943 to 1971. He was responsible for the development of the blood transfusion service, and became its regional director during the war. He played an important role in the evolution of the health service and devised a scheme whereby university medical staff could be employed under a joint appointment system. He was a member of the General Medical Council for 28 years, chairman of the Standing Medical Advisory Committee to the Ministry of Health, Northern Ireland, for six years, chairman of the Northern Ireland Council for Postgraduate Medical Education for eight years, and a member of the Cameron Commission which investigated the causes of political unrest in Northern Ireland. For many years he served on the Senate of the University and finally became pro-chancellor, a post he held till his death in May 1979. He was the recipient of many honours, none of which he consciously sought. He was awarded the CBE in 1948, the KBE in 1967, and several honorary degrees and honorary fellowships from his own and other universities and colleges.

His work on behalf of various charitable organizations was unremitting, and, in different capacities, he was associated with the Homes for the Blind, the Marie Curie Beaconfield Home, the Mental Health Association, the British Empire Cancer Campaign, the Muscular Dystrophy Association and the Multiple Sclerosis Society.

To list Sir John's activities gives only an impression of his enormous capacity for hard work. The value of his contribution to the advancement of medicine in the Province is inestimable. Yet, despite his innumerable commitments, those of us who worked in his department realized that he remained a pathologist at heart, keeping abreast of the literature, maintaining his interest in research, never losing contact with his students, fulfilling the entire lecture programme in pathology, available to his staff on all occasions, and rarely delegating his duties as head of the Institute of Pathology.

All who have written of him since his death have stressed his great love for his profession, his humanity and kindness, his courage and wisdom – a man without equal and whom generations of students will never forget.

As the vice-chancellor declared in his funeral oration, Queen's had lost the greatest contemporary Queensman of them all, Northern Ireland had lost a great citizen, Ulster had lost its greatest doctor and medical educationalist, the Kingdom had lost the doyen of its pathologists, and Ireland had lost a great son.

He died as he would have wished, still in active service at the age of 73, whilst attending a meeting of the General Medical Council in London. He was survived by his wife Isobel, his son Denis, also a pathologist, and daughter Rosemary, a general practitioner in Scotland.

EFMcK

[*Brit. med. J.*, 1969, **1**, 1718; *Lancet*, 1979, **2**, 53]

BIGGINS, Richard Maxwell *b.*15 Oct 1907 *d.*17 Jan 1977
MB BS Melb (1930) MD (1938) MRCP (1939) MRACP (1940) FRACP (1951) FRCP (1967)

Max Biggins was born in Launceston, Tasmania, the son of Montague Herbert Biggins, publican, and his wife May Biggins (née Tynan). He received his early education at Launceston High School after which he attended De La Salle College, Malvern, Victoria, and Melbourne High School. Following graduation from the University of Melbourne in 1930, he had appointments as resident medical officer successively at St Vincent's Hospital, the Children's Hospital, and the Eye and Ear Hospital in Melbourne. Subsequently he entered general practice in Echuca, a country town in Victoria, situated on the river Murray.

In 1938 he married Mary Lilian Harding, the daughter of John Harding, a farmer and grazier. Together they travelled to England in 1938 in order to develop Max's ambition to become a consultant physician. He was admitted to membership of the Royal College of Physicians of London in 1939 and then returned to Australia, securing appointments as honorary physician to outpatients at St Vincent's Hospital, which is a clinical school in the Faculty of Medicine of the University of Melbourne. As was commonly the case in Australia at that time, he also resumed general practice, this time in the Melbourne suburb of Hampton, while he built up a successful practice as a consultant physician in Collins Street, where most of the specialist practitioners had their consulting rooms at that time. In 1942 he joined the Australian Army Medical Corps and served until 1945, attaining the rank of major.

From his earliest days at St Vincent's, Max Biggins excelled as a teacher and found great enjoyment in this vocation, extending beyond his rostered sessions at the hospital to additional tutorials where the students were fascinated by his encyclopaedic knowledge. In 1964 he accepted an appointment as dean of the clinical school at St Vincent's Hospital and in 1966 became an associate dean (clinical) within the Faculty of Medicine.

He was a man of great integrity, noted for his kindly manner in all his conversations with patients, relatives, students and staff. Of all the etimates one heard of him, it was his kindness which was most frequently the subject of comment.

His wife Lilian was a lively, intelligent woman, and their marriage brought great strength and happiness to Max, as did their two children John and Rosemary. Contented at home and in his professional activities, he developed his varied interests with quiet enthusiasm. He was an expert gardener, excelling in the growing of azaleas and camellias, and had a fondness in his garden for English trees. He loved furniture, china and fine music, and gradually acquired a superb collection of original Australian paintings in the traditional style.

When Max was dean of the clinical school at St Vincent's he established a Dean's prize as a personal gift, selecting for the award a student who had not only high academic distinction but who had also revealed those qualities most likely to promise the future development of a generous and conscientious physician. After his death his family ensured that the annual award would be continued by establishing the RM Biggins prize in medicine in final year. JJB

BIRCH, Charles Allan *b*.30 Apr 1903 *d*.20 Sept 1983
MB ChB Liverp (1925) MRCS LRCP (1925) MD (1928)
DPH(1928) MMSA (1929) MRCP (1930) DCH (1935) FRCP (1945)

Allan Birch, son of a Wigan clothing manufacturer, was educated first at the Wesleyan School, and then at Wigan Grammar, from where he won the Sir Francis Sharpe Powell scholarship to the University of Liverpool. There he gained medals in physiology, pathology, and clinical medicine, and qualified with first class honours. After resident posts at the Liverpool Royal Infirmary and the Maternity Hospital, he became senior medical tutor and registrar at the Liverpool Royal Infirmary, and at the same time was elected honorary assistant physician to the Royal Albert Edward Infirmary, Wigan.

In 1932 he was awarded a Dorothy Temple Cross travelling fellowship, and for twelve months studied tuberculosis at Sea View Hospital, Staten Island, New York, and at the Royal Victoria, Montreal. Allan enjoyed taking exams, as his long list of qualifications shows, and while in America he came first out of hundreds in the diploma of the National Board of Medical Examiners of the USA. It was whilst he was in America that he met and married Marjorie Bold, an artist, also there on a fellowship.

Returning to Liverpool, he found that no vacancies in the honorary staff were expected for some years, and since great developments were promised in the Middlesex County Hospital Medical Service, he secured the first appointment of staff physician, attached to the North Middlesex County Hospital. Here at first virtually single-handed, he had to deal with such a wide range of acute illness, that Hamilton Bailey, his friend and teacher, urged him to write a book on emergency medicine; but this had to wait for some years.

On the outbreak of war Allan and two surgical colleagues were seconded to Chase Farm and rapidly transformed the old orphanage buildings into an Emergency Medical Service (Sector 2) Hospital linked with the London Hospital. He wrote later 'Whilst there were excellent dormitories and kitchens there was no equipment, so 50 gallon water tanks were converted into sterilisers, biscuit tins made into dressing drums and cow troughs into bedpan washers. The bakehouse became the dispensary. The hospital was functioning completely 10 weeks after war started, with 600 beds, and after one incident dealt with 350 casualties in the space of three days'. In his spare time he 'dug for victory' in the allotments between the wards and his son remembers helping him turn an occasional anti-aircraft shell on a lathe in the hospital workshop which was given over to the war effort. After succeeding Robert Galloway as medical superintendent, Allan was appointed consultant physician to Chase Farm Hospital at the inception of the NHS.

Allan had an eye for a gap in the publishing field. In 1948 he at last brought out the first edition of his book *Emergencies in Medical Practice* that covered every conceivable situation. It was very well received and gradually gained world wide recognition for the author and his hospital. It was translated into many languages and Allan saw it through to its 10th edition in 1976. Under a new editor it has now fittingly become *Birch's Emergencies in Medical Practice*. His other books *Common Symptoms described for Nurses*, *The House Physician's Handbook* 1st Edition 1955, 5th Edition 1980, and *Medicine in Britain - a guide for Overseas Doctors* were also highly successful.

As a man Allan was shy, gentle and unassuming. He rose early and did all his writing before breakfast. He was not much interested in sport and although he belonged to a golf club he was 'no great shakes'. He was, however, an expert bee keeper, and was president of the local association. He took exercise by cycling to work to 'help his joints' as he suffered from rheumatoid disease for many years. For this his registrars were sometimes privileged to inject a dose of gold. He never complained but confided that the best place for the prescribed corset was the back of the wardrobe. In time the bicycle gave way to a moped, and later still to a small motorbike. He used his car for domiciliary consultations and for holidays. He and his wife were great travellers and went to most countries of the world, often by caravan and always with his Minox camera.

Throughout his subsequent time at Chase Farm Hospital he insisted on being a *general* physician, as in his view, specialization was for teaching hospitals. He was a perfectionist to the end; one of his chiefs had called him a 'hundred per-center'. Challenged by a sceptical HP, he showed that he still enjoyed examinations by passing the ECFMG at age 60! Also at an age when others would have rested on their laurels he learned from Sir Francis Avery Jones how to do gastroscopies, and had his wife paint the mucosal pictures in water colour – until photography became possible.

Allan was a fine teacher and a great clinician who kept abreast of all modern developments. He was wholly committed to the NHS and considered that private practice detracted from the service. But perhaps his greatest attribute was to ensure that commonsense prevailed at the bedside. He felt patients needed to be protected from 'enthusiastic young surgeons'. Despite his eminence he delighted in repeating a patient's overheard remark 'You see that old codger? That's Dr Birch. They bring him round every Thursday on a refreshment course'!

Allan took a fatherly interest in his younger colleagues, and gently suggested a broadening of their activities, acting almost as a talent scout for the various local, regional and national organizations in which he was interested. He was founder member then president of the Middlesex County Medical Society, president of the whole time Consultants Association, chairman of the Enfield and Potters Bar division of the BMA, member of the North East Metropolitan Regional Hospital Board, examiner in medicine for the University of Liverpool, and after retirement member of the Lord Chancellor's Pensions Appeal Tribunal.

On retirement in 1968 he moved first to Hastings where he worked actively as honorary librarian to the Postgraduate Medical Centre and continued to study and write. He published *Names we remember: 56 eponymous medical biographies* and a year before he died *How to Survive your Holiday*. He had plans for rewriting the description of Parkinson's disease from which he suffered for the last 16 years of his life, and he was collecting information for a series of articles on hospitals named after famous people and on the medical history of Hastings.

With sadly increasing disabilities Allan and Marjorie later moved to North Wales to be near their daughter. Perhaps his one disappointment was that neither of his children followed him into medicine, but he was pleased to coach a nephew who is now a teaching hospital consultant surgeon.

For such a mild-natured man one can only wonder at the determination that fired Allan Birch to live his life so fully and to encourage his wife (who also suffered in later years a chronic progressive neurological disorder) to do the same. Clearly they supported each other strongly through their many years of marrige. He is remembered with great affection, respect and admiration. PEM

[*Brit. med. J.*, 1983, **287**, 1312, 1559, 1639; *Lancet,* 1983, **2**, 1095; Photo]

BISHOP, Peter Maxwell Farrow *b.*14 Aug 1904 *d.*19 Jan 1979
BA Oxon (1926) BM BCh (1929) DM (1943) MRCP (1951)
FRCP (1957) FRCOG (1967)
Hon Dip Acad of Med Barcelona (1949)

Peter Bishop was born in Harrogate, Yorkshire, the son of a medical practitioner, Thomas Henry Bishop, and of his wife, Sarah Grace (née Williams), herself the daughter of an iron master. He was educated in Berlin, at Charterhouse, and then at Trinity College, Oxford, from whence he came to Guy's Hospital for his clinical training.

After he qualified in 1929, Peter Bishop was appointed, in turn, to be assistant house surgeon, outpatient officer, and house surgeon at his own hospital, then resident obstetrician to Frank Cook, whose influence later played a considerable part in shaping his career. In 1930 he was appointed demonstrator in the physiology department and also acted as assistant anaesthetist at Guy's, until the post of lecturer in physiological chemistry became available in 1933. By now he was writing and lecturing on the endocrine control of the female sex cycle, and developing what was to be a lifetime interest in gynaecological endocrinology. He became a clinical assistant in the gynaecological department and, in 1936, the first clinical endocrinologist to Guy's Hospital. To this were added other appointments – deputy superintendent from 1938 to 1945, medical officer in charge of the hospital Emergency Medical Service during the war years, endocrinologist at Chelsea Hospital for Women in 1944, senior lecturer in applied physiology and Guy's consultant endocrinologist in 1946, and senior lecturer in the gynaecological aspects of endocrinology at the Postgraduate Medical School at Hammersmith in 1948.

Peter Bishop's main publications included numerous papers on the clinical uses of sex hormones, some early work on corticosteroids, a very lucid and pioneering book on *Gynaecological Endocrinology* and a singlehanded review of *Recent Advances in Endocrinology* (1954). As a stylish and stimulating lecturer, writer and teacher, he influenced an entire generation of undergraduate and postgraduate students throughout the medical world. He was an energetic man but, as Sir Arthur Sims travelling professor in Australia in 1964, he found himself in such demand, both as a lecturer and socially, that it was as much as he could do to maintain the pace. There was no escape from the demands made on him as a lecturer – in Madrid, where he was made an honorary member of the Endocrine Society; in London, where he was Rolleston lecturer of 1965; and in Oxford, where he was Litchfield lecturer. He had the unusual distinction of being elected a fellow of both the Royal College of Physicians and the Royal College of Obstetricians and Gynaecologists, became medical consultant to the Family Planning Association, and was at various times chairman of a number of organizations that were concerned with endocrinology and fertility. Perhaps the appointment which gave him the greatest pleasure, however, was his appointment as master of the Society of Apothecaries in 1967, the year of his retirement.

Peter Bishop's home life was a very happy one. He enjoyed good company and had a ready wit, which was perhaps best brought out in his amateur theatrical productions, as author of three Guy's Hospital residents' plays, and producer of five. In 1937, he married Phyllis, the daughter of a surgeon, Edward Owen Thurston. They had a son and two daughters, who had the rather unusual experience of spending part of World War II in the Warden's House at Guy's, while their father was spending as much time administering the emergency service, or shovelling incendiary bombs off the hospital roof, as he did with his family.

His outside interests never deflected him from the serious purpose of his life, which was to develop hormonal forms of treatment, during a period in which the majority of his colleagues were totally sceptical, both of their value and their potential. Perhaps the breakthrough came in 1938 when, at the request of the Therapeutics Trials Committee of the Medical Research Council, he undertook the first clinical trial of the earliest synthetic oestrogen, diethylstilboestrol, synthesized by EC Dodds and his colleagues in 1938. He became enthusiastic, but his experiences led to the warning that 'we may expect some more surprising effects than nausea and vomiting from the promiscuous use of this compound'. His studies led to a better understanding of gonadal dysgenesis and of menstrual disorders. They also led on to the combined forms of treatment from which the contraceptive pill was eventually developed. His warning about high doses proved timely, after a large number of complications emphasized the importance of controlled dosage. These problems were subsequently overcome through the work of others, but, in a world which is still beset by the problems of population control, his studies had a seminal role in stimulating the development of major areas of continuing research.

MHL

[*Brit. med. J.,* 1979, **1**, 691; *Lancet,* 1979, **1**, 281, 394; *Times,* 19 Nov 1979; *Daily Telegraph,* 20 Jan, 23 Jan 1979; *Nature,* 1979, **278**; *Guy's Hospital Gazette,* **94**, 2289; *Brit. J. Family Planning,* **5**, (1); Photo]

BLANDY, Anthony Charles *b.*25 Jan 1911 *d.*24 Nov 1978
BA Cantab (1932) MRCS LRCP (1935) BChir (1937) MRCP (1948) FRCP (1970)

Anthony Charles Blandy was born in Nottingham and, except for a brief period as surgeon lieutenant commander in the RNVR during the second world war, he served his home county all his life. His father, Wilfred Boothby Blandy, was a general practitioner in Nottingham and his mother, Ethel, was the daughter of a publisher, Charles William Redin. Anthony was educated at Grosvenor School, Nottingham, and Wellington College. From Wellington, he went up to Christ's College, Cambridge, and undertook his clinical training at the London Hospital.

After several house posts at the London, he joined the RNVR in May 1940, and served throughout the war. On demobilization, he returned to the London Hospital as supernumerary registrar in the children's department. As early as 1939, while a house physician in the children's department at the London, he had become especially interested in paediatrics, and in 1950 he returned to Nottingham to take up an appointment as consultant paediatrician to Nottingham Children's, Mansfield General, and Newark Hospitals. He was also appointed consultant paediatrician to Notts County Infant Welfare and School Services.

From 1958 to 1964, Blandy served on the management committee of Mansfield Hospital, and on the management committee of the Nottingham No 2 Hospital from 1965 to 1970. He was president of the Nottingham Division of the BMA in 1966, a member of council from 1965 to 1970, and a member of council, Nottingham Medical Chirurgical Society, from 1960 to 1965.

He married Catherine Annie, daughter of John Watson Brown, a colliery sales manager, in 1940, and they had two children; a son and a daughter. Anthony Blandy had few interests outside his work and his family, and he devoted much of his spare time to serving the Mansfield Hospital, and Notts Children's Hospital, in an administrative and teaching capacity; he was clinical tutor at the latter for some five years. GW/VL

[Photo]

BOLTON, John Richard *b*.30 Oct 1913 *d*.25 Dec 1977
MBE (1944) MB BChir Cantab (1939) MRCP (1945) MD (1947) FRCP (1959)

John Richard Bolton was very much a West Country man. He was born at Plymouth, the son of George Howe Bolton, a company secretary, and May, daughter of Richard Curtin McCarthy. He was educated at first at Plymouth Grammar School, from where he won a scholarship to Blundell's School. Here he showed great distinction, leaving as a scholar for Trinity College, Cambridge, where he read mathematics for two years and then changed to medicine.

He made his clinical studies at the London Hospital, where he qualified at the outbreak of the second world war. Before he joined the RAMC he held a house physician's appointment at Poplar Hospital. His Army service was primarily in Malta during the siege, and for great devotion to duty he was appointed MBE in 1944. He later served in Italy in the rank of major and became a full medical specialist, having progressed to membership of the College.

He returned to the London Hospital on demobilization and worked for a short period in the receiving room before becoming first registrar to the professorial unit and then, in 1948, assistant director of the unit to Clifford Wilson. He worked on problems of hypertension and diabetes and a great future at his old hospital seemed assured, yet he yearned to return to his native West Country. In 1952 he was appointed as physician to the Bath Clinical Area, where he undertook the establishment of a geriatric department.

For 25 years he devoted himself to a life's work at St Martin's Hospital, Bath, and in return he earned the devotion and unstinting personal respect of everyone with whom he came in contact. He was personally and clinically wise, and part of his great charm came from the humility and gentleness with which he worked. He was never heard to speak harshly of anyone but, nevertheless, even if his points of view were unpopular, he never deviated from his rigid principles of upright conduct. He was a popular teacher, with great clarity of exposition, and he had a large following of juniors who flocked to work with him and who learnt to emulate his careful and thorough bedside approach, and to appreciate his quizzical sense of humour. John Bolton retired early to his Cornwall home at Padstow where he was set to enjoy his painting, sailing and bird watching, but this was all cut short by a tragic accident at sea. He left a widow, Elsie, and three sons, two of whom are doctors. DWP

[*Brit. med. J.*, 1978, **1**, 116; Photo]

BOMFORD, Richard Raymond *b.*15 May 1907 *d.*30 Jan 1981
CBE (1964) BA Oxon (1928) BM BCh (1931) MRCP (1935)
MD (1938) FRCP (1942) MA Oxon (1963)

Richard Bomford was born near Evesham. His family had long farmed in Worcestershire and his father and brothers were well known in agricultural circles. He was educated at Bromsgrove School and Wadham College, Oxford. He went to the London Hospital in 1928, winning prizes in medicine and obstetrics before qualifying in 1931. After two years of house appointments and one in the Institute of Pathology at the London, he spent a year as Sir Halley Stewart research fellow before spending two years as medical first assistant. There followed a Rockefeller travelling fellowship spent at the Rockefeller Hospital for Medical Research in New York City before appointment as physician to the London Hospital in 1938 and, shortly afterwards, to Poplar Hospital. By that time he had made important contributions on refractory anaemias and was soon to publish a valuable paper on poisoning by methyl mercury compounds jointly with Donald Hunter and Dorothy Russell.

In 1940, Dick Bomford joined the Army as a medical specialist with the rank of major. He was soon promoted to lieutenant colonel and went to West Africa in charge of a medical division, returning to the United Kingdom in 1942, from whence he went to Normandy in 1944 and then to India. In 1945, he was promoted to brigadier and, as consultant physician, went with the 14th Army to Burma and Malaya. He was mentioned in despatches in 1946.

Returning to London after the war, Dick was for a period consultant physician to Mile End and St Andrews Hospital as well as to the London and Poplar. Though a countryman born and bred, he had become extremely fond of the East End in which he had lived since his arrival at the London as a clinical student. He knew it intimately and it was said that before the war there was no one living within walking distance of the London who did not know him. He played the organ in most of the churches in the East End and at All Hallows by the Tower, and his piano accordion, which went with him and the 14th Army into Burma, was greatly appreciated in the public houses of Whitechapel in the late 1930s. In 1958, Dick gave up his rooms in the West End and set up his consulting rooms in a house on the London estate in Whitechapel, which we shared for ten happy years.

Dick was punctilious in the fulfilment of the daily responsibilities of a busy and most caring physician and teacher. Along with a shy gentleness and genuine modesty, unhurried movements, a memorable smile and an infinite capacity to listen quietly to others, went an agile, questing mind, a rare sensibility and, almost in contrast, an ability to come quickly to decisions, and the will and courage to put them into effect. These qualities won him the trust of both patients and colleagues and endeared him to students and the young doctors who worked with him. He remained always a generalist, taking an active interest in the development of psychosomatic medicine, calling on his considerable experience of tropical medicine, running diabetic clinics in several hospitals and serving as consultant gastroenterologist to the Army and consultant physician to Dr Barnardo's Homes. For many years, he edited *Clinical Methods*.

Dick was a member of the General Nursing Council and, for twenty years, consultant adviser in medicine to the Ministry of Health. He was chairman of the Armed Services Consultants Approval Board (Medicine and Medical Specialties) from 1962 to 1970 and a member of the (Platt) working party on hospital staffing. In 1951, he succeeded Charles Hill (later Lord Hill of Luton) as the BBC's radio doctor and regularly for six years broadcast sound information, good sense and much wisdom to an eager public.

Dick Bomford was secretary of the Medical Pilgrims, treasurer of the Royal College of Physicians from 1957 to 1970, and chairman of the medical council of the London Hospital from 1964 to 1970, having previously been its secretary for many years. He was well fitted to help organizations, founded long ago, to adapt to the very different and rapidly changing circumstances with which they were confronted in his time. He was not driven by any reforming or crusading zeal but sought only to do his best for institutions which meant much to him and in the importance of which he firmly believed. He had an abiding faith, not in himself, but in values and standards which, though he would never proclaim them to the world nor ever demand allegiance to them from others, were, no matter how much he might question them, those by which alone he himself could live.

Dick would reach decisions in his own mind as to the direction change should take, which of the old ways ought to be abandoned and which translated into terms more appropriate to the present. He would force them on no one, but offer them only as what seemed best to him, but because of his integrity, his concern, his values, his respect for the past and obvious dislike of change for the sake of change, his judgement was trusted. Thus, as treasurer of the College, he played an immensely important role in its removal from Pall Mall to Regent's Park, responsible for much of the work involved and giving careful, but imaginative, thought to every detail. He had a most important influence, too, on the building committee, his firm and enthusiastic support for Lasdun's design doing much to overcome the doubts of older members. Dick loved the College and took endless trouble quietly to maintain and raise the standard of facilities available to fellows and especially the quality of College dinners.

At the London, to which also he was devoted, through thirty years of constantly changing and increasingly difficult circumstances, Dick Bomford stood steadfast in the midst of a hospital community which, like so many others, was confused and uncertain; contributing to deciding the direction of change but, with infinite patience and constant consideration for all, controlling its speed. His early retirement in 1970 was a great loss but he felt the need to engage, while he could, more completely in the care of the acutely ill and took an opportunity offered by the Shah of Iran to become physician to the Reza Shah Kabir Hospital in Tehran. He equipped himself with a dormobile, drove there and, while there, drove around the whole country, getting to know the people, liking them and feeling it a privilege to care for them. Ironically and inexplicably, as he was about to return home on leave, he was attacked in his quarters by unknown assailants and badly beaten up. Despite this, he accepted an invitation to help a new medical school and returned to Iran only to find on arrival that the school authorities had changed and he was no longer wanted. He returned to England and, for some time, was an adviser to the British Postgraduate Medical Federation. He served on medical appeal tribunals, and was working for the Samaritans at the time of his sudden death at home in Roxwell, Essex.

Despite his many and varied commitments, Dick remained always a relaxed, unhurried, kind and happy man with time and abundant energy for the enjoyment of a full like. The pleasure he got from music, painting, gardening, cooking, wine, reading, travel, even his poultry farming, he shared with many friends, along with his love of beauty and nature. He had an unquenchable zest to live life to the full – without haste, without contention, with goodwill to all men and without selfishness of any kind. Few men can have had more friends in every walk of life, or been more thoughtful for them. He had a genius for helping, for encouraging, and for the exactly right timing of an act of kindness. JRE

[*Brit. med. J.*, 1981, **282**, 662; *Lancet,* 1981, **1**, 397; *Times,* 7 Feb 1981; *College Commentary,* Jan 1981, **15**, 39-41; Photo]

BONSER, Georgiana May (née Duthie) *b.*5 May 1898 *d.*9 June 1979
MB ChB Manch (1920) MD (1923) MRCP (1945) FRCP (1954)

Born in Manchester, where her father, Ogilvie Duthie, was director of education for Salford, Georgiana Duthie was educated at Manchester High School for Girls, Manchester University and King's College Hospital, London. After house appointments, which included the distinction of being the first woman house surgeon at the Manchester Royal Infirmary, she proceeded to a demonstratorship in anatomy under Professor Stopford.

She was awarded the MD with distinction in 1923, and became the first Dickinson travelling scholar, University of Manchester, selecting the Pasteur Institute in Paris as the centre for her overseas study. It was whilst working in Paris that she met her future husband, Kenneth Bonser, whom she married in December 1927.

On her return from Paris, she was appointed demonstrator in pathology at the University of Leeds under Matthew Stewart, and in 1927 became research fellow and lecturer in the newly established department of cancer research. She was promoted reader in 1950. Her initial research was concerned with the possible role of genetic factors in the formation of tumours, particularly tumours of the breast in mice. This experimental study was combined with a clinical follow-up of the sibs of a cohort of patients treated for cancer of the breast. Her second major research interest was stimulated by a request to make an epidemiological study of cancer of the bladder in men employed at the ICI dye works, Huddersfield. This study was pursued with the help of chemists, particularly DB Clayson and JW Jull, and with the surgical skill of LN Pyrah, who assisted with the animal experimental work. They made an exhaustive study on the effects of beta-naphthylamine and associated aromatic chemicals with carcinogenic properties. With the outbreak of World War II and the virtual closure of the department of cancer research, she was appointed morbid anatomist to Pontefract General Hospital in 1942, and in 1948 transferred to St James's Hospital, Leeds. The latter appointment she continued part-time until her retirement. Even after retirement she continued, with the co-operation of her clinical colleagues, to run a clinic for the study of the effects of hormones in the treatment and control of cancer of the breast and tumours of the testicle. Her researches led to her being in great demand nationally and internationally, and she visited many countries – Holland, Italy, India, Israel, Egypt, Turkey, Greece and Japan – to participate in symposia and to lecture.

She was a member of the scientific committee on toxic substances in agriculture and food storage, Ministry of Agriculture, of the carcinogen panel of the Ministry of Health and of the scientific committee appointed by the chemical industry to enquire into the cause and prevention of papilloma of the bladder.

Georgiana Bonser was deeply concerned that women medical graduates should play an important role in professional matters. She was the first woman chairman of the Leeds Division of the British Medical Association, and president of the Women's Medical Federation (1959–1960). She and her husband kept open house for women medical undergraduates at Leeds, and she was always available to discuss with them problems arising during their course and to counsel them concerning their postgraduate career. She did much to encourage medical women to continue in practice, and was able to find employment for a number of distinguished women graduates in the cancer department to the mutual benefit of both.

Despite a full and active professional life she found time to study art and languages, and was able to participate in her husband's archeological activities. Many are the miles they drove and tramped together in the north of England searching for the drovers' roads in preparation for a book by her husband. RET

[*Brit. med. J.*, 1979, **1**, 1789; **2**, 402; *Daily Telegraph*, 12 June 1979; Photo]

BOURNE, William Arthur *b.* – 1900 *d.*1 Feb 1976
MRCS LRCP (1925) MA MB BChir Cantab (1927) MRCP (1927) MD (1936) FRCP (1947)

William Arthur Bourne was born at Moira, near Ashby-de-la-Zouch, the only son of Moses Bourne whose family had been closely linked with the collieries in the West Midlands since at least 1842. Moses Bourne was a strict Methodist and married a Miss Edith Bacon. Their son William continued as a Nonconformist, going first to the grammar school at Ashby-de-la-Zouch and then on to Mill Hill School. From there he won an open scholarship to Christ's College, Cambridge, where he took a full part in college life, playing cricket, football, and becoming a keen beagler. He also spent some time writing verse and novels.

From Cambridge he went to St Bartholomew's Hospital, where he qualified with the Conjoint diploma in 1925. He became house physician to Sir Percival Horton-Smith-Hartley, then house surgeon at the Metropolitan Hospital, later spending a year in gynaecology under Malcolm Donaldson. In 1928 he went into a general practice at Bedford, bought for him by his grandparents, later moving to Exmouth, and then in 1935 to Hove. General practice gave Bourne the fullest scope for his versatile talents, and he turned his hand to many different interests as well as becoming an exceedingly skilful and experienced practitioner. He kept the fullest notes about his patients and read widely in medical literature, as well as continuing to write poetry. He was never idle and became keen on sailing, golf, sketching and photography.

During the 1939–1945 war he was – to his disappointment – not allowed to join the Forces but was appointed honorary physician to the Royal Sussex County Hospital (1942) and to the Hove General Hospital in 1946. At this time he gave valuable help on the committee of the Royal College of Physicians which was concerned with the introduction of the National Health Service, and himself began to specialize in gastroenterology. He was one of the first physicians in England to acquire and use the semi-flexible gastroscope, which had been introduced from Germany.

He was elected FRCP in 1947, by which time he had become an expert in his specialty, contributing papers on the oesophagus, gastric cancer, anaemia, and other subjects. He was elected president of the section of medicine of the Royal Society of Medicine and also of the clinical section, and in 1963 of the British Society of Gastroenterology.

Bourne was a fine clinician; a man of the widest general interests and knowledge, and immensely popular with his patients and friends. In build he was a big man, appearing to some as taciturn, reticent and even forbidding, but he was in fact a man of deep sympathies and a delightful sense of humour. He had a remarkably good memory, fine powers of observation, and abounding energy and enthusiasm. It was largely Bourne's work which started the idea of day hospitals, which followed his formation of 'An Outpatients' Club', which he described in *The Lancet* in 1950.

He married Joyce Postle, who was a nurse at Bart's and daughter of an old Norfolk family. He had two sons, one of whom became medically qualified, and two daughters, one of whom followed her mother as a nurse at Bart's. The other daughter died tragically in a sailing accident which seemed to precipitate Bourne's own death in 1976, as he lay for some months paralysed and speechless after this shock. TCH

[*Brit. med. J.*, 1976, **1**, 775, 843; *Lancet,* 1976, **3**, 757; *Times,* 10 Feb 1976; Photo]

BOYD, *Brig. Sir* **John (Smith Knox)** *b.*18 Sep 1891 *d.*10 Jun 1981
OBE (Mil 1942) KHP (1944–46) Kt (1958) MB ChB Glasg (1913)
MD (1948) MRCP (1950) FRCP (1951) FRS (1951)
Hon LLD Glasg (1957) Hon FRCP Edin (1960) Hon FRSM (1965)
Hon FRCPath (1968) Hon DSc Salford (1969)

The Boyds are an ancient lowland clan and John was very proud of his Scottish ancestry. He was born at Largs in Ayrshire, where his father was an agent at the Royal Bank of Scotland. He left the local school in 1908 and, with the aid of a grant from the Carnegie Trust (which he repaid with his first earnings) went to Glasgow University to study medicine. He graduated with honours in April 1913, receiving the John Paterson bursary and the Brunton memorial prize as the most distinguished graduate of the year.

Boyd served as house surgeon to the cardiologist John Cowan and then went as ship's surgeon on a voyage to Rangoon. On his return in the summer of 1914, war was declared; John applied for a commission in the RAMC, was called up in October and went straight to the Ypres salient with a Field Ambulance of the 27th Division. In May 1915, the 27th, reduced in numbers from 20,000 to 4,000 men, was transferred to Armentières, the Somme, and finally to Salonika, where John became MO to the Engineers and trekked widely through Macedonia. He had to tackle severe epidemics of dysentery and malaria, acquired a deep interest in tropical medicine and applied for a regular commission in the RAMC. In 1920 he went to India, working in pathology laboratories in Nasirabad and Mhow. From 1923 to 1929 he taught pathology at the RAM College in Millbank and then, in the rank of major returned to India where he was in charge of laboratories in Bangalore and Poona. He made a detailed study of bacillary dysentery, reclassified the causative organisms, described new strains and settled the laboratory diagnosis. He loved India and its peoples, and travelled widely.

In 1936 he returned to Millbank and was put in charge of vaccine production. He set about preparing enough TAB vaccine for the protection of British troops in the shadow of war. He also worked with the Wellcome organization in the development and use of tetanus toxoid and, through his efforts, tetanus was not a problem for the British Army in World War II. In 1940, in the rank of colonel, he went to the Middle East as deputy director of pathology, organized the service there, and collaborated with Sir Neil Hamilton Fairley in the control of malaria. With GAH Buttle, he introduced sulphaguanidine for the treatment of bacillary dysentery and established an effective blood transfusion service that saved countless lives during the Mediterranean campaign.

In 1943 he was recalled from Cairo and put in charge of pathology for the 21 Army Group. He organized the laboratory and blood transfusion services for the Normandy landings, and also established the optimum methods of using penicillin in wound surgery. He was promoted brigadier in 1945. In 1946 his colleagues in the RAMC hoped that he would become their director general at the War Office, but John Boyd had had enough of full time administration and longed to get back to the bench. He accepted the directorship of the Wellcome Laboratories of Tropical Medicine in Euston Road and supervised the research programme for the next nine years. His own distinguished work was centred on bacteriophage, which he regarded as a promising model for the study of the relationship between cells and viruses in human infections. In 1955 he became a Wellcome Trustee, and reinforced the interest of the Trust in diseases of the tropics.

He retired in 1966 but continued to take an active interest in the affairs of the RAMC and of the Royal Society of Tropical Medicine and Hygiene. He acted as the Society's secretary, its president, was elected an honorary fellow, and received its highest award, the Manson medal. In May 1981 in his 90th year, a special meeting was arranged for him at Manson House, where he enjoyed meeting many of his old friends and colleagues; two months later, he died.

John Boyd served on numerous committees and received many honours. He was created Knight Bachelor in 1958. Almost all who had the good fortune to work with him admired and loved him. Long after the war, his team of Middle East pathologists continued to meet, and in 1962 they presented him with his portrait, by Norman Hepple, as a mark of their esteem. This now hangs in the RAMC Headquarters Mess at Millbank.

Sir John was a wonderful chief, astute and circumspect and inclined to conservatism. But once he made up his mind on a course of action he was vigorous, straight and true and never wavered. A memorial service was held at the Chelsea Hospital in October 1981, and Major General MHP Sayers said of him 'He had the outward appearance of a soldier, yet spoke like a fellow of the Royal Society. If ever a man happily harmonized the rival calls of Mars and Aesculapius, it was John Boyd'.

He was twice married; Elizabeth (née Edgar) died in 1956 and Mary (née Murphy) died in 1967. There were no children. LGG

[*Times*, 13 June 1981; *Brit. med. J.*, 1981, **283**, 314, 445; *Lancet*, 1981, **2**, 482; *Biogr. Mem. roy. Soc.*, 1982, **28**, 27-57; Photo]

BOYD, William *b.*21 June 1885 *d.*10 Mar 1979
CC (1968) MB ChB (1908) MD (1911) DPM (1912)
MRCPE (1912) FRCP* (1932) FRCSC (1949) Hon FRCPE (1955)
FRS Canada†

Distinguished as a teacher and writer in the field of pathology – both medical and surgical – Boyd was acclaimed by thousands of medical students wherever English was read.

His early education in Glasgow and at Trent College in Derby prepared him for entry into the University of Edinburgh where he graduated MB ChB in 1908 and MD in 1911. The following year he took his qualification in psychiatry. He never gave up his interest in the human nervous system, and was an admirer of the pioneer work of Rio-Hortega and the Spanish school.

After serving for a year in a field ambulance with the RAMC he accepted the chair of pathology at the University of Manitoba in Winnipeg, following by twenty years the gifted Frank Fairchild Wesbrook, a Cambridge colleague of Sherrington, and first full-time professor, unpaid! Boyd loved to reminisce about his own occupancy of the professorship, and hoped that his early students had long since forgiven him his initial lectures. He claimed to have prepared these on the ocean liner taking him to Canada, and once established in Winnipeg he said he was only one lecture ahead of his students!

Whatever his beginnings as a teacher of pathology, three generations of students came to know him as an engaging lecturer – witty, wise and never petty. He was a showman with a flair for understatement – asking more questions on a subject than he could possibly answer. He saw himself as a humble fellow student, but his elegant turn of phrase gave him away. To say that he was 'the students' friend' would be too trite. Students in Winnipeg (1915 – 1937), Toronto (1937 – 1951), and finally in Vancouver (1951 – 1954) worshipped him, as their philosopher sent to make pathology thrilling and meaningful. He never disappointed them.

Boyd wrote volumes for surgeons (1925), internists (1931), and then his *Textbook of Pathology: Introduction to Medicine* in 1932. It went into its eighth edition when he was 85 years of age. There can have been few students who were not transported by the beauty and appositeness of his prose.

A keen interest in pathology museums brought Boyd into contact with Maude Abbott and other Oslerians. Four such teaching facilities bear his name in North America. The superb library of the Academy of Medicine in Toronto was named in his honour. Honorary degrees and decorations pleased 'the Professor' but did not change his sterling simplicity. He was a particularly 'unsplenetic' man, and had no time for jealous gossip.

He suffered the removal of a parotid cancer during his busy life, and blindness at the end. Nevertheless he was a most buoyant soul, of the kind that makes a medical school an inspiration for young minds. In his long and happy life he was the touchstone of innumerable practitioners and researchers, generous in his praise, comforting in adversity. WCG

[*Brit. med. J.*, 1979, **1**, 959; Photo]

BRAID, Frances *b*.5 Dec 1892 *d*.26 Jan 1981
MB ChB St And (1917) MD (1921) MRCP (1923) FRCP (1938)

Frances Braid was a Scot, the younger daughter of Francis Braid, chief sanitary inspector in Kirkcaldy, and his wife Jessie Winter Cant, whose father was a crofter. She was educated at Kirkcaldy High School, St Andrews University and Dundee Royal Infirmary where she obtained her first medical appointment. Later, at the Edinburgh Royal Hospital for Sick Children, she came under the influence of John Thomson and decided to devote her life to paediatrics. To gain further experience in the specialty she moved to Birmingham Children's Hospital to work with Leonard Parsons, at first as house physician and then as resident medical officer. In fact she was destined to remain in Birmingham until she retired, for she was appointed assistant physician to the Children's Hospital in 1923 and consultant physician in 1929.

Frances Braid was one of the first full-time paediatricians in England, and one of the first women to be elected a member of the British Paediatric Association, in 1945. Her pioneer work with new born infants had proved a major contribution to paediatrics and she soon became a familiar and much consulted figure at annual meetings of the Association. She was appointed paediatrician at Birmingham Maternity Hospital in 1928 and, making good use of her clinical skill, her obstinacy and her Scot's charm, she succeeded in breaking down the barriers which divided obstetricians and paediatricians; the team which she brought into being had a markedly beneficial effect on neonatal morbidity and mortality. The value of her work with her consultant colleagues at the Maternity Hospital was greatly increased because she took full advantage of the opportunity to study normal new born infants, as well as those who were diseased, and because she appreciated how important to the health of the neonate was the role which could be played by general practitioners and medical officers at the maternity and child welfare clinics of the city. She made them all feel that they were an integral part of her team, infecting them with her enthusiasm, giving them much needed support, and encouraging them to come to her ward rounds and outpatient clinics at the Children's Hospital. In these ways she initiated a form of postgraduate activity which foreshadowed later developments in neonatal care and community paediatrics.

She wrote a number of papers on diseases of the newborn and their sequelae and, in 1950, she was invited by the University of Birmingham to deliver the Ingleby Lectures, choosing to speak about hypothyroidism in infancy and later childhood. Frances Braid did not marry, and when she retired she returned to Scotland to live with her sister in the family home in Edinburgh. CGP

[*Brit. med. J.*, 1981, **282**, 662; Photo]

BRAMWELL, John Crighton *b*.4 Mar 1889 *d*.8 Sep 1976
BA Cantab (1910) MA (1921) MB ChB Manch (1915) MD (1923)
MRCP (1929) FRCP (1929) Hon FRCPE (1960)

John Crighton Bramwell was born in Edinburgh, the son of Byron Bramwell and his wife Martha Crighton. His father, later Sir Byron, an outstanding clinical teacher and scientist in Edinburgh, was for many years Scotland's leading physician; and his eldest brother Edwin became a well known neurologist and professor of clinical medicine in the University of Edinburgh. Both were Fellows of the College.

He was sent to his father's school, Cheltenham College, and entered Trinity College Cambridge as an exhibitioner, where he obtained a first class in the Natural Sciences Tripos. In 1912 he embarked on his clinical medical training with a scholarship at the University of Manchester, chosen by his father instead of Edinburgh so that the two brothers would not compete with each other in later years. At that time consultant posts at Manchester Royal Infirmary were almost invariably filled by selection from local graduates. Moreover the Infirmary drained patients from the largest populated area in the country. On the outbreak of the first world war Bramwell volunteered for service overseas and joined the 1st East Lancashire Territorial Field Ambulance in Egypt. The following year he was granted leave for two months to sit his final examination, after which he was posted to the 23rd Division in France and Italy, at first with a Field Ambulance, later as DADMS to GHQ, Italy.

When demobilized Bramwell became GR Murray's house physician, and medical and cardiographic registrar at Manchester Royal Infirmary. While at Cambridge he had come under the influence of Keith Lucas, and in Manchester he collaborated with AV Hill in the University department of physiology, which resulted in several papers on pulse wave velocity and arterial elasticity. In 1923, as Rockefeller fellow of the Medical Research Council, he studied at Washington University and the Rockefeller Institute of Medical Research, New York. On his return to Manchester in 1925 he was appointed assistant lecturer in experimental physiology. After five years devoted to clinical teaching and physiological research, during which time he obtained his MD with gold medal, in 1926 he was elected to the honorary staff of Manchester Royal Infirmary and entered consulting practice as a cardiologist. He was appointed professor of systematic medicine in the University of Manchester in 1940, a post he vacated in 1946 to permit the appointment of Robert Platt as full time professor of medicine. In its place Bramwell became professor of cardiology, a post he held with distinction until, on retiring in 1954, he was made professor emeritus by the University.

Throughout his professional life Bramwell was a tireless worker, and published on cardiovascular topics, pulse wave velocity, aneurysmal dilatation of the left auricle, bundle branch block, quinidine therapy, the heart of athletes, gallop rhythm, the alcoholic heart and on blood pressure and myocardial infarction. He was the author of several textbooks including *Heart Disease and Pregnancy*

(1938), and *Principles and Practice of Cardiology* (1942) written jointly with King of Baltimore.

Tall and slim, Bramwell had a distinguished and cultured appearance which, with his innate courtesy and charm, made him a popular consultant in practice. His kindness and consideration towards his subordinates was invariable; even under provocation he was controlled and urbane. His success as a clinician however was due to the amalgam of a shrewd clinical sense and an extensive knowledge of the scientific basis of cardiology. As a teacher he was popular, since he had the peculiar gift of the greatest teachers of rendering difficult topics simple. He was an ideal examiner, and much sought after as a lecturer and speaker. He was recognized by his contemporaries as one of the leading cardiologists of his time, and a clinician of the first rank, who built up an outstanding department of cardiology in Manchester. Bramwell's flair for writing led to many demands on his time. He was editor, and later senior editor, of the *Quarterly Journal of Medicine* and a member of the editorial board of the *British Heart Journal* for many years. In 1956 a special number of this journal was dedicated to him. He was president of the Association of Physicians and the Cardiac Society in 1955.

Bramwell was active in College affairs, holding office as councillor, censor and senior censor. In 1937 he was Lumleian lecturer and in 1956 gave the Harveian Oration.

When he retired Bramwell resided permanently near Ambleside in the Lake District, where he was occupied with his leisure activities of gardening and fly fishing. His later years were marred by increasing difficulty in getting about and much to his chagrin the loss of a leg was very restricting.

In 1929 Bramwell married Elsa Violet, daughter of James Risk, distiller, of Edinburgh. They had two sons, one of whom carried on the family medical tradition into the fourth generation when he became a general practitioner, and a daughter who went into medical publishing. HTH

[*Brit. med. J.*, 1976, **2**, 764; *Times,* 11 Sept 1976; *RCP Edin. Chronicle,* Jan 1977, **7** (1); Photo]

BROCK, *Lord* **Russell Claude, Baron Brock of Wimbledon**
*b.*24 Oct 1903 *d.*3 Sept 1980
Life Peer (1965) Kt (1954) MB BS Lond (1927) FRCS (1929)
MS (1931) FRCP* (1965) Hon FACS (1949) Hon FRACS (1957)
Hon LLD Leeds (1965) Hon ScD Cantab (1968)
Hon FDS RCS (1969)†

Russell Brock, the son of Herbert Brock, a professional photographer, and his wife Elvina Carmen, was born in London. As a small boy he was sent to Christ's Hospital School, leaving in 1921 at the age of 17 with an arts scholarship for entry to Guy's Hospital Medical School. Here he won many prizes, and qualified as a doctor in 1927. The year before he qualified, Russell married Germaine Louise

Ladevèze, a lady of Swiss origin, and by her he had three daughters. After Germaine died, Russell married Christine Jones, who had been his faithful secretary for many years.

Soon after qualifying, Russell embarked on a career in surgery and in 1928 became a fellow of the Royal College of Surgeons. He soon devoted his interests to thoracic and cardiac surgery, and in 1929 was awarded a Rockefeller travelling fellowship which enabled him to work under the great thoracic surgeon, Evarts Graham in St Louis, Missouri.

After his return from America, he obtained the mastership of surgery of London University and became, in 1932, a registrar and tutor at Guy's and a research fellow of the Association of Surgeons of Great Britain. In 1935 he was appointed thoracic surgeon to London County Council and, in the same year, won the Jacksonian prize for his essay on new growths of the lung. In 1936, Russell Brock was appointed consultant surgeon to both Guy's and the Brompton Hospital. In 1938, he became a Hunterian professor and in 1949 he was appointed a member of the council of the Royal College of Surgeons, serving as vice-president in 1956, having been knighted in 1954, and president from 1963 to 1966, becoming a Life Peer in 1965. In 1957 Russell had given the Bradshaw Lecture and in 1961 the Hunterian Oration.

In being invited to 'prepare a short biography' for Munk's *Roll*, the author is provided with some details of the subject which may be referred to and which are entered by the subject himself. In Russell's case, these are characteristically brief and to the point. For instance, under the heading 'Principal publications, with dates', he writes 'Articles too numerous to give'! This brief observation is true, pungent and typical. He omits to mention the many articles which he wrote for the Guy's Hospital Reports, of which he was editor for many years, and to which he gave a quality which assured the dispatch of this paper to most medical centres throughout the world. There are, however, four papers which he regards as worthy to be mentioned in Munk's *Roll: The Anatomy of the Bronchial Tree* (1946); *The Life and Work of Astley Cooper,* (1952); *Lung Abscess* (1952); *The Anatomy of Congenital Pulmonary Stenosis,* (1957). These four papers are the results of careful investigation and are of outstanding value in the message which they convey.

As already mentioned, in February 1961, he delivered the Hunterian Oration. This was a contribution which illustrated vividly the breadth of Russell's interests, for here, instead of the details of a technical analysis, we have a historical story which embraces not only Hunter, but references to Sir Astley Cooper, Lord Lister, Wood Jones, Grey Turner, Sir Charters Symonds and others. In his introduction to this oration, he writes 'As my chief executive office in the College is chairman of the Museum and Research Committee, I intend to speak about the duty and policy of the College in regard to the Hunterian museum and to research. Both of these meet on the common ground of Hunter's life; both are important in the life of the College now and in the future'. The last part of this now almost historic oration deals with policy in research and the laws against vivisection wherein he observes, 'The scientific spirit engendered by Hunter continued into the early decades of the 19th century, but England was soon to lose her position in the van of surgical research as the development of surgery proceeded along more vocational lines. In contrast, tremendous advances were being made in physiology, chemistry, physics, pathology and other sciences ... this (contrast) was principally due to the restrictive legislation placed on animal experimentation by which medicine was placed in the absurd position of defending the labours necessary for its advancement.'

Finally, there is a section on 'Research and Inspiration' in which he says 'The vocational and the scientific attitude can often be usefully combined, and some great advances have resulted from this. I suppose one of the most notable is that of the introduction of vaccination by Edward Jenner'.

Now perhaps we may pursue a more personal picture of Russell's life. In some respects it is easy to speak about him because what is abundantly clear is that he was a man of absolute integrity, immense energy on behalf of his patients, and a thinly veiled concern and devotion to those who were under his care.

It is a truism that his determination was that only the very best was good enough for his patients, that the care of their lives and health was the essence of his happiness, and that nothing would allow him to accept anything but the maximum endeavour on their behalf; this was the star which he followed throughout his life.

Many will know of his great work in the operating theatre and the ward, of his teaching qualities, and the advances which must have saved many lives and alleviated so much misery and distress. Russell was revered by his colleagues and his students. To both he was an inspiring figure. This was due as much to his manner of address as to his position at the summit of the world of surgery. On the other hand, if anyone was in pain or trouble, the façade of sternness was discarded and, in its place, stood a man of infinite kindness who could give consolation and advice, and whose very presence and attention were healing.

One, who worked for him many years ago, wrote 'He was immensely considerate, kind and polite to every patient and we learnt a lot from him, not only the principles of surgery, but also how to be 'a doctor' – the title by which he invariably addressed the most junior students at the bedside'.

It was, however, with his work at Guy's Hospital, as with his work at the Brompton, that he helped to build a reputation which made these hospitals a pillar of thoracic surgery throughout the world. Of his hobbies, little was known, but in his entry in *Who's Who* it was revealed that these were 'writing, reading, antiquities and the topography of London', to which might be added – history, bibliography and gardening. Russell's interest in so many spheres, and his wide knowledge, made him a most interesting and delightful person to talk to. For instance, he was responsible for renovating the old operating theatre in St Thomas' Street shared by St Thomas'

Hospital and Guy's, where Sir Astley Cooper operates; a historic memorial to surgery in the eighteenth century which is on view to those interested.

If this picture of his character so far has seemed only one of grave study, reading and work, I am sure he would wish it to be mentioned that he was, in his early days, a long-distance runner.

Those who knew him will continue to think of him with affection and respect and many will thank him in their hearts and minds for the care which he took of them. HA

[*Brit. med. J.*, 1980, **281**, 814, 952, 1013; *Lancet*, 1981, **2**, 600; *Times*, 5 Sept 1980; Photo]

BROCK, John Fleming *b.*27 Mar 1904 *d.*3 July 1983
BA Cape Town (1925) BA Oxon (1928) MRCP (1932)
MA DM (1935) MA Cantab (1937) FRCP (1938) Hon FACP (1966)
Hon DSC Natal (1971) Wits (1965) UCT (1979)

For many years the department of medicine at the University of Cape Town was headed jointly by John Brock and Frank Forman, and they made a formidable team. Forman was an outstanding, brilliant clinician; Brock's great strength lay in research and administration. But he was also sound, careful and thorough at the bedside, displaying a deep sense of compassion and sympathy for his patients, and he was an excellent clinical teacher.

Brock was born in Port Elizabeth, South Africa, the son of John Brock, a general medical practitioner who qualified at Bart's and emigrated to South Africa from Paignton, Devon. His mother, Edith Ethel (née Fleming) was the daughter of a Presbyterian minister. He received his early education at the Grey Institute, Port Elizabeth, graduated BA from the University of Cape Town and then went to Oxford as a Rhodes scholar. His early career took him to the London Hospital where he was intern, registrar and research assistant to Donald Hunter and HM Turnbull. From 1932 to 1934, as a Leverhulme research scholar of the College, he worked under GR Minot in the Thorndike Memorial Laboratory at Boston City Hospital, concentrating on iron deficiency and hypochromic anaemia. In 1934 he became the first medical assistant at the Postgraduate Medical School, Hammersmith; moving in 1936 to Cambridge as assistant director of research in medicine under JA Ryle.

Two years later he was appointed to the chair of the practice of medicine at the University of Cape Town and joint head of the department of medicine, Groote Schuur Hospital. He at once recognized a lack of interest in research which he knew was essential to a good clinical department; he established a group to work in clinical nutrition, and gathered round him men of the stature of Eales, Bronte-Stewart, Hanson and Truswell. His 1952 WHO monograph on kwashiorkor remains a classic in the field. He extended the department's nutritional interests to include the role of dietary fats in the pathogenesis of atherosclerosis and the consequences of vitamin deficiency. Driven by his emphasis on research and the organizational flair with which he nourished it, the department in Cape Town soon became one of the world's leading centres. He achieved international recognition in medical education and community health, especially as related to nutrition.

When Frank Forman retired from the chair of clinical medicine in 1953, Brock became professor of medicine and head of department. He belonged to the senate of the University for thirty-seven years, was a founder member of the College of Physicians, Surgeons and Gynaecologists of South Africa and its president from 1965–1968. He retired in 1970, when he was made emeritus professor of medicine and honorary professor of the history and philosophy of medicine.

He married Ruth Mary, daughter of Henry Lomberg, a mining engineer and manager, in 1933 and they had four children, two sons and two daughters. He was a quiet, modest and gentle man, a little hard to get to know. He had been a prominent sportsman in his youth, representing his school, university and hospital in rugby and athletics, and he continued to play tennis and squash until a late age. He drove himself hard, seldom appeared to relax or take time off, and rarely indulged in small-talk. He was a courteous and sympathetic listener, always willing to advise, and he could be firm when he needed to be. Working in a Government hospital, he felt it would be wrong to state publicly his views on apartheid, but as soon as he retired he joined what was then the Progressive Party and declared his detestation of racial discrimination. RH(4)/GW/VL

[*Lancet,* 1983, **2**, 1093-4; *UCT News*, University of Cape Town, July 1983, 10; Photo]

BROMLEY, John Frederick *b.*13 Dec 1899 *d.*3 June 1981
OBE (1946) MB ChB Manch (1923) DMRE Cantab (1925)
MRCP (1937) FFR (1947) FRCP (1953) FRCR (1975)

John Bromley was born at Ashton-under-Lyne, the son of Frederick William Bromley, a solicitor. He was educated at Sedbergh, where in 1913 he was a Scholar and in his last year won the quarter mile. On leaving school he joined the Royal Garrison Artillery as a subaltern and as such served for the last nine months of the first world war. Thereafter he entered medicine at Manchester, graduating in 1923.

After a house surgeon's appointment, he was appointed assistant medical officer in the X-ray department at the Manchester Royal Infirmary, and in 1925 obtained the DMRE at Cambridge. He achieved his first consultant appointment as radiologist to Crumpsall Hospital and Booth Hall Children's Hospital in Manchester. From there he moved to the North Staffordshire Royal Infirmary as radiologist and served many other hospitals in the Potteries in the same capacity. In 1934 he was appointed assistant radiologist at the Birmingham General Hospital and three years later was elected to the

Membership. His experience at Stoke and in Birmingham led to most valuable papers on occupational diseases of the lungs and skin malignancy.

At the outbreak of war he joined the medical services of the RAF, in which he served for six years, achieving the rank of group captain and being appointed OBE in 1946. On return to civil life Bromley became the first director of the department of radiotherapy at the United Birmingham Hospitals, an appointment he held until his retirement in 1965. He also accepted the duties of adviser in radiotherapy to the Birmingham Regional Hospital Board, and consultant in radiotherapy to the Royal Hospital at Wolverhampton. He was lecturer in clinical radiology in the University of Birmingham, and in 1948 was appointed an honorary consultant to the RAF. His academic interests continued and he published important papers on chorion carcinoma and myelomatosis.

In 1947 Bromley became a Fellow of the Faculty of Radiologists, having been secretary for the previous two years. He was a member of the council and president of the radiological section of the Royal Society of Medicine and a member of the council of the British Institute of Radiology and the British Association of Physical Medicine. In 1953 he became a Fellow of the College, in 1959 a Fellow of the College of Radiologists of Australasia and in 1973 a foundation fellow of the Royal College of Radiologists.

Bromley had wide interests outside medicine. He was a keen Johnsonian and Shakespearean, and in 1960–1961 was president of the Birmingham Central Literary Association. His other major leisure occupations were music, campanology, and swimming, in which he continued to engage every day at the Queen Elizabeth Hospital in Birmingham until the last few weeks of his life.

Bromley was a naturally happy man, always friendly and helpful. His wide culture, his pleasant manner and charm made him a wonderful companion, and his great professional success did not alter a naturally modest and unassuming personality.

He married in 1929 a medical colleague, Sarah Walker, who unhappily died four years later. In 1935 he married Edith Mary, the daughter of the Revd James Neale, who survived him together with one of the three daughters of the marriage. AGWW

[*Brit. med. J.*, 1981, **282**, 2145, **283**, 239]

BROWN, Edward Hilton *b.*15 Oct 1920 *d.*11 Apr 1977
BA Oxon (1941) BM BCh (1944) MRCS LRCP (1944) DCH (1945) MA (1948) DM (1949) MRCP (1954) FRCP (1973)

Edward Hilton Brown was consultant physician at Hither Green Hospital. For a man always fit, and endowed with much energy and drive, the knowledge that he had carcinoma of the pancreas was indeed a cruel blow. In the normal course of things, he should have had many years of useful work ahead of him. He bore the last months of his illness with courage and extraordinary will-power, supported by his wife and daughter. He had married, in 1951, Faith Ella Brown (Sherry), daughter of John Henry Sheridan, an Army officer, and they had one daughter, Lesley.

Edward Hilton was born at Bristol, the son of Albert Edward Brown, a customs and excise officer, and his wife Mabel, daughter of Thomas Hornsby Hilton, a boot and shoe manufacturer. He was educated at Bristol Grammar School and the University of Oxford. He graduated at Oxford and undertook his clinical training at Bristol Royal Infirmary, winning the Suple prize medal in surgery and the Sanders scholarship and silver medal.

After house jobs at the Bristol Royal Infirmary, during which time he took his DCH, he became assistant medical officer at Lewisham Hospital in 1945. The post included not only general medicine, paediatrics and anaesthetics, but also the care of 150 infants at Ladywell Residential Nursery. The latter provided much of the material for his DM thesis on giardiasis, and probably sowed the seeds of his life-long interest in infectious diseases. His National Service was spent in various military hospitals in Germany, and on its completion in 1950, he returned to Lewisham Health District as senior registrar in infectious diseases and general medicine at Hither Green Hospital. Apart from a year as senior registrar at the Royal Free Hospital, 1954–1955, he remained at Hither Green and became consultant physician there in 1959. He was smallpox consultant for the Ministry of Health, on the advisory board of the Fellowship of Postgraduate Medicine, and an active member of the council of the Association for the Study of Infectious Diseases (now the British Society for the Study of Infection). He was also lecturer in infectious diseases at Guy's Hospital medical school.

He wrote little, but his papers were of the highest quality. He was especially interested in the prevention and control of hospital-generated infections. He was devoted to Hither Green Hospital; its welfare, and that of its patients, was always uppermost in his mind. He taught generations of students the basic principles of infectious diseases. He was first and last a perfectionist; working extremely hard himself, he had little time for slackers.

Outside his work, his interests lay in his family, gardening, bridge and reading. GW/VL

[*Brit. med. J.*, 1977, **1**, 1222; Photo]

BROWN, George Malcolm *b.*16 July 1916 *d.*19 May 1977
OC (1976) CD (1946) MD CM Queen's (1938) DPhil Oxon (1940)
MRCP (1943) FRCPC (1946) FACP (1949) FRCP (1961)
FRSC (1966) MACP (1973)†

George Malcolm Brown was born in Campbellford, Ontario, Canada, the second son of the Revd Dr George Andrew Brown and his wife, Elizabeth Stewart. The family shortly thereafter settled in Kingston, Ontario, where George Brown was called to the ministry of Chalmers Presbyterian Church, a charge he held for 25 years until his retirement in 1950.

After matriculating from Kingston Collegiate and Vocational Institute with high first class honours at the unusually early age of 16, Malcolm Brown entered medical school at Queen's University in Kingston. He received numerous honours and prizes throughout his medical course. His outstanding abilities were recognized by the award of a Rhodes Scholarship, which he held at Balliol College, Oxford, from 1938 to 1940. Here he studied experimental hypertension under BG Maegraith and, later, Sir Howard Florey. In 1940, he obtained the degree of D Phil and then pursued the study of internal medicine at the Radcliffe Infirmary under LJ Witts, gaining the MRCP.

From August 1943 to August 1946, Brown served with the Royal Canadian Army Medical Corps in the United Kingdom, Italy and Northwest Europe, attaining the rank of major. For two years of this period he was seconded to the RAMC to serve as physiologist with the malaria research unit.

In 1946, he joined the department of medicine at Queen's University, Kingston, as associate professor. In addition to his clinical and teaching duties, he organized and, for several years, led the Queen's University Arctic Expedition, to study the Canadian Eskimo. Early papers by Malcolm Brown and his colleagues, arising from his studies of man's adaptation to cold, still find their place in comprehensive texts on the subject.

He was appointed full professor of medicine in 1951, and remained in the department until 1965, when he resigned to become the president of the Medical Research Council. During those years Brown's contributions to Canadian medicine, both within and outside Queen's University, were many and substantial. The possessor of a superb and logical mind, a lively, if often well-hidden, sense of humour, and an unlimited capacity for hard work, he set the very highest standards both for himself and for all those who worked with him. Formidable in debate, he made many good causes appear the better because of his advocacy. He was an excellent general internist, but his particular interests lay in the fields of gastroenterology and haematology, in both of which he set the stage for the development of subspecialty practice at Queen's. As a teacher, he gave an example of clarity and logic which will be remembered by a generation of undergraduate and graduate students. At the same time Brown pursued significant personal research, while working to create facilities and opportunities for research as new members were recruited to the department. He was elected to membership of the American Society for Clinical Investigation in 1955 and the American Clinical and Climatological Society in 1965.

Meanwhile, he was making his mark in other organizations. For some years a member of the council of the College of Physicians and Surgeons of Ontario, the provincial licensing body, he served from 1956 to 1958 as its president. He was awarded his Fellowship in the Royal College of Physicians of Canada in 1946 and worked hard as an officer of that body, ultimately achieving its presidency from 1962 to 1964. A Fellow and, ultimately, a Master of the American College of Physicians, he served as a member of its board of Regents from 1965 to 1972. In 1966, he was elected a Fellow of the Royal Society of Canada and the following year was named to the board of trustees of Queen's University. The latter appointment, which continued until his death, gave him particular pleasure, for his father had served before him on the board; their combined and, in part, overlapping service spanned an unbroken period of 50 years. He served as a member of the Science Council of Canada from 1966 to 1970, and at the time of his death was an associate member of the National Research Council of Canada, and a member of the council of trustees of the Institute for Research on Public Policy.

As president of the Medical Research Council, Malcolm Brown's accomplishments were once again recognized across Canada and beyond. His dealings with the medical schools of Canada were always even-handed, and demonstrated his concern to see medical research developed strongly and equitably in all Canadian Health Sciences Centres. He set a standard of erudition and fairness that won the admiration of his colleagues, and he served Canadian biomedical science with distinction, wisdom and foresight. Under his leadership the Medical Research Council continued to develop as a prestigious organization with the highest standards. In 1976, Brown was appointed an Officer of the Order of Canada.

His publications included some 70 papers in scientific journals in the fields of malaria research, cold physiology, haematology, and gastroenterology.

Malcolm Brown married in 1950 Helen Louise Gatch, daughter of Gordon G Gatch of Toronto, by whom he had two daughters, Alison and Alexandra, and a son, Malcolm. JCL

[*Brit. med. J.*, 1977, **1**, 131, 270; *Lancet,* 1977, **2**, 274; Photo]

BROWNE, Richard Charles *b.*6 July 1911 *d.*3 Mar 1980
BA Bristol (1934) BM BCh Oxon (1937) MRCP (1940) DM (1946) FRCP (1964) FFOM (1978)

Richard Charles Browne came to distinction in what was then King's College of the University of Durham in 1946, as professor of industrial health, a chair newly created by the Nuffield Foundation with the active support of the dean of medicine, RB Green, and the rector of King's, Lord Eustace Percy.

Browne was born in Bristol, where his father was in a general practice in an industrial area. After school at Clifton, he went on to Wadham College, Oxford, and then to Bristol Medical School, where he gained an honours BA in physiology and was Theodore Williams Scholar in pathology. House appointments in LJ Witt's medical department at Oxford (where he had Douglas Black, later president of the Royal College of Physicians as a colleague) and in Bristol followed the BM in 1937. His thesis for the Oxford DM in 1946 was based on work carried out while in the RAF medical service in Cambridge, for the Flying Personnel Research Committee.

In his inaugural lecture in Newcastle he defined industrial health as 'the reciprocal relationship between job, home, and health'. He was adept at anticipating future trends in the University and he successfully piloted the senior common room into enlarged premises as its chairman, thereby fostering better integration of all the faculties. Into the medical faculty he brought a number of innovations in advance of other departments, introducing medical statistics, now a separate department with its own chair; pulmonary physiology, and occupational hygiene, from both of which have come contributions to research and teaching in the University; and an occupational health service mainly to industry in the north-east of England, and further afield.

It was his firm view that 'There is not or should not be any such thing as "academic" industrial health uninformed by field practice; a service stands in the same relationship to such a department as do hospital beds to its purely clinical counterpart. It provides a good deal of the basic material on which the department runs.' Perhaps his most significant contribution to the advancement of occupational hygiene as an academic discipline was made a few years before his retirement when, in 1973, he established in his department a postgraduate course leading to the degree of Master of Science in Occupational Hygiene.

In his writing, teaching and professional activities, Richard Browne consistently supported the idea that occupational health problems are best solved by the team approach, in which physicians, hygienists and engineers are involved as equal partners. His research covered a wide range of problems, including ergonomics, pneumoconiosis and nystagmus in coal miners, vanadium poisoning, acid decalcification of teeth, and shipyard accidents. Latterly he conducted a major survey of sports injuries in the North of England for the Sports Council. From the earliest days he used local industry as his source of field work, as the inspiration for two books on occupational medicine, and to enhance the quality of departmental teaching for medical and engineering students. His closest personal contact with industry was through his consultant and committee work with the electricity boards, which continued after his retirement.

Browne was a delightful person to work for; it was his policy to be readily accessible to all members of his staff and to encourage and support them. He enjoyed both travel and being at home. Abroad his expertise was much in demand, and he visited widely in Africa, Europe, and Turkey. At home he delighted in his family, his garden, and the seventh-century church in his village of Corbridge upon Tyne. He was survived by his wife Barbara, a son, and three daughters.

RIMcC

[*Brit. med. J.*, 1980, **280**, 1057; *Lancet*, 1980, **1**, 725; Photo]

BURT, Hugh Armitage *b.*16 Mar 1911 *d.*12 Mar 1976
BA Cantab (1932) MRCS LRCP (1935) MB BChir (1937)
MRCP (1941) MA (1952) FRCP (1952)

Hugh Burt, who had been director of the department of physical medicine and rheumatology at University College Hospital since 1947, died shortly before his sixty-fifth birthday. He was born in Buxton, where his father, Dr J Barnes Burt, had laid the foundations of a distinguished rheumatological practice, before moving to Bath. His grandfather was also a doctor, and Hugh had a keen interest in continuing the family tradition, his special talents allowing him to play a critical role in the transitional years faced by physical medicine after 1945. His mother was Dorothy Armitage, whose grandfather, Sir Elkanah Armitage was Lord Mayor of Manchester and knighted by Queen Victoria in 1849. He was educated at Westminster School and gained an exhibition to Trinity College, Cambridge, where both his great grandfather and great great grandfather had read mathematics and become wranglers. He subsequently entered University College Hospital Medical School and, after preliminary appointments at UCH and at the West London Hospital, enlisted in the RAMC, becoming lieutenant colonel in due course, so beginning a long association with the Army which he continued to serve as adviser in physical medicine to the War Office until his death.

His deep concern with the mechanisms and relief of pain in his field of work, coupled with innate organizing ability, led to his making a large contribution to the establishment of physical development centres, convalescent depots, and other military rehabilitation services. These qualities were deployed to the full as he built up his department at University College Hospital, gathering round him a group of loyal physiotherapists and other colleagues; his championship of the paramedical remedial professions was furthered by his work on the council of the Professions Supplementary to Medicine. His unobtrusive but firm leadership was valued by his colleagues, whom he served as vice-chairman of the medical committee and as member of the board of governors. He took endless trouble over his patients, yet found time to edit the *Annals of Physical Medicine*, to act as examiner in physical medicine for the Royal College of Physicians, to become president of the British Association of Physical Medicine and of the section of physical medicine of the Royal Society of Medicine and to serve in more than one capacity on the Empire Rheumatism Council. He contributed chapters to two books and wrote many practical articles, mostly on the subject of back pain, and the part that physical medicine had to play in its relief.

He was a quiet, unassuming man whose wide reading was reflected in his understanding of Tudor history and his interest in English literary style, but the qualities valued most highly both by his friends and by all those who came to him for help were his patience, kindliness and shrewd humorous observation of the human scene, which enabled them to see their troubles in proper perspective. In the last years of his life he developed a taste for gardening, which he shared with his old friend and surgical colleague, Doreen, daughter of Simeon Nightingale, engineer and company director of Stockton, whom he married a few days before he died in University College Hospital.

JFS

[*Brit. med. J.*, 1976, **1**, 966; *Lancet*, 1976, **1**, 704-5; *Rheumatology Rehab.*, 1976, **15**, 126]

BUTTLE, Gladwin Albert Hurst *b.*11 Apr 1899 *d.*3 May 1983
OBE (1942) BA Cantab (1922) MRCS LRCP (1924) MA (1927)
MB BChir (1967) FRCP* (1970) Hon MD Louvain (1945)

Gladwin Buttle, affectionately known to many simply as 'B', was a pioneer in the use of sulphonamides, a one time regular officer in the Royal Engineers, and an outstanding wartime leader in the development of blood transfusion services. He was born at Woldingham in Surrey; his father, William Buttle, was a solicitor and his mother, Mary, was the daughter of William Henry Ward, a builder. Gladwin started school at a Miss Brown's of Warlingham, went on to Whitgift Grammar School in Croydon and from there to the Royal Military Academy, Woolwich. In 1918 he became a second lieutenant in the Royal Engineers, intending to make his career in the regular army. However, after only one year he decided to go up to St John's College, Cambridge, to study medicine. He remained on the reserve of the Royal Engineers until 1939, and throughout his career retained an engineer's skill in improvisation, ability to overcome practical difficulties, and a habit of storing away any bit of equipment 'in case it might come in useful'.

At Cambridge, Gladwin had the intellectual capacity and maturity to profit richly from the great teachers of the time, including not only Ernest Rutherford, Adrian, Joseph Barcroft, Langley and Gowland Hopkins, but also Arthur Quiller-Couch, whose style and elegance in English were to serve as a model in writing to Gladwin throughout his life. His partner in the practical work was RA McCance, and the small class included Jack Gaddum, who became one of Gladwin's closest friends. They went together to University College Hospital, London, where they were excited by the teaching of Sir Thomas Lewis on the conduction of the cardiac impulse and the action of histamine on capillaries, and soon after qualifying Gaddum persuaded Buttle to join him at the Wellcome Physiological Laboratories in Beckenham. Gladwin was to stay for 14 years, working first on the mode of action of digitalis and local anaesthetics, but soon turning to the control of streptococcal infections by antisera and drugs. He obtained Prontosil from Domagk and tested it on mice infected with type C streptococci, which unluckily were not susceptible. Soon afterwards there was a meeting at the Royal Society of Medicine at which Dr Hörlein of Bayer put forward spectacular results and Buttle, to Hörlein's disgust, spoke of his own failure to repeat his successes. Gladwin said later that Alexander Fleming made the comment at that meeting that no drug was effective against streptococci – an odd remark in 1934 for one who was to enjoy a few years later the fame of his 1929 discovery of penicillin. Gladwin next tried Prontosil against virulent streps provided by Leonard Colebrook from cases of puerperal sepsis, this time with strikingly good effect, and he arranged for the treatment in 1936 – with the active part of the dye, sulphanilamide, – of a woman dying of puerperal sepsis, who recovered, although she spent a month in a mental hospital as a result of the enormous trial dosage used. Further exciting experiments followed in the use of sulphanilamide and its derivatives in the treatment of meningococcal and gonococcal infections, and in investigations which were to prove of importance in leprosy. In 1937 Gladwin tried diamino-diphenyl sylphone (dapsone) on himself, obtaining antibacterial properties in his blood, with only a trace of methaemoglobinaemia, but his paper on the value and safety of a low dose of the sulphone was unfortunately overlooked, in regard to its significance for the treatment of leprosy, for many years.

At the outbreak of the second world war Gladwin was persuaded by Lionel Whitby to transfer from the Royal Engineers to the RAMC, in the newly formed Army Blood Transfusion Service. So began a major part of B's career which has, in my opinion, never been adequately recognized; his OBE in 1942 acknowledged his outstanding leadership of No 1 Base Transfusion Unit in Cairo, but should surely have been just the prelude to higher awards. Gladwin's invariable custom of giving all possible credit to others probably hindered wider recognition of his own supreme contribution to war medicine. Heneage Ogilvie was to write afterwards that 'the greatest surgical advance of the war, more important even than penicillin, (was) the development of the transfusion service ... and (it was) lieutenant colonel GAH Buttle who taught us how to use it'. Plasma was being produced in large quantities in England, but for casualties on the field of battle it was the replacement of whole blood which enabled early and effective surgery to be carried out under anaesthesia. The UK did not agree and would not send equipment. Buttle, with his devoted team in Cairo and the Middle East Forces, had to improvise the local manufacture of rubber tubing, bungs, drip-chambers and needles, and their adaptation to many hundreds of gin and whisky bottles – not all of which lost their original contents before B generously sent them forward to the Field Transfusion Units in the boxes of blood and plasma. Gladwin's initiative and determination, against the declared wishes of the War Office, were protected by JSK Boyd (*q.v.*), who later said 'it was much easier to give Buttle what he wanted straight away, than to be forced to do so a week or two later and have to apologize for the delay'. Countless men must owe their lives, or their freedom from more severe disabilities, to Gladwin Buttle: he set a magnificent example of never taking 'no' for an answer, and never saying 'no' to any request for help.

At the end of 1943 Gladwin had the honour of being summoned to Carthage to help treat Churchill's bronchial infection; the Prime Minister, despite his illness, wanted an explanation of the mode of action of penicillin, and an assurance that adequate supplies of the 'wonder drug' would be available for the invasion of Normandy. Gladwin was also involved, with Frank Ellis, in saving Orde Wingate's life by blood transfusion after Wingate had cut his throat during the insanity of an attack of cerebral malaria.

As soon as the war was over Gladwin was appointed to the Wellcome chair of pharmacology in the school of pharmacy, London University, continuing his own research on the chemotherapy of bacterial diseases, and extending his investigations into the induction of resistance to experimental tumours in animals, work which unfortunately could not be extended successfully to human beings. For ten of these years Gladwin was also teaching pharmacology at Bart's. For a short time, in 1968, he worked in Mexico on behalf of the FAO, as consultant in the pre-clinical teaching of veterinary students. There followed a spell as professor of pharmacology in Addis Ababa (1972–1974) and in Riyadh (1974–1978). He was actively teaching up to the age of 79, and remained insatiably curious about every advance in biology and medicine up to the very last days.

Gladwin's other selfless task in life was to accept from his remarkable brother, Frank, responsibility for the work of the Buttle Trust for Children. Frank was an Anglican clergyman who combined a personal poverty with a flair for stock market investment. He made a fortune which the two brothers devoted, through the Trust, to the education and welfare of illegitimate, abandoned or deprived children. Gladwin was chairman of the Trust from 1953 to 1974 and under his guidance it grew in national importance, dispensing around £1m a year for the welfare of children.

Gladwin married Eva Korella, a talented painter, in 1936, bringing her to England from the threatened city of Danzig where her father was professor of botany and curator of the museum. During all the 47 years of their marriage, and particularly since his retirement, Gladwin – so often oblivious of his own welfare – would have been lost without the secure home life and love which Eva provided. They had one child, Richard.

Gladwin has been described as a 'force of nature', a man larger than life in the breadth of his intellectual scope, the depth of his scientific curiosity, in his personal courage, humour and determination, and above all in his infinite kindness and practical sympathy. He was a robust, heavily built but agile man, with a prominent lower jaw, who chewed out his words with an accent others loved to imitate; an accent which was just as evident when he was speaking French, German, Spanish or Arabic, and who had – as a sort of signature tune – a loud, boisterous, heaving laugh, so infectious that many found themselves helplessly laughing without any idea of what the original joke had been. GW

[*Brit. med. J.*, 1983, **286**, 1758 & **287**, 138, 370; *Lancet,* 1983, **1**, 1232; *Times,* 9 May 1983; Mem. Service Univ. Church of Christ the King, London, *Address*; Photo]

BUZZARD, Edward Miller *b.*13 Mar 1909 *d.*9 Mar 1976
BA Oxon (1930) MRCS LRCP (1934) BM BCh (1935)
MRCP (1937) FRCP (1949) MA (1960)

Edward Buzzard was born at 76 Wimpole Street the residence of his father E Farquhar Buzzard, FRCP, later Sir E Farquhar Buzzard, Bart, regius professor of medicine at Oxford. His mother before marriage was May Bliss, daughter of Edward Bliss, of Edgbaston. His elder brother, Anthony, had a distinguished career in the Royal Navy and retired as a rear admiral. One of his sisters married Harold Gardiner-Hill, FRCP *(q.v.)* physician to St Thomas's Hospital.

Buzzard, always known to his family and friends as Teddy, was, like his father, educated at Charterhouse School, Magdalen College, Oxford, and St Thomas's Hospital, where he was house physician to Sir Henry Tidy and registrar to Sir Maurice Cassidy. He also worked at the Brompton Hospital.

At the time of the Abyssinian crisis in 1935 his strong sense of duty made him join the Royal Navy Volunteer Reserve. In 1937 he married Sylvia Fordham, daughter of Dr JW Fordham of Leicester. They had three daughters and one son.

Teddy's career was interrupted by service in the RNVR throughout the war from 1939 to 1945, in Africa and Ceylon, with the rank of surgeon lieutenant commander. After the war he was appointed a supernumerary registrar at the Radcliffe Infirmary, and two years later was elected to the honorary staff. His main life's work was spent in the service of the Oxford hospitals, where he gave meticulous and sympathetic care to all patients, whether in hospital or private practice. He examined at the universities of Oxford, Cambridge and London, and for the Conjoint and Membership examinations of the College. He was appointed a lecturer in medicine at Oxford in 1957.

Teddy Buzzard was a tall, good-looking man with great charm, in the best sense of the word. He was one of the last of the general physicians, with a wide and deep knowledge of medicine. He had a special interest in respiratory diseases. Everybody liked him; no one could quarrel with him. Lord Richardson, an old friend, wrote of him: 'His lifelong response to his wonderful endowments of body and mind was to show to all consideration, which derived from his innate modesty. Although he seemed to be personally detached from the failings, and most of the weaknesses, of us all, he understood them and was always kindly about them. His company was restful, his standards strengthening, and his courage inspiring. In him was greatness.'

Apart from his professional work, Teddy showed remarkable versatility. A natural athlete and ball-games player – a Buzzard family trait – he represented his university at lawn tennis and squash rackets. Such was his skill, character and prestige that he was selected at the age of 20 to captain the combined Oxford and Cambridge lawn tennis team that visited the United States of America in 1929. He played in the Wimbledon tournament for several years and succeeded in defeating one or two well known players. Although he came from a school that favoured the association game, he captained St Thomas's at rugby. He was also an ardent naturalist and ornithologist. His cottage in Cornwall was a great joy, where he indulged in what he called 'gentle beachcombing'. Despite his many accomplishments and a large circle of admiring friends, he remained totally unspoilt. He retired in 1974 and went to live at Frilford Heath, a few miles outside Oxford. His last years were clouded by a long and distressing illness, which he bore with characteristic fortitude. AMC

[*Brit. med. J.*, 1976, **2**, 904, 1023, 1225; *Lancet*, 1976, **1**, 819]

BYROM, Frank Burnet *b*.14 Feb 1902 *d*.14 Oct 1976
MRCS LRCP (1923) MB BS Lond (1924) MD (1926) MRCP (1926) FRACP (1940) FRCP (1953)

Frank Byrom was born in Wigan, the son of Thomas Henry Byrom FRIC FCS, chief analytical and research chemist of the Wigan Coal and Iron Companies, and lecturer at the Mining and Technical College. He came of an old Lancashire family which, in the 17th century, produced John Byrom, composer of the carol 'Christians Awake'. From the Stationers' Company's school Frank entered the London Hospital medical college, where he had a distinguished student career, carrying off most of the undergraduate prizes. He was awarded honours with distinction in medicine in the London MB, and proceeded to hold a long sequence of house appointments at the London Hospital, including house physician to the medical professorial unit and resident accoucheur. From 1927 to 1930 he was medical first assistant to Leyton-Riddoch and during this period he acted as demonstrator in physiology, and carried out research on blood phosphorus in health and disease with HD Kay FRS.

This was followed by a Rockefeller research fellowship at the University of Chicago, where he became interested in electrolyte and water metabolism. He returned to the medical unit at the London as Beit memorial research fellow, and over the next three years published studies on fluid and electrolyte balance in myxoedema, diabetes and epilepsy. At this point he joined forces with Clifford Wilson, who had visited Goldblatt's laboratory (USA) where experimental hypertension was produced in dogs by renal artery constriction. There were, at the London, no facilities for working with dogs, but an ample supply of Wistar rats. Wilson and Byrom devised the tail plethysmograph method for making repeated blood pressure measurements in the rat. This ingenious invention opened up a whole field of research, since the rat, in its hypertensive behaviour, was found to resemble man more closely than did any other experimental animal. Constriction of one renal artery by an adjustable silver clip led to severe hypertension, with the production of vascular and glomerular lesions in the opposite kidney closely resembling those occurring in malignant hypertension in man. These experiments established the role of high blood pressure, whatever its cause, in producing renal vascular damage. They led to a concept of a vicious circle in hypertensive renal disease, and provided a rationale for medical and surgical measures calculated to lower the blood pressure.

In 1940, Byrom was appointed director of the postgraduate pathological unit at Prince Henry Hospital, Sydney, and during the war years he assisted in the building of a plant for freeze-drying plasma. He maintained his interest in experimental hypertension, and by a brilliant technique of micro-surgery he succeeded in implanting acrylic windows in the rat's skull through which the superficial cerebral arteries of the hypertensive animal could be studied and photographed. He showed (contrary to existing theory) that cerebral arteries and arterioles were capable of focal and diffuse vasoconstriction, and that 'vascular crises' (resembling hypertensive encephalopathy in man) were associated with cerebral oedema and arterial necrosis.

Byrom returned to England in 1957 and, with a personal grant from the MRC, made his third outstanding contribution, namely the study of the responses of the retinal arteries to hypertension. Working with Peter Daniel at the Maudsley Hospital, and later returning to the London, he devised a technique for photography and ciné-photography of the retina of the anaesthetised rat. The results confirmed and amplified his earlier findings, and formed the basis of his view that hypertensive vascular damage results from dilatations of muscular deficient zones in the arterial wall. The techniques, results and conclusions, were published in his monograph: *The hypertensive vascular crisis*, which (wrote TF Fox, his life-long friend) 'is a model of scientific writing; it illustrates his clinical approach, logical thinking and lucid expression; he was as elegant on paper as in the laboratory'. In appreciation of his outstanding contribution to our understanding of high blood pressure Byrom was invited to give the Volhard lecture in 1976 (in his 74th year) to the International Society of Hypertension. At times working under great difficulties in terms of staff, finance and accommodation, Frank was greatly sustained (and even given technical help) by his wife, Kathleen, daughter of artist Percival Stanger Prichard, and by his gifted family. Of their five children (three boys and two girls), two qualified in medicine at the London, and one of these married Frank John Goodwin FRCP, renal physician to the London Hospital.

Byrom retired to Sandgate and built himself a laboratory dedicated to the restoration and repair of early English clocks, which he collected and displayed with great success and enthusiasm. At the bottom of his garden was the Channel where he and his wife bathed at all seasons.

CW

[*Lancet*, 1976, **2**, 1146]

CADMAN, Ewan Frederick Braithwaite *b*.19 Dec 1919 *d*.28 Sept 1980

MB ChB Liverp (1943) MRCP (1945) DCH (1945)
MD Wash St Louis (1946) MD Liverp (1954) FRCP (1970)

Ewan Cadman was born in London, the son of Frederick Cadman, a civil servant, and his wife Jennie Braithwaite. The family moved to Southport, Lancashire (now Merseyside) and Ewan was educated at King George V School, commencing his medical studies at Liverpool University in 1937. His studies were interrupted by a move to the United States in 1941, where he was awarded a Rockefeller Scholarship which enabled him to spend two years at an American university. Ewan spent these years at Washington University, St Louis, where he successfully sat the American final examinations, but the regulations governing the scholarship meant that the degree could not be conferred until the British qualification was obtained. He returned home and qualified MB ChB at Liverpool University in 1943, followed by the DCH and MRCP and MD(Liverpool).

After qualifying at Liverpool, he held appointments as house physician at the Liverpool Royal Infirmary and the Hospital for Sick Children, Great Ormond Street, London, and later became medical officer at the Heswall Branch of the Royal Children's Hospital. During his period of National Service, from 1946 to 1948, he served in the RAMC and then took up an appointment as medical registrar at the Liverpool Royal Infirmary. He was appointed lecturer in medicine in the University, a post which entailed clinical duties and carried the rank of senior medical registrar. It was about this time that, when being medically examined for life insurance, he was found to be hypertensive. This fact made him modify his future plans, as he had previously entertained ideas of a career in academic medicine.

In 1953 he was appointed consultant physician to the Southport Hospital Group, returning to his home town. It must not, however, be thought that he entertained any ideas of an easy life. He was determined to make his unit efficient, and he displayed notable drive in introducing new developments, including a coronary care unit. He also played a prominent part in forming a postgraduate centre associated with the Southport General Infirmary.

Ewan Cadman possessed the gift of clear thinking and quickly identified the essentials of a problem, either clinical or administrative. He was also extremely practical. He was very much a general physician and his interests were varied and wide-ranging. His publications included papers on lupus erythematosus, fainting, and phaeochromocytoma.

His political views could, perhaps, be described as somewhat left of centre, but in his hospital activities he was always impartial and worked for what he believed to be best for patients and hospital staff alike. He was chairman of the Southport Branch of the BMA from 1969 to 1970, and president of the Southport Medical Society in 1973. Outside his profession, his interests were archaeological and mainly devoted to local history. But he enjoyed swimming and could sail a yacht effectively.

His friends believed that he pushed himself too hard. It was only a year before his death, after he had suffered several setbacks in health, that he decided to reduce his activities and consider an early retirement. The end, however, came quickly and he died in the unit which he had been instrumental in starting.

In June 1951 he married Margaret, daughter of James R Armour, director of a timber firm. They had met at the Liverpool Royal Infirmary. They had three sons, the second of whom is medically qualified. An uncle is a consultant chest physician at St Bartholomew's Hospital.

WHRC

[*Brit. med. J.*, 1980, **281**, 1645]

CALVERT, Edwin George Bleakley *b*.21 Jan 1893 *d*.3 Aug 1976
MB BCh BAO Belf (1915) MD (1920) DPH (1920) MRCP (1923) FRCP (1941)

Edwin Calvert was the eldest of the four children of James Calvert of Lyndhurst, Lurgan, Co. Armagh, and his wife, Anne, née Armstrong, daughter of George Armstrong, of Tullyweel House, Creagh, Fivemiletown, Co. Fermanagh. Both families had extensive farms, but James Calvert was not a farmer and became clerk of the union (a local government office) at Lurgan.

All the children took up the study of medicine. Edwin became a physician; his sister, Evelyn, became an anaesthetist and she married FMB Allen, the first professor of paediatrics at Belfast; the second son, Cecil, became a distinguished neurosurgeon, first at Belfast and later in the British army during the 1939 war – he was afterwards killed in a motor accident; the youngest brother, Howard, never qualified, as he left his medical studies in 1915 to join the army and was shot dead by the IRA during the rebellion in Ireland in 1916. The children's interest in medicine was undoubtedly due to the influence of their mother; as a young married woman, she had taken a local child, who had been bitten by a rabid dog, to Pasteur's clinic in Paris, where he was given a course of anti-rabies treatment. She had remained in Paris for the period of the inoculations and had been very kindly looked after by Pasteur.

Edwin Calvert was educated at Methodist College, Belfast, and entered the Queen's University in 1910; there he had a brilliant academic career, obtaining a gold medal in anatomy and gold medals at the MB and MD examinations. On qualifying in 1915 he went into the army, and subsequently served with the 6th battalion Northumberland Fusiliers till the end of the war. After demobilization he returned to Belfast and was appointed lecturer in the department of physiology, where he worked chiefly in biochemistry. In the following year he obtained an appointment as assistant in the newly established professorial unit at St Mary's Hospital, London, under Frederick Langmead, and remained there for five years, his work including the biochemistry and other clinical pathology of the unit; during this period insulin was introduced, and in 1923 Calvert published an improved method of estimating blood sugar (*Biochem. J.*, 1923/24).

In 1925 he resigned from St Mary's and obtained appointments as honorary physician first at the Temperance Hospital and then at the Northern (later Royal Northern) Hospital, and to both of these he gave a lifetime of devoted service; he was also consulting physician to the Samaritan and City of London Maternity Hospitals.

For many years he contributed to successive editions of *Pye's Surgical Handicraft* the chapters on examination of the urine and on kidney function tests, and his writings in various journals were on diabetes, kidney disease, endocrine disorders and rheumatoid arthritis.

Calvert continued in private practice long after retirement from his hospitals, but late in life he went to live at Barton-on-sea where he enjoyed his golf and gardening and took up painting. He died in consequence of a head injury which he sustained on the previous day by tripping on the kerb in Barton village.

Calvert was a gentle and modest person, very thorough in all his work, and somewhat slow of speech even for an Ulsterman. He married in 1928 Nancy, daughter of CW Narsden of Sydney and (temporarily) of Park Place, St James's, and the ceremony took place at All Souls', Langham Place, where his uncle had formerly been rector. They had one son and two daughters. JPM

CALVERT, Rowland James *b.*12 Oct 1918 *d.*23 June 1978
BSc Glasg (1939) MB ChB (1943) DPH Birm (1947) MRCP (1949) PhD Lond (1956) MD Glasg (1956) FRCP (1970)

Rowland Calvert was born at Brampton in Cumberland (Cumbria). His father was the Reverend George Calvert of the Presbyterian Church, and his mother Isobel Broach, daughter of James Graham, a farmer.

He was educated at Greenlaw in Berwickshire and Coatbridge High School in Lanarkshire, and while a pupil there he played soccer for the Scottish schoolboys' team.

He entered Glasgow University for the BSc in agriculture in 1937, transferred to the BSc in pure science, and graduated in 1939. In October, 1938, he registered as a student in the faculty of medicine of that university and qualified MB ChB in 1943. He was a member of the Glasgow University teams in soccer, badminton and tennis.

After qualifying he was house physician at Glasgow Royal Infirmary, and in 1943 joined the RAMC. He saw service overseas in Italy, Austria, Greece and Germany and left the RAMC in December, 1946, with the rank of captain.

After the war he worked at Hammersmith Hospital as a house physician and then went to University College Hospital, where for two and a half years he worked in wholetime clinical research with HP (later Sir Harold) Himsworth, Max (later Lord) Rosenheim and Andrew Wilson. He had taken the DPH at Birmingham in 1947 and the MRCP in 1949. He was senior medical registrar at Whipps Cross Hospital from 1951 to 1954, then at the North Middlesex Hospital, after which he did some consultant locums before being appointed consultant physician in Burnley. During this period he published no fewer than twenty papers on a variety of subjects. He also took the PhD at London University and the MD with commendation at Glasgow in 1956. He was elected FRCP in 1970.

Calvert had an encyclopaedic knowledge of medicine and was particularly interested in metabolic disorders. Unfortunately, a few months after he moved to Burnley he suffered an extensive myocardial infarction, but made a remarkable recovery, due in no small measure to his wife, Gwen's, devoted and selfless care.

He was a chairman of the Burnley Division of the BMA and a president of the Burnley Caledonian Society.

Rowland Calvert always had an interest in medical education, and was appointed to the post of postgraduate clinical tutor to the Group in 1965. The opening of the Mackenzie Medical Centre in Burnley in 1966 added a new dimension to the whole of medical practice in the district. Ever since, there has been a full programme of lectures, symposia and unit specialist meetings almost every day of the week. The initial and continued success of the medical centre was largely due to Calvert's organization, his widespread contacts and, above all, his personality and unique handling of the meetings. He had a deep and lasting love for the English language and for rhetoric, often in its more florid and picturesque form.

Rowland was a large man physically, with a personality to match, and was greatly beloved by his colleagues and patients. He was married to Gwendoline May, widow, daughter of AEA Clark, but they had no children. WT

[*Brit. med. J.*, 1978, **2**, 285; Photo]

CAMERON, Alister James Victor *b.*11 Sept 1916 *d.*2 Jan 1980
MA Glasg (1936) MB ChB (1940) FRFPS Glasg (1942)
MRCP (1944) MD (1952) FRCPG (1964) FRCP (1964)

Alister Cameron was born at Stenhousemuir, Stirlingshire, and brought up in Clydebank. His father, a cost accountant, was also called Alister James Victor Cameron, and his mother, Mary, was the daughter of John Adam, a foreman iron grinder. He was educated at Clydebank High School, where he was dux medallist, and obtained a bursary to Glasgow University, where he graduated MA in the humanities in 1936. He then transferred to the faculty of medicine on a Stewart bursary and graduated MB ChB in 1940, obtaining prizes in clinical medicine and surgery. After resident appointments in the Western and Royal Infirmaries, he joined the EMS and was appointed medical registrar at Gartloch Emergency Hospital, Glasgow, in 1942, and later became assistant physician to the outpatient department. In 1945 he was appointed acting physician in charge of the medical unit at Ballochmyle Hospital, Ayrshire.

Glasgow University awarded him the Christina Hansen research scholarship in medicine in 1946, when he started his research in cardiology, particularly vector cardiography, of which he was a pioneer, in the department of JW Wright. In 1947 he was appointed assistant physician to the outpatient department of Glasgow Royal Infirmary, and proceeded MD in 1952. At the end of this year he spent four months in France at the Clinique Cardiologique de la Faculté de Médecine, University of Paris, under the direction of E Donzelot, where he studied cardiac electrophysiology with particular reference to vector cardiography. This was an extremely happy period of his life: his wife, Janet, whom he had married in 1949, was a medical graduate of Edinburgh University and she was able to join him in Paris for the latter part of his visit. She was the daughter of Hugh Bryden Murdoch, a science teacher at Trinity Academy, Edinburgh, who later became headmaster of the David Kilpatrick Secondary School, Edinburgh.

In 1953 Alister became consultant cardiologist to the Western Infirmary, a post he held until his death. During this period he built up the department of cardiology and planned its further development in phase one of the Western Infirmary. His work in the field of vector cardiography was internationally recognized, and demonstrated his ability in mathematics and statistical analysis. Early in the 1960s he carried out an excellent controlled clinical trial of hyperbaric oxygen in acute myocardial infarction. In the last 25 years of his life it became clear that his main strength was in clinical and teaching aspects of cardiology.

He was a member of the British Cardiac Society, and of the first European Congress in Cardiology in 1952; a member of the Association of Physicians of Great Britain and Ireland; a fellow of the RSM, a member of the International Society of Internal Medicine, the Scottish Society of Physicians, the Scottish Society for Experimental Medicine and the Royal Medico-Chirurgical Society of Glasgow. He was elected a fellow of the College, and of the Glasgow College, in 1964.

Alister Cameron was a gentle and modest man. He was also an excellent raconteur, which made him a popular student and postgraduate teacher, and a natural scholar. He never lost his love for Latin and Greek, and his interests included Russian literature and East European culture. He travelled widely in Europe, America and Canada, and it was after a trip to Eastern Europe that he took up the study of Russian. He also had a great love for the poetry and history of his native land, and a deep appreciation of music which was shared by his wife and his daughter. Until the onset of his illness in 1970 he also enjoyed golf and tennis. Despite indifferent health following the first attack of myocardial infarction, he continued to work. After the tragic loss of his wife in 1976 he sublimated his intense grief in his work for the medical student organizations in the university, and in 1977 he became president of the student Medico-Chirurgical Society in which he took a very active interest. He was a man who made close and lasting bonds with friends and colleagues, and despite the many vicissitudes of his later years he remained cheerful, and always thoughtful of others. AG(1)

[*Brit. med. J.*, 1980, **280**, 324, 728; Photo]

CAMPBELL, *Sir* **David** *b*.6 May 1889 *d*.30 May 1978
Kt (1953) MC (1918) BSc Glasg (1911) MA (1911) MB ChB (1916) MD (1924) FRCP* (1956)†

David Campbell was born at Patna, Ayrshire, and educated at Ayr Academy and Glasgow University, where he graduated with honours in the faculties of both arts and medicine, with the addition of a BSc from the science faculty. As a student in three faculties he took an active part in student affairs over a number of years When he graduated in medicine in 1916 he went straight into the RAMC, where he served with distinction in France and was awarded the Military Cross. On completing his military service in 1919 he was appointed assistant to the professor of materia medica and therapeutics in his old university, and it was in this field of medicine that he made his career and reputation as a distinguished teacher, physician and administrator.

In 1924, when he was Pollok lecturer in pharmacology and therapeutics, his MD thesis was awarded first class honours and the coveted Bellahouston gold medal. From 1925 to 1926 he was one of the first of a distinguished line of Rockefeller fellows who made Johns Hopkins University their US base. In 1930 he moved to Aberdeen to become the regius professor of materia medica and therapeutics and a consultant physician in Aberdeen Royal Infirmary. Within two years his drive and clear-headed shrewdness had won him the respect of his colleagues and he was elected dean of the Faculty of Medicine, a post to which he was re-elected at three-yearly intervals for the next twenty-seven years! He was the doyen of an able, self-confident and autocratic group of Glaswegians who dominated the Medical Faculty of Aberdeen University in the '30s and '40s – John Cruickshank and John Young (from the 'Bobby' Muir stable), James Learmonth and, last in time of appointment but not least, Dugald Baird. It was this team under David Campbell's leadership that diluted the north-eastern parochialism of the medical faculty and enhanced its well deserved national and international reputation for excellence.

David Campbell was nominated to represent the University of Aberdeen on the General Medical Council in 1936 and continued to do so for the next twenty-five years, the last twelve of these as its president. His effectiveness as an administrator lay in careful selection and preparation of items for the agenda of the many committees which he chaired, a shrewd knowledge of his colleagues' personalities, and an uncanny sense of timing. It is probably apocryphal, but credible, that, on occasions when he had to catch the night train to London immediately after a faculty meeting, he would draft the minutes *before* the meeting and they rarely had to be altered.

As a teacher he belonged to the old school of pharmacologists, whose lectures took the student through a pharmacopoeia dominated by tinctures, powders, pills and compounds. His own *Handbook of Therapeutics* was a classic of its time. He never used notes other than the sheets extracted from the pharmacopoeia and circulated to the class. These had to be memorized, and disaster awaited the student who did not know the doses of nostrums that have long since disappeared from chemists' shelves. His classes were fully attended and few dared sleep in the 2–3 p.m. lectures given throughout the summer term. His watchful eye, quick wit and pawky humour were helpful stimulants. In spite of his administrative commitments he retained full responsibility for patients in his medical wards, and his remarkable memory, acute observation and attention to detail made him an able and respected physician.

He had many honours bestowed upon him. He was knighted in 1953 and was an LLD of Aberdeen, Dublin, Glasgow and Liverpool, and DCL of Durham, and a fellow of the Royal Colleges of Physicians of London and Glasgow, and a fellow of the Royal Society of Edinburgh.

His recreation was golf, at which he was a creditable performer, and for many years he could regularly break '80' and defeat most members of the faculty. On one occasion returning by train from a match between the Senates of Glasgow and Aberdeen at Prestwick he regaled the carriage with a detailed account of every one of the 78 shots he had played to defeat his opponent!

He married in 1921 Margaret, only daughter of Alexander Lyle of Kerse. There were no children. He died at the age of 89 at his home in Milltimber, Aberdeenshire. EKC

[*Brit. med. J.*, 1978, **2**, 61; *Lancet*, 1978, **2**, 55; *Times*, 15 June 1978; Photo]

CANDAU, Marcolino Gomes *b.*30 May 1911 *d.*25 Jan 1983
MD Rio de Janeiro MPH Johns Hopkins USA FRCP* (1961)
Hon degrees†

Marcolino Gomes Candau was one of the greatest figures in medicine during the 20th century. He became a world figure almost irrespective of his nationality because his main professional work was outside his own country. He was a Brazilian, born in Rio de Janeiro in 1911, educated there and holding his first public appointments in that state's Department of Health. He also became assistant professor of hygiene in Rio and he obtained the MPH of Johns Hopkins USA. He emerged from the State Health Department onto the wider scene as director of division in the Serviçio Especial de Saúde Pública, which did so much good work in North Eastern Brazil from 1940, and moved on to WHO as head of division in the Regional Office for the Americas in 1950. A year later Candau became assistant director general of WHO before returning to the Regional Office, from which he was chosen as director general by the World Health Assembly in 1953. There were other more widely known candidates in that election and the choice of Candau was a surprise to many. That choice was quickly vindicated beyond any doubt, and Candau remained director general for 20 years. He chose to retire in 1973 when many hoped he would accept another term, but again his timing was impeccable, and he made an admirable succession possible without the confrontation between developing countries and main contributors which many had feared.

In 20 years Candau, as he was universally known, brought WHO from a struggling aid agency in the UN family to a position of great influence and real achievement. He managed to do this without alienating any of the large political entities involved or ever being suspected of bias. It was obvious that the developing countries had his sympathy – as they should – but he did not use the political strength they could have given him in a way that alienated the major contributors to the budget – the USA nearly one third and the USSR nearly one seventh. One could not fail to admire his dexterity and never doubted his honesty. In 20 years inevitably there were failures as well as successes. The malaria eradication programme attempted too much, but still achieved a great deal. The smallpox eradication programme was a magnificent success. The promotion of training erred for a long time on the side of medical schools, which developing countries wanted but could not always afford or service, while they did not produce staff with a more simple training that would have been of greater use. But the sovereign states would not be denied, and it was not at Candau's inspiration that they sometimes over-reached. Candau always sought to develop a more simple infrastructure and mostly he succeeded. His successor's policy was only possible because of the ground work Candau had done. Candau's reaction to the Assembly's rejection of his scheme for a world biomedical research centre was typical of him. He accepted it loyally in principle as in detail, and applied that same principle in helping to deflect the grandiose project for a world cancer research centre into the modest and rational Lyons-based WHO subsidiary, the International Agency for Cancer Research, which has done so much to develop the epidemiology of cancer.

WHO is probably the most respected of all the international agencies and the least disrupted by political differences. For that we largely have to thank Candau and the deputy he chose, also a Fellow, Pierre Dorolle (*q.v.*).

Candau was an urbane, unpretentious, friendly man. He could fight fiercely in defence of his staff, but utterly lacked consciousness of his own dignity. He was a charming host and a welcome and delightful guest. His intellectual quality was of the highest, but he was never the condescending expert some people of high attainments become. He was fluent and idiomatic in at least three languages with odd little quirks in pronunciation that endeared him the more to Assemblies. When he died suddenly at 71, nearly a decade after his retirement, he was mourned by the many at the ensuing Assembly who remembered him and his work, but also by uncountable numbers in the health field throughout the world.

Looking back through three quarters of the 20th century which encompassed his life there might be a very small number of doctors of comparable stature, but none who could equal his contribution to disease prevention, health promotion and, most of all, the care of people. He received innumerable honours, but he certainly valued most of all the informal and universal approval successive Assemblies gave him. He was twice married and the two sons of the first marriage, and his second wife, survived him. GEG

[*Times*, 28 Jan 1983; *Lancet*, 1983, **1**, 369, 487; WHO Jan 1961, *Biographical Notes*; Photo]

CANT, William Howard Pinney *b.*31 Jan 1906 *d.*30 August 1981
MRCS LRCP (1930) MB BS Lond (1930) MD (1936) MRCP (1936) FRCP (1959) DO Dubl (1976)

William Cant was the maternal grandson of the Revd Charles Pinney who was vicar of Coleshill, Warwickshire for many years. He was born at Coleshill where his father, Arthurt Cant, one of the first medical graduates of the University of Birmingham, was in general practice for more than half a century. William was educated at West House Preparatory School in Birmingham, Shrewsbury and the University of Birmingham, but he graduated from the University of London in 1930, proceeding MD six years later and being elected a member of the College in 1936. After house officer appointments, Cant was resident medical officer at the Birmingham Children's Hospital, and later he was assistant clinical pathologist and in charge of the diabetic clinic at the Birmingham General Hospital, until 1938, when he returned to the Children's Hospital as clinical pathologist. Soon after the outbreak of war he was placed in charge of the blood transfusion service in the Midlands, where his supremely efficient work was responsible for the later success of the West Midlands Regional Blood Transfusion Service, established with the National Health Service in 1948.

After the war he was appointed physician to the Birmingham Children's Hospital, and as such was one of the first to specialize wholly in paediatrics; he was also elected paediatrician to the West Bromwich and District Hospital and the Lickey Grange School for Blind Children, and to these three institutions he gave devoted and unselfish service for the next twenty-four years of his life. Always friendly, unassuming and anxious to help others, Cant was enormously popular, particularly with his students and residents, in whose welfare he took a great interest, but he knew all the nurses, porters, technicians and other workers in the hospitals where he worked, and each regarded him as their friend. For his patients and their parents he always seemed to have all the time they wanted, and he made each child, and the parents, feel that they were his most important problem.

Cant was a member of the British Paediatric Association, secretary and later president of the Midland Regional Paediatric Society, a lecturer and examiner in paediatrics in the University of Birmingham and also the university's postgraduate clinical tutor in paediatrics. His work in this latter appointment was so highly regarded that when the postgraduate medical centre at the Children's Hospital was opened it was named after him. When he reached the age of 65, and in consequence had to retire from his consultant appointments, Cant was still full of energy and anxiety to serve his fellow men. His work at the Lickey Grange School for Blind Children had given him a keen interest in ophthalmology, and he took the Diploma in Ophthalmology in Dublin and became a clinical assistant in ophthalmology at the Birmingham and Midland Eye Hospital. Within a very short time he was the most respected and best loved person in the hospital, and he continued to work there until his death, doing an outpatient session on the morning of the onset of his fatal illness. Despite his age, his death cast a gloom over the whole hospital greater than any other event could have provoked.

Cant married in 1939 Isabel Martineau, a fellow medical student and daughter of CE Martineau, who held the chair of accountancy in the University of Birmingham. Their marriage was supremely happy and they had one daughter and one son. Cant's wife came from a family with a tradition of unselfish and magnificent public service to the city of Birmingham, and her own splendid personality complemented her husband's contribution to everything with which he was associated. Totally devoid of ambition, always humble and gentle, Cant's life was devoted to helping others. He became a fellow in 1959 but took no great part in College affairs, though his life and his work were everything of which the College could be proud.

Cant was somewhat eccentric in the informality of his attire and his dedication to physical exercise. Despite increasing respiratory disability he continued to run and to play tennis until the end of his life. His interests were wide, and at the time of his death he was president of the Central Literary Association. AGWW

[*Brit. med. J.*, 1981, **283**, 798; Photo]

CAPPELL, Daniel Fowler *b.*28 Feb 1900 *d.*13 Feb 1976
CBE (1958) MB ChB Glasg (1921) MD (1928) FRFPSG (1947)
MRCPE (1958) FRCPE (1960) MRCP (1958) FRCP (1960)
FRCPG (1962) FRCPath (1963)†

Daniel Fowler Cappell, professor of pathology in the University of St Andrews and pathologist to the Royal Infirmary and other hospitals in the Dundee region 1931 – 1945; professor of pathology in the University of Glasgow and pathologist to The Western Infirmary 1945 – 1967, was born in Glasgow, the second son of Robert Cappell, pharmaceutical chemist, and Annabella, daughter of Daniel Fowler, haulage contractor, Glasgow.

From Glasgow Academy, as dux of the VIth class, he followed his youngest uncle to Glasgow University in 1916, by which time his brother and uncle were in France; the latter died on active service as a chaplain. His performance in the anatomy class was such that the professor (TH Bryce) prevented his enrolling as a surgeon probationer and retained him as a part-time teacher. During this period he was asked to map out the neurovascular hila of the limb muscles. This was incorporated in Quain's *Anatomy*, gained the Struther's gold medal and prize (usually won as the result of postgraduate research), and its utility in relation to wounds (World War II) was recognized in Professor Brash's book on the *Neurovascular hila*. He also did locum house officer jobs, including five months with Sir William Macewen, obtained the medal in pathology, and passed his finals with honours in 1921.

Cappell's potential had been noted by CH Browning, who had returned to Glasgow to occupy the chair of bacteriology, and he saw to it that Cappell got the McCunn Scholarship in pathology and encouraged him to study Goldmann on intra-vital staining and learn German thereby. This work was continued when, in 1923, he became assistant to Robert Muir, along with JS Young (later professor at Belfast and then Aberdeen), the one lecturer being JWS Blacklock (later professor at Glasgow Royal Infirmary and then at St Bartholomew's, London). A notable feature of his busy life at this time was his steady acquisition of experience of the appearances of disease as seen by the naked eye and through the microscope; from this mental thesaurus he could years later retrieve with phenomenal certainty. Many pathologists thought that Cappell at the microscope was the most accurate diagnostician in Britain, and his opinion was widely sought, the only cost involved being the loss of time for his own research. The 'surgicals' were always a prime obligation, and here Cappell's passion for quality led to a cooperation with the technicians, providing harvests to this day. The outward mark of this was the honorary fellowship of the Institute of Medical Laboratory Technology (1950), and in 1956 the award of the Sims Woodhead medal for his conspicuous service to medical laboratory technology. He was delighted when DS Fraser, the boy he started to train in Dundee in 1931, was capped in 1975 by HM The Queen Mother, as Chancellor of the University of Dundee, with the honorary degree of master of medical science. Cappell stressed on his junior colleagues the duty and value of cooperation with technicians, even to the extent of knowing the technical problems. Of these colleagues seventeen have become professors, fourteen in pathology, two in medicine and one in surgery.

As teacher, Cappell was at his best with small groups, and in his early years at Dundee he enjoyed the contact with the students. The class of 1935–1936 had only 40 students; of these, 34 became consultants in one field or another. His skill in all aspects of communication increased with his knowledge, and Cappell was therefore Sir Robert Muir's natural choice for the editorship of his *Textbook of Pathology*. From Cappell's hand came the 6th, 7th and 8th editions, and then jointly with his successor, JR Anderson, the 9th edition in 1971.

His research on intra-vital staining was published in papers that occupied most of the July 1928 issue of the *J. Path. and Bact.*, and formed the basis of an MD thesis, awarded honours and the Bellahouston gold medal. This work, along with that of JW McNee (later Sir John), was a further illumination from Muir's juniors of the emerging concept of the reticulo-endothelial system of Muir's friend, Aschoff. Later in Dundee, with his assistant Sheila Callender, he identified the mechanism of the so-called pernicious anaemia of pregnancy. Then, before the outbreak of war, he had established a blood transfusion service in the Dundee region, the model for the rest of the country, and was ready to meet the problems of the Rhesus factor, becoming pre-eminent in the elucidation of the Rh-antigens.

Characteristically, as soon as he saw the practical possibilities of this new knowledge, he turned his endeavours in that direction, and played a major part in communicating the necessary information to the medical and nursing professions.

Recalled to the Glasgow chair in 1945, on the death of J Shaw Dunn, he planned a regional scheme of pathological services, as a close and friendly partnership of the University laboratories with the others. He joined the Association of Clinical Pathologists, later to be president and chairman of council, and helped to disperse the suspicion with which academic pathologists were regarded by other pathologists, especially in England. As a peace-maker his precise objectivity made him valuable and valued, and along with Cuthbert Dukes and Geoffrey Hadfield, he helped to engender the unexpected amity that attended the formation of the College of Pathologists. In the College, as vice-president and chairman of the examining board, he set the standards of examination to be a realistic measure of knowledge and of diagnostic accuracy.

Following Sir James Paget's dictum, 'never to refuse duties or offices which come in the plain course of events', he accepted such obligations if they concerned education or the study of disease. His combination of wisdom and perception of the way forward, combining the Argus and Briareus of Bacon's essay, resulted in a massive demand for his services, even after retirement, as an adviser, examiner or as a committee member. He seemed tireless when on duty-bound, possibly because he was objective enough to know his ambition for excellence in study, and especially the study of disease, had to be a long-term plan. His objectivity occasionally suffered some diminution when he realized a colleague's planning was for self-advancement.

Homo antiqua virtute ac fide, he pursued excellence in his work, in his planning and in his human relationships, creating notable loyalty among those who shared his high intent and dedication to the morality of accuracy. It could well be said of him as Carlyle wrote of Lord Jeffrey: '... a man, intrinsically of veracity; was in earnest too, though not "dreadfully in earnest"...'. Indeed, one never knew when a flash of gratuitous cheerfulness would break in. In close alliance with his friend JH Dible he helped to create, from the start in 1950, the warm and valuable relationship binding Dutch pathologists with the British.

He married in 1927 Audrey, daughter of Charles Alfred Griffin, manufacturer's agent in Glasgow, and although they had no children the door was always open at their hospitable home. Her life-long interest in social work was mirrored in the cheerful catalytic influence she provided in the Cappell's Blood Transfusion Service, still remembered with joy and pride in the Dundee region. They were both skilled anglers and shared this, as they did their special claret, with juniors as well as coevals. 'Without her he might have flown as high, but he could not have stayed so long on the wing.' He died, after a few hours illness, in Stracathro Hospital, near Edzell in Angus, to which they had retired in 1967. ACL

[*Brit. med. J.*, 1976, **1**, 528; *Lancet*, 1976, **1**, 496; *J. Path.*, 1977, **122**, 175-183; Photo]

CARMICHAEL, Edward Arnold *b*.29 Mar 1896 *d*.9 Feb 1978
CBE (1942) MB ChB Edin (1921) MRCP (1925) FRCPE (1926) FRCP (1932) Hon DSc Edin (1963)

Arnold Carmichael was the son of Edward Carmichael MD, who was born and went to school in Edinburgh, graduated from its University, and practised medicine in the city as a family doctor until his death. Arnold Carmichael's education followed that of his father at Edinburgh Academy and Ediburgh University, where he obtained the MB with the Annandale Gold Medal in 1921. His University was to award him the DSc *hom. causa* in 1963, too. He became a Fellow of the Edinburgh College six years before election to the London Fellowship in 1932. All his junior medical and surgical house appointments were, not surprisingly, at the Edinburgh Royal Infirmary.

His medical education was interrupted by combatant service in the infantry in the world war of 1914–1918. What was surprising was that, with a life grounded in Edinburgh and steeped in American medicine, he should, as soon as possible, have migrated to London to study neurology, for there was then in Edinburgh a strong school led by Edwin Bramwell, whom he knew well and respected.

Arriving at the National Hospital for Nervous Diseases, Queen Square, he became one of four residents, the others there being Macdonald Critchley, Hugh Garland and Esmond Rees, all of whom became Fellows. There began his association with Godwin Greenfield also a Fellow, with whom he collaborated in a text book on the *Cerebrospinal Fluid* and afterwards in several clinico-pathological papers, mainly in *Brain*. He then became registrar in neurology at St Bartholomew's Hospital, and during that time was attracted by the methods of Sir Thomas Lewis, who had just founded the journal *Clinical Science.*

Returning to the National Hospital as honorary assistant physician he became interested in the effects of the autonomic nervous system on blood vessel control. After a short time, he was appointed to the new post of director of the Neurological Research Unit of the Medical Research Council in that hospital, a post which he continued to hold until his retirement at 65.

Carmichael's major contribution in those years was not so much in the weight or substance of his personal research, but in the influence he had upon the thought and attitudes of the increasing number of young postgraduates in all the neurological specialties who came to Queen Square from the then Empire, the Commonwealth, and the Western World. He was an enthusiastic, evocative teacher with a compelling quirk which appealed especially to those from the New World, his clinical teaching being by lively free discussion. Clinical observation was closely linked to physiological and pathological observations.

His formal ward rounds and seminars became essential parts of each postgraduate student's week, at a time when Kinnear Wilson, Gordon Holmes, George Riddoch, and Charles Symonds were teaching in the same small postgraduate medical school in Queen Square. His emphasis on the physiological approach to medicine of Sir Thomas Lewis, and the physiologically orientated attitude of the Medical Research Society was, though, rather out of step with his colleagues' more direct bedside or purely clinical approach. This aspect of his career was admirably described in the obituaries in the *Lancet* and the *British Medical Journal*.

After retirement he continued to teach neurology in several medical schools in North America and in the national institutes in Washington, where his old students eagerly welcomed him. He was elected an honorary alumnus of the Neurological Institute of New York in 1966.

He was happier there in an atmosphere which suited his personality than at home, in what he seemed to feel a repressive or reactionary environment. Perhaps he was right, but he found difficulty in accepting his clinical colleagues for what they had to give, and gave well, without reservations. It was this restraint which kept him from more widespread recognition at home. He was not, for instance, elected president of the Association of British Neurologists as expected, though he had been its excellent secretary for several years, and whilst he edited the British Medical Association's *Journal of Neurology and Psychiatry* he held no post on the journal *Brain*, which he would have liked.

But when he was 80 a birthday dinner was held in Hove near his home, and eminent research workers from all parts of Britain and from several overseas countries assembled there.

A lasting material monument to him is the Rockefeller Building of the National Hospital, which was erected entirely through his initiative to house his research unit and wards, as well as the neuro-surgical unit, a fact which was forgotten unfortunately in the turmoil of World War II which began shortly afterwards. During those years he worked for the Medical Research Council in personnel research for the fighting services, for which he was awarded the CBE. DJW

[*Brit. med. J.*, 1978, **1**, 513; *Lancet*, 1978, **1**, 398; *Times*, 11 Feb 1978; Photo]

CARSON, James *b*.13 May 1907 *d*.9 Nov 1978
MB BCh BAO Belf (1930) DPH (1934) MD (1935) DCH (1941) MRCP (1946) FRCP (1970)

James Carson was born in Ballybay, County Monaghan, Ireland, the son of David J Carson, a merchant, and Martha, daughter of Thomas McMurry, also a merchant.

He received his early education at Campbell College, Belfast, whence he proceeded to the Queen's University, Belfast, where he graduated with second class honours in June 1930.

He then held house appointments in the Ulster Hospital for Children and Women, Belfast, the Royal Victoria Hospital, Belfast, and Purdys Burn Fever Hospital in Belfast.

In 1934 he went to Vienna and completed his medical education there; and also spent a period working as a ship's surgeon. In 1936 he was appointed RMO at the City Isolation Hospital and Sanatorium, Leicester, and in 1937 he moved to Manchester as deputy medical superintendent and RMO at Bootle Hospital, beginning a connection with the north west of England which lasted until his death. In 1941 he was appointed deputy medical superintendent physician at Withington Hospital, Manchester. From 1942 until 1946 he served in the RAMC, obtaining the rank of lieutenant colonel and serving as OC medical division in various military hospitals in India, SEAC and BAOR.

He returned to his post in Manchester in 1946, and in 1950 was appointed consultant physician to the South Cheshire Group of Hospitals, where at first he filled the role of physician, paediatrician, geriatrician and occasional psychiatrist.

He devoted his life to the medical work of South Cheshire and the Manchester Region, giving much of his time to the hospital management committee and to various regional commissions and committees. He played a major part in the establishment of the specialist medical services in an area where none had existed before the National Health Service.

James Carson was a pragmatic and essentially practical physician with great clinical skills. His opinion was widely sought. He gave a great deal of his time to voluntary work within the local community, notably to the St John's Ambulance Association of which he was chairman of the Crewe Division and was made a serving brother of the Order of St John of Jerusalem in 1969; to his Parish Church of which he was for many years a church warden, and to the Crewe Disablement Advisory Committee, which he served as chairman for many years.

His interests encompassed gardening, at which he was greatly skilled, country pursuits, including beagling, which activity he continued until two or three years before his death, and music and the arts in general.

He had a generous personality and, although a life-long bachelor, enjoyed a special relationship with young people, particularly the children of his many friends and colleagues in whose careers and activities he took an active interest.

He retired in 1972, after having taken a major part in the planning of the new hospital at Leighton, near Crewe, but promptly put himself back to work again; firstly with attachments to the geriatric unit, and fulfilling many appointments as locum for his consultant physician colleagues during their holiday absences, and latterly in developing an occupational health service for the NHS staff within the District. He remained active in this way until very shortly before his death.

RDC

[*Brit. med. J.*, 1979, **1**, 60; Photo]

CARTER, Frederick Stephen *b.* 12 June 1918 *d.* 1 Dec 1977
MRCS LRCP (1942) MB BChir Cantab (1942) MA MD (1949) DCH (1947) MRCP (1950) FRCP (1976)

Frederick Stephen Carter was born at Nutfield, Surrey, the son of

Robert Leonard Carter, a stockbroker. There were family connexions with Elizabeth Fry. He was educated at St Lawrence College, Ramsgate, and Queens' College, Cambridge, proceeding to the Middlesex Hospital, where he qualified in 1942.

Carter spent some time in the Merchant Navy and then joined the Colonial Medical Service, serving in Kenya, Sierra Leone and Aden. He retired from the Service in 1963 and took a post as senior lecturer in medicine at Khartoum University. On his return to England he became consultant paediatrician to the Romford group of hospitals. He moved to Jersey in 1971, where he was appointed consultant paediatrician.

Carter wrote several papers on paediatric problems in the tropics, his last paper being a comparison of the growth and development of baby gorillas with human infants, at birth and during the postnatal period.

In 1947 he married Nym, daughter of William Wilson Grantham JP. They had two sons and a daughter; one son entered the medical profession. In his leisure time he enjoyed singing in a male voice choir, and cycling and swimming. GW/VL

[*Brit. med. J.*, 1977, **2**, 1676; Photo]

CHAIN, *Sir* **Ernst (Boris)** *b.*19 June 1906 *d.*12 Aug 1979
KCB (1969) D Phil Berlin (1930) PhD Cantab (1943)
MA Oxon (1945) FRS (1949) PhD Liège (1946) Bordeaux (1947)
Turin (1954) Paris (1959) Yeshiva (1961) Chicago (1965)
Hon FRCP (1965)

Ernst Chain was born in Berlin to parents of different origins. His father, Dr. Michael Chain, was a chemist and industrialist who originated from Russia, while his mother, Margarete Eisner, had been born in Germany. After studying at the Luisengymnasium, Ernst Chain entered the Friedrich-Wilhelm University, Berlin, in 1924, where he graduated in chemistry and physiology, obtaining his PhD in 1930. He then worked for three years in the department of chemical pathology of the Charité Hospital, Berlin, under Peter Rona. In the early part of 1933 Ernst Chain came to England, almost immediately after Hitler's accession to power in Germany. He spent a few months in the department of chemical pathology at University College Hospital Medical School, London, under Charles Harington, but their temperaments were somewhat incompatible and, later that year, Chain joined Sir Frederick Gowland Hopkins in Cambridge, where he remained until 1935. Chain had apparently been introduced to Hopkins by JBS Haldane, who had just come to London to accept a chair at University College. Hopkins had a great influence on Chain, which persisted throughout his life. HW Florey (later Lord Florey) had taken up in 1935 the chair of pathology in Oxford, and was anxious to recruit a biochemist into his research group. Hopkins was approached indirectly with a request to recommend one of his scientists for the Oxford appointment, the post was offered to Chain, and he moved to Oxford, where he remained until 1948. During this period the important work on penicillin was done which led to the award of the Nobel prize for physiology and medicine to Fleming, Chain and Florey in 1945. Chain and Florey had been frustrated in the beginning of their penicillin work by lack of support from the Medical Research Council, and even after the penicillin work had been completed, Chain was unable to get what he considered adequate support for his further research in Oxford. When in 1948 the headship of a department in the Istituto Superiore di Sanita, Rome, was offered to him, he accepted the post both with alacrity and regret, feeling that this new post gave him greater opportunity to expand his research than had been possible in Oxford.

In 1958 PMS Blackett (later Lord Blackett) discussed on a visit to Rome the possibility of Chain setting up a department of biochemistry at Imperial College, London. This idea was further explored by Sir Patrick Linstead, who was then rector of Imperial College, and as a result of combined efforts by Chain and Linstead, support by the Wolfson Foundation and the Science Research Council was obtained to set up the Wolfson Laboratories under Chain's direction. Thus, in 1964 Chain returned to London to take charge of the new facilities which were given to him. Chain retired from his chair in 1973, but he continued to be active in many different directions until his death.

During his Cambridge period Chain worked on the biochemical basis of the action of snake venoms, and made a significant contribution to our understanding of their biological action. When he moved to Oxford he worked on a variety of topics, but of particular importance was his demonstration, together with Duthie, of the 'spreading factor', being identical with hyaluronidase, as the enzyme which splits a well-defined linkage in the hyaluronic acid molecule. Chain also showed that lysozyme was an enzyme, and he defined to some extent its mode of action.

However, his most outstanding achievement was his participation in the isolation of penicillin. There has been much argument about the relative contributions of Fleming, Chain and Florey, and the complicated story is told in an objective manner by Gwyn Macfarlane in his biography of Florey, but Chain's contribution was vital and his enthusiasm and devotion were of decisive importance for the successful solution of an important piece of work. The isolation of penicillin and its introduction into medicine were to prove a milestone of great importance in therapy, and ultimately led to the discovery of many other antibiotics.

Of almost equal importance to the isolation of penicillin was the preparation of new penicillins, which was to a very large extent due to Chain's imaginative and persistent efforts. In 1954, on the advice of the late Sir Charles Dodds, the chairman of the Beecham Group, Henry Lazell, approached Chain to help Beechams with their plans to enter the field of antibiotics. Chain, who had been interested in the development of plants for fermentation, decided to cooperate with Beechams in a research programme aimed at modifying *p*-aminobenzyl-penicillin. The discovery was made that under certain conditions a precursor of penicillin, namely 6-aminopenicillanic acid, accumulated in the fermentation fluid, and this was decisive in opening up the possibility of making on an industrial scale new penicillins of a desired structure.

In recent years Chain became increasingly interested in animal and human biochemistry, particularly in the field of carbohydrate metabolism, the action of insulin, cardiovascular disease, and some problems of nutrition. Some of this work was jointly done with his wife, Dr Anne Beloff-Chain, a distinguished biochemist in her own right.

Ernst Chain was an accomplished person with many interests, full of vitality, and possessed of an unbounded energy. He had a passionate belief in the causes he embraced, and was not given to easy compromise. Thus, he believed strongly that the present emphasis on molecular biology was mistaken, and that the future in biology and especially in biochemistry would lie mainly with those who were working on the whole organism or whole cells. He tended to push these views to extremes, and he could be intolerant of those who were prepared to follow a more moderate line. Chain also felt strongly that the pharmaceutical industry was serving the community extremely well, that attacks on it were unfounded, and that academic scientists should collaborate closely with industry. Chain himself cultivated such contacts throughout his life. He was particularly critical of what he considered was the narrow-minded attitude of the academic establishment on these matters, and again he occupied a somewhat extreme position.

Chain had many interests outside science. He was an expert pianist, and he performed together with his elder son in public. Music was one of his major concerns, and indeed he had considered at one time entering on a musical career. He was closely involved with the Weizmann Institute in Israel, as well as with many other scholarly institutions in that country. Chain had great loyalty towards friends, and was unusually generous to those who were in need or in personal difficulties.

He married Anne Beloff, sister of Max (later Lord) Beloff, in 1948, and they had two sons and a daughter. He was extremely happy in his married life, and greatly enjoyed the success of his children. AN

[*Biogr. Mem. roy Soc.*, 1983, **29**, 43-91; *Brit. med. J.*, 1979, **2**, 505; *Lancet*, 1979, **2**, 427; *Times*, 16 Nov 1979; *Daily Telegraph*, 14 Aug 1979; *Guardian*, 15 & 27 Aug 1979; Photo]

CHESTERMAN, *Sir* **Clement (Clapton)** *b.*30 May 1894
*d.*20 July 1983
Kt (1974) OBE (1918) MRCS LRCP (1917)
MB BS Lond (1917) DTM&H Cantab (1920) MD (1920)
MRCP (1928) FRCP (1952)

Born into a large and happy Bath family, with strong Christian connections going back to Neuchatel in Switzerland and to the West country, Clement Chesterman was a debonair and adventurous lad who early showed promise of great strength – of body, of character and of intellect. He had four years at Monkton Combe School, before entering Bristol Medical School in 1911. His interest in tropical medicine began when, as a medical student dresser in Serbia during the first world war, he treated victims of various tropical scourges. It was stimulated enormously during his apprenticeship to Major Philip Bahr in Palestine, where, as a lieutenant, Chesterman was responsible for a malaria diagnostic service and saw much typhus and dysentery. After demobilization, he enrolled for the last course in tropical medicine to be given at the London Dock Hospital, thereafter taking in his stride the Cambridge DTM&H and the London MD in tropical medicine.

Chesterman had two heroes – David Livingstone and Albert Schweitzer. He treasured 'a few dead leaves' from a tree in Central Africa under which Livingstone's heart was buried, and some more leaves from a mango tree in Ujiji, where Livingstone met Stanley. His association with 'le grand Docteur' began in 1923, when, having read *On the edge of the Primaeval Forest*, he wrote a letter of appreciation to Albert Schweitzer as from his mission station at Yakusu, 2000 miles east of Lambarene, in the former Belgian Congo. Chesterman drew up an imaginary hospital case-sheet of a patient named Lazarus. Schweitzer acknowledged this missive and sent Chesterman a photograph inscribed 'a mon collègue d'Afrique'.

Chesterman had turned his back on a promising academic career to follow in the footsteps of David Livingstone; he offered to serve as a Baptist medical missionary, and was appointed to Yakusu, near Stanleyville (Kisangani). He had caught his first glimpse of Africa as he travelled by ship to and from Serbia in 1915; this continent was to hold for him an irresistible fascination.

As he passed through Kinshasa in 1920, he was given a supply of a new drug for trypanosomiasis, in case he should find any cases in the district to which he was going. He did, indeed. In some of the riverside villages near Yakusu, a third of the population was suffering from the infection. Using tryparsamide carefully and methodically, Chesterman was soon hailed as a powerful medicine-man who could even conquer the dreaded *bosingisi*, and who could moreover do miracles with 'the work of the knife'.

It was his early experiences in controlling sleeping sickness and in training medical auxiliaries that determined Chesterman's whole orientation and his views on the role of a medical service in tropical Africa. Prevention is better *by* cure, he advocated, and the only way to encourage the adoption of Western medicine is by developing a programme of simple health posts manned by trained and supervised medical auxiliaries. In this respect, he was 50 years ahead of his time.

In 1936, Chesterman was called by the Baptist Missionary Society to leave his beloved Yakusu, and to assume the office of medical secretary with a base in London. With real reluctance, but with profound professional satisfaction, he left Yakusu: the whole of the Upper River was a healthier and happier place than when he had arrived in 1920. With trypanosomiasis almost eradicated, and yaws controlled (in the days before penicillin), and with thriving schools for the training of public health auxiliaries (*infirmiers*) and nurse-midwives, he had done a marvellous pioneering job. He had become very fluent in the local African language, Lokele, into which he had translated the well known hymn 'At even, e'er the sun did set, the sick, O Lord, around Thee lay'.

Although feeling somewhat restricted in his new administrative post, Chesterman entered into its duties with enthusiasm. He went to the World Council of Churches meeting in Madras in 1938, and managed to persuade a reluctant Ida Scudder to upgrade the Vellore Women's Medical College and to admit men students, thus qualifying for government recognition.

At the outbreak of World War II, Chesterman joined a general practice in Buckinghamshire, but afterwards resumed his interest in tropical medicine and became a much respected consultant in this subject, greatly in demand by the Colonial Office, foreign governments and insurance companies. He was appointed lecturer in tropical medicine at the Middlesex Hospital, and was a very active member of the Royal Society of Tropical Medicine and Hygiene, taking every opportunity of contributing to the discussions at the monthly scientific meetings. He was elected vice president of the Society in 1951-1953, and president of the Hunterian Society in 1966-1967. His *Tropical Dispensary Handbook* went through seven English editions, and sold well in French, Spanish and Portuguese translations. His knighthood in 1974, a little belated, gave tremendous satisfaction to his many friends, as did an honorary fellowship of the Royal Academy of Music.

Sir Clement was active in many ways quite apart from his large consultant practice in tropical medicine. He found time to be an active president of the Medical Missionary Association, and vice president of the Leprosy Mission; he was a faithful supporter of the Friends of Vellore, and was the indefatigable chairman of the Albert Schweitzer Hospital Fund in Great Britain. A great thrill to Chesterman came in 1955 when he organized the itinerary of Albert Schweitzer in England, which included a visit to Buckingham Palace (to receive the Honorary Order of Merit), to Cambridge University (to receive an honorary LLD) and to the Royal College of Physicians of London.

Chesterman was a great man, and a good man. He was blessed with a wonderful helpmeet of a wife, who predeceased him by two years, and gifted sons and daughters.

He was master of the clever verbal quip and often amused himself during tedious committees by doodling and rhyming, and then entered the discussion with some apt phrasing that neatly embodied the decision that his fellow committee members were painfully groping towards.

He was a tireless and eloquent advocate of Christian medical missions; his book entitled *In the Service of Suffering* contained much of his thinking along these lines.

He was a great encourager. He stimulated Charles Fisher to investigate a Yakusu-based *Schistosoma (intercalatum*), an investigation that earned Fisher a Bristol MD.

Clement Chesterman died full of years, and full of good works. He was one of the last of the great medical missionaries. SGB

[*Brit. med. J.*, 1983, **287**, 435; *Lancet*, 1603, **2**, 353; *Times*, 27 July 1983; Photo]

CLARK, *Sir* **George (Norman)** *b.* 27 Feb 1890 *d.* 6 Feb 1979
Kt (1953) MA Oxon (1916) DLitt Oxon (1947) Hon FRCP (1965)†

Sir George Clark was the son of James Clark CBE JP, a draper, and Mary, née Midgeley. Born at Halifax, he was educated at Bootham School, Manchester Grammar School and Balliol College, Oxford, where he gained first classes in *Literae Humaniores* and modern history. Elected a Fellow of All Souls College in 1912, his career was interrupted by the 1914 – 1918 war. He served with the Post Office Rifles, was wounded twice and taken prisoner. To relieve the tedium of the prison camp he learnt Russian and wrote plays to be performed by his fellow prisoners, one of which was later put on at the Haymarket Theatre.

On return from the war he became lecturer, fellow, tutor and librarian of Oriel College. In 1929 – 1930 he served as proctor. His main writings included *The Dutch Alliance and the War against French Trade; The Seventeenth Century; The Later Stuarts; Science and Social Welfare in the Age of Newton; Guide to English Commercial Statistics 1696 – 1782; The Colonial Conferences between England and the Netherlands; The Wealth of England 1498 – 1760; Early Modern Europe; War and Society in the Seventeenth Century,* and *The Campden Wonder*. His last book, published when he was over 80, was the highly acclaimed *English History. A Survey*. In addition, he did much editorial work for the *English Historical Review*, the *Home University Library*, and the immense undertakings of the *Oxford History of England* and the *New Cambridge Modern History*.

In 1929 he was elected professor of economic history at Oxford and again became a fellow of All Souls. Two years later he was appointed to the regius professorship of modern history at Cambridge, with a fellowship at Trinity College. In 1947 he returned to Oxford as provost of Oriel College. Unlike most historians he did not have a 'period', but could write and speak on Greek, Roman, Byzantine, mediaeval or modern history with equal facility.

His connexion with the Royal College of Physicians began when Lord Moran invited him to undertake a definitive history of the College. This was an entirely new field to him, which he greatly enjoyed, and there resulted two notable volumes, entitled with characteristic understatement *A History of the Royal College of Physicians of London*. Sir George was also a trustee of the British Museum, a member of the University Grants Committee and president of the British Academy. Academic honours came to him from all over the world. He held honorary doctorates from the universities of Aberdeen, Cambridge, Colombia, Dublin, Durham,

Hull, Sheffield and Utrecht, as well as membership of numerous learned societies.

In person he was a short, neat man with striking blue eyes. To the end of his life he kept a photographic memory, a most acute mind and a lively sense of humour. Despite his immense learning and distinction in many fields he was the most modest of men.

He married Barbara, daughter of WB Keen; they had one son and one daughter. AMC

[*Daily Telegraph,* 7 Feb 1979; *Times,* 19 Nov 1979; Photo]

CLARKE, Owen *b.* 24 July 1915 *d.* 20 Sept 1977
MRCS LRCP (1940) MB BChir Cantab (1941) MA (1947)
MD (1950) MRCP (1952) FRCPC (1970) FRCP (1974)

Owen Clarke was educated at Sherborne School, Dorset, Clare College, Cambridge University, and the London Hospital. He graduated in medicine in 1940, immediately joining the Indian Medical Service and serving in SE Asia for five years. While there he met a Queen Alexandra's Royal Army Nursing Service nurse, Sister Kitty O'Leary, and they were married at Secunderabad in 1945.

On return to Britain he did resident hospital appointments at Papworth and the Brompton, and was later appointed a clinical assistant at the Brompton, an appointment he held until 1969. In 1948 he was appointed medical consultant to the Province of Ontario Immigration Medical Services in Britain. This was his first contact with Canada, working under the late Clair Brink. He visited Canada for the first time in 1949. He was responsible for the medical surveillance of thousands of prospective immigrants to Canada.

In 1950 he was appointed consultant chest physician to the South East Metropolitan Regional Hospitals Board. His headquarters were at the Canterbury Chest Clinic, where he looked after patients in the Isle of Thanet region of SE England. It was during this period that Owen Clarke's tremendous qualities as a compassionate, deeply concerned and sympathetic physician became widely known and respected by his medical colleagues. Each one of his large number of patients, many of them with long-term distressing respiratory disease, loved him as 'my doctor'.

Clarke was very active in local and national medical affairs, was a keen member of the British Tuberculosis Association, and was its honorary secretary for many years. He was an active member of the Canterbury Rotary Club.

In 1953 Owen Clarke was awarded the Canadian Fellowship of the National Association for the Prevention of Tuberculosis. He spent four months visiting Canada and the United States, where he made a great impression.

In 1967 he was invited by the former Canadian Tuberculosis Association – now the Canadian Lung Association – to visit Canada as a 'Centennial Lecturer' and to give a series of lectures across the continent, to commemorate 100 years of Canadian Confederation.

With his wife Kitty, he travelled from coast to coast; together they made a great success of this tour, during which Clark made a major contribution to Canadian medicine through his clear, lucid and concise lectures.

Shortly after returning to Britain he was invited to head the chest unit at the new University Hospital in London, Ontario. So in 1969 he returned to Canada for the fourth time, and he and Kitty made their home in London. He was appointed associate professor of medicine, University of Western Ontario, and consulting physician to the Westminster Hospital.

Besides his university activities, he quickly became active in national affairs, was a member of the executive committees of both the Canadian Tuberculosis and Respiratory Disease Associations and the Canadian Thoracic Society. He was chairman of a national commitee on standards and classification of respiratory disease. He was an active member of the International Union Against Tuberculosis and the College of Chest Physicians and participated in their programmes in Africa, Asia and North and South America.

He was consultant to the Canadian International Development Agency and advised on programmes in Africa and Asia, where his wide knowledge of medical affairs, and of providing health programmes relevant to the country, were invaluable.

He was survived by his loving wife Kitty in London, Ontario; his daughter Janet, a research scientist in Ottawa; son John, a business consultant in Saudi Arabia, and son Robert, an actor with the Royal Shakespeare and the Chichester Festival Theatres.

Owen Clarke was a dedicated physician, an international authority on health, and a loving husband and father. CWLJ

[*Brit. med. J.*, 1977, **2**, 1228; Photo]

CLEAVE, *Surg. Capt.* **Thomas Latimer** *b.*8 Aug 1906
*d.*15 Sept 1983
MRCS LRCP (1927) MRCP (1936) FRCP (1976)

Son of a Royal Navy captain and engineer, Peter Cleave (as he was always known) was born in Exeter and educated at Clifton College. Entering the Bristol Medical School at the age of sixteen, he passed his primary FRCS at eighteen but decided to be a physician. He finished his training at St Mary's Hospital and went straight into the Royal Navy. There he was a medical specialist in various hospitals at home and abroad, ending up as surgeon captain and director of medical research until he retired in 1962.

In the 1970s Cleave received international acclaim as the father of the dietary fibre hypothesis, but for twenty years before that he had been an obscure and ridiculed writer. As a boy he had become convinced of the importance of diet to health. His desire to prevent as well as to treat disease was strengthened by his eight-year- old sister's death from perforated appendicitis. At medical school he was taught by Rendle Short, who propounded that appendicitis is caused by lack of cellulose in the diet. At this time also he was profoundly influenced by the writings of Charles Darwin, and henceforth he built all his theories on the rock of the adaptation of species to their environment. His great vision was to see that the human body must be maladapted to the artificial foods of civilization of which the most artificial were the refined carbohydrates, chiefly sugar and white flour. He reasoned that if man avoided unnatural foods he would surely avoid unnatural diseases, that is, diseases absent in wild animals or primitive communities. He spent his life gathering evidence and developing arguments to support this view, which culminated in his grand hypothesis of a range of diseases caused by maladaptation to the foods and drinks containing refined carbohydrate. These diseases included obesity, diabetes, coronary heart disease, peptic ulcer, dental caries, constipation, appendicitis and varicose veins. Since they all had a common cause he viewed them as a single master disease, the *Saccharine Disease*. His book of this name, published in 1974, sold many thousands of copies. His previous books were *A Molecular Conception of Organisms and Neoplasms* (3rd edition 1955); *Fat Consumption and Coronary Disease* (1957); *On the Causation of Varicose Veins* (1960); *Peptic Ulcer* (1962); and *Diabetes, Coronary Thrombosis and the Saccharine Disease* (1966), jointly with GD Campbell; (1969) jointly with GD Campbell and NS Painter. The last of these had a wide readership; the rest were ignored.

Cleave was slow to achieve recognition for several reasons. At a time when others were learning to trust only randomized trials and probability values he trusted in the lessons of nature and logical argument. He was recording differences in disease patterns over time and space long before the epidemiology of chronic diseases was a recognized discipline. He looked for big differences and had no use for statistical analysis. He painted with broad strokes on the biggest possible canvas when others were focussing on ever more minute areas of investigation. At his own expense, he published his lofty ideas and findings in books, while ordinary mortals submitted humbly to peer review and the rule of editors. In his crusade he bombarded would-be converts with letters. His letters were always colourful. Sometimes they had the impact of grapeshot, if not a broadside. Sensitive colleagues and admirers became alienated. He expected complete loyalty and hated criticism.

Cleave's most effective advocate was Denis Burkitt FRS, already famous in another field, and the meeting of the two men in 1967 was the turning point in the fortunes of Cleave's hypothesis. Burkitt's connections with 150 Third World hospitals enabled him to confirm many of Cleave's epidemiological observations and even to add to his list of Western diseases which can be explained by refined carbohydrate. In articles and spell-binding lectures, Burkitt woke doctors and scientists all over the world to the idea that diets depleted of fibre are harmful to health.

The idea of fibre depletion is inherent in Cleave's concept but he preferred to emphasize the dangers of sugar, the fibre depleted extract of sugar cane and sugar beet. Burkitt and his East African physician colleague, Hugh Trowell, tended to emphasize the positive virtues of a high intake of fibre and especially of bran. But Cleave was the pioneer here too because in 1941 he had been one of the first to advocate raw bran in medical practice. While serving on the battleship *King George V* he had sacks of bran brought on board to combat the constipation which was prevalent in the sailors, deprived of fresh fruit and vegetables. Bran was so effective the Cleave became known throughout the navy as 'the bran man'. Research has shown that bran has other valuable properties and its use has spread widely. But it is a serious distortion of Cleave's idea to call it the bran hypothesis. His message is not that we should add fibre to our food (unless we need a laxative) but that we should stop taking fibre out of it.

1979 was his *annus mirabilis*, when he was awarded the Harben gold medal of the Royal Institute of Public Health and Hygiene (previously awarded to Pasteur, Lister and Fleming) and the Gilbert Blane medal for naval medicine, which is awarded jointly by the Royal College of Physicians and Surgeons but never before to a retired man. A few months later, the Royal College of Physicians published its report *Medical aspects of dietary fibre* which largely vindicated Cleave's theory and summarized the large body of research which it has stimulated. But the full implications of overnutrition, and the role of fibre-depleted foods in causing it, have not received the emphasis which Cleave believed they deserved. His last work, published in 1977, was an article entitled *Overnutrition, now the most dangerous cause of disease in westernized countries*.

Cleave was certainly one of the most original medical thinkers of the twentieth century. His rare combination of panoramic vision, piercing logic and bulldog tenacity deserves the title of genius. He had his weaknesses (he utterly rejected a role for animal fat in coronary heart disease) and many of his ideas will be modified, but he was a true pioneer who started a major revolution in scientific thought.

His main relaxations were gardening, which he did with military precision, originality and great success, and also fly fishing and pigeon shooting.

Cleave married twice and was survived by a medically qualified son and a daughter from his first marriage as well as by his second wife, Helen. He was always very close to his younger brother, Hugh, also a retired surgeon captain.

KEH

[*Brit. med. J.*, 1983, **287**, 1145, 1480; *Lancet*, 1983, **2**, 862; *Times*, 21 Sept 1983; Photo]

CLEGG, Hugh Anthony *b*.19 June 1900 *d*.6 July 1983
CBE (1966) BA Cantab (1922) MB BChir (1928) MRCP (1929) FRCP (1944) Hon MD Dubl (1952) Hon D Litt Belf (1962)

Hugh Clegg's qualities came from both parents. His intellect came from his father, a prep school headmaster in East Anglia whose tutoring in the classics enabled Hugh to win scholarships to Westminster and Trinity College, Cambridge, as well as giving him a lifelong interest in Latin and Greek and English style. His energy, ability, and eagerness to do everything himself probably came from his mother. All these attributes combined to make him a formidable editor, an innovator as well as an upholder of standards, even if he was not always easy to live, or work, with.

Having got a first class in the Natural Sciences tripos, Clegg went to Bart's, where he qualified in 1928. After house jobs there and the Brompton Hospital he became resident medical registrar to Charing Cross Hospital. Passing the MRCP in 1929 he was tipped for a post on the staff, but times were hard, he wanted to get married, and he had no private means. Whether Clegg had the sympathy or the suavity to make a hospital consultant in private practice will never be known, but his defection from clinical work was journalism's gain.

Throughout most of Clegg's days as a junior on the staff of the *BMJ* Gerald Horner, the chief editor, was a sick man. Much of the quality and independence that Horner's predecessor, the great Sir Dawson Williams, had won for the *BMJ* was lost in the 1930s and the journal showed it, degenerating virtually into a parish magazine which, as legend put it, occupied less space in the wastepaper basket if it was left in its wrapper. Clegg bided his time and learnt his craft; besides an energetic routine subeditorial role, he wrote and edited some pamphlets and books and played an increasing part in the gentler medical politics of those days. Travelling as often as he could, he formed friendships with people such as the journalist Frederick Voigt, the typographer Stanley Morrison, and the statistician (Sir) Austin Bradford Hill. By the time the second world war broke out he was virtually at the helm (although he was not appointed editor until 1947). He ran the journal with only one or two other helpers, coped with wartime Home Front duties such as firewatching, and found the time to launch what became the medical department of the British Council, as well as a regular bulletin of abstracts of medical articles, and to take an increasing part in the debates on the Beveridge and other reports.

Once appointed editor, Clegg's energies were used to the full. With Stanley Morrison's help, the *BMJ* was redesigned. Prodded by Bradford Hill, Clegg tightened up the refereeing of the original articles, particularly the statistical aspects. The immediate postwar years were those of the great large-scale clinical trials (on antibiotics, for example) and epidemiological studies (such as on smoking and lung cancer), which the journal published week after week, together with explanatory anonymous leading articles written by authorities as well as equally knowledgeable juniors who were nurtured for the future. A whole bevy of new specialist journals was launched, making the BMA at one time the largest medical publishing house in the country. Clegg also found the time to sponsor the first two world conferences on medical education (as well as to edit the proceedings), to become involved in the affairs of the World Medical Association, and to start a concern with medical ethics that was eventually to lead to the Declaration of Helsinki on human experimentation.

Such omelettes cannot be made without breaking many eggs, and Clegg was hardly a finicky cook. His staff tended to pass through sine waves of personal relationships: successively extreme approval, disapproval and withdrawal of work, and renewal of esteem. Whole issues of the *BMJ* already ready for Tuesday press might be torn apart and reassembled on a Monday afternoon (but the printers loved the hassle). Articles that a subordinate had already accepted might be rejected (usually with good reason) and the junior left to explain matters. Editorials might be rewritten at the printers on press day itself, particularly at the time of the debates on the NHS Bill, when his thoughtful and well-argued leading articles often helped to create BMA policy. On the other hand, Clegg was often generous to his juniors, encouraging them to write or to develop special interests and defending them if they over-reached themselves.

Clegg's intellect and debating skills, let alone the help of friends in high, and modest, places, were never more needed than in what became known as the 'Gold-headed Cane' affair. His editorial of that name, published in 1966, questioned whether the then president of the Royal College of Physicians should not stand down for a younger man. Sir Russell Brain, as he then was, had, however, been appointed to lead an important delegation to the Government in which the BMA was prominently represented. Resenting his authority and standing, Clegg's enemies at the Association seized their chance and claimed that his editorial had violated BMA policy. At a meeting of the Council he was censured and ordered to show all future medicopolitical editorials to the chief officers for approval. Clegg refused this stipulation (as did his colleagues on the *BMJ*) and was looking for a suitable post in general practice when the Annual Representative Meeting of the BMA vindicated his attitude, when it overthrew a motion: 'That this Representative Body instructs the Council to take steps to ensure that leading articles in the *British Medical Journal* reflect the policy of the Association'.

This affair was more than a domestic storm: Clegg's victory established that to obtain a journal of international standing its owners (even if a trade union) must allow its editor complete freedom, reserving the right to dismiss him if he grossly abused it. Widely publicized, the repercussions of this debate were felt in many quarters inside and outside medicine, and they helped other organizations and their editors to clarify their roles. Certainly the BMA learnt a lesson and left the *BMJ* alone to run its own affairs. Never one to shirk the truth, Clegg hammered this principle home time after time, even in his farewell speech to an audience which included many of his erstwhile opponents, who had acknowleged his genius with the award of the BMA gold medal. Though some questioned the propriety of raking over old history on such occasions, his successors have had reason to be grateful for his candour.

Short and stocky, Clegg had an almost military bearing and a rasping voice; he was interested in food and wine, travel, books and conversation, but little else and as a result became bored throughout his 18 years of retirement. Missing the 'platform' he had had while editor, he tended to brood on two occurrences: his honour of a CBE compared with the knighthood conferred on his counterpart at the *Lancet* – a relative neglect he shared with another great, and difficult, man, Leslie Witts – and the fact that he had missed call up in the first world war by only a month. Almost everybody respected him and many adored him; his foibles, strengths, and weaknesses were well summed up by a former junior colleague John Rowan Wilson, who drew on him (along with several others of the *BMJ* staff) for Suvarov, the director of a Siberian research centre, in his novel *The Side of the Angels*. Certainly without Hugh Clegg postwar British medicine in general and the *BMJ* in particular would have taken different courses.

In 1932 Clegg married Baroness Kira Engelhardt of Smolensk, Russia, who survived him with a son, and a daughter who specialized as a psychiatrist. SPL

[*Times,* 7 July 1983, *Lancet,* 1983, **2**, 175; *Brit. med. J.*, 1983, **287**, 166, 220; Photo]

COHEN, *Lord* **(Henry)** *b.*21 Feb 1900 *d.*7 Aug 1977
1st Baron Cohen of Birkenhead (1956) CH (1974) Kt (1949)
MB BCh Liverp (1922) MD (1924) MRCP (1926) FRCP (1934)†

Henry Cohen was born in Birkenhead and was educated at the Church School of St John (where the fees were 2d a week), then proceeded as a scholar to the Birkenhead Institute. From there he won a scholarship to Oxford, but on grounds of expense he transferred it to Liverpool, and even there he felt obliged to walk to and from the ferry each day to cut down his expenses.

His original intention had been simply to study medicine in order to become a criminal lawyer, but as his work continued he realised that medicine alone had enough to offer him. He graduated in 1922 with first class honours and distinction in every subject in the curriculum, and obtained the MD with special merit in 1924. In the same year he was appointed assistant physician to the Liverpool Royal Infirmary, where he remained on the staff until his retirement 41 years later.

To obtain such a post within two years of qualifying shows not only the exceptional brilliance of Cohen, but also the remarkable perspicacity of those who elected him and, as will be seen, his subsequent career showed that they were fully justified. By 1934 it was clear to his seniors that he was the obvious choice for the chair of medicine at the University of Liverpool and from this time to the end of the war he rose to eminence in the conventional way; election to the FRCP in 1934, later an examiner to the College and member of Council 1943 to 1946.

Of the same standard as his great clinical competence was his ability to speak in public, and his lectures and orations were brilliant resonant performances, showing originality, breadth of vision, erudition and wit. Towards the end of a long series of named lectures came the Harveian Oration at the Royal College of Physicians in 1970, on the motion of blood in the veins.

Another aspect of his greatness was his grasp of administration, particularly as chairman of committees, and it was this capacity which was to be of special use after the introduction of the NHS. He had little or nothing to do with the original idea of the Service, yet once the scheme turned into reality, he became one of the principal expert and voluntary advisers to the Ministry. He became more and more a regular part of the advisory machine, and before long a quite indispensable pillar of the system. He was the first vice-chairman of the Central Health Services Council when it was formed in 1949, and became chairman in 1957. His great contribution to the NHS was that he brought to the Ministry the professional knowledge of the active clinician, so that the administration was kept closely in touch with the outside medical world – a service that its desk doctors could not hope to provide. In recognition of his talents he received a knighthood in 1949, and it was as Sir Henry Cohen that he was elected president of the BMA in 1951.

Many people nowadays think that there is a sharp distinction between the clinician and the medical administrator, and it is most stimulating to reflect that Henry took both in his stride. As his Reader, it is as a clinician that I remember him – I always attended his rounds and was amazed at the skilful way he logically unravelled difficult clinical problems, and how well he could hold his own in any branch of medicine. To the undergraduate his teaching and his lectures were a delight, and many generations remember him with affection.

Brilliant as he was, it was hard work which contributed greatly to his success. Not for him the Friday exodus to Wales, but rather outpatients for many years on Saturday afternoons. He knew too the meaning of stress. His humble origins and rapid rise led to jealousies, and he once told me that anyone worth his salt must inevitably have enemies.

In 1952 he was seriously ill with a coronary thrombosis over which, after several anxious weeks, he triumphed with characteristic intelligence. Unlike most doctors, he strictly adhered to the medical advice he was given, and on recovery gave up his vast private practice and dedicated himself to the national work of the organization and advancement of British medicine. He presided over countless committees and was a household name to general practitioners, who had good reason to bless the Cohen categories as they struggled with the drugs to be used in the NHS. One of his most important scientific contributions arose by virtue of his chairmanship of the committee dealing with the organization of poliomyelitis vaccination in this country. He also played a large part in the preparation of the reports on the medical care of epileptics and on staphylococcal infections in hospital, to mention just two among many. His remarkable memory and powers of exposition made him a formidable figure in the councils of the Ministry of Health, and the debt owed to him by successive Ministers and departmental heads was immense.

For these great administrative talents he was created a peer in 1956, the first physician from the provinces to be raised to the House of Lords. When he made his maiden speech on the subject of vivisection, Lord Silkin, deputy leader of the Opposition, said that he had never heard a more effective maiden speech in the House. The *Lancet* of the day, in congratulating him on his title, spoke of 'his union of quietness with brilliance, of delicacy with endurance', and said of his advice to all the Ministers of Health since the NHS started that 'no explorer of this part of medicine can go far without finding the tracks of some pioneer Cohen committee in the sand'.

It was appropriate that his great grasp of medicine and his legalistic bent were harnessed together when he became president of the General Medical Council in 1961, and anyone reading his summings-up cannot fail to appreciate his humanity – the cold analyses of the facts were not followed up by harsh judgments.

It is said that, during his presidency, the young increasingly came to regard him as symbolizing rigidity in the Establishment, but it may well be that when the dust has settled, his most criticized actions will be seen to have been fully justified.

Another honour which Cohen enjoyed shortly before his retirement was his election (in 1964) to the presidency of the Royal Society of Medicine. Here he took his place in a long line of distinguished men, and he was awarded the gold medal of the Society in 1971. He received honorary degrees from several universities, and was an honorary fellow of many medical colleges and societies both at home and abroad. In 1970 he became chancellor of Hull University.

Outside medicine, his first love was the theatre, and he took an active part in the running of the Liverpool Playhouse. He personally helped to select the plays, and, as he was no starry-eyed intellectual but a shrewd business man, the Liverpool repertory company was one of the few in the country to make money. His favourite theatre story was that when, as a small boy, he had taken the part of the first watchman in *Much Ado About Nothing*, it had been reported in the local press that 'the first watchman had two lines to speak and both were inaudible'. His later distinction as an orator showed that the words of the critic had not fallen on stony ground.

His other great love outside medicine was the collection of old silver, and when he was president of the Liverpool Medical Institution in 1954 his inaugural lecture on the subject delighted his medical and lay audience. As he said, it satisfied the intellect as well as the aesthetic senses as a leisure occupation. Nevertheless, his pastimes were not all intellectual; he enjoyed his television sporting programmes, and when talking to patients he always knew the results of the Reds and Blues football matches in Liverpool. His publications included *New Pathways in Medicine* (1935); *Nature, Method and Purpose of Diagnosis* (1943); *Sherrington: Physiologist, Philosopher and Poet* (1958); and *The Evolution of Modern Medicine* (1958), besides numerous contributions to journals and medical books.

He was unmarried.

CAC

[*Brit. med. J.*, 1977, **2**, 525, 647, 1094; *Lancet,* 1977, **2**, 413; *Times,* 9 Aug 1977; *Guardian,* 9 Aug 1977; *Brit. J. Alcohol and Alcoholism,* 1977, **12**, 151; Inc. Liverp. School of Trop. Med., *Annual Report*, 1976-77; Photo]

COLE, Leslie Barrett *b.*23 Feb 1898 *d.*2 June 1983
MRCS LRCP (1922) MB BChir Cantab (1923) MRCP (1925)
MA MD (1926) FRCP (1933)

That a resident assistant physician at St Thomas's Hospital should leave London for the provinces was thought astonishing in 1927. If Cole was setting a precedent then, he set two others later. In 1957 he became the first dean of the Cambridge postgraduate medical school, and in 1964 the first of our College's vice-presidents under new Bye-Laws.

His father, Samuel Barrett Cole, was a Swindon clothier who retired early and sent his two sons to Leighton Park, the Quaker school near Reading. Leslie, the elder, spent his twentieth birthday as a Gunner officer at Hyderabad (Sind). Transferred to Mesopotamia for active service, he was recalled to England in June 1918 to go on with his medical studies. The coming shortage of doctors was causing anxiety.

At King's College, Cambridge, he was given an exhibition, and at St Thomas's he won the Mead medal and the Toller prize. The return to Cambridge was a venture; for Addenbrooke's Hospital was below London standards, though the university connection gave it potential. Cole did much to revitalize it, working for a day when it should be the clinical centre for the Cambridge medical school.

Meanwhile he had to earn fees, by convincing general practitioners that his opinion was worth getting. And this he soon did. Besides a steadily increasing knowlege, especially of diabetes and diseases of the heart, he had instinct and judgement, and his advice was clear and practical. Though deeply interested in diseases, he cared even more about the people who had them, and about the situation of those people. He was very kind, and his views on such subjects as diet and rest in bed were refreshingly sensible.

In due course he joined the staffs of the West Suffolk Hospital and Papworth.

As a young consultant he sometimes felt that 'clinical observation has about reached its limit', and wondered whether he had come to a dead end. But these thoughts were the prelude to his becoming for a time the foremost British authority – indeed, a world authority – on the treatment of tetanus.

This infection, rare though it was, kept turning up in East Anglia, and he was all too often confronted with patients, in distress and danger, whose best treatment was uncertain. His early hopes of curare were dashed, but in time his experience of many methods enabled him to write with confidence on what should and should not be done. His summary in Robert Hutchison's *Index of Treatment* (1948) was a model.

In 1939 Addenbrooke's supplied most of the senior staff of the 20th General Hospital, and Cole became lieutenant colonel in charge of the medical division. A tented hospital was set up at Dannes-Camiers in January 1940, but it was little used, and on the night of 21 May he had to march his men to Boulogne, with some walking wounded, to take ship for England. When the hospital was re-established in Northern Ireland he still felt almost useless, and he was thankful to be sent back to Addenbrooke's, which had doubled its beds and needed him badly. On 18 June 1941 he wrote: 'I have more than fifty beds and terrific outpatients, a moderate amount of private work and a number of odd things as well. I hope that the work will get heavier and heavier as it probably will. I don't ever really get tired of clinical work'.

But he also enjoyed writing – a substitute for the teaching he would have liked to do more often. Three short postwar papers – significantly entitled 'Diagnosis and the Patient', 'Treatment and the Patient', 'Prognosis and the Patient' – contain more useful advice than most textbooks, and much of it is still timely.

Seeing the doctor as responsible for the entire patient, he had always practised 'holistic' medicine. Concern over a cardiac infarct should not, he felt, mean lack of concern for a corn that is also causing pain. Repeatedly he drew attention to the noxious anxieties that can be aroused by investigation, by treatment, and by silence; and to the care needed to prevent them.

'The more thorough an examination ... the greater can be the influence of the final summing up. There is perhaps no part of treatment in which serious mistakes are more commonly made or harder to set right ...'

'With reservations, the aim should be to tell the truth or at least as much of it as is compatible with comfort and hope. This should be done with conviction and without hesitation, and to do this the physician must have confidence in himself ... Lack of confidence in a doctor is communicated to his patient in the same way as nervousness in a rider is communicated to his horse. The results in both cases are often disastrous ...'

'The second aim should be to tell a patient nothing that is likely to frighten him either directly or by evasion. Very little is ever gained by doing this, and yet it is perhaps the cause of more distress and illness than all the other mistakes in medicine and surgery put together'.

Cole insisted that whatever is said should be said in words the particular patient can understand. Communication matters so much that 'the ability to say things clearly should be recognized as one good reason for going in for medicine'. Those in charge of medical education should realize that 'the study of the English language is as important as the study of anatomy and physiology, because it is the vehicle which makes or mars all the rest of diagnosis and treatment and indeed can often make or mar research'.

With vigour of mind went vigour of body. The strenuous tennis he played at St Thomas's continued till his late seventies; and in his eighties he was still taking the daily cold bath of his schooldays. He loved riding, and before the war he hunted regularly with the Cambridgeshire foxhounds. But the occupation that fitted his personality best was cruising at sea in small boats, for he liked both decisive action and tranquil contemplation, as well as the danger and beauty of the sea. Only in his fifties did he discover his considerable talent for painting. Here too he was an enthusiast, and his enthusiasms were lasting – whether they were for butterflies, for Vermeer, Picasso, and his Japanese prints, for his colleges in Cambridge and Regent's Park, or for his friends.

Taught at Addenbrooke's by Sir Clifford Allbutt, Cole never wavered in his wish to see it a major academic centre. The National Health Service made it a teaching hospital, and in 1957 when the university created the school of clinical research and postgraduate medical training, he appropriately became its dean. In this post till 1965, he did much to arrange the courses, for specialists and for general practitioners, which set a national example at a time when the expansion of postgraduate training had scarcely begun.

For many years the undergraduate medical students at Peterhouse had his tutorial help, and from 1958 to 1965 he was an assessor for the Cambridge MD degree. By this time he was an examiner of long and varied experience: for Cambridge in pharmacology and medicine; for Oxford and Bristol in medicine; for the Conjoint Board in medicine and pathology; and for the MRCP. In this role as in others, he was well informed, thorough, sagacious, and reliable. At the College he became a councillor in 1950 and a censor in 1960, and in 1964 and 1965 he was senior censor and senior vice-president.

Cole's mother was Annie, daughter of Ebenezer Gammon. He married in 1927 Mary, daughter of the late Surgeon Captain HW Finlayson DSO. They had three sons, two of whom followed him to King's College and all three into the medical profession. They are RHL Cole of Barnstaple, RB Cole FRCP of Newcastle-under-Lyme, and PH Cole of Northampton. He died at his last home, at Flore, near Northampton. TFF/JW/NDC

[*Brit. med. J.*, 1983, **2**, 436; *Lancet,* 1983, **2**, 115; Photo]

COLLINS, Vernon Leslie *b.*10 Nov 1909 *d.*24 Mar 1978
CBE (1973) MB BS Melb (1933) MD (1936) MRCP (1940)
DCH Lond (1940) FRACP (1962) FRCP (1968)

It is relatively easy to chronicle a man's achievements, but difficult to write about him as a person. Most people only know a man by the way he communicates with them in personal relationships. Vernon Collins was not an easy man to know; he had a natural reserve and dignity and did not readily communicate his feelings. A man's character is often revealed when he is faced with adversity: in later life Vernon Collins was stricken with a disabling illness which made it difficult for him to carry on his job but, though often under great stress, it never occurred to him to quit. He had great courage, persistence and purpose and never complained about his illness, which progressively restricted his bodily movements and speech but did not impair his mind. He learned how to live with his crippling disorder and continued to retain his interest in people, and in all aspects of medical, social and political life.

'Vern', as he was known to his friends, was born at Nhill, Victoria, Australia, to John and Susan Collins. His father was a farmer and his mother was the daughter of John Hann, also a farmer. He was educated at Horsham High School and the University of Melbourne, where he graduated in 1933. In 1934 he served as junior resident medical officer at the Royal Melbourne Hospital, being promoted senior medical officer in 1935. He then became resident medical officer and registrar at the Children's Hospital, Melbourne, where he was appointed medical superintendent in 1937.

At the beginning of the second world war he came to England, serving as physician and gastroenterologist at the North Middlesex Hospital and he was also responsible, under the EMS, for organizing the blood transfusion service for the area. In 1940 he obtained his membership of the College and his DCH. This was a momentous year for Vernon Collins, for apart from academic achievements he married Josephine O'Shea and began what was to be a long and happy married life throughout which he was constantly inspired, encouraged and supported by his wife. They had two sons of whom they were justifiably proud.

He returned to Australia in 1945 and was appointed honorary physician to outpatients at the Children's Hospital, Melbourne; becoming honorary physician to inpatients in 1948. In 1949 he was appointed as medical director and physician to the Hospital, a post which he held until 1959. This was the first full time appointment of a medical director to a teaching hospital in Melbourne. When making the appointment the committee of management realized that many changes were needed to meet the demands of the community and keep abreast of medical advances overseas, and this phase of Vernon Collins's career was probably the most important in his professional life. It was certainly one of the utmost significance for the hospital which he was to serve so loyally and diligently. To implement changes in a very old, totally inadequate Victorian-style hospital was a formidable task, and only made possible by a man who had a broad perspective and understanding of the changes necessary in hospital administration, policy and staffing, and the will to carry them out. Opposition was inevitable but his foresight, equanimity and purpose, gradually influenced and drew support from the majority. He was directly responsible, in 1953, for the introduction of salaried sessional staff, thus creating the necessary openings for many young people. He was instrumental in introducing unrestricted visiting of children by their parents; personal interviewing of parents on the death of their child; concern for the underprivileged, and respect for the dignity of child and parents whatever their social status. He was a great administrator and an excellent teacher, but it was this personal concern and sensitivity for the sick child and his, or her, family which made him a good and loved physician. After his appointment to the chair of paediatrics at the University of Melbourne, in 1959, he continued to serve the hospital as a member of the senior medical staff.

In addition to his duties at the University, he remained active in the promotion of modern medicine. He was involved in the planning of a new hospital at Parkville; the Tweddle Baby Hospital and the School of Infant Welfare and Mothercraft. He had a strong faith in the value of social education and made a notable contribution to the department of social studies at the University; for a period of six months in 1964 he was acting head of this department. Later, as chairman of the board of social studies, he played a considerable part in establishing social studies as a four-year university course.

Vernon Collins was a physician moulded on the Oslerian tradition, and the last phase of his career was characterized by the development of sound, broad training in clinical paediatrics for undergraduates: a training which always stressed the value of compassion, courtesy and humanity, when caring for patients.

He spent his last days in the home he loved, in the garden he had created, with his books and his music. He was not afraid of death, only fearful that he might be obliged to go into hospital before the end. Thanks to the superb nursing skill and devotion of his wife, his fears proved groundless. GW/VL

[*Aust. Paediatr. J.*, 1978, **14**, 128-130; 1974, **10**, 255-257; Photo]

COLSON, Guy Malcolm *b.*29 May 1920 *d.*11 Jun 1981
MA BM BCh Oxon (1944) MRCP Lond (1946) FRCP Lond (1972)

Guy Colson was born in Letchworth, Hertfordshire, the son of Richard Henry Colson, banker, and his wife Winifred Violet, the daughter of William Henry Cotton, bespoke shoemaker. He was educated at St Edward's School, Oxford, and later at Trinity College, Oxford, where he was successively secretary and captain of the University rugby team. He continued his studies at the Middlesex Hospital, London, where he became captain of the Middlesex Hospital RUFC. He qualified in 1944 and remained at the Middlesex Hospital successively as house physician, casualty medical officer and medical registrar. During the latter appointment he passed his membership examination and also published a paper on phalangeal metastases in bronchogenic carcinoma (*Lancet,* 1948, **1**, 100-102). The next two years were spent in the RAMC as medical specialist with the rank of captain, and in 1949 he was appointed senior medical registrar first to the Royal Devon and Exeter Hospital and then to the Bristol Royal Infirmary, where he remained until 1954, when he was appointed consultant physician to the Bolton Group of Hospitals.

Once established in his permanent appointment, Colson's flair in both clinical and administrative fields rapidly became apparent. He was successively secretary and chairman of the old medical advisory committee, and continued as chairman of the medical records and pharmaceutical sub-committees over a period of many years. He was secretary and subsequently chairman of the medical division after the NHS reorganization in 1974. Despite his flair for administration, it was in clinical fields where Colson excelled, maintaining an exemplary standard of practice in wards and outpatient clinics, as well as establishing a flourishing private practice. Colson helped to train a succession of junior residents, many of whom have reason to be grateful to him for his efforts on their behalf. He was a regular contributor to the proceedings of the Bolton Postgraduate Centre and readily accepted his part in the training of medical students from nearby Manchester University.

Guy Colson's energy and enthusiasm extended to his leisure pursuits, being particularly fond of fishing, sailing, shooting, cricket and squash. He was a member of two cricket clubs, the Northern Nomads and the Gentleman of Cheshire, and at one time belonged to two shoots, one in Lancashire and one in Scotland, and was seldom happier than when tramping the moors with a gun under his arm. At home he was a keen and successful gardener who particularly enjoyed his spells in the greenhouse.

Guy's friendly manner and gregarious disposition won him many friends from all walks of life in the north west, where he did much to enhance the reputation of his profession. Because of ill-health he decided to retire from the hospital service at the end of 1978, but he continued with his private work, and found a fresh interest in the newly opened St. Ann's Hospice where he was honorary consultant.

Colson was married twice, first in 1945 to Pauline, by whom he had four sons. In 1966 he married Audrey, daughter of James Stewart, engineer, of Bolton, who survived him. PJDS

[*Brit. med. J.*, 1981, **283**, 389; Photo]

CONYBEARE, Ernest Thomas *b*.25 Nov 1903 *d*.2 Apr 1979
CBE (1964) BSc Lond (1926) MRCS LRCP (1928) MB BS (1930) MRCP (1931) MD (1933) FRCP (1938)

Ernest Conybeare was born in Plymouth, the only son of William Conybeare, a coachbuilder, and his wife, formerly Edith Mary Miller. He was educated at the Hoe School and the Plymouth and Mannamead College in Plymouth, from where he went to Guy's Hospital, qualifying in 1928. He had earlier taken the London BSc, with first class honours in physiology. When he proceeded to the MD in 1933, he was awarded the University gold medal.

At Guy's he was assistant house surgeon, outpatient officer and house physician and, in 1931, was given a Rockefeller foundation fellowship, which he held at Johns Hopkins University, where he was John D Archbold Fellow in medicine. He returned to Guy's Hospital as medical registrar from 1932 until 1936 and then joined the medical staff of the Ministry of Health, later the Department of Health and Social Security, where he remained for nearly forty years, attaining the rank of principal medical officer. In the earlier part of his time at the Ministry of Health he functioned mainly as an epidemiologist and, among other tasks, was closely concerned with the investigation of the outbreak of typhoid in Croydon. Later he became an expert in the field of pharmacology and therapeutics. Most of his publications reflect these periods of his work, and among the more important are papers on 'Encephalitis after Vaccination' (*Monthly Bull. Min. Public Health & Public Health Lab. Service,* 1948, **7**, 72, and 1956, **15**, 40) and on 'Tetanus' (*Brit. med. J.*, 1951, **1**, 504 and *Proc. Roy. Soc. Med.*, 1959, **52**, 112). He was a skilful writer and for the last five years of his career he was associate editor of *Prescribers Journal*.

His excellent clinical knowledge, combined with considerable skill as a medical administrator, made him one of the most valued members of the medical staff of the Ministry of Health, and he received the CBE in 1964. He was a charming and helpful colleague to whom one could always turn for advice, and the value of his contributions was increased by the accuracy which distinguished all his work.

He was an enthusiastic player of tennis and hockey, activities which he pursued well into his fifties, and he also had an interest in music and the theatre. His manner was quiet, but he was the possessor of a delightfully dry sense of humour.

In 1938 he married Marjorie Deacon, daughter of Alexander John Blaikley, a banker; his brother, John Blaikley, was an obstetrician and gynaecologist and was superintendent of Guy's Hospital from 1958 to 1966.

He had two sons and two daughters, one of the sons being a consultant orthopaedic surgeon. TJBG

[*Brit. med. J.*, 1979, **1**, 1223; Photo]

COWEN, Edward Derek Huxley *b.*1 Mar 1917 *d.*23 July 1982
BA Cantab MB BChir (1941) MRCS LRCP (1941) MRCP (1943) MD (1947) FRCP (1968)

EDH Cowen – known always as Tim (from a childhood nickname referring to his then tiny stature!) – came from an illustrious scientific background. He was related to the great TH Huxley whose sister married a Cowen: thereafter the family name became Huxley Cowen. His paternal grandfather, George Huxley Cowen was a general practitioner in New Malden, Surrey, and died in 1923. George's son, Edward George Huxley Cowen (Tim's father) was a successful and much loved GP in Sutton, Surrey, and during the first war served in the RAMC. After the war, at a comparatively late age, he took his Membership and became consultant physician to the J Arthur Rank film organization, where he organized one of the first industrial medical departments in the country.

Tim Cowen was born in Blackpool, and he never had any other ambition than to become a doctor. After attending Wellesley House School and Canford School, Dorset, in due course he took his medical degree at Pembroke College, Cambridge, and afterwards qualified at St Thomas's Hospital. He had suffered a severe mastoid infection as a boy of 13 which impaired his hearing in one ear. Later, early in the war, he had another mastoid infection (sadly before the days of antibiotics) and his other ear was seriously affected. It was considered unlikely that he could carry on his medical career, as he became almost totally deaf in one ear, and had only very limited hearing in the other. He was therefore unable to join the Forces, but worked throughout the war as registrar in Westminster Hospital, under very unpleasant conditions owing to the frequent bombings – the hospital being hard hit on many occasions through the war. He had then a hearing aid, and was determined to overcome all the seemingly impossible barriers to his becoming a consultant. After the war he held the Elmore medical research studentship at Addenbrooke's Hospital in Cambridge, to work on the development of phonocardiography, which was reported to the Cardiac Society in June 1948. He than became senior registrar and honorary medical tutor to John McMichael (now Sir John) at the postgraduate medical school, Hammersmith. His great interest in hearts remained with him throughout his career, although it was in diabetes that he specialized later. Finally he obtained the post of consultant physician at the Lister Hospital, Hitchin, and the St Albans City Hospital in 1950. At that time, having put in for every consultant post in or near London (along with 60 or so other equally well-qualified applicants) he had begun to feel that his deafness was a real bar to his advancement. But this was not so; in fact his deafness, although imposing a great strain on his general health, was never an apparent disadvantage to him in his career. He became very skilful at lip-reading and always asked his staff at the hospital to look at him while speaking and not to mumble. He found, however, that very few junior members of his team ever remembered to do this for him – perhaps out of shyness; he therefore took to speaking very loudly to them in the hope that it might result in their reciprocating by shouting back. But the marvel was that he managed so well, and that many of his patients and acquaintances never realized that he was deaf at all.

Tim Cowen was over 30 years at Lister Hospital and St Albans, and saw and initiated many developments. The distance between these two hospitals was nearly twenty miles, and one day was spent at one hospital and the alternate day at the other; so that there was quite a heavy amount of travelling as well as a large number of beds and clinics to deal with. There was only one colleague (who was already there), and between the two of them they were responsible for the heavy work load of both in and outpatients. Fortunately, both Tim Cowen and his colleague were lucky in having good junior medical staff, because quite experienced men had just been demobilised from the Services and wanted junior posts at first. The work load was so heavy however that there was little time for clinical research, although later Tim Cowen started a diabetic clinic at the Lister Hospital which he continued right up until the time of his retirement, and made this one of his special interests. In those days there was little in the way of supporting consultants, and Tim Cowen and his colleague covered not only general medicine but also neurology and physical medicine. In due course, however, specialist consultants were appointed, which relieved the pressure on the two general physicians, although the work load remained heavy in view of the area covered. In addition there were three cottage hospitals that were liable to call on their services at any time. Tim Cowen and his colleague were also available for domiciliary visits – not infrequently when the day's work at hospital was done, people were visited with their doctor (which was the customary thing in those days), often to see two or three patients fairly late at night. The general practitioners soon learnt to respect Tim's opinion and knew that his integrity was such that unless things were done in a proper professional manner he did not want to have anything to do with it.

Tim Cowen was an excellent teacher and many of his junior staff got good consultant posts in various parts of the world. His patients felt confidence and affection for him, and his straightforward manner and integrity made him a reliable and loyal colleague.

In 1948 he married Rosamund Rieu, the daughter of EV Rieu, who was amongst other things a translator of the classics, in particular of Homer's *Odyssey* and *Iliad*, and who started, with Sir Allen Lane, the Penguin Classic Series, and was editor for many years. Tim Cowen had five children by the marriage, three daughters and two sons. The scientific trend remains strong in the family. The eldest son, John, is a GP in private practice in London; his second son, Huxley, (named after TH) took a degree in marine biology at London University, and his youngest daughter, Bryony, studied biochemistry at St Andrews University. Tim's family and his home became the great joy of his life.

For the last twelve years of his life, he had a villa in the Monchique mountains in the Algarve, Portugal, which became his other great joy, and a place where he spent nearly all his holidays – repairing, mending, painting and generally keeping himself happy and occupied. He was never so happy as when employed on the many different 'odd jobs' in the house and garden, and apart from carpentry, plumbing, electrics etc., he had a remarkable knowledge of mechanics and regularly repaired and serviced many pieces of machinery, from cars down to mowing machines and kitchen appliances.

He was a keen shot and enjoyed a week-end's grouse shooting in Yorkshire, and pheasant and partridge week-ends in Hampshire or Northumberland. His other interests included golf, which on his retirement (only two months before he died) he had decided to take up more seriously – his colleagues had presented him with a fine new set of golf clubs as a retirement present. He also loved music and most evenings put on a record or two – very loud, so as to get the maximum impact. He particularly loved operatic arias, and in moments of high spirits could often be heard holding forth with some favourite snippet of opera in full voice.

As regards his character, one of his outstanding qualities was his capacity to combine a wicked, often outrageous sense of humour with tremendous humanity and warmth. In the words of a nephew 'he was one of the few great humorists I have ever met who gave one at all times the clear sensation that he was very much in love with the world and with people – he loved to laugh with the world rather than against it'. He could be disconcertingly candid and was gravely suspicious of charm or facile conversation in others. He had very little regard for his own popularity, and did not hesitate to criticize or be ruthlessly frank if he considered it would help that person.

He referred to Casa Rosa, his villa in Portugal, as his paradise on earth, and it was fitting that it was there, overlooking the magnificent view down to the Algarve coast, and reading his favourite author, Laurens van der Post, that he suffered the brain haemorrhage which was to take him within a few hours perhaps to another kind of paradise.

PJWM

[*Brit. med. J.*, 1982, **285**, 819; Photo]

COXON, Robert Victor *b*.14 Nov 1914 *d*.2 June 1980
MRCS LRCP (1938) MB BS Lond (1938) FRCS (1940)
MRCP (1940) MD (1942) DPH (1946) DPhil Oxon (1952)

Robert Victor Coxon was a reader in human physiology at Oxford for almost 30 years. He was born in London, the son of Robert Cecil Coxon, a local government official, and his wife Beatrice Annie Phillips, and was educated at St Dunstan's College, Catford. He entered Guy's Hospital as a War Memorial scholar in arts, took his MB BS London in 1938 and, after house appointments at Guy's, took the FRCS and MRCP in 1940. After two years as medical registrar, he served in India as a medical specialist in the RAMC for three years, where he investigated the therapeutics of malaria and dysentery. It was in India that he met and married Mary Wynne Bowen, daughter of a schoolmaster, and herself a doctor in the RAMC.

After a year in chemical pathology, he became Betty Brookes research fellow at Oxford and worked for a DPhil on the carbohydrate metabolism of the brain under Sir Rudolph Peters. He continued to work on biochemical problems of the brain for the rest of his career, working for a year in the United States with Van Slyke. He retained academic contacts in the USA, working also with Baird Hastings and Chaikoff. Their influences were apparent in his work on CO_2 transfer using radioactive markers, on diuresis in dogs, and in critical accounts of the reliability of various physical instruments in physiological use.

In 1951 he was appointed reader in human physiology, fellow and lecturer, and later professorial fellow of Exeter College. He was appointed adviser to preclinical students – a post which at Oxford takes the place of a preclinical dean.

Coxon was a member of the General Board of Faculties for over 20 years; served on the Nuffield Committee and was chairman of the Board of the Faculty of Medicine. On two occasions he was acting head of department between appointments, and was relied on for advice on university administration and politics by three heads of department. As preclinical adviser he was very helpful to undergraduates who were trying to get into clinical medical schools. Some of his strongly held conservative views were unfashionable, often preceded by a deprecating 'I may be Blimpish but...', but they were to the point and often convincing. He stoutly defended the tutorial system and the independence of tutors. He had high standards in research, and feeling that physiology was becoming more quantitative, he took up a degree course in mathematics with the Open University at the age of 60.

Victor Coxon was excellent company in college and obviously derived great pleasure from his fellowship there. He had a long-standing love of France, and particularly of Brantôme, where he bought a cottage. His fluent French enabled him to be quickly welcomed by the local community, and one lawyer wrote to his daughter; 'Il était un sage'. In spite of a heavy burden of ill health in later years he retained his sharpness of mind and clarity of thought. He also had a mischievous sense of humour; he loved a good witty tale and delivered them skilfully. He was the centre of a happy family; there were three children of the marriage, one son and two daughters. His son is also in medical practice. GW/VL

[*Brit. med. J.*, 1980, **281**, 688, 878; *Times*, 12 June 1980; Photo]

CRAIB, William Hofmeyr *b.*17 May 1895 *d.*10 Apr 1982
MC/bar MB BChir Cantab (1923) MRCP (1928) MD (1930) FRCP (1936) Hon LLD Cape Town (1962) Hon MD Wits (1966) Hon DSc Natal (1969)

'Don' Craib was born in the small Karoo town of Somerset East, South Africa, and educated at Gill College where his Scots father, Professor James Craib, was a teacher. A bursary enabled him to study engineering at the South African College in Cape Town, where he took his BA in mathematics and physics. He resigned from a post as lecturer in the University in order to volunteer for service in Europe (1914–1918) and enlisted in the Royal Field Artillery. His exceptional courage and gallantry as a battery commander in France gained him the Military Cross and bar. After the war, he decided to study medicine and was admitted to Caius College, Cambridge, and later entered Guy's Hospital, London, where he graduated in 1923. He was one of the earliest recipients of a Rockefeller fellowship, which enabled him to work at Johns Hopkins Hospital, Baltimore from 1925 to 1926, during which time EP Carter encouraged him to undertake fundamental work on the electrical forces in the heart. On returning to England, he joined Sir Thomas Lewis's electrocardiographic work. He wrote three papers during this time, the first being a study of the electrical fields surrounding active heart muscle, in 1927; the second a study of the electrical fields surrounding skeletal muscle, in 1928; and the third a Medical Research Council monograph on the electrocardiogram, in 1930. Whilst in America, Craib had a feeling that his work was being ignored because it posed too much of a challenge to the accepted electrocardiographic theory of the day, and this feeling grew during his work for Lewis. The two men had increasing disagreements about the research being undertaken – it is said that they argued all day and every day – and eventually Craib was forced to resign his post and return to South Africa.

In essence Craib had challenged the accepted negativity hypothesis, at that time, of the genesis of the ECG current, and showed that myocardial excitation entailed movement along the muscle fibre, not a wave of negativity, but of an electrical doublet. FN Wilson of Ann

Arbor later refined this work and named it the dipole hypothesis. In spite of their disagreement, Lewis was generous to his junior colleague and wrote in 1929 'by the doublet hypothesis the interpretation of electrical responses from excitable tissues in general is reduced to a state of much greater simplicity and accuracy'. Later in life, however, Craib came to believe his work had been unfairly neglected and opposed, both in America and also in England, by ED Adrian of Cambridge in addition to Lewis, and he wrote for private publication a monograph entitled 'In Defence of Honour', in which he was the defendant in an imaginary court scene, charges being levelled against him. Although this monograph was written in a humorous style there is no doubt that it showed a decided streak of paranoia. This was unnecessary because in addition to Wilson and Lewis, Craib's work was praised in print by the ECG pioneer D Sodi-Pallares in 1970. On returning to South Africa, Craib occupied the post of professor of medicine at the University of Witwatersrand in Johannesburg for fourteen years. This however was a part-time post and offered him no opportunities for research. Or if it did, he certainly did not take them up, because he never wrote another word on the electrocardiogram, and the papers that he did publish after leaving Britain were of a minor nature.

In the second world war Craib was a senior physician in the South African Army, and on his return to the medical school he had a disagreement with the Senate, resigned and started practice in Port Elizabeth. In his later years, several honorary degrees were bestowed on him in South Africa, and in addition he was appointed vice-president of the Council for Scientific and Industrial Research there, and was elected to life-time membership of the Johns Hopkins Society of Scholars. In 1976 he had the great satisfaction of having his research publicly praised at the Seventh European Congress of Cardiology.

Personally, he was a very pleasant person to meet and talk with, and Sir George Pickering once said 'if you meet Don Craib, please give him my love – I was very fond of him'. He was survived by his wife, Doris Eileen Vevers of Bristol, a professional 'cellist before her marriage, and their two daughters; Gillian Mary, a senior nursing sister at the Provincial Hospital in Port Elizabeth, and Patricia Gwynne, a qualified radiotherapist who trained under John Hodson at UCH. Patricia (Patsy) married John Skinner, professor of zoology at Pretoria University and director of the Mammal Research Institute.

AH

[*Lancet,* 1983, **1**, 1232; *SA Med. J.,* 1982, **62**, 37; *Somerset Budget (SA),* 30 Apr 1975; *Johns Hopkins Med. J.,* 1976, **138**, 279-288; Photo]

CRANE, Walter Alfred James *b.*27 June 1925 *d.*29 Dec 1982
MB ChB Glasg (1947) MD (1959) MRCPG (1966) MRCP (1967) FRCPath (1971) FRCPG (1972) FRCP (1975)

Bill Crane was born at Kilmarnock, Scotland. He entered the

University of Glasgow in 1942, and graduated MB ChB with commendation in 1947 and MD with honours and a Bellahouston gold medal in 1959.

After his house jobs, Crane spent two years as a pathologist in the Royal Army Medical Corps in the Mediterranean and Middle East. As an undergraduate, he had been noted by Tom Symington and Alastair Currie (later Sir Tom and Sir Alastair), who encouraged him to consider a career in pathology; and he subsequently (in 1950) became Hansen research scholar in pathology in the University department of pathology at the Royal Infirmary, Glasgow. It was soon obvious that he was highly gifted both as a teacher and as a diagnostic histopathologist; and he also quickly demonstrated an outstanding talent for research, tackling problems in man and in experimental animals with vigour and imagination. He was appointed registrar in 1952 and lecturer in 1954. When he started his career the Royal Infirmary Department was an adrenal-centred environment, and he was soon drawn into this field. He concentrated on the role of the mineralocorticoids in hypertension, an interest which he retained throughout most of his subsequent career. He rounded out his training in the basic sciences by spending a year (1956 – 1957) as assistant professor with Dwight Ingle, in the Ben May Laboratory for Cancer Research (of which Charles Huggins was director) at the University of Chicago, USA, returning there for some months in 1962 as associate professor in the department of physiology. In 1959 he moved from Glasgow to a senior lectureship, with honorary consultant status, at the University of Sheffield. He was first assistant to Douglas Collins, and when Collins died in 1964 Crane predictably succeeded him as Joseph Hunter professor of pathology and head of department. He was also appointed honorary director of cancer research, and as such he increasingly turned his attention to aspects of tumour pathology. For many years he served on the executive and finance committee of the Yorkshire Cancer Research Campaign.

Crane was a fine speaker with good 'presence', and an outstanding teacher. With his warm and friendly personality he attracted able young graduates to a career in pathology, and others came from abroad to train under him, including a succession of young Greek pathologists. He had little difficulty in building up a large and successful department. He played a considerable part in the development of the multidisciplinary division of laboratory medicine at Sheffield, and in the development of laboratory services throughout the Trent Region. He was much involved in the planning and building of the new Hallamshire Teaching Hospital, particularly during his period of office as dean of the medical school (1976 – 1979).

His reputation in research led to his being invited by the Medical Research Council to serve on its Systems Board from 1974 to 1977, and on one of the Board's grants committees.

Crane's gentle, courteous personality, backed by a fine intellect and good judgement, made him a highly respected and popular member of any organization which he served; and not surprisingly his experience and talents were in ever-increasing demand, nationally and internationally. He gave generously of himself and his time to many spheres of activity. He was a staunch supporter of the Pathological Society of Great Britain and Ireland, and his term of office as its scientific secretary from 1969 to 1974 was both happy and successful. During it the links with the Netherlands Pathological Society were greatly strengthened, and in 1976 the Dutch pathologists showed their appreciation by making him an honorary member of their Society. In 1975 he helped to found the Association of Professors of Pathology of Great Britain, becoming its first secretary. He was an examiner for the Royal College of Pathologists for many years and a member of its Council from 1970 to 1973. He served as an external examiner in pathology to many universities in this country. Through his deep interest in medical education, he was appointed a member of the medical sub-committee of the University grants committee in 1978 and was still serving on it at the time of his death. He represented the University of Sheffield on the General Medical Council from 1979, when he was also elected a member of its education committee. He became a member of the executive committee of the Council in 1980.

Crane travelled extensively abroad, particularly to the United States of America, Greece, and the Far East. In 1975 he spent several months helping the medical school at Salisbury, Rhodesia. In 1982 he visited Oman as a member of the Teaching Hospital Advisory Committee of Muscat in the Sultanate of Oman; and later that year, on behalf of the British Council, he visited some twenty medical centres in Japan to discuss the organization of undergraduate and postgraduate medical education.

Crane had a coronary thrombosis in 1977, exactly five years prior to the second and fatal attack. He displayed great courage and determination in recovering from it, and gradually resumed his wide-ranging activities, both professional and social. He was pleased to have completed his term of office as dean of the medical school. There is no doubt that had he lived further opportunities for service would have been open to him.

Although a fine swimmer, his main way of relaxing was social – an evening's bridge gave him particular pleasure. Throughout his life he had exhibited a striking capacity for forming strong and enduring friendships; as the following quote from a letter from one of his Greek trainees (Professor Delides of Athens) illustrates clearly: 'Throughout the years of my association with Professor Crane, he was an inspiring teacher and sincere friend; and his human and academic qualities shall for ever remain engraved in my remembrance and in that of his friends and colleagues in Athens.'

No man was prouder of his family, and they reciprocated his feelings. He was survived by his wife, Yvonne, whom he married in 1952; a son, Peter, training to be a surgeon; and a daughter, Susan, a school teacher. His many friends were saddened by his premature death.

RCC

[*Brit. med. J.*, 1983, **286**, 403; *Lancet*, 1983, **1**, 252; Photo]

CROFT, Charles Richard *b*.1 July 1902 *d*.4 Sept 1981
TD (1945) BA Oxon (1923) MRCS LRCP (1926) BM BCh (1926) DM (1930) MRCP (1934) FRCP (1967)

Born in College Street, Winchester, though to his later discomfort never registered, Charles Richard Croft was the youngest of the four children of William Bleaden Croft, the first science master at Winchester College and known to generations as 'The Bleeder'. WB Croft went up to Pembroke College from Christ's Hospital with a classical scholarship, taking a first class in mathematics (though unclassified in the compulsory classics papers) in 1873. Winchester appointed him to teach mathematics but soon afterwards sent him back to Oxford to read Natural Science (physics and chemistry) in which he was again placed in Class 1. He came to enjoy a considerable reputation away from Winchester, serving as external examiner at Oxford and was the first to demonstrate successfully in this country, at the Physical Society in 1893, Branly's coherer which was the early detector of Hertz's radio waves of 1888.

There was already a tradition of medicine in the family. Croft had had two great-uncles in the profession. His grandfather, Charles Ilderton Croft (1813 – 1860), who was apprenticed to one of them, Dr James Croft of George Lane, qualified Lic. Soc. Apoth. in 1834, was Freeman of the City in 1856 and FRCS in 1857. He practised as a surgeon at 6 Lawrence Pountney Hill in the City. Among his nine children were EO Croft, the first professor of gynaecology at Leeds University. A grandson of Croft's great-uncle, Gilmore Croft, was the successful London surgeon, John Croft, a St Thomas's surgeon who collaborated with Florence Nightingale in the establishment of the Nightingale Nurses Training School, and who brought plaster of Paris ('The Croft Splint') to England.

At Charterhouse, Croft took the traditional classics course and was accepted by Trinity College, Oxford, but in the interval he rapidly learnt up the necessary sciences at a London crammer and was thus able to start straight away on medicine at Trinity, where his tutor was EGT Liddell, later professor of physiology. After Oxford he went to St Thomas's for his clinical training and there he won medical prizes (Toller and Wainwright) in 1925 – 1926. On qualifying he was appointed house surgeon to Cyril AR Nitch and PH Mitchiner at St Thomas's. The latter, who had held high rank in the Army during the first world war, suggested that he should make a career in the RAMC. Instead, he moved to Oxford as the house physician at the Radcliffe Infirmary, (there being only one at that time), and worked with Alec Cooke FRCP, who was the one medical registrar there in 1927.

His next appointments, as junior and senior obstetric house surgeons at St Thomas's, were perhaps to determine his future. He was involved with a distressing case of contraction ring of the uterus in which the foetus was trapped leading to death of the baby and mother, the usual outcome of this condition at that time. He found in the literature a new treatment from Germany using amyl nitrite. At this point, for family reasons, he decided to go into general practice.

Arriving in Plymouth for the interview he was met at the station by the senior partner, who was worried by a case of delayed labour. Croft was at once able to diagnose contraction ring and successfully treated the patient with amyl nitrite. For a time this treatment was known as the Croft method. Not unnaturally, he got the job and this case, and subsequent experimental work at the Marine Biological Laboratories in Plymouth, formed the basis of a successful thesis for the Oxford DM in 1930. He married, settled in Plymouth and built up a very successful general practice. In 1934, on the basis of his thesis and publications, he was made MRCP without examination, an unusual distinction. He was subsequently appointed medical registrar at Plymouth and was made consultant physician to South Devon and East Cornwall Hospital there in 1937. He was thus one of the last of the general practitioners to become a consultant physician, a common and honourable route to consulting practice before the turn of the century.

As a Territorial, he was called up at the onset of World War II in which he had a distinguished record, being twice mentioned in despatches. Starting with the campaign in Greece, he went to Crete where, during the evacuation from Heraklion, he arranged to move wounded soldiers under his care, in caves in the hills, onto a ship which, much to his distress, was bombed with the loss of his patients. He then went to Palestine and got together a civilian mobile ambulance which had been given to the British Army by American philanthropists. This collection of vehicles and tents he commanded as the Number One Mobile Military Hospital throughout the African desert campaign. He claimed at that time to be an expert on tentpoles! This hospital, with full operating theatres, was used between casualty clearing stations and base hospitals, being regarded with circumspection by the Army establishment as it did not conform to a standard Army pattern. After the war, Croft was asked for a report on it which was published in the *RAMC Journal*, as his unique experience with a mobile hospital was felt useful for planning for modern warfare. He ended the war a full colonel with command of a general hospital in Rome.

He returned to Plymouth, worked up his old practice from a basement in Devonport and, in 1947, just before the National Health Service came in, he sold it and moved to consulting work full time. He ran a rheumatology clinic, was a member of the Heberden Society and an active supporter of the Arthritis and Rheumatism Council. He was a brilliant diagnostician and in domiciliary practice his colleagues also appreciated his background as a general practitioner. He had an interest in clinical endocrinology and was president of the Plymouth Medical Society 1966–1976. In addition to scientific and clinical papers, he wrote on Sir William Osler and Sir Richard Croft, the Royal obstetrician, who was not an ancestor but who, he felt, had been wrongly accused of the death of Princess Charlotte and the potential heir apparent.

He was a kind and gentle man whose Christian beliefs were enhanced by Freemasonry in which he rose to high levels. His own general practitioner, an Irishman with a mischievous sense of humour, claimed that he was the only English gentleman that he had ever known! In 1928 he married Phyllis Mary Lee, whose ancestors included an early eighteenth century physician, Dominic Lee of Louth, Lincolnshire, who had emigrated from Kilkenny near Dublin, qualified MD in Louvain in 1715 and who married a cousin of Sir Isaac Newton, Robert Boyle the chemist, and Thomas Warton, a poet laureate. Two of his three sons qualified from Oxford and St Thomas's and both took a DM (Oxon), the second being marked in 1973 by a dinner in Christ Church. The company included six FRCPs, one being the regius professor of medicine, Sir Richard Doll. His eldest son is physician at St Thomas's Hospital. He died at home in Kingsclere, Hampshire, where he moved after retirement. DNC

[*Brit. med. J.*, 1982, **284**, 62; Photo]

CROFT, Peter Basil *b.*14 June 1922 *d.*23 July 1981
BSc Oxon (1946) MA (1947) BM BCh (1947) MRCP (1951) FRCP (1970)

Peter Basil Croft was born in Ashton-under-Lyne. His father, Harold William Croft, was a civil servant and his mother Kathleen Luscombe, was the daughter of a headmaster. He was educated at Bristol Grammar School and then won a scholarship to Keble College, Oxford. He was one of the few students who were allowed to do a full course in physiology in wartime Oxford, and he gained first class honours in Natural Science (physiology). In 1943 and 1944 he did research on the metabolism of thermal burns in animals in the department of biochemistry, University of Oxford, under Sir Rudolph Peters. This work formed the subject of a BSc thesis which he obtained in 1946. After qualification he did various house jobs, including that of house physician to LJ Witts on the medical unit at the Radcliffe Infirmary, Oxford. Early in his career he decided he wanted to do neurology, working first with Michael Ashby at the Whittington and later with Lord Brain at the London Hospital. There he was to take part in much of the research in that distinguished department, his particular interest being in the remote effects of cancer on the nervous system. On this subject he wrote many papers including some with Lord Brain, Ronald Henson, Marcia Wilkinson and Henry Urich. In one (1963) he and his co-worker examined 1500 patients with cancer in an effort to find the incidence of the various types of carcinomatous neuromyopathy. Another important paper was that on 'Abnormal Responses to Muscle Relaxants in Carcinomatous Neuropathy' (1958) in which he pointed out the dangers of giving relaxant drugs to patients with cancer. He was an industrious worker and a keen observer and wrote papers on a wide variety of neurological topics, including the metabolism of thermal burns, familial hypertrophic polyneuritis, spontaneous spinal subarachnoid haemorrhage and ocular myopathy.

He became consultant neurologist to the Prince of Wales's

Hospital, Tottenham, in 1958, the Bolingbrooke Hospital in 1959, the Lister Hospital in 1961, the Queen Eizabeth II Hospital at Welwyn Garden City in 1964, and the Whittington Hospital in 1964, resigning his appointments at the Bolingbrooke and the Lister when he became director of the neurological unit at the Whittington Hospital. In 1970 he became honorary consulting neurologist to the Jewish Home and Hospital. With his remarkable memory, kindness, unflagging devotion and balanced judgement he rapidly made his mark as a most valued friend and colleague, and was often asked to give a second opinion on a difficult case or to see members of his colleagues' families. He was a hard worker and nothing was ever too much trouble – on one occasion when a colleague was going to lecture in America he spent the entire night trying to find a vital piece of film.

During his time as neurologist at the Whittington he played a prominent part in initiating and organizing the now world famous membership course held there. He was renowned as a brilliant teacher and many generations of registrars, house officers and students have reason to be grateful to him for the sound training he gave them. Above all things he was a clinician and to him the patient always came first. Schooled in the Radcliffe and London Hospital tradition, careful history-taking and examination of the patient were important to him, and he had no sympathy for those who did not come up to his high standard.

In addition to his clinical duties he was a great attender of meetings, and until his last illness never missed a meeting of the Association of British Neurologists. He served on numerous committees, including the finance committee of the Royal College of Physicians. For many years he was secretary of the neurologists and neurosurgeons committee of the North East Thames Area, and was a keen and able secretary and member of the Council of the neurological section of the Royal Society of Medicine. He was a keen photographer and gardener, and roses were his special joy.

In 1954 he married Patricia, whose father, Frederick George Fox, was a tea planter, and they had two sons and two daughters.

MIPW

[*Brit. med. J.*, 1981, **283**, 624; *Times*, 28 July 1981]

CROOKS, James *b.*22 Mar 1919 *d.*3 Jan 1983
CBE (1982) MB ChB Glasg (1951) MD (1959) FRFPS (1954) MRCP (1956) MRCPE (1956) MRCPG (1962) FRCPE (1963) FRCPG (1964) FRCP (1969) MFCM (1979)

James Crooks was born in Glasgow, where his father was a post office worker. He was educated at North Kelvinside School, but an important part of his early training took place in the Life Boys and the Boys Brigade. From the age of 7 to 16, participation in both of these organizations was a major part in his development, and undoubtedly enabled him to withstand his later experiences as a prisoner of war. In the Boys Brigade he was influenced by the radiologist, Fergus Leslie

Henderson, the 'Doc', who was in charge of the 69th Boys Brigade Company. It was here that he took part in organized games, bathing, boating, fishing, hill-climbing, cycle tours, nature study and various excursions. He became a leader of his squad, developed an interest in literature, took a principal part in an opera, and captained the first eleven at cricket and won the bronze award which he treasured throughout his life. When he was 16 his father died and he had to leave school to help support his mother and younger sister. He entered a firm of stockbrokers as a clerk and during this period began to write short stories, some of which were published, and he attended night classes for further training in writing.

Jim joined the territorial army at the time of the Munich crisis, and a few days before war broke out he was called up to the Royal Corps of Signals as a sergeant. After Pearl Harbour he was sent out with the 18th Division to Singapore, landing a few days before it surrendered to the Japanese. For the next three and a half years he was a prisoner of war in the notorious Changi prison and worked on the Burma railway. He was always reticent about this period but it was at this time that his qualities of leadership began to emerge. His training in the Boys Brigade and his early acquired maturity after the death of his father stood him in good stead. He initiated a primitive social service by which squares of stamped paper acted as a 'money reward' shared with those who were too unwell to work. He also contributed to courses in the 'university of Changi'. After being posted as missing for 19 months he managed to get a postcard through to his wife and childhood sweetheart, Betty, whom he had married in 1940. He returned to Glasgow in 1945. His experiences in the Far East, exposed to disease and death, had made him ferociously determined to become a doctor, but he was without any entrance qualifications. He managed to squeeze about two and a half years work into three months and remarkably gained a place in medicine in the University of Glasgow in 1946.

From this point in James's life everything seemed easier. After a distinguished passage through medical school he graduated in 1951. He spent his junior medical years in Glasgow hospitals, in particular a period in the Southern General Hospital where he wrote his first papers on canicola fever. In 1954 he moved to the Western Infirmary, Glasgow, to the department of medicine under Sir Edward Wayne. Their partnership was a most effective one. Sir Edward sparked off his enthusiasm in the statistical approach to medicine and therapeutics and in thyroid disease, and this work on thyroid disease culminated in 1960 in the Bellahouston medal gained for 'eminent merit of an MD thesis'. These interests formed the basis of distinguished work in his post as senior lecturer in the department of materia medica and therapeutics in the University of Aberdeen from 1960 to 1969, and from then as professor of pharmacology and therapeutics in the University of Dundee.

Jim Crooks was always interested in medical teaching both at an individual level and in the development of medical curricula. As a senior registrar he would take under his wing the unfortunate undergraduate or postgraduate who had difficulty in passing the clinical exam, and in this he almost had a 100% success rate. He played important parts in the planning and implementation of the new medical curriculum in Aberdeen, and in the development and establishment of a centre for medical education in Dundee. His approach to any problem was essentially pragmatic and practical. His methodology was always thorough and painstaking and communicated with a beguiling simplicity, a product of his skill in writing and teaching. Throughout his career his wide research interests were not only in clinical pharmacology, therapeutics and endocrinology, but also in the application of computers in medicine, and the place of health economics and audit in medical practice. In particular his work on drug handling in the elderly, for which he was co-director of an MRC programme, on drug metabolism and on adverse drug reactions, were all of high distinction. His work on the drug kardex system was a model of simplicity, as was his hospital formulary, both of which were widely copied elsewhere. He maintained throughout his life his interest in thyroid disease and initiated the Scottish Automated Follow-Up Register (SAFUR), which is a computer based follow-up system for thyroid disease in Scotland. It was as chairman of the Undergraduate Medical Education Committee of Dundee Medical School that Jim Crooks played an important part in developing the medical curriculum and setting up the centre for medical education in Dundee. He was a most valued member of the Committee on Safety of Medicines from 1977 until his death; of the Chief Scientist Committee of the Scottish Home and Health Department, and of numerous other committees and subcommittees in the Health Service; he was a member of the Tayside Health Board, and its policy and resources and general purposes committees; a member of the BBC medical advisory committee; the University representative on the General Medical Council; regional adviser to the Medical Council on Alcoholism; a leading member of Tenovus Tayside; he was also a consultant in the World Health Organization. His knowledge and experience were widely sought in Canada, the United States and Russia. His initiative and drive earned him numerous research grants and contracts, culminating in the establishment of Drug Development (Scotland) in Dundee in 1982. He hoped this would become a model of collaboration between university and industry, and a means of generating funding for medical research. His outstanding work received acclaim, and several awards, in 1982. He received the first Lilly prize for outstanding contributions to clinical pharmacology over a period of years, and in November 1982 he gave the second annual Glaxo/Strathclyde lecture. In the New Year's Honours List he was awarded the CBE.

He was a man of great strength of character, accompanied by a modest and compassionate personality. He always exuded good sense, hopefulness and humour. His experience as a prisoner of war undoubtedly played an important part in his development, although he was well trained for this in his association with the Boys Brigade in Glasgow. He never showed the slightest bitterness about his experiences as a prisoner of war and in fact was happy to welcome Japanese colleagues to his department. He played ball games well, enjoying the competitive aspects of tennis and badminton and, more recently, golf – he was a member of the Royal and Ancient. His marriage to Betty in 1940 was a source of great strength to him. They had one son, who is also a doctor. AG(1)

[*Brit. med. J.*, 1983, **286**, 312; *Lancet*, 1983, **1**, 253; *Times*, 13 Jan 1983; *Daily Telegraph*, 4 Jan 1983; Photo]

CROWTHER, Joseph Stanley *b.*2 Dec 1907 *d.*22 Aug 1981
BA Cantab (1930) MRCS LRCP (1944) MB BS Lond (1944) MRCP (1949) MD (1950) FRCP (1971)

Stanley Crowther was born in Bradford, the son of Thomas Edward Crowther and his wife, Mary Hannah, née Baines. After attending school in his home town, he went to Cambridge to read chemistry, physics and mathematics. When he graduated he became a buyer at Harrods, but he later turned to medicine and entered University College Hospital in 1939, where he was awarded the senior clinical medicine prize.

After a variety of hospital jobs in London, and two years with the RAMC in Nigeria and Germany, he began to specialise in thoracic medicine and worked at Clare Hall Hospital and Paddington Chest Clinic. In 1956 he went to Chesterfield as a senior hospital medical officer, and in 1961 he was appointed consultant chest physician to Ransom Hospital in Mansfield and the Nottingham Chest Clinic. Later he also had duties at the Nottingham City Hospital, and he occupied these posts with distinction. When he retired in 1972 he worked at the Nottingham University Health Centre, and maintained a lively interest in medicine until he died. He was throughout a meticulous, skilled and kind physician.

At Cambridge Stan won a Blue for football. In later life he was a keen walker on hills and on mountains, as well as 'Ban the Bomb' marches from Aldermaston. He travelled widely and he was always interested in the customs and ways of other nations. In 1936 he married Ellen, daughter of John Wilson, and they had two sons.
DD

[*Brit. med. J.*, 1981, **283**, 1067]

CUDWORTH, Andrew Gordon *b.*16 Mar 1939 *d.*11 Oct 1982
MB ChB Liverp (1963) MRCP (UK) (1971) FRCP (1978)

As a medical student in Liverpool, with a young family, Andrew Cudworth was short of money, and joined the Army Cadet scheme. After he had qualified in medicine in 1963, and done his house jobs, he accepted enthusiastically the responsibilities he had incurred, and signed on as a Regular Army medical officer for five years, on a short service commission, rising to the rank of major. He was fond of the

Army, and made and retained many friends there. After returning to civilian life he continued as a Territorial until he resigned in June 1982. It seems a strange beginning for someone who was to prove one of the outstanding figures in British academic medicine – but it gave him an experience of life and maturity of judgement which perhaps contributed later to his notable success as an organizer and administrator, as well as a scientist.

He returned to Liverpool and became a medical registrar at the age of 30, and got his Membership in 1971, at the age of 32. It is astonishing to reflect that the whole immense span of his work in academic medicine was crammed into the next 10 years. He joined the department of medicine in Liverpool, and published his *first* paper – a case report with immunological overtones – in 1972. His *second* paper – another case report, this time of a diabetic patient, was published in 1973, when he was 34. To these twin scientific threads – immunology and diabetes – was added a third, when his interest in the inherited basis of disease was stimulated by Cyril Clarke and Joseph Woodrow. He and Woodrow, with another group in Copenhagen, were independent and virtually simultaneous discoverer of a genetic marker which was linked to the severe, insulin-requiring form of diabetes. Patients with this disease had a characteristic inherited 'fingerprint' (as it were) – recognizable by a blood test. This discovery overnight changed a disease, which though common had been quite mysterious, into one which became amenable to proper study.

Andrew at once became a well-known figure in the field of diabetes, and in 1977 was appointed consultant physician to St Bartholomew's and Hackney Hospitals, and senior lecturer in the medical college. In the short time that remained to him, his achievements were phenomenal. He had immense powers of concentration and hard work, allied to great scientific originality.

He realised that if the genetic prediposition to diabetes could be refined, quantified and made exact, it would become possible to predict, amongst people who had not yet developed the disease, which ones would do so. By the close study of his own patients in the district, and by collaboration with many other physicians in and around London, he was able to refine the genetic markers of the disease, and from a single blood sample establish with a very high degree of certainty two separate 'axes' of susceptibility, and one of non-susceptibility, or resistance to the disease.

He realized that the exemplary childhood diabetic register established at and around Windsor by John Lister and his colleagues, provided a wonderful opportunity for capitalizing on his genetic discoveries. For the first time it became possible to predict with virtual certainty which children in diabetic families were at risk. Thus he could watch by means of further relatively simple tests the progress of the illness, and find out the details of the process by which the body turned upon itself, and destroyed the vital insulin-producing cells in its own pancreatic gland.

His work in diabetes was wide, and he made notable contributions to many aspects, but his immunogenetic work was outstanding. It revealed the unexpected and exciting fact that childhood diabetes, which hitherto had seemed to have a sudden onset, in fact developed quite slowly, over many years. This opened up new vistas of study, particularly the use of various types of 'immune-suppressing' drugs during the long incubation period of the disease. Andrew Cudworth's discoveries also paved the way for genetic counselling, and other more radical approaches to the prevention of this common illness.

Cudworth, of course, became in increasing demand as a speaker and organizer at international meetings, and in 1980 was appointed editor-in-chief of the international diabetic journal, *Diabetologia*. Early in 1982 he was the guest of honour of the American Juvenile Diabetes Foundation, which awarded him its much coveted prize for his original discoveries. London University recognized his distinction by the award in January 1982, of a personal chair in human metabolism.

Although he was outstanding in research, he also took care of very many patients who already had diabetes, collaborating with David Galton in the diabetic clinic at Bart's. At Hackney he set up a model and comprehensive diabetic service, and quickly established a great reputation throughout London as a caring as well as technically masterful clinician. Patients came from far and wide to seek his help, which was always freely given.

He was highly valued by Bart's medical students and postgraduates as a teacher, in which role he was also outstanding. In particular, he encouraged his students towards study in depth of medical problems. The regular scientific presentation sessions he made them prepare – and which he attended and criticized – were very popular.

Amazingly, he was also a gifted administrator, largely because he gained and kept the complete trust of all his colleagues. The respect and trust of these colleagues were shown, amongst other things, by his appointment in 1981 as secretary of Bart's Medical Council, and as chairman of the District Medical Division.

During his long and distressing illness (a right parietal lobe glioma) his personal courage and inner resources became inspiringly apparent. He realized at once, after diagnosis, that he had probably only a matter of months to live. Andrew had always lived each day as if his last – and he seemed to be possessed of almost superhuman equanimity as well as energy. Characteristically, he never complained about his fate – nor indeed did he ever spontaneously mention his illness to others. He needed less than any man the advice that Dylan Thomas gave his father:

'Do not go gentle into that good night...
Rage, rage, against the dying of the light.'

He carried on working with undiminished energy and enthusiasm up to his death. Just two days before he died, he was making helpful and imaginative comments about the possible cause of a mysterious sequence of illnesses in a patient whose problems had been discussed with him, and was anxious that this line of enquiry should be followed up.

He was survived by his wife, Mary, two sons and a daughter.

None of those who knew, respected, admired and loved him, will ever forget Andrew Cudworth, whose name will live on through his important scientific contributions. CJD

[*Brit. med. J.*, 1982, **285**, 1434-35; *Lancet*, 1982, **2**, 996; *The Times*, 22 Oct 1982; Photo]

d'ABREU, Alphonso Liguori *b.*5 Aug 1906 *d.*19 Apr 1976
CBE (1968) OBE (1944) MRCS LRCP (1929)
MB BCh Birm (1929) FRCS (1932) ChM Birm (1935)
FRCP* (1968)

Alphonso d'Abreu was elected a Fellow of the College under the provisions of Bye-Law 39(b) in 1968. He was one of the most outstanding members of the profession of his time. The son of John Francis d'Abreu, a general practitioner in Birmingham, he was educated at Stonyhurst College and the University of Birmingham, from which he graduated in medicine in 1930. Two years later he was elected FRCS, and from then until 1939 he perfected his surgical skills in the teaching hospitals in Birmingham and Cardiff.

During the 1939–1945 war he served with distinction at home and overseas with the RAMC, and was appointed OBE in 1944 and mentioned in despatches the following year. After the war he was acting professor of surgery in the University of Wales for a year, before being appointed to the part time consulting staff of the Birmingham United Hospitals. He quickly became the leading surgeon in the Midlands and soon gave up general surgery in order to devote himself entirely to cardiothoracic work, which was always his major interest. His *Practice of Thoracic Surgery*, which ran to four editions, became the standard work of reference, and he was one of the pioneers of the surgery of congenital heart disease, rheumatic heart disease and bypass surgery.

His great energy and surgical skill, his strikingly handsome appearance and his wonderful charm and kindness cast a spell over everyone with whom he come in contact, and from his earliest years it was obvious that he would achieve distinction in the profession.

From 1959 to 1963 he was professor of cardiac surgery, and from 1963 to 1971 Barling professor of surgery in the University of Birmingham. He was dean of the Faculty of Medicine in Birmingham (1959–1963), and at the Royal College of Surgeons he was twice Hunterian Professor, a member of the court of examiners (1956–1962), and of the council (1963–1975) and vice-president. He was a member of the medical subcommittee of the University Grants Committee (1963–1972), president of the section of surgery of the Royal Society of Medicine (1966–1967), a member of the Central Health Services Committee of the Ministry of Health (1964–1971), president of the Thoracic Society (1968–1969) and of the Society of Thoracic and Cardiovascular Surgeons of Great Britain and Ireland (1969–1970). In 1967 he was visiting professor of surgery at Harvard.

He was honorary colonel of the medical services of the 42nd Division (TA) (1963 – 1966) and consulting surgeon to the British Army (1964 – 71). He was appointed CBE in 1968 and was a Deputy Lieutenant for Warwickshire. He married Elizabeth, daughter of Lieutenant Colonel Courtney Throckmorton, and there were three daughters of the marriage.

'Pon', as he was always called, had intelligence, elegance, energy and manual dexterity to a degree only encountered once in every two or three generations. His enormous success and achievements were inevitable, as were the many honours thrust upon him, but he remained ever modest and unassuming, gentle, courteous, considerate and kind to everyone. He did more for British medicine than almost anyone of his generation and in return he was one of the best loved and most respected members of the profession. Unhappily his later years were clouded by illness and disability, which he bore with a fortitude, courage and cheerfulness that was admired by all who knew him.

AGWW

[*Brit. med. J.*, 1976, **1**, 1078, 1155; *Lancet*, 1976, **1**, 1028; Photo]

DALRYMPLE-CHAMPNEYS, *Sir* **Weldon** *b.*7 May 1892
*d.*14 Dec 1980
Bart CB (1957) MA Oxon (1921) BM BCh (1922) DPH (1923)
MRCP (1925) DM (1929) FRCP (1935)

Weldon Champneys was born in London, the son of Sir Francis Champneys, first baronet, an eminent gynaecologist who played a large part in securing the regulation of the training of midwives and was the first, and longest serving, chairman of the Central Midwives Board and a Fellow of the College. His mother, Virginia Julian, was the only daughter of the late Sir John Warrander Dalrymple, seventh baronet of North Berwick. Weldon assumed the additional surname of Dalrymple by deed poll in 1924, and succeeded his father as second baronet in 1930.

He grew up in a medical household, attending Gresham's School, Holt, and then went to Oriel College, Oxford, and later for his clinical training to St Bartholomew's Hospital Medical College. Although he joined the Grenadier Guards as a combatant and served throughout the war, being wounded, earning the 1914 – 1915 Star and remaining on the reserve of officers till 1938, Weldon returned to complete his medical training. After house posts at the Brompton and Victoria Park Hospitals and the Neasden Fever Hospital, he joined the staff of the Willesden Public Health Department, serving with George Buchan, one of the most distinguished medical officers of health between the wars. Weldon obtained the Oxford DPH and was one of that considerable group of able men who after World War I deliberately chose preventive medicine as a career, possibly influenced by the new value accorded to that specialty by the Dawson Report of 1920. Sadly that kind of recruitment did not continue, perhaps because Dawson's Advisory Council was disbanded, and later generations of leading hospital clinicians had not his insight into health care and health promotion.

Weldon was with Willesden only three years, and in 1927 he joined the medical staff of the Ministry of Health, He was promoted to one of five new, short-lived, senior posts designed for a peacetime regionalization of the medical staff. After less than a year, on the retirement of Thomas Carnwath, he became the third holder of the post of deputy chief medical officer. He remained in that grade till his retirement in 1956, and was then created Companion of the Bath, having previously served for three years as honorary physician to the King. He was Milroy lecturer in 1950, awarded the Neech prize of the Society of Medical Officers of Health in 1948 and was chairman of a joint committee of WHO and FAO on brucellosis. He was a member of Council of the Royal College of Veterinary Surgeons and for a time its vice chairman. He was a vice president of the Royal Society of Health and president at various times of the sections of epidemiology, comparative medicine and history of medicine of the Royal Society of Medicine. His principal publications concerned undulant fever, of which he had made a special study in England.

Weldon's career was almost entirely in the Ministry of Health, where he worked mainly on prevention and supplies, including drugs. He followed the usual path of a recruit of his time, making special enquiries and reporting within the Ministry on such subjects as sick-bays in public schools, undulant fever, supervision of milk pasteurising plants, and production of sterilized catgut. He was active in the Royal Society of Health. As DCMO he was chairman of numerous working groups on supplies, notably one on artificial respirators, but apart from this he was little involved in the main preoccupation of the Ministry in the NHS. In 1940 shortly after Weldon's promotion to deputy, Sir Wilson Jameson had been brought into the Ministry as chief medical office, and four years later a second DCMO, John Charles, MOH of Newcastle, was brought in to work on the NHS. Sir John Charles, as he became, succeeded Sir Wilson and Weldon was disappointed a second time. It says much for his loyalty that he never allowed any sign of resentment to appear.

Weldon was an elegant, able man with many interests outside medicine. He was a superb photographer; he travelled widely; he was a considerable expert on herpetology; he spoke four languages fluently; he had an exhaustive knowledge of brucellosis in Britain; he was an excellent chairman of international groups with his linguistic skill. He had a full social life, closely linked with the charitable work of his first wife. All this meant that the intense preoccupation with health care that engulfed his colleagues from the time of the 1944 White Paper on the NHS largely passed him by. He had qualities and capacity that were not fully used, and that was not wholly the fault of the Ministry. At the end of an official career of thirty years there had to be some disappointment. Weldon was a loyal colleague and charming friend to the few who were at all close to him. It should have been possible for him to make a larger mark, but he seemed not to have the drive.

Weldon married in 1924 Anne, daughter of Colonel Spencer Pratt, who died in 1968 without children. In 1974 he married Norma, widow of AS Russell and daughter of Colonel R Hull Lewis. In retirement he lived latterly in Oxford, but still attended College functions. GEG

[*Brit. med. J.*, 1981, **282**, 159; *Times*, 16 Dec 1980; Photo]

DAVIDSON, Samuel Whately *b.* 25 May 1896 *d.* 30 Aug 1976
MB BS Durh (1920) MD (1923) MRCP (1923) FFR (1938)
FRCP (1942) Hon FCRA (1957)

Samuel Whately Davidson's father, Joshua, was a provision merchant and importer in Newcastle upon Tyne, and his mother, Lucy Clara Unsworth, was the daughter of a master clockmaker in the same area. Davidson was at school at Rutherford College in Newcastle. He lost his father when he was ten years old. His father had always hoped that his son would become a medical missionary, but his guardian pressed him into a career in pharmacy. Whately was not happy working in a pharmacy, and he finally prevailed upon his guardian to let him enter the local medical school.

As a student he served in the Royal Navy as a temporary surgeon probationer. After qualifying he intended to make a career as a physician, but in 1925 at the suggestion of his chief, William Hume (later Sir William), he became honorary assistant physician to the X-ray, massage and electrical department of the Royal Victoria Infirmary. He became head of the department in 1930 and held this post until his retirement in 1961.

His career as a radiologist was outstandingly successful. He established X-ray services in many hospitals in the north east of England, including that at the Newcastle General Hospital in 1929. From 1938 until 1966, when he was 70, he was consultant radiologist to the regional thoracic surgery unit at Shotley Bridge Hospital. He would arrive at the hospital at 6.30 a.m. complete his reporting, and return to the Royal Victoria Hospital by 9.00 a.m., to start a full day's work. Between 1948 and 1951 a new department of radiology was planned and built at the RVI. It is still a superb department, and it is a lasting memorial to Whately Davidson's vision and energy.

He served as an examiner in radiology to many universities and boards from 1937 to 1966. He held many important offices both locally and nationally, serving as president of the Faculty (now Royal College) of Radiologists, president of the section of radiology of the Royal Society of Medicine, president elect of the British Institute of Radiology, and as a member of the Standing Medical Advisory Committee of the Ministry of Health for six years. In 1968 he was elected a fellow of the British Medical Association.

Whately Davidson maintained his interest in the Navy, being mobilized in 1938 and released for duty in the EMS the following year. He was at one time a district commissioner of the Boy Scouts, and received the Medal of Merit of the Scout movement.

In his long career he had witnessed and played a material part in the emergence of diagnostic radiology as a specialty. After his official retirement he was almost continuously employed doing locums in the north east, and at the time of his death he was a locum consultant radiologist to the Queen Elizabeth Hospital, Gateshead. For over ten years after his sixty-fifth birthday he regularly gave tutorials (for which he would take no payment) to FFR (FRCR) candidates. For a long period he was a most successful chairman of the Regional Committee for registrars and senior registrars.

Whately had a most attractive personality and was beloved by a wide circle of people. He was always ready with a smile or a greeting for the patient lying on a stretcher in the corridor. He was a staunch Presbyterian, with a high sense of humour. Many will recall his twinkling blue eyes and his cheerful face surmounting a figure somewhat reminiscent of a Toby jug – often telling a joke against himself, sometimes at a piano playing the Blaydon Races, sometimes dressed in deerstalker, anorak and knickerbockers, energetically beagling.

In later years he was a frequent visitor to the consultant's dining-room at the RVI, and he made many new friends among the staff appointed after his retirement.

Whately Davidson married in 1936 Elizabeth Brenda Mason, the daughter of a wirerope manufacturer. There were two sons and a daughter of the marriage; the daughter married a son of William Gilchrist Patterson, FRCP. CKW/GW

[*Brit. med. J.*, 1976, **2**, 705; *Lancet*, 1976, **2**, 750; Photo]

DAVIDSON, *Sir* **(Leybourne) Stanley (Patrick)** *b.* 3 Mar 1893
d. 22 Sept 1981
Kt (1955) MB ChB Edin (1919) MD (1925) FRCPE (1925)
BA Cantab (1926) MRCP (1936) FRCP (1940)
Hon MD Oslo (1946) Hon LLD Edin (1962)
Hon LLD Aberd (1971)

Leybourne Stanley Patrick Davidson, the second son of Sir Leybourne Davidson, was born in Ceylon and died in Edinburgh after a series of distressing illnesses which afflicted him following his retiral from the chair of medicine at Edinburgh University in 1959.

He had led an active life both physically and academically, and was a well-known 'character' on the Edinburgh medical scene. It was not uncommon for his colleagues to greet each other with 'Have you heard the lastest story about Stanley?', before launching forth on an account of some new unorthodox episode in his activities at home or overseas.

He was educated at Cheltenham College and then at Trinity College, Cambridge, transferring to Edinburgh University to read medicine. His family home was at Huntly Lodge, Aberdeenshire, and in August 1914 he interrupted his studies to become a combatant in the Gordon Highlanders, a regiment which had been raised in 1794 by the Marquess of Huntly. He served for three years, chiefly in France and Belgium. Twice wounded, the second time so seriously that he was thought to be dead, he was rescued after having laid in the open at Festubert for twenty-four hours, and admitted to the gas-gangrene ward of the base hospital at Boulogne. His experiences during the first world war made him think deeply about his future activities, and when he returned to Edinburgh in 1917 to resume his medical studies he became a hard worker who managed to obtain first class honours on graduation in 1919. Having fought alongside representatives of all levels of society, he had a fresh outlook on the problems of his fellow men.

First, he became assistant to the professor of bacteriology and had clinical experience at the Royal Infirmary and Leith Hospital. In 1925 he was awarded a gold medal for his MD thesis on immunisation and antibody reactions. With George Gulland he produced, in 1930, a 300 page book on *Pernicious Anaemia*, at a time when liver therapy had just been introduced. The smallest section is on therapy, because most of his patients had been treated with arsenic or hydrochloric acid, but an account is given of the great advance that had just been made by the discovery of the value of feeding liver, and there is mention of the early use of liver extracts given by injection. Stanley Davidson was now launched, at a most suitable time, on the main research interest of his career, with expansion later into other aspects of nutrition and the study of rheumatic disorders.

In 1932 he was appointed to the regius chair of medicine in Aberdeen, but in 1938 he returned to the chair of medicine in Edinburgh. This appointment was regarded as controversial by some staid colleagues who were still thinking in terms of Victorian days, and were somewhat alarmed by the return of this outspoken, unpretentious young professor to whom all patients were equal, and who had no time for private practice. He was determined to reorganize hospital medicine throughout the city, and eventually did so, largely by bringing in consultants who had been trained south of the border. During the second world war he was an adviser to the Department of Health on the organization of hospitals in wartime, and gave advice to the Ministry of Food about rationing. In 1941 the Polish School of Medicine was founded in Edinburgh, and Stanley Davidson acted as head of the department of medicine until it closed down in 1949. The Order of Polonia Restitutor was conferred on him in 1945 by the President of the Polish Republic. He was created a Knight in 1955. From 1947 to 1952 he was physician to King George VI in Scotland, and from then until 1961 he served the Queen in a similar capacity. He attempted, in vain, to establish a Royal College of Physicians in Scotland by a merger of institutions, but, despite the temporary divisions that occurred over this issue, he was elected president of the Royal College of Physicians of Edinburgh from 1953 to 1957. He received the honorary degree of LLD from Edinburgh University in 1962 and from Aberdeen University in 1971. He had been given an honorary MD by the University of Oslo in 1946.

Most of his writings related to haematology or rheumatic disorders, and the textbooks which he edited alone or with colleagues were the *Textbook of Medical Treatment*; the *Principles and Practice of Medicine*, and *Human Nutrition and Dietetics*.

In his day his sports included golf, tennis, shooting and fishing, and he claimed to know the rivers of New Zealand rather better than those of Scotland. His cautious attitude to financial matters was legendary. It was, for example, impossible to persuade him that it was necessary to purchase a still at £9 with departmental funds in order to obtain distilled water. His solution to the problem was to ask the department of bacteriology to supply it daily, free of cost, in 8 oz. bottles. Fortunately, it was possible to have the still installed when he was away shooting on 'the twelfth', and to put the account through when he was fishing. Despite this caution, he made generous financial contributions to the Universities of Edinburgh and Aberdeen, and to the Royal College of Physicians of Edinburgh.

It was particularly sad that his wife, Peggy, died in 1979, and that he had to finish his days in a nursing home. Unfortunately, too, he had no children. RHG

[*Brit. med. J.*, 1981, **283**, 993, 1131; *Times,* 2 Oct 1981; Photo]

DAVIES, Charles Edwin *b.* 14 June 1914 *d.* 26 Nov 1979
BA Oxon (1935) MA BM BCh (1943) MRCP (1945) DM (1951)
FRCP (1963)

Charles Edwin Davies, formerly consultant physician at the Royal Hospital, Sheffield, was born at Milford Haven and went to Haverford West Grammar School. In 1933 he went up to Wadham College, Oxford, on an open scholarship, to read classics and was admitted to an honours BA in 1935; then immediately entered the Oxford School of Jurisprudence and was admitted to a degree in this subject in 1937. Without ado, he began to study medicine, and qualified BM BCh in 1943, after clinical studies at the Radcliffe Infirmary. In the meantime, he had completed his legal training and was called to the bar of Gray's Inn in 1942.

His first house appointment was at the British Postgraduate Medical School, Hammersmith, working with J McMichael (later Sir John) and EP Sharpey-Schafer, an appointment that gave him an enduring and fruitful interest in the clinical physiology of chest disease. After a second house appointment in Salisbury, early in 1944 he became assistant to Professor Barnes in the Royal Infirmary, Sheffield, where he rapidly established a brilliant reputation as a teacher of bedside medicine (the 25 students of the school paid him a rare tribute by asking for his teaching time to be increased). In that same year he joined the medical branch of the RAF and served for some time in Germany as officer-in-charge of the medical division of a general hospital, returning to Sheffield in 1946 as lecturer in medicine, with CH Stuart-Harris (later Sir Charles).

In the five year period before he became senior lecturer in 1951 (when he received the degree of DM) he pursued with great energy his research interest in cardio-respiratory disease; he established the technique of cardiac catheterization in Sheffield, and encouraged the development of blood-gas analysis methods. He made several original and important contributions to the clinical physiology of pulmonary heart disease, especially in the role of the renal circulation as a cause of congestive heart failure. He also made the original observation that administration of oxygen to patients with anoxic cor pulmonale increases the cerebrospinal fluid pressure considerably.

Davies left the University department of medicine in 1956 to become a National Health Service consultant physician in medicine, with special interest in diabetes, at the Royal Hospital, and remained in this post until he retired in 1975. A member of the College since 1945, he was elected to the fellowship in 1963 and was for many years a member of the British Cardiac Society and the Association of Physicians.

Charles Davies was a man of many parts and much talent, as his early career – embracing the classics and law as well as medicine – reveals. Possessor of an outstandingly sharp intelligence, he had a clarity and fastidiousness of thought, speech and literary style, that made him a superb teacher in the learn-for-yourself style, with a slight vein of benign mockery. Though he took some knowing, the effort was supremely worthwhile, for his friendship once given was warm, unshakable and generous. Quick to detect and scourge arrogance or pomposity in his peers, he would laugh off and stoutly defend the worst foibles of his junior staff who, to a man, developed affection, loyalty and respect for him. An intensely sharp, irreverent sense of humour and a dry wit made him a most amusing companion; a true intellectual, he had a phenomenal knowledge of motor car performance and specification, but never changed a sparking plug.

He married Mary Elayne, daughter of John Hugh Gee, in 1942, and they had two daughters, Catherine and Helen.

Charles Davies was not your common man, and there must be many who find the world a duller place without him. TH/JJD

[*Brit. med. J.*, 1980, **280**, 1546; Photo]

DAVIES, David Lewis *b.*16 Apr 1911 *d.*24 Oct 1982
CBE (1982) BA Oxon (1933) BM BCh (1936) DPM (1943)
MA (1944) DM (1948) MRCP (1964) FRCP (1970)
FRCPsych (1971)

David Davies was a psychiatrist of distinction, and a man who inspired loyalty and very special affection. It was the match of professional and personal qualities that made him such an influential figure.

Davies went up to St John's College, Oxford, as a scholar and, after gaining a first in animal physiology, he completed his clinical training in Manchester, qualifying in 1936. During the war he served as a major in the RAMC, and had gained useful psychiatric experience in this setting before arriving at the Maudsley in 1946.

He was, from that moment, until his retirement in 1976, to be crucially involved with the fortunes of the Maudsley and Bethlem Royal Hospitals, and with the post-war development of the Institute of Psychiatry. He was on the consultant staff of the Joint Hospital from 1948 and, from 1950–1966, he was dean of the Institute, responsible for turning Aubrey Lewis's vision of a centre of excellence into a reality. The partnership between the two men was based on mutual respect, and on Davies's absolute identification with Lewis's ideal of eclectic scholarship and insistence on high standards of patient care. Davies exerted his influence through his role in the design of the Maudsley's training courses, and by his very personal example as an astute clinical teacher. Those who were selected to serve as his registrars were likely to receive both the commiseration and envy of their colleagues: he was known to be tough and exacting and likely to be moved to a characteristic silence in the face of an inadequate case presentation, but he was known also to be a clinician who combined unusual knowledge of the literature with remarkable and down-to-earth commonsense. Working for him was especially enjoyable because of his own amused and forgiving enjoyment of human behaviour in all its quirkiness.

Davies's other important professional achievement lay in his work on alcoholism. In 1956, he published with Michael Shepherd and Edgar Myers a two-year follow-up of 50 alcoholics, together with an analysis of prognostic factors, and this article can in retrospect be seen as a model for that type of investigation. But his international reputation in this field was born overnight when, in 1962, he published a short paper reporting on seven 'alcohol addicts' who had allegedly returned to normal drinking. This was, of course, at that time a revolutionary claim, which ran starkly counter to the dictum 'Once an alcoholic always an alcoholic'. The paper was one of the most influential single contributions to the literature on alcoholism of this century. From then on 'Davies' meant 'return to normal drinking'. Although subsequent research suggests that some of his findings were faulty, and the interpretation to be put on those findings more complicated than he supposed (for instance, not all his patients may have been 'addicts' or, in later terminology, 'dependent on alcohol'), the fundamental importance of this report in opening the way for new thinking cannot be doubted. He was also very creative in his setting up and fostering of the Alcohol Education Centre, a voluntary organization which, during its all too short existence, was remarkable for its achievements in interdisciplinary education. In 1979 his contributions to alcohol research were recognized by the award of the Jellinek memorial prize. He was elected president of the Society for the Study of Addiction, and sat on the editorial board of the *British Journal of Addiction*.

Davies's other interests were many – a student of psychotic art who wrote on Louis Wain and Victorian flower painting; a craftsman in woodwork; a keen gardener, and a dedicated supporter of Chelsea Football Club. After retiring from the Maudsley, he became chairman of the Attendance Allowance Board, for which work he was, in 1982, awarded the CBE.

But behind all these achievements was the man. His quiet enthusiasm; his sense of curiosity; his chuckling humour, the warmth only just hidden behind the shyness, made any chance encounter with

Davies a moment of pleasure. His largest memorial is, perhaps, that by his professional energy and personal magnetism he helped to turn alcoholism studies in this country from an area of academic neglect into a very active field of interdisciplinary research. JGE

[*Brit. med. J.*, 1982, **285**, 1434; *Times*, 30 Oct 1982; Photo]

DAVIES, John Owen Fisher *b*.8 Apr 1908 *d*.4 Mar 1978
CBE (1964) QPH (1965) MRCS LRCP (1931) MB BS Lond (1931) DPH (1934) MD (1935) DRCOG (1935) MRCP (1964) FRCP (1970)

Jof Davies, as he was always known, was born at Fochriw, Mid-Glamorgan, and spent his childhood in Wales. His father, Eleazar Davies, was a general medical practitioner and his mother, Annie Rosaline, was the daughter of William Owen Morgan, a local headmaster. Eleazar died when Jof was only eight years old and his mother returned to her profession as a school teacher in order to support him and her other child, Jof's sister. From an early age Jof was determined to follow his father into the medical profession and as a first step his mother coached him successfully for entrance to grammar school in the best Welsh tradition of educational self-reliance. Thereafter, never lacking his mother's encouragement and emotional support, Jof had to win his education competitively. He obtained a place at Epsom College and his education there resulted in his being eligible for Cambridge, which had been his ambition. The expense, however, was beyond the family's resources and he eventually commenced his medical education at the Middlesex Hospital where he was Freer Lucas scholar. He played rugby enthusiastically, graduated MB BS in 1931 and subsequently obtained a London MD.

Between 1931 and 1935 Jof held a series of house officer posts at the Middlesex, St John and St Elizabeth, City of London Maternity, North Eastern Fever and Willesden Maternity Hospitals. He obtained the DRCOG and by 1934 had entered his chosen field of public health by obtaining a post as assistant medical officer to Staffordshire County Council. He moved to a similar post in the Borough of Willesden in 1936, obtained a DPH and was promoted to principal medical officer, Middlesex County Council, in 1939. This county council was particularly renowned for its health services, local authorities having wide scope in those days. Jof stayed in Middlesex throughout the war years, administering emergency services and acquiring the skills he was later to apply to his work in the National Health Service. In 1947 he was appointed deputy senior administrative medical officer to the new North West Metropolitan Regional Hospital Board in readiness for the commencement of the National Health Service in 1948. He held this post for three years and was then appointed senior administrative medical officer to the Oxford region.

Jof was in charge of the Oxford region for seventeen years, apart from a two-year secondment to the Ministry of Health from 1961 to

1963 as a senior principal medical officer. During all that period he never ceased his attempts to measure the performance and outcome of hospital care and to use his considerable powers of persuasion to obtain change and improvement. Some aspects of his work and ideas were published by the Nuffield Provincial Hospitals Trust – *Towards a measure of medical care*, 1962, and *Problems and progress in medical care*, 1964. By far the greatest evidence of his abilities and personal leadership, however, was the achievement of changes in the way hospital services were delivered in the Oxford region. Jof would define and measure a problem, pilot a solution and, if successful, would demonstrate the value of a new method of working to his clinical colleagues, convincing them that a change was worthwhile. This personal approach, undertaken with intellectual skill but also with charm and humour, earned him both respect and friendship. The Oxford region became notable for quality, enterprise and efficiency in its hospital services. Jof was honoured, being made CBE in 1964 and QHP in 1965.

He had not much enjoyed his secondment to the Ministry of Health – he found this period useful but irksome and preferred his own personal style of administration to that of a Government department. He was nevertheless prepared to take another step in his career, and when he was invited to become secretary to the new Central Committee on Postgraduate Education he accepted with enthusiasm, becoming secretary to the Council in 1967. He had contributed to the development of postgraduate education from the time of the first Oxford Conference and was anxious that the administrative machinery should be effective. His loss from the Oxford region was keenly felt but he gained new friendships which he greatly valued. He retired in 1975.

In 1951 Jof had married Alison, daughter of John Lawson who was a merchant banker. It was a second marriage for both of them and they made a family home and farmed at Chiselhampton, near Oxford. They had two daughters and Alison had two children – a son and a daughter – by her previous marriage. Early happiness at Chiselhampton was marred by the tragic death of Alison's son who was killed at the age of 14 when the tractor he loved to drive overturned. This accident caused great sadness but they later spent many happy summer holidays in Spain where they had a villa near Marbella, and Jof acquired the ability to relax in that wonderful climate. He would have wished to be remembered for his home life and family as much as for his professional life of distinction and success. He was a kind and generous man who attributed much of that success to his family and to his colleagues. He helped everyone around him to flourish and prosper. ERR

[*Brit. med. J.*, 1978, **1**, 723; *Lancet*, 1978, **1**, 619; Photo]

DAVIS, Leslie John *b.*6 Aug 1899 *d.*31 Oct 1980
MB ChB Edin (1924) MD (1930) MRCP (1937) FRCPE (1941) FRCP (1945) FRFPS (1946) FRCPG (1962)

Leslie Davis was born in Kent, the son of John Davis and Rosa Helena Pethebridge. His father, a man of independent means, appears to have been somewhat erratic in the management of his business affairs, with the consequence that Leslie's education was haphazard. He attended St George's, Eastbourne, and University College School, London, but left without a formal university entrance qualification. He served at sea in the Naval Auxiliary Service during 1917–1918.

Undecided whether to seek his future career in agriculture, engineering, or medicine, he attended a 'crammer' course and gained admission to study medicine at the University of Edinburgh where he graduated in 1924, being awarded the medal in clinical surgery. After a house appointment in surgery at the Royal Infirmary, Davis spent some months in general practice in Britain and Egypt. On his return to Edinburgh he joined Sir David Wilkie in the newly opened laboratories for surgical research, and the training he received there was to influence his career. He was awarded a research studentship, and an assistantship, in the Wellcome Bureau of Scientific Research. In 1927 he was appointed to the staff of the Wellcome Tropical Research Laboratories in Khartoum, where for the next three years he practised laboratory and clinical medicine under tropical conditions. His MD thesis in 1930 was on the effect of experimental splenectomy in certain protozoal diseases with special reference to feline piroplasmosis.

From 1931 to 1939 Leslie was professor of pathology in the University of Hong Kong, and he was instrumental in establishing a free pathological service for small hospitals in South China. During this time he also served as principal medical officer in the local RNVR, with the rank of lieutenant commander. In 1939, Davis became medical director of the Medical Laboratories of Bulawayo, Southern Rhodesia, but 1940 saw him back in Edinburgh where he volunteered for military service but was not accepted. He subsequently joined the staff of LSP Davidson's university department of medicine in the Royal Infirmary as temporary physician and Crichton research scholar. In 1945 he was appointed Muirhead professor in the University of Glasgow and physician in charge of wards in the Royal Infirmary, Glasgow. He held this appointment until he retired in 1961.

The University took a risk in appointing someone of Davis's unorthodox background and experience to a clinical professorship, and particularly so to one in the Royal Infirmary where, up to that time, more respect had been paid to a man's practical skill in his craft and his acceptability as a consultant than to his contributions to research and scholarship. To the undiscerning the dice might have seemed loaded against him. Somehow, as a laboratory worker, he was expected to maintain the reputation of his University clinical unit for first class clinical practice and teaching, and at the same time he was expected to initiate research based on sound scientific principles, despite the fact that no laboratory facilities were available to him.

The closure of the extra-mural medical schools, specifically St Mungo College, shortly after his arrival in Glasgow, provided Davis with the opportunity to set up a laboratory based department of medicine in accommodation adjacent to the Infirmary. He was therefore able to apply the scientific skills he had learned in the laboratory to clinical practice. He must have derived a great deal of personal satisfaction from this development in his career, which also allowed him to achieve a second reputation as a clinical haematologist.

His department prospered and attracted able young men who became active in research and in due course came to occupy senior academic appointments both at home and abroad. Davis set them a fine example in the meaning of service and the obligations of responsibility. Glasgow medicine, and particularly the Royal Infirmary, is largely indebted to him for introducing the scientific method into academic internal medicine. The climate of opinion he created in his hospital was favourable to innovation, the development of sub-specialization and the introduction of research.

He published some sixty original papers and articles, mainly on pathological and haematological themes.

Leslie Davis was a shy and sensitive man. His aloofness could be off-putting on first acquaintance but beneath the reserve, and despite the occasional embarrassing volatile irascibility, which diminished over the years, those who got to know him well found a kindly and considerate character who never bore grudges and who respected those who had the courage of their convictions.

Davis retired to the Isle of Wight in 1961, but he kept in touch with Glasgow and made an annual pilgrimage to meet old friends and to cast a benevolent eye on his former department and its staff. He had probably never greatly enjoyed the administrative responsibilities of his appointment. He gave the impression that he would have preferred to shun them, but from a sense of duty he played a full part in the activities of the faculty of medicine, the senate, the board of management of the Royal Infirmary, and the Western Region Hospital Board. He was for many years a member of the Inter-university council. For a time he was honorary physician to the Royal Navy in Scotland, an association which gave him a great deal of pleasure.

Outside medicine, Davis's main interests in his active years were sailing and carpentry. He sailed on the Clyde during the season; building and sailing a number of craft which he kept in fastidious trim and which were among the fastest on the west coast. He continued sailing around the Isle of Wight for a number of years after he retired. As the years went by he became more involved with the less strenuous activity of precision engineering, for which he had a special flair, and he developed a professional expertise. His success in this hobby provided him with a third career and virtually fulfilled a youthful ambition to be an engineer.

Leslie Davis married Marjorie Adelaide, daughter of Arthur Cleveland, an accountant, in 1938. There were no children of the marriage.
EMMcG

[*Brit. med. J.*, 1980, **281**, 1503; *Lancet*, 1980, **2**, 1148; Photo]

DAVISON, George *b.* 21 May 1910 *d.* 23 Mar 1983
MB BS Durh (1932) MD (1935) MRCP (1935) DCH (1935) FRCP (1953)

George Davison was the son of George and Ann Isabelle Davison. His forebears were Northumbrian, from both north and south of the Tyne, with long roots in seafaring, railways and mining.

He was educated at Edward VI Grammar School, Morpeth, and at Durham University College of Medicine and its associated hospitals in Newcastle upon Tyne. Graduating, with first class honours, in 1932, he held resident appointments in the Royal Victoria Infirmary, Newcastle, made a short but prophetic sally into London medicine at the Hospital for Sick Children, Great Ormond Street, returned to Newcastle in 1935 as medical registrar to the Infirmary, and in 1938 became paediatric registrar to the newly established children's department of the Newcastle General Hospital.

From then until his retirement as senior consultant in 1974 this was the centre of his professional life. His attitudes and style of practice were influenced by two outstanding men: James Spence who brought him into paediatrics, and William Hume who kept him a physician in the mainstream of medicine.

Davison believed deeply in the importance of the general clinician, and demonstrated this so convincingly that his counsel was widely sought by colleagues and general practitioners alike. He was a doctor's doctor. Reluctant at first to accept administrative responsibilities, he became an effective and trusted member of the Medical Advisory Committee of the Northern Regional Hospital Board.

He had two wider interests: the British Paediatric Association, of which he became a member in 1945 and an honorary member in 1974, and professional examinations. He loved the friendships of the first and in return, through his photographic skill, provided the Association with a remarkable pictorial record of personalities and meeting places over many years. The second developed from his concern for high standards in clinical teaching; if knowledge and skills were to be measured, methods must be relevant and as precise as possible. This brought him especially to the MRCP examining board and to question-setting in medicine and in paediatrics; it involved him also for many years in the Diploma of Child Health, and in adapting it to changing needs.

In his priorities, research gave place to clinical care and teaching; yet his careful studies established the general prevalence of congenital pyloric stenosis, and increased our understanding of urinary tract infection in childhood and adolescence.

He had wide personal interests – environmental conservation, photography, scouting, boys' clubs – preferring private support rather than public involvement. He was a governor and vice-chairman of the board of governors of his local high school.

What were the inner springs of his untiring commitment? These were fed in a happy childhood by his parents, especially his father. A gifted headmaster, he consistently expressed high standards of achievement and enjoyment; George made these his own not only in medicine but in mathematics, electronics and music. Order, precision, humanity were his watchwords, nurtured by rich involvement and delight in his family.

In 1938 he married Maud Hope; she died in 1959 leaving two daughters both of whom became doctors. In 1964 he married Eleanor Pamela Price-Jones, a paediatrician in training; she with their daughter and son survived him.

Slight in build, seemly in dress, welcoming in appearance, upright in behaviour, he was a man in the mould of Chaucer's 'verray parfit gentil knight'. SDMC

[*Brit. med. J.*, 1983, **286**, 1522-1523; Photo]

DENNY-BROWN, Derek Ernest *b.* 1 June 1901 *d.* 20 April 1981
OBE (1942) MB ChB NZ (1924) D Phil Oxon (1928)
MRCP (1931) FRCP (1936) MD (1946)

Derek Denny-Brown was born in Christchurch, New Zealand. He was educated at the New Plymouth High School and Otago University. In 1925 he went to Oxford, where he matriculated through Magdalen College, simultaneously with JC Eccles and JZ Young. All three were later awarded the Rolleston memorial prize (Denny-Brown sharing it with WAH Rushton in 1930), and all three became honorary fellows of Magadalen. As Beit memorial fellow he worked with Sir Charles Sherrington from 1925 – 1928. He then went to the National Hospital, Queen Square, where he was successively resident medical officer and registrar to outpatients. The major influence during that period was Sir Gordon Holmes. He was subsequently registrar to Sir Charles Symonds at Guy's Hospital, and in 1935 was appointed consultant both to Queen Square and St Bartholomew's Hospital. In 1936 he received a Rockefeller travelling fellowship to work with John Fulton at Yale. He returned to London in 1937, but in 1939 he was appointed director of the neurological unit at the Boston City Hospital. His appointment there was interrupted for two periods by the second world war in which he served with the British Army. In 1946 he became James Jackson Putnam professor of neurology at Harvard University; he became professor emeritus in 1967. He was Fogarty International scholar at the National Institutes of Health, Bethesda, Maryland from 1972 to 1973.

Denny-Brown was a man of immense energy with a remarkable capacity for sustained hard work. His Saturdays at the Boston City Hospital gave an examplar of the man. Coffee was first taken in the sparse surroundings of the laboratory. At 10 a.m. the grand round began in the rather small conference room, which was packed with his own staff and visitors from other departments and other hospitals. Distinguished visitors from abroad were often there. After a case had been presented, Denny-Brown would then discuss the problem exhaustively, drawing on his encylocpaedic knowledge. Diagnosis was not his forte, and he spent little time on it. Standing, his tall figure slightly stooped, wearing a short white coat and with his bright, altert eyes partly closed and, as it were, focussed inwards, he would explore the pathology and the normal and pathological physiology which the case exemplified. He spoke clearly, with an inflection that showed his New Zealand origins, and had a characteristic way of hestitating for a moment in mid-sentence before making an important point. His thought was complex and his utterance (like his writing) at times obscure. But his insights were compelling. At noon he took a leisurely lunch at which the conversation was witty and enriched from his fund of anecdotes. The mood then changed abruptly as he went to the laboratory with one or two of his fellows to work with the monkeys. His experimental method was fundamentally clinical: successive focal lesions were made and for many weeks the animals were systematically examined and the observations recorded on cine film and in his own clear handwriting. If the assistant who operated the camera did not respond immediately to his softly spoken instruction 'go' or 'stop', reproof was swift; neither time nor film was to be wasted. During these sessions, which often lasted until after 5 p.m., his concentration was absolute. He discouraged comments and questions and responded irritably to interruptions from man and monkey.

At home, he was warm and hospitable, and visitors from all over the world were charmed by the old-world courtesy with which he and his wife Sylvia greeted them. He was a good conversationalist, having wide intellectual interests and a real sense of fun.

Denny-Brown's influence on neurology was profound. With his physiological background his emphasis was on mechanism. At Oxford he made observations on the physiology of the motor unit and of the postural background to movement which were of lasting importance. He was subsequently responsible for important insights into diseases of mucle, peripheral nerve, the basal ganglia, higher cerebral function and the cerebral circulation. His later years were devoted to the study of motor control and its breakdown in disease, and the mechanisms of compensation for its deficits. His approach to training was disseminated throughout the United States by his pupils, a considerable number of whom came to head departments of neurology. His influence was scarcely less important in Britain. In his appreciative but trenchant letter declining the invitation of his former colleagues in 1960 to become the first professor of neurology at Queen Square, he set out his principles of neurological training and defined the role of the academic department of neurology. Knowledge of the existence of this letter and its contents played an important part in securing the change in attitude which led to the transformation of Queen Square in the 1960s and 70s.

Denny-Brown's contribution to neurology was recognized by honorary degrees from universities in North and South America, the United Kingdom and New Zealand. He was made an honorary fellow of the Royal Society of Medicine in 1958 and of Magdalen in 1976. He gave the Goulstonian lecture to the College in 1937 and the Croonian lectures in 1960. He gave the Sherrington lectures at Liverpool in 1963 and was awarded the Sherrington medal of the Royal Society of Medicine in 1962. He received the Jacoby award of the American Neurological Association in 1968.

Derek Denny-Brown had married Sylvia Summerhayes in 1937. They had four sons. WIM

[*Brit. med. J.*, 1981, **282**, 2146; *Lancet*, 1981, **1**, 116; *Times*, 28 Apr 1981; Photo]

DENT, Charles Enrique *b.* 25 Aug 1911 *d.* 19 Sept 1976
CBE (1976) BSc (1931) PhD (1933) FRIC (1943)
MRCS LRCP (1944) MB BS (1944) MRCP (1945) MD (1949)
FRCP (1954) FRS (1962)†

Charles Dent was born in Burgos, Spain. He was the son of Franklin Dent, who studied chemistry in Leeds before acquiring his PhD in Munich and later working in Spain, where he met his wife. Charles' mother was Carmen Colsa De Mira y Perceval who came from a well established Spanish family. In 1915 the family settled in Bedford where Charles received his early education. Later they moved to Wimbledon where Charles went to Wimbledon College, a Jesuit foundation. In 1927 he left school and was first employed as a bank clerk in Tottenham Court Road, but he did not enjoy this work and decided to study chemistry. He left the bank, obtained a post as laboratory technician and studied at evening classes in the Regent Street Polytechnic. In 1930 he was admitted to Imperial College as a student in chemistry, graduating with first-class honours in 1931 and proceeding immediately to a PhD with a thesis on copper phthalocyanin, a blue pigment resembling haem, which he wrote in 1933. In 1937 he entered University College London as a medical student. His clinical studies were interrupted several times by the war but he completed his course in 1944. In the same year, he became house physician to Sir Thomas Lewis, obtained the MRCP in 1945 and was appointed assistant to the medical unit at University College Hospital Medical School.

His war service was varied and distinguished. He served in France, was besieged at Arras, mentioned in despatches, and evacuated unharmed from Dunkirk. He returned to his medical studies, but was recalled by the War Office and appointed consultant in chemistry. He worked in the scientific department of the British censorship, where his chemical knowledge helped in the detection of secret chemical messages, and was of value in uncovering a spy ring. While involved in this work he was sent to Bermuda, where he met his future wife, Margaret Ruth Coad, the daughter of an Anglican clergyman who was also working in the intelligence field. They married in 1944, the year he qualified in medicine.

After the war he engaged at once in clinical research, initially in the field of amino acid metabolism. He appreciated the enormous possibilities of partition chromatography, then a new technique, for the study of biological fluids and the elucidation of clinical metabolic disorders. He was a pioneer in this field and helped to define a number of 'inborn errors of metabolism'. In 1946 he was awarded a Rockefeller scholarship and studied for a year in Whipple's department in Rochester, NY, USA, where he became impressed by the opportunities, in terms of quantitative measurements, afforded by a metabolic ward. He persuaded his hospital to set up a metabolic ward in 1951. Colleagues now scattered all over the world remember the excitement and stimulus which for the next quarter of a century flowed from his work in this ward at University College Hospital.

During these years he was appointed reader in medicine in 1951, and professor of human metabolism in 1956. By 1953 his research interests had broadened to include the study of clinical disorders of calcium and phosphorus metabolism. He soon developed from a laboratory scientist, who was principally interested in the biochemical manifestations of disease, to a clinician for whom the study of the diseases as such, and the welfare of the patients, were the chief considerations. These patients came to be numbered among his many admirers. He was a gifted teacher who was both liked and respected by his students. He did not take lovingly to committees, though he played an important part in the general activities of his school and hospital.

He received many honours and distinctions, being elected FRCP in 1954 and FRS in 1962, the year in which he gave the Humphry Davy Rolleston lecture. He received the Gairdner Foundation award in 1965 and was made an honorary MD of Louvain in 1966 and of Uppsala in 1974. In the 1976 New Year's Honours List he was appointed CBE.

His remarkable qualities of tenacity and strength of character sustained him superbly during a long illness. Almost to the end he found the energy to play squash, which he enjoyed so much. Other beloved hobbies included wine-making and viniculture, for he grew his own grapes.

Charles Dent and his wife had five daughters, and one son who followed a medical career. LW

[*Brit. med. J.*, 1976, **2**, 88; *Lancet*, 1976, **2**, 813, 918; *Times*, 21 Sept 1976; *Biogr. Mem. roy. Soc.*, 1978, **24**, 15-31; Photo]

DEUCHAR, Dennis Charles *b.* 20 Sept 1924 *d.* 19 May 1977
MB BS Lond (1948) MRCP (1951) MD (1952) FRCP (1968)

Dennis Deuchar, physician in charge of the cardiac department at Guy's Hospital, died at the early age of 52. During his entire life, from the age of 18, he suffered from repeated episodes of illness but these were never allowed to interfere with his professional work, and he never complained. He underwent several courses of radiotherapy as well as many painful operations, but his enormous courage, and a very close family, enabled him to present an unchanged appearance under conditions which would have been impossible for a lesser man. His wife, Daphne, daughter of Raymond Stanley Knowles, and his two sons were a constant source of strength to him.

Dennis was born in London, the son of Charles William Deuchar and his wife Eva Lily, daughter of Thomas Levett Hart. He was educated at Finchley Catholic Grammar School and, after the family moved to Bexhill-on-sea, at Bexhill Grammar School. He entered Guy's Hospital Medical School in 1943, where he took many undergraduate prizes before qualifying in 1948. The MRCP followed in 1951, and the MD in 1952. Apart from a year spent at Johns Hopkins Hospital in Baltimore, USA, as a Howard Hughes foundation research fellow, he served Guy's Hospital during the whole of his working life.

After house appointments at Guy's, he became research student in congenital heart disease, and as early as 1949 became involved in developing the cardiac catheterization laboratory at the hospital, together with HE Holling and GA Zak. Much of the apparatus had to be built personally, and it was at this time that he acquired his lifelong interest in bioengineering. He became a founder member of the Biological Engineering Society in 1961, and also served as a council member for three years. It was at the Johns Hopkins Hospital that he first developed his interest in ballistocardiography. He contributed regularly to the literature on this subject, and became president of the Ballistocardiographic Society in 1967. He was appointed assistant physician to the cardiac department at Guy's in 1958, and succeeded Charles Baker and Ralph Kauntze as physician-in-charge in 1971. Although he was supreme as an expert on the haemodynamic aspects of cardiovascular disease, his wide experience of medicine, together with his judgment and humanity, made him a superb clinician.

Dennis Deuchar was a great supporter, and later editor, of *Guy's Hospital Reports*, to which he made many contributions. He also served the *British Heart Journal* as a member of the editorial committee, and was associate editor at the time of his death. His book *Clinical Phonocardiography* was published in 1964 and has become a standard work.

He set high standards, and his capacity for clear, logical thought, his scrupulous weighing of clinical signs and investigations, and his ability to see straight to the crux of a problem made his opinion often sought by his colleagues. It is characteristic that a few days before his death he was planning the expansion of his department.

His interests outside medicine were wide, and he particularly enjoyed music, cinema and theatre, good food and wine and good company. He had a modest, gentle nature and a soft spot for the eccentrics of this world. His sense of humour made him excellent company, his approach to life enlivened any occasion, and he had the ability to make acquaintances feel like friends. He inspired respect and loyalty among all who came into contact with him, and continued working right to the end, in the full knowledge that recovery was impossible. GW/VL

[*Brit. med. J.*, 1977, **1**, 1421; *Lancet*, 1977, **1**, 1164; Photo]

DICKS, Henry Victor *b.* 27 Apr 1900 *d.* 12 July 1977
MRCS LRCP (1926) MB BChir Cantab (1927) MRCP (1927)
MA MD (1930) FRCP (1947) FRCPsych (1971)

Henry Dicks was my close colleague and friend for over thirty years. In expressing what he meant for me, I know I shall say something of what he was for all of us, for Henry was a remarkably well defined person. He was not the kind of man who tended to be one person in one setting and another man in a different one; he was his whole self wherever he was. And the wholeness stemmed from his most outstanding trait – Henry Dicks was a very happy man to the core of his being.

After the shock of learning of his death, and when the edge of the sorrow and loss blunted, I began, both when I was recalling him and also thinking of Maud and their family, to get a pervasive feeling of this happiness. It was not just the recall of his sense of enjoyment and fun in so much of his living. There was much more. There was the feeling of one whose happiness came from a joyous commitment to life, to what he did whether at work or in leisure, and to those with whom he shared it. This happy involvement, combined with the effective and fruitful way in which he used his talents and his energies throughout his life, gave him a realistic serenity and perspective that was so much valued by so many.

I have heard colleagues, on first or limited acquaintance with Henry, comment on his unfailing charm and courtesy as though these were acquired mannerisms. With further experience, however, they realised that these qualities were deeply-rooted features of the man. Henry Dicks loved life and people to a quite unusual degree; they were of endless interest to him, and almost everything he did was with or for others. It was never truer of anyone that his style was the man.

Henry was born in Pernau, Estonia (then a part of the Russian Empire) being the youngest of six children. His father, Julius Dicks, had left London in the 1870s for this town in which he became a prosperous timber merchant, ship owner and, later, British Vice Consul. His mother, Magda von Plath, came from a cultured Baltic German family, her father having been a university lecturer in Russian philology. Henry's boyhood was a happy one in this very stimulating family environment. With his mother speaking German at home and his father using English, he was bilingual from an early age. His mother was eager that he should have a wider experience than the small town could provide, so after a few years in a German school in Riga, Henry went to the foremost Russian private school in St Petersburg. Here, in addition to a classical education, he became a devotee of the opera and the ballet, and acquired a love for the

Russian people and their culture. In these school years, too, he learned the violin, and his love for music, and for that instrument, was such that he seriously thought of becoming a musician.

When the Russian revolution broke out in 1917, Henry was there to share in the excitement and relief of the February uprising. He heard Lenin and Trotsky speak to the crowd, and later he witnessed the shelling of the Winter Palace which ended the Kerensky Government. Towards the end of the year he was evacuated with other British people to Finland, where they were trapped for some weeks by the civil war before going on to Sweden, then Norway. When he reached Britain at the age of 18 he was promptly enlisted into the army.

Attached at first to the Artists' Rifles, he was transferred to intelligence because of his knowledge of Russian and German. Later he went off to North Russia as an interpreter with General Denikin's unsuccessful campaign against the Bolsheviks, and after its withdrawal he was moved to South Russia in a similar capacity with the Allied Expeditionary Force. When this, too, failed, Henry was among those evacuated to Egypt, where he was lucky not to die from a severe attack of typhus at the El-Kantara camp. He was reunited in Egypt with one of his brothers who had been in central Russia, and together they returned to England to be demobbed. The rest of the family went back to Pernau to re-establish the family business, but at this point Henry, with his mother's encouragement in particular, began to concentrate on a medical career in England. Unfamiliar with the English educational system at first, he went to crammers and then to St John's College, Cambridge, where he very quickly distinguished himself academically and as a tennis player (in which game he played for his college and later for Bart's). He was never to return to live in Estonia, though he several times visited for the summer before the surviving members of his family had to leave the country in 1939.

At Bart's, Henry maintained his academic brilliance and had as his first post that of house physician in the medical professorial unit under Sir Francis Fraser (as he later became).

With his widely cultured background and his interest in the personal and social behaviour of man he quickly responded to the emerging growth of psychological medicine under the influence of Crichton Miller at the relatively newly established Tavistock Clinic. Henry took the great risk at that time of becoming a clinical assistant at the Tavistock, even when a distinguished career as a physician seemed so certain, especially with his appointment as chief assistant to Lord Horder's firm at Bart's. His broad perspective was also the important factor in his decision to train at the Tavistock rather than with the psychoanalysts.

By 1931, his commitment to psychological medicine had become dominant and he was soon fully engaged in it, partly in private practice and partly in the Tavistock Clinic.

The professional uncertainties of those early years were made tolerable by the devoted support and encouragement of his wife. Henry had met Maud before going to Cambridge, when he had attended a party given by an Army friend from the Russian campaign, and they were married in London in 1927, on 19 November, a year after he qualified in medicine. The date is one, too, with a special poignancy; had he lived for a few more months we should all have shared in the joy of their golden wedding.

His talents for his new field of study were quickly manifested, and within a few years he was assistant medical director under JR Rees, with responsibility for the clinical training programme. From further experience he published his *Clinical Studies in Psychopathology* in 1939, which for ten years was a highly popular textbook. It is of interest today to note how articulately alive he was then to the constrictive materialistic philosophy in medicine, especially in neurology. Within his more comprehensive philosophy of the nature of man, he offered as a sheet anchor to those confronting the complexities of psychological conflict the view that: 'every patient with mental illness was more afraid then he could tolerate when he was a baby, and the faults in his psychic structure represent the gallant attempts to allay this intolerable feeling by the inadequate means at his disposal'. The prescience of this generalisation is an excellent indicator of the extent to which all of his work evolved from a wisdom that contrasts notably with the limitations of more doctrinaire attitudes.

When World War II broke out, Henry went with some of his colleagues to the EMS Neurosis Centre at Stanborough, whence in 1941 he joined the Army as a psychiatrist specialist, being command psychiatrist, London District, for a time. The landing of Rudolf Hess in this country, however, soon started him on a new line of work. With his unusual facility in German, he was placed in medical charge of this highly important prisoner, an experience he subsequently described in three of the chapters of *The Case of Rudolf Hess*. During the next four years, with the rank of lieutenant colonel, he was adviser to the Army on German morale, to SHAEF on psychological warfare, and the Control Commission on German personnel.

After the war Henry Dick's professional activities followed three main streams. The central one was, of course, his clinical work. His status was such that in 1946 he was invited to be, and became, the first Nuffield Professor of Psychiatry at Leeds University. Two years later, however, his cultural interests and his involvements in a variety of research studies drew him to return to London and back to the Tavistock Clinic. Here for the next twenty years he played a major part in stimulating fresh viewpoints in clinical work, and in providing a broad vision for the consideration of the implications of clinical work for social measures. It was characteristic of his ever lively mind that he took up therapeutic work with marital problems long before this work achieved its current popularity, and from this experience he wrote in 1967 *Marital Tensions*, one of the most valued books on this subject.

For the many members of the staff who joined the Tavistock after the last war, it was a special pleasure to have Henry Dicks as a senior colleague. He shared to the full all the new ideas that were then emerging, and so was a splendid bridge between the old and the new. As a member of the council of the original Clinic for thirty years, a body which his foresight preserved, he was particularly gratified when through its continued existence it was able to claim a substantial legacy from a grateful patient. His long and intimate knowledge of the Tavistock made him the obvious choice when this Council invited him to write for its jubilee in 1970, *Fifty Years at the Tavistock Clinic*.

In parallel with his clinical work were the two other streams. One was the expression of his lifelong interest in the study of man as a social being. It led after the war to his collaboration with many distinguished anthropologists in Europe and the United States in projects on culture and personality carried out for UNESCO. This interest was also expressed in his work for the Tavistock Institute of Human Relations, on whose council he served most of his last decade. In more recent years he was a senior research officer at the Columbus Centre in Sussex University for research in collective psychopathology, from which post he produced *Licensed Mass Murder*, a study of some of the SS killers.

The third stream of work reflected Henry's active concern for the development of his profession. The urbane, humorous *joie de vivre* he radiated, along with his wisdom, tolerance and far-sighted vision, made him very much sought after as a contributor to the resolution of conflict situations, and he responded by giving a great deal of his time and energy to many professional and scientific bodies. He was chairman of the medical section of the British Psychological Society and a member of its council. He was also a member of the council of the National Association for Mental Health and the World Federation of Mental Health; and he was chairman of the training committee on marital dynamics of the Family Planning Association. For twenty years he served in various capacities in the Royal Medico-Psychological Association before he was elected president, an office he held shortly before that body became the Royal College of Psychiatry. His many contacts with universities and learned bodies in the United States led to his election as a Distinguished Fellow of the American Psychiatric Association.

Another aspect of his professional and humanistic concern was his activity in the now widely publicized issue of Soviet maltreatment of dissidents, and abuse of psychiatric hospitals for this purpose, and this must surely have represented a full circle for Henry, bringing him back to close involvement in Russian affairs. It gave him scope for approaching Soviet officials in their own language, which few Western psychiatrists of his stature could have done, or were willing to do. He was one of the first, and most energetic, supporters of this cause in Britain, and he had the satisfaction of knowing that much had been achieved towards the aims of publicizing the abuses.

It will have become clear that Henry Dicks was a remarkably gifted, productive and rounded person. His outstanding natural abilities had been given a fortunate background for the development of all of them – intellectual, artistic, cultural and athletic. He found an almost inifite range of things in this world enormously enjoyable, and amongst his leisure activities playing his violin probably gave him most pleasure. He had innumerable musical friends and partners in duets, orchestras and – what he enjoyed most of all, like many musicians – a string quartet, in which he played less than a fortnight before his death.

It was characteristic of Henry Dicks that his gifts and personal qualitities were equally prominent in the devoted enjoyment of the life he had with his wife, his four children and his five grandchildren.

JDS

[*Brit. med. J.*, 1977, **2**, 322; *Times*, 18 July 1977; Photo]

DIMSDALE, Helen Easdale (née Brown) *b.* 2 July 1907 *d.* 20 Apr 1977
MRCS LRCP (1933) MB BChir Cantab (1937) MRCP (1939) MA MD (1949) FRCP (1949)

Helen Dimsdale was born at Stretford, the daughter of John Harold Brown, chairman of textile and steel companies, and his wife Ellen Carse, whose father was William Easdale, a linen manufacturer and property owner in Belfast. She was a descendant of the famous dissenting divine, Dr John Brown of Bedford, a first cousin of Sir Geoffrey Keynes and a niece of Sir Walter Langdon Brown. Educated at Culcheth Hall and Hayes Court, she proceeded to Girton College, Cambridge, where she was placed in the first class in the Natural Sciences Tripos in 1929. After this she went to University College Hospital for clinical studies, qualifying with the Conjoint diploma in 1933 and passing her MB BChir in 1939. House appointments at Windsor, University College Hospital and Elizabeth Garrett Anderson Hospital followed. She was medical registrar at the Elizabeth Garrett Anderson from 1938 to 1939, when she obtained the membership.

Helen pursued a training in neurology and neuropathology at Maida Vale, the London, and Chase Farm Hospitals from 1941 to 1946. She served the Elizabeth Garrett Anderson Hospital as a physician from 1946 to 1952. She was appointed physician at Maida Vale in 1947 and at the Royal Free Hospital in 1950; she continued thus until ill-health brought about her premature retirement in 1967. Elected to the fellowship of the college in 1949, she served on council from 1961 to 1963.

Helen Dimsdale was medical tutor at the Royal Free from 1951 to 1954, and a recognised teacher both there and at the Institute of Neurology. She published a number of useful papers, and examined in neurology for the Diploma of Psychological Medicine at Durham and for the FRCS in medical ophthalmology.

She was the first woman to be appointed to the consultant staff at Maida Vale Hospital and indeed to a clinical neurological consultancy in Britain. A careful, conscientious clinician, she had an alert and enquiring mind. Helen Dimsdale also possessed administrative ability, serving as chairman of the planning committee for the new Royal Free Hospital in the 1950's and as treasurer of the Association of British Neurologists from 1961 to 1966. Her later years on the staff were clouded by chronic ill-health, which prevented her from scaling the heights she might have expected to conquer.

Helen was an active sportswoman in her younger days; she played tennis for her college and lacrosse for Southern Schools and was also a keen sailor. In 1930 she married Wilfrid Dimsdale, son of a fellow of King's College, Cambridge, and descendant of Dr Dimsdale, who vaccinated the Empress Catherine of Russia and was rewarded with a barony. They had one son, an economist and fellow of Queen's College, Oxford. RAH

[*Lancet,* 1977, **1**, 1018; *Times,* 23 Apr 1977]

DOBBS, Richard Heyworth *b.* 10 May 1905 *d.* 21 Aug 1980
MRCS LRCP (1930) BChir Cantab (1932) MB (1934)
MRCP (1936) MD (1941) FRCP (1947)

Richard Heyworth Dobbs was educated at Bedales School, Downing College, Cambridge, and the London Hospital where he qualified in 1930. Enterprisingly, he persuaded the dean of the London to allow him to go for a year of his clinical course to Vienna, which was then living largely on its pre-first world war reputation as a great medical centre. Extraordinary indeed were the scenes he recounted of those times.

When a boy of ten years, Richard had a severe nephrotic illness and Sir Frederick Still was called in. Still asked him what he intended to be when he grew up and Richard replied 'I want to be a children's doctor like you, sir'. Their next meeting occurred some 15 years later when Still happened to examine him for the MRCP and was able to recall their earlier conversation. Richard Dobbs' paediatric training included a spell in the USA at the Children's Hospital, St. Louis, and a first assistantship at University College Hospital, before he was appointed to the three hospitals at which he was to work for the next 30 years – the London Hospital, the Queen Elizabeth Hospital for Children, Hackney, and Southend General Hospital. At 'the Queen's' the building of the Hayward block – which opened in 1972 – owed much to his leadership at that time. During the war years he served in the RAMC as lieutenant colonel in charge of a hospital medical division in the Middle East.

For 15 years Richard was editor of *Archives of Disease in Childhood*, during a period in which the journal was actively expanding in size and scope. He was president of the British Paediatric Association in 1970.

In middle age Richard took up sailing and, despite minimal experience, sailed his 45ft *Natasha* in ocean races. On one notable voyage he carried a crew of paediatricians to Copenhagen, to attend the International Congress of Paediatrics. Largely dispensing with the bothersome mechanics of formal navigation methods, he was surprisingly adept at finding his way about the sea, apparently relying on an inborn talent for recognizing a coastline, allied to a characteristically happy-go-lucky attitude to the kind of lurking hazards that are apt to keep other less intrepid yachtsmen in a state of mild chronic anxiety. He had also learned to ski at the age of five years and represented the University during his time at Cambridge, thereafter managing to get to Switzerland each year until he was 65.

When he reached retirement age in 1970, it seemed that he might have difficulty finding adequate outlets for his still abundant energies and capabilities. The first requisite for a happy retirement is good health, and with this he was blessed well into his mid-70s. The second is for the individual to define what he enjoys doing and arrange his life accordingly. Richard decided that looking after sick children was what he enjoyed best, and he spent six months with the Grenfell Mission in Labrador, where he acquired such skills as how to erect an igloo in under ten minutes, before going to Nigeria as professor of paediatrics at Ahmadu Bello University, Zaria. This was to be his and his wife's home for the next five years, and his enthusiasm and sound judgement of priorities proved just what was needed to build up the recently established children's unit there. His natural friendliness made him a popular teacher of students, while his many contacts in Britain and elsewhere enabled him to bring in a regular supply of keen young paediatricians at registrar level to enliven and strengthen the unit.

His wife, Phyllis, also a doctor, was his companion for over 60 years, from the time they were school fellows at Bedales and medical students together at Cambridge and the London. Their home, which they built on the summit of Hampstead Hill, was the scene of great hospitality to friends from all over the world. They had a son and a daughter. Richard's particular quality was his outgoing friendly personality, and this enabled him to get quickly on easy terms with people of all sorts – patients, colleagues, foreigners, the young and the old. DG/GW

[*Brit. med. J.*, 1980, **281**, 752; Photo]

DORMANDY, Katharine Marian (née Baker) *b.* 20 Apr 1926 *d.* 30 May 1978
MB BS Lond (1951) MRCP (1954) MRC Path (1964) MD (1970) FRCP (1977)

Katharine Marian Baker was born in Oxford, daughter of Air Marshall George Brindley Baker. In 1951 she married Thomas Dormandy, clinical pathologist at the Whittington Hospital. They had three children. Katharine studied medicine at the Royal Free Hospital and qualified in 1951.

From 1951 to 1954 she held house officer and registrar posts at the Royal Free Hospital and Central Middlesex Hospital, and from 1954 to 1956 research posts at the Central Middlesex Hospial and at St Mary's Hospital, Paddington. She became senior registrar in haematology at the Hospital for Sick Children, Great Ormond Street in 1959. During this appointment her life long interests in blood coagulation, haemostasis and the treatment of haemophilic patients began. In 1964 Katharine Dormandy was appointed senior lecturer and honorary consultant in haematology at the Royal Free Hospital and in 1970 she became university reader in haematology.

Immediately after Katharine had been appointed to the Royal Free Hospital she set about organizing a haemophilia centre. At first this was housed in a caravan, which was located at the Lawn Road Hospital, donated by the Haemophilia Society. Determined to establish a first class haemophilia centre, Katharine Dormandy set up an appeal fund to finance a purpose designed building. This centre was completed before her death but sadly she was too ill to undertake its direction. It was to become one of the foremost haemophilia reference centres in the United Kingdom. Katharine undertook many research projects, and she was particularly interested in those topics likely to improve the care of haemophilic patients at home and in hospital, to prevent crippling joint deformity; the treatment of patients having anti-factor VIII antibodies; and statistical surveys of the progress of haemophilic children during their school years and after.

Her main characteristics were the energy which she devoted to the welfare of others and her practical approach to all problems. It is difficult in fact to know how she managed to live such an active life. No time seems to have been taken from work during the infancy of her children. Each day started at 6.30 a.m. and she arrived at work by 8 a.m. to have a little time to deal with outstanding problems before everyone else arrived. She seldom got home before 6 p.m. to prepare supper. At work all the problems that she considered had for her interconnecting and often conflicting side issues; for example, when conducting a statistical survey most scientists are content to obtain accurate figures, but for Katharine each statistic turned out to be a real live patient with problems that must be solved.

Her great courage in the last painful years of her life was an inspiration to her friends and patients. It was entirely characteristic that even in her last months she was more interested in the Haemophilia Society, the new haemophilia centre, and her patients and family, than in her own health. In 1977 she was awarded the first gold medal of the Haemophilia Society. This medal, inaugurated in honour of RG Macfarlane, was given to Katharine Dormandy particularly on account of her outstanding work for the social and physical welfare of haemophilic patients. RB

[*Brit. med. J.*, 1978, **1**, 1703; *Lancet*, 1978, **1**, 1320; *Times*, 6 June 1978]

DOROLLE, Pierre-Marie *b.* 14 Nov 1899 *d.* 13 Nov 1980
MD Bordeaux (1924) Hon MD Geneva (1969) FRCP* (1970)†

Pierre-Marie Dorolle was born at Wassy, Haute Marne, France, the son of Maurice Léopold Dorolle, a professor of logic and philosophy, and his wife Marie Luce, daughter of Elphège Lefèvre, a barrister. He first intended to read science at the University of Marseilles, but his studies were interrupted by the first world war, during which he served as a health worker.

At the end of the war he decided to take up a medical career and studied first at the University of Paris, and then at the École du Service de Santé de la Marine at Bordeaux. On qualifying in 1924 with the degree of Doctor of Medicine, and the distinction of Lauréat de la Faculté, he spent a year working in hospitals in Marseilles and then joined the French Marines. He was sent to French Indo-China and served there as specialist in public health and administrator until 1950.

During these 26 years of his colonial service Pierre Dorolle held a number of important posts. He was director of health services of the city of Hanoï, chief medical officer of the Saigon-Cholon area, lecturer at the Faculty of Medicine of Saigon, director of health of Annam, and then director of public health at the French High Commission. In the last mentioned capacity, Dorolle took part, after the second world war, in the negotiations for the transfer of power between France, Viet Nam, Cambodia and Laos. This in turn led to his accompanying, as adviser, the delegations from the three last-mentioned countries to the Third World Health Assembly, which admitted these countries to the membership of the World Health Organization.

Before joining in 1950 the staff of the World Health Organization, Dorolle participated in many international activities: he took part in the deliberations of the Consultative Committee of the Eastern Bureau of the League of Nations' Health Organization; he was rapporteur of the Inter-Governmental Conference on Rural Hygiene, organized by the League in Bandung in 1937; he was appointed chief technical expert and representative of the secretary-general of the League for technical collaboration with China from 1937 to 1940, and he took part in the allied meeting on nutrition in Singapore in 1947 and in the FAO rice meetings in Rangoon, Baguio and Bangkok from 1948 to 1950. As deputy director general of the WHO, Dorolle served with three directors-general and was closely associated with their work: Brock Chisholm, MG Candau and H Mahler. He witnessed the growth of the Organization from 71 members to 138, took part in numerous meetings of regional committees, assisted the presidents of twenty-three World Health assemblies, and an equal number of chairmen of the executive board, represented WHO and the director-general at a great variety of intergovernmental and nongovernmental meetings, and lectured at numerous universities and other institutions.

He retired from the World Health Organization in 1973 but continued to live in Geneva. He was married twice; there is one daughter of each marriage.

Pierre Dorolle was doctor *honoris causa* of the University of Geneva, laureate of the National Academy of Medicine in Paris, fellow of the Royal College of Physicians (England), honorary fellow of the Royal Society of Health of Great Britain, and member of the Société de Pathologie Exotique of Paris, as well as of numerous other learned societies.

In assessing Pierre Dorolle's service to his own country and to the World Health Organization it would be difficult to improve on an obituary written by Sir George Godber, one of Dorolle's former colleagues and friends: 'for 23 years he was an important influence on World Health assemblies and the executive board; always unobtrusive, courteous, and scrupulously fair, never intruding his own opinions, but always alert and attentive at innumerable long meetings. His knack for producing a helpful turn of phrase in a draft took international bodies round many awkward corners. No one ever saw him display impatience, much less irritation, and his ability to speak French and English was invaluable in removing inconsistencies between texts – which always seemed to emerge at inconvenient moments. Dorolle knew the constitution and procedure in minute detail and seemed to be able to find the way through any bureaucratic obstacle, something that was invaluable when the representatives of the Netherlands and the United Kingdom finally managed to get a resolution on family planning through the WHO executive board.

But Pierre was not just a skilful international bureaucrat: he felt deeply the importance of international health work, he could give an address of commanding erudition at any function in the French or English speaking worlds, using a text of his own devising and not merely a speech drafted for him. He was trusted implicitly by delegates and experts of every nation at WHO. No one doubted his impartiality or integrity. His field experience was mainly in less developed countries, but he was no less at home with the technical experts.

The WHO family of nations has every reason to be grateful to this physically slight and unassuming man for his long service at the highest level. A World Health Organization that is universally accepted and admired is a monument to Pierre Dorolle as much as to anyone, and it was his special virtue that he did not know that. Most men are less modest'.

Dorolle's last public function was at the commemoration in Marseilles on 3rd October 1980 of the 75th anniversary of the Institute of Tropical Medicine of the French Armed Services, where Pierre Dorolle – a former student – was one of the honoured guests.

A great specialist of tropical public health, a brilliant international civil servant, a generous host, a faithful friend, a refined and distinguished Frenchman with an admiration for British culture, Pierre Dorolle's memory will be cherished by all who had the privilege of knowing him. LJB-C

[*Brit. med. J.*, 1980, **281**, 1645; 1981, **282**, 79; *Lancet*, 1980, **2**, 8205; Photo]

DOUST, John William Lovett *b.*9 July 1914 *d.* 25 June 1980
BSc Lond (1939) MRCS LRCP (1942) MB BS (1942)
MRCP (1943) FRCPC (1954) FRCP (1969)

John Lovett Doust was born in London, the son of William Henry Lovett Doust, a wool broker, and his wife Florence Jane, the daughter of Henry Walter Coltman, a company secretary. He was educated at Strand School and the University of London and his clinical studies were undertaken at King's College Hospital. After house appointments at King's and Horton Hospital, he joined the RAMC in 1943 and served for four years, first as a specialist in chemical pathology and then as medical specialist in military hospitals in the

UK, France, Belgium and India. In 1947 he was appointed medical registrar at the Maudsley Hospital, and received a Nuffield travelling scholarship in 1948 which enabled him to spend two years in the United States. On his return to England in 1950 he was appointed senior lecturer at the Institute of Psychiatry, and honorary consultant to the Bethlem Royal and Maudsley Hospitals.

On the invitation of Aldwyn Stokes, Lovett Doust emigrated to Canada, and assumed a series of research responsibilities at the Toronto Psychiatric Hospital and the Queen Street Mental Health Centre. In 1966 the Toronto Psychiatric Hospital was closed and he joined the Clarke Institute as head of the clinical physiology unit, and head of the research section of psychophysiology. He also continued as head of research at the Queen Street Mental Health Centre. Failing eyesight forced him to resign as chief of services of the Clarke's Institute but, despite his disability, he continued to direct the work of the psychophysiology research section, producing a number of publications. At the time of his death he was professor of psychiatry at the University of Toronto, due to retire at the end of June, and named as professor emeritus in the department of psychiatry, to take effect on July 1, 1980.

In 1947 he married Katherine Louisa, daughter of Bernard deGrave Mourant, a tea planter. They had one son and four daughters. Lovett Doust was a soft-spoken, dignified and literate man. His interests included oriental medicine, philosophy and comparative religion.

FHL/GW

DOW, James Findlay *b.* – 1911 *d.*24 Sept 1983
BA Cantab (1932) MB BChir (1936) MRCP (1938) FRCP (1948)

James Dow's connection with St George's Hospital spanned almost forty years and there is no doubt that he exerted a major influence over the Hospital and the School, becoming for many people a very special friend.

He was born in Glasgow, educated at Strathallan School and St John's College, Cambridge, receiving his medical training at the Middlesex Hospital, and graduated in 1936. After house appointments at the Middlesex and Brompton, he was appointed resident assistant physician at St George's in 1939; an appointment which was to mark the beginning of a lifelong association. During the war years, in the absence of many physicians who had Service commitments, or EMS obligations at sector hospitals outside London, James Dow found himself virtually running medicine at St George's, with a heavy load of ward, outpatient, and teaching duties. It gave him the opportunity to exercise his outstanding administrative skills and under his direction St George's continued to function smoothly through the 'blitz'. He also had occasion, later in the war, to organize the medical support for the surgical teams sent to Cosham, near Portsmouth, to receive casualties from the D-day beach head invasion. Mercifully, casualties were few and James found time to do some teaching, at which he excelled, and to enjoy a little relaxation in the sun on the nearby beaches. At that time bombs were falling on his battle scarred colleagues at Hyde Park Corner, which led to the famous telegram: 'From the trenches of Hyde Park we salute the heroes of Cosham!' – much to James's amusement.

In 1946 James was appointed honorary assistant physician at St George's and, after two years of National Service in the Army, settled down to pursue his medical career. He was soon in great demand for he had an extraordinary clinical acumen, a deep knowledge of medicine in general and gastroenterology in particular. He was a superb teacher and remained a wise and valued friend to his junior staff in their later careers, being one of the most sought after medical opinions in London. He was compassionate and caring with his patients, who in turn recognized that they were in safe and sympathetic hands.

Having kept St George's afloat during the war years, his talents were now employed in the development of the new St George's Hospital. Together with a few of his colleagues he had the vision to see that the future of the hospital lay elsewhere than Hyde Park Corner: a teaching hospital ought to function as a general hospital serving a large and varied population. In 1950, James Dow moved his firm to the Grove Fever Hospital, Tooting, and rapidly established a first class medical and gastroenterological unit there. Reluctantly, and with some self-sacrifice, he returned to Hyde Park Corner when some medical units had to be sent back there to facilitate the building of the new medical school at Tooting. It was a sad and frustrating time for him for by then the hospital at Hyde Park Corner was in its death throes. However, as chairman of the medical advisory committee James Dow guided the hospital safely through its many difficulties, and his wisdom, foresight and fairness proved inestimable in making this committee an effective administrative tool. He also served St George's as a member of the board of governors and as one of the special trustees.

James Dow loved internal politics; he was a great schemer and his schemes were nearly always winners. He was a brilliant committee man and a great chairman, with an invaluable gift of timing. A brief intervention from him nearly always cleared the air and led to a decision. He was indeed so much a part of St George's that it was particularly sad when his deteriorating health made it impossible for him to attend the 250th anniversary celebrations of the Hospital, held at Westminster Abbey.

St George's was James's first love, but he also served Wimbledon Hospital, was chairman of the medical committee of King Edward VII Hospital for Officers (Sister Agnes), and an examiner in medicine at Cambridge and the College. He was adviser to the London Life Assurance, and a member of the Association of Physicians of Great Britain and Ireland.

In his younger days James was a great sportsman, being captain of the Middlesex Hospital Medical School rugby team and a good all rounder at golf, cricket and squash. In later years he was especially fond of fly fishing. He loved good food and wine, and the company of his friends and family, for he was a devoted family man. His first marriage ended tragically with the early death of his wife Moira, who left him with an infant daughter. His second wife, Jean, a consultant radiologist, survived him, as did their four children, one of whom is a medical graduate. JB/GW/VL

[*Brit. med. J.*, 1983, **287**, 1386; *Lancet,* 1983, **2**, 1096; Photo]

DOWLING, Geoffrey Barrow *b*.9 Aug 1891 *d*.1 June 1976
MB BS Lond (1920) MRCP (1921) MD (1921) FRCP (1933)†

GB Dowling, consulting physician to the department for skin diseases at St Thomas's Hospital and to St John's Hospital for Diseases of the Skin, died peacefully at St Thomas's Hospital at the age of 84. He had long been an internationally revered authority on his specialty and the doyen of British dermatologists. He had been in failing health for several months, happily without lessening of his intellect, humour or courage. In the month before his death he attended, with obvious enjoyment, the annual oration and dinner of the club which bears his name, and also a dinner to mark the 250th anniversary of the founding of Guy's Hospital.

Geoffrey Barrow Dowling was born in Cape Town, where his father was first organist of the cathedral and a leading figure in the musical life of Cape Province. Educated at the Diocesan College in Cape Town, at Exeter Cathedral Choir School, Dulwich College and Guy's Hospital, his medical training was interrupted by two years' service as a cavalry trooper in the first world war. In 1920 he graduated MB BS with honours in medicine and soon became MRCP. At Guy's he held several house officer and registrar appointments in medicine and pathology, and his outstanding ability was soon recognized. His decision to specialize in dermatology owed much to the influence of HW Barber. In 1926 Dowling was appointed physician to St John's Hospital for Diseases of the Skin, a post to which later was added the charge of the Goldie Leigh Hospital for the treatment of skin diseases in children, including fungus scalp infections. In 1927 he was appointed assistant physician to the skin department at Guy's. He was also in charge of the skin department of the West London Hospital, resigning these two latter posts on his appointment to St Thomas's Hospital in 1933. In addition, he was civilian consultant in dermatology to the Royal Air Force.

Dowling was largely responsible for the renaissance of dermatology in the United Kingdom, and many would hold that his influence has been unequalled in the past century. He was a superb clinician with an exceptional talent for distinguishing between the significant and the irrelevant. He realized the importance of exact observation and description, and in this respect perhaps the French school ranked highest in his esteem. To an even greater degree his influence was manifest in the clarity of his thinking, whether in individual diagnosis or in investigative studies, which were at that time predominantly clinical. With his formidable and occasionally devastating critical faculty he drew a sharp distinction between speculative theory and proven fact, while appreciating that some well tested empirical observations would have to await a rational explanation. With his keen and enquiring mind he perceived that in many fields further advances would have to rely on experimental investigation, which at that time was in its infancy and limited to a few brilliant workers such as Haxthausen, for whom he had a lasting respect and affection. His early experience in pathology led him to encourage the study of the histopathology of the skin. This encouragement was within a few years to ensure its pre-eminence in this country. When, in 1952, Dowling was appointed the first director of medical studies at the Institute of Dermatology, he greatly encouraged investigative studies particularly in photobiology and in contact sensitivity, the results of which were to achieve world wide fame.

His original contributions were outstanding. They began with the investigations which he carried out with JHH Macleod on the role of *Pityrosporon ovale* in seborrhoeic dermatitis. Later, in conjunction with Freudenthal, he became interested in the relationship between dermatomyositis and scleroderma. This culminated in his authoritative Watson-Smith lecture to the Royal College of Physicians in 1953. His greatest contribution was the demonstration in 1945 of the efficacy of massive doses of calciferol in the treatment of lupus vulgaris. This was no chance discovery but the outcome of simple and logical deduction from the knowledge that the only previously significant treatment had been concentrated ultraviolet rays, a technique devised by Finsen, very time consuming and available to few. The same therapeutic advance was introduced independently and simultaneously by Charpy in France, but neither knew of the other's work until after the war. Although calciferol was soon superceded by other anti-tuberculous drugs, Dowling's treatment gave the first hope for the majority of sufferers from this age old and often grossly disfiguring disease, which at that time was still not uncommon. His colleagues deeply regretted that he did not receive the public honour which he so justly merited.

His retirement from his hospital appointments in 1956 signalled the beginning of a second period of unrelenting professional activity, during which he became an almost legendary figure. For many years he gave invaluable service as a locum consultant, with very busy clinics at Lewisham General Hospital and at Farnham Hospital in Surrey. For him the enjoyment of the work more than compensated for the difficulties of public transport, often having to leave his house before dawn. Even in his late seventies he retained an undiminished interest in dermatology, continuing to make valuable and often original contributions.

By the mid-1950s over half the dermatological consultants appointed in the United Kingdom during the previous decade had been trained by him. Many of the papers written by his registrars, some attaining international recognition, derived from Dowling's suggestions and help. His reputation also attracted first class postgraduates from overseas, particularly from Australia and South Africa. It was also characteristic of Dowling that he did not restrict his help to his own registrars. He initiated the regular Saturday morning meetings at St John's Hospital for Diseases of the Skin, open to all junior dermatologists, which now enjoy an international reputation.

Much of the immense influence that he was to have on dermatology in this country and overseas began in 1948, when he started an informal journal and travelling club which was later to bear his name. The object of the club has always been to promote knowledge and friendship among younger dermatologists and it now includes members from most European countries, the Middle East, Africa, North and South America. To commemorate the great service rendered by its founder, the club contributed generously to a fund to establish an annual Dowling oration. The British Association of Dermatology also paid him the unique tribute of founding a Dowling Fellowship for young dermatologists to undertake research projects for upwards of a year.

In his earlier years it was not always easy to the newcomer to detect the qualities which made him so pre-eminent and beloved. His kindly and scholarly bearing were obvious to all, but modesty and intense concentration sometimes made him appear preoccupied, an appearance enhanced in the clinic by a magnifying visor which temporarily rendered him incommunicado. His abhorrence of appearing to patronize often led him to overestimate the erudition of his audience, and with a less than perfect enunciation his observations were not always clear to the uninitiated. For these reasons he was perhaps less than successful as a teacher of undergraduates, to whom he nonetheless endeared himself by his great kindness and occasional mannerisms. In middle life Dowling appeared older than his contemporaries and to generations at St Thomas's he was affectionately known as 'Daddy Dowling'. With a great appreciation of music, his interest in the students' welfare found a happy expression when he became president of the St Thomas's Hospital Musical Society, which was actively sponsored for many years by Ralph Vaughan Williams who dedicated a composition to the Society.

The tolerance that he showed to his juniors did not always extend to his contemporaries, and occasionally his judgements were less than fair. He had a very keen sense of humour but on occasion he was known to mistake the friendly badinage of a colleague for an attack on dermatology itself. The occasion when a new nurse mistook him for the barber caused him much amusement as it embarrassed the present writer, then his house physician. The friendly title of 'Headmaster' which he soon acquired after the founding of the Dowling Club initially gave him some misgivings, until he realized it was a token of affection. In committees, which he greatly disliked and avoided if possible, he was not very successful, and he had no taste for intrigue.

Dowling was a man of wide culture with an extensive knowledge and appreciation of literature, music and painting; his interest in the latter being greatly stimulated by the accomplishments of his family. He was very interested in many branches of sport. In his youth he was no mean rugby player and later became a competent golfer. The motorcar held little attraction for him except as a means of transport. His style of driving was unorthodox and perhaps, on occasion, perilous but accidents were few and trivial. In his seventies he became an enthusiastic and proficient cook, a hobby which afforded him much pleasure.

Socially, his gentle and benevolent charm at once endeared him to the newcomer and to his friends of all ages and all nationalities. His gregarious habits and sense of fun astonished the stranger as much as they delighted his friends. The prodigious stamina that was such a feature in his professional life extended also to his social activities.

Many professional honours came to him. He was president of the British Association of Dermatology and was later made an honorary member. He was president of the dermatological section of the Royal Society of Medicine and was later elected honorary fellow of the Society. All the major dermatological societies of the world conferred on him their honorary fellowships. He was president of St John's Dermatological Society and gave the Prosser White oration in 1958. An honorary doctorate of medicine was conferred on him by the University of Utrecht in 1957 and, in 1959, he received an honorary doctorate of medicine from the University of Pretoria. In 1972 he was awarded the Alfred Marchionini gold medal.

He married, in 1923, Mary Elizabeth Kelly, who died in 1965. They had two sons and two daughters.

[*Brit. med. J.,* 1976, **1**, 1474; *Lancet,* 1976, **1**, 1359; *Times,* 3 June 1976; *Brit. J. Derm.,* 1976, **95**, 677; Photo]

DOWNIE, Ewen Thomas Taylor *b.*22 Apr 1902 *d.*1 Aug 1977
MB BS Melb (1925) MD (1929) MRCP (1928) FRCP (1945)
FRACP (1938)

Ewen Downie (he rarely used his middle names) was the son of Thomas Taylor Downie and Katherine Maude Smith. His father was a well known obstetrician in Melbourne. Ewen graduated from the University of Melbourne in 1925 and spent a two-year period as a resident and registrar at the Alfred Hospital, one of the teaching hospitals of the University of Melbourne. He made the conventional medical pilgrimage to London where he was a clinical assistant (probably unpaid) to Francis (later Sir Francis) Fraser at St Bartholomew's Hospital. He spent two years in London and became a member of the Royal College of Physicians, a *sine qua non* for ultimate success as a specialist physician in Australia.

Downie started practice as a consultant physician with a particular interest in diabetes. He worked for two or three years as a research fellow at the Baker Institute for Medical Research and developed a clinic at the Alfred Hospital for the special care of the diabetic. This was one of the earliest diabetic clinics in Melbourne, and diabetes was to remain one of Downie's principal and abiding interests for the rest of his life. In 1932 he was appointed as physician to outpatients at the Alfred Hospital, and in the same year he became sub-dean of the Alfred Hospital Clinical School. He continued his interest in student and educational affairs for the next 25 years. After his return from the war he became dean of the Clinical School, and was for two years (1947 – 1948) Stewart lecturer in medicine at the University of Melbourne, which at that time had no clinical professors; the appointment to the Stewart lectureship was a *de facto* professorial appointment.

Downie continued to promote the interests of the diabetic, and encouraged many younger graduates in this specialty. By the mid-1950's he had created a small team of researchers, for whom he established an environment in which a productive amalgam of clinical and basic research could be undertaken. This medical unit was first called the diabetic and metabolic unit, but in 1968 was named after him, and it still bears his name: the Ewen Downie Diabetic and Metabolic Unit. His contributions to diabetes were recognized by invitations to give a Banting lecture in Toronto in 1955, and a Lilly lecture to the American College of Physicians in 1957.

His interest in diabetes and metabolism resulted in the birth of endocrinology as a distinct sectional specialty of internal medicine in Australia. This led to the formation of the Endocrine Society of Australia in 1958; Downie was the first president of the Society (1958 – 1960) and was made a life member in 1967. He was a member of the American Endocrine Society, and of the American and British Diabetes Associations, and was a consulting editor for the journal *Diabetes*.

Like many of his contemporaries, he served in the Australian Army during the second world war. He held senior posts in the Army as a specialist physician, and was ADGMS in Washington, DC, in 1944, where he made many friends who became part of his international network – people to whom he could and did refer his younger protégés for training and advice. He ended his Army career as a colonel.

In addition to his responsibilities as a physician to the Alfred Hospital, he was elected to the board of management of the Hospital in 1952, and remained on the board until he retired in 1962. He was vice president of the Hospital for the two years prior to his retirement. Thus, he had been associated with the Alfred Hospital from the time he entered as an undergraduate medical student in 1922 until he retired in 1962.

Downie continued to practise almost until his death. The latter years of his practising life were hampered by a serious physical disability (laryngectomy). Notwithstanding his problem of speech, he participated in public meetings and never lost interest in the affairs of the diabetic. His fortitude during these latter years was a source of admiration from friends and critics alike. Downie did have his critics. He could be quite acidic in conversations with colleagues and others who had not gained his respect. He did not tolerate fools. He believed in the establishment and order of events, and was without mercy on those who created disorder. Downie was intensely loyal to those who served him well; he would spare no personal effort to help younger people in their professional careers, or young diabetics who needed great moral support during their developing years to cope with their disability.

In 1932 he married Muriel Mary, daughter of John Cumming, a member of a well known Victorian pastoralist family. They had one son (Ewen Jr), and one daughter. BH

[*Photo*]

DRURY, *Sir* **Alan (Nigel)** *b.*3 Nov 1889 *d.*2 Aug 1980
Kt (1950) CBE (1944) MB BChir Cantab (1916) MA MD (1920) FRS (1937) FRCP* (1951)

Sir Alan was a very punctual and regular man, and it seems clear that he got these habits from his father, who worked for the Great Eastern Railway and eventually became superintendent of the line. Sir Alan wrote of his father: 'Unpunctuality in life meant to him a waste of one's own and other peoples' time. In addition, he believed that it was possible to achieve more if life was lived in a regular manner'.

Alan's interest in learning developed only during his last year at school, but after that he advanced very rapidly. Although he did not get an entrance scholarship to Cambridge, he was awarded a scholarship as a result of exams which he took after his first year, and he went on to get a first in both parts of the Natural Sciences Tripos. He was also awarded a special studentship by his College and a prize for the best all round performance. His physiology class included Adrian and Rudolph Peters, and they were taught by Joseph Barcroft; with them he formed lifelong friendships.

After service with the RAMC in India in the first world war, he was offered a job by Sir Thomas Lewis, whom he had met briefly during his first few months in the RAMC. He worked with Lewis for what he described as 'six breathless years'. Alan gave a vivid and entertaining account of these years in a paper which he published in the University College Hospital magazine in 1955. He described how the whole work of Thomas Lewis's circle was conducted in an unattractive basement, dark, crowded with equipment and uninviting. He wrote: 'into it came patients for electrocardiography, dogs for experiments, trays with coffee and buns for lunch. It was hot and dusty in summer and cold in winter. The scientific peaks were the only scenery and it was our job to try to find the pathways to the top'. There is no doubt that Alan found this period extremely stimulating, and that even if he found Lewis rather a hard taskmaster, he would never hear anything critical said about him without reminding one of all his strong points.

In 1926, Alan applied for the chair of physiology at St Bartholomew's Hospital. However, while waiting for the result of his application he developed pulmonary tuberculosis and, although the hospital offered him the post, he had meanwhile decided that he should seek work outside London, and turned the offer down. From 1927 until 1940 he worked in Cambridge as an external member of the MRC Scientific Staff. HR Dean gave him accommodation in the department of pathology, and was doubtless influential in getting him a fellowship at Trinity Hall. He now entered on a period when he collaborated with some very interesting people, two of whom, Szent-Györgyi and Florey, later received Nobel prizes. With typical modesty he wrote: 'a few visitors came to work with me and I had a useful and interesting life'. In 1937 he was elected a fellow of the Royal Society.

In early 1940 the sort of opportunity which he had been hoping for came his way, when the MRC asked him to join their headquarters staff, and he found himself in charge of the four London Blood Supply Depots. He remained at the MRC head office until 1943, when he was invited to become director of the Lister Institute.

The years 1940 to 1945 were probably the busiest in Alan's life; apart from serving as a member of the Medical Research Council and the Colonial Medical Research Committee, he was chairman of committees on blood transfusion research, traumatic shock, and several related to nutrition. Incidentally, he always attributed some particularly favourable development in his career to the help of someone else, and in this case it was his old friend Sir Landsborough Thomson who got the credit. In 1952 he entered on the last period of his professional career, when he was nearing retirement age at the Lister Institute. He moved to Babraham to take charge of the department of experimental pathology. Most remarkably, he took up a new line of research, and with Betty Tucker he opened a new field of work relating to blood groups and red cell survival in sheep. In his middle sixties, he retained all his enthusiasm for research. He would come to the lambing pens late in the evening when there was an important lamb to be studied, and go on working throughout the night.

Although his own research work was extremely valuable, Alan's greatest contribution surely came from his tremendous impact on the scientific development of blood transfusion. The work which he fostered had an influence throughout the world, wherever blood transfusion was practised. His interest in the subject began just before the outbreak of World War II, when he encouraged RIN Greaves to apply his knowledge of freeze-drying to the preparation of dried serum for transfusion. Alan kept in close touch with this work, and was responsible in 1942 for securing a substantial grant from the Wellcome Trustees, which led to the setting up of a plant in Cambridge capable of drying enough plasma for virtually the whole country. As director of the Medical Research Council Blood Transfusion Research Committee, he brought together everyone who was in a position to influence the development of the subject, and through his guidance the Committee initiated projects on a very wide range of topics. From about 1941 onwards it was true to say that the United Kingdom was leading the field not only in many scientific aspects of blood transfusion but also certainly in the efficiency with which supplies of blood and plasma were provided.

As soon as the war ended, Alan instituted a series of moves which consolidated the gains which had been made during the war. He persuaded the Medical Research Council to set up several units working on different aspects of the subject, and he himself became honorary director of the Blood Products Research Unit, which soon made great strides in plasma fractionation. The Lister Institute, under his directorship, also gave hospitality to Dr Race's Blood Group Research Unit and Dr Mourant's Blood Group Reference Laboratory, and the predominance of the United Kingdom in this field lasted for at least the two subsequent decades.

Although Alan was a man of great achievements he was the most 'unpompous' person you could meet. He had a rather diffident manner, athough he could speak out very firmly and pungently when the occasion rose. He treated everyone alike, and although he knew so many famous and influential people he was the very antithesis of a name-dropper. He had the admirable habit of giving you his whole attention and you never felt that he was looking over your shoulder to see if somebody more important was passing by. One particularly endearing characteristic was his constant action behind the scenes to help his protégés. The fact that he was trusted by many eminent scientists of his day made him a powerful patron and a recommendation from him would always be taken seriously. Although, to many people, he appeared reserved, he behaved with great warmth to those who had come to know him, and he was the most constant of friends.

Alan married Daphne Marguerite Brownsword in 1916, and there was a son and a daughter of the marriage. His wife died in 1975.

PLM/GW

[*Brit. med. J.*, *1980*, **281**, 568; *Lancet*, 1980, **2**, 378; *Times*, 5 Aug 1980; *Biogr. Mem. roy. Soc.*, 1981, **27**, 173-198; Photo]

DUNLOP, *Sir* **Derrick (Melville)** *b.*3 Apr 1902 *d.*19 June 1980
Kt (1960) BA Oxon MB ChB Edin (1926) MD (1927) FRCPE (1932) FRCP (1960) FRSE (1960) QHP (1961)

Son of GHM Dunlop MD FRCPE, Derrick Dunlop, who was to become a doyen of British medicine, was educated at Edinburgh Academy, Brasenose College, Oxford, and Edinburgh University where he qualified in 1926. After working as a house surgeon at the Royal Infirmary of Edinburgh, Dunlop went into practice (with morning suit and top hat) in London, but soon returned to Edinburgh to study tuberculosis under Sir Robert Philip. He became an assistant physician in 1934 and in 1936 Christison professor of therapeutics and clinical medicine at Edinburgh University and a senior physician in the Royal Infirmary. For twenty-five years he served these institutions with deep commitment, rare distinction and unique panache.

A gentle, thoughtful doctor – rightly beloved by his patients, to each of whom he gave with his great charm immeasurable confidence – Dunlop's interests were primarily in clinical endocrinology, metabolism and nutrition. But he was a notable diagnostician in all areas of medicine and, of course, a quite superlative teacher.

He held generations of medical students in thrall. His was a household name for all who graduated and practised in Edinburgh.

Sunday morning after Sunday morning – regardless of travelling through the snow from his lovely sixteenth century castle – he would hold court in his wards, when 50 or more general practitioners would come, some from long distances, to hear this great clinical teacher. His enthusiasm in demonstrating his exceptional clinical skills would be hard to match and certainly has not been seen in Edinburgh since. The care he took in the preparation of his lectures, often great discourses, was only overshadowed by the brilliance of his exposition. His lectures on therapeutics were perhaps his greatest achievement as an undergraduate teacher. He loved our language, rolling out the most eloquent of phrases and adjectival clauses. A *prima donna* – vain and elegant – who rose magnificently to each occasion; he was very self-critical and distressed if his message was not always perfect.

With 'Stanley' (Sir Stanley Davidson) and Rae Gilchrist, he upheld and extended the great traditions of the Edinburgh Medical School and attracted many devoted colleagues to his staff. In addition to many papers, he wrote with CP Stewart *Clinical Chemistry in Practical Medicine* and his better known *Textbook of Medical Treatment* with Sir Stanley Davidson and Sir John McNee.

Sims Commonwealth professor in 1957, this cultured man received many honours – knighted, physician to the Queen (1961–1965) and extra physician after this, he was awarded honorary degrees in Birmingham, National University of Ireland and Bradford. He was both a Lumleian and Croonian lecturer of this College. He was an honorary fellow of the American College of Physicians and an honorary fellow of the Royal College of Physicians of Edinburgh.

Dunlop retired from his chair when he was 60. He was then invited to become the first chairman of the Medicines Commission, which became known for many years as the Dunlop Committee. His sagacity, tact and diplomacy were fully employed in persuading the pharmaceutical industry and the medical profession to collaborate. Mainly due to him, this experiment in voluntary controls was a remarkable success. Industry agreed not to market new drugs without asking the advice of the committee, and the medical profession for its part agreed to the collection and analysis of adverse reactions to drugs. Time has shown that his vision was right, with the need for establishment of the authority of the Committee on Safety of Medicines, even although he would have preferred continuation of voluntary agreement to legislation.

Edinburgh medicine has not been the same since this outstanding man, so loyal to his juniors and students, left the scene. In his retirement, he was awarded by the Royal Society of Medicine its triennial gold medal, and Winthrop Laboratories instituted a travelling scholarship in his name – both gave him much pleasure. But what gave countless others great pleasure was his wit and marvellous oratory: his Harveian oration at the Royal College of Edinburgh in 1957 led to a standing ovation, an unique event for the dour Scots! Similarly, his colourful address on Edinburgh medicine to the Association of Physicians in 1977 will be treasured by many. An

Anglicized Scot, he knew them well, laughing a little and caring a lot.

He married Marjorie Richardson, daughter of a lawyer, and she was a superb foil for his extravagances of mood and a wonderful supporter at all times. They had a son and daughter. MFO

[*Brit. med. J.*, 1980, **281**, 66, 316; *Lancet,* 1980, **1**, 1425, **2**, 324; *Times,* 20 June 1980; *RCP Edin. Chron.*, Oct 1980, **10**, pp.6-8; Photo]

DUKE-ELDER, *Sir* **(William) Stewart** *b.*22 Apr 1898
*d.*27 Mar 1978
GCVO (1958) KCVO (1946) Kt (1933) GC St J (1960) K St J(1948)
MA BSc St And (1919) MB ChB (1923) FRCS (1924) MD (1925)
PhD Lond (1925) DSc St And (1927) FRS (1960) FRCP* (1962)†

Stewart Duke-Elder was born in Dundee, the second of three sons of the Revd. Neil Stewart Elder, minister of the United Free Church of Scotland, and Isabelle, née Duke, who was the daughter of the Revd. John Duke, also a minister of the United Free Church, who lived at Camsie, Stirlingshire. The Elder family lived at the manse in Tealing, a village nestling in the Sidaw Hills.

His early education was taken at the Morgan Academy, Dundee, where he was usually top of his class and gained the Dux Medal in 1914 – 1915 and also gold medals for English, Greek, Biology and Religious Knowledge. He entered the St Andrews Bursary competition in which he came top of the list, with the result that he was given the first foundation scholarship, with a bursary of £50 a year for four years. In 1919 he graduated MA with first class honours in natural sciences, and passed the examination for the BSc with distinction in physiology. He was a demonstrator in physiology in the 1918 – 1919 session at St Andrews and a demonstrator of anatomy in 1920 – 1921 at University College, Dundee, where he finished his medical course. He was a member of the council of the Students Union and was its president in 1921 – 1922. He played rugby football and also took part in motor-cycle racing.

Duke-Elder qualified in medicine at St Andrews in 1923. After graduating, he went to London to do house appointments at St George's Hospital, but *en route* he took a locum post for a Dr Arthur, a general practitioner in Wellingborough, Northants. At St George's he gained the post of resident casualty officer for three months, and then became house physician for six months. He worked as a clinical assistant in the eye department in 1924, and in the same year passed the final examination for the fellowship of the Royal College of Surgeons of England.

At this stage he became interested in research concerning the physiology of the eye, and on the advice of Sir John Parsons FRS, a senior ophthalmic surgeon at University College Hospital, London, and Moorfields, he started research work at University College under the direction of Professor Starling FRS in the department of physiology and of Dr Drummond in the department of biochemistry. With the help and advice of Parsons, Duke-Elder obtained in 1925 a part time MRC grant to work in the physiology department, where Parsons had the use of a laboratory and the benefit of the help of three professors of physiology, Ernest Starling FRS, who was the Foulerton research professor, AV Hill, FRS, who was second Foulerton research professor, and C Lovat-Evans FRS, who held the chair of physiology.

Duke-Elder also had help and advice from three successive secretaries of the Medical Research Council, Sir Walter Fletcher, Sir Edward Mellanby and Sir Harold Himsworth.

His thesis entitled *Reaction of the Eye to Change in the Osmotic Pressure of the Blood* won him in 1925 the MD of St Andrews and the gold medal. In 1927, his thesis entitled *The Nature of the Intraocular Fluids and the Pressure Equilibrium in the Eye* gained him the DSc (St Andrews). He collected a number of prizes and research fellowships during this period including the Henry George Plimmer research fellowship, the Sir Francis Laking research scholarship and the BMA Scholarship. In 1926, at the early age of 28, he was appointed assistant ophthalmic surgeon to St George's Hospital, and five years later was promoted to the full status of ophthalmic surgeon, later becoming consultant ophthalmic surgeon when he retired from hospital work in 1963.

At Moorfields Eye Hospital he became clinical assistant to Sir John Parsons, and he was also appointed medical officer in the ultra-violet ray department. He became surgeon at Moorfields in 1928 but subsequently retired from the hospital staff in 1936 on account of ill-health, and because of the many other commitments in which he was involved. However, many years later he was appointed consulting surgeon to Moorfields.

The year 1928 was a happy one for Stewart Duke-Elder because a certain young doctor came on the scene who was studying ophthalmology at Moorfields. She was Phyllis Mary Edgar. It was a short romance and they got married within a few months. In 1930, Phyllis accompanied Stewart on his first visit to the USA, where he had been invited to give the Howe Lecture at Harvard University. In the States they made many friends, with whom they were to keep in touch throughout their lives. Phyllis Duke-Elder was a great help to her husband in his work, especially when he was writing papers and books. She was frequently to be seen sitting in the library of the Royal Society of Medicine, looking up references and making abstracts for him. Unfortunately she developed pulmonary tuberculosis, which involved her in having to submit herself to operations on the chest and to be away in Switzerland for long periods of convalescence, but they took it all in their stride, and eventually Phyllis was again able to join Stewart in all his activities.

The rapidity with which Stewart Duke-Elder achieved fame was quite remarkable. Less than three years after he had gained his FRCS he was an author in the *Recent Advances* series, producing the first edition of *Recent Advances in Ophthalmology*. This was followed by an excellent work entitled *The Practice of Refraction*. His private practice grew apace, especially in 1932 when, after joint consultations with senior colleagues, he operated upon the then Prime Minister,

Ramsay Macdonald, for glaucoma. But despite his long lists of operations and his many patients he found time to work hard at the first volume of his *Textbook of Ophthalmology*, which dealt with the development, form and function of the visual apparatus. In the preface Duke-Elder worte 'It seems to me anomalous that no reference textbook of ophthalmology should exist in our literature, and it is in order to make such a work available that I have written this book'. He stated that hitherto ophthalmologists had confined their interests to the structural ruins which disease had left behind, but now the tendency would be to probe more deeply and examine the more subtle nature of the initial defect, and to pass from the study of structures composed of cells to the study of cells composed of atoms and molecules, and to look beyond anatomy and pathology to biophysics and biochemistry. 'This first volume' he wrote, 'is entirely devoted to the fundamental sciences upon which alone a thorough understanding of clinical ophthalmology can rest'. The book was one of the most valuable contributions that Duke-Elder made to ophthalmology.

After the death of King George V in 1936, to whom Sir Richard Cruise had been surgeon oculist, Duke-Elder was given the Royal appointment to King Edward VIII, and subsequently was appointed surgeon oculist to King George VI and then to the present queen Elizabeth II, until he retired from the post in 1965, having occupied it for 29 consecutive years.

In the second world war Duke-Elder joined the RAMC in 1940, starting with the rank of lieutenant and then rapidly becoming promoted to colonel, and subsequently to brigadier in the Army Medical Service, when he was appointed to the post of consultant ophthalmic surgeon to the Army. His wife volunteered for service with the Red Cross and was in charge of the Zachary Merton Convalescent Home at Kingswood, Surrey, which had been taken over by the Red Cross and was essentially used by Duke-Elder as a place where he could refer problem cases from the Army for whom special investigation and treatment might be needed. Whilst Duke-Elder was engaged in army duties visiting hospitals in various theatres of war, his private practice was looked after partly by his wife and partly by his colleague Allen Goldsmith, whose general health prevented him from joining the Armed forces. Goldsmith continued to work in private practice with Duke-Elder until illness overtook him, resulting in his death in 1977.

After the second world war, Duke-Elder was the leader of a number of ophthalmologists including Sir John Herbert Parsons and Miss Ida Mann, who were anxious to improve the standard of British ophthalmology, especially in the context of education and research. With this end in view they planned to amalgamate the three main ophthalmic hospitals in London, Moorfields, the Royal Westminster and the Central London. The Central London Hospital became the Institute of Ophthalmology, where research laboratories, a library and a lecture room were set up. Also included in the Institute was a large department of pathology under the direction of a full time pathologist, Norman Ashton (later Professor Norman Ashton, FRCP, FRS). The other two hospitals confined their attentions to inpatients' and outpatients' care and clinical teaching. With Duke-Elder as director of research, the Institute soon became well known for the excellence of its work, and many young doctors and scientists came to work there from universities overseas. It was largely his work at the Institute that won for Duke-Elder a distinction now rarely conferred upon members of the medical profession who are primarily engaged in clinical work, namely the Fellowship of the Royal Society. When he retired from the post of director of research at the Institute in 1965, he was appointed its life president, and emeritus director of research. Apart from his research work at the Institute, Duke-Elder was instrumental in collecting money from numerous charitable organizations for the 'Fight for Sight' campaign, helped by Ashton and the secretary of the Institute, Clifford Seath.

There is little doubt that the establishment of the Institute, a year before the National Health Service, was a great stimulus to the development of scientific ophthalmology in the United Kingdom, and so was the inauguration in 1945 of the Faculty of Ophthalmologists, with its headquarters at the Royal College of Surgeons of England in Lincolns Inn Fields. The Faculty persuaded the College to initiate a special examination for an FRCS in ophthalmology. (Such an examination already existed, but no-one was allowed to take it until he or she had first passed the FRCS in general surgery, and only one man, FA Williamson Noble had ever taken the exam - and he passed with distinction.) Duke-Elder was the first president of the Faculty and occupied the post for four years. He was also one of the first examiners for the new ophthalmic fellowship.

One of the appointments that Duke-Elder much enjoyed was that of 'Hospitaller of the Order of St John', where he succeeded Lord Webb-Johnson. His duties in that capacity involved being in charge of the St John Ophthalmic Hospital in Jerusalem, which at that time was situated in makeshift conditions in the Old City; Duke-Elder was determined to set up a much better and thoroughly up to date building. He also conceived the idea of inaugurating research work at the hospital in order to discover more about the organism causing trachoma, and to find a method of prevention and cure. He aroused the interest of many influential people, including the rulers of several of the Gulf States, with the result that six years later – in 1960 – a splendid well equipped St John Ophthalmic Hospital had been built on the Nablus Road in Jerusalem. But already, five years before the new hospital started its clinical work, the trachoma research project had been going on in conjunction with the Medical Research Council and the Institute of Ophthalmology in a set of laboratories which had been built in the grounds of the hospital. For various reasons the work had to be transferred to the Gambia in West Africa, and subsequently to Iran, where it was for many years under the direction of Barrie Jones of the Institute of Ophthalmology (London), and fulfilled its purpose most satisfactorily.

But of all the useful things Duke-Elder did in his busy life there is no doubt that his contribution to ophthalmic literature was the most important. His *Textbook of Ophthalmology* in seven volumes (1932–1954) was a stupendous piece of work by a man who wrote every word himself before it was submitted for typing. This won for him the Fothergillian prize awarded by the Medical Society of London, for the best contribution to the whole of British medical literature for the current decade. But having finished this book and realizing that some of it needed to be brought up to date and to be rewritten, he decided to write a much larger work entitled *A System of Ophthalmology* in 15 volumes, of which the first volume appeared in 1958 and the last in 1976. For most of these volumes he enlisted the help of certain of his colleagues, but there is no doubt that the inspiration and direction of the work were entirely his. The speed and high quality of his output of medical books and articles were phenomenal. This was partly because early in his life he had learnt to depend upon fewer hours of sleep than most people need – indeed it was not unusual for him to write steadily throughout the night and then begin an arduous day's work without any sleep at all. But that is only part of the explanation of his amazing output of learned papers and books. Duke-Elder had a tremendous power of mental concentration. He had the ability to read a mass of scientific papers and reports, extract the essential facts and then put them into an orderly form which was easy to read and understand. Altogether he published some 147 scientific articles and papers and gave no less than 12 eponymous lectures. He was also editor-in-chief of the *British Journal of Ophthalmology* and of *Ophthalmic Literature.*

Duke-Elder was constantly in demand to travel overseas to give lectures, especially in the USA where he had many medical friends. He was awarded no less than 17 medals in recognition of his work. With such a high reputation his private practice became enormous. His opinion was regarded as the best that could be obtained in the entire world, and patients were referred to him from every continent.

After the 1939–1945 war he was civilian consultant to the RAF, ophthalmic adviser to the Ministries of Health, Supply and Labour, and to the London Transport Board, and he was honorary member of virtually all the ophthalmological societies of the world and of many other scientific bodies. The XVI International Ophthalmological Congress held in London in 1950, of which he was chairman, was a successful and happy occasion. He was subsequently elected president of the International Council of Ophthalmology and held that post for 12 years (1950–1962), at the termination of which he was made honorary life president. In 1958, at the request of the International Council of Ophthalmology, Duke-Elder wrote a history of the activities of the International Council during its first 100 years: *A Century of International Ophthalmology 1857–1957.* Of all his honorary degrees the one that gave him the greatest pleasure was the LLD of his old college, St Andrews. He was president of the Ophthalmological Society of the UK in 1965 and 1966. During those years, the Duke-Elders were well known for the hospitality in their home in London to vast numbers of ophthalmologists and their wives, from the British Isles and from most countries overseas.

Stewart Duke-Elder was a warm-hearted Scot with an informal manner, his sense of humour and his charming smile would at once put strangers at their ease. He was invariably cheerful and never pompous. He was a good listener and always took a great interest in the personal problems of his colleagues, especially those of the younger generation. He was, however, reserved and reticent about himself. Throughout his professional life he was fortunate in having love, support and help from a marvellous wife. She took an important part in all his activities and was an ideal hostess. TKL

[*Biog. Mem. roy. Soc.*, 1980, **26**, 85-105; *Brit. med. J.*, 1978, **1**, 993; *Lancet,* 1978, **1**, 834; *Times,* 3 Apr 1978; Institute of Ophthalmology *Annual Report*, 1977-78; Photo]

EDINGTON, George Millar *b.*18 Apr 1916 *d.*26 Jan 1981
CBE (1970) MBE (1958) MB ChB Glasg (1939) DTM&H (1949)
DCP (1951) MD (1953) MRCP (1960) FRCPath (1963)
FRCP (1969) Hon DSc Ibadan (1972)

George Millar Edington was born in Glasgow, where his father, George Edington, was a merchant, and his mother, Catherine Murray, was the daughter of John McDougall, a schoolteacher who held a headmastership.

George's schooling, both primary and secondary, was at Glasgow High School, where he captained the school at tennis and played for two years in the first fifteen at rugby. He had no problems in obtaining entry to the Faculty of Medicine at Glasgow University in 1934. During his undergraduate years he played rugby not for the University but for Glasgow High School Former Pupils, which was at that time one of the leading Scottish clubs. He graduated in 1939, and subsequently spent two years as a resident house officer at Stobhill Hospital in Glasgow, before joining the RAMC. He served first with a Field Ambulance (No 147) in the UK, and as RMO with the First Battalion of the Highland Light Infantry, but the subsequent years (1943 to 1946) were spent in Burma with field dressing stations and the 5th Field Ambulance. He was demobilied in 1946, and it was then that he joined the Colonial Medical Service and entered on his formal training in tropical medicine and pathology, gaining his DTM&H in 1949.

In 1948 George married Mary Jane Hamilton, whom he had met when she was working on the cabin staff of aeroplanes in which George travelled so frequently between London and West Africa. They remained a devoted, though childless, couple for the remainder of his life.

George was posted to the staff of the Medical Research Institute in the Gold Coast and in 1950 he was appointed specialist pathologist in charge of the Institute. It was during the six years when he held that appointment that he and his colleagues described for the first time the pathological nature of sickle-cell disease. There can be no doubt that it was the publication of these papers from the Gold Coast that triggered off world wide research on this subject, with outstandingly important results.

In 1956, when the Gold Coast became independent (Ghana), George Edington was released from the Colonial Medical Service, and in 1958, in belated recognition of his service in the Gold Coast, he was awarded the MBE.

On returning to England in 1957, George obtained an appointment as consultant pathologist at the Whiston and Rainhill Hospitals in the Liverpool Region. He did not enjoy his stay in this appointment, for he missed the opportunities for research, teaching and organization that had dominated his work in Africa, and confessed to being bored with purely routine diagnostic histopathology. He had developed a real love and understanding of the native populations of West Africa, and back in England he missed the sense of pioneering that his work in Africa had afforded.

In these circumstances it was not surprising that when, in 1958, the chair of pathology in the young University of Ibadan, in Nigeria, became vacant he jumped at the opportunity, and took up the appointment with enthusiasm. At that time the Ibadan Medical School was just gaining its independence from London University, and the ambitious University College Hospital was nearing completion. Edington saw it as his task to set up a modern team of doctors and scientists to bring the best of service and research in laboratory medicine to West Africa, but with the main intention of training the local population to be able to take on these duties themselves. High quality undergraduate teaching was amongst his objectives from the start. In the early days he attracted active young workers from the UK and other western countries to estabish teams covering all the appropriate aspects of laboratory medicine, but long before he left Ibadan he and his colleagues had been able to train up African graduates to take over an increasing proportion of the work.

The civil war which broke out in Nigeria in 1968 led to serious disturbances at Ibadan University, as a result of which Edington was appointed as acting vice-chancellor. This appointment demonstrated the complete confidence that the University had in his integrity and ability, and Edington was able to restore order and keep the University going efficiently during a most difficult three-year period. It was in recognition of this outstanding work that he was promoted to CBE in 1970.

By 1971 peace was restored in Nigeria, and the reorganized Republic was opening up new universities in many of the more outlying states. A new vice-chancellor was appointed at Ibadan, and Edington accepted the challenge of moving to the chair of pathology in the recently established medical school at Ahmadu Bello University in the northern state of Zaria. In a remarkably short time medical graduates – now trained specifically with local practice in mind – were being produced. Soon Edington felt that he could hand over the department to Nigerians, and so he accepted, at the age of 62, the further challenge of moving even further north to take up the post of provost and professor of pathology at the embryonic College of Medical Sciences which was being established there in 1979. The dual responsibilities of teaching in his own subject and of organizing the establishment of clinical departments must have been formidable. Much of Edington's time was spent in staff recruitment, and it was while travelling in the USA in 1980 on a combined scientific and recruitment exercise, that symptoms of his final illness developed. Regrettably these symptoms were neglected till the tour was completed and brought him to London, where he naturally reported to the Hospital for Tropical Diseases. An advanced colonic carcinoma was disclosed at operation, and after a stormy post-operative period George was able to join his wife at the *pied-à-terre* which they maintained at Bexhill, on the Sussex coast. They were able to enjoy some weeks of autumn sunshine together, but George was far from well, and in October he was admitted to University College Hospital and found to have peritoneal spread of the tumour. Only palliative treatment was possible and George soon understood that he had not long to live. Nevertheless, he always mustered a smile to greet his visitors, and was full of praise for the doctors and nurses looking after him. Four days before the end, he was keen to know if one of his papers was in the current number of a journal.

One of George's most remarkable achievements was the way he maintained his personal research and educational work, in spite of the enormous load of administrative and organizational work in which he was involved during the last 12 years of his life. His published papers exceeded a hundred in number, and he contributed to the proceedings at countless meetings and conferences in all parts of the world. His priority in describing the pathology of sickle-cell anaemia has already been mentioned. Other subjects to which he made notable contributions included cancer epidemiology in Africa, Burkitt's tumour and other lymphomas, tumours of liver, bowel, uterus and breast, endomyocardial fibrosis, and parasitic disease and infections, including Lassa fever. His textbook (published with HM Gilles in 1969) on *Pathology in the Tropics* has become a standard work.

All who visited the Edingtons in Africa will recall the happy atmosphere of their home, and particularly the total absence of 'colour consciousness'. TF

[*Brit. med. J.*, 1981, **282**, 577, 828, 1081; *Lancet,* 1981, **1**, 452, 567, 623; Photo]

EDMUNDS, Albert William Blair *b.*1 Oct 1916 *d.*28 Feb 1982
MB ChB Edin (1939) MRCPE (1947) MRCP (1950) FRCPE (1962) FRCP (1972)

Blair Edmunds was born in Swatow, South China. His father, Alfred William Edmunds, was initially a civil engineer and later a teacher at the Missionary College, Swatow. His mother, Dorothy Paton, also of a missionary family, was a teacher.

Blair Edmunds was educated by his mother up to the age of nine years and then at George Watson's Boys' College, Edinburgh, and the

Medical School, University of Edinburgh. After a short period in general practice he saw service in the RAMC in Africa, Ceylon and Burma.

At the start of the National Health Service in 1948, Blair Edmunds was appointed medical registrar and later senior registrar at the Memorial Hospital, Darlington. In 1952 he was appointed consultant physician to the Darlington and Northallerton Group of Hospitals, the post he held until his retirement in October, 1981.

Blair Edmunds gave devoted service to his hospitals and to the local community; he was renowned for his hard and conscientious work and for his kindness to patients and colleagues. He took a very active part in administration, in the development of postgraduate facilities and in new techniques of medical management. One of his greatest achievements was the development of a coronary care unit in Darlington, in 1968, long before most other hospitals in the Northern Region.

Blair Edmunds always retained a touch of the missionary, and a love of Africa. In 1975 he took leave of absence from National Health Service duties and worked for two years in Gabarone, Botswana, for the Government Medical Service.

In 1947 he married Grace Vivian, daughter of Henry William Turnbull Bermeaud of Aberdeen, and they had two sons and a daughter. JH

[*Brit. med. J.*, 1982, **284**, 1638; Photo]

EVANS, Ernest Hywel *b.*5 Nov 1907 *d.*23 May 1982
BSc Wales (1926) MB BCh (1929) MB BS Lond (1931) MD (1933) MRCP (1935) FRCP (1967)

Ernest Hywel Evans was born in Cardiff, the son of David Evans, professor of music at University College Cardiff, and his wife Mary, an accomplished violinist and singer, daughter of Richard Thomas, a steel worker. He was educated at New College School, Oxford, Cardiff High School and University College Cardiff, pursuing his clinical studies at University College Hospital, London. He qualified MB BCh (Wales) in 1929 and held house posts at Cardiff Royal Infirmary from 1929 to 1930, becoming a demonstrator in pathology and bacteriology at the Welsh National School of Medicine in 1931, and assistant to the professor of medicine from 1932 to 1934.

In 1937 he entered general practice at Hastings, becoming physician to the Buchanan Hospital, St Leonards-on-Sea, and to the East Sussex Hospital, Hastings. During the second world war he served in the RAMC as medical specialist, and later as officer commanding a medical division. He saw service in Malta, Palestine, and North Africa, subsequently serving under Brigadier Max (later Lord) Rosenheim in Sicily and Italy. He was proud of being able to look after Max when he was ill, and they always remained firm friends. He later joined the RAMC Territorial Army, gaining the TD, and retired with the rank of colonel.

In 1947 he was appointed physician in acute medicine to Glamorgan County Council. With the implementation of the National Health Service in 1948 he became consultant physician to the Rhondda HMC and to the advisory committee of the Welsh Hospital Board. From 1948 to 1973 he was a member of the medical panel of the Medical Appeals Tribunal, Wales. He was a fellow of the Royal Society of Medicine, president of the Rhondda Medical Society from 1955 – 56, and president of the Society of Physicians of Wales, 1958. He played a large part in the development of medical services in the Rhondda, and was elected an honorary fellow of the Rhondda Medical Society shortly before his death.

In 1939 he married Mary Margaret Mackenzie (Mac), who was also a doctor and daughter of Edgar Llewellyn, a general practitioner in Cardiff. They had two children, a son and a daughter, Sarah, who became medically qualified.

He was a man of much energy and enthusiasm, devoted to his work; always ready to add extra sessions to his already heavy work load. He had a keen intellect and a marked sense of humour, being forthright when necessary but devoid of malice, though he would not tolerate any petty bickering between his consultant colleagues. He was an accomplished pianist and music was a source of great pleasure to him all his life. In his beautiful home at Cyncoed, Cardiff, his musical evenings had the character of 'master classes'. His family life was especially happy, his wife and children being devoted to him and sharing his love of music. They enjoyed entertaining, his wife being an excellent cook and he being an expert on wines, of which he had a good store. He read widely and enjoyed foreign travel. His hobbies included hockey, playing for Cardiff University College and the County, and sailing. He also qualified as a pilot after the war.

DAW/GW

[*Brit. med. J.*, 1982, **285**, 67-68; Photo]

EWAN, William John Strachan *b.*5 Sept 1913 *d.*10 Feb 1981
MB ChB Aberd (1936) MRCP (1940) FRCP (1970)

Bill, as he was affectionately known, was born in Tottenham, London, where his father, William John Strachan Ewan, was in general practice. He was the only son and youngest in a family of four children who became orphans within seven years of his birth. The children were fortunate in that their aunt, Mary Ewan, who lived in Aberdeen, willingly undertook the responsibility of their upbringing. Her courage and considerable personal sacrifice were rewarded by gaining the love and affection of all four children. Bill was educated at Fettes College and the University of Aberdeen, where he graduated in medicine in 1936, pursuing his clinical work at Aberdeen Royal Infirmary. Following house appointments at Aberdeen Royal Infirmary, he took up senior resident posts at Hackney and Hammersmith Hospitals, London, becoming a member of the College in 1940.

Bill joined the RAMC in 1940 as a medical specialist and served in the Middle East and Italian campaigns, the latter part in command of a medical division. In 1943 he was appointed medical officer to the Cairo Conference. While in Egypt he met and fell in love with a charming girl, equally dedicated to the medical profession, and they were married in Rome in 1944. Joan Mary, daughter of Frank Thatcher, a clerk in Holy Orders, was a nursing sister in Queen Alexandra's Imperial Military and Naval Nursing Service. They had one daughter, Rosie.

In May 1946 Bill was appointed physician to the Rush Green Hospital and physician superintendent to the Harold Wood EMS Hospital. The latter was a dormitory sector unit, and Bill Ewan had the responsibility of developing it into a district general hospital, to serve the needs of a rapidly increasing local population and a new town development at Harold Hill. Ewan undertook a daunting task with almost obsessional dedication and resolve, so that it became his life's main work. A wiser appointment could not have been made, for Bill was not only an outstanding physician but also a superb administrator. He sought to provide a service of excellence for the patients and, by example and precept, a spirit of harmony and dedication throughout the entire hospital staff. By sheer unselfish hard work Ewan succeeded where many less determined would have given up in despair and frustration. A perfectionist, he demanded of his staff the same high standards and, if need arose, he reprimanded them in private but loyally supported them against outside criticism, and was always concerned with their welfare.

Bill's wise counsel was constantly sought by his colleagues, but he never considered undertaking private practice, and remained firmly committed to the National Health Service. He would have been the first to admit that without the staunch support of his wife, Joan, much of this endeavour would not have been possible. In his later years he was affectionately referred to by his juniors as 'Uncle Bill', and it is strong testament to his popularity and esteem that no less than 80 of his former junior staff attended a dinner in honour of his retirement in 1979.

Bill Ewan was shy and reserved in character and frugal in habit, but he was a very good companion. He was also discreetly generous to those in need of help. He had little time available for recreation and family life, and consequently it was all the more precious to him. He allowed himself only one holiday a year, when he disappeared with his family into the Highlands of Scotland for four weeks. In early years he had represented his university at rugby and golf. He had a natural ability for the latter game and at his best played off an enviable handicap of plus two. Time did not change his beautiful rhythmical swing, but his work load only allowed him the occasional game. JET

[*Brit. med. J.*, 1981, **282**, 1389]

FAIRLEY, Keith Douglas *b*.25 July 1898 *d*.19 Dec 1977
MB BS Melb (1920) MD (1922) MRCP Lond (1924) FRCP (1935) FRACP (1938)

Keith Fairley was born in Victoria, Australia, the son of James Fairley, a bank manager.

He was educated at Melbourne Church of England Grammar School, where he obtained his colours for tennis and athletics. At school he was quiet but cheerful but above all he showed a dogged determination to achieve his goal: to be a successful scholar. This pattern of life continued over the years. He excelled at his studies and in 1915 was awarded the Henry Berthon and Warden's scholarship to enter Trinity College, University of Melbourne.

At the University he studied medicine and met with early success, obtaining the exhibition in physics and first class honours in biology, chemistry and anatomy. His success as a scholar continued during his medical course, which ended at the Melbourne Hospital in 1920 with the exhibition in medicine and the Jamieson prize in clinical medicine.

Keith was appointed house physician and then registrar at the Melbourne Hospital, where he set the pattern of his future medical life: a life dedicated to the care of his patients and to medical research. He was confronted immediately with a medical emergency, to treat severely ill patients suffering from the panepidemic of influenza, which was raging in Melbourne. His patients were housed in a huge Worth's Circus tent, as the hospitals were overcrowded. He recalled that some deaths occurred in the younger patients who refused to rest – 'toxic myocarditis'.

Returning to the Melbourne Hospital, he worked in the wards and in the neighbouring laboratories of the Walter and Eliza Hall Research Institute under the Director, Charles Kellaway.

In the Institute he joined his brother Neil Hamilton Fairley, Charles Kellaway, Harold Dew and Fanny Williams in a study of hydatid disease which was infecting workers on the sheep stations in Victoria. From 1923 to 1933 this team carried out splendid researches into the diagnosis and management of the disease, and were greatly aided by the hydatid complement fixation test improved by Neil Fairley. In 1923 and 1930 Keith Fairley and Williams reported the value of this test in detecting a recurrence after operation. Based on these researches, Dew (later Sir Harold Dew, Professor of Surgery, Sydney University) wrote in 1928 his fine Australian classic, *Hydatid Disease: Its Pathology, Diagnosis and Treatment*.

The brother, later Sir Neil Hamilton Fairley, left the Institute to become director of a tropical diseases institute in India, and later was appointed consulting physician to the School of Tropical Medicine, London. During World War II he was consulting physician to the Australian Imperial Forces. His doctor son Gordon inherited his father's great ability, but tragedy came – he was killed by a terrorist bomb in London.

Keith and Neil Fairley's two other brothers were doctors. James died in World War I; Ronald died in 1974 after a most rewarding life as a general practitioner in the country town of Corowa, New South Wales.

In 1923 Keith Fairley worked with FM Burnet (later Sir Macfarlane Burnet) on the treatment of typhoid fever with intravenous typhoid vaccine. Fairley reported that, if given in the early stages of the illness, there was a pronounced reaction followed by improvement. However this method was not used by others owing to the reactions.

In the Institute, Burnet studied the antibody response to the typhoid infection and to typhoid vaccines given prophylactically. He was impressed with the potentialities of these studies and in 1971 he wrote, 'In all probability it was this interest in Keith Fairley's work that mapped out the general course of my own research, which started with two papers on the antibody response in typhoid fever'.

In 1924 Keith went to London to work for his MRCP examination. During his successful studies he took time off to play tennis with his medical colleagues, James Officer Brown (later Sir James, a leader in thoracic surgery in Australia) and Eccles MacKay, a surgeon. They were fine players and enjoyed representing the Cumberland Lawn Tennis Club. Fairley and MacKay visited Leonard Plews at Buxton, to play tennis, and fell in love with his two charming daughters – Fairley married Eileen at Buxton, and later MacKay married Vivienne who played a distinguished role in the Australian Red Cross during World War II. Eileen took a keen interest in ballet and fostered it in Melbourne.

Keith and Eileen Fairley had two sons and two daughters. Their doctor son Kenneth FRCP, married Priscilla Kincaid-Smith FRCP, in London: later in Australia they became famous for their researches in kidney diseases. A second son, Ian, had a successful career as a restaurateur in Melbourne and Greece, but to the family's great sorrow he died in Sri Lanka from septicaemia.

Keith Fairley was proud of his membership of the College and felt greatly honoured by being promoted to Fellow in 1935. He played a leading role in the establishment of the Royal Australasian College of Physicians, being elected Fellow in 1958 and vice president in 1959.

During his association with Kellaway, Fairley studied lead poisoning. The incidence of chronic nephritis in Queensland children was high and was attributed to lead ingestion, first noted in 1892 by Gibson and his colleagues. In 1929 Nye described the lead painted Queensland houses, and the hand soiling of the children playing on the painted verandas. In an excellent review in 1958, DA Henderson stated that in 1934 the Queensland Government asked the Hall Institute to report on the problem. Fairley was appointed and, after exhaustive enquiry, supported his Queensland colleagues in recommending prohibition of lead paint on the surfaces exposed to children. This was adopted and the incidence of chronic nephritis fell. Fairley continued his interest in lead poisoning, and was appointed medical adviser to the Mobil Oil Company. For many years he recommended safeguards for those associated with lead-containing fortified petrol.

In later years Fairley studied thyroid disease and the indications for surgical treatment. He was concerned by the occasional postoperative complications and welcomed the coming of carbimazole and I^{131} treatments. He and his colleagues soon established the advantages of I^{131} in the treatment of diffuse toxic goitre, as it avoided some of the dangers of operation. They accepted the problem of determining the optimum dosage. Douglas Hicks, pathologist at the Royal Melbourne Hospital ('Royal' after 1935), recalled, 'In later years, when I reviewed with Keith Fairley the pathology of his thyroid cases, he revealed a deep understanding of the fundamental processes involved and displayed qualities of mind on a plane well beyond his peers'.

He was a fine lecturer at the University of Melbourne and tutor at Trinity College. In 1927 he was appointed physician to the outpatients department of the Melbourne Hospital and in 1943 was promoted to inpatients. He enjoyed his teaching on his ward rounds – his orderly mind and erudition stood him in good stead. His meticulous bedside examinations were a memorable lesson to all who accompanied him, young and old. His method of teaching was time consuming and lacked some of the sparkle and gaiety of his more flamboyant colleagues – but he gained immeasurably from this thoroughness and from his warm and generous personality.

Tennis continued to fill his leisure hours. He was a fine player, obtaining his blue at the University and later representing the State of Victoria, when he contested some of the 'greats' – O'Hara Wood, Wertheim, Clemenger and Fitts. In later years he continued to play with his less skilled medical colleagues, who cherished his company but feared his aggressive service.

Advancing years and some rheumatic discomfort reduced his activity, but he continued to treat his loyal and grateful patients, and to enjoy the affection of his family and friends. He passed away with confidence and courage, having served his profession and his country well.

IW

[*Photo*]

FEINMANN, Elozor Leslie *b.*3 July 1917 *d.*25 July 1983
MB ChB Manch (1941) MRCP (1949) FRCP (1971)

Being born into a Jewish ghetto in Manchester, of a Russian speaking mother and Lithuanian German father, proved to be a good beginning. Rebecca, his dentist mother, was a refugee of the first Russian revolution. Morris, his father, anticipating the future, had ventured to Lerwick; there he used selling herrings to find a hospitable community from whence to start afresh. Leslie grew up in an atmosphere of thrift, hard work and, through the British Refugee Council, service to refugees to which his father literally gave his life; the Morris Feinmann Home is a memorial. His premature death, following that of Rebecca, was a powerful formative influence. Leslie Feinmann won a scholarship to the Manchester Grammar School, thence to Manchester University where he graduated in medicine in 1941. After a brief spell as house surgeon he joined the 8th Army in Egypt and served throughout the North African and Italian campaigns; the subsequent tales to his children lost nothing in the telling.

Feinmann returned to Salford as RMO, then registrar to Ronald Lane from whom he acquired an enduring interest in occupational medicine. His first significant paper, which was on diabetic neuropathy (*BMJ* 1953, **1**, 1408), dates from this time. From Manchester Feinmann moved to Newcastle as SHMO and assistant chest physician at the General Hospital and Newcastle West Chest Clinic. He developed a single breath carbon dioxide test of lung mixing, and set up the Hugh-Jones standardized exercise step test, visiting the MRC pneumoconiosis unit to learn the practical details. An application for a Prophit scholarship of the College was almost successful, but talking too much at the interview tipped the balance against him; he therefore lost an experience of research which he was to miss later on. Instead he went as consultant chest physician to Gateshead, combining treatment of tuberculosis and practical exercise testing with active involvement in the issues of the day. He became chairman, North Region CND, vice chairman, Newcastle North Labour Party, and was not averse to leading a procession of witness or presenting a petition when this seemed appropriate. The emphasis was on measures to better the working man, based on Humanism which had replaced the Judaism he had grown up with.

By now Feinmann's medical opinion was well regarded, so with eight papers to his name he applied for a consultant post in Newcastle. Sadly, the prejudices aroused by his non-medical activities damaged his chances and he had too much integrity to countenance manoeuverings that might have benefited him. This incident may have been in his mind when, many years later, he gave his presidential address to the North of England Thoracic Society on the subject of ethics; then all who heard him were moved by his sincerity and the depth of his insight.

In 1955 tuberculosis was still quite prevalent but in Gateshead in 1968 it was very much diminished; the workload was less and Feinmann became part-time physician at the Regional Thoracic Centre, Shotley Bridge, with charge of the regional lung function laboratory. Subsequently he found himself with time on his hands and empty beds at his disposal but confronted by much chronic geriatric illness. However, the impulse to alleviate the attendant suffering ran up against the conventions of the times; geriatric medicine remained with the geriatricians. Now in his sixtieth year, Feinmann could honourably have settled for a quiet life. Instead he applied for and secured a consultant post in general medicine, by then vacant for a year, at the Sunderland General Hospital. His new and mainly younger colleagues watched sceptically as he reorganized the chest department, built up the district lung function laboratory at Ryhope Hospital and played a full part in teaching medical students. Was he now going to reorganize them? In fact he observed and commented but did not advise, and his puckish sense of humour did the rest. The move was both successful and happy. The traditional chest physician had made the adjustment to modern medicine which eluded so many of his contemporaries.

A high proportion of the patients in Sunderland were shipyard workers and amongst them Feinmann diagnosed many cases of emphysema. Was this due to welding fumes? The Boilermakers Union thought so and there was possibly cause for redress. Feinmann secured the agreement of Messrs Austin and Pickersgill to undertake a survey, and promises of help from the Employment Medical Advisory Service (EMAS), many colleagues and the regional statistician. EMAS backed out, but with help from the present writer the study went ahead, albeit on a shoestring. A screening survey was undertaken, followed by exercise and other tests on a selected sample of 200 men. By bad luck the analysis took time and extended into Feinmann's retirement from the NHS in 1982. To secure continuity he became medical officer (part-time) to the shipyard. Incredibly, and most woundingly, this led to the accusation of self-seeking from the Union, but the misunderstanding was resolved. Subsequent to his death the study continued, but it was the big unfinished business of his life.

Retirement brought time for reflection; the vision of peace on earth and the need for self-sacrifice to achieve it. At this point near catastrophe befell: a cardiac arrest during investigation for abdominal pain. After three days unconscious in coronary care, almost his first words were 'they made the wrong diagnosis'. The damage was not mortal, but priorities now had to be defined. Before long, accompanied by his wife, Sylvia, he was visiting Russia on behalf of the medical campaign against nuclear weapons and planning a further expedition for which he was elected leader. A former colleague at Sunderland fell ill with cancer and he visited him daily to comfort and support him during the terminal illness. He wrote about the meaning of life. He was concerned that his children should live adventurously and not accept too readily the apparently secure futures his and Sylvia's genes and example had secured for them – Mary, now deputy head teacher, Jane, medical journalist, Richard and Charlotte, physician and psychiatrist respectively, Sarah, artist, Mark, clinical psychologist. The first priority was to live life to the full, so both in Newcastle and at his home in Grasmere he daily extended the range of his activities ... one mile on the level, a thousand foot climb, 2000 ft., a swim in Grisedale Tarn, but despite a heatwave the water was icy and precipitated a further arrhythmia ... Now a lovingly built cairn overlooks the spot.

Leslie Feinmann was a remarkable man; enthusiastic but not without self-doubt, totally unselfish and idealistic but with his feet just on the ground, compassionate, not sentimental, a skilful physician and almost everyone's friend. JEC

[*Brit. med. J.*, 1983, **287**, 768; *Lancet*, 1983, **2**, 637]

FFRENCH, Geoffrey Ernest *b.*25 Nov 1917 *d.*25 Jan 1980
BA Cantab (1939) MRCS LRCP (1942) MB BChir (1942)
MD (1948) FRCPC (1954) FACP (1964) FRCP* (1976)

Geoffrey Ffrench led a peripatetic life till 1968, when he established himself at the Central Middlesex Hospital as consultant physician in industrial medicine. He was born in Dublin, the son of Ernest George Ffrench, a physician and member of the College, and was educated at Harrow and Trinity College, Cambridge. He graduated from St Bartholomew's Hospital in 1942, taking his MD in 1948.

In 1942 Ffrench joined the RAF, seeing service in Burma, where he wrote the basis of his MD thesis on *Acute and Chronic Diseases of the External Ear*. He returned to settle down at Tenby until 1948, when he went to the Camp Hill Hospital, Nova Scotia, as junior physician. This was followed by a few years in the Kolar goldfields in South India, and a spell as consultant physician in Oakville, Ontario, Canada, from 1953 to 1959. This wide experience of all sorts and conditions of men made him a sound choice to assist in the opening of a medical school in Ghana in 1960. Unfortunately, for political reasons, the project did not get off the ground.

In 1961 his interest in occupational health was stimulated by his appointment as consultant in medicine to the Kuwait Oil Company. He held this post until 1968, when he returned to England to take up his appointment at the Central Middlesex Hospital. In 1979 he retired from the directorship of the unit but continued as a consultant. In this busy general hospital, surrounded by extensive light industries, he was invariably helpful in resettling the chronic bronchitic, the diabetic and the heart cases. He had wide general medical knowledge and fresh ideas, bringing light into the life of many colleagues. His papers ranged from ankylosing spondylitis to toxoplasmosis. His last volume on occupational disease did not command the medical interest it might have, being directed towards the enlightened business manager. This would have been rectified in a new book which he was preparing at the time of his death.

Geoffrey Ffrench had a large presence, not only mental but physical, which inspired confidence, and his personality was warm and charming. He had great vitality and wide interests. He was a fellow of the Royal Geographical Society, a member of the Medical Geography Study Group of the Institute of British Geographers, and enjoyed travel, writing, and woodwork. He was especially interested in geographical diseases and the part played by trace elements.

In 1942 he married Marjorie Grace, daughter of William Ewart Godfrey, and they had four children: two sons and two daughters. Despite his total commitment to his professional life, he was able to enjoy a happy family life with his wife and children in rural Kent. In the face of the overwhelming nature of his final disease he was an optimist, working and planning for the future, and extracting a wry humour from the fact that the rare sarcoma of the lung, which eventually killed him, stimulated medical interest. He was brave, interesting, and interested, to the end. JGB/GW

[*Brit. med. J.*, 1980, **280**, 728, 875; *Lancet*, 1980, **1**, 496; Photo]

FOREMAN, Harold Mason *b*.1 Dec 1913 *d*.19 Apr 1976
MBE (1946) MB ChB NZ (1937) MRCP (1947) FRCP (1963)

Harold (Bill) Foreman was born in Auckland, the second son of Robert James Foreman, an accountant, and his wife Hettie Elizabeth (née Mason). He was educated at Beaumont Primary School, Takapuna, and was a foundation pupil of Takapuna Grammar School. He entered Otago University in 1932, briefly living at Knox College, and graduated in 1937. He played rugby for Otago in 1936–1937 and for Auckland University in 1938. He was a member of the NZ University side in that year.

In 1938 he joined the staff of the Auckland Hospital. He volunteered for service abroad at the outbreak of the second world war and left New Zealand with the 1st NZ General Hospital in May 1940. The unit, intended for the Middle East, was deflected to the UK where it was established at Pinewood. In December 1940 they were transferred, by way of Cape Town, to Cairo as a 'canvas hospital' at Heliopolis. In March 1941 Foreman went, with his unit, to North Greece where it was set up at Farsala. In the ensuing debacle and retreat he was captured with patients on 26 April 1941, at Megara. The tales of his many adventures, of the POW Hospital at Corinth, and of the one in Athens to which all Crete casualties were flown; of his journey across eastern and central Europe to upper Silesia in 1941, and of his volunteering to care for Russian POWs in appalling conditions at Neuhammer, January–May 1942, are detailed in *Despite Captivity: a Doctor's Life as a Prisoner of War* (Borrie,J, W Kimber & Co., London, 1975). At Neuhammer, he himself contracted typhus fever and was fortunate to survive. After recovery, from 1942 to 1944, he was physician to Cosel POW Hospital, with charge of both British and Russian prisoners. At the end of 1944 he returned to the Central Hospital at Lamsdorf Camp, near Breslau. During February–March 1945 he was in charge of 2500 sick POWs taken on a 10-day journey across a broken Germany to Hammelburg, near Frankfurt-am-Main. In this venture his integrity, high moral code and insistence on the preservation of decency, ensured that those on the march, and others who joined them, were not mercilessly removed by retreating Nazis back to Nuremberg. Much diplomatic skill was required at that time, and Foreman revealed a flair for it. It was his humanity, his dogged persistence and his utter belief in what was 'right', that would not accept 'no' for an answer, which earned him the high regard of those he led. For his military services to POWs he was awarded the MBE.

In London, after the war, he obtained appointments as house physician, resident medical officer and registrar at the Brompton Hospital, serving at the hospital for six years and gaining his MRCP in 1947. He entered fully into the life of the hospital at Brompton, contributing to the team spirit and becoming a thoroughly trained physician with special knowledge and experience of chest disorders.

In 1951 he became physician-superintendent of Sully Hospital, Glamorgan. For most of Foreman's time this hospital had a central position in cardiothoracic medicine and surgery in South Wales. He knew all the staff personally, introducing many amenities for them, and for the patients and their relatives. With the later development in Cardiff of the Welsh Medical School, it was a great sorrow to him to see the facilities at Sully run down. An early member of the Thoracic Society, he served on the Council and was successively assistant secretary, secretary, and president in 1972 at the time of the second Cardiff meeting. At that meeting there were many colleagues from his Brompton days and physicians and surgeons from Poland, Texas, Portugal, Australia, New Zealand, Rhodesia and South Africa.

Harold Foreman was always known as 'Bill'. He bore the exacerbations and exhausting treatment of his last illness with the highest courage, rejoicing in its remissions. It was the greatest pleasure to him, and to many old friends, to be at the Otago Medical School centennial celebrations in February 1975. He married Pamela Mary Villar in 1948 and had a family of four daughters and two sons. A younger brother, Joseph Maxwell Foreman, also an Otago graduate in medicine, died in 1969. KR

[*Brit. med. J.*, 1976, **1**, 1346; *Lancet*, 1976, **1**, 1087; Photo]

FORMAN, Frank *b.*16 Feb 1898 *d.*9 Mar 1980
BA SAfr (1915) MB ChB Aberd (1922) MD (1932) MRCP (1932) FRCP (1942) Hon MCPSA (1970)

Frank Forman was born in Paarl, Cape Province, S Africa and had his schooling at the Paarl Gymnasium. He matriculated in 1916 with a first class pass, and was awarded the Gould Adams medals for top marks in the Union of S Africa in physics and mathematics.

As there was no medical school in S Africa at that time, he took a BA degree (majoring in anatomy and physiology) at the South African College, and then went to Aberdeen where he graduated with distinction from Marischal College, sharing the James Anderson gold medal in clinical medicine. He did his internships in Aberdeen and London and then, in 1923, returned to Cape Town, to the posts of lecturer in bacteriology and clinical tutor in medicine. These combined to make the first full time university clinical post in S Africa.

In 1932 he went to London for postgraduate study at the National Hospital for Nervous Diseases, Queen Square, and in the same year was awarded the MD (Aberdeen) for a thesis on pain. Later in 1932 he returned to Cape Town, to be appointed assistant to the professor of medicine (Falconer). In 1938, when Falconer became principal of the university, Forman was appointed professor of clinical medicine.

In 1954 he resigned his chair to become full time senior lecturer in the department of medicine, until he reached the age of compulsory retirement in 1963. Nevertheless he remained at Groote Schuur Hospital working full time as honorary consultant and lecturer in medicine until 1971, when he emigrated to Israel. There, he was appointed to an honorary consultantship in medicine, with part time teaching duties at the Tel Hashomer Hospital, Tel Aviv, a post which he held up to his death.

Frank Forman was an outstanding example of the general physician. Although neurology was a special interest, he was equally at home in all the branches of internal medicine. He devoted his whole attention to every patient and had an astonishing 'case' memory. Years after seeing a patient he could quote detailed points in the history or examination which illustrated some diagnostic principle. When reminiscing with past members of his staff he would frequently say 'Do you remember Mrs B. 3rd on the left in D1..'.

Frankie, as he was affectionately nicknamed by his students, shone as a bedside teacher. His obvious sympathy and sincerity, his quiet dignity, his transparent honesty and modesty were examples to generations of medical students. These qualities, combined with his outstanding clinical skills, made him a legend in his lifetime.

It is surprising that despite his early promise in mathematics and physics, he showed little interest in either a numerical or technological approach to medicine. He made few research contributions, but went out of his way to support his juniors in research. In the late 1940s his departmental budget was minescule, and there was no laboratory or office, only a bench in a ward sideroom. He fought for and obtained a laboratory for his juniors and somehow provided money for equipment.

In 1934 he married Golda Selzer, a medical graduate of Cape Town University who became a distinguished pathologist. They had two sons, Arthur and Robert. The former became a theoretical chemist and the latter a cardiologist. Frankie was a keen gardener and usually wore a miniature rose in his buttonhole. He and Golda loved walking, especially on Table Mountain, and they knew all the many rare orchids that grew there, and their haunts. In Israel too he enjoyed walking, and despite his frail appearance, when over 70, he could still outpace men 50 years his junior in the desert heat.

Frankie had no thought of personal gain. Although as professor he was entitled to private practice, he never accepted a fee. His early retirement from the chair and later honorary work in S Africa and Israel were characteristic. In his last years he often visited Cape Town, and it was on his way back to Tel Aviv from one such visit that he developed a myocardial infarction and died soon afterwards in Israel, the country that he loved so well. GB

[*Brit. med. J.*, 1980, **280**, 949, 1381; *Lancet*, 1980, **1**, 834; *Cape Argus* SA, 15 May 1954, 6 Dec 1963; *Cape Times* SA, 28 Apr 1954; *Friend* SA, 7 Dec 1963; Photo]

FORREST, Alistair Douglas *b.*17 Oct 1924 *d.*10 May 1979
MB ChB St And (1947) DPM (1949) MRCP (1955) MD (1959)
MRCPE (1967) FRCPE (1970) FRCPsych (1973) FRCP (1977)

Alistair Forrest became nationally known as a psychiatrist in Britain because of his work at the Royal Edinburgh Hospital, to which he was appointed as a consultant in 1960. He became the physician superintendent of Gogarburn Hospital in addition in 1971, developing the 'Scottish pattern', then newly introduced, of having general psychiatrists work in the field of mental subnormality. Forrest succeeded in transforming the hospital and its service with a new spirit of optimism. He went as visiting professor to the University of Saskatchewan in 1976–1977, and then left Edinburgh to become a professor in the department of psychiatry at Saskatchewan. He died tragically early in Saskatoon of a brain tumour.

His professional and academic achievements were considerable. He won the Gaskell gold medal of the Royal Medico-Psychological Association in 1959. (As a medical student he was awarded a gold medal for zoology at St Andrews University.) He was lecturer in the department of psychiatry at the University of Edinburgh from 1958 to 1960. He developed a computer assisted follow-up service for schizophrenic patients in 1971. He was a chief author of a much quoted follow-up study of schizophrenic patients in 1963. He was the first editor of the Edinburgh textbook *Companion to Psychiatric Studies* published in 1973.

A friendly, cheerful, immensely approachable and kind colleague, Alistair Forrest was genuinely interested in his patients and his associates, with a warmth and spontaneity which sometimes seemed to disguise his firmness of purpose, his great energy, his resolute capacity for hard work; his many drug trials were conducted and papers written with no evidence of strain or pressure.

His father had been an actuary in an Edinburgh firm in Bombay, where Alistair was born. The father retired to Edinburgh where he died at the age of 96 years in 1979; Alistair only knew his father as a comfortably off retired gentleman. His mother, the youngest of twelve children, had a father who was a ship's chandler in Leith, owning a fleet of boats trading around the Scottish islands. She married when nearly 40, her husband then having attained the status which his firm considered appropriate to marriage. She died in Edinburgh aged 87 years.

The older of the two children is Bertram (now an anaesthetist in Yorkshire). The boys were sent at the age of four to a boarding school in Edinburgh for children of parents living abroad. As a schoolboy Alistair was chosen to play schools rugby for Scotland, but he broke an ankle before the international when fifteen. He then did his first serious studying, winning a scholarship to St Andrews, where he left his medical studies with first class honours, also playing rugby, gaining a hockey Blue, and as middleweight boxing champion. (He later campaigned to have boxing stopped in public schools.) He also edited the University magazine.

He was married twice, and had three children. His widow lives in Canada. He became a member of the Royal College of Physicians in 1955 and a fellow in 1977. He was also a fellow of the Edinburgh College, and of the Royal College of Psychiatrists. He had a vigorous, productive and useful life, not without stresses but also with much happiness. He could surprise those who knew him with bold, unexpected and novel undertakings, such as the decision only a few years before he died to go to Canada. HJW(2)

[Photo]

FOWLER, Frank James *b.*1 Oct 1911 *d.*2 Apr 1981
CBE (1974) OBE (1945) TD (1938) MB ChB Birm (1935)
MRCP (1970) FRCP (1976)

Frank Fowler was a medical administrator of high calibre, whose influence on the National Health Service during the formative phase, and again after its reorganization, was considerable.

He was born in Smethwick and educated at King Edward's School, Birmingham, and at Birmingham University, where he graduated in 1935. He was elected MRCP under Bye-Law 117 in 1970 and FRCP in 1976. He held house appointments at the Birmingham General Hospital and in other hospitals in the Midlands. His first appointment as a medical administrator came early in his career: as a locum medical superintendent in Hall Lane Hospital, West Bromwich, where he had held a house appointment earlier. No doubt this helped to shape his very distinguished career in the Army Medical Services, along with his experience in his university's officers' training corps, where he rose to the rank of sergeant-major.

At the beginning of the war he became medical officer to a unit of the Royal Engineers, as a territorial, and was evacuated from France in 1940. From then on he progressed rapidly through various staff appointments to the post of ADMS Allied Command in the Mediterranean, reaching the rank of full colonel at the age of 33, and being awarded an OBE in 1945, on top of the Territorial Decoration which he had received in 1938, with clasps in 1951 and 1957.

After demobilization and a period of clinical postgraduate training, again in the Midlands, his gifts as a medical administrator led him almost as a matter of course into the higher administrative strata of the developing National Health Service. He began in the Oxford Region in 1948, became deputy senior administrative medical officer of the North East Metropolitan Hospital Board in 1951 and senior administrative medical officer of the North West Metropolitan Board in 1958.

Unlike some of his colleagues, Frank readily accepted the importance of fully collaborating and integrating with his fellow chief officers, and particularly with his administrative colleagues. This was a major reason for his being so well informed about what was happening in the Regions, although he himself did not venture out a lot into the field. One of his administrator colleagues has described him as 'being able to see around every corner'. This capacity, along with its directness at times and his sense of humour, which was misinterpreted by some as sarcasm, undoubtedly made him some enemies.

In the 1974 reorganization of the National Health Service he was transferred, as regional medical officer, to the Yorkshire Region. This was not of his own volition, but his experience and outstanding capability were highly appreciated in the North, where his successful adaptation seemed to give him a new lease of life. When he retired at the age of 65 he and his wife returned to London. He was re-employed at DHSS for some four years with the nominal rank of senior medical officer, but with far greater knowledge of and influence on the service than his rank would suggest. During this period he suffered a severe heart attack one night, and characteristically would not allow his wife to call a doctor until the morning, and not before he had shaved.

Frank influenced the national scene in many ways. He was for some time chairman of the Group of Senior Administrative Medical Officers and later of the Group of Regional Medical Officers. In 1974 he was awarded the CBE.

When the formation of the Faculty of Community Medicine was mooted in 1968, he was one of the two regional medical officers in the small group which prepared the ground. He played an invaluable part in the formative years up to 1972, and as first treasurer of the Faculty was one of its most influential members in the early years.

Frank's personality presents something of an enigma. He appeared as a very modest and reserved man, yet his years as a medical student present a very different picture. Treasurer of the hospital carnival, secretary of the Student's Union and of the Guild of Undergraduates, and a member of the court of governors two years before he qualified. His assessment of others, an essential prerequisite for his post, was searching and fair, his integrity and discretion were absolute. Jo (née Kennedy), his charming wife, sums him up like this: 'My own memory of him is of a very private and shy man, but, oh, what fun to be with!'.

WGH

[*Brit. med. J.*, 1981, **282**, 1883; Photo]

FOWWEATHER, Frank Scott *b.*- 1893 *d.*25 Feb 1980
MSc Liverp (1915) MB ChB (1922) DPH (1924) MD (1925)
MRCP (1934) FRCP (1943)

Born in Bolton, Lancashire, Frank Fowweather had an elder brother and two sisters. His father owned a cutler's shop in nearby Blackburn. He attended the local elementary and grammar school where he had an excellent academic record; he then went to Liverpool University to study medicine. Emerging with an MSc in chemistry, at the beginning of the first world war, he was appointed chief chemist to a firm making explosives in Huddersfield. During this period he also travelled to Manchester to give evening lectures in mathematics. At the end of the war he returned to Liverpool and became a partner in a small firm of consulting analysts, but then decided to take up medicine and began studies at the Liverpool Medical School. During this time he retained his position as an analyst, working on a part time basis. Following his success in obtaining a medical qualification, he studied further and obtained the Liverpool Diploma in Public Health. Working next as a general practitioner in Ellesmere Port, he numbered among his patients many bargees and their families, and often commented on the difficulties of practising medicine in the cramped conditions of a barge.

In 1924 he was appointed lecturer in the department of pathology at Leeds University. Berkeley (later Lord) Moynihan wrote the foreward to a book called *Handbook of Clinical Chemical Pathology* written in 1929, by the then Dr Fowweather, on the basis of lectures given to medical students in his capacity as head of the chemical pathology section. As a lecturer Frank Fowweather was clear, concise, and precise. Publications of his original work were appearing in scientific journals on such subjects as the determination of fat in faeces (1926), and the determination of urea clearance (1934). This latter work led to some controversy. Fowweather advocated giving the patient 15 g of urea orally and determining the blood urea level during the second hour, when he argued the level was effectively constant. Opponents of the idea of administering urea pointed out that to produce a changing urea level just at a time when a constant value was required negated any analytical advantage. In 1931 Frank Fowweather was promoted reader in chemical pathology. He was made a Fellow of the College in 1943. About this time the department moved from the General Infirmary at Leeds to the new, nearly completed, Institute of Pathology. During the second world war he continued with his university duties, and served as medical officer to the North East Leeds Home Guard. He became professor of chemical pathology in 1946.

The following year saw some expansion of his department with a modest increase in staff, but Frank Fowweather failed to seize the opportunity, made available by increased demand for clinical biochemical work at that time, to expand both the routine and research aspects of the department's work. He largely confined it to the provision of a basic biochemical service to the Infirmary. This stemmed in no small way from his lack of ability as a negotiator, committee man and diplomat. He was outright in his condemnation of things of which he did not approve, and failed to lend support to colleagues' projects when reciprocal support for his own department would, undoubtedly, have followed. A further consequence of this was that he numbered few of his clinical or university colleagues as close friends. He continued, however, to exercise his undoubted skill as an analyst. He also conducted a study of orthostatic albuminuria occurring in young men being medically examined for service in the armed forces (1953). His ability at accurate manipulation was further emphasized at this time when he took up bookbinding as a hobby. He bound the many separate issues of scientific and medical journals in his possession into a series of annual volumes; beautifully bound and gold lettered, the books were a tribute to his skill and care. He retained a connection with Liverpool University by continuing his membership of the University Masonic Lodge where, after serving as Master, he was given Provincial Honours.

Ill health precipitated his retirement in 1956 at the age of 63, when he was created emeritus professor. He left Leeds to live at Wirral, where he had family connections and friends, and most of his time was spent quietly at home with his wife. There were no children of the marriage. His hobbies were golf and fox terriers. ATH

[*Photo*]

FRASER, Thomas Neilson *b.*2 Feb 1910 *d.*2 Dec 1976
MB ChB Glasg (1933) FRFPSG (1936) MRCP (1936) MD (1948) FRCP (1952) FRCPG (1962) MRCPE (1964) FRCPE (1967)

Fraser was born in Glasgow, son of Malcolm Fraser, stockbroker, and Mary Jane Stewart, daughter of Duncan Stewart, a master coppersmith. He was educated at Glasgow Academy and Morrison's Academy, Crieff. His medical school was Glasgow whence he graduated in 1933. He married Mabel, daughter of Trevor Griffiths, a dental surgeon, in 1940, by whom he had a son and daughter. His daughter Alison Elliman became MRCP 1968 and is a consultant physician.

After house officer posts in the Western and Victoria Infirmaries of Glasgow Fraser had a period of ill health, which later precluded his serving in the Forces. He was chosen for the Hall fellowship in medicine in the professorial unit at the Western Infirmary in 1936 and also was appointed an assistant physician to outpatients. Subsequently he was promoted an assistant to the professor in 1945 and in the following year appointed physician in charge of the rheumatism unit at Killearn Hospital near Glasgow. In 1948 he was appointed consultant to the Western Infirmary and honorary lecturer to the University of Glasgow. Seven years later, in 1955, he was appointed to administrative charge of wards, a position held till his retirement in 1975, when he was the senior medical consultant. He was on the board of examiners of the Royal College of Physicians and Surgeons of Glasgow for the Membership, and examiner for the MB ChB of Glasgow University. For a period he was a member of the board of management of the Western Infirmary, to which he gave wise counsel.

Fraser was a general physician of great ability, but from an early stage in his career his interest was in rheumatology, and he was responsible for the first controlled trial of gold in the treatment of rheumatoid arthritis. For this and other important contributions to the subject he was awarded the doctorate of medicine with honours.

While at the University he was an all round sportsman, obtaining colours for rugby and cricket and also enjoying golf and shooting. He was a keen and skilful angler, much of his fishing being in the river Lyon in Perthshire. In 1932 he rescued a woman from drowning in that river, for which he was awarded the certificate of the Royal Humane Society.

Fraser, being possessed of an even temperament and a nice sense of humour, was the best of company. He was a good teacher, well liked by his students and very popular with his colleagues. As an administrator in charge of a medical unit he carried out this not always easy task well. Essentially he was a very kind man; a quality much appreciated by his patients, and indeed by his many friends. JBR

[*Brit. med. J.,* 1977, **1**, 114; *Lancet,* 1976, **2**, 1419; *Glasgow Herald,* 8 Dec 1976; Photo]

GAAFAR, Mohammad Mohammad *b.*23 Oct 1902 *d.*2 Jan 1982
MB ChB Cairo (1925) MRCP (1931) MD (1932) FRCP (1963)

Mohammad Gaafar was born in Zifta, Egypt, the son of Mohammad Ahmed Gaafar, a merchant, and his wife Zeinab Abd El-Rayek, daughter of a farmer. He was educated at Saidia School, Cairo, and the University of Cairo, pursuing his clinical studies at the Kasr El Eini Hospital. Following graduation in 1925 he held various house appointments at the hospital and, from 1927 to 1928, was medical officer to the Egyptian Ministry of Public Health. In 1930 he joined the Egyptian Education Mission to London, spending a year on postgraduate work at St Bartholomew's Hospital and obtaining his membership of the College in 1931. He then returned to Egypt and took his MD (Cairo) the following year. In 1935 he was appointed physician and medical tutor to the Kasr El Aini Hospital, and became assistant professor of general medicine in the faculty of medicine, University of Cairo, in 1939. He was promoted to professor in 1943, becoming head of the medical department in 1957. He wrote numerous papers, published in the *Journal of the Egyptian Medical Association*, and was elected president of the Egyptian Society of Endocrinology in 1960.

Mohammad Gaafar married Samaâ Mohamad Ahmad, daughter of a government official, and they had three sons and two daughters. One of his sons, MA Gaafar, is presently professor of medicine and endocrinology at the University of Cairo. Outside medicine, his interests included tennis, fishing and gardening. He was also a member of the Egyptian Shooting Club. Sadly, his later years were clouded by ill health, and he died after four years of a prolonged illness. GW/VL

[Photo]

GAINSBOROUGH, Hugh *b.*16 June 1893 *d.*31 Dec 1980
MRCS LRCP (1917) MA Cantab (1919) MB BChir (1921)
MRCP (1922) FRCP (1929)

Hugh Gainsborough was in some ways an unlikely person to be on the staff of a West End hospital in the 1930s. Unmistakably semitic, he had no time for the affectations sometimes thought necessary for successful private practice. He had a questioning intelligence which refused to accept uncritically the medical dogma of the day, and as a first class scientist he engaged actively in biochemical research, often in association with John Addyman Gardner, the distinguished St George's biochemist. Not surprisingly his main clinical interests were in disease where laboratory studies had an important role, and particularly in renal disease and diabetes mellitus. He established special diabetic clinics at St George's and at the London Jewish Hospital, and was one of the first physicians to use insulin in treatment. In spite of his commitment to science, his care for his patients, and particularly for the sick members of the nursing staff, had earned him a high reputation as a sympathetic and widely competent doctor during his time as resident assistant physician at St George's. It was this quality more than any other which endorsed his election to the staff as assistant physician in 1927.

As a teacher Hugh Gainsborough made little impact on the average undergraduate. He was an appalling formal lecturer and on ward rounds he seemed either 'too scientific' or later, as his psychosomatic interests developed, 'too vague and indecisive' for those who were looking for the kind of didacticism which would help them to pass their qualifying examinations. His house physicians and registrars gained a truer picture, and learned as much from his insistence on the importance of rather intangible personal and social factors as they did from his critical use of laboratory data.

Always a compassionate doctor, his friendship with Emanuel Miller and his collaboration with Eliot Slater on a survey of psychological factors in gastrointestinal disease encouraged his interest in psychiatry. He cared little for the formal categorization of mental diseases, but immersed himself enthusiastically in psychodynamic concepts with all their implications for diagnosis and treatment. He pursued his beliefs in studies of obesity and chronic bowel disorders.

Hugh Gainsborough's real influence at St George's became apparent during the war, when he was senior physician and one of the senior members of the staff remaining at Hyde Park Corner. Together with Hugh Gordon, then acting dean, he strongly supported the view that St George's should be rebuilt at Tooting instead of at Hyde Park Corner, as had been originally proposed. He had already submitted detailed suggestions for planning that hospital, so that inevitably he became chairman of the medical planning committee which was set up to advise on the ultimately abortive project at Springfield. In conjunction with his architect nephew he put forward a number of new ideas on hospital design, some of which came to fruition when the new hospital was eventually built at Tooting Grove in the 1970s. Essentially he saw the future St George's as a district hospital serving a large neighbourhood community, with a medical school having a far stronger academic base than it had had in the past. Ideally he would have liked the hospital to be staffed by whole-time salaried clinicians dividing their time between patient care, teaching and research, instead of engaging in private practice, but he was realistic enough to know that this was unlikely to be immediately possible. He therefore supported the allocation of a substantial number of beds and suitable clinics for private practice, in the hope that it would enable the majority of the staff to be 'geographically wholetime'.

Hugh Gainsborough's determination to introduce a clinical academic presence into St George's first showed itself when he established a twenty-bedded gastroenterological unit at Atkinson Morley's Hospital, Wimbledon, in 1942, and again in the 1950s when he gave enthusiastic support to the formation of teaching units in medicine and surgery, with part-time directors but with at least one whole-time teacher at lecturer or senior lecturer level in each. In spite of some opposition from other members of the staff who feared, correctly enough, that they would lead in the fairly near future to the establishment of professorships for which Hugh would almost certainly have a candidate in mind, the units came into being. Hugh himself became part-time director in medicine. Too honest to be devious, it was usually obvious that all his projects had some secondary objective dear to his heart. Normally this was to secure a job for one of his protégés. With a ready sympathy and keen, perhaps over keen, eye for the underdog he would give unstinted (and sometimes unjustified) support to those he thought likely to be 'discriminated against' because of their race or their sex. It was a mark of his standing among his colleagues that so many of them accepted this foible with tolerant good humour.

As senior physician, Hugh Gainsborough organized regular meetings, often over dinner, with his fellow physicians. Discussions on these occasions were uninhibited and often ranged far beyond their ostensible purpose, so that the business in hand was sometimes scantily treated or even overlooked, but even those who disagreed with his reputedly 'leftist' politics and were sceptical of some of his ideas, learned much from this sensitive and private person. After his retirement, casual meetings with his former colleagues and visits to the College as senior fellow kept him in touch with medicine and with St George's. A small dinner party to celebrate his 80th birthday enabled most of those he had known and worked with to acknowledge their debt and to demonstrate their affection.

In 1926 Hugh married Maia Pilikowski, who died in 1939. They had no children. MIAH

[*Brit. med. J.,* 1981, **282**, 487; *Lancet,* 1981, **1**, 169; *Times,* 1 Jan 1981; Photo]

GARDINER-HILL, Harold *b.*14 Feb 1891 *d.*25 Mar 1982
MBE (Mil) BA Cantab (1912) MRCS LRCP (1915) MB (1915) MRCP (1920) MA MD (1928) FRCP (1929)

Harold Gardiner-Hill was educated at the Westminster School, Pembroke College, Cambridge, and St Thomas's Hospital, where he graduated in 1915. He served in the RAMC until 1918, and then returned to St Thomas's to join the newly formed medical unit under Hugh McLean as a research assistant. His interest was endocrinology, and this came at a time when it was becoming possible to measure the biochemical abnormalities in the clinical and pathological disorders which had already been described. After a brief appointment as assistant physician to the Royal Free Hospital in 1928, he was elected to the staff of St Thomas's in 1929 and retired in 1956. He was elected MRCP in 1920, FRCP in 1928, and was the Oliver Sharpey lecturer in 1937.

He soon abandoned academic medicine for private practice, in which he was notably successful on account of his good opinion, dedication to the work, and his capacity to please both patients and general practitioners. He joined the staff of many small hospitals round London, which was then a recognized method of getting to know general practitioners, and for the same reason he lectured widely throughout the country.

He was a dapper little man with an affable manner and a sense of obligation towards his juniors. These friendly characteristics tended to obscure his intellectual capacity. They also concealed a somewhat contorted character beneath, and several of his colleagues found to their dismay that some casual remark had touched off a deep resentment in his mind, and were never spoken to again.

He was a notable golfer and half his obituary in *The Times* was devoted to these activities. He played for Cambridge University 1911–1912 and became a member of most of the best clubs in the British Isles. He was captain of the Royal and Ancient in 1956 and chairman of the Rules Committee 1949–1952.

He married Margaret Helen, daughter of Sir Farquhar Buzzard, also a physician to St Thomas's Hospital, by whom he had three sons, all of whom went into commerce. JBH

[*Brit. med. J.*, 1982, **284**, 1202; *Times*, 30 Mar 1982; Photo]

GARDNER, Arthur Duncan *b.*28 Mar 1884 *d.*28 Jan 1978
BM Oxon (1911) FRCS (1912) DM Oxon (1913) FRCP (1949)

Arthur Duncan Gardner was born at Rugeley, Staffs, the youngest of the three children of James William Gardner, a successful solicitor, and Mary, daughter of David Wrigley of Liverpool, a cotton merchant. He was educated at Rugby School, University College, Oxford, and St Thomas's Hospital. His all round abilities were soon confirmed by his achieving second class honours in Law after two years' study instead of the usual three, and by obtaining the FRCS after one year, and the DM two years from qualification. Also he played hockey for Oxford and his county and was a considerable gymnast.

After house appointments, his first post was as junior pathologist at St Thomas's, and it seemed that his career was to be in that discipline. He was awarded the Radcliffe travelling fellowship and the Radcliffe prize for medical research. On the outbreak of war in 1914 he failed to gain entry to the RAMC for the strange reason that it was 'full', so he joined the Red Cross and served as a surgeon with the BEF in France.

On returning to civil life he was invited back to Oxford by the professor of pathology, Georges Dreyer, and became successively lecturer, reader, and professor of bacteriology. For over 20 years he was in charge of the Medical Research Council's Bacteriological Standards Laboratory. Here he did some of his most important scientific work, notably improvement of the antigenic properties of the vaccines for cholera and whooping cough. Later, he carried out the bacteriology that was indispensible for the work of Florey and Chain on penicillin.

In 1927 he was elected a fellow of University College, where he was a much loved Steward of Common Room for many years, and exercised a soothing influence on colleagues with differing political views. He enjoyed teaching and was the author of three successful books – *Microbes and Ultramicrobes* (1931), *Bacteriology for Medical Students and Practitioners*, 4 editions (1933–53), and *Penicillin as a Chemotherapeutic Agent* (jointly, 1940).

In 1948 his career took an entirely new turn when he was appointed regius professor of medicine, and at a very difficult time. He was at once faced by a daunting array of problems, including the aftermath of the war, the advent of the National Health Service, the question of the continuance of the clinical medical school, and the relationship of the university to the hospitals. In addition, there was friction, if not warfare, between personalities and between departments. He faced all these formidable difficulties with equanimity, good humour, resolution and skill. He left the medical school in a much better state than he found it. His success in dealing with people derived from his transparent honesty, a complete lack of self-interest, and scrupulous fairness. A clear and attractive speaker, he gave the Rede lectures at Cambridge on 'The Proper Study of Mankind is Man', the Litchfield lecture at Oxford, and at the age of 93 a memorable lecture at the fiftieth anniversary celebrations of the Sir William Dunn School of Pathology at Oxford. As regius professor he was *ex officio* a student (= fellow in other colleges) of Christ Church, and was paid the compliment of election to an honorary fellowship at his old college, University. He once described his hobbies as reading, writing and arithmetic, but they also included literature and music. Like his mother he had an excellent singing voice.

Age never bent his back or his spirit. He once remarked that if he were young again he would certainly volunteer to go to the moon. A delightful sense of humour, unobtrusive kindnesses and generous hospitality were other endearing traits. He married Violet, daughter of John Fowler Newsam of London, a shipping broker. There were three children of the marriage, two of whom predeceased him. His surviving son became a consulting surgeon at Torquay. AMC

[*Brit. med. J.*, 1977, **1**, 447; *Lancet*, 1977, **1**, 456; *Times*, 30 Jan 1978; Photo]

GARMANY, Gerald *b.*24 Apr 1914 *d.*17 July 1979
BSc Manch (1935) MB ChB (1938) DPM Eng (1942)
MRCP (1945) FRCP (1956) FRCPsych (1971)

Gerald Garmany was the son of David Garmany, an engineer, and had his early education in his native town of Stockport at the grammar school. He qualified in medicine at the University of Manchester in 1938, having previously obtained a BSc degree in physiology and anatomy. After hospital resident posts and basic training in general medicine, he volunteered to serve in the Royal Navy soon after the outbreak of World War II. He had close contact with Desmond Curran, then consultant psychiatrist to the Royal Navy, and this influenced his decision to specialize in psychiatry. He qualified DPM in 1942, and became a graded consultant psychiatrist in the Naval

Medical Service. His achievements during the war are well illustrated by a paper on reactive war-time anxiety states, published in the *Lancet* in 1944. His large experience of war-time anxiety resulted in 88% success in management, with return to full combatant duties.

He was helped and supported during these difficult years by a happy marriage in 1939 to Margaret Joyce Garmany (nèe Stafford), who was a fellow medical student at Manchester, and who also specialized in psychiatry. Joyce was the daughter of a school master, and her personal support together with that of their two sons, one now in general medical practice, was a major factor in Gerald's life. After demobilization early in 1946, Gerald had a period as assistant lecturer in psychiatry at the University of Bristol and later as regional psychiatrist to the South West Metropolitan Regional Hospital Board.

Garmany was appointed as consultant psychiatrist to Westminster Hospital and Westminster Children's Hospital in 1948, and immediately had a profound influence on the teaching and practice of psychiatry at the medical school. He was one of the pioneer psychiatrists, who assisted in removal of patients from long term incarceration in vast mental asylums, and concentrated on remedial therapy in general hospital wards. During this period, he wrote an excellent manual on the use of muscle relaxation as an aid to psychotherapy, and contributed useful scientific articles to medical journals. He was a pioneer in the use of chlorpromazine in psychiatry, and reported that all cases of psychoneurosis in which mental tension was a prominent feature were amost uniformly improved. Garmany considered that abreactive techniques had an important place in acute reactive anxiety states during war, but had a much more limited use in peacetime, being chiefly of value for acute dissociative states. He stressed the importance of anxiety states in practice, and reported that this was the diagnosis in 28% of consecutive referrals to his hospital outpatient department. Constitutional predisposition to anxiety was found to be of greater importance than operative stress factors. He considered that a rigid division of depression into the endogenous, reactive and involutional types could not be entertained in general psychiatric practice.

Garmany was a clear, common sense teacher of psychiatry, and was a popular exponent of his specialty to generations of Westminster medical students. Soon after his appointment at Westminster Hospital, he started a day hospital, and extended inpatient psychiatric care to All Saints' Hospital in Lambeth. In the latter half of his fifties he suffered from a period of gradually failing health, and was forced to retire prematurely from his hospital appointments in 1972.

Throughout his active life, Gerald Garmany was a psychiatrist of great personal drive and organizing ability. His hobbies included the games of golf and chess, and throughout his adult life he maintained an expert knowledge of civil law, and was, for many years, a member of Lincoln's Inn. He will long be remembered with fondness by his hospital patients, numerous Westminster medical graduates, who benefited from his superb psychiatric tuition, and his colleagues at

Westminster, who missed his clear and practical approach to psychiatric problems. MDM

[*Brit. med. J.*, 1979, **2**, 452; Photo]

GARROD, Lawrence Paul *b.*7 Dec 1895 *d.*11 Sept 1979
BA Cantab (1918) MA (1921) MB BChir (1921) LMSSA (1923) MRCP (1923) MD (1933) FRCP (1936)

Lawrence Paul Garrod was the son of an Exeter draper, Cubitt Garrod. His mother was Gertrude Darelly, daughter of Samuel Davey. He was a second cousin of Sir Archibald Garrod who preceded him on the staff of St Bartholomew's Hospital. Lawrence was at school at St Peter's, Exmouth, going from there to Didcot School and then to King's College, Cambridge. His medical education at Cambridge and Bart's was interrupted by service as a surgeon sub-lieutenant RNVR in 1917 and 1918. At Bart's he was an outstanding student, winning the senior medical prize, the Brackenbury scholarship. In 1924 he became chief assistant to Morley Fletcher, and at that stage seemed bound for the staff of the hospital as a physician. But in 1925 he turned to pathology and ultimately to bacteriology. He was a reader in the University of London in 1929 and professor in 1934, a post that he held with that of bacteriologist to the hospital and bacteriologist to the City of London, until his retirement in 1961.

At Bart's he was a well known and respected figure, and his opinion was frequently sought. With his clinical background and his very extensive laboratory experience, he did much to direct bacteriologists towards the much more clinical role of the medical microbiologist today. Not the easiest of men to know, he had a disconcerting manner that discouraged some of the senior and junior staff, and although it was probably due to shyness, he could appear aloof. At home he was very different, and in his letters expressed himself more freely than he did in conversation at work.

For the thousands of Bart's men who passed through his hands Garrod may well be remembered best as a teacher. His lectures were lucid and were illustrated by anecdotes, some of which were passed down as part of student folk-lore. A meticulous attender at his practical classes, he enjoyed demonstrating his own very considerable technical ability.

From his early days, Garrod had an enquiring mind, and before the war he had, by chance, become interested in disinfectants and their actions. In this field, that attracts the serious attention of few doctors, he rapidly became one of the country's recognized experts, and his name was attached to a standard test. This early training left him ideally placed for the examination first of the sulphonamides, and then antibiotics. The war years were spent in relative exile at St Albans, running a clinical pathology laboratory, but despite this he continued his active engagement in research, and with the introduction of penicillin he began his extensive contribution to the literature of chemotherapy. For many years, with his assistant, Pamela Waterworth, each new antibiotic was studied and its properties and actions described. *Antibiotic and Chemotherapy*, written first with Mary Barber and then with Francis O'Grady, enabled him to show his thorough grasp of this extensive subject.

Apart from papers on chemotherapy, Garrod's literary contributions to medicine were remarkable, both for their size and quality. With Geoffrey Hadfield, he was responsible for five very successful editions of *Recent Advances in Pathology*, and with REO Williams and others he was an author of *Hospital Infection – Causes and Prevention*. For many years he edited the *British Journal of Experimental Pathology*. As a critic of a paper he had few rivals, and it is possible that this ability hampered the freer expansion of his own research work. Probably his influence extended most widely through his work for the *British Medical Journal*. From 1931 until shortly before he died he was in constant demand for leading articles, annotations and book reviews, which he wrote, in the Editor's words, with 'effortless ease, precision of style, accuracy of fact and a certain marked honesty that has been vastly refreshing'. His opinion was frequently sought on the suitability of papers submitted for publication, and for a time he was chairman of the Journal Committee. Retirement did not slow his pen, and he continued writing and responding to the many calls to lecture in this country and abroad.

Professional recognition came his way with honours and appointments. He was a member of committees of the Department of Health, the Medical Research Council and WHO. As an examiner he served the Universities of London, Oxford and Cambridge. He was elected president of his section of the Royal Society of Medicine, vice-president of the British Medical Association, president of the Institute of Medical Laboratory Technology, consultant in antibiotics to the Army, and on retirement, honorary consultant in chemotherapy to the Royal Postgraduate School. Glasgow awarded him an honorary doctorate of law, the University of Louvain conferred on him the title of honorary alumnus, and the Royal College of Pathologists elected him an honorary Fellow.

In 1922 he married Marjorie, daughter of Bedford Pierce MD, FRCP, superintendent of The Retreat, York. They had a daughter and three sons, two of whom qualified as doctors. RAS

[*Brit. med. J.*, 1979, **2**, 740; *Lancet*, 1979, **2**, 647; *Daily Telegraph*, 12 Sept 1979; Photo]

GARROD, Oliver *b*.22 Jan 1915 *d*.23 Sept 1983
MBE (1945) MRCS LRCP (1939) MB BS Lond (1946)
MRCP (1947) MD (1948)

Oliver came from a family with distinguished medical predecessors, including Sir Alfred Garrod his great grandfather and Sir Archibald Garrod his great uncle. Sir Lawrence Paul Garrod, the bacteriologist, was a distant uncle. His father was an organic chemist. Oliver's sister, Hilary, married AC Frazer FRCP.

When he left Bradfield College where he was captain of athletics, he went to St Bartholomew's Medical College and as a student he won the Brackenbury scholarship in medicine and wrote an outstanding essay on 'The life of Samuel Jones Gee' for which he won the Wix prize. It was published in Bart's hospital reports.

He qualified in 1939 with the conjoint degree just before war was declared. He was already a member of the Territorial Army and immediately war broke out he went into the RAMC, first serving as regimental medical officer to a motor cycle battalion of the Kings Royal Rifle Corps, subsequently volunteering to go overseas. Whilst on training with the regiment in Derbyshire he met his future wife, Barbara Morrison, and they were married on New Year's Day 1941. The next day he sailed to India. He was posted to Rawalpindi where he had the opportunity to buy a number of Persian rugs, a hobby that had started in England and continued for the rest of his life. In the summer of 1941 he was sent to the Persian Gulf and served first in Basra and then Shaiba where he was staff captain medical.

He had a great longing to visit Persia and went there on leave twice in the winters of 1941 and 1942 respectively, travelling on the trans-Iranian railway. From Tehrán he reached the Caspian Sea on the second visit. He later did a course in malariology and subsequently worked in a field laboratory on malaria, based in Baghdad, surveying the incidence of this disease in northern and central Iraq.

In 1943 he was invited to form a medical dispensary to work amongst the nomadic tribes of south west Persia. This had both political and medical implications. The ulterior aim was to keep the tribes on the side of the Allies at a time when German infiltration in Persia was rife. He and his Persian interpreter with three British other ranks penetrated deep into the mountain ranges of south west Persia and stayed with the chieftains of several nomadic tribes. He collected a considerable amount of material about the tribes which he communicated to the Royal Central Asian Society after his return to England in 1945.

When his health broke down (he contracted pneumonia after infective hepatitis and malaria) he returned to Tehrán to act as medical officer to the British legation for three months prior to repatriation. For his invaluable services he was awarded the MBE in 1945.

After demobilization he returned to Bart's to resume a broken appointment as house physician to the medical unit and subsequently became chief assistant to AW (Patrick) Spence, who specialized in endocrine diseases, and Neville Oswald, chest physician.

During the two years 1946–1948 Oliver passed in succession MB BS, MRCP and MD. He became interested in diabetes insipidus and worked with Joseph Cates on this subject, publishing articles in *Clinical Science* and other journals. On the conclusion of the appointment at Bart's he went to the Royal Postgraduate Medical School, Hammersmith, working with Russell Fraser, who also specialized in endocrine diseases. In 1951 he obtained a Rockefeller foundation scholarship to visit the United States for one year, and spent this working under Cecil Loeb at the Columbia Presbyterian Hospital in New York.

After returning to the United Kingdom, he went to the Middlesex Hospital where he worked in the clinical research department under Professor Kekwick. He worked on primary aldosteronism, with Tait and Simpson, and published several important papers on this subject. He continued this attachment at the Middlesex, after he had been appointed consultant physician to Barnet General Hospital in 1955, up till 1959. He remained at Barnet and Potters Bar Hospitals until retirement in 1980. He started a clinic for treating and supervising patients with hypertension in the early days of drug therapy for this condition, and he also organized a first class diabetic service. Oliver was an excellent clinician and had great compassion for his patients.

He was a member of several medical societies, being secretary and vice-president of both the endocrine and clinical sections of the Royal Society of Medicine and a keen member of the Medical Society of London. He was very attached to the Hunterian Society to which he was in succession secretary, orator and president. He made his Hunterian oration on 'Hibernation of mammals' which was a landmark in the history of that society. He was inspired by John Hunter's interest in this subject. He contributed regularly to the *Medical Annual*, writing the chapter on endocrine diseases.

His interest in Persia continued. He was a member of the Iran Society and a loyal friend and counsellor of the Royal Society for Asian Affairs, formerly the Royal Central Asian Society. He went on a number of expeditions with that society to Anatolia and Afghanistan but did not return to Persia until 1978 when he helped to organize a three week tour. Although Oliver travelled extensively throughout the world, his first love was Asia to which he repeatedly returned. His last visit was to India and Nepal with the Society in 1980, shortly after retirement.

His interests were wide and he had a great knowledge of the arts. His home became a gathering place for friends who went to admire his lovely garden, his antiques, Persian miniatures and particularly his Oriental rugs. He loved Bach and Mozart and was a keen pianist. Oliver and his wife were very hospitable, she as an excellent cook and Oliver with his choice vintage wines. After meals it was his custom to show his colour slides of his most recent holiday. His slide presentations were also a regular feature of the Ladies' Benevolent Fund functions in Barnet. He had a keen interest in gardening: all his plants were choice.

Going round to his home at lunchtime from the hospital he would do a little weeding whilst drinking a glass of sherry with his houseman. How unfortunate for Bart's that they did not appoint him when they had the chance to do so; they obviously did not recognize the strength behind his bland manner.

His last two and a half years brought out his fundamental courage in face of adversity, already shown in his career and particularly during the war years. A brain biopsy operation was followed by a total left hemiplegia from which he never fully recovered and he led a wheelchair existence thereafter. Although radiotherapy helped to a certain extent he remained an invalid, and during the early months of

1983 it was apparent that his disability was steadily progressing.

He had many friends in many walks of life. His wife Barbara, his son who is a lecturer in psychology at Glasgow University and his daughter, an architect, who also lectures in English at Zurich, survived him.
KWGGH

[*Brit. med. J.*, 1983, **287**, 1559; Photo]

GAVEY, Clarence John *b.*20 June 1911 *d.*7 Sept 1982
MRCS LRCP (1934) MB BS Lond (1934) MD (1936) MRCP (1936) FRCP (1948)

Clarence Gavey was born in Guernsey, the son of Walter John Gavey, Jurat of the Royal Court of Guernsey. After his early education at Queen Elizabeth College in Guernsey, he came to the London Hospital as a student in 1929. His record as a prize winner at the London is evidence of his success as a student and he very early decided on a career in clinical medicine; he qualified in 1934 and by 1936 had obtained his MRCP and, less than six months later, his MD. In 1939 he began his lifelong interest in cardiology when he published, with Sir John Parkinson, an important paper on the treatment of heart failure in the first issue of the newly founded *British Heart Journal*.

At the beginning of the war he went to Westminster Hospital as medical registrar but left before very long to serve in the RAMC, mostly in the Middle East. By this time he had begun the practice he continued throughout his career of recording and keeping personal notes on many of the patients he saw; these notes were referred to on many occasions in his later career when he was confronted by a similar problem. He returned to Westminster after the war and was soon appointed to the consultant staff. A year after his election to the fellowship of the College in 1948, he gave the Goulstonian lecture on 'The Cardiology of Old Age'. Further publications followed, one of the most notable being his essay on *The Management of the Hopeless Case* with which he won the Buckston Browne medal of the Harveian Society of London in 1950.

Gavey served on the staff of Westminster for thirty years, acquiring greater and greater responsibilities. He was a member of the board of governors and of the academic board of the Medical School and was chairman of the committee which supervised the building of the Page Street Wing of the hospital. He was physician in charge of the cardiac department, a department he largely created, and was also physician to Moorfields Eye Hospital. His interest in and deep knowledge of medical ophthalmology added an unusual interest to the work of the general medical firm he headed.

He had always seemed to be in robust health throughout his working life and it was a great sadness to his family and all who knew him that, very shortly after his retirement in 1976, the first episode of the heart failure, from which he eventually died, occurred. Despite this, he returned, as he had planned, to Guernsey to take up his many interests. These included painting in oils, philately, playing the organ and acquiring and reading a great many books – mainly biographies and autobiographies. His greatest pleasure, however, was in his native island and he enjoyed studying its archaeology and discussing its affairs, particularly with his brother who had succeeded their father as Jurat. Although his retirement was blighted by ill health he retained his enthusiasms up to a short time before his death and kept up a correspondence with colleagues at Westminster, being always eager to learn the latest news of his old hospital.

Gavey's career spanned a period of great change and progress in cardiology and, though not a great innovator himself, he always encouraged his younger colleagues to develop their ideas to the full. His own particular strength lay in his attention to detail in the clinical management of patients. His insistence on accurate and comprehensive clinical notes led to his being regarded as a demanding chief until his juniors realized that, however high the standards he required of them, those he set for himself were higher still. Those who worked for him for any length of time knew that, behind his stern, even forbidding manner, lay kindness itself, a very great personal and professional integrity and an unshakeable loyalty to those with whom he worked.

In 1937 he married Marjorie Guille, also from Guernsey, who survived him as did their three daughters. PRF

[Photo]

GIBBENS, Trevor Charles Noel *b*.28 Dec 1912 *d*.27 Oct 1983
CBE (1977) MRCS LRCP (1938) MB BChir Cantab (1939)
DPM (1946) MD (1947) MRCP (1966) FRCPsych (1971)
FRCP (1974)

Trevor Gibbens was the eighth son of a civil servant. Two of his brothers became doctors, but medicine was not in fact Trevor's first choice as a profession and it required the persuasive powers of Edward Glover and Sir Cyril Burt to steer him in that direction. He was educated at Westminster School and went up to Emmanuel College, Cambridge, where he began to read history, but later switched to medicine. He did his clinical training at St Thomas's Hospital.

At the outbreak of war in 1939 Gibbens was at the Maudsley Hospital, but as soon as it became possible, he was commissioned in the RAMC. He was posted abroad with the British Expeditionary Force, but as a consequence of the military debacle on the Continent of Europe, he was taken prisoner. He was directed to a prisoner of war camp where his job was to look after Russian prisoners. He decided to escape and, accompanied by a friend, made a gallant attempt to do so, but was recaptured when within an ace of success. He was severely punished for his pains and kept in solitary confinement for six weeks. He was later transferred to a British POW hospital.

There can be no doubt that his experiences as a prisoner of war, and as an escapee, had a profound influence on him and were in no small measure responsible, not only for the way his subsequent career came to be shaped but also for the deep, and lifelong sympathy he felt for the underdog. It was in fact the notes he kept of his clinical experiences in the POW hospital, where he had to cope as best he could with prison psychoses, that were to serve later as the basis of his MD thesis.

On his repatriation after five years in captivity he was appointed MBE for his outstanding services to the troops in Germany. Then, for a time, he served at Larbert POW rehabilitation unit and, after demobilization, he was appointed as registrar at Hammersmith Hospital.

In 1946 Gibbens resumed his psychiatric training at the Maudsley Hospital. In 1948 he was awarded a Nuffield travelling fellowship which allowed him to visit forensic institutions and prisons in the USA. On his return from the States he was appointed senior lecturer in forensic psychiatry at the Institute of Psychiatry located at the Maudsley Hospital and, in the goodness of time, he was the obvious choice for the chair of forensic psychiatry when it was established at the Institute. This post he held with distinction from 1967 until his retirement in 1978 when, sometime later, he was appointed emeritus professor.

Trevor Gibbens, in the course of his long career, was actively engaged in a host of research projects all of which bore his personal stamp of originality, thoroughness and academic integrity which earned him universal respect: he was without question the outstanding academic forensic psychiatrist of his day. Of his major research projects mention must be made of his surveys of Borstal lads, of cruel parents, and of the clients of prostitutes, and his study of shoplifting, all of which are classics in their own right.

But his interests and work spread far beyond the purely academic field: his services, nationally and internationally, were in constant demand and willingly given. He was, for example, a member of the Streatfield Committee in 1958, and a member of the Royal Commission on Penal Reform from 1964 to 1966. In 1967 he served as president both of the British Academy of Forensic Sciences and of the International Society of Criminology. For three years, from 1972 to 1975, he was a member of the Parole Board. In addition, he acted as adviser to the World Health Organization, the Probation and After-Care Advisory Board, and to the Institute for the Study and Treatment of Delinquency. He was vice-chairman of the Howard League for Penal Reform from 1975 until his death. He was promoted CBE in 1977.

In 1950, Gibbens married Pat Mullis by whom he had three children: a daughter who qualified as a doctor, and two sons. For a man as deeply committed as he was, Gibbens found comfort and relaxation with his family in his home in Dulwich, and latterly in his cottage in the Dordogne.

Trevor Gibbens left his mark on British forensic psychiatry, a mark as indelible, indeed, as the mark he made on the minds and hearts of those of us who were privileged to know him and to learn from him.

HRR

[*Brit. med. J.*, 1983, **287**, 1636; *Lancet*, 1983, **2**, 1262; *Times*, 8 Nov 1983; Photo]

GIBSON, Kenneth Burgoyne *b.*7 May 1914 *d.*2 May 1982
MBE (1945) MB ChB Liverp (1938) MRCP (1947) MD (1948) FRCP (1975)

Kenneth Gibson was born in Liverpool, the son of Samuel Henry Gibson, an insurance official. He was educated at the Liverpool Institute and the University of Liverpool, graduating in 1938. After a short period, first as house surgeon at the David Lewis Northern Hospital, and then as assistant resident medical officer at the Walton Hospital, Liverpool, and the Cleaver Sanatorium, Cheshire, he joined the RAMC in 1940. He served both in the field of battle and in administration and rose to the rank of lieutenant colonel as ADMS Land Forces, Greece.

On demobilization he was appointed senior physician to the hospital at Childwall, Liverpool, and in 1949 became consultant physician superintendent to the Newsham General Hospital, Liverpool. In 1955 he left his home territory to take up an appointment as consultant geriatrician at St Albans City Hospital, Hertfordshire, and he also served the Abbots Langley Hospital. He published a paper on 'Work of a geriatric unit – a survey of 13,500 patients' in the *Lancet*, 1955, **1**, 960.

Kenneth married Jean Brough Brocklehurst in 1947 and they had two daughters. His wife died in 1972. His hobbies included music, reading, travel, and the French language. GW/VL

GLANCY, James Edward McAlinney *b.*9 Feb 1914 *d.*20 Apr 1980
MB BCh BAO NUI (1937) DPM RCP&S (1943) MD (1948) MRCP (1948) FRCP (1970) FRCPsych (1971)

James Glancy, son of Michael James Glancy, a general practitioner, and Anne Teresa McAlinney, was born in Brideswell, Eire. He received his school education first at the Convent of La Sainte Union, County Kildare, and then at Blackrock College, Dublin, before entering medicine. After graduating with first class honours from the National University of Ireland, he came to England, where he spent all of his professional life. He practised psychiatry at Goodmayes Hospital, Essex, from 1942 until his retirement in 1979, and was its last medical superintendent. Always a competent physician, he was alert to the importance of general medicine for psychiatry, but he also realized that psychological and social factors were as essential as the physical.

As well as being an astute clinician, he was an effective administrator and negotiator. He was an enthusiastic member of the BMA, served on its Council and on its mental health committee. He chaired the psychiatric advisory committee for the North East Thames Regional Health Authority for a number of years, and was the master of the Guild of Catholic Doctors from 1970 to 1973. Towards the end of his professional life his fund of experience and abilities were recognized when he was invited to serve as a principal medical officer to the Department of Health and Social Security; while there he chaired the working party on security in NHS psychiatric hospitals, which reported on the care of disturbed mentally ill patients.

James Glancy was a man of great kindness and understanding, with a delightful sense of humour, which qualities enhanced everything he did. He married in 1945 Margaret Mary Redgrove. They had a daughter, who became a clinical psychologist, and a son who entered medicine.

GJG

[*Brit. med. J.*, 1980, **281**, 67; Photo]

GOLBERG, Boris *b.*27 Jan 1922 *d.*28 June 1980
MB BCh Wits (1944) MRCP (1948) DMRD Eng (1960) FFR (1962) FRCP (1976)

Boris Golberg, a learned and distinguished radiologist, died at his home in Bushey, Herts. at the age of 58. Born in Cyprus, his father, Aron Golberg, was a watchmaker of Russian origin. His mother, too, came from Russia. The family moved to South Africa in 1924, and there he remained until coming to England in 1947. He was educated at Jeppe High School, and graduated at the University of Witwatersrand in 1944, with subsequent house officer posts at the Johannesburg General Hospital until 1946, when he joined the S A Medical Corps for 18 months.

After coming to England he embarked upon a career in respiratory medicine with posts at the Hammersmith and Central Middlesex Hospitals, and a senior registrarship at St Charles' Hospital and the Paddington and Kensington Chest Clinic. Between 1952 and 1954 he worked in the field of pulmonary tuberculosis for the World Health Organization in Bandung, Indonesia, with subsequent posts in Bristol and Ashford, Middlesex.

He inevitably developed great interest and expertise in radiology, and in 1958 he took the first of a series of promotions in this specialty at the Middlesex Hospital, leading to his appointment as consultant radiologist at Edgware General and associated hospitals in 1964, a post that he held until his death. He played a large part in creating a first class unit, with his own particular interest in the field of arteriography.

He was a widely read and learned man, and published many excellent papers. His sense of humour is demonstrated by two of his most recent publications, 'The department of inappropriate investigations' and 'Lateral chest radiology or a chicken in every pot' (*Brit. med. J.*, 1977, **2**, 124; 1980, **1**, 909).

He married Joan, the daughter of David Scott, an electrical engineer, in 1947. His wife, two sons and a daughter survived him. His brother, Leon Golberg, became professor of toxicology at South Carolina in the USA and was Milroy Lecturer at the College in 1967.

GSCS

[*Brit. med. J.*, 1980, **281**, 233, 138; Photo]

GOLDSMITH, Kenneth Leslie Grant *b*.15 Aug 1920 *d*.3 July 1976
MRCS LRCP (1943) MB BS Lond (1943) PhD (1959)
MRCP (1969) FRCP (1976) MRCPath (1963)

Kenneth Goldsmith, who came of Scottish forebears, was born in Orpington, Kent, the son of Leslie Harold Goldsmith, a teacher, and Lillus Jane, daughter of William Grant. He attended the Roan School for Boys, Greenwich, whence, with a London County Council senior county exhibition (medical), he entered King's College, University of London, in 1939 and spent the years 1941 to 1943 at the Westminster Hospital Medical School. Because of the war, the student body was dispersed, and Goldsmith received part of his medical undergraduate instruction in Glasgow and Birmingham.

After qualifying, he was house physician at the South Middlesex EMS and Fever Hospital 1943–1944, and deputy medical superintendent of this hospital 1944–1946. He did national service as a flight lieutenant in the RAF Medical Service, 1946–1948. Upon demobilization he became supernumerary registrar, department of pathology, Westminster Hospital, 1948–1949. He then served as registrar in the hospital's blood transfusion department from 1949 to 1951.

It was in this post that his interest was awakened in blood transfusion generally and, in particular, the relationship of blood groups to anthropology. From 1951 to 1955 he was senior registrar in the blood transfusion department, Westminster Hospital, and senior hospital medical officer from 1955 to 1960. During the latter appointment, he was awarded the degree of PhD (London) in 1959 for a thesis on 'The blood groups of Somali tribes, with special reference to anthropology'. This was one of the first studies on the blood groups of the Somalis, the field work for which he did himself in what was then British Somaliland.

In 1960 Goldsmith joined the staff of the Medical Research Council Blood Group Reference Laboratory. He became deputy director in 1962 and succeeded AE Mourant FRCP FRS, as director in 1965. During the period 1960 to 1965, Kenneth Goldsmith consolidated his reputation and established himself as an expert blood group serologist.

The Blood Group Reference Laboratory, one of the two central laboratories of the National Blood Transfusion Service, was the first laboratory of its kind. In addition to being the national reference point for all blood group serological problems submitted by regional transfusion centres and hospital pathology laboratories, it prepared blood grouping sera for the regional transfusion centres from human sera they supplied, and undertook the preparation of certain blood grouping reagents in animals. In the early 1950's the laboratory had assumed, at the request of the World Health Organization, the responsibilities of acting as the WHO International Blood Group Reference Laboratory.

Goldsmith thus became director of an already active laboratory with a wide range of responsibilities. Under his directorship the laboratory extended the scope of its work. He introduced new techniques, and shortly before he died he and his staff assumed an active role in organizing quality control applied to blood group serology in regional transfusion centres and hospital laboratories. The very high quality characterizing hospital transfusion and ante-natal serology in Britain owes much to the standards expected – and exacted – by the Blood Group Reference Laboratory. In August 1975 the laboratory assumed an additional responsibility when it was designated the WHO Collaborating Centre for Reference on the use of Anti-D immunoglobulin for the prevention of Rh-sensitization in pregnant women.

One of his constant objects was to raise and maintain the standard of blood group serology, viewed in its widest context. Consequently many of his publications were concerned with the preparation and quality of blood grouping reagents and the quality control of red cell grouping technique, including, particularly, the importance of the use of standard reference preparations of haemagglutinins. A paper, written jointly with RA Kekwick FRS and JM Jones and entitled 'The Influence of Polymers on the Efficacy of Serum Albumin as a Potentiator of "Incomplete" Rh Agglutinins' (*Nature* 1969; **224**: 510) was important because it contained the first report of a possible basis for this potentiating effect of albumin, although the effect had been reported some 20 years before. Kenneth Goldsmith quickly appreciated the practical importance of the Gm-groups in blood group serology: three important papers are Brazier,DM, Goldsmith,KLG, Gunson,HH and Loghem,E van, 'The first human example of anti-Gm (17): Gm(Z)', *Vox Sang* 1971,**21**,558; Brazier,DM and Goldsmith,KLG, 'Frequency of certain Gm and Inv factors in UK' *Nature*,1968,**219**,193; and Simmons,M, Stapleton,RR, Brazier,DM and Goldsmith,KLG, 'An example of an anti-antibody causing difficulty in ABO grouping', *Vox Sang* 1971, **21**,284.

Pre-eminent among his other interests was teaching. He lectured frequently: he devoted much time to preparing his material and his lectures were carefully organized and clearly delivered. One result of this interest was that many of his publications were reviews of different aspects of transfusion.

He acted as chairman or secretary of several Medical Research Council and DHSS working parties, and was chairman of the joint albumin working party of the International Society of Blood Transfusion and the International Committee for Standardization in Haematology.

Goldsmith was an ideal man to direct the activities of the Blood Group Reference Laboratory. He was an internationally recognized expert in blood group serology: he had abundant energy and enthusiasm and was always cheerful and imperturbable, even when facing problems which would daunt most. He was immediately ready to help anyone who brought him a problem. He never spared himself and was usually accessible at any hour of the day or night. He inspired the devotion of his staff, of whom he demanded much, yet in such a friendly, unassuming and unselfish way that the laboratory was a very happy one. He will also be remembered with particular affection by the many doctors and technicians who came to his laboratory to be trained, many of them from parts of Africa and the Far East, which he had visited on behalf of WHO.

He gave the impression of being a man who had found for himself a niche in professional life for which he was ideally suited.

He had several hobbies – photography, bird watching, gardening and, in particular, horology and radio.

He married in 1950 Pamela Aileen, daughter of Paymaster Commander Thomas Moffatt Fitzgerald, RN(Ret) of Seaford, Sussex, and formerly a sister at the Westminster Hospital. They had two sons, and later adopted two Chinese orphan girls from Hong Kong.

W d'AM

[*Brit. med. J.*, 1976, **2**, 308; *Lancet*, 1976, **2**, 212; Photo]

GOODMAN, Neville Marriott *b*.22 Apr 1898 *d*.30 April 1980
CB (1961) MRCS LRCP (1923) MB BChir Cantab (1925)
MA MD (1933) DPH Lond (1933) FRCP* (1950) PhD (1952)

Born at Kingston upon Thames to Louisa and Roger Goodman, MD Cantab., Neville Goodman was educated at Mill Hill and Sandhurst. An only child, bespectacled and interested in wild flowers, he was an unusual candidate for a Regular Army commission, but he had (when he chose) a parade-ground voice; his mother's father, Hunt Marriott, had been a colonel; and he did well at the Royal Military Academy.

He joined a regular battalion of the Worcester Regiment in 1917 and, though badly wounded, survived to see further service in France, Belgium, and Germany. At 20 he was a captain.

From Pembroke College, Cambridge, he went to the London Hospital, where he later held four house appointments, one to Sir Robert Hutchison.

The next seven years were spent in practice at Lymington; and had he had a family he might, like his father, have remained a general practitioner. But his marriage, in 1928, was childless, and in 1932 he took up public health.

After field experience in Surrey, he joined the Ministry of Health in 1934, and presently found himself becoming an expert on international health regulations. From 1938 he was British delegate to the Office International d'Hygiène publique and a member of the Health Committee of the League of Nations. With his friendliness, good sense, and aptitude for languages, he was quickly at home in these semidiplomatic circles.

The war stopped all that and the Ministry's depleted staff had to cope with evacuees, probable epidemics, and the need to keep hospitals going despite the 'blitz'. When the bombing of London began, Goodman was (central) responsible for health in the air-raid shelters at Westminster, Stepney, and Whitechapel, and at first their condition was sometimes appalling. As a sideline he was made inspector of anatomy, and in 1944 he gave an Arris and Gale lecture to the Royal College of Surgeons on the supply of bodies for dissection.

The same year saw him back in international work – now concerned less with regulations than with keeping people alive. To care for 'displaced persons', to restore brokendown health services, and to prevent the spread of diseases, the United Nations had set up a Relief and Rehabilitation Administration (UNRRA), and the Ministry of Health seconded Goodman to it as director of health for Europe. This was at a time when a European journey was often an adventure in itself. In 1947 he was given the Médaille de la Reconnaissance Française.

That same year, when the new World Health Organization (interim commission) made him director of its field services, his travels were still wider. He now lived near Geneva, and for a year he acted as assistant director-general of WHO. If he had not been slightly deaf, which handicapped him in committee, he might well have become director-general.

Rejoining the Ministry of Health in 1949, he took a full share in getting the National Health Service off the ground. Though a lifelong Liberal, he preferred planning to letting things just happen. From 1955 he was the principal medical officer concerned with hospital and local authority services in the four Metropolitan regions, and from 1960 he was one of Sir George Godber's two deputies. As such he proved invaluable: he provided contrary opinions when needed; he helped his juniors; and he never stood on his dignity. Whether as colleague, friend, or Fellow of the College (to which he was elected under bye-law 39b), he was generous and loyal.

From 1934 to 1960 Goodman lectured on public health at his old hospital, and in 1935 he wrote the St John Ambulance Association's manual on *Hygiene*. After his return from Geneva, the London School of Hygiene and Tropical Medicine made him its lecturer on international health, and his standard work on *International Health Organisations* appeared in 1952. His light touch made him a welcome lecturer, and his biography of his former chief, *Wilson Jameson, Architect of National Health*, is refreshing as well as instructive. As a writer, his style was unadorned but, on paper as in person, he was almost always interesting – because he was himself so interested and in so much. Over the years he made some 350 unsigned contributions to *The Lancet*, 'ranging from very good sense to very good nonsense.'

Before and after his retirement in 1963, official requests for advice took him to Ethiopia, the Sudan, Turkey, Iran, and Afghanistan; and his own inclinations took him to North America, Mexico, the Caribbean, Egypt, and Israel.

An amateur botanist and ornithologist from childhood, he had become a gardeners' gardener, with a country garden at Wadhurst in Sussex – with a wood, a stream, and kingfishers – and a town one at his lovely 17th-century home in The Grove, Highgate Village. Also he collected bronzes, now mostly in museums.

His first wife, Beatrix Warr Edwards, died in 1970, and in 1979 he was greatly pleased by election to an honorary fellowship at her college at Oxford, Lady Margaret Hall.

In 1971 he married Phyllis Bucknell, a former colleague in UNRRA and the Ministry; and their house at Sandwich drew old friends and new. To the last, he was excellent company. TFF

[*Brit. med. J.*, 1980, **280**, 1232, 1325; *Lancet*, 1980, **1**, 1040; Times, 3 & 10 June, 1980; *WHO Chronicle*, 1980, **34** (7/8); Photo]

GORDON, Christie Wilson *b*.13 Dec 1911 *d*.9 Aug 1979
TD (1948) QHP (1974) MB ChB Aberd (1938) DPH Eng (1946) DPH Johns Hopkins (1947) MRCP (1966)FRCP (1971) FFCM(1972)†

Christie Gordon was born at Buckie in Banffshire, the son of John Wilson Gordon, social security officer for the county of Banff. After scholastic education at Buckie Academy, he went into banking but disliked his choice and entered medicine as an undergraduate at Aberdeen, graduating in 1938. He held house officer appointments at the Royal Infirmary in Aberdeen before joining the RAMC at the outbreak of war, serving with distinction in India, Persia, Iraq and the Middle East and achieving the rank of lieutenant colonel and the Territorial Decoration.

On demobilization Gordon was Rockefeller fellow at Johns Hopkins 1946–48, where he was awarded their doctorate in public health. From 1949 to 1952 he was lecturer in hospital administration at the London School of Hygiene and Tropical Medicine. In 1950 he was appointed deputy senior administrative medical officer to the Birmingham Regional Hospital Board, and seven years later he was appointed senior administrative medical officer, which post (changed in 1974 to regional medical officer) he held with dedication and success for 19 years. His was the largest region in the National Health Service and he administered it with such ability, courtesy and charm that everyone involved in the hospital service with him became his friend and admirer. He built up the consultant and junior staffs in the hospitals under his jurisdiction to the highest level of excellence; where buildings were inadequate or obsolescent as at Coventry, Burton, Stoke, West Bromwich and Birmingham itself, he carried out enormous rebuilding programmes; he did much to develop the Robert Jones and Agnes Hunt Hospital and the Birmingham Accident Hospital as centres of excellence; he grasped the need for increased postgraduate educational facilities and was the first SAMO to develop postgraduate centres in his region; he appreciated the vital importance of close links with the board of governors of the United Birmingham Hospitals and the University of Birmingham, and both regarded him as one of their most valued friends.

When he retired he donated a retirement gift from his colleagues to the University, which used it to found a 'Christie Gordon lecture', the first of which was given by Lord Hunter of Newington FRCP, and the second by Sir George Godber FRCP.

Christie Gordon was one of the great medical administrators of his day and his achievements stemmed, apart from natural ability and knowledge, from tenacity, charm, gentleness and persuasion. The University of Birmingham showed their appreciation of his achievement by the award of an honorary LLD.

During the war he married Robina Alice Munst, daughter of a writer in the Town Clerk's department at Aberdeen. There was one son of the marriage who became a solicitor. Christie's brother, Ian Gordon, was a physician of great distinction on the staff of Aberdeen Royal Infirmary.

Active and interested in the University of Birmingham, his friends and his church, until a few days before his death, Christie suffered a cerebrovascular accident of such magnitude that survival was impossible. AGWW

[*Brit. med. J.*, 1979, **2**, 506; *Lancet*, 1979, **2**, 428; *Daily Telegraph*, 14 Aug 1979]

GORDON, Ian Ronald Simson *b.*15 June 1915 *d.*12 June 1979
MB BChir Cantab (1939) MRCP (1942) MA MD (1944)
DMRD (1952) FRCP (1970) FRCR (1975)

Ian Gordon was born at Bath, the son of Ronald Grey Gordon, a medical practitioner, and his wife, Agnes Theodora, daughter of George Henderson, a farmer. He was educated at Charterhouse and Cambridge, graduating from the London Hospital in 1939. At the outbreak of the second world war, Ian Gordon was considered unfit for military service, and from 1940 to 1942 he was house physician and registrar at the Royal United Hospital, Bath. In 1950 he transferred to Bristol to train as a radiologist, and thereafter he spent the remainder of his working life in Bristol, becoming one of the most important radiologists in Britain in a rapidly developing specialty.

Ian married Diana, daughter of Alan Alexander Geekie, a dental practitioner, in 1947. They had a large family of six children; four sons and two daughters. He and his wife were extremely hospitable, and many of the overseas trainee radiologists who came to Britain remember the quiet warmth and genuine welcome extended to them in the Gordons' country home.

Within the teaching group in the University of Bristol, Ian took over responsibility for the Children's Hospital and the Maternity Hospital, and in due course became one of the leading paediatric radiologists, not only in Britain but also in Europe. He was a founder member of the European Paediatric Radiologists Club, and never missed its annual meeting. He was also a founder member of the radiologists group within the British Paediatrics Association, which held a very successful first meeting at York in 1979. For many years he was secretary of the medical staff committee of the Children's Hospital and later its chairman, and he was largely instrumental in creating the Bristol Bone Dysplasia Registry. Cases were sent to him from far and wide for his opinion. His book *Diagnostic Radiology in Paediatrics*, published jointly with FGM Ross, became the standard book on paediatric radiology in Britain.

As a teacher, Ian Gordon was indefatigable in stimulating younger people to think. He always had time to stop what he was doing and explain. He held innumerable regular weekly sessions with paediatricians and surgeons, and others, which were enormously popular as teaching and learning sessions with both undergraduate and postgraduate students; he took an active part in all the department's regular teaching sessions, contributing cases to the Tuesday lunchtime case discussion seminars and, for 25 years, he also organized the weekly academic lecture. He was greatly admired and respected at Bristol, and held in deep affection.

Ian was an unassuming man. He and his wife were intrepid travellers and caravaners, driving to many remote parts of Europe for their holidays. He had a heart attack in 1963, followed by a second five years later. He refused, however, to make an invalid of himself and lived a full professional, family and social life until the end. He died while playing tennis. GW/VL

[*Brit. med. J.*, 1979, **2**, 557]

GORDON, John Everett *b*.18 June 1890 *d*.27 June 1983
BSc Chicago (1916) PhD (1921) MD (1925)
Hon AM Harvard (1943) FRCP* (1943)

John Gordon was professor of preventive medicine and epidemiology at the Harvard School of Public Health from 1938 to 1958, and subsequently emeritus professor. He was also senior lecturer at the Massachusetts Institute of Technology until the time of his death.

He was born in Austin, Minnesota, the son of Fanny and Newton Gordon. His father was a journalist, and his mother was the daughter of a farmer. The family later moved to Barron, Wisconsin, where his father became a newspaper editor, a fact that affected his son's approach to manuscripts all his life. John was educated at the local High School, the University of Chicago, and the Presbyterian Hospital, Chicago. On graduation in 1916 he enlisted as a first lieutenant in the Sanitary Corps, assigned to work on meningitis and influenza, returning to the United States at the end of hostilities. He took his PhD at the University of Chicago in 1921, and for a short time he taught bacteriology in Chicago and at the University of Western Ontario. This experience was a formative influence for it kindled a lifelong interest in infectious diseases and, in particular, the interplay of nutrition with infection.

In 1925 he gained the MD at Rush Medical College, Chicago, and became assistant superintendent of the Municipal Contagious Diseases Hospital in Chicago, and medical director of the Herman Kiefer Hospital, Detroit. These posts, however, did not satisfy his thirst for a deeper knowledge and understanding of the aetiology and causation of disease and, after serving for a few years as epidemiologist to the City of Detroit, in 1933 he accepted an appointment as field director for the Rockefeller Foundation, departing with his family to Romania to direct a study which aimed to determine why scarlet fever persisted in virulent forms in that part of the world. It was while he was in Romania that he was invited to become Charles Wilder professor of preventive medicine and epidemiology at Harvard, a post he accepted in 1938, but he had hardly begun his new career when he was asked to organize and direct a field hospital unit in Britain. This was during the second world war, and he left America in 1940 with John R Mote of the American Red Cross, arrived in England in the middle of the battle for Britain, and established the American Red Cross-Harvard Field Hospital unit at Salisbury. The unit had a threefold purpose: hospital care for the patient, clinical and epidemiological research, and field studies of communicable diseases under wartime conditions. This was the beginning of a six-year tour of duty, most of it as chief of preventive medicine for the US Army in Europe. The end of the war found him in the Pacific area. For his wartime services he received the Distinguished Service Medal, the Legion of Merit, the Order of the British Empire, the Croix de Guerre avec Palme, the Liberty Cross of Norway, and the medal of the US Typhus Commission.

On cessation of hostilities, John Gordon returned to America with strong new confirmations of the relevance of communicable disease epidemiology, such as the triumphant control of typhus in Europe by application of the new DDT to everyone crossing the Rhine river from east to west. Back at Harvard, he was elected head of the department of epidemiology in the graduate school and was soon at work on several applications of epidemiological concepts and techniques to non-communicable diseases; to diabetes, congenital deformities, mental disease, traumatic accidental injuries, etc. He also foresaw the need for epidemiologists to be concerned with the problems of overpopulation, and joined with two of his former students, John Wyon and Carl Taylor, in starting one of the first major projects in this field – the Khanna project in India. From the seven years of field work, followed by ten years of data analysis and reporting of findings, about thirty-five papers emerged and, in 1971, a book describing the Khanna Study. A follow-up study of the same villages was incorporated in the findings in the book, and John Gordon dedicated much hard work to these publications, although it was only one task among many.

At Harvard he invariably gave the introductory course in epidemiology himself, illustrating one of his principles by waving in the air a shellalegh club he had picked up in Ireland, and announcing that the job of the epidemiologist is to spot the most cogent relationship and hit it on the head. He ran a year-long weekly seminar known as Epidemiology 15, for ten students only, and by the end of the year all the participants had designed their own field projects.

He wrote sections of the medical history of the United States forces in the second world war, wrote two articles a year for the *American Journal of Medical Sciences*, edited the American Public Health Association's *Control of Communicable Diseases*, regularly every three years contributed the chapter on the then original concept of 'Weanling Diarrhoea' to the WHO monograph on *Interactions of nutrition and infection*, and numerous other publications. His interest in nutrition had deep roots and a paper with Harding Le Riche in 1950 was the first to deal with the application of the epidemiological method to nutrition.

In 1959 he was invited to the Institute of Nutrition of Central America and Panama in Guatemala, to assist in the design and interpretation of field studies of the interaction of nutrition and diarrhoeal disease. He and his wife Miriam then visited Guatemala for long stays each year for the next ten years, where they were both loved and he became a legend. John also undertook long-term studies of intestinal diseases in the Arctic, and consulted on studies of the effect of the atom bomb on Hiroshima – all in addition to the Khanna Study.

In his later years at Harvard, John Gordon developed a partial hearing loss but did not allow this to disable him. On the contrary, he turned it to his advantage when presiding over the then curriculum committee and other bodies; it has been said that motions were carried by votes of John Gordon for, and six against: a perfect example of the interaction of host and environment about which he spoke so frequently.

Following his retirement from Harvard, John accepted a senior lectureship in the department of nutrition and food sciences at the Massachusetts Institute of Technology, which he held, and worked at until a few months before his death. While at the Institute, at the age of 79, he was asked to investigate the problem of aflatoxin produced by *Aspergillus flavus*, a potentially serious problem in the foodstuffs of tropical developing countries. He eagerly accepted and went to Thailand, criss-crossing the country in a jeep at the hottest time of the year, wearing out both Thai and American colleagues who were his juniors by many decades. Out of this came an experimental design for examining the relationship between the aflatoxin content of foods, Reye's syndrome in children, and carcinoma of the liver in adults. At about this time he was invited to become a member of the NAS/NRC expert committee on the history of medicine and he participated actively in its meetings. The major scholarly task of his last five years was the writing of a book on nutritional epidemiology in collaboration with Nevin S Scrimshaw. Despite his eagerness to complete this book he developed great patience with Nevin Scrimshaw's over-commitments and extensive foreign travel which made it impossible for him to do his share. He left behind drafts of all the chapters, most of them revised for the fourth, fifth, sixth and seventh time. The most striking feature of the last years of his life was his continued enthusiasm for new editorial tasks, new intellectual challenges, and any opportunity to train additional students in the field of epidemiology. Even in rain and snow, he drove the twelve miles from Wellesley to the Institute to be at his desk, editing and keeping in contact with students. It was only at the age of 83 that he finally consented to go to Ipswich for summers, but it did not interrupt his editing. During his last year, his hours at the Institute became a little shorter and if the weather was too severe his wife was sometimes able to dissuade him from driving the twelve miles from Wellesley, but there was no loss of enthusiasm or willingness to take on new tasks.

John Gordon had a great influence on American and Pan-American epidemiology over a period of almost fifty years. He was clear headed, thinking far into the future, and a tyrant for knowing the facts of the present. He loved to clarify principles, savouring the details of each case. He always searched for a more holistic view of his cases; he bewildered biologists with his demands for behavioural facts, and behavioural scientists with his vigorous and deeply practical biological mind. Although he did not appear to follow any specific religious doctrine, he lived a life which any aspiring saint might envy – not by what he said, but by what he did. He could be sharp and acerbic at times, but he had a genius for handling people.

He married Miriam Louise, daughter of Charles Herman Lapham, a merchant, in 1921 and they had a son and a daughter. Much of his strength came from their close relationship and her constant care of him. His deep distress and concern when she became ill showed that his concept of synergism was not just an epidemiological one. A highlight of his final years was his arrival at the Faculty Club of the Institute for what he expected to be a simple dinner for his 90th birthday, but which – with Miriam's conspiratorial assistance – turned out to be a celebration with friends and colleagues not only from the Boston area, but also from elsewhere in the United States and abroad. It was a joyous occasion, with John Gordon in full command of his intellectual powers and sense of humour. The following day he was back at work as usual.

John Gordon's breadth of experience and intuitive sense for what was important brought simplifying insight to complex issues. He was without doubt one of the most experienced epidemiologists of the century.

NSS/GW/VL

[*Memorial Minute,* Harvard University, Feb 1984; *J. Tropical Pediatrics,* 1969, **15**, 71-75; Photo]

GOUGH, Jethro *b.*29 Dec 1903 *d.*16 Feb 1979
BSc Wales (1924) MRCS LRCP (1926) MB BCh (1927)
MD (1930) FRCPath (1963) FRCP* (1967)

Jethro Gough was born in Mountain Ash, Glamorgan, the son of Jabez Gough, a hay and corn merchant, and of Ellen Matilda, the daughter of Eli Mortina, a baker and shopkeeper. He went to school in Mountain Ash and then on to the University of Wales at Cardiff, and the Welsh National School of Medicine. He was one of the first group of students to qualify from the new clinical school. His student career was noteworthy for distinctions in physiology, pathology, obstetrics and gynaecology and for winning the Alfred Sheen prize and McLean medal.

He went to Manchester as demonstrator in pathology under Shaw Dunn, returning to Cardiff in 1929 as lecturer in pathology. He became senior lecturer in pathology under JB Duguid at Cardiff, and when Duguid moved to Newcastle in 1948 Gough succeeded him as professor.

Jethro Gough took a keen interest in the problems of clinical medicine, and in early years often joined senior teaching rounds. His interest in clinical pathology was responsible for the development of the excellent postgraduate training of clinical pathologists at Cardiff, as witnessed by the success of these consultants in Wales and many countries. He demanded a high standard of diagnostic histopathology. All this did not lessen his devotion to research and academic pathology.

During the 1939–1945 war, he remained in Cardiff, having the evacuated students of University College London under his care, and additional responsibilities in the blood transfusion service and in the control of infection in war wounds.

Between 1929 and 1939 he published a number of papers on various topics in clinical pathology; then in 1940 came the first of the series of brilliant papers on pneumoconiosis of coalworkers, in the paper *Pneumoconiosis in Coal Trimmers*. With Mr Wentworth, a senior member of the technical staff, Gough developed the Gough-Wentworth large lung section technique now in world-wide use in the study of many organs. The method was described in 1949 and greatly advanced knowledge of pneumoconiosis and of many lung disorders. Gough's work on coalworkers' lung disorders led, in 1969, to his being invited to give evidence before the Committee on Labor and Public Welfare of the United States Senate, a distinction of which he was most proud. He was called to assist the State of West Virginia to establish legislation on compensation for coalminers. In Wales his work was especially recognized by the National Union of Mineworkers and many associated bodies, and by the establishment in 1974 of the Jethro Gough prize in pathology, to be awarded annually in his own medical school.

Jethro Gough was one of the founders of the Royal College of Pathology and was a council member and vice-president. He was responsible for the expansion of the Institute of Pathology in Cardiff and, until his retirement in 1969, was active in the planning of the new University Hospital of Wales.

He was particularly helpful to other research workers in the school, to the Pneumoconiosis Research Unit (MRC) at Llandough Hospital, and the Asthma Research Unit at St. Davids and Sully Hospitals. He took a practical interest in studies of pulmonary heart disease. His advice was sought by many European centres working in the field of pulmonary disorders, and he participated in a number of Ciba Foundation symposia.

Jethro Gough's work was also his hobby, which perhaps was a pity for a man with such a sharp inquiring mind. He was survived by his wife, who gave him devoted care over a long period of failing health. They had two sons, one an academic physicist and the other a pathologist in Jethro's own school, the University Hospital of Wales.

AJT

[*Brit. med. J.*, 1979, **2**, 507; Photo]

GRANT, Leon Julian *b*.13 Jan 1915 *d*.15 Mar 1982
MRCS LRCP (1938) MB BS Lond (1938) MRCP (1949)
FRCP (1971)

Eldest son of the Reverend Nehemiah Grundstein, Leon Grant was born in East London and was educated locally at the Raine's Foundation School, one of those élite grammar schools, alas now vanished, which nurtured an abundance of talent among the first generation of poor Jewish immigrant families from Eastern Europe.

He qualified in 1938 at the London Hospital, having entered with distinction as Price scholar. After qualification he was appointed demonstrator in pharmacology at the London Hospital Medical College. Various house jobs followed until 1942 when he was commissioned in the medical branch of the Royal Air Force. He served in England and in the Middle East, being graded temporary specialist in radiology.

Returning to civilian life in 1946 he chose chest diseases as his special subject and served as senior medical registrar at the London Chest and National Temperance Hospitals. He was admitted to the membership of the Royal College of Physicians in 1949.

In 1951 he was appointed consultant physician to the Kensington and Chelsea Hospital Group. In 1967 a further appointment as consultant physician to the National Temperance Hospital was followed in 1969 by appointment to the staff of University College Hospital. Despite his abiding involvement with pulmonary conditions, Leon was to remain one of the dwindling band of general physicians in an increasing age of specialization, and generations of medical students and general practitioners were to benefit from his help and advice, both of which he gave with unstinting generosity.

The last few years of his life were clouded with misfortune. He never quite recovered from the consequences of open heart surgery, and from the loss of his devoted wife Patricia from a brain tumour. There were no children of the marriage, and a small circle of close friends assisted by the Herculean efforts of his amazingly dedicated secretary, Mary Thompson, managed to lighten the burden of his prolonged terminal illness which he bore with great fortitude.

Leon Grant apart from his professional achievements had many and varied interests. From his father he inherited a magnificent baritone voice, which was equally at home in renderings of ancient Hebraic melodies or Schubert lieder. He was an accomplished linguist and was proud of his ability to read medical papers in their original language. He had a large library, much of which was devoted to medical history, and an encyclopaedic knowledge of Georgian silver, many fine examples of which adorned his home.

Above all else he was a pious and learned man of unusual sensitivity, possessed of a love and reverence for knowledge for its own sake, and to whom his Jewish religion was all important.

One can say that he aspired, in the words of the psalmist, to 'Ascend the mountain of the Lord, and stand in His holy place, with clean hands and a pure heart'. MJ

[Photo]

GRAVESON, George Stanley *b*.10 May 1915 *d*.16 Apr 1976
BA Cantab (1936) MB BChir (1939) MRCP (1941) MA MD (1947) FRCP (1959)

Stanley Graveson, as he was known to his medical colleagues, was born at Farnworth, Lancashire, into a non-medical family. He was educated at Farnworth Grammar School, from whence he went to St John's College, Cambridge. He studied for the Natural Science Tripos, taking Part II in pathology. His medical training was subsequently continued at Manchester, where he qualified in 1939.

Junior appointments were held at his own teaching hospital, the Manchester Royal Infirmary. In 1944 he joined the Royal Air Force, serving as a specialist in neuropsychiatry until 1947; leaving with the rank of wing commander. It was during his medical service in the Forces that he gained much of his experience for his MD thesis on *Nutritional Neuropathy* (Cambridge, 1947). He also changed his main interest from that of forensic psychiatry to neurology, which was to be his future work.

After demobilization, he spent a short period at the National Hospital, Queen Square, London, but, later in 1947, returned to Manchester as lecturer in neurology at the University. In 1950, he was appointed as the first consultant neurologist to the Western Area of the SW Metropolitan Regional Hospital Board; in 1959, this became the Wessex Regional Hospital Board. It was planned to have a neurosurgical service and he laid the foundations of this. Colleagues – medical, surgical, radiological, pathological, physiological – joined him in subsequent years and, in 1965, the Wessex Neurological Centre was opened at the General Hospital, Southampton. The subtle change in title was an indication of the persuasive charm he possessed, and the determination his colleagues had, to build a well co-ordinated and efficient unit.

Stanley Graveson took a major share of the service load in the region. He began by providing, alone, a service to Southampton, Portsmouth, Bournemouth, Winchester, Salisbury and Dorchester. He had an exceptional capacity for work. Short of stature, quiet of manner, he possessed a North Country shrewdness and a great facility for quickly summing up the important points of a clinical problem. His incisive, quick mind was not satisfied with the diagnosis, but also with treatment and future management of the problem.

He was a most loyal colleague, always trying to see the best in people. This enabled him to get many people to work together and reach conclusions more quickly and happily than they would have done without his practical and sound advice. The widespread commitments of his appointment precluded him from attending many committee meetings, but he was the first chairman of the Cogwheel Division of Neurological Sciences in Southampton, where his quiet, calm manner and native common sense were of inestimable value.

He was a member of the committee on neurology of the Royal College of Physicians, and an examiner for the Membership. He was a member of the Association of British Neurologists and of the

Association of Physicians of Great Britain and Ireland. He had served on the council of the section of neurology of the Royal Society of Medicine, and on the council of the Association of British Neurologists, as well as being a member of the medical panel of the Multiple Sclerosis Society.

His work was so absorbing that he had little time for hobbies, but he was well informed about local activities and, on holiday, was a keen walker, enjoying the Lakeland fells and maintaining a particular affection for the North Lancashire valleys.

In 1940, he married Margaret Joyce, daughter of Professor John Waugh Scott. They had three sons, one of whom became a general practitioner. His wife died in 1972, and he was survived by his second wife, Jeanne.

PKR

[*Brit. med. J.*, 1976, **1**, 1223; *Times*, 28 Apr 1976; Photo]

GRAY, Malcolm Kennedy *b.*30 Apr 1898 *d.*30 Mar 1978
MB ChB NZ (1921) MRCP (1924) FRACP (1938) FRCP (1954)

Malcolm Gray was born in Nelson, New Zealand, the son of the Revd. RS Gray, a noted Baptist clergyman, and Mary Alice Gray. He attended several different schools including Otago Boys' High School. After graduating from Otago Medical School he became a resident at the Trentham Army Hospital, and in 1924 went to England for postgraduate training. For a year he worked with Sir James McKenzie at St Andrews University, and this laid the foundation for his future career as a cardiologist. After an appointment at Queen Mary's Hospital at Stratford, he returned to Christchurch Hospital as a junior physician in 1926, and retired 32 years later as director of medical services.

He as an incisive teacher who insisted on punctuality and discipline. For many years he was sub-dean of the branch medical faculty of Otago University, the forerunner of the Christchurch Clinical School. He became a foundation fellow of the Royal Australasian College of Physicians in 1938 and was chairman of the Dominion Committee, but declined higher office. The Cardiac Society of Australia and New Zealand was one of his main professional interests, and he became a life member.

From 1940 to 1944 he served in the Middle East and Italy as officer in charge (major) of the medical division of No 2 New Zealand General Hospital in Cairo, the Western Desert and Italy. He was invited to be an examiner in medicine for the University of Cairo.

Gray was a skilled pianist, having become an associate of Trinity College, London at the age of 18 and gained a gold medal. Sport played an important part in his life. He enjoyed bowls and duck-shooting, and was a low handicap left-handed golfer and a very hard man to beat.

Mac Gray was Christchurch's first cardiologist, and established electrocardiography at Christchurch Hospital. He was a good diagnostician and set high clinical standards. He was proud that Paul Wood was once his resident at Christchurch Hospital, and perhaps some of his forthright and dogmatic teaching style rubbed off on the younger man.

In 1927 he married Constance, daughter of George Fishlock, a guardian of a poorlaw institution, of Woodstock, England. They had a son and two daughters. DRH

[Photo]

GREEN, Francis Henry Knethell *b.*27 Aug 1900 *d.*30 Apr 1977
CBE (1949) MRCS LRCP (1924) MRCP (1925)
MB BS Lond(1926) MD (1928) FRCP (1942)

Frank Green was educated at Highgate School and St Bartholomew's Hospital, London. He was the son of a stockbroker; his maternal grandfather, Henry Hicks MD FRS, was a physician and geologist. It was Frank's own ambition to make a career as a physician. Despite his promising start, the worsening of the asthma, from which he had suffered from childhood, prevented his doing so. Having by this time developed an informed interest in the progress of medical knowledge, and having a natural flair for administration, he therefore elected for a career with the Medical Research Council. Joining its headquarters staff in 1929, he rose progressively until he occupied the third place in its hierarchy. By then his reputation was such that it was taken for granted that when his immediate superior retired he would succeed him as 'chief of staff'. Unfortunately, his ill-health had progressed to the extent that he did not feel able to undertake such a physically demanding post.

It so happened that the Wellcome Trust had just decided to recruit a scientific secretary and its chairman, Sir Henry Dale, having worked with Green, pressed him to come. So he went to this post in 1955. There he remained until 1963 when, his ill health having again overhauled him, he retired. Nevertheless, he did not retire completely. He undertook to act as part-time scientific adviser to the British Heart Foundation and this he did until he finally had to cease work in 1967.

Thus, Frank Green's career spanned the formative years of organization for medical research in this country, and he played a notable part in forwarding this in each of the three posts he held. It was not only that he had an admirable judgment of research in the biomedical field and an encyclopaedic knowledge of those engaged in it, nor even that he had a heartening disregard for administrative punctilio; rather it was that, for him, the research worker always came first. Not that his standards were easy. He had an unerring eye for the meretricious or slipshod, just as he had in the context of his other great interest, modern painting. But he responded with enthusiasm to a well-done piece of research, or a well conceived proposal for further investigation, and he would spare no effort to promote it. It was this that set the tone of all his dealings with research workers. It was no wonder therefore that they gave him, and the institutions he served, their confidence.

Frank Green gave the Bradshaw lecture in 1954. He was survived by his wife, Joyce (née Hinde), whom he married in 1933. HH

[*Brit. med. J.*, 1977, **1**, 1288; *Lancet*, 1977, **1**, 1067: *Times*, 4 May 1977; Photo]

GREENAWAY, *Sir* **Thomas Moore** *b.*1 June 1902 *d.*30 Oct 1980
Kt (1968) MB ChM Sydney (1925) MRCP (1934)
FRACP (1938) FRCP (1951)

Thomas Greenaway was educated at North Sydney Boys High School, Australia, gaining his leaving certificate at the early age of 15, and winning a University exhibition. In 1918 he enlisted in the AIF, when only 16 years old, and reached France before the war ended. On demobilization, he entered the Faculty of Medicine, University of Sydney in 1920, graduating in 1925. From 1925 to 1926 he was resident medical officer at the Royal Prince Alfred Hospital, afterwards entering general practice with CC McDonald at Hurstville, where he remained until 1934. He was appointed clinical assistant in medicine at the Royal Prince Alfred in 1928, and honorary assistant physician in 1929.

'TMG' married Lavinia Figtree, daughter of a local medical practitioner. They had three children; a son, John, now a senior physician at the Royal Prince Alfred Hospital, and two daughters, Judith and Patricia. They were a very happy family, extremely loyal to one another, and held open house for generations of students and residents, whom 'TMG' was always ready to help and advise.

In 1934 he came to London for postgraduate study, obtaining his MRCP in the same year. On his return to Sydney he practised as a consultant physician in Macquarie Street. He retained his appointment at the Royal Prince Alfred, and was also appointed consultant physician to Marrickville, Ryde and St George Hospitals. As a consultant he was much sought after, being regarded by his peers, patients and students as an outstanding clinician and teacher. He was a foundation fellow of the Royal Australasian College of Physicians and helped to shape it.

During the second world war he was selected to remain at the Royal Prince Alfred Hospital, running his own unit, and filling in for some of his colleagues and serving part-time in the Army. After 1946 the department of medicine underwent an active period of development, in the initiation of sub-specialty units and postgraduate activities, and 'TMG' played an important part in this. He was a first class general physician with a special interest in endocrinology. In 1944 he was appointed to the board of censors of the RACP, was censor in chief from 1954 to 1958, a member of council for eight years and president from 1960 to 1962. From 1963 to 1973 he was a member of the Medical Board of NSW, and was appointed honorary fellow of the Royal Australian College of General Practitioners in 1968. He was knighted for his services to medicine and medical education in the same year.

'TMG' was a brilliant, well balanced physician, with enormous clinical expertise, an excellent teacher, lecturer and examiner, and a keen advocate of continuing medical education. Significant features of his personality were courtesy and a keen sense of humour. He was said 'never to have a mean thought in his head'. He was a student of the Bible and Shakespeare and loved to quote passages at appropriate times. At his memorial service in the hospital chapel, Geoffrey McDonald quoted St Paul's words 'Luke, the beloved physician'. They were well applied to Thomas Greenaway. SJMG/GW

[Photo]

GREENE, Charles Raymond *b*.17 Apr 1901 *d*.6 Dec 1982
BA Oxon (1924) MA (1927) MRCS LRCP (1928) BM BCh (1929) MRCP (1943) FRCP (1964)

Raymond Greene was born into a united and talented family. Of his brothers, one was to become the distinguished author Graham Greene and another was to be Sir Hugh Carlton Greene, one time director general of the BBC. Like his brothers, Raymond was educated at Berkhamsted School, where his father was headmaster. He went up to Pembroke College, Oxford, as senior open scholar and Theodore Williams scholar in medicine. From there he went to the Westminster Hospital with a scholarship in anatomy and physiology. He graduated in 1927 and did a number of resident jobs at the Westminster Hospital. He was offered a registrarship in paediatrics but had to refuse this on financial grounds as his father had been forced by illness to retire early. A brief spell with a well organized general practice in Wisbech gave him an enthusiasm for family doctoring and he happily joined Dr Counsell in a large practice in Oxford. Here he loved the social mix of his patients and developed his skills as a very personal doctor. Dr Counsell proved to be a most accommodating senior partner, as he allowed Raymond to continue his career as a mountaineer. Raymond had learnt from his father how to climb in the Lake District and he had spent much of his undergraduate time climbing in the Lakes and the Alps. So it was not surprising that he joined the Himalayan expedition to Mount Kamet in 1931. He proved to be a strong climber and an equable team member. As a doctor he developed an interest in the problems of high altitude and cold. In pursuing this subject he was Schorstein research fellow of Oxford University from 1932 to 1934. The highlight of his career as a climber came with his membership of the 1933 Everest expedition. These experiences led to his training of commandos during the second world war, and his appointment by the Royal College of Surgeons as Hunterian professor in 1943 when he lectured on injury due to cold.

Returning to general practice after the Everest venture, he married Eleanor Craven of the USA and achieved his DM (Oxon) in 1935. His interest in endocrinology gradually grew, at first by working as clinical assistant at the Radcliffe and the endocrine clinic of the Westminster

Hospital. When war came he started his career as a hospital physician, being attached to a sector hospital in Aylesbury and teaching medicine to the students of the Middlesex Hospital. He still found time for personal study and passed the MRCP examination in 1943. At the end of the war he set up practice in Harley Street and became physician to the Metropolitan Hospital. When the National Health Service was inaugurated he had become consulting physician to the Royal Northern Hospital and to the thyroid clinic at New End Hospital, Hampstead. This clinic had been set up by the LCC and developed by Jack Linnell and Sir Geoffrey Keynes.

With the expert surgical help of Jack Piercy, Raymond made New End into a leading centre for the study and treatment of thyroid disease, and then expanded the unit to cover the whole of endocrinology. At the Royal Northern he continued to be a very general physician and was elected FRCP in 1954. Inevitably his practice drew more and more patients with endocrine disorders. Raymond's own contributions to thyroid research were mainly his study of lymphoid changes in the thyrotoxic thyroid and their implication in the development of postoperative myxoedema (this preceded the discovery of auto-immune thyroiditis), and his work on the solitary thyroid nodule for which he was rewarded with a second Hunterian professorship. More important, he attracted a steady flow of overseas experts to New End and a mass of patients with every variety of thyroid disease. He encouraged others' research with steady fund raising and personal support. In due course he was to be chairman of the International Goitre Conference held in London in 1960, and vice-president of the European Thyroid Association, which he did much to form.

Raymond was one of that small band of physicians who made endocrinology a respectable specialty in this country. He was a founder member of the section of endocrinology of the Royal Society of Medicine and later its president. But he was always the patient's doctor rather than the specialist. He looked back at his 'ten years before the mast' in general practice as essential training for a consultant physician and regarded endocrinology as a bastion of general medicine.

By temperament and physique he was an imposing character. His air of succeeding without really trying irritated some, but it belied a rigid discipline of hard work. He endured a most painful treatment of a pharyngeal cancer with stoic courage, only taking pride in the fact that he continued to work throughout that time. He liked doing things himself, a trait well exemplified when appointed personal physician to General de Gaulle on his State visit to this country as president of France. Raymond organized all the medical details of the visit with minimal recourse to the authorities. The award of the Cross of the Legion of Honour he described as 'undeserved and unexpected'.

As befitted the Greene family, Raymond had a great love of the English language, using the spoken and written word with meticulous artistry. He had a long association with Heinemann Medical Books, as a director for 20 years and as chairman for a decade. His autobiographical sketches showed his skill as a raconteur and were aptly titled *Moments of Being*; he really enjoyed being alive. In the Johnsonian sense he was a most clubbable man. His colleagues saw him best when relaxing over a pint at the local pub. He would lead the conversation over a dazzling variety of subjects with a wealth of anecdote and a wit that was polished if sometimes mordant. For those who worked closely with him there will be an abiding memory of unobtrusive support and a quiet steadfast loyalty given without question. Beneath the public man there was the husband and father who rejoiced in family life. He was survived by his wife, one son and one daughter. ASM

[*Brit. med. J.*, 1983, **286**, 69; *Lancet,* 1983, **1**, 136; *Times,* 8 Dec 1982; Memorial Address, All Souls, Langham Place, 2 Feb 1983; Photo]

GRESSON, Christopher *b.*9 July 1917 *d.*8 June 1982
MB ChB Otago NZ (1941) MRCP (1948) FRACP (1961)
FACD (1967) FRCP (1975)

Christopher was born at Christchurch, New Zealand, the son of Maurice James Gresson, a barrister. He was educated at Medbury Preparatory School, Christ's College, and the University of Otago where he graduated in medicine. From 1943 to 1946 he served Christchurch Hospital as house physician, medical registrar and assistant medical superintendent; he was also lecturer in anatomy at the University of Otago Medical School. He was appointed visiting physician to Christchurch Hospital in 1955; visiting physician to Middlesmore Hospital, Auckland in 1969, and visiting dermatologist to Auckland Hospital in 1974.

In 1952 he married June Marie, daughter of Arthur Clifton, a bank official, and there were three daughters of the marriage. He had no special interests outside medicine and his family. GW/VL

[Photo]

GRICE, Kenneth James *b.*23 Mar 1915 *d.*6 Sept 1980
MB BS Melb (1939) MRACP (1943) MD (1946)
MRCP (1946) FRACP (1952) FRCP (1965)

Kenneth James Grice was the son of JH Grice of Brisbane, Queensland. He was educated at Brisbane Grammar School and Melbourne University, obtaining honours in each division of the medical course and being awarded exhibitions in anatomy and in obstetrics and gynaecology. After one year as resident medical officer to the Royal Melbourne Hospital he joined the Australian Army Medical Corps, with which he served in the Middle East and in New Guinea. In 1946 he was appointed as physician to the Royal Melbourne Hospital, and as a Nuffield travelling fellow he proceeded to the United Kingdom to study cardiology at the National Heart Hospital and the London Hospital. On return to Melbourne in 1948 he entered private consulting practice with his major interest in cardiology. In 1960 he toured India as a Colombo Plan fellow to advise on the development of cardiology, and in 1967 he visited Papua New Guinea on behalf of the Australian Government to undertake a survey of cardiac disease. From 1961 to 1970 he was a director of the National Heart Foundation. He served also as a visiting physician to the Heidelberg Veteran's Hospital from 1948 until his death.

Grice was undoubtedly happiest in his role of clinical teacher, especially of undergraduates. His concern for their needs was always apparent, and it was his appointment as dean of the Clinical School at the Royal Melbourne Hospital from 1959 until his retirement for health reasons in 1979 that gave him the greatest satisfaction. For twenty years he was a member of the Faculty of Medicine of Melbourne University and chairman of the Board of Studies of his own clinical school. His influence over years of rapid changes in curriculum content and teaching methods was both wise and far reaching. However, he was always willing to bow to majority decisions and to implement the wishes of his Board of Studies, even if they were not wholly as he had hoped. His counselling of students and young graduates was never done grudgingly, was always compassionate, and never looked for easy ways out of problems if they were not the appropriate ones.

In 1941 he married Dulcie, the daughter of E Olsen of Brisbane. They had one son and one daughter. By nature he was reserved and even shy, and rarely talked about himself. His recreations lay in fly-fishing, music and reading. On all of these matters he was a ready and witty talker, but on his own achievements he was totally reticent.

WMcLR

[Photo]

GROSSMAN, Morton Irvine *b*.4 May 1919 *d*.26 May 1981
BA Ohio (1939) MS Northwestern (1942) PhD (1944) MD (1944) FRCP* (1981)

Morton Grossman was born in Massilon, Ohio, USA, the third and youngest child of Russian immigrants; by the time he was growing up, his father had made a fortune and lost it by unwise investments. Morton's mother profoundly influenced his development; she was a loving but stern and austere perfectionist who drove her children to strive for the highest standards of achievement. At 16, he enrolled in Ohio State University, supporting himself by sparetime jobs. On graduation (1939) he entered the School of Medicine but after two years was advised to transfer to Northwestern University Medical School, Chicago. During his clinical studies there he began research in gastrointestinal physiology with Andrew Ivy, then at the height of his reputation in this field. After army service (1944–1946 and 1951–1955) chiefly in nutritional research, Morton trained in clinical gastroenterology and became chief of gastroenterological services of the Veterans Administration (VA) Centre, Wadsworth Hospital, Los

Angeles. In 1962 he was appointed one of the first senior medical investigators of the VA, a highly prestigious permanent fulltime research appointment, which he held for the rest of his life. In 1965 he was persuaded to combine this with chairmanship of the department of physiology of UCLA, but he relinquished the latter after only four months. From 1974 he was the first director of the Centre for Ulcer Research and Education (CURE) in Los Angeles, a multicentre project funded by the National Institute of Health and private benefactors.

Morton Grossman was universally regarded as one of the outstanding figures of this century in investigative gastroenterology. The broad theme of his research, expressed in hundreds of publications by himself and more than forty pupils from many countries, was the integration of nervous and hormonal influences in the control of the gastrointestinal secretions in health and disease, notably peptic ulcer.

Of prodigious energy, great intelligence and possessing an encyclopaedic memory, his interests were of vast range, not only within the biological and medical sciences, but in literature, art, music and philosophy; he was interested in everything. His day in the laboratory began at 4–5 am and ended at 5–6 pm; he needed only little sleep and his evenings were spent mostly at home in leisure pursuits with his family. Apart from his research, he exerted over many years a unique and worldwide influence on standards of research and teaching in gastroenterology by his writings and eponymous lectures, participation in international meetings (he loved travel) and refereeing of countless papers submitted to gastroenterological journals in the USA and other countries; his editorial association with *Gastroenterology*, the journal of the American Gastroenterological Association (AGA), extended over 21 years. His many honours and awards included presidency of the AGA (1967–1968), honorary membership of the British and Canadian Societies of gastroenterology, membership of the American Academy of Arts and Sciences and of the Association of American Physicians; he received the Anniversary Medal of the Swedish Medical Society (1970), the Friedenwald Medal of the AGA (1978), and posthumously the Beaumont Triennial Prize of the AGA (1981), shared with Sir James Black FRS.

Morton Grossman was a warm, gentle, generous, modest man, fond of laughing at himself; the best things in his life, he thought, were his family and what he had done for the advancement of his subject and his pupils. He bore his terminal illness with exemplary fortitude. He married Dorothy Armstrong in 1957; they had one child, David. Details of his life and work, including part of a taped autobiographical interview, are found in *Gastroenterology* **75**, 1978, and (Memorial Number) **83**(2), 1982.

RAG

GUEST, Isidore Arthur *b*.9 Sept 1911 *d*.3 Aug 1978
MRCS LRCP (1937) MA MB BChir Cantab (1937) MRCP (1940)
MD (1945) FRCP (1970)

He was born in Birmingham, his father Harry Guest being a toy merchant and his mother Rosetta, née Goldberg, daughter also of a toy merchant in Birmingham.

Guest was educated in King Edward's School, Birmingham, which he entered on a foundation scholarship. From there he went to Emmanuel College, Cambridge, where he first studied for the Bachelor of Arts degree by way of the Natural Sciences Tripos. He received his clinical education in Birmingham, from where he qualified MB BChir in 1937. His early postgraduate training was followed by the MRCP in 1940, and in the war he served in the RAMC, where he was a graded specialist with the rank of major.

He was concerned a good deal with maritime troop transport, and conducted research into ways of preventing seasickness. He invented the combined cannula and needle which revolutoinised intravenous treatment. He was modest about it, and though it retained the name Guest cannula, few people seemed to know that it was he to whom medicine owed a great debt for conceiving this simple yet brilliant idea and giving it a practical form. His methodical mind inclined him early on to neurology and he was strengthened in that resolve by a registrarship at the National Hospital, Queen Square. He proceeded MD Cambridge and in 1947 joined the staff at Selly Oak Hospital, Birmingham, at first as a general physician with special interest in neurology. Later he devoted himself entirely to his first love, and while continuing to serve Selly Oak Hospital also did sessional work at the East Birmingham Hospital and the Midland Centre for Neurosurgery and Neurology.

He retired from the NHS in 1977, and in the period before his death he engaged in some locum consultant work.

Guest was a clear lecturer, and to witness a clinical demonstration by him was an experience never to be forgotten. He was a member of the Association of British Neurologists and was elected FRCP in 1970. His outside interests included cybernetics and research into the refinement of colour television, which he took up with great zeal after his retirement. Essentially a reserved man, his integrity and loyalty to the institutions in which he worked were exemplary, and his patients were invariably appreciative of his kindness and gentleness. He married Nancie, née Barnett, in 1950 and there was no issue of the marriage. AMN

[*Brit. med. J.*, 1978, **2**, 904; Photo]

GUTTMANN, *Sir* Ludwig *b*.3 July 1899 *d*.18 Mar 1980
Kt (1966) CBE (1960) OBE (1950) MD Freiburg (1924)
MRCP (1947) FRCS (1961) FRCP (1962) FRS (1976)†

It was thanks to Ludwig Guttmann's drive and personality that the

Spinal Injuries Centre at Stoke Mandeville Hospital developed rapidly. Starting with six beds in a twenty-bedded ward, it expanded over some fifteen years to a hundred and ninety-two beds, with an international reputation second to none. Guttmann saved and made worthwhile the lives of many thousands of severely disabled people all over the world, for he and his staff trained a very large number of colleagues from many countries in the specialized treatment of the paraplegic and tetraplegic patient.

Ludwig was born at Tost in Upper Silesia, Germany, the son of Bernhard Guttmann, a manufacturer, and his wife Dorothy, daughter of Marcus Weissenberg, a farmer. He was educated at the Grammar School in Königshütte and the University of Freiburg, Breslau, obtaining his MD in 1924. His first intention was to be a paediatrician but, by lucky chance, the one solitary job available in this specialty at Freiburg Hospital attracted a large number of applicants. He made a lightning decision and walked upstairs to apply for, and obtain, a junior post in the department of neurology where he worked under the distinguished neurologist, Otfrid Foerster. Foerster was a demanding boss, expecting complete dedication from his colleagues seven days a week, and this training was reflected in the demands and expectations which Ludwig Guttmann always exhibited throughout his working life. From 1928 to 1929 he worked in the department of psychiatry at Hamburg University, and founded the first neurosurgical department in a German mental hospital. He returned to Breslau to be Foerster's chief assistant, also becoming a reader in neurology, but he relinquished the position four years later as a protest against the Nazis. He was then elected reader of the department of neurology and neurosurgery at the Jewish Hospital, Breslau, and by 1937 had become medical director and was responsible for medical and nursing education, as well as being chairman of the Jewish Medical Association.

During the years that followed, he was able to help many people – Jews and Christians – to leave the country. After the 1938 pogroms, in which the Jewish Hospital was involved, and during which the Gestapo arrested many doctors, Guttmann was ordered by the Nazis not to leave Breslau. He left in March 1939.

Before the outbreak of the second world war, he had spent some time in Oxford, working with Trueta, and researching on peripheral nerve lesions under the auspices of the Medical Research Council. Later, he and Whitteridge published an original paper on the pronounced cardiovascular changes in patients with lesions at or above the level of T5 during distension of the urinary bladder. All this was to prove the prelude to his life's work, which began in 1944 when the Government asked him to start the first special centre for spinal injuries at Stoke Mandeville Hospital, on the recommendation of George Riddock, then neurologist to the British Army. Shortly afterwards, paraplegic patients from the D-day landings were admitted, and the National Spinal Injuries Centre was launched. It is as well to remember that all the great advances in this field have been made since the second world war, before which an injury of the spinal cord was virtually a death sentence. Ludwig tackled this unpromising subject and, at first by himself and later with a small but increasing group of colleagues, effected a complete transformation of the dismal scene. The centre at Stoke Mandeville became the Mecca for all those interested. Ludwig Guttmann had the vision to realize that these patients could not only be kept alive but also rehabilitated to earn their own living, fulfil themselves, and not be 'confined to the scrap heap'. In 1948 he founded the Annual Stoke Mandeville Games for the Paralysed, which in 1952 achieved renown as an international sports event for paralysed people. During the Olympic Games in Melbourne in 1956, the Olympic Committee awarded the Fearnley Cup to the organization of the Stoke Mandeville Games. It was the first time this particular Olympic award had come to Britain, and the first time it had been given to a sports organization for the severely disabled. Coincident with the games, a scientific meeting was inaugurated, and from this developed the International Medical Society of Paraplegia, of which Ludwig was the first president and the first recipient of the annual medal. Carried forward by his enthusiasm and dedication, the next logical step was the journal *Paraplegia*, of which he was editor until his death. In 1979, the May edition of this journal was entirely devoted to special papers and appreciations from present and previous colleagues to commemorate his 80th birthday. In this volume are numerous stories of his many kindnesses.

Guttmann was truly indefatigable; his hard work and dedication to Stoke Mandeville did not prevent him from finding time to lecture and advise on the treatment and rehabilitation of paraplegia in over thirty countries. As a result, special centres for the treatment of spinal cord injuries were set up in many of them; the centres in Spain and Germany bear his name, as does a street in Holland. He was appointed OBE in 1950, CBE in 1960 and knighted in 1966. He received numerous decorations and honours from all over the world, and was elected a Fellow of the Royal Society in 1976. After his compulsory retirement from the NHS in 1966, he continued to devote his energies to the service of paraplegic patients, and still worked a sixteen hour day. His research interests continued to the last, and he made some 150 contributions to medical literature.

In 1927 Ludwig Guttmann married Else, daughter of Solly Samuel, and they had a son and a daughter. Throughout his life he was supported by his wife, a woman of considerable personality and a great humanitarian. His son, Dennis, also became a specialist in medicine.

Ludwig Guttmann was a man of dedication of purpose, a tireless searcher after truth, and intolerant of carelessness, inefficiency, or low standards. He was a fighter in any cause in which he believed, and he did not usually lose a fight. At the same time, he had a kind and genial personality, always responding generously to appeals for help or advice. He was also a brilliant neurologist; his policy set the standard by which other methods were judged, and his results were unrivalled. He was an excellent psychiatrist with a profound insight into the effects of disability. Affectionately known as 'Poppa', his opinions were respected and his displeasure feared. It is said that when Sir William Osler was leaving the United States to take up the chair at Oxford, he remarked: 'I have loved no darkness, sophisticated no truth, nursed no delusion, allowed no fear'. These words well describe the life of Ludwig Guttmann. Men of his calibre are rare.

GW/VL

[*Biogr. Mem. roy Soc.*, 1983, **29**, 227-244; *Brit. med. J.*, 1980, **280**, 950, 1021, 1057, 1233; *Lancet,* 1980, **1**, 724-5; *Paraplegia,* May 1979; *Koroth,* June 1980, **7**, 11-12; *Times,* 20 & 29 Mar 1980; Photo]

HADDOW, *Sir* **Alexander** *b.*18 Jan 1907 *d.*21 Jan 1976
Kt (1966) MB ChB Edin (1929) PhD (1937) MD (1937) DSc (1938) FRS (1958) FRSE (1961) FRCP* (1968) Hon Dsc Edin (1968)

Alex Haddow was born at Leven in Fifeshire, but while still an infant his family moved to Broxburn, West Lothian, a shale mining town, where his father, William Haddow, was the landlord of the Green Tree Tavern, and his mother, Margaret Docherty, who had been in domestic service, was the daughter of a coachman.

Young Haddow did well at his local school and the Academy, but his interest in medicine resulted from his admiration for the local practitioner, Alexander Scott (1875 – 1956), an impressive character, who had looked after Alex in two serious illnesses and incidentally had written an excellent report on shale miners' occupational cancer.

Haddow graduated from Edinburgh in 1929 and was house physician to Murray Lyon, but had already determined on a career in cancer research. TJ Mackie was looking for an assistant to work on tumour immunology, so Haddow was appointed as assistant lecturer in bacteriology, also to a Davidson research fellowship, which was followed by a Laura de Saliceto studentship. His first paper (1933) was on the morphology of certain fish neoplasms, followed by work on various experimental neoplasms, but in 1935 he made the significant observation, sometimes known as the 'Haddow phenomenon', that carcinogenic hydrocarbons inhibit the growth of implanted tumours, whereas structurally similar but non-carcinogenic compounds lack this growth inhibiting property. It was clear that Haddow's enthusiasm for experimental oncology could not be satisfied in a department of bacteriology, with a heavy teaching and diagnostic load, so in 1936 he moved to London to the Research Institute of the Royal Cancer Hospital. It was in this Institute that Sir Ernest Kennaway, with his research team, was studying the synthetic and naturally occurring polycyclic hydrocarbons, initially identified as the carcinogenic constituent of tar; but Sir Ernest was struggling against Parkinsonism and his caustic humour and intolerance rendered it an unhappy department, with jealousies and suspicions amongst the staff. It was in this atmosphere that Haddow continued to study the growth inhibiting and other biological effects of carcinogenic agents, chiefly working with his former Scottish colleagues. In 1943, stimulated by Charles

Huggins' work on the hormonal treatment of prostatic cancer, he became interested in cancer chemotherapy, and collaborated with Edith Paterson of Manchester in a study of possible hormonal inhibiting effects on breast cancer and other tumours.

In spite of the tense relationship with the director, Haddow's enthusiasm and idealistic outlook was having an effect on the Institute and when, in 1946, Sir Ernest Kennaway retired, there was general agreement that Alex should become director of the Chester Beatty Institute, as it had become, and he was also appointed professor of experimental pathology in the University of London.

Not only was there a change in atmosphere at the Chester Beatty, but of philosophy; collaboration with other Institutes, even industrial laboratories, was encouraged. It was the work on urethane with Dr Sexton of Imperial Chemical Industries that led to its recognition as a therapeutic agent in leukaemia and myelomatosis, while collaboration with Haddow's own colleagues on 4-amino-stilbene brought about the introduction of the chemotherapeutic agents myeleran, chlorambucil and melphalan.

However, the breadth of the Institute's activities – the research station at Pollard's Wood, the creation of the Institute of Cancer Research, cooperation with the clinical research departments – all meant less and less time for bench work, in spite of the fantastic hours that Haddow worked. So his papers tended to become admirable reviews or critical essays, but Alex was always accessible to every member of the Institute and knew precisely what was going on, their excitements and their worries.

His work was universally recognized - he became FRS in 1958, and received many other honours both at home and abroad. From 1962 until 1966, as president of the International Union against Cancer, he travelled widely, proving an admirable ambassador for the needs and achievements in the cancer campaign. Sir Alexander Haddow – he was knighted in 1966 – did not restrict his endeavours to the world of cancer. He served as chairman, or on the council, of the Society of Visiting Scientists, the Press Council, the Science Consultative Group of the BBC, the Ciba Foundation, and the Association for World Government, from which the Pugwash Movement evolved, but he lost enthusiasm for these two latter bodies as they broke into differing political factions.

Unhappily Sir Alex's intellectual drive was impeded by the physical disabilities of diabetes; rapidly failing sight necessitated his retirement from the directorship in 1969, and he soon became totally blind – the first shock of which he met with astonishing courage, taking the chair at a scientific committee without revealing his sudden, total incapacity. Nevertheless, as was understandable, Haddow became overwhelmed with feelings of bitterness and disappointment, but as the strain and exhaustion of the last few years receded, with the support of his wife Feo, and many blind friends, he regained his equanimity. The Institute had given him the Lodge at his beloved Pollard's Wood, the research station near Chalfont St Giles, and here he continued to write and prepare lectures, which were magnificently delivered. He gave the opening address at the 10th International Cancer Congress at Houston, Texas, before a vast unseen audience; the Karnofsky lecture; the presidential address at the initial meeting of the Oncology section of the Royal Society of Medicine, and for the Sidney Farber award; while *Perspectives in Biology and Medicine* published some remarkable essays written in his last few years, though his unfinished autobiography remains in typescript.

Sir Alex was a complex personality. To his colleagues and staff he was kindly, and generous to a fault, indeed there was some criticism of his laissez-faire attitude for the Institute, though he believed that research workers should find their own pace and their own problems. On the other hand, he was very jealous of his directorial rights and responsibilities, and would brook no interference from outside, whether professional or administrative; over the years there were many personality clashes, but he bore no grudges. In his leisure, when he allowed himself to find it, he was a listener rather than a talker, appreciative of good food and wine and the fine arts, while his opportunity to visit many countries and peoples delighted his natural curiosity.

Sir Alexander Haddow was twice married. In 1932 to Lucia Black of Castle Douglas, a medical practitioner and daughter of a master mariner, and they had one son born in 1937. Lady Haddow died in 1968 when ill-health was overwhelming Alex, but more than a year later he married an old Scottish friend, Feo Standing, a widow with two children, who proved a wonderful companion and support during the years of his ebbing strength. AHTR-S

[*Biogr. Mem. roy. Soc.*, 1977, **23**, 133; *Brit. med. J.*, 1976, **1**, 287, 408, 470; *Lancet*, 1976, **1**, 260; *Nature* (Lond) 1976, **260**, 179; *Times*, 22 Jan 1976; *UICC Bulletin*, 1976, **14**, 6; *Canc. Res.*, 1974, **34**, 3159-3164; Photo]

HALL, Gilbert Steward *b.*-1902 *d.*6 Sept 1976
MB ChB Birm (1926) MRCP (1932) FRCP (1948)

Gilbert Steward Hall was the son of Benjamin Hall, a solicitor in Wolverhampton. He was educated at Wolverhampton Grammar School and the University of Birmingham, from which he graduated in medicine in 1926. After holding junior hospital posts at the General Hospital, Birmingham, he served for three years at the National Hospital for Nervous Diseases, Queen Square, first as a house physician and then as resident medical officer. He became a member of the College in 1932 and then returned to his old hospital in Birmingham as medical registrar and resident medical officer. Greatly influenced by Stanley Barnes, the distinguished Birmingham neurologist, whose personal and professional example he always emulated, he became first assistant to the department of neurology in the Birmingham United Hospitals, consultant neurologist to the Birmingham and Midland Nerve Hospital, the United Birmingham Hospitals and the Royal Institute for the Blind.

Hall was a superb clinical neurologist and a devoted and

conscientious doctor. Naturally he had an enormous practice, but he gave magnificent service to all the hospitals he served, and in addition found time for research; his contributions on tuberose sclerosis, the neurological complications of polyarteritis nodosa and Wilson's disease being particularly valuable. During the 1939–1945 war he served in the RAMC with the rank of lieutenant colonel, being command neurologist to the Southern, Western and Scottish and Northern Ireland Commands and, for a year, adviser in neurology at Allied Force Headquarters in the Central Mediterranean.

Gilbert Hall was a member of the Association of British Neurologists and the Association of Physicians of Great Britain and Ireland, in both of which he was a most popular figure. He made an enormous contribution to British neurology and to the hospitals on whose staff he served. By nature kind, generous and unselfish, everyone and every organization with which he was associated was his debtor, for he was essentially a giver and not a taker. Towards the end of his professional life he had two episodes of cardiac arrest. Providentially the first occurred at a meeting of the West Midlands Physicians Association at Dudley Road Hospital, and the second outside the telephone room at the Queen Elizabeth Hospital, when a very efficient staff nurse was only two paces behind him, and on both occasions he was successfully resuscitated. He liked to say wryly that he had 'gone one better than Lazarus'.

After the second episode he retired prematurely and went to live at Seaford, where he enjoyed ten years of seclusion with his charming wife (also a doctor, née Mary Gould), eventually dying from a stroke at the age of 74. There were four sons and a daughter of the marriage, and one of the sons is a solicitor in the family legal practice at Wolverhampton. Hall was slightly eccentric, old fashioned and forgetful, but a magnificent doctor and colleague, and a lovable man who never had an unkind or disloyal thought, and never did an unkind deed.

AGWW

[*Brit. med. J.*, 1976, **2**, 705, 765; *Lancet*, 1976, **2**, 751; *Bull. Fac. Med. Birm. Univ.*, 1976; Photo]

HALL, Stephen Barton *b.*25 Oct 1899 *d.*11 Oct 1978
MB ChB Liverp (1922) MD (1930) DPM (1931) MRCP (1950)
FRCP (1964) FRCPsych (1971)

Stephen Hall was the only son of Webster Hall, a clergyman whose forbears were tailors and landowners in Great Eccleston in the Fylde, Lancashire, and Clara, only daughter of William Barton of Ambleside in the Lake District, who was connected with buying and selling property and was a great fell walker.

Stephen was born in Liverpool and educated at Liverpool College and the University of Liverpool, where his medical studies were interrupted by military service. As a student he was a champion three miler and an expert oarsman. Qualifying MB ChB in 1922, he pursued postgraduate studies in the psychological aspects of medicine at the

Maudsley and other London hospitals. In 1924 he married Muriel Pickering Jones, who later gained international recognition as a child psychiatrist, and who co-operated with her husband in many of his professional activities.

In 1924 Stephen established the Liverpool Psychiatric Clinic (renamed the Liverpool Psychiatric Day Hospital in 1948) – a pioneering venture of which he was honorary physician (consultant psychiatrist) until his retirement in 1964. In 1929, together the Halls started the Liverpool Child Guidance Clinic, of which Stephen was honorary psychiatrist and director from 1929 to 1932, and Muriel, honorary psychiatrist from 1931 to 1938.

In 1930 he was appointed honorary consultant psychiatrist to the Liverpool Royal Infirmary. He was consultant psychiatrist to the Borough of Birkenhead from 1934 to 1939, and to the North-West Regional War Neurosis Centre (Emergency Medical Service), Aintree and Southport, from 1940 to 1946.

His publications reveal his wide concept of the role psychological medicine should play in the care of patients, and, indeed, in the conduct of society, covering, as they do, psychological aspects of organic disease, of disorders of speech and the special senses, of physiological processes such as adolescence, of social adjustment, and of air raids and of the re-armament programme. It was on the basis of his publications, particularly his book *Psychological Aspects of Clinical Medicine* (1949), that he was elected a member of the College.

In the University of Liverpool he was appointed lecturer in psychological medicine in 1944; and in 1952 a department of psychological medicine was established, with Stephen its first director of studies. He was devoted to his department, which grew steadily during the twelve years of his direction. He aimed to 'approach psychological medicine as an integral part of general medicine rather than a special or separate subject', as he states in the introduction to his book, and to that end he sought to establish links with other departments in the Faculty of Medicine. The link with the department of child health was especially fruitful. His wife, Muriel, consultant psychiatrist to the Royal Liverpool Children's Hospital since 1947, was appointed lecturer, part-time, in his department in 1955 and, following her untimely death only nine months later, Stephen arranged that her successor should also be a child psychiatrist, with duties in the children's hospitals and University department of child health as well as his own department – a highly satisfactory arrangement and one of the first of its kind in this country. He was also quick to realize the contribution his discipline might make to the study and teaching of normal psychology, especially to psychologists in clinical practice. The appointment of a senior lecturer in clinical psychology in his department, and the provision of a course in clinical psychology for psychologists, the first in this country, soon necessitated the establishment of a sub-department of clinical psychology within the department of psychological medicine. Stephen was always concerned that a Chair should be established for his successor, and on his retirement in 1964 that hope was realized.

Following retirement, he taught in his former department, was for many years a member of the University Court, and in 1972, as youthful and energetic as ever, undertook a lecture tour of the United States and Canada, visiting several centres where former students of his were working. In March 1977 he went to live in Aynhoe in Oxfordshire.

As a clinician, Stephen was methodical and sincere, and capable of a degree of detachment which greatly enhanced the value of his clinical judgement. He was a quiet, retiring man whom few knew well, but in conversation and committee he was a good listener, considerate and modest - attributes which, together with his quiet sense of humour, contributed greatly to his friendly and fruitful co-operation with colleagues.

He had many interests, including fast cars and ice skating, and he shared with his wife a love of the countryside, bird-watching, and landscape and rock gardening. Nevertheless, they both accepted hotel life for many years for the sake of their work, and it was sad that Muriel's rapidly fatal illness supervened within a year of their building a house with a garden in Mollington, near Chester. They had no children.

JDH

[Photo]

HALLPIKE, Charles Skinner *b.*19 July 1900 *d.*26 Sept 1979
CBE (1958) MRCS LRCP (1924) MB BS Lond (1926)
MRCP(1926) FRCS (1931) FRCP (1945) FRS (1956)

Charles Skinner Hallpike was born in Muree, in what is now Pakistan, about 30 km north east of the present capital, Islamabad. He was a descendant of Lieutenant Colonel James Skinner CB, whose remarkable exploits with his irregular cavalry 'Skinner's Horse' (which became the First Bengal Cavalry) facilitated the British conquest of India at the end of the 18th and beginning of the 19th century.

Hallpike was the son of Frank Robert Hallpike and Rosamund Helen Skinner. When he was three years of age, his family came to London. Thereafter followed a misfortune that affected the whole of his life. He developed Perthes disease. This was so severe that his school life was gravely interrupted by periods of recumbancy. Nevertheless, he became a classical scholar at St Paul's School. He entered Guy's Hospital with an entrance scholarship in Arts, became Beaney Prizeman in pathology and qualified in 1924.

Resident appointments in ENT were held, first at Guy's Hospital, where he was house surgeon in the aural department, and then at Cheltenham General Hospital. In 1929 he was appointed Bernhard Baron research fellow at the Ferens Institute of Otology, Middlesex Hospital, London. The following year he was awarded the Duveen travelling studentship of the University of London. In 1931, he became a Rockefeller travelling fellow, and in 1934 he was Foulerton research fellow of the Royal Society. In 1940, Hallpike left the Ferens Institute to take up an appointment as director of the Medical

Research Council's Otological Research Unit, and as assistant aural surgeon at the National Hospital for Nervous Diseases. This hospital redesignated him aural physician in 1944. From 1948 to 1952 he was ENT consultant to University College Hospital. On his retirement he returned to the Ferens Institute to become director of research and stayed there until 1968.

Debarred from active service in the Armed Forces because of his physical disability, Hallpike was able to place his immense knowledge and expertise at the service of the Air Ministry, being a member of the Flying Personnel Research Committee from 1938 to 1955. His almost unique knowledge of ear function in health and disease played a major role in overcoming the otological problems associated with the rapid development of military aviation.

Above all, Hallpike was a perfectionist and a man of the highest integrity, who could not suffer fools. Nevertheless, he did not fail to give credit where credit was due and with his wisdom, shrewd judgment and single-mindedness of purpose, he inspired that combination of dedication and loyalty which characterized his successful research team.

Charles Hallpike published 241 papers. The most important of these were on such subjects as Ménière's disease, vestibular function, optokinetic and caloric nystagmus, and inner ear degeneration.

Hallpike had a good knowledge of precision engineering and was an ingenious designer of equipment. Much of the equipment in his laboratory had been built to his designs. This included apparatus for sectioning the temporal bone, a rotating chair for testing vestibular function and a monocular ear microscope. The latter was adopted by poultry farmers for sexing day-old chicks.

A number of honours were bestowed on him as a result of his and his team's work. He twice received the Gamble Prize of the Royal Society of Medicine (in 1938 and 1947); the William J Muckle fellowship of the University of London in 1941; the Dalby prize of the Royal Society of Medicine in 1943; the Hughlings Jackson lectureship and medal of the Royal Society of Medicine in 1947; the Shambaugh prize of the Collegium Otorhinolaryngologicum Amicitiae Sacrum in 1955; the Bárány medal of the University of Uppsala in 1958, and the Guyot medal of the University of Groningen in 1959.

In 1960, Hallpike became the joint founder of the Bárány Society, 'an International Society devoted to developing and propogating knowledge of disorders of vestibular and associated functions'. He was also elected an honorary fellow of the Royal Academy of Medicine in Ireland.

The orthopaedic disability which hampered him in so many ways could not deter him from competitive sport. In his younger days he was an excellent billiards player, and he captained the Public Schools Veteran Shooting Team at Bisley. He played the violin, taught himself the piano, and was fond of classical music.

In 1968 he retired to West Moors, Dorset, where he still continued to win prizes – for growing roses. He also continued to take an interest in neuro-otology. He was a member of the organizing committee for the 1977 meeting (in London) of the Bárány Society, which was perhaps the last scientific meeting at which he gave an address. He died in the South Western Hospital, Southampton.

In July 1935, Charles Hallpike married Barbara Lee Anderson, who survived him. There were three children: two sons and one daughter. The elder son, Jeremy, born in 1936, also read medicine and belongs to this College; he became a consultant neurologist in Adelaide, South Australia. The younger son, Timothy, born in 1946, is an officer in the Royal Navy. The daughter, Janet, took an honours degree in English and Theology at Girton College, Cambridge, but died in 1966.

RH(3)

[*Brit. med. J.*, 1979, **2**, 1444; *Lancet*, 1979, **2**, 805; *Times*, 19 Nov 1979; *Daily Telegraph*, 27 Sept 1979; Photo]

HAMILTON, Charles Keith Johnstone *b.*17 Apr 1890 *d.*5 July 1978

MC (1916) BA Oxon (1913) MRCS LRCP (1920)
BM BCh (1920) MRCP (1923) FRCP (1933)

Keith Hamilton was born at Laura, South Australia, the son of Charles Wolf Hamilton, medical practitioner, and his wife Sarah Henrietta, daughter of Alexander George Patton, also a medical practitioner. He was educated at Queen's School, Adelaide, and Lincoln College, Oxford, where he took an honours degree in Natural Sciences. He then went to St Thomas's Hospital, London, for his clinical studies.

On the outbreak of the 1914–1918 war he joined King Edward's Horse as a trooper, later getting a commission in the Royal Field Artillery. After being awarded the MC he was severely wounded, needing two laminectomy operations, and thereafter was forced to walk with the aid of two sticks.

He returned to St Thomas's Hospital, qualifying in 1920, under very great physical handicap, and was then casualty officer and resident anaesthetist, house physician, and house physician to the children's department; all at St Thomas's Hospital. From 1923 he was house physician to the Hospital for Sick Children, Great Ormond Street. He was John Temple research fellow at St Thomas's, and published articles on *Principles of infant nutrition* (with KH Tallerman) and *Heart disease in Childhood* (with HB Russell). In 1925 he was appointed assistant physician to the Infants Hospital, Vincent Square, Westminster, and in 1927 physician to the children's department at Charing Cross Hospital, and consultant paediatrician to the LCC.

Keith Hamilton was a man of medium height with black hair and dark, sunken eyes. His most obvious characteristics were his reticence and modesty. He rarely spoke at committees. He was vice-dean of Charing Cross Hospital for some years, and it was in personal relationships with students and junior members of staff where he was most helpful.

When the 1939–1945 war broke out he insisted on being physician to Charing Cross Hospital itself, when it had a small staff in central London, most members of the staff being distributed around the Charing Cross sector. He and his wife lived at the hospital throughout the war including, of course, the period of heavy bombing. Those at the hospital will remember him walking quietly through the wards, a source of inspiration and courage to patients and staff.

Soon after the end of the war, Keith Hamilton resigned, was appointed honorary consulting physician to the children's department, and went to live in Somerset on the edge of Exmoor. He gradually improved in strength, was able to take up riding again and even hunted. Hamilton was always a keen and expert horseman. When in the Royal Field Artillery he took great pride in training his men and horses and got together a famous team known as the Galloping Blacks. It was after an inspection of the Galloping Blacks that King George V sustained a bad fall from his horse, which resulted in some injuries, causing great anxiety at the time. Hamilton used to ride through the moor to reach a car which would take him to Taunton, where he had started a fine children's department in the Taunton and West Somerset Hospital. After the death of his wife in 1959, marking the end of a very happy marriage, he continued to live on his farm on Exmoor, looked after by a faithful man and wife.

An appreciation of Hamilton and his work in the Charing Cross Gazette, when he retired, ended with the words 'He spoke little, but wrought mightily'. **RAH(2)**

[*Times*, 8 July 1978; *Brit. med. J.*, 1978, **2**, 507; *Charing X Hosp. Gaz.*, Winter 1969/70, 67 (2); Photo]

HARE, Patrick James *b.*18 Jan 1920 *d.*5 Apr 1982
MB BS Lond (1944) MD Johns Hopkins (1944) MRCP (1949)
MD (1954) FRCP (1964) FRCPE (1970)

Patrick Hare was born in Dunfermline, the son of John Henry Hare, owner-actor manager of the local theatre, and Isabella (McIntyre) Hare. He spent his early schooldays at Malcolm Canmore School, ending them at Westminster City School, London. His medical education was undertaken during the war years at University College, London, where he was Andrews scholar, and at University College Hospital Medical School. He spent his final undergraduate year as a Rockefeller student fellow at Baltimore, USA, and obtained dual medical qualifications at Johns Hopkins and the University of London.

After qualifying he joined the RAMC, serving as a graded dermatologist in Burma and Singapore between 1945 and 1948. Although the antithesis of the traditional army man, he counted his service time as good experience and seldom mentioned its gruesome aspects. On his return to London in 1948 he became registrar in the skin department at University College Hospital under WN Goldsmith, and it was here that W Freudenthal fostered what was to become a lifelong interest in histopathology of the skin. During this period he also acted a a clinical assistant at St John's Hospital for Diseases of the Skin. In 1951 he was awarded a London University postgraduate travelling fellowship and worked in Paris under Tzanck and Rivalier, and in Zürich under Miescher. He was appointed consultant dermatologist at University College Hospital in 1952, took charge of the department in 1959, and in the same year was appointed to the staff of the Whittington Hospital. In 1966 he was exchange professor in the department of medicine at McGill University, Montreal. He was appointed to the Grant chair of dermatology in Edinburgh in 1968, and retired in 1980, when the title of emeritus professor was conferred on him.

From 1958 to 1968 he was editor of the *British Journal of Dermatology*, a real one-man show in those days. It was sometimes hard to persuade dermatologists to write articles for his journal and then he often had to rewrite and proof read them. However, there is no doubt that, during this period, the journal grew in stature as a result of his tact and editorial skills. He was chairman of the specialist advisory committee on dermatology of the Joint Committee for Higher Medical Training from 1974 to 1978, and was president of the section of dermatology of the Royal Society of Medicine in 1978.

Paddy Hare's research interests included comparative pathology, embryology and the history of medicine. He presented papers mainly on clinical or histological themes and wrote two books *The Skin* and *Basic Dermatology*. He was not a laboratory man and indeed had sometimes to be coaxed into a lab to see the merits of the latest acquisition. Nevertheless, realizing the importance of basic dermatological research, he encouraged others to develop electron microscopy, tissue culture and immunological methods in his department. His interest in comparative dermatology led to the formation of the Skin Biology Club, of which he was a founder member and a most distinguished and popular president from 1969 to 1979.

Paddy was an avid reader and could always be called upon as a reliable reference source. He was also invaluable as a translator who spoke German, French and Italian. His love of books extended beyond dermatology and medicine and he was a much respected and effective convenor of the central medical library committee of Edinburgh University from 1972 to 1980. He played a major part in the planning of the new Erskine medical library at Edinburgh, which was opened shortly after his retiral.

Paddy hated missing a single clinic and seldom sacrificed one for committee work. He was at his best teaching informally in the clinic, or at the other end of a double-headed microscope. He rarely repeated himself, and as he spoke quietly and to the point he had to be listened to with care. He disliked pomp in any guise, and cant. He had little time for formal lectures and made no secret of this, showing a puckish response to concern that his own lectures sometimes received a moderate rating from students. Colleagues soon came to admire his great erudition and ability to focus quickly on the relevant points at issue. His case notes were succinct, and he was amused when told by one doctor that the longest part of a letter from him was sometimes the patient' address.

Although dogged by angina for a number of years before his early retiral, Paddy was devoted to his patients and his department. He took a close interest in the welfare of the staff and was justifiably proud of keeping his door always open for colleagues in difficulty. He was delighted to be able to act as a clinical assistant at a weekly dermatological clinic when he retired to live in Bath in 1980, and worked until a few weeks before his death.

Paddy had a wonderful family life. His marriage to Mary Bridges shone with happiness. She knew that Paddy's life was his work and she supported him and encouraged him in all that he did, even though she knew he was often pushing himself beyond his physical reserves. The Hare home was a very happy and welcoming place and no one joined the department without experiencing the warmth of their hospitality at an early stage. Paddy and Mary shared many interests including their enjoyment of gardening and wild flowers. There were two sons; John, a medical physicist in London, and Kenneth, a general practitioner in Edinburgh. JAAH

[*Brit. med. J.*, 1982, **284**, 1482; *Lancet*, 1982, **2**, 1136; *Brit. J. Derm.*, 1982, **107**, 719; Photo]

HARRIES, John Thomas *b*.24 June 1934 *d*.27 Mar 1983
MB BS Lond (1958) MRCP (1965) MD (1971) MSc Bioch (1972) FRCP (1978)

John Harries was born in Llanelli, Wales, the son of William John, a farmer, and was buried 48 years later in the cemetery overlooking the farm where he had spent his childhood. He was deeply proud of his Welsh ancestry and spoke Welsh fluently. He gained a choral scholarship to the Cathedral Choir School in Hereford and though over the years his singing voice lost is melodious quality, he always enjoyed singing, particularly after a good dinner with his friends. He was deeply moved by choral singing, particularly of a Welsh choir.

As a medical student at King's College Hospital Medical School he was better known for his colourful pranks than for his academic achievements. During a period in the Navy on short service commission he visited countries in the Middle and Near East, and gained a deep understanding of, and affection for, Arab cultures. This was to help him greatly during the last few years of his life when he forged links between the Ministry of Health in Oman and the Institute of Child Health and Great Ormond Street Hospital, with the aim of strengthening the health services for children in that country.

John Harries was a great sportsman. He represented Llanelli and Wasps rugby football clubs and the Navy at rugby and cricket. His enthusiasm for rugby continued and his association with Llanelli and Wasps remained close. He knew what loyalty to a team means, and later in his professional and academic life he felt the same unwavering loyalty to the institutions he served, and to the team of which he was to become a leader. Young research fellows working with him knew that he was always ready to spend time with them, discussing their work. They learnt more from him than just science, becoming life-long friends.

His interest in paediatric gastroenterology was kindled during his early appointments at Great Ormond Street, where he served as house physician to Sir Wilfred Sheldon (*q.v.*) in 1966. With the exception of a period spent as research fellow at St Bartholomew's Hospital, in order to learn techniques used in the investigation of adults with gastrointestinal disorders, he worked at the Institute of Child Health for the rest of his life. Though fascinated by the study of the physiology and pathology of the gastrointestinal tract in infancy and childhood, he was aware of the need to maintain close links with 'adult' colleagues. He became a member of the British Society of Gastroenterology and served on the editorial board of *Gut*.

In his researches, John Harries contributed to many aspects of paediatric gastroenterology. He edited *Essentials of Paediatric Gastroenterology* and at the time of his death was preparing the second edition. His greatest interest lay in the application of modern biochemical methods to the investigation of patients, and to the elucidation of problems in the physiology and pathology of gastrointestinal function. He recognized the questions which, with the use of sophisticated techniques, were ready for answers. If a particular technique was not available in his laboratory he or one of his colleagues would visit a laboratory at home or abroad to learn it. Thus sprang up an international network of friends engaged in gastrointestinal research. Because he had so many friends abroad his membership of the European Society for Paediatric Gastroenterology and Nutrition meant much to him, and during the last few years of his life he was a greatly valued member of the council of that Society. He was aware of the need for close cooperation with biochemists and for medical scientists working in paediatric gastroenterology to acquire more than superficial knowledge of biochemical principles and techniques. In his own training he took an MSc in biochemistry, and encouraged his younger co-workers to do the same. His pride, when they succeeded in the examination, was great. If one wanted to single out a particular area of research where he excelled it would be the inborn errors of metabolism of intestinal absorption and secretion. He knew that detailed investigation of these rare conditions would throw new light on the physiology of the gut. He had the original mind that allowed him to make the very best use of the partnership of Great Ormond Street, with its unique clinical opportunities, and the research laboratories in the Institute of Child Health. He edited a monograph in the series *Clinics in Gastroenterology* entitled 'Familial Inherited Abnormalities', a volume which serves as an apt memorial of his great contributions in this field.

John did not find the proliferation of committees, so much part of today's medical scene, to his liking and avoided them whenever possible. When he felt it necessary to attend, in order to persuade his colleagues of the need for a certain development, he was not at his best and would present a rather sullen mien, an unbending stance, and often an air of intense boredom. He preferred his research and clinical work and discussions with his friends in the local pub over a pint. He was an individualist with strongly felt loyalties and profound sympathy for those in trouble, whether patients, their parents or friends, but one had to know John well to become fully aware of his deep compassion. OHW

[*Brit. med. J.*, 1983, **286**, 1292 & 1452; *Lancet*, 1983, **1**, 1116; *Times*, 16 Apr 1983]

HARRIS, Kenneth Edwin *b*.3 May 1900 *d*.23 Oct 1981
BA Cantab (1921) MRCS LRCP (1924) BChir MA (1925)
MRCP (1926) MD (1929) FRCP (1934)

Kenneth Harris was born in Manchester where his father Thomas Harris MD FRCP, who died age 46, was a consultant physician at the Royal Infirmary. Through his mother, Isabel Maud Brockbank, he was related to two Fellows, namely his uncle Edward M Brockbank and his cousin William Brockbank.

Education at Shrewsbury led on to Gonville and Caius College, Cambridge, and University College Hospital Medical School, where he gained two prizes and two medals. After house appointments to TR Elliott and CC Choyce (1924–1925), he became assistant to the Medical Unit 1926–1929, and then medical registrar to UCH from 1929–1932, being also clinical assistant to TF Cotton at the National Heart Hospital. He did research under Sir Thomas Lewis and jointly published 13 papers, chiefly on vascular responses of the skin. He married a fellow student, Edith Abbott, in 1932; they had no children. Also in 1932 he was appointed physician at UCH and he became senior physician at the age of 39, a post he held for 26 years. An appointment to the Royal Chest Hospital lasted from 1933 to 1945. His papers on heart disease included an important contribution on 'Heart Disease in Pregnancy'.

His clinical work was in general medicine, with a special interest in cardiology, and he conscientiously looked after a large in and out patient practice at UCH, where he was especially noted for his excellent vocational teaching. His ward visits were always crowded, and students had to enter their names on a waiting list in order to take cases on them. He did much work as an undergraduate examiner in London, Bristol and Cambridge and to the Society of Apothecaries, and his involvement with the MRCP led to his election as a Censor in 1950 and Senior Censor in 1953. He was much in favour of there being an Academy of Medicine in London, and was disappointed when others in the College aborted what he thought was a unifying concept. He developed a special interest in therapeutics and successfully campaigned for the retention of heroin in the pharmacopoeia, at a time when there was strong pressure to ban it from clinical practice because of the growing drug addiction problem.

He founded the Physician's Dining Club at UCH, which was

valuable in bringing together the academic and the hospital staff, and presided over it for several years. He and his wife had a great interest in the welfare of the students and junior staff, and their hospitality was generous. In spite of this he was not really close to either staff or students, due partly to lack of a sense of humour, and his colleagues often referred to him as the headmaster.

He had a large private practice and when he had patients in the UCH Private Wing, he meticulously paid his juniors for any services they rendered there. He and his wife died within one week of each other and they left £500,000 in their will, half of which went to the North London Collegiate School. AH

[*Brit. med. J.*, 1982, **284**, 754; Photo]

HARRIS, Ruth Freda *b.*27 May 1926 *d.*26 Mar 1980
MRCS LRCP (1950) MB BS Lond (1950) DCH (1952) MD (1977) MRCP (1977)

Shortly before she died Ruth Harris's name had been included in the recommendations of Council to Comitia for election to Fellowship. She was born at Stoke Newington, London, where her father Judah Harris was a shoe factor; her mother, Annie, was the daughter of Soloman Swerdloff, a cabinet maker.

She was educated at the Parliament Hill Grammar School and the Royal Free Hospital Medical School, where she received several undergraduate awards, qualifying in 1950. Her first post was that of obstetric house surgeon at the Royal Free Hospital, and thereafter she held four resident posts in paediatrics – mainly in London hospitals. For the next two years she was a research assistant in the chemical pathology department at the Hospital for Sick Children, Great Ormond Street, where, under the guidance of WW Payne (*q.v.*), she studied the metabolic effects of treating fibrocystic disease with pancreatin, and laboratory guides to the prognosis of acute nephritis.

The foundation of her life's work in electroencephalography was laid in the neonatal department of the Institute of Child Health at Hammersmith Hospital where, following a course of instruction at Queen Square, she worked from 1956 until 1960. She was the first British physician to study the EEG in healthy and sick newborn babies. In that research she displayed the technical expertness, the keen powers of observation and the scrupulously accurate reporting which characterized all her future work in electroencephalography – a subject that has not lacked its over-imaginative exponents.

From 1960 to 1967 she underwent her apprenticeship proper in electroneurophysiology under the guidance of G Pampiglione, as senior registrar at Great Ormond Street and for a further year at the National Hospital, Queen Square. In 1968 she was appointed consultant neurophysiologist to the Bethlem Royal Hospital and the Maudsley Hospital, and (from 1973) to the Queen Mary's Hospital for Children, Carshalton. In both hospitals she enthusiastically developed the clinical neurophysiology departments, greatly increasing their versatility and usefulness. She still held these appointments at the time of her death, when she had built up a solid reputation as one of the very few experts in this country on the electroencephalogram in infancy, childhood and adolescence. At the Maudsley Hospital she was reponsible for all the electromyography and peripheral neurophysiological work in adults as well as in children.

Ruth Harris published, alone or in collaboration, upwards of forty papers and chapters in books covering many aspects of the electroneurophysiology of infancy and childhood. It would be untrue to say that most of her work displayed great originality; instead it was painstaking, thorough and above all accurate; work that had to be done and was done supremely well. She wrote extensively on the EEG in mental retardation, degenerative disease of the CNS and psychosis in children, showing in the latter that the EEG might sometimes reveal unsuspected epileptic phenomena, and that these children improved with appropriate anticonvulsant therapy. The subject of the thesis for which she was awarded the London MD in 1977 was that of the EEG in children with infantile spasms treated with ACTH. In the same year she was elected MRCP under Bye-law 117.

She wrote a number of thoughtful and admirably critical review articles. She was a frequent contributor at meetings of the EEG Society and was well known and respected internationally.

In 1952 she married Sidney Ernest French who for many years was Secretary of the Surrey Branch of the Communist Party of Great Britain until, a few years before his death in 1979, he resigned to form the New Communist Party, the philosophy of which was to the left of the parent body. Husband and wife were a devoted couple and Ruth Harris, whose father was also a communist, shared the ideals that informed their political views. However, she had taken no active part in politics for many years. They had one daughter and one son.

Although most of Ruth Harris's working life had been devoted to electroneurophysiology, she had all the qualities of a first-rate clinician – a profound knowledge of clinical paediatrics, astute judgement and splendid common sense. As a young woman she displayed admirable presence of mind in the case of Sisera's syndrome when acting as doctor to a boys' summer camp. The victim had fallen on the sharp end of a large metal tent peg and driven it into his skull up to the hilt. The case was thus named and successfully treated by Antony Jefferson, neurosurgeon in Sheffield.

Ruth Harris was the anonymous author of an article entitled 'On Having Cancer' (*Lancet*, March 1st, 1979, pp.715-716). This is worthwhile reading both as an account of the horrors – and the at least temporary efficacy – of chemotherapy for disseminated malignant disease, and also because it conveys a flavour of the woman herself – her courage, her modesty, her honesty, her consideration for the feelings of others and her robust sense of humour.

PT/AAJ

[FRCP nomination withdrawn at her death, but included in Munk's *Roll* by consent of the College Officers.] [Photo]

HARTFALL, Stanley Jack *b.*27 Feb 1899 *d.*31 Dec 1982
TD BSc Leeds (1923) MB ChB (1926) MRCP (1930) MD (1931)
FRCP (1940)

Stanley Jack Hartfall was born in Salisbury, Wiltshire. In the days before the 1914–1918 war a good education was not easily come by; he was educated at a Church School in Salisbury but always said that his real education began when he joined the army, at the age of 17, during the first world war. He trained as a cavalryman, but later became a gunner in the field artillery. After falling a victim to gas warfare and sustaining scalp wounds, he was posted back to England from the battle front, largely on account of his youth. On demobilization he embarked on a course of intensive study which resulted in his matriculation and, in 1920, he became a student at the University of Leeds, where he graduated BSc in 1923. His intention was to become an analytical chemist, but his main interest was in biochemistry and this eventually led to medicine. He obtained his MB ChB in 1926. His first years in medicine were spent as house surgeon to JF Dobson, and as house physician to Maxwell Telling. He also became a keen disciple of Maxwell Stewart. He was later appointed RMO, medical tutor, and registrar (the only one in those days), and shortly after 1931 he left Leeds to take a post as medical assistant to Sir Arthur Hurst and LJ Witts at Guy's Hospital, London. Between the two world wars he served as medical officer to the Yorkshire Hussars, and studied in Berlin and Copenhagen on travelling fellowships, working with von Bergman, Morowitz and Meulengracht.

At the outbreak of the second world war he was called up for service and posted as lieutenant colonel in charge of the medical division of a general hospital, formed almost entirely from medical personnel and staff of Leeds Infirmary and local general practitioners. The hospital was evacuated just before Dunkirk, and Hartfall was transferred to Malta where he established a third general hospital on the island.

Hartfall's main clinical interests were haematology and gastrointestinal disease. In 1935 he was appointed professor of therapeutics in the University of Leeds, a post he held until after the war, when he was transferred to the chair of clinical medicine. He became chairman of the medical faculty in 1961, retiring in 1964. In his later years he specialized in rheumatology, and he published papers on anaemias, blood and gastrointestinal diseases, arthritis and rheumatism. He was honorary physician and consulting physician to the General Infirmary at Leeds, Leeds Regional Hospital Board, and Harrogate Royal Bath Hospital.

In 1931 he married Muriel Hunter, a nursing sister at Leeds General Infirmary, and they had a son and a daughter. The son, William Guy, became a surgeon at Guy's; sadly, the daughter died while still in her twenties. They also had an adopted son. Outside medicine Hartfall's major preoccupation was his family, and he was a superb host, although he was greatly incapacitated by increasing blindness in later years. Their house at Bramhope was surrounded by a beautiful garden and he was extremely proud of the profusion of rhododendrons, though he confessed that he was not 'green-fingered'. He had a life-long interest in sport and at one time was captain of the Medical School cricket team. Strangely, although he was a member of his local golf club he never played. When asked about his game he replied that on a voyage to Malta during the war the ship had been torpedoed and, although passengers and crew were saved, his golf clubs had not survived. He never replaced them. GW/VL

[Univ. of Leeds Medical Magazine, **4**, 9-11, 17; Photo]

HARTSTON, William *b*.26 Nov 1904 *d*.7 July 1980
MRCS LRCP (1926) MB BS Lond (1926) MD (1928) MRCP (1929) DPH (1933) DTM&H (1946) FRCP (1969)

William Hartston was born in London, the son of Lewis Hartston, a timber merchant. He was educated at Parmiters School and the University of London, where he studied medicine at the London Hospital, qualifying with the Conjoint in 1926, and soon after graduating MB BS with honours and a distinction in medicine. During the next five years he held a series of junior positions at the London, as house physician, house surgeon, house physician to the skin department and then as clinical pathologist. A period of further clinical experience followed as resident medical officer at the Mile End Hospital and at the Queen's Hospital for Children, and as medical registrar at St John's Hospital for Diseases of the Skin. During this time, be obtained the MD in 1928 and the MRCP in the following year. His interest then turned towards preventive and social medicine; after obtaining the DPH in 1933 he held the posts of assistant MOH in the Rhondda, and later at Scunthorpe, where he developed his enthusiasm for diseases of the chest and tuberculosis.

In the second world war he served five years in the RAMC, first as a deputy director of hygiene and later as principal medical officer to GHQ Middle East Command, with the rank of lieutenant colonel. Following demobilization, he obtained the DTM&H in 1946 and continued his career in the field of public health, first as MOH in Cambridge, and in 1947 as deputy MOH to the Middlesex County Council. Finally, in 1950, he was appointed principal medical officer to the London County Council (later the Greater London Council) and he remained in this post until his retirement.

It was at the LCC that he was able to pursue his special interest in the control of tuberculosis which, in the post-war years, was prevalent and posed a problem to the public health. He was successful in creating a comprehensive tuberculosis service and, before the general introduction of anti-tuberculosis drugs, he was involved in a major programme of BCG vaccination of London schoolchildren and young persons. For many years he held the post of clinical assistant (research) in the chest department of St Thomas's Hospital, where his earlier experience of the pathology of skin disease (in particular, the micro-circulation of the skin), combined with his interest in tuberculosis, enabled him to pursue his researches into tuberculin, BCG as well as the Kveim test in sarcoidosis. For many years he contributed an update on diseases of the chest and tuberculosis to the *British Encyclopaedia of Medical Practice*. He was especially fond of his association with the Acid Fast Club and the British Microcirculation Society. In 1964, the MRC awarded him a Dorothy Temple Cross research fellowship, and he went to Nigeria to study leprosy. After his retirement from the GLC in 1969, he did not give up work, but was consultant physician to the Boroughs of Camden and Islington, and he continued his clinical attachments at St Thomas's chest department and the London Hospital skin department.

Bill's medical achievement was, however, merely one aspect of his much wider interest in social welfare. His great passion, especially in his later years, was for medical history in its relation to social history; in particular the history of the Poor Law, the London dispensaries and the life of James Parkinson. He was a popular lecturer at the diploma course in the history of medicine at the Society of Apothecaries, as well as a leading light in the history of medicine section of the Royal Society of Medicine, where he had a successful term of office as president.

Bill was a well-rounded personality, with both the scientific and artistic sides of his nature displaying themselves harmoniously. He was no mean oil painter, enjoyed pottery and prided himself on his culinary skills.

Usually genial, but occasionally a little abrasive, there was always an underlying genuine kindness. His first marriage to Marjorie White in 1932, ended in 1945. He then married Mary Roland and they had one daughter and one son, the latter (also a William Hartston) being a famous chess player.
AS

[*J. roy. Soc. Med.*, 1980, **73**, 694; Photo]

HASLETT, Thomas Bones Hamilton *b*.8 Mar 1907 *d*.27 Jan 1980
MB BCh BAO Belf (1929) BSc (1933) MD (1933) DPH (1934) MRCP (1938) FRCP (1966)

Ham Haslett was born in Larne, Northern Ireland, the son of JA Haslett, linen factory manager, and Alice Hamilton, the daughter of the Town Clerk of Larne.

Ham went to Larne Grammar School, after which he had a distinguished career in Belfast, where he obtained first class honours in 1929 at the Queen's University, followed by a first class BSc in pathology, and MD with gold medal in 1933. He was Rockefeller research fellow and lecturer in pathology at Queen's University from 1931 to 1934, in which year he decided against a career on the teaching staff in Belfast in favour of a more clinical career in England, and obtained the appointment of pathologist to Cheltenham General Hospital, and soon afterwards consultant physician to Cheltenham and other Gloucestershire hospitals.

As would be expected with this background, his main interests as a physician were in diabetes and blood diseases, the former particularly being remembered in the pioneering work he did in founding the Diabetic Clinic in Cheltenham (the first in Gloucestershire) which became the largest single medical clinic in the hospital. He was also blood transfusion officer for North Gloucestershire. Despite these special interests he was always in demand as a general physician, and his thoughtful, wise and considerate opinion was sought by his hospital colleagues and a large circle of general practitioners in Gloucestershire and neighbouring counties. In addition to Cheltenham, he gave devoted service as consultant to Winchcombe, Evesham and Bourton-on-the-Water Hospitals and to Cheltenham College and Dean Close School. His stature as a wise counsellor was perhaps best reflected in his outstanding chairmanship of the Cheltenham Medical Staff Committee from 1954 to 1957. At the same time he was president of the Gloucestershire branch of the BMA.

In addition to his distinguished university academic career, Ham represented his university for three years at hockey and five years at golf. Golf continued as his main sporting activity throughout his consultant career, with a handicap of scratch for several years, and the winning of innumerable medical golfing trophies. As with so many Irishmen, horse racing was in his blood, and he was an enthusiastic and active member of Cheltenham racecourse.

Ham retired as a consultant in 1969. Unfortunately ill health prevented the pursuit of his more active hobbies during retirement, but by way of compensation he was able to turn to his old love of music – he had a fine baritone voice as a young man. His wife Jean (by whom he had two daughters) was fortunately able to continue to give him the support she had given throughout his years of work as a consultant.

He died at his home at Chipping Norton.

On a personal note, Ham is remembered by the warmth of his friendship and the quiet modesty of his opinions; on a practical note, his memorial is the Diabetic Clinic at Cheltenham Hospital.

RFJ

[*Brit. med. J.*, 1980, **280**, 727; Photo]

HAWE, Albert Joseph *b.*20 Mar 1901 *d.*25 Feb 1979
CBE (1959) OBE (1953) MRCS LRCP (1923)
MB ChB Liverp (1923) DTM&H (1926) MD (1930) MRCP (1930)
FRCP (1949)

Albert Hawe was honorary professor of medicine at Ghana Medical School, Accra (formerly the Gold Coast), and a senior consultant physician in Ghana. He was born at Rossmore, Ireland, and studied medicine at the University of Liverpool, where he graduated in 1923. After house appointments, he obtained the DTM&H in 1926, winning the Liverpool University Milne memorial medal in tropical medicine. He subsequently joined the Colonial Medical Service, arriving in Ghana in April 1926, where he was to spend the rest of his life.

Albert was a leading authority on tropical diseases and one of the most respected, skilful and competent physicians in Africa. His ward rounds were calculated to inspire high standards, for his first concern was the well being of his patients, irrespective of colour. He loved Ghana and her people and they in turn loved him dearly. Most of the senior members of the Ghana medical profession worked under him, and he played an important part in shaping their future. He was personal physician to President Kwame Nkrumah, an office he held with distinction. Only members of the Ghanian medical profession would appreciate how much personal trust, patience and medical expertise was needed in this appointment, and Albert Hawe possessed them all in full. He was awarded the John Holt medal for meritorious service by the University of Liverpool, and Ghana honoured him with the Grand Medal in recognition of his selfless service to their country. He was appointed OBE in 1953 and CBE in 1959.

He married Margaret Mary, a Ghanian; a quiet, unselfish woman who cared lovingly for him and their family. Albert was a practising Christian, and his name will remain a household word in Ghana, even in the villages. During his leisure hours he enjoyed gliding, sailing and flying. He obtained his pilot's licence in the 1920s. GW/VL

[*Brit. med. J.*, 1979, **1**, 902; *Lancet*, 1979, **1**, 682; Photo]

HAYWARD, Graham William *b*.7 June 1911 *d*.26 Nov 1976
MRCS LRCP (1935) MB BS Lond (1935) MD (1937) MRCP (1937) FRCP (1946)

Graham Hayward was born in Cardiff, the son of William George Hayward, who worked in the educational department of the Ministry of Health, and of his wife Mary Louise, née Holland. His grandfather, 'Hayward the Silent', had been superintendent of police: so noted for his huge size that he had been locally unique in being able to patrol the dockland single-handed. These attributes appear to have been hereditary, as also had been the extra brain-power which gave him and his sister such excellent academic careers. The two attended Cardiff High School, where she ran away with all the prizes: he subsequently went to St Bartholomew's Hospital, and at his final MB examination achieved distinctions in all five subjects then available (medicine, surgery, pathology, midwifery and gynaecology, and forensic medicine and hygiene), a feat never previously achieved. Whilst a student he played for the Bart's first XV, and also boxed heavyweight for London University.

After qualification in 1935 and house appointments to the medical professorial unit (LJ Witts q.v.), he held the post of resident medical officer at the National Hospital for Diseases of the Heart, and cardiology became his special interest thereafter. A Rockefeller travelling fellowship took him to America in 1937 for a year – where he met his wife. In 1939 he was awarded the Mackenzie McKinnon research fellowship of the Royal College of Physicians to work on pulmonary congestion and oedema, but the war came and he was enrolled in the Emergency Medical Service to work on transfusion. In

1941 he enlisted with the New Zealand Expeditionary Force, travelled to Italy and the Middle East, and became an expert on amoebiasis, leaving with the rank of brigadier.

After the war he joined the staff of Bart's and worked with Geoffrey Bourne to establish the new department of cardiology, and to set cardiothoracic surgery going. He remained in charge of the excellent and progressive department until his retirement in 1976, but also remained fully active as a general physician, running a general medical firm and participating in all hospital affairs. At the same time he was a very active staff member of the National Heart Hospital, was its dean from 1948 until 1961, and was therefore largely responsible for its rise to preeminence in the post-war cardiological world. One of his own special interests within cardiology was subacute bacterial endocarditis, and his early work with Cates, Christie and LP Garrod (q.v.), laid bare the critical importance of achieving adequate bactericidal antibiotic levels; in 1974 he summarised much of the work and elaborated on the subsequent developments in his notable Croonian lectures.

As a man Graham was a big, stalwart, reliable figure, modest and peace-loving but of unassailable integrity. As a teacher he was supreme: he never missed a round, and his students rarely missed them either. Always enthusiastic, he had a breadth of outlook that prevented him from any errors of over-emphasis; he had a fine gift of lucidity, and the greatness never to indulge in sarcasm. He ran a very happy teaching unit and was much respected as an uncannily faultless physician.

His work in the hospitals and private practice was heavy, but he was also an excellent and vigorous gardener. He was surrounded by great affection in his personal and family life, though tragedy struck early, and his eldest son died while still quite young. He was survived by his widow, by a married daughter, and by two sons.

He retired from the NHS on his 65th birthday, but continued in busy private practice until his death, from coronary heart disease, only six months later.

HWB

[*Brit. med. J.*, 1976, **2**, 1458; 1977, **1**, 175; *Lancet*, 1976, **2**, 1314; *Times*, 1 Dec 1976]

HENLEY, Wilton Ernest *b*.28 May 1907 *d*.9 Oct 1981
CBE (1967) MBE (1946) BA Oxon (1932) BM BCh (1935)
MRACP (1941) DM MA (1945) MRCP (1946) FRACP (1951)
FRCP (1960) Hon LLD Auckland (1972)

Wilton Ernest Henley was born at Napier, the son of Dr EAW Henley who died while Wilton was still a boy. He was educated in Napier and at Wanganui Collegiate, where his prowess in rugby became evident and he later played for the Hawkes Bay team. In the first year of his medical course at the University of Otago he was selected as a Rhodes scholar. Henley continued his medical course at the University of Oxford and went to St Mary's Hospital, London, for his clinical years, qualifying in 1935. After a period as house officer at

St Mary's Hospital he became a Radcliffe travelling fellow in 1937, and a Lady King scholar in 1939, gaining experience in general medicine.

Henley returned to New Zealand in 1940, and from then until 1944 was physician to the Waikato Hospital, Hamilton. Between 1944 and 1946 he was with the RNZAMC, first in Italy with the 2 NZEF, and then with the British Commonwealth Occupation Force in Japan, rising to the rank of lieutenant colonel and being appointed MBE. After demobilization he had a period of refresher study in Britain.

On return to New Zealand he was appointed senior physician, first at Middlemore Hospital, Auckland, and then at Auckland Hospital. He became extensively involved in the work of the NZ Committee of the RACP, and he was sub-dean of the branch faculty at Auckland of the University of Otago Medical School 1956–1961. Indeed he became over-committed, and it was not too difficult for the Auckland Hospital Board to persuade him to become superintendent-in-chief in succession to Selwyn Kenrick in 1961. The potentialities of the position were immense, as it was likely that Auckland would eventually be given planning permission to have a medical school. Henley was to be the right man in the right place, when finally at the end of 1964 the setting up of the medical school was authorized. He was given a year off by the board and seconded to work with the University Grants Committee and the various government departments concerned, planning in detail the new venture for which there were few national guidelines. Henley's work in guiding the planning exercise, before the arrival of Cecil Lewis as dean in 1966, was an achievement of a very high order. He had the necessary personal authority, both in Auckland and with the government, to carry this towards a successful launching. It was fitting that the School of Medicine was subsequently to name a lecture theatre after him as it did to its other founding fathers, Sir Douglas Robb and Cecil Lewis.

Wilton Henley married Wilhelmina Muriel Jean Barns-Graham in 1936 and she survived him, as did two sons who are doctors and a daughter.

Henley was a first rate sportsman all his life. As a student he was a rugby blue at Oxford University and St Mary's Hospital, and he played in an Irish trial. He was an outstanding place-kicker; his interest in the game never waned and he followed the All Blacks with critical enthusiasm to the end. Also he was a first-rate golfer and was an excellent fisherman.

Wilton Henley was known to friends and colleagues as 'Chook'. He was a spare man with a commanding presence, treating all with the utmost courtesy. He was a doctor in the great clinical tradition, being meticulous in history-taking and physical examination, and his astute comments at grand rounds were legendary. Every patient and the relatives received the greatest consideration, and he came to stress the advantages of physical contacts and the healing power of simply laying on hands. He had little bent for research; but he was early in the field of special care for over-weight babies of diabetic mothers whose control he managed in a special clinic at the National Women's

Hospital, with results that were ahead of the times.

Henley retired in 1973, and he returned to the clinical field when he became a senior medical officer in the Kingseat annexe to Raventhorpe Hospital. This is the long term psychiatric block, and he was able to bring his clinical talents to bear so that cases were adequately characterized, and many seemingly hopeless cases recovered to return to the community. Active to the end he was stricken with a massive stroke, with a gross aphasia. With characteristic fortitude he declined any attempts at treatment and he died after a fortnight's illness.

Henley shone in committees, where his comments were always succinct and would usually bring a tedious discussion to a quick decision. As a chairman he was superb; the meeting began precisely on time and he had mastered the agenda before the meeting.

As Dr Michael Gilmour said at the service in St Mark's Church, Remuera on 13 October: 'An obligation a Rhodes scholar accepts is "to esteem the performance of public duty as the highest aim"'. Wilton Henley surely obliged. JLN/GW

[*NZ Med. J.,* 24 Mar 1982, p.197; *RACP College Newsletter,* Dec 1981, **13**, 3; Photo]

HETZEL, Kenneth Stuart *b.*26 Sept 1897 *d.*24 Mar 1979
MB BS Adelaide (1920) MD (1926) MRCP (1923) FRACP (1938) FRCP (1946)

Ken Hetzel was born near Tanunda in South Australia. His grandfather, Carl Hetzel, migrated to Adelaide from Silesia, and his father, Frederick, had a dairy and cheese factory. He was educated at Gawler High School and subsequently at Prince Alfred College, where he was a prefect in his final year. He had a brilliant career at the Adelaide Medical School, graduating top of his year in 1920.

His initiative and ability earned him research assistantships with TR Elliott and CR (later Sir Charles) Harington after he travelled to London in 1922. Regrettably illness prevented him from subsequently accepting a Beit fellowship to continue research in London, but after several more years in Adelaide in general practice, and as assistant physician to the Adelaide Children's Hospital, he worked with the leading world figures Minot and Castle at Thorndike Laboratory, Boston, while holding a Rockefeller travelling fellowship. Again however, his hopes of an academic career were frustrated, this time by the world depression.

A foundation fellow of the RACP, he rapidly established himself as a leader in medicine in Adelaide. He was director of medical studies and subsequently dean of the Medical Faculty in the Adelaide University, and presided over the unprecedented expansion of that Faculty and the appointment of its first four clinical professors. He was also a member of the University Council for 15 years. He was responsible for securing approximately $700,000 in donations to the University of Adelaide from several benefactors, and had the pleasure of seeing his elder son Basil appointed to the inaugural Michell chair of medicine at the Queen Elizabeth Hospital.

In 1945 he travelled through China for 12 months for UNRAA as travelling professor of medicine.

Although he retired from his position as senior honorary physician at the Royal Adelaide Hospital in 1957 at the age of 60, his energy and interest in medicine carried him on in active community medical service up to the age of 80. A well organized, efficient and charming man, he would willingly come in to offer assistance to his hospital interns at any time of the day or night. In 1922 he married Elinor Watt; they had two sons both of whom have themselves achieved eminence in medicine. RH(2)

[Photo]

HICKMAN, John Anthony *b*.9 Apr 1940 *d*.23 Jan 1979
BChir Cantab (1964) BA MB (1965) MRCP (1966) FRCP (1978)

John Anthony Hickman, one of twins, was educated at Greshams School, Selwyn College, Cambridge, and the Middlesex Hospital, where he qualified in 1964. He held a number of junior appointments at the Middlesex, obtaining the MRCP in 1966. Rather unusually for a physician he then held a post in the department of surgical studies for two years. During this time he carried out original research in fibrinogen metabolism, and developed a new technique for the quantitative estimation of fibrinolysis. This was followed by an appointment as senior medical registrar at the Brompton Hospital. Returning to full time clinical medicine, his clinical acumen and mature approach to medical problems soon became evident there. He had always been interested in teaching, and this manifested itself most obviously at the Brompton by the efficient yet self-effacing part he played in the organization of the Monday clinical meetings.

In November 1972 he was appointed consultant physician to the London Hospital and the London Chest Hospital at the early age of 32. He immediately threw himself wholeheartedly into the life of both hospitals. In particular he was most active in the teaching of the undergraduates at the London Hospital Medical College. He became a clinical tutor and often entertained students at his home. He took great pride and pleasure in this teaching and never hesitated to rearrange his increasingly busy schedule to fit in a student lecture.

In addition he was consultant physician to the Post Office and Civil Service Sanatorium Society and medical adviser to the Midland Bank. He was a member of the British Thoracic and Tuberculosis Association. After his death a memorial fund was set up at the London Hospital Medical College to endow a student prize and an annual lecture in his memory. The first such lecture was given in October 1981.

John married Anne Veronica, daughter of Herbert Walmsley Higginson, a solicitor, in 1968 and they had three sons. His busy life did not leave him much time for leisure activities, but he was an excellent golfer and enjoyed playing at Sandwich and Brancaster. They had a cottage at Salthouse, where he would enjoy bird-watching and walking on the beach with his sons. He developed acute leukaemia in November 1977. He bore his illness with great fortitude and equanimity. He had the most modern treatment of total body irradiation, followed by a marrow transplant from his twin, medical brother, Roger. Throughout this time he remained his usual self and still found time to think of others, and for a time the transplant seemed to be successful. Sadly, he relapsed tragically about a year after the initial onset of his illness. He was looked after at home during his final months, receiving tremendous support from his wife and twin brother. Although he knew the end was in sight he faced this without remorse and indeed with serenity. Two days before he died he was still asking about the hospital and actively planning for the future. In five years he made a great impression, and many friends, in the hospital and medical school at the London. He was characteristically modest about his achievements, and a typical remark of his when thanked for a postgraduate lecture he gave overseas was to reply 'I came to teach you, but it was you who taught me'. DH/GW

[*Brit. med. J.*, 1979, **1**, 418; Photo]

HIGHTON, Thomas Cecil *b.*3 Oct 1917 *d.*26 Apr 1976
MB ChB Liverp (1942) MRCP (1945) MRACP (1961)
FRACP (1966) FRCP (1970)

Tom Highton was associate professor of rheumatology at the University of Otago, New Zealand. He was born at Johannesburg, South Africa, the son of Thomas Highton, who was employed by the South African railways, and his wife, Caroline, daughter of Johannes Karl Langman, an hotel owner. When he was nine years old he came to England with his parents, where he attended the King George V School at Southport. He proved to be a student of considerable promise, but the early death of his father led to hard times for the family, and it was necessary for him to obtain scholarships to complete his education. These he attained, and he entered Liverpool University as a medical student in 1936, graduating in 1942. He distinguished himself as a student, gaining distinction in pharmacology and therapeutics, the medal in forensic medicine, and the Owen T Williams prize for the highest aggregate marks in medicine, surgery and obstetrics.

Owing to the outbreak of the second world war, Tom Highton held various house posts while still an undergraduate, at the Liverpool Royal Infirmary. This was invaluable experience and, after graduation, he was appointed house physician at the Walton Infirmary, where he was responsible for acute medical wards with some 129 beds. In 1943 he joined the Royal Navy as surgeon lieutenant and served in combined operations on a troop carrier in the Mediterranean and, later, with the Home Fleet. While on active service he took his MRCP, and the close of the war found him as a physician at the Royal Naval Hospital, Haslar.

On demobilization he was appointed senior medical registrar at the West London Hospital. It was here that he began his long and rewarding career in rheumatology. He came under the influence of Will Copeman and, subsequently, of Eric Bywaters, obtaining a Nuffield fellowship in chronic rheumatic diseases. He was Saltwell Scholar in 1949. This enabled him to continue his training in rheumatology at the West London and Hammersmith Hospitals, and it was at this time that he became friendly with two other pioneers of New Zealand rheumatology, Chris Gresson and Moore Tweed. These were friendships which were to last his life time, and stimulated his interest in their country.

In 1951 he accepted an appointment as research medical officer at the Queen Elizabeth Hospital, Rotorua, NZ, a post which was both challenging and frustrating. Although there was ample scope for his talents as a physician, rheumatology was not then recognized as a valid medical specialty, and he had to be very persistent to have his skills accepted. He was the first to realise that gout was a common complaint among the Maoris, and he pioneered the use of intra-articular corticosteriods in New Zealand. Research, however, was limited, for there was barely enough time and money for essential patient care. In 1957 he accepted a Medical Research Council post at the University of Otago. In due course, his research began to flourish, and he established an international reputation for his electron microscopic studies of synovial tissue, for his investigations of the nature and role of mucopolysaccharides in connective tissue, and for his careful therapeutic trials of anti-inflammatory drugs. He published over 40 papers in scientific journals and built up a large and active research group during his 19 years at Dunedin. He also established a first class clinical rheumatology service in the Dunedin and Wakari Hospitals.

Tom Highton was elected a fellow of the Royal Australasian College of Physicians in 1966 and a fellow of this College in 1970. He was president of the New Zealand Rheumatism Association, a councillor of the International League against Rheumatism, vice-president of the South East Asian and Pacific Area League against Rheumatism, and an honorary member of the American and Indian Rheumatism Associations. At the time of his death he was chairman of the ILAR standing committee for International Clinical Studies. He served on the executive of the Faculty of Medicine, and on the Medical Advisory Committee of the Otago Hospital Board and its ethical sub-committee, on the council of the Otago Medical Research Foundation, and as president of the Otago University Medical Research Society. In 1975 he was awarded a personal chair in medicine by the University.

He married Roberta Sibyl Janette, daughter of Joseph Samuel Baker, an engineer, in 1949, and they had four children; two sons and two daughters. John, Penelope, Paul and Clare. Clare also entered the medical profession, studying at Cambridge, and taking her MRCP(UK) in 1980.

Outside his professional work, Tom Highton's interests lay in photography, boating and trout fishing, but he was also very active in promoting the welfare of disabled people. He was president and vice-president of his local Disabled Citizens Society for some years, and a ministerial nominee representing disabled people on the Dunedin District Committee of the Disabled Reestablishment League.

GW/VL

[*NZ Med. J.*, May 1976, **83**, 376-7; Photo]

HILL, *Sir* Ian (George Wilson) *b*.7 Sept 1904 *d*.5 May 1982
Kt (1966) CBE (1945) TD MBChB Edin (1928) FRCPE (1933) MRCP (1952) FRCP (1956) Hon LLD (1970)†

Ian Hill was born in Shotts, Lanarkshire, the son of a banker, Alexander Wilson Hill, JP and his wife, Jean Robertson, daughter of George Lockhart Malcolm. His early childhood in South Uist fostered his love of nature and his skill as a fly fisherman. A schoolboy prodigy at George Watson's College in Edinburgh, he foreshadowed his later distinctions when he addressed the British Association on the subject of lepidoptera. He graduated with honours at Edinburgh University, winning the Ettles scholarship as the most distinguished medical graduate of the year. His early career was influenced by WT Ritchie and Sir Edward Sharpey-Schaefer, and a Rockefeller travelling fellowship enabled him to work with Frank N Wilson, the world authority on electrocardiography at the famous Heart Station in Ann Arbor. This was probably the happiest time in his life and certainly one of the most important. He became deeply involved with a team of enthusiastic young men who were pioneering the use of electrocardiography in the study of myocardial infarction, and all of them later achieved distinction. He next travelled to Vienna to work with Karl Wenckebach. His German was fluent and his Viennese pursuits were cultural as well as medical. There followed lectureships in Aberdeen with Stanley Davidson, and in Edinburgh with Derrick Dunlop. His academic career was interrupted by the second world war. A keen territorial, he was mobilized at its outbreak and served throughout, mostly in the Middle East, India and Burma. By 1945 he was a youthful brigadier, consultant physician to the XIVth Army and to the Allied Land Forces, South East Asia, and had been appointed CBE. On returning to Edinburgh he resumed work as an assistant physician at the Royal Infirmary, and also became consultant physician at the Deaconess Hospital. His prominence in the field of cardiology (he had already introduced the use of unipolar (V) ECG leads to Britain) was recognized by an invitation to give the Gibson lecture at the Royal College of Physicians of Edinburgh.

He had quickly established a successful private consultant practice, but in 1950 he sacrificed that to return to academic life when he succeeded Adam Patrick as professor of medicine in the University of St Andrews. At its medical school in Dundee, he was one of a group of newly appointed wholetime professors charged with raising academic standards and initiating research. He soon built up a department with young lecturers who, under his guidance, were to carry out notable work in cardiology, endocrinology and diabetes, nephrology and neurology. He regarded his chief task as that of undergraduate education, but he also attracted postgraduate students from overseas, particularly the USA, India and Hong Kong. He was a master clinician over the whole field of medicine and a brilliant and memorable undergraduate teacher, whether in the vivid declamatory formal lecture, the professorial grand round or the less formal discussions in an over-crowded seminar room, where he would light a cigarette and enthrall his undergraduate and postgraduate students with illustrative anecdotes.

Having established a secure base in Dundee he was able to embark on extramural activities. He was appointed physician to the Queen in Scotland and gave valued service to the Royal Family on several occasions. He was elected president of the Royal College of Physicians of Edinburgh (1963 – 1966) and travelled widely on its behalf in Australasia, India, Africa and the Far East. Among his other distinctions were the presidencies of the Scottish Society of Physicians and the Association of Physicians of Great Britain and Ireland, and the chairmanship of the British Cardiac Society. His continued military interests led to an honorary colonelcy of the 2nd Scottish General Hospital (1947 – 1958) and he was appointed consulting physician to Scottish Command (1965 – 1970). When he retired from his chair in 1969 the University of Dundee acknowledged his service by the award of an honorary LLD.

The phenomenal energy which Ian had shown throughout his career did not flag, however, and he went on to spend a year as visiting professor in the University of Teheran and two years as dean of the Faculty of Medicine in the Haile Selassie I University of Ethiopia.

Ian Hill was short and slight in build but his military bearing, superabundant energy, ceaseless striving, penetrating intellect, erudition and witty repartee commanded attention in all circles. He was a front-line fighter, not a back-room diplomatist. Fearless in his beliefs, he did not hide his contempt for pretension or his irritation at incompetence. But the rather prickly manner concealed – perhaps too well – a sensitive and warm-hearted man, deeply compassionate, who inspired loyalty and returned it. In Vienna Wenckebach once said to him 'Cardiology is your first love: it will be your last love'. And so it was: his last paper in a medical journal in 1980 surveyed the treatment of heart disease over half a century. It may have given him secret satisfaction to reflect that in that time he had brought hope and succour to many thousands of patients of all ages afflicted with heart disease.

He married, in 1933, Ellen Audrey Lavender, the daughter of an industrial chemist, who had trained as a nurse at Edinburgh Royal Infirmary. They had one daughter and one son, Alasdair, whose appointment as QC gave Sir Ian much pleasure. Lady Hill died in 1967 and he later married his cousin, Anna. Her constant companionship brought him great happiness, in Iran and Ethiopia, and eventually in their retirement to a charming cottage in Crail. The number of friends and former students who visited them from all over the world was a tribute to them both, and the cordiality of their welcome was a legend.

DE-S/KGL

[*Brit. med. J.*, 1982, **284**, 1637 & 1779; *Lancet*, 1982, **1**, 1257-58; *RCP Edin. Chronicle*, Nov 1982, **12**,(4); Photo]

HILL, *Sir* (John) Denis (Nelson) *b.*5 Oct 1913 *d.*5 May 1982
Kt (1966) MRCS LRCP (1936) MB BS Lond (1936) MRCP (1940) DPM (1940) FRCP (1949) FRCPsych (1971)

Denis Hill, emeritus professor of psychiatry, University of London, and one of our country's most distinguished psychiatrists, died suddenly in his sixty-eighth year. Born and brought up in the Manor House at Orleton, Herefordshire, his father was Lieutenant-Colonel JA Hill. He was educated at Shrewsbury School and thereafter at St Thomas's Hospital Medical School. A childhood interest in the new 'wireless' developed into a lifelong interest in the clinical applications of electronic amplification, which was then to provide such great impetus to the development of psychiatry. In 1936, whilst house physician to Russell Brain at Maida Vale Hospital, he saw Grey Walter's homemade EEG, the first in this country, and soon realized its potential for psychiatry and for the field of epilepsy. During the war, by which time he was working in psychiatry, he set up one of the first EEG laboratories, developed a close relationship with the medical services to the armed forces, and was largely responsible for electroencephalography becoming recognized as an important technique of neuropsychiatric investigation. At this stage he wrote and published extensively in the medical literature, making fundamental contributions to our understanding of temporal lobe epilepsy and psychopathy in particular. He was inevitably drawn into the forensic field and throughout the 1960s and 1970s was widely consulted by the profession and by Government on such matters. In particular, he was an influential member of the Aarvold Committee in 1972, and of the Butler Committee on Mentally Abnormal Offenders, 1972–1975. The current therapeutic approach to such offenders owes a great deal to him, and also reflects his parallel interest in the social mainsprings of disordered behaviour. At a time when it was unfashionable to support psychotherapy, he championed it.

He also played a fundamental role in medical education in this country. Appointed to one of the first chairs in psychiatry located at an undergraduate school (the Middlesex) in London University, he led the fight to get the subject of psychiatry properly established in the undergraduate curriculum of that university. In 1966 he moved to the postgraduate chair at the Institute of Psychiatry, where he stayed until his retirement in 1979. In the early stages of this last appointment there was considerable conflict because of his determination and success in establishing psychotherapy as an academic and clinical discipline, alongside the many other developments at the Institute of Psychiatry which now stand as such great tributes to his foresight. He had a marvellous capacity for synthesis, and always strove to keep his subject firmly within medicine. He was a very active College man, a council member, and chairman of the committee on psychological medicine prior to the formation of the Royal College of Psychiatrists. A member of the General Medical Council from 1961 until his death, he rapidly became one of its elder statesmen, and was largely responsible for the development of the present health procedures in relation to fitness to practice.

Denis Hill shunned the highest offices which others tried to persuade him to pursue. He preferred instead to work tirelessly and constructively behind the scenes. He was shy, and intolerant only of humbug and mediocrity. He was at one and the same time a great all-rounder and a scholar in academic medicine. Never gratuitously forthcoming, he would nevertheless generously share his ideas with anyone showing serious interest.

He first married Phoebe Elizabeth Wade, with whom he had a son and a daughter. His second marriage was to Lorna Whellan, consultant child psychiatrist at King's College Hospital, and they also had a son and a daughter. ACH

[*Brit. med. J.*, 1982, **284**, 1481; *Lancet*, 182, **1**, 1136; *Times*, 14 & 18 May 1982; *Middx. Hosp. J.*, Oct 1966, **66** (5), 174-5; *Bethlem Maudsley Hospital Gazette*, Dec 1966, **8** (4), 16-19; *World Medicine*, July 1966; *Brit. med. J.*, 1960, **2**, 1681; *Lancet*, 1960, **2**, 1259; *Univ. Lond. Gazette*, Dec 1960, 289; *GMC Annual Report for 1982*, Sept 1983, 7]

HILL, Leslie Charles *b*.30 Aug 1900 *d*.30 May 1983
MB ChB Birm (1924) MD (1927) MRCP (1928) FRCP (1946)

Leslie Hill was born in Wolverhampton. He was of Yorkshire stock, his father Alfred Charles Hill being manager of a steel works. He was educated at Wolverhampton School where he had a brilliant career both academically and on the sports field. He was awarded an exhibition in classics at Worcester College, Oxford, but to his lasting regret, was unable at the end of the 1914–1918 war to take this up, due to a temporary decline in the family fortunes. He decided on a career in medicine and entered Birmingham University, where he qualified from the General and Queens Hospitals in 1924; there then followed house appointments to James Russell and to Ball and Wilkinson at the Children's Hospital, where he became resident medical officer to Sir Leonard Parsons and from whom he acquired a lifelong interest in children's cardiac disorders.

In 1930 he was appointed physician to the Devonshire Royal Hospital, Buxton, where he remained until 1937. His work here gave him experience in the rheumatic diseases, and after a period at Hammersmith he was appointed, in 1938, registrar and later physician to the Royal United Hospital, and also to the Royal National Hospital for Rheumatic Diseases at Bath, where he spent the rest of his life.

During the war he served in the RAMC in North Africa, Sicily and Italy, where he commanded a medical division in a military hospital in the rank of lieutenant colonel. He was seriously ill with typhoid and invalided home, and, after convalescence, he took up once more his hospital appointment at Bath.

Leslie Hill was a popular consulting physician and his opinion was widely sought in neighbouring West Wiltshire, where he visited the hospitals at Devizes, Chippenham, Warminster and Malmesbury, always travelling in a series of vintage Bentley motor cars. With the advent of the National Health Service in 1948, he threw himself into its organization and was a founder member of the Bath Hospital management committee. He was a member of the South West Regional Hospital Board from 1953 to 1962. He had wide administrative interests and was an excellent committee man, for which services his colleagues at Bath and in the region were always grateful. A good chairman, he was always courteous and fair; in spite of radical leanings, he displayed a conservative approach.

In 1957 he delivered the College's Lumleian lectures, on systemic lupus erythematosus.

Leslie Hill was a great sportsman and a good cricketer – he played regularly until he was 55 for the Lansdown Cricket Club and was president of the club – one of the oldest in the country and whose ground adjoins the Royal United Hospital – until his death. He enjoyed his membership of the MCC and travelled as a fervent supporter on many of the tours in Australia, South Africa and the West Indies. He never missed a test match. He was also an expert dry fly fisherman and an excellent shot. His hobbies were essentially physical and in the field; as he grew older and suffered the disabilities of age, he felt himself deprived, and he then sought to immerse himself in his reading.

He was always supported up to the hilt by his devoted wife, whom he married in 1930. Emma Marion Robertson was the daughter of the famous jam and marmalade manufacturer. On her death he was a lonely figure, but was faithfully supported by his only child and daughter Alison and her husband Anthony – they were his lasting joy.

DWP

[*Brit. med. J.*, 1983, **287**, 768; Photo]

HILSON, Don *b.*8 May 1918 *d.*16 Oct 1983

BA Cantab (1939) MRCS LRCP (1942) MA (1944) DCH (1947) MRCP (1948) MB BChir (1949) FRCPE (1968) FRCP (1973)

Don Hilson was born in Johannesburg, South Africa, of emigré Jewish parents in 1918, and was educated there at Parktown Preparatory School and Witwatersrand University, before coming over to England to read medicine at Cambridge. He qualified from the Westminster Hospital where he was Wander scholar in 1942, winning the Sturges gold medal and the Frederick Bird prize.

After serving as paediatric registrar in the Westminster Hospital, house surgeon at Great Ormond Street, RMO at the Alder Hey Children's Hospital, and Queen Mary's Hospital Carshalton, he moved back to Capetown in 1945 as professorial medical assistant, but in 1950, not liking the kind of government that white South Africans had chosen for themselves, he returned to England for good, and after a period as senior registrar in Liverpool was made the first consultant paediatrician to serve the children of Oldham, Ashton, Hyde and Glossop in 1951, a post in which he served until his retirement.

One cannot imagine a translation more drastic than from the sunlit Rand to the rainy foothills of the Pennines, but Hilson took it in his stride (his forebears had after all managed the transition from Russia and Switzerland to South Africa with success) and rapidly established himself in the already languishing cotton towns, where he brought energy, flair and imagination to a paediatric service in a locality that had never had one before.

A man of parts, with musical, artistic and sporting interests, he combined the social and intellectual polish of his University, the slightly exotic physiognomy of his forebears, the uninhibited practicality of his country of origin, and the down to earth common sense of his adopted city, informing all of them with a nimble mind, a genuinely kind heart and an idealistic outlook. These qualities were evident in the book that he wrote on practical paediatrics in 1963, which was well received and proved very useful. He became in time a fellow of the Royal Society of Medicine, a member of the British Paediatric Association, an associate fellow of the South African Medical Association (in recognition of a series of working visits to the New Republic), and a prominent member of his local branch of the BMA and of the Manchester Medical Society, which he served when his turn came round as president of its paediatric section. He was also active in adoption, being chairman of the Ashton under Lyme Adoption Society for many years, and in postgraduate and undergraduate medical education. He was made an honorary lecturer in paediatrics by the University of Manchester in 1969, and postgraduate tutor in 1964.

As a physician Hilson was diligent, extremely well informed and generally popular with his patients and their parents. He was particularly good to his junior colleagues, trying to ensure that they undertook original work and that they were not bypassed by teaching hospital colleagues on the consultant ladder. He did not like to be crossed, and was perhaps over-ready to resent what he saw as patronage or interference on the part of colleagues in the Manchester teaching hospitals, where in fact he was held in considerable respect, despite his apparently idiosyncractic and not always orthodox practice. His ideas, though off-beat at first hearing, were usually based on sound biological instincts and often turned out to be ahead of their time, but it is difficult for a single handed paediatrician to pursue original ideas in a peripheral hospital in the North West of England.

Asked how it was that South African medical schools turned out so many able and indeed brilliant graduates, one of them once replied 'pedantic Scots professors, imaginative Jewish students and lots of sick Africans'. Don Hilson was a good example of a physician brought up in this tradition, and the children of Oldham and its surrounding conurbation benefited over many years from his learning, his originality and his ability, single-handed, to minister to their needs.

Hilson's wife Lena was also a physician, and shared his interests and concerns from the time of their marriage in 1941 until retirement and death. JAD

[Photo]

HINDEN, Elchon *b*.30 Nov 1908 *d*.27 July 1977
BA Cantab (1929) MRCS LRCP (1931) MA (1932)
MB BChir (1933) MRCP (1934) MD (1946) FRCP (1970)

Elchon Hinden was born in Liverpool, to Israel Lewis Hinden,a Lithuanian draper of that city and his wife Florence Henrietta (née Cohen), whose father, Joseph, was a shopkeeper.

Hinden was educated initially at the local Rathbone School and proceeded to the Liverpool Collegiate School, from where he gained a major entrance scholarship to Cambridge University, becoming senior scholar at Trinity College. He gained first class honours in Part I of the Natural Sciences Tripos and proceeded BA in 1929. His clinical studies were undertaken at St George's Hospital, London, and he qualified in 1931; an MD was obtained in 1946, with a thesis on aetiological aspects of gastroenteritis.

Elchon Hinden was successively casualty officer, house surgeon and house physician at St George's Hospital from 1931 to 1932, and then assistant medical officer at various hospitals in London until 1941, when he joined the RAMC, serving in West Africa, Belgium and India. He was demobilized in 1946, with the rank of temporary major as a medical specialist. There followed a period as assistant to the paediatric department at Guy's Hospital and then he was appointed paediatrician to Whipps Cross Hospital, London, in 1947, with responsibilities as visiting paediatrician to Thorpe Coombe Maternity Hospital and Forest Gate Maternity Hospital, both in East London. Hinden was the first paediatrician appointed to Whipps Cross Hospital and remained as such until his retirement in 1973. During all but the last eight months of those 26 years, he was a 'single-handed' consultant.

Among many arduous duties, he found time to be a member of the advisory committee of the National Association of Mental Health, and served on the case committee of the Independent Adoption Society. With great insight into the needs of children, he brought paediatrics and the concept of child health into the community in East London, long before 'community paediatrics' became fashionable.

Elchon Hinden was a wise man. He spoke eloquently and wrote with great clarity. He enjoyed travel, photography and, most of all, his collection of books. His intention on retiring was to spend his time amongst his books, but always tireless he spent part of his retirement working as a clinical medical officer in north-west London, amongst the children he cared for.

In 1933 he married Rita Gesundheit, daughter of Jacob, an orange grower. As Gerda Cohen, she was an eminent writer and journalist, sharing Hinden's belief in true socialist principles. They had a daughter and a son. Their son embarked on a medical training, to the delight of his father, but soon found that music was his true vocation.

Elchon Hinden was active until his death. He collapsed after a morning swim in north London and died shortly after. He would, perhaps, like to be remembered for his memorable dedication in his book, *A Primer of Paediatrics*, for it sums up the tenor of his professional life: 'to the children, the original, long-suffering teachers of paediatrics'.

BWL

[*Brit. med. J.*, 1977, **2**, 709]

HOBSON, Jack Abbott *b.*22 Apr 1910 *d.*27 Feb 1977
BSc Manch (1931) MB BCh (1934) DPM (1936) MD (1941)
MRCP (1947) FRCP (1961)

Jack Hobson was born at Rossendale, Lancashire, the son of Frederick James Hobson, architect, and his wife Sarah Elizabeth. He spent his early years in Rossendale and attended Bacup and Rawtenstall Grammar School, where he gained a state scholarship to the University of Manchester medical school. He had a brilliant career both at school and university, gaining many prizes. After appointments as house physician at the Manchester Royal Infirmary in 1935, and assistant medical officer at the Cheadle Royal Infirmary 1935–1936, he began his career in psychiatry, first at the Prestwich County Mental Hospital in 1936, and later that year as assistant medical officer at St Luke's Woodside Hospital, where he was to spend most of his professional life. In 1939 he was awarded the Gaskell gold medal and prize of the (then) Royal Medico-Psychological Association. This medal and prize he shared with Eliot Slater; 1939 was a vintage year for British psychiatry.

He joined the Royal Navy Volunteer Reserve in 1939 as a specialist in neuropsychiatry. He served until 1946, attaining the rank of surgeon lieutenant commander. After leaving the Navy he served for two years as chief assistant in the department of psychological medicine at St Mary's Hospital until 1948, when he was appointed consultant psychiatrist to the Middlesex Hospital and St Luke's Woodside Hospital, becoming senior consultant psychiatrist in 1960, until his retirement in 1975. St Luke's Woodside Hospital was a private non-profit making hospital, which elected to join the Middlesex Hospital when the National Health Service came into existence in 1948, and it then became the inpatient psychiatric department of the Middlesex Hospital.

Hobson's special interest in psychiatry was forensic psychiatry, also alcoholism and drug abuse. His main ambition was to achieve the abolition of capital punishment, and he was a founder member of the Society for the Abolition of Capital Punishment with Koestler, Lord Gardiner, Victor Gollancz and Mr Silverman. In the 1950s, Jack Hobson took a prominent part in some of the most notorious murder trials, particularly those of Christie and Straffan. His behaviour in the Court Room was impeccable, and he withstood attacks from prosecuting counsel much more effectively than many of his contemporaries engaged in other notorious trials. The degree of diligence and thoroughness he displayed in the investigation of these cases can be appreciated only by those who were intimately associated with him at the time.

His early writings were on the use of d-Tubocurarine in the control of electrically induced convulsions, and he was a pioneer in the use of muscle relaxants. He also wrote papers on the treatment of sequelae of head injuries, the treatment of alcoholic patients and termination of pregnancy.

Psychiatry was by no means the whole of Jack Hobson's existence; indeed he was a tremendously gifted man. He took part in archery, including the making of bows; he was interested in mountaineering and speleology, repeatedly visiting the caves of his beloved Lancashire; he dabbled in musical composition, and was always interested in chess, where he reached county levels. He played bridge and reached international standards. He painted in oils and pastels. Another interest was antique navigational and scientific instruments, which he restored with meticulous accuracy, and he also restored antique furniture. He was fascinated by the American West, and he invented a game based on the town plan of Tombstone. Yet another interest was Shakespeare, and he wrote a couple of papers on Shakespeare's Falstaff. He was always keen on sport; he swam and boxed for the University. he was a first class player of snooker, a competent skiier and towards the end of his life took up golf. This immense list of interests illustrates another of Jack Hobson's traits, that of taking up a subject, pursuing it with immense vigour until he had achieved a high degree of expertise, and then transferring his attention to something different.

His chief quality was his pursuit of truth, whether in religion, ethics, philosophy or science, and this involved him in the precise meanings of words. He was intrigued by words and language and the correct expression of ideas and concepts, and this meticulousness restricted his own literary output.

He married three times. He had a daughter Diana by his second wife. His third wife was Doreen Mary, née Bottone, by whom he had three children —Sarah, Prudence and Jack.

Soon after he retired on 1 September 1976, he developed the illness from which he died six months later in the Middlesex hospital which he loved and served so well. It was indeed tragic that he did not have more years in which to develop further his multitudinous talents, and to enjoy the company of his wife (also a consultant psychiatrist) and his family.

AWB

[*Brit. med. J.*, 1977, **2**, 130]

HOGARTH, James Clancey *b*.27 Mar 1908 *d*.25 Oct 1979
MB ChB Glasg (1933) DPH Eng (1938) MD (1941) MRCPE (1949) MRCP (1949) FRCPE (1956) FRCP (1968)

James Clancey Hogarth was the son of Arthur James Hogarth, a distiller, and Elizabeth Clancey, who was the daughter of Richard Christopher Clancey, an 'average adjuster' in shipping insurance. Their home was near Glasgow. He was in fact born two months prematurely while his parents were on holiday in Devon. Part of his early life was spent in Devon where his parents built a family house overlooking Torbay, but such was their attachment to Scotland that all the stone and building materials were sent down from Scotland. His father was initially in business with Sir Alec Walker at the Johnny Walker distillery, and later became a director of Distillers, which took over the Johnny Walker firm.

James Hogarth went to Glasgow High School, and undertook his medical studies at Glasgow University and the Royal Infirmary, Glasgow. He qualified in 1933, having been the Cullen medallist and the Muirhead prizewinner in medicine. His first appointments were as house physician and house surgeon, respectively, to the professors of medicine and surgery at Glasgow Royal Infirmary. After further house appointments, Clancey, as he was generally known, came south to London, where he worked at the LCC Eastern Fever Hospital, Hackney, and where he was co-author of a textbook on *Fevers* with Maurice Mitman.

He went next to the Southern General Hospital until 1943, when he joined the RAMC. He became major (medical specialist) serving first on the hospital ship *Dorsetshire*, later as officer in charge, medical division, Stover Military Hospital, Devon, until 1947. He then resumed his previous appointment at the former Southern Hospital, Deptford, working as consultant physician and also as deputy medical superintendent. He soon became consultant physician to the Dartford Group of Hospitals.

In addition to general medicine, Clancey built up a special interest in rheumatology, a choice which may have been influenced by the fact that his mother had had severe rheumatoid arthritis. He was a keen photographer and became an excellent clinical photographer, much contributing to the value of his clinical records. He became a greatly respected, very experienced and a very kindly physician. Furthermore, his skills as an administrator contributed much to the efficiency of the hospital as it was building up under the National Health Service.

Clancey's interest in mankind was paralleled by a strong interest in nature, particularly in the preservation and support of bird life, and also in the conservation of wild animals. At home he was a keen gardener and became a considerable authority on roses. He had a fine interest in classical music, and with his excellent auditory memory he developed his linguistic abilities. Above all he was a family man. He had married Harriette Ruth Lewis, whose father was an American farmer who served in the United States Army in the Philippines and in

China. Having graduated in 1936, Harriette studied nursing at the University of Buffalo and at the Mayer Memorial Hospital. When the second world war broke out she volunteered for overseas duty with the American National Red Cross, which was how she met James Hogarth in 1944. They married three years later at Paignton, Devonshire, and had two sons and one daughter. The eldest son, Arthur, became an analytical chemist, the second son, Roderick, went into business administration, and the daughter, Judy, took up nursery nursing and became a play therapist. Altogether he had an exceptionally happy married life.

Throughout his professional life in England he retained his characteristics as a rather dour and quiet Scotsman, one who could always be relied upon as a friend, and as a superb physician.

FAJ

[*Brit. med. J.*, 1980, **280**, 124; Photo]

HOLMAN, Portia Grenfell *b.*20 Nov 1903 *d.*16 May 1983
MB BChir Cantab (1941) DPM (1941) MRCP (1944) FRCP (1961) FRCPsych (1971)

Portia Holman was born in Sydney, Australia. Her father, William Arthur Holman KC, was the first Labour premier of New South Wales, 1914–1918. Her maternal grandfather was a journalist. The late Lord Platt (PRCP 1957–1961) was her third cousin. She was educated at Shirley School, Sydney, and took a degree in English at a Sydney college. Her father's work as an international lawyer often took him to Europe and Portia accompanied him. She came to Newnham College, Cambridge, in 1923, and took a good degree in economics in 1926. During the next two years she attended the Sorbonne, Paris, studying at the Institut de Psychologie Appliqué and later at the London School of Economics; followed by nearly three years as a lecturer in the moral sciences department of St Andrews University, Scotland. An increasing interest in psychology led to a decision to study medicine, and to help pay for this she lectured at adult education centres.

In 1933 she returned to Newnham to study medicine and did her clinical training at the Royal Free Hospital. After qualifying in 1939 she made up her mind to study psychiatry and after house appointments at the Elizabeth Garrett Anderson Hospital, at Great Ormond Street and the Mill Hill emergency hospitals, she took the DPM. She was appointed director of the first child guidance clinics at Twickenham and Ealing in 1944; psychiatrist to the West Middlesex Hospital in 1945, and consultant psychiatrist to the Elizabeth Garrett Anderson in 1946. She then relinquished her posts at Twickenham and the West Middlesex, but continued in Ealing where she worked for a further twenty-five years. She remained an adviser to Ealing Borough until 1977. After retiring from the Ealing child guidance clinic in 1970 she worked at St Bernard's Hospital, Ealing, and was closely associated with the Cavendish School for maladjusted children and the special withdrawal unit at the Faraday School, Alton.

Portia wrote several papers on her specialty and her contribution to psychiatric literature included: 'Family vicissitudes in relation to personality development', Chap 2, *Foundations of Child Psychiatry* (1968); *A hospital school experiment in therapeutic recreation* (1971) with Anne Sycamore Sebastians; and *Children who wet their beds* (1957), a London Family Health publication. She gained her Cambridge MD with a thesis on 'Some factors in the aetiology of maladjustment in children' and this was subsequently published in the *Journal of Mental Science* (1933), and won her the Burlingame prize of the Royal Medico-Psychological Association. At a later date she chaired the section of child psychiatry of the Association, and she became a founder fellow of the Royal College of Psychiatrists.

In the late 1940s Portia helped to establish the Mulberry Residential School for maladjusted children, near Oxford. In 1953 she became a founder member of the Association of Workers for Maladjusted Children. Her professional distinction was recognized by election to the fellowship of the College, an honorary membership of her former medical school, and her election as president of the London Association of the Medical Women's Federation. In 1965 she served on the Church of England board of social responsibility committee on abortion.

She was a loyal and vigorously involved member of the Labour party; no doubt this was fostered by her father in her early years. At Cambridge, she knew Maynard Keynes and later, during the happiest years of her life, when she lived in Bloomsbury, she was part of a circle of left-wing intellectuals. She was a trade union member (ASTMS) and canvassed for the Labour party in elections. She strongly supported the introduction of the National Health Service, and had many friends among members of Parliament and Labour peers.

When Portia was convinced of the justice of a cause she took action in a positive way, without aggression. She interrupted her medical studies and went to Spain as a medical auxiliary during the Spanish civil war to help the Republican side. Among many other causes, she championed the struggle to prevent the closure of the Elizabeth Garrett Anderson Hospital and, at the age of 73, joined other demonstrators in a 'sit down' protest in Euston Road. She was an active member of the Campaign for Nuclear Disarmament and joined the demonstrations at the Greenham Common base a few weeks before her death. Throughout her life she had a keen nose for injustice and a deep sympathy for the underdog. Her innate sensitivity enabled her to distinguish between the good and the truly excellent both in people, the arts, and everyday affairs. Her vast range of interests, her gift for friendship and her understanding, brought out the best in her wide circle of friends from all walks of life. She remained unmarried and lived alone.

She wrote fluently and lucidly, with an attractive handwriting, and was much valued as an editor of papers, especially memoranda. She was proud of her fellowship of the College and when she lived in Prince Albert Road, Regent's Park, she enjoyed being near enough to attend lectures and classes. Just previous to her death she was enjoying French classes run by the College.

Portia made herself readily available to help colleagues and patients night and day, but in spite of a busy professional life, and so many other activities, she had the time and energy to enjoy cultured recreations. She loved theatre and opera, enjoyed good food and wine, and was an accomplished hostess. She had a beautiful home, took pride in her garden, and collected modern pictures and fine glass. She had a distinctive stylish manner and certain eccentricities; the latter were endearing to her friends but deterred others from appreciating her worth. As a motorist she was notorious for her alarmingly dangerous driving.

In 1982 she left London to live in Oxford to be near special friends. She was preparing to go for her annual, and much valued holiday in France and to attend the College French course in Paris, when she died suddenly following a cerebral haemorrhage while visiting the Cavendish School in Ealing. It was comforting to many of her friends to know that she did not endure a long illness, and it was fitting that she – who had succoured so many so selflessly – was among close friends when she died. JL

[*Brit. med. J.*, 1983, **286**, 2066; *Lancet*, 1983, **1**, 1342; Photo]

HOLZEL, Aron *b*.27 Jan 1909 *d*.28 Oct 1978
MD Prague (1933) DCH (1947) MRCPE (1964) MRCP (1965)
FRCPE (1969) FRCP (1970)

Aron Holzel was born in the Austro-Hungarian province of Galicia which is now part of Rumania, the son of Solomon Holzel, a Jewish farmer and accountant, and of Bertha Fiderer, daughter of Isaac Fiderer, a merchant. He was educated at the Maximilian Grammar School, Vienna, and at the German University of Prague, qualifying with distinction in 1933. From 1934 to 1939 he worked in Prague as a children's physician, holding junior posts in the Babies' Hospital, the German Children's Hospital and the University Polyclinic for Children's Diseases. After the occupation of Czechoslovakia by the Germans he escaped to England, and worked in Warwick during the war as resident assistant physician.

At the end of the war he was appointed locum consultant in paediatrics. He moved to Manchester in 1948 to join Wilfrid Gaisford in establishing the new academic department of paediatrics, and as lecturer in child health worked successively at the Royal Manchester Children's Hospital, the Duchess of York Hospital for Babies, and Booth Hall Children's Hospital. In 1955 he was made senior lecturer and in 1962 reader. In 1971 he was awarded a personal chair, and on his formal retirement in 1974 he was made professor emeritus and appointed dean of postgraduate medical studies. A member of the British Paediatric Association from 1951, he was appointed to its Council and Academic Board in 1966. He was also a member of the German, Swiss, French and Japanese Paediatric Societies, and a founder and one-time president of the European Society for Paediatric Research. In 1973 he became the first paediatric president of the Manchester Medical Society.

He died as he would have wished, after giving a paper on his favourite topic of milk allergy in babies.

Medicine was the major interest in Aron Holzel's life, but his knowledge encompassed a wide range of cultures and disciplines. Within medicine his contributions were wide ranging, spanning medical history and philosophy, the description of new physical signs and the exploration of new aspects of pathophysiology. His most recent research was on the founding fathers of Manchester paediatrics.

Aron Holzel was a masterly clinician, observant, devoted and careful in everything he did. His research work stemmed in the first instance from clinical observations interpreted in the light of his wide embracing knowledge of pathophysiology. He was perhaps the first paediatrician to recognise the importance of milk allergy; he was the first to demonstrate the existence and nature of lactose intolerance, and he initiated the studies that led to the elucidation of the enzyme defect in galactosaemia. He was also among the first to demonstrate the role of the respiratory syncytial virus in bronchiolitis, and of staphylococcal infection in toxic epidermal necrolysis. Cystic fibrosis and infant nutrition were subjects which particularly interested him.

As a colleague he was stimulating, approachable and inexhaustibly good-natured. He could, however, be disconcertingly outspoken when he felt anyone was not living up to his professional and personal standards of conduct. Holzel was as widely respected locally as he was in the wider circles of European and world medicine, and universally liked. He brought to Manchester medicine, with its tradition of down-to-earth competence, a wider vision. His contributions to medical knowledge were on a par with his concern for his patients, and his influence lives on.

Aron Holzel married Dr Frieda Salus, daughter of Dr Richard Salus, in 1941, and their daughters are Dr Ruth Holzel, who obtained a PhD in chemistry, and Dr Helen Holzel, who became a microbiologist.

JAD

[*Brit. med. J.*, 1978, **2**, 1504, 1567; *Lancet*, 1978, **2**, 1060; *Times*, 4 Nov 1978; Photo]

HOOD, *Lt.Gen., Sir* **Alexander** *b.*25 Sept 1888 *d.*11 Sept 1980
GBE (1946) CBE (1939) KCB (1943) CB (1941) KCVO (1953)
MB ChB Edin (1910) MD (1931) Hon FRCSE (1941)
FRCP* (1944) DCL Durham (1945) LLD Edin (1945)
Hon FRFPS Glasg (1947)†

Alexander Hood was born at Leith, Edinburgh, the son of Alexander Hood and Agnes Marshall (née Cunninghame). He was educated at Leith Academy, George Watson's College, and Edinburgh University. After qualifying in 1910 he spent a year as house surgeon in the Royal Infirmary of Edinburgh. In 1912 he joined the Royal Army Medical Corps serving with Indian troops in France and

Belgium in the first world war, and immediately afterwards on the north-west frontier of India and in Afghanistan. Continuing as a regular officer he studied pathology, achieving specialist status in 1923. During the years 1922–1937 he served on the Rhine, in India and in Egypt, mainly as a pathologist, and is credited with introducing the Khan Test to the Army, and having performed original work on cerebrospinal meningitis and pneumonic plague. He gained the MD of Edinburgh in 1931.

He was called from his specialty to administration at an early stage to become ADMS (later DDMS) HQ British Forces in Palestine and Trans-Jordan during 1937–1939, and it was here that he gained such a reputation as an administrator that he was marked as a future director-general. His skill was also acknowledged by a CBE and mention in despatches. He did not have to wait long to assume the highest office. After service in France 1939–1940, in 1941 he was promoted from the substantive rank of colonel direct to that of lieutenant-general, passing over scores of his seniors to become director general of Army Medical Services for the remainder of the second world war.

In this post Hood's contribution to the war effort was second only to those of the great military commanders, and his work in directing the Army Medical Service towards prevention of disease and reduction of pain and suffering and disability, was probably the greatest contribution of any doctor. He was of large commanding presence, powerful personality and of great intellect, dominating and bending to his will the few regulars and many distinguished civilians who formed his medical directorate team at the War Office. He obtained complete loyalty, and by delegating heavy responsibility extracted from all the greatest possible contribution. Thus no innovation or advance in medicine was neglected, but was rapidly examined for its relevance to field or hospital work. If his experts gave favourable opinions, Hood's administrative and executive ability ensured the minimum time lag between discovery and practical application. A directorate of medical research was set up to cooperate with the Medical Research Council, and to assist and support its operational units. Hood decided, against many pressures, that research by doctors upon soldiers should be directed solely to promoting health and preventing and curing disease and alleviating injury in the individual. His guidelines remain for the use of, and have been applied by, his successors in office.

He was always extremely proud of his contributions to the United States Forces – how he assisted them on their first entry to the war, and the close collaboration he ensured with their medical leaders, to the great benefit of both nations. Among his many achievements were the reorganization of field medical units; the provision of forward surgery on the field of battle; the organization of a first-class blood transfusion service; the rapid introduction of new chemotherapeutic agents, such as antimalarials and antibiotics; and the placing of Army psychiatry on a sound basis.

His success ensured that he held the appointment of DGAMS for three years after the war, but his dream of being the first head of a combined medical service for Navy, Army and Air Force was not realized. After a year in the Ministry of Health, Hood was appointed in 1949 Governor and Commander-in-Chief Bermuda, and his tenure was until 1955. In 1953 he acted as host to Churchill, Eden and President Eisenhower during their Bermuda conferences.

He was a very fine golfer, being the RAMC champion; gaining an Army Championship trophy; and winning the coveted Queen Victoria Jubilee Vase of the Royal and Ancient Club, St Andrews, in 1953.

His first marriage was to Evelyn Dulcia, daughter of George Ellwood of Kensington, and of this there were one son and two daughters. His second marriage was to Mrs Helen Winifred Wilkinson of Hamilton, Bermuda. He died in Bermuda. JPB

[*Brit. med. J.*, 1980, **281**, 1149; *Lancet*, 1980, **2**, 654; *Times*, 15 Sept 1980; Photo]

HOPE, Elinor Oliver Steenson *b.*11 Aug 1939 *d.*19 May 1982
MB ChB Edin (1963) MRCP(UK) (1969) FRCP (1980)

Elinor Hope was born in a small town in the south of Scotland and studied medicine at Edinburgh University. After qualifying she decided to specialize in general medicine and soon gained her membership of the College. As a junior, she was highly regarded by her consultants when she trained in chest medicine.

In 1973 she was appointed a consultant physician (with a major interest in chest medicine) at the Aylesbury Group of hospitals, at the age of 33. She was based initially at Tindal Hospital, running the chest department with Elizabeth Hills. This department was later transferred to Stoke Mandeville Hospital and integrated with the division of medicine.

She was an extremely competent and conscientious doctor, highly regarded by both patients and staff. She was a member of the British Thoracic Society, and took an active part in hospital medical administration. Although she was a private person she had a lively personality and a strong sense of humour. She was unmarried and remained very close to her family. She loved country life and had a keen interest in walking, gardening, ornithology, and travel. Her sudden, tragic death after depression at the age of 43 was a great shock to her colleagues, family and friends. PC/GW

HORWICH, Leon *b.*29 July 1924 *d.*4 Feb 1977
MB BCh Liverp (1953) MRCP (1963) MD (1966) FRCP (1974)

Leon Horwich was born at Southport, Lancashire, the son of Isaac Horwich, a master tailor, and Amelia, daughter of Leon Fincklestein. He was educated at King George V School, Southport, and Liverpool University. During the second world war he served in the Royal Army Medical Corps, joining as a private in 1943 and rising to the rank of sergeant by the time of his discharge in 1947. He then entered

Liverpool University Medical School where he qualified in 1953.

After a series of resident and registrar appointments at various Merseyside hospitals, he was appointed Nuffield research assistant at the department of medicine, University of Liverpool. Two years later, in 1966, he was appointed physician superintendent at Whiston Hospital but in 1972, with the changed administration, was designated consultant physician to Whiston and St Helen's Hospitals. He became the first chairman of the medical executive committee of St Helen's and Knowsley Area Health Authority, an appointment he held until June 1976.

As a general physician with special interests in neurology and gastroenterology, Leon Horwich contributed notably in the decade he spent at the two large hospitals with which he was chiefly associated. His attributes of gentle patient care, well recognized diagnostic acumen, and unobtrusive hard work made him a valuable and trusted colleague.

In 1965 he pioneered studies in the use of carbenoxolone (Biogastrone) in the treatment of gastric ulceration, and his publications became widely quoted internationally. He contributed original articles on the use of chloroquin in the treatment of rheumatoid arthritis, the influence of ABO blood groups in duodenal ulceration, and studies in peripheral nerve conduction in disease, and many other publications in scientific journals. In his role as hospital administrator he commanded general respect and admiration for his tactful and effective approach to many inevitably perplexing problems.

In the last few months of his life he bore his distressing illness with great fortitude. At the height of his troubles he was able to tell a friend that two things in particular had been revealed to him – that he was able to endure pain, and that he had learnt with apparent surprise that he was held in such devotion by so many friends and relatives. It was indicative of his general lack of pomp and circumstance.

NB-J/GW

[*Brit. med. J.*, 1977, **1**, 719; Photo]

HOWARTH, Frank Hugo *b*.18 July 1916 *d*.1 Jan 1981
MRCS LRCP (1941) MA MB BChir Cantab (1941) MRCP (1948) DMRD (1950) FRCP (1966)

Frank Howarth was born at Pelsall, Staffordshire and received his scholastic education at Queen Mary's School, Walsall. From there he went to Corpus Christi College, Cambridge, where he achieved a double first in the Natural Sciences Tripos and was awarded numerous exhibitions and prizes. In addition, while at Cambridge he obtained the primary FRCS and played rugby for the Cambridge University Medical Society. From Cambridge he went to the London Hospital and graduated in 1941. Thereafter he served with distinction in the RAMC in Burma and Arakan, achieving the rank of major and the grade of medical specialist and officer in charge of medical division despite the fact that he was only in his twenties. Returning to civil life he was medical registrar to the president of the College, Lord Brain, and the Treasurer, Dick Bomford, at the London, and obtained the membership in 1948. He also became supervisor of studies in physiology at his old college, Corpus Christi.

However, in 1948 he decided to devote his life to diagnostic radiology, and after five years of increasingly responsible posts at the London Hospital, and a period of postgraduate study in Stockholm, he was appointed consultant radiologist to the Queen Elizabeth Hospital in Birmingham, and lecturer in radiological anatomy in the University of Birmingham in 1954. In these appointments he spent the remainder of his working life and made a contribution that cannot be overestimated. He pioneered the use of the Seldinger technique in angiography in Great Britain, but this was the least of his achievements. His training as a physician and his great intellectual capacity made him a radiologist towering above his colleagues. Whenever asked for help, he would immediately grasp the problem and identify how much he might contribute to its solution. In cases of especial difficulty or complexity he was always the final arbiter. The Queen Elizabeth Hospital never had a more devoted servant, nor one who was so universally respected for his humility, his kindness and his invariable courtesy as well as for his expertise and leadership. The many radiologists he trained are a lasting reminder of a man whose attributes may never be equalled. He died suddenly from a heart attack on New Year's Day 1981, at the age of 64.

Frank had married Lucy Hopkins, once a theatre sister at the London, in 1946, and they had two sons. AGWW

[*Brit. med. J.*, 1981, **282**, 328; *Lancet*, 1981, **1**, 228; *Times*, 7 Jan 1981]

HOYLE, John Clifford *b*.4 July 1901 *d*.10 Feb 1976
MB BS Manch (1925) MD (1929) MRCP (1931) FRCP (1938)

Clifford Hoyle was born in Brierfield, Lancashire, where his father, John Hoyle, was a much loved general practitioner. His mother, Esther Brierley, was the daughter of a soap manufacturer. Clifford was educated at Sedburgh Preparatory, Rydal, and Manchester University, where he graduated in 1925. For three years he was a first assistant at London Hospital, subsequently being appointed a consultant at King's College Hospital, the Brompton, and King Edward VII Hospital, Midhurst.

Hoyle had worked with WE Dixon at Cambridge before serving under Sir John Parkinson and William Soares at the London, so that he brought a special knowledge of pharmacology to the practice of cardiology. Perhaps his most important achievement was the establishment of the department of medicine at King's College Hospital, which he was appointed director, and which he handed over when a professor of medicine was appointed. His teaching ability was considerable. He brought to the bedside a healthy distrust of the use of drugs without proper proof of their efficacy. He sometimes deliberated a long time before making a firm diagnosis, but then rarely did he alter it, and he was at his best when teasing out clinical problems at the bedside. His command of English was such that he would sacrifice many hours in correcting the grammar and syntax of the papers of many of his juniors. His Lancashire accent persisted throughout life.

Hoyle was interested in the history of medicine, and at the time of his death was preparing a biography of Laënnec. His other great interests were opera, photography and gardening, greatly enjoying the latter on his retirement to Cornwall, his wife's native county.

In 1931 he had married Mary Irene Rosewarne, the daughter of a Cornish mining engineer. They had two sons. SO/GW

[*Brit. med. J.*, 1976, **1**, 591; *Lancet*, 1976, *1*, 497; *Times*, 20 Feb 1976; Photo]

HUBBLE, *Sir* Douglas (Vernon) *b*.25 Dec 1900 *d*.6 Nov 1981
KBE (1971) CBE (1966) MRCS LRCP (1924) MB BS Lond (1926) MD (1934) MRCP (1950) FRCP (1954)

Douglas Hubble was born on Christmas Day, the son of Harry Edward Hubble and Agnes Kate, née Field. He received his medical education at St Bartholomew's Hospital, qualifying with the conjoint diploma in 1924 and graduating from the University of London two years later. Thereafter he entered general practice at Derby where he rapidly acquired a considerable reputation. In 1932 he was elected to the consultant staff of the Derbyshire Children's Hospital, and in 1934 he obtained his MD. He became deeply interested in paediatric endocrinology and published a number of excellent papers on the subject, which gave him a national reputation. The combination of general practice and consulting paediatrics continued until 1942 when he was elected physician to the Derbyshire Royal Infirmary and the Derby City Hospital. An increasing consulting practice and the advent of the National Health Service led to his withdrawal from general practice in 1948; it was not however until 1950 that he obtained the membership of the College and four years later he became a Fellow.

Numerous universities invited him to accept their chairs of medicine or paediatrics and in 1958 he eventually chose the paediatric chair at Birmingham. In this he was supremely successful, developing the Institute of Child Health and becoming Public Orator in the University and dean of the Faculty of Medicine, 1963–1968. His services were so highly valued that he was retained for three years beyond the normal retiring age. In 1968, still young in heart and with abounding energy, he went to Addis Ababa as dean of the Faculty of Medicine in the Haile Selassie I University. On his return to England he went to live in retirement near Newbury, where he devoted himself to literary work and scholarship. He was appointed CBE in 1966 and KBE in 1971. In the College he was councillor, examiner, Langdon Brown lecturer and Osler orator, but he also gave valuable service to many other bodies. From 1958 to 1968 he served on the British Pharmacopoeia Commission, and on the General Medical Council

(1965 – 1969), where his great achievement was the drafting of the requirements for the preregistration year. He served on the clinical research board (1962 – 1966), and the tropical medicine research board (1965 – 1969) of the Medical Research Council, and was chairman of the council for Investigation of Fertility Control (1963 – 1968). He was president of the paediatric section of the Royal Society of Medicine in 1956, and served on the executive committee of the Association of Physicians of Great Britain and Ireland (1957 – 1960). He was the recipient of many professional honours, including the James Spence medal of the British Paediatric Association, the Dawson Williams prize of the British Medical Association, and numerous lectureships; the Burns at the Royal College of Physicians and Surgeons of Glasgow (1957), the Honeyman Gillespie of the University of Edinburgh (1958), the Felton at the Royal Children's Hospital, Melbourne (1961), the Lawson Wilkins at Johns Hopkins University (1965), the Lloyd Roberts at the University of Manchester (1966), the Tisdall of the Canadian Medical Association (1967), the Osler of the Society of Apothecaries (1968), and the Leonard Parsons of the University of Birmingham (1971).

Hubble was an enthusiastic Johnsonian, a member of the Johnson Club and in 1956 president of the Lichfield Johnson Society. Only a year before his death he contributed an excellent paper to the British Medical Journal entitled 'O Absolom', in which he recounted some of the eccentricities of the Gosse and Sitwell families. He was also a fine orator, but his greatest attributes were his kindness, his unselfishness, his urbanity and his capacity to live in amity with everyone with whom he came into contact, as well as to inspire their admiration and affection.

During his latter years he became very deaf, and he died, from multiple myelomatosis, at the home of his daughter in Edinburgh. In 1928 he had married Marie Arnott Bryce, who predeceased him by a few months. There were three daughters of the marriage. AGWW

[*Brit. med. J.*, 1982, **283**, 1408, 1495, 1618; **284**, 62; *Times*, 16 Nov 1982; Photo]

HUGHES, Richard Osborne *b.*20 Dec 1939 *d.*19 June 1983
BSc Liverp (1960) MB ChB (1963) MRCP (1967) FRCP (1982)

Richard Hughes was born at Preston, Lancashire, and educated in Birkenhead before studying medicine at Liverpool University, where he qualified in 1963, having obtained BSc with honours in physiology in 1960. Apart from a year in Leeds, his junior posts were in the Liverpool hospitals and at one stage he was senior house officer to CA Clarke (now Sir Cyril), who was later elected president of the College. From 1969 to 1974 he was senior registrar to the Liverpool hospitals. In 1974 he was appointed consultant to the geriatric department at Clatterbridge Hospital, Wirral.

Richard's father was David Osborne Hughes, a consultant chest physician. In 1964 he married Jennifer Jane, whose father, William

Bryan, was an optician and pharmacist. Pharmacy was closely associated with the family, for his own grandfather and aunt had followed this profession, and so did his wife and her brother. He and his wife had two children; a son and a daughter.

When he came to Clatterbridge in 1974 he had a few sessions in general medicine, but the majority were in geriatric medicine and he joined two other physicians in this specialty, which had grown rapidly in the 1960s owing to the activity of these two doctors and the general political and emotional atmosphere reigning in the country at that time. In general medicine he shared a ward with another physician who had already been there for 20 years with the same nursing staff, which must have been a demanding and daunting experience. Fortunately, they were both tolerant men, both possessed a sense of humour and perhaps a slightly cynical understanding of the politics of medicine, so that a happy relationship quickly developed. At first Richard Hughes showed a partiality for finding rare conditions, but he eventually found that sparrows were more common than hoopoes. At a time when there was no such common knowledge, he was particularly interested in the interaction of drugs, clearly the result of his close relationship with the pharmacological profession. Later, he realized the need for an endoscopy clinic in Wirral, and with very little financial backing, and in somewhat primitive conditions, he established one. Hughes became adept at the technique and very knowledgeable about gastroenterology, and he instilled his enthusiasm in his junior colleagues, so that his successive registrars carried on his techniques when they progressed to other hospitals. Sadly, he had no very clear ability to tell the time, and so much of the work was done when the blood sugar of patients, medical and nursing staff, was low, but despite this they were all enthusiastic and glad to be his patients and pupils, and perhaps also intrigued by some of the revelations produced by intravenous diazepam.

He was somewhat diffident and insecure at first, and had difficulty in communicating with those under his care. But as time passed he developed a real interest in his patients, their problems and their welfare. Perhaps seeing the modest results which could be obtained by applying the very demanding disciplines of rehabilitation to the elderly, he felt that they could be more successful when applied to the young disabled person. He threw himself into this project with great enthusiasm, in a specially built unit for this work, and was once again rewarded by the respect and liking of those he treated.

Richard Hughes then entered the jungle of medical politics, becoming chairman of the medical advisory committee of Clatterbridge Hospital, chairman of the district consultants advisory team and consultant representative on the district management team. No doubt he realized that if major modifications had to be made in the local application of medicine, it was there that power and influence dwelt. Such modifications were, indeed, badly needed, because the commissioning of a new and over-large district hospital, and the consequent down-grading of the previously excellent Clatterbridge Hospital where he worked, produced unhappy results in the field of hospital medicine.

Unhappily, his life was too short for him to achieve his full potential. He died following a major car accident, enduring a month in the intensive care unit, stoical to the end. MWWW

[*Brit. med. J.*, 1983, **287**, 369]

HULBERT, Norman George *b*.3 Jan 1911 *d*.9 Nov 1982
MRCS LRCP (1934) MA MB BChir Cantab (1935) MRCP (1937) MD (1940) FRCP (1964)

Norman George Hulbert was born in India, his father Joseph George Hulbert being a lieutenant colonel in the Indian Medical Service. His mother, Elsie Frances, was the daughter of Alexander Brooke, a merchant of the City of London and Handford, Cheshire. He was educated at Wellington, Trinity College, Cambridge, and St Bartholomew's Hospital Medical School, qualifying in 1934. He spent several years in the cardiology department at Bart's, and then at the Royal Chest Hospital, before making neurology his special interest. Throughout his career, however, he successfully and proudly remained a general physician. He was a brilliant teacher, and medicine continued to be fresh and exciting for him all his days.

Hulbert was formerly consulting physician to the West End Hospital for Neurology and Neurosurgery, the Metropolitan Hospital, the Royal National Throat, Nose and Ear Hospital and the Mildmay Mission Hospital. He was also chief medical officer of the Sun Life Assurance Society. The favourite among his hospitals was the Mildmay and, one way or the other, he gave it 42 years of faithful service. Deeply valuing the spirit of Christian vocation and service that permeated the hospital, he fought hard for its retention when it was threatened with closure. As a teacher he had an endless flow of instructive anecdotes, but what emerged most strongly was his warmth and his ability to inspire hope. Committees gave him less pleasure, but he did not spare himself from hospital meetings, enlivening them with his wit and shortening them with his clarity of thought.

In 1936 he married Joan Margery (Primrose Rostran, the writer) daughter of Owen Frances Grazebrook, JP, at St George's, Hanover Square. They had two children: a son and a daughter, and six grandchildren.

He never sought to own a car, maintaining that public transport was quicker and cheaper, so that it was by bus and tube, with bowler hat and furled umbrella, that he reached his numerous and scattered appointments. In his early days he had a bowler for Bart's and a trilby for his East End hospitals, but he later kept to the bowler, which he said would serve as protection if he should be coshed. He greatly enjoyed being photographed by tourists. Since he found medicine so entertaining he hardly needed diversions, but in his younger days he followed beagles, and he enjoyed fly-fishing. He was also an excellent fencer, and was elected a member of the Epée Club in 1957.

GW/VL

[*Brit. med. J.*, 1982, **285**, 1753; Photo]

HUMBLE, Joseph Graeme *b*.10 July 1913 *d*.10 June 1980
CVO (1955) MRCS LRCP (1937) MRCP (1959) FRCPath (1964) FRCP (1970)

Joseph Humble was born at Mansfield, Nottinghamshire, the son of Wensley Taylor Humble, a caterer of the town, and of Louisa Anne Humble, née Witham, the daughter of a publican. There is no record of any medical connection in the family at that time, nor in previous generations.

Joe Humble, as he was always called, was educated at the preparatory school to Queen Elizabeth Grammar School, Mansfield, but was later a pupil at Bedford Modern School. He enrolled as a pre-clinical medical student at King's College, London, in 1932, and from 1934 to 1937 was a clinical student at Westminster Hospital at its previous site at Broad Sanctuary, opposite Westminster Abbey. He was thus one of the last generation of students to be trained in the old medical school and hospital. Joe qualified in 1937 and for the next 41 years, until his retirement as emeritus professor, was continuously on the staff of Westminster Hospital and Medical School. He was house physician to the children's department from June 1937 to January 1938, and for the remainder of his career was on the staff of the pathology, and later of the haematology departments, of the medical school, being junior assistant pathologist 1938–1939, acting assistant pathologist 1940–1946, haematologist 1946–1949, senior lecturer in haematology (University of London) 1949–1964, reader in haematology 1964–1972, and professor of haematology 1972–1978.

Joe's main interests in haematology were in the fields of leukaemia, aplastic anaemia, and marrow transplantation, but in addition he wrote many useful articles on other aspects of his specialty, e.g. 'The mechanisms of petechial haemorrhage formation' *Blood*, **4**, 69-75, 1949, using *in vivo* microscopical techniques; 'Diphyllobothrium infestation and anaemia in Great Britain' *Brit. med. J.*, **2**, 188, 1950, 'A family illustrating the double inheritance of the sickle cell trait and of Mediterranean anaemia' *J. clin. Path.*, **7**, 201, 1954, as well as many interesting and informative case reports.

In collaboration with RJV Pulvertaft, he published many articles on marrow culture, and the study of living cells by phase-contrast micro-cinematography. They were particularly interested in the interaction of lymphocytes and other cells, and first described the phenomenon named by them 'emperipolesis', in which the lymphocytes became adherent to other cells, or apparently passed over or into the interior of these cells. This work was greatly helped by the excellent department of medical photography at Westminster Medical School under the direction of Peter Hansell, an old friend of Joe's.

Joe Humble's enduring fame in haematology will undoubtedly rest on his pioneering work in marrow transplantation in this country. His interest was first alerted in the mid-1950s, when he developed techniques for obtaining and infusing marrow, and in methods of cryopreservation of marrow samples. On the clinical side, he was greatly helped by collaboration with KA Newton, consultant oncologist, and in the laboratory aspects of preservation of marrow by

DE Pegg. Marrow was obtained by aspiration from pelvic bones and sternum into heparinized tissue culture fluid. After removal of fat and particles capable of causing embolism, the concentrated cells were infused intravenously into the recipient, to settle spontaneously in the bone marrow. Cryopreservation was chiefly by rapid freezing of replicable cells in liquid nitrogen. These methods have resisted the changes imposed by time and modern refinements, and are still widely employed throughout the world. In the early 1960s, Joe pioneered the techniques of autotransplantation in the management of malignant disease, but the use of marrow from donors was hampered by current lack of knowledge of tissue antibodies and immunity, and by the poor available methods for combating rejection episodes.

The break-through in hetero-transplants came in 1971, when transfer of marrow from a sib was successful in a case of immunodeficiency, and later from a father to an affected child. In 1973, success occurred in a transplant from a completely unrelated donor, proved potentially compatible by tissue typing techniques. Joe was actively engaged in improving and facilitating marrow transplantation in haematological diseases, cases of immunodeficiency, and in metabolic hereditary disorders in which essential enzymes were absent, until the time of his retirement in 1978. His skill, knowledge, and encouragement undoubtedly had a great influence in making Westminster Hospital and Medical School one of the leading centres for marrow transplantation in the world.

He was honoured by being created CVO in the New Year's Honours list of 1955 for personal services to the Royal Family.

Joe Humble was a concise and conscientious teacher of his specialty. Many generations of Westminster graduates will remember with gratitude their excellent grounding in the important principles of haematology. He was a kind and gentle man, and was obviously often distressed at the serious prognosis of many of the blood diseases which were his main interest.

In his own student days, Joe was a keen sportsman, playing rugby for the Westminster team, and association football for the United Hospitals. In the cricket field, he was a skilled wicket keeper and later demonstrated his prowess in many staff-versus-student matches. His hobby was medical history, and in collaboration with P Hansell he published an excellent history of Westminster Medical School and Hospital. In his short retirement, he wrote the biography of James Guthrie, a distinguished Westminster graduate and Peninsular Army surgeon in Wellington's forces.

He had a supremely happy married and family life. In 1942 he married Elsie May Hunt, the daughter of a farmer, who however was always referred to as Ann Humble. They had three sons, one of whom is, like his father, a specialist in pathology, and another a gifted historian and writer.

It is no secret that Joe died of chronic lymphatic leukaemia, a fact published in several obituaries. The diagnosis must have been a great shock to him, as it was found when testing a new Coulter counter with a blood sample obtained from himself. Joe remained in good health until his retirement in 1978, but sadly did not long enjoy a much deserved retirement. The disease steadily reduced his powers of immunity, and his last year was marred by repeated and ever more serious bacterial and fungal infections. His fortitude in the face of adversity was a great example to his friends and colleagues. It was a deep pleasure to Joe to attend for a short period the occasion of the 100th Anniversary of Westminster Dining Club, but his obvious ill-health was a sad reminder to his many friends and admirers that his days were numbered. For many of us, he epitomized the Westminster man – trained at Westminster, married to a Westminster nurse, his whole working career without interruption carried out at Westminster, where he finally died. For almost half a century in work and in play he added distinction, lustre and warmth to the life of the School and Hospital which he so loved. MDM

[*Brit. med. J.*, 1980, **280**, 1624 *Times,* 14 June 1980; Photo]

HUNT, Thomas Cecil *b.*5 June 1901 *d.*22 Dec 1980
CBE (1964) BA Oxon (1923) BM BCh (1926) MRCP (1928)
DM (1930) FRCP (1935)

Thomas Hunt was born in Guildford. His antecedents are of considerable interest. His great-grandfather was William MacMichael, who received from William IV the gold-headed cane 'for curing him of the gout'. Thomas's father, on the other hand, was much less well-off – he was a clergyman and classical scholar – and having educated the two eldest boys, there was not much left in the till when the time came for Thomas's education. So this was won the hard way, with scholarships to St Paul's, Magdalen College (Oxford) and St Mary's. He still felt the pinch after leaving the University, for during his first year at St Mary's he used to travel to Oxford each week, to do physiology tutoring and demonstrating for Charles Sherrington. After qualifying he won a Radcliffe travelling fellowship, which had also been won more than 100 years earlier by his great-grandfather. He opted for Vienna, where he studied endocrinology, and his teacher there was Bauer whom he was later to repay when, in Nazi-ridden 1938, Bauer had to be got out of Austria.

TCH was appointed to St Mary's in 1930, and this coincided with his marriage to the actress Barbara Todd. TCH said 'I fixed the marriage, but not the appointment', and the meaning of this had its origins in sport. He was a good wicket-keeper and narrowly missed a blue at Oxford. He was also an occasional batsman, and on a cricket tour in Guernsey the gods were with him. The girl of his choice was watching, and he hit 50 in four overs. Barbara's theatre career was reduced to tatters, but it was worth it as they lived happily together for fifty years, their golden wedding being celebrated shortly before his death, and they had a most distinguished family.

Other appointments held by TCH were physician to the Royal Masonic Hospital, Paddington Hospital, King Edward VII Hospital for Officers, and chairman of the Medical Sickness Annuity and Life

Assurance Society.

Gastroenterology became Thomas's specialty by chance rather than design. After his appointment at St Mary's (which at that time was, of course, honorary) he was awarded a Mackenzie McKinnon fellowship which gave him a £400 p.a. grant to study duodenal intubation. His papers on the subject greatly impressed Arthur Hurst, and in 1936 Hurst invited Thomas and one or two others to dinner at the Athenaeum and suggested that they form a gastroenterological club. This was the beginning of what, in 1945, was to become the British Society of Gastroenterology. Later on, when *Gut* became its official journal, Thomas was a member of the editorial board.

In January 1940 Thomas joined the RAMC, and his lifelong love of travel was fully satisfied over the five years of war. One of his early appointments was consulting physician in Freetown, which gave him the chance of going aboard almost every troopship in the Merchant Navy. Later, as a brigadier, he was consultant in Algeria and Iraq, and with his headquarters in Baghdad he visited most countries in the Middle East as well as India.

After the war he played an important part in the early stages of the European and Mediterranean Society of Gastroenterology, and presided at the London Congress in 1956. The World Congress of Gastroenterology also greatly appealed to him, and he was its president from 1962 to 1966. Aged 70 and still very active, he organized the British Digestive Foundation to raise funds for research into gastrointestinal disorders, and a special appeal was made on the 100th anniversary of Hurst's birth. He had a wide interest in epidemiology and nutrition, and was chairman of an international working party on environmental factors in alimentary cancer. He made a continuing contribution to gastroenterology for nearly fifty years.

A characteristic of Thomas's was his great enthusiasm when championing causes, and one of the most important of these was visiting and advising universities in the new countries of the Commonwealth (often with Professor Kinmonth), and he was closely connected with the new medical school at Ibadan, and also in the West Indies. It could have been surmised that he would have preferred to have lived a hundred years ago, when the map was still red, but this was not so. With his mental toughness he found multiracial societies far more exciting – they were a great challenge to his ability to handle difficult situations and to bring peace.

With his own upbringing, and his marriage to someone of wide artistic tastes, it is not surprising that his house should reflect the sensibility and discrimination of both of them. Their delightful hospitality is a very happy memory. They had a splendid collection of Nymphenburg china, and among their books an almost complete set of first editions of Somerset Maugham, and a volume by William MacMichael describing his journey from Russia to Constantinople on his Radcliffe fellowship in 1817. Thomas and Barbara also did a great deal, both on the professional and artistic side, for the Medical Society of London, of which he had been president.

Thomas was a great RCP man, having been senior censor and senior vice-president. He was a considerable force on the Conjoint Board, and had strong views on the merit of the examination. The soft voice *could* also be very firm and come down most decidedly on one or other side of the fence, and on two occasions he changed the course of history. Before the war Churchill often consulted him, and one day the leader-to-be rang up asking for an appointment at 4.30 pm. Thomas was quite firm – he had another patient at that time. Winston was nettled and switched to Charles Moran, and thereby hangs another story [Moran, *Winston Churchill: the struggle for survival 1940 – 1965 . . .* (1966)]. The second occasion was when it was left to TCH (with two others) to decide whether or not Anthony Eden's health was robust enough for him to remain in office as the prime minister. The answer was a regretful but entirely firm 'No'.

His strong interest in medical history was reflected in his Harveian Oration in 1973 at the College, *Digestive diseases: the changing scene*, and in his Lettsomian lectures to the Medical Society of London in 1973, *Doubt, Dogma and Dyspepsia*.

He was, above all, a medical diplomat both at home and overseas. One of his outstanding qualities was his ability to understand and often reconcile conflicting opinions. His sincerity, charm of manner, his gift as a conversationalist, his eloquence as a speaker, his wide artistic interests and considerable ability as a linguist, made him one of the most distinguished physicians of his time. CAC/FAJ

[*Brit. med. J.*, 1981, **282**, 234, 397; *Lancet*, 1981, **1**, 110; *St. Mary's Hosp. Gaz.*, Mar/Apr 1962; *Commemoration of Dr. Thomas Hunt*, St. Mary's Hosp. and Med. School & Brit. Soc. Gastroenterology, 21 Jan 1982; Photo]

HUNTER, Donald *b.*11 Feb 1898 *d.*11 Dec 1978
CBE (1957) MRCS LRCP (1920) MB BS Lond (1920) MD (1922) MRCP (1923) FRCP (1929)

Donald Hunter was born in London, the son of George Hunter, deputy engineer-in-chief of the GPO, and lived there all his life. His mother was a remarkable woman, whose personal sacrifices enabled all her five sons to obtain scholarships to grammar school and university. All were to achieve doctorates in their chosen disciplines, but Donald was the only one who chose medicine. He entered the London Hospital in 1915, but interrupted his studies in order to serve as surgeon-probationer RNVR in HMS *Faulknor*, a flotilla-leader in the Dover Patrol. After the end of the 1914–1918 war he returned to the London, where he qualified in 1920. After a series of house appointments, he became first assistant to Lord Dawson of Penn. He was appointed assistant physician to the London Hospital in 1927 and became a fellow of the Royal College of Physicians in 1929, giving the Goulstonian lecture in 1930 and the Harveian Oration in 1957. He served the London Hospital as physician, teacher and research worker for 36 years, until he retired in 1963.

Donald Hunter earned great renown as a teacher of clinical

medicine, being richly endowed with what he himself called 'fire in the belly'. He had a passion for his subject, and for accuracy and clarity. He employed an indescribable mixture of something like free association, a touch of Russell Howard's instruction by abuse, with a vein of humour all his own. Others might have combined these attributes without producing the peculiar effect Donald had on his audience. The secret lay perhaps in his ability both to surprise and inspire, much that he said being unexpected but everything being important. Nor will his students easily forget the demonstrations given in the museum of the London Hospital Medical College, of which he was curator for 30 years. In his teaching he was at his best, for he appreciated that good general medicine was the bedrock foundation of sound doctoring. He restocked and modernized the museum until it housed more than 8000 specimens, representing almost all that is worth having in morbid anatomy. In addition, he mounted whole series of annotated clinical photographs.

Outside the London, he served on the British Pharmacopoeia Commission, the Poisons Board, and as editor of the *Quarterly Journal of Medicine* and the *British Journal of Industrial Medicine*, being the founder editor of the latter.

Hunter was director of the MRC department for research in industrial medicine at the London Hospital, and in 1957 he was made a CBE in recognition of the work his MRC unit had done in occupational medicine. In 1955 his book *The Diseases of Occupations* was published, and immediately became a classic. The fourth edition was published in 1969. He wrote all 1000 pages of the book in 18 months by getting up at 5 am every day. Donald and his team of doctors, chemists, physicists, engineers and technicians determined, or helped to determine, the following additions to the schedule of prescribed diseases under the Industrial Injuries Act: poisoning by organic phosphorus compounds, organic mercury compounds, tri-cresyl and tri-phenyl phosphates, beryllium and cadmium, as well as bagassosis and mesothelioma of the pleura and peritoneum. Donald did outstanding work on hyperparathyroidism and made a long series of contributions to industrial toxicology. He examined for many universities, for the RCP as Censor and Senior Censor and then, for many years, on the panel of examiners for the membership. Candidates sometimes found him rather formidable and perhaps a little unpredictable, but fellow-examiners considered him to be very fair.

He travelled widely for the World Health Organization, for various governments and medical societies, and visited many foreign medical centres as a member of the Medical Pilgrim's travelling club.

After he retired from the London in 1963 he worked for four years at the Middlesex, and then for three years at Guy's. Even at 70 years of age he continued to display the old characteristic enthusiasm and fire in teaching students, and this was undoubtedly his real love in medicine. In later years, his practice was almost confined to patients whose medico-legal claims arose from chronic poisoning in the various dangerous trades. During his time at Guy's a colleague brought him a sick man employed by a pest control firm. In Donald's own language 'this unfortunate man, while working in the Pool of London, became the victim of acute methyl bromide poisoning. From a tiny boat he had the task of manipulating a cylinder containing enough of this deadly poison to kill the whole population of London: the target was, in fact, three maggots – no less. They were attempting to attack a cargo of five tons of dried peaches contained in a lighter anchored in mid-river. No doubt the maggots died. The patient was seized with giddiness, headache, double vision and slurred speech. He escaped the fate of the maggots only because of God's good west wind blowing down river in some force at the time. It's surely time that pest control experts, so-called, should cease to behave as if their aim were to crack a hazel nut with a ten-ton hammer'.

In his later years he also took great interest in anti-pollution measures, and deplored the fact that the Press consistently failed to point out how Britain led the world in this field.

He was deeply disappointed by the little interest shown in preventive and community medicine. He felt that public health doctors should hold university chairs in environmental medicine, and be given beds and clinical clerks of their own. To call a man a professor of social medicine simply because he was a wizard with figures made no sense to Donald. He called them 'arithmetic doctors'. The student body should be shown the conditions in which men and women lived and worked, and not merely fed with statistics.

While working as first assistant to Lord Dawson of Penn, he met and married Mathilde Bugnion, one of his students at the London, whom he coached for the Oxford BM examination. 'Thilo' was the daughter of a Swiss pastor in Lausanne. They had two daughters, one of them a doctor who followed her mother to Somerville College and qualified in 1957; and two sons, the younger of whom went to King's College, Cambridge, and qualified in medicine in 1963. The marriage was a very happy one, and he delighted in the fact that his wife was more than a match for him in intelligence, and a splendid help in his life's work.

Donald was certainly an individualist, who could inspire the utmost devotion and, on occasion, the most violent opposition. He would never have claimed to be a saint and, indeed, delighted in telling the story of a house physician who came to bid him farewell, presenting him with a copy of *For Sinners Only*. In a letter to RR Bomford, in 1970, enclosing some notes for his own future obituary, he wrote 'Hippocrates is dead, Osler too, and I don't always feel very well myself. Therefore I enclose material suitable for my obituary in the College . . . and now to cheat all of you by living to 95!'. He was a great character, who well deserves his place in the history of the London Hospital and British medicine.

GW/VL

[*Brit. med. J.*, 1979, **1**, 60, 134; *Lancet*, 1978, **2**, 1390; *J. Soc. Occup. med.*, 1979, 29(2), 81; *Times*, 19 Nov 1979; *Daily Telegraph*, 15 Dec 1979; Photo]

HUNTER, Mark Ian Alastair *b*.18 June 1909 *d*.5 Dec 1983
MRCS LRCP (1933) MRCP (1935) MB BChir Cantab (1937)
MD (1945) FRCP (1947)

Alastair Hunter came from a medical family. His father was a general practitioner in Sussex, and he was educated at Winchester and Trinity College, Cambridge, before going on to St George's Hospital, from where he qualified in 1933.

He soon gained stature as a physician, rising through the medical ranks at St George's and starting to develop his specialty of cardiology. He was a disciple of John Parkinson at the London Hospital, where he was Paterson research scholar in the cardiac department. He served as an EMS physician at the London Hospital 1939 – 1945 and then went to the Far East as a medical specialist in the RAMC. He returned to St George's in 1947 to set up the cardiac department, where Aubrey Leatham later joined him. He continued to do medicine and cardiology during the whole of his long career at St George's, but also became increasingly involved in the vast transition which that hospital and its associated medical school were about to experience and was, in fact, one of the formative figures responsible for those changes. He, Ken Robson (*q.v.*), James Dow (*q.v.*) and others had the vision, in the early 1950s, to see that the teaching hospital would be better placed in the centre of an ordinary population rather than as it was, at Hyde Park Corner, and they set in train the events which led to the development of school and hospital at Tooting.

For fifteen years from 1956, Hunter was dean of the medical school. In this job his remarkable gifts came to the fore. He knew all the students, their strengths and weaknesses and knew too how to recognize and bring out their latent attributes. His judgement of people was phenomenally precise, and appointments committees usually had the good sense to follow his lead. An accurate judge, but also totally free from malice, and with another gift, for friendship, so that generations of St George's graduates look back on his role there with gratitude. On the larger scale, he steered the school through some of the biggest changes in its history and set it on the course towards the large independent medical school which it has now become.

He became an important influence beyond St George's, especially in the University of London. He was a member of the senate and the academic council, and he became chairman of the conference of metropolitan deans. At the College, he served as assistant registrar (1950 – 1957), censor (1971 – 1973) and vice-president and senior censor (1974 – 1975).

Hunter was a cultivated man of wide learning. One of his special talents was for modern painting, of which he made a notable collection. The Fitzwilliam Museum, Cambridge, benefited from his guidance and his generosity. The College, too, was much helped by his artistic knowledge and judgement when it moved to Regent's Park.

Alastair Hunter had many other gifts: an all round sportsman for whom cricket, squash and cross-country running were perhaps his favourites, but soccer and golf too were not neglected. It happened that the first bit of the new St George's medical school actually built was the squash courts, a cause of much amusement among visitors. He was running and playing cricket into his seventies and continued, too, an active working life after retirement, helping to plan the Cambridge clinical school and advising the Association of Commonwealth Universities. He had a cardiac operation and had, after a bad patch, returned nearly to his normal health when he died suddenly.

Alastair was unmarried. His sister Diana survived him. HPL

[*Brit. med. J.*, 1984, **288**, 573; *Lancet*, 1984, **1**, 116, 236, 295; *Memorial Address*, Sir Denis Logan, St Paul's Church, 9 Feb 1984; Photo]

HUNTER, Richard Alfred *b.*11 Nov 1923 *d.*25 Nov 1981
MB BS Lond (1946) DPM (1951) MD (1952) MRCP (1953)
FRCPsych (1971) FRCP (1972)

Richard Hunter was born at Nuremberg; his father was Ernst Hirschmann, a merchant, and his mother was Ida, daughter of Sigmund Wertheimer, also a merchant. The shadow of the Nazi revolution persuaded his mother to bring Richard, with his brothers, to England. Here he began his education at The Hall, Hampstead, before going to St Paul's School and thence to St Bartholomew's Hospital. He qualified in 1946, and between house posts at St Bartholomew's and the Maudsley Hospitals, he served as a captain in the RAMC from 1948 to 1950. He was initially attracted to surgery, being house surgeon to Sir Geoffrey Keynes, but later turned to psychiatry. He held posts at Napsbury and Guy's Hospitals before being appointed to the National Hospital, Queen Square, as senior registrar in psychiatry in 1957, and in 1960 physician in psychological medicine. Three years later he became consultant psychiatrist to Friern and Whittington Hospitals.

It was at Friern that Richard Hunter was able to put into practice what history and research had taught him. He had the gift of being able to relate to patients immediately, and to make them aware of his sincerity and determination to find out what made them ill. He believed that the abnormal mental state was not a disease in itself, but an epiphenomenon, a sign of dysfunction within the brain. Convinced of the importance of nursing care in a patient's recovery, he supported his nursing staff in every possible way. They knew this and were devoted to him.

It was a paper on William Battie (*Practitioner*, 1955, **174**, 208-215) which not only revealed Richard Hunter's interest in medical history, but also marked the start of his book collecting. Aided and abetted by his mother, (Ida Macalpine: see Vol. VI, pp.304-5), he indulged this passion to such effect that over the succeeding eight years he had built up a library of psychiatric literature which was second to none, and comprised several thousand volumes. Moreover this formed the basis for their *Three hundred years of psychiatry, 1535 – 1860* (1963), a treasure house of extracts from contemporary works, enhanced by penetrating comments. Three years later a paper in the *BMJ* (1966, **1**, 65-71) in which they set out to show that the 'insanity' of George III was a classic case of porphyria, aroused some controversy. This was to some extent rebutted by their *George III and the mad business* (1969), for which painstaking research produced much new evidence, including the medical history of the forebears and descendants of George III.

President of the sections of psychiatry and of the history of medicine at the Royal Society of Medicine, Richard Hunter was much in demand as a lecturer; he lectured for the Faculty of the History of Medicine and Pharmacy of the Society of Apothecaries, and was visiting Trent lecturer at Duke University, North Carolina, Sloan professor at the Menninger Foundation, Topeka, Kansas, and Hannah visiting professor in Toronto. The enthusiasm which he had brought to his book-collecting showed through in his public utterances, giving rise to a certain forcefulness and often an acerbity which aroused opposition among his colleagues. He never was, and never could be, all things to all men; he was too much of an individualist for that. He did not suffer fools gladly – and he showed it. He was, however, a kindly man, modest and generous, almost impulsively so; in conversation with his friends he liked to have his pipe of tobacco.

The death of his mother in 1974 brought about a complete change in his lifestyle. A year later he married Thea Bostick, superintendent radiographer at Queen Square, and bought a house in Essendon, where for six years he revelled in tending his poultry and very large garden, and basked in the love of his wife and three children. Major surgery suddenly became necessary in the summer of 1981, and after a chequered convalescence, he died in Queen Elizabeth II Hospital, Welwyn Garden City. LMP

[*Brit. med. J.*, 1981, **283**, 1616-17; 1982, **284**, 131; *Lancet*, 1982, **1**, 58; *Times*, 1 Dec 1981; Photo]

HURST, Edward Weston *b*.22 June 1900 *d*.16 Dec 1980
BSc Birm (1920) MB ChB (1922) MD (1924) DSc (1932)
MRCP (1932) FRCP (1940) DSc Adelaide (1941)

Edward Weston Hurst was born in Birmingham, the son of Edward William Hurst and his wife Clarinda, daughter of Thomas Wem. He was educated at King Edward VI School and the University of Birmingham, where he graduated in 1922. In 1926, after house appointments at the National Hospital, Queen Square, London, he was appointed clinical pathologist to the Miller General Hospital, and became pathologist to the International (Millbank) Fund for Research on Poliomyelitis at the Lister Institute in 1928. He spent two years, from 1932 to 1934, in the United States as associate at the Rockefeller Institute for Medical Research, Princeton, New Jersey, returning to the Lister Institute as a member of the research staff. In 1935, at the early age of 35, he became William Withering lecturer at the

University of Birmingham.

In 1936 the South Australian Government decided to set up an Institute of Medical and Veterinary Science which, among other things, would take over the role of the Adelaide Hospital laboratories of pathology and bacteriology. Weston Hurst was selected as foundation director, but his initial appointment was as director of the hospital laboratories, so that he might play an active role in preparing the regulations for the new Institute. The IMVS Act was passed in 1937, and he took up his dual appointment as director of the Institute and Keith Sheridan professor of experimental medicine in the University of Adelaide. His initial appointment was for five years. Shortly after his reappointment in 1943 he resigned and returned to England, where he became a member of the research staff of Imperial Chemical Pharmaceuticals Limited, in Manchester, and later a member of the research staff of the Central Toxicological Laboratory of ICI, until his retirement in 1967.

As a young man he enjoyed alpine walking and photography, and his love of Italy led him to study Italian intensively. He was a member of the Institute of Linguists. On retirement, he and his wife went to live in Malta, where he continued his interest in photography. He was married twice: first to Phyllis Edith, daughter of JG Picknett MA, in 1926. They had three daughters. Phyllis died in 1940, and in 1942 he married Barbara Ternent, daughter of WT Cooke DSc, of Adelaide; they had a son and a daughter.

Weston Hurst was a strict disciplinarian and an excellent teacher, greatly appreciated by his students. He contributed a number of papers on pathology and allied subjects to European and foreign journals, and was a lifelong member of the Pathological Society, and, for some years, a member of the British Neuropathological Society.

GW/VL

[*Neuropath. appl. Neurobiol.*, 1982, **8**, 191; Photo]

HYLAND, Herbert Hylton *b*.3 Nov 1900 *d*.1 Aug 1977
MD Toronto (1926) MRCP (1929) FRCPC (1934) FRCP (1962)

After graduation in medicine, at Toronto in 1926, Herbert Hyland served as an intern at the Grace Hospital, and as an assistant in general practice in Stratford, Ontario. Then, encouraged by Duncan Graham, he studied for two years in London, England, where he soon acquired his MRCP, and found his lasting interest in neurology at the National Hospital for Nervous Diseases, Queen Square. He returned to the staff of the department of medicine at the Toronto General Hospital in 1930. He instilled new vigour and interest in neurology through being a popular and keen teacher, clinical investigator and consultant. His lectures and published works were always of top calibre, and he collaborated effectively in several projects with his colleagues in medicine, neurosurgery and neuropathology. His pre-war papers included studies of subacute combined degeneration of the spinal cord, anorexia nervosa, frontal lobe tumours, poliomyelitis and intracranial aneurysms. Like most neurologists of his era, Hyland included in his activities the study and treatment of psychoneuroses, and he continued this psychiatric part of his practice throughout his career.

Soon after the outbreak of World War II in 1939, he enlisted with No 15 Hospital, RCAMC, and a few months later was seconded to No 1 Canadian Neurological Hospital, with which he served in Basingstoke, England, from June 1940 until December 1942. He was promoted to lieutenant colonel and was in charge of the medical side of that very busy and successful neurological hospital.

After his return to the Toronto General Hospital, Hyland resumed an important leading role in a rapidly growing and changing scene of neurology in the department of medicine. With his resident and staff colleagues, he again produced good clinical studies and publications, including further work on intracranial aneurysms, brainstem tumours, cerebral venous thrombosis, cerebellar ataxias, hemiballismus, and the cerebral changes of hypertension. At the same time, he was for many years head of psychiatry at the Toronto General Hospital, and at the Wellesley Hospital when it was a division of the TGH from 1949 to 1960.

He was recognized nationally and internationally, being elected a fellow of the Royal College of Physicians of London in 1947 and a member of the American Neurological Association. He was a charter member and an early president of the Canadian Neurological Society.

It was a great loss to his associates and the department when Hyland retired from most of his University duties in 1960. He did carry on actively as a consultant neurologist for several more years. In 1968 he was appointed to the consulting staff of the Queen Elizabeth Hospital, and finally served as physician-in-chief of that hospital from 1970 until 1973, when poor health forced him into complete retirement.

The contributions of Hyland to medical neurology were numerous, and deserving of tribute and thanks from the Toronto General Hospital and the University of Toronto. In a more personal way, we who worked closely with 'Bob' Hyland, as he was known by his friends, cherish memories of his delightful and inspiring companionship and leadership. Until his retirement, he was never satisfied with doing only routine clinical and administrative chores and teaching. He constantly had some clinical investigation and writing under way. With that he regularly involved and stimulated his colleagues. His papers show the surviving value of clinical studies and of clinicopathological correlations, even in this age of advanced scientific research technology.

He married Mary Ruth, daughter of Robert Patterson, an accountant, in 1938. They had two sons and two daughters, the elder son becoming a chest physician at the TGH and at the Wellesley Hospital. JCR

[*Can. J. Neurol. Sci.*, Feb 1978, **5** (1):51; Photo]

INGELFINGER, Franz Joseph *b.*20 Aug 1910 *d.*26 Mar 1980
MD Harvard (1936) FRCP* (1975)

Franz Ingelfinger, late professor of medicine at Boston University, USA, and editor of the *New England Journal of Medicine* from 1967 to 1977, was born in Dresden, Germany, where his father, Joseph, was a physician and his mother was an American schoolteacher. At the age of twelve, Franz was taken to the United States, becoming an American citizen in 1931 and taking an arts degree at Yale University in 1932. He began his career by helping with his mother's English students, but soon decided to study medicine. He went to Harvard Medical School where he graduated in 1936, and as there were only two practising gastroenterologists at Boston at that time he decided to become one himself. He trained at Philadelphia, becoming interested in problems of intestinal motility and absorption, and in 1940, four years after he had qualified, he was appointed chief of gastroenterology at the Evans Memorial Hospital, Boston. With his colleagues, Kramer and Bradley, he embarked on a long career as a clinical gastroenterologist. He was active in research and was credited with playing a major role in transforming gastroenterology from a largely empirical specialty into one with a sound scientific basis. He did original work in the motions and contractions of the œsophagus and intestines; in the role of the liver in many diseases, and in the occurrence of megaloblastic anaemia after total gastrectomy.

While professor of medicine at Boston University he also taught at Harvard and Tufts, and former students remember him as a brilliant, charismatic teacher and a superb diagnostician.

In 1967 he succeeded Joseph Garland as editor of the *New England Journal of Medicine*. The journal then had a circulation of 105,978 and a national reputation for the technical competence of its articles. Ingelfinger acquired the necessary business knowledge very quickly and set out to broaden the scope of the journal to include social and ethical problems affecting medicine and society, and he developed the correspondence section into a lively forum for new ideas. He applied more stringent criteria to papers submitted for publication, and they would be rejected if medical data had already appeared substantially in the lay press. On the other hand, he was always ready to publish outspoken articles on politically sensitive topics, and made a courageous attack on laetrile, the quack cure for cancer. Ingelfinger was known for his wit, commitment to accuracy, prolific writing and drive, and he loved controversy and new challenges. When he retired, the journal's circulation had reached 169,873 and had editions in Europe. The number of articles submitted increased by 140%. The journal was first issued in 1812 and since then the publication has become essential to most doctors; at the time of Ingelfinger's death the circulation had reached 205,000.

In 1941 he married Sarah Parson, daughter of Arthur Asahel Shurcliff, a landscape architect, and they had a son and a daughter. The son, Joseph A Ingelfinger, is a physician in Boston.

In 1975 he became gravely ill and was operated on for adenocarcinoma of the œsophagus. The operation was successful and he survived for over four years and continued to lecture and write, despite the disabling effects of radiation treatment. In 1977 he retired from his post as editor of the *New England Journal of Medicine* and was succeeded by Arnold S Relman. He died three years later, survived by his wife and children. GW/VL

[*Brit. med. J.*, 1980, **280**, 1057; *New York Times*, 27 Mar 1980; *Forum on Medicine*, Apr 1980, 294-295]

ISDALE, Irwin Colin *b*.29 Jan 1924 *d*.22 Nov 1982
MB ChB NZ (1948) MRCP (1956) MRACP (1957) FRACP (1968) MCCMNZ (1980) FRCP (1981)

Irwin Isdale was born in Ngaruawahia, New Zealand, and educated at King's College, Auckland, He and his sisters followed in their father's footsteps at Otago University, where his own two daughters have since, in their turn, qualified in dentistry and medicine respectively. During his early postgraduate years at Christchurch Hospital he met and married his wife, Lynn. He had a natural vocation for medicine, and his outstanding contributions began at an early age, when he was working with EGL Bywaters at Taplow and Hammersmith, and produced definitive papers on the pathology and natural history of the exanthemata of Still's disease and Henoch-Schönlein's purpura. Subsequently in 1956 he joined the team at Queen Elizabeth Hospital as rheumatologist and physician; and continued his research despite a heavy service load. He was the clear choice for the post of medical superintendent when this became vacant in 1971, and he continued to lead the team there for the rest of his life.

His active interest in paediatric rheumatology stayed with him, and he wrote extensively on this topic; as well as on adult rheumatism. He was in great demand as a conference speaker and many times shouldered the burden of office in the New Zealand Rheumatism Association, of which he was a past president. He gave generously of his time to the Crippled Children's Society, and was lately a vice-president of the South East Asia and Pacific Area League against Rheumatism. It is certain that he would still have had much to offer and achieve had he been spared.

Irwin was a keen gardener and an enthusiastic skier. An amateur interest in Egyptology was climaxed by a trip up the Nile, a voyage from which he derived great fascination. No discussion with him ever lasted long without revealing his puckish sense of humour. He was attending a conference in Amsterdam when his final sudden illness came, and he died in London shortly afterwards. He was fortunate that Lynn was with him to provide her warm-hearted support and companionship when his lifetime of good-natured commitment to medicine was ended so far from home. REW-StC

[*NZ Med. J.*, 1983, **96**, 64; Photo]

ISRAËLS, Martin Cyril Gordon *b*.25 Sept 1906 *d*.14 Apr 1979
BSc Manch (1928) MSc (1929) MB ChB (1932) MD (1935)
MRCP (1938) FRCP (1949)

Martin Israëls, the son of a Dutch father, Herman, who came from The Hague, and an English mother, Jeannette (née Gordon), was born in Manchester and educated at Manchester Grammar School. He was a student at Manchester University, where he graduated BSc with first class honours and subsequently MB ChB in 1932. From 1933 to 1936 he held the Lady Tata research scholarship and in 1933 was appointed assistant director of the laboratory for clinical investigation. In 1940 he was awarded the Foulerton research fellowship of the Royal Society. He served in the Royal Air Force from 1940 to 1945 and reached the rank of wing commander. With the exception of those five years he spent all his working life in Manchester Royal Infirmary, where he will long be remembered with affection and respect. On his discharge from the RAF he returned to Manchester Royal Infirmary as a lecturer in haematology, and in 1948 he was appointed consultant physician to the United Manchester Hospitals. In 1962, on the retirement of JF Wilkinson, he became director of the department of clinical haematology, and in 1970 he was appointed the first professor of clinical haematology at Manchester University. He retired in 1971, but continued to live in his beloved Cheshire.

In the field of haematology Martin Israëls became a household name. He was one of the first haematologists to combine his laboratory skills with clinical acumen. He was a pioneer in the study of bone marrow changes in blood diseases, and the application of tissue culture techniques to bone marrow cells. His qualities as a teacher were outstanding and in 1964 he became the dean of postgraduate studies at Manchester University, a post which he held for five years. He was the author of many scientific papers and of several textbooks in haematology, and he was in great demand as a writer of leading articles for medical journals. His colleagues honoured him by electing him president of the Manchester Medical Society in 1971. For many years he served as an examiner for the Royal College of Physicians.

He was a quiet, cultured man with a great love of the arts. He was a member of a distinguished Dutch family of artists which included Joseph and his son, Isaac Israëls, and it was a great pleasure and privilege to be conducted round the Amsterdam art galleries by Martin Israëls. In 1935 he married a kindred spirit in the form of his beloved wife, Ivy (née Wray), who herself was a devoted and accomplished artist. They had one daughter.

IWD

[*Brit. med. J.,* 1979, **1**, 1349; *Lancet,* 1979, **1**, 937; *Manchester med. Gazette,* Oct 1979, **50**(1); Photo]

JACOBS, John Harry *b.*19 Aug 1915 *d.*14 Nov 1979
MA Cantab (1940) MRCS LRCP (1940) MB BChir (1946)
MRCP (1948) FRCP (1972)

John Harry Jacobs was born in London, the son of Nathaniel Jacobs, a company director, and Ann Nancy, daughter of John Abrahams, a manufacturer. He was educated at University College School, Hampstead, and the University of Cambridge. He qualified in medicine at St Thomas's Hospital with the Conjoint in 1940, graduating MB BChir in 1946. The period between the Conjoint and his graduation was covered by service in the RAF during the second world war. He held the rank of squadron leader and was mentioned in despatches. On demobilization he decided to specialise in rheumatology and was senior registrar in the rheumatology unit at St Stephen's Hospital, Chelsea, from 1948 to 1952. From 1952 to 1956 he was first assistant physician in the department of rheumatology and physical medicine at the Royal Free Hospital. In 1955 he was appointed consultant in charge of the department of physical medicine and rheumatology at the North Middlesex Hospital, where he remained until he retired in 1975. He was a member of the Advisory Committee of the North East Regional Board on physical medicine and neurophysiology.

Ill health obliged him to give up his hospital work nine months before his official retirement, but he later did part-time sessional work at Kingston and Ealing, up to the time of his death.

Harry Jacobs was an active member of the Thames Sailing Club, serving both as secretary and commodore. His other interests outside medicine were music and gardening. He never married. GW/VL

[*Brit. med. J.*, 1980, **280**, 1233; Photo]

JEFFERSON, Keith Edmund *b.*18 Apr 1923 *d.*23 Oct 1977
MB BChir Cantab (1946) MA (1947) DCH (1949) DMRD (1950)
MRCP (1950) FFR (1953) FRCP (1967) FRCR (1975)

Keith Jefferson was educated at Oundle School and studied medicine at Clare College, Cambridge, and Guy's Hospital, qualifying in 1946. He served for a short while in the RAMC after holding house appointments at Guy's Hospital, Tunbridge Wells, and at the Miller Hospital in Greenwich. After obtaining the DCH and the MRCP, he specialized in diagnostic radiology at St George's Hospital. He was appointed a consultant at St George's Hospital in 1956, and also in the same year at the Brompton Hospital.

During his radiology training Keith Jefferson had become interested in cardiac radiology, just as selective angiocardiography was becoming an accepted procedure. In the late 1950's he visited the Cleveland Clinic in Ohio and learned from Mason Sones the technique of selective coronary arteriography, bringing this knowledge and expertise back to England. Image intensification, which made cinéradiography possible, was becoming available and he became one of the first radiologists to recognise the value of this tool in the diagnosis of cardiac lesions. He won the Barclay prize of the British Institute of Radiology in 1960 for his paper on 'Thoracic Aortography and Cinéradiography of the Aortic Valve'.

Though he contributed to the radiology of chest diseases, especially interstitial pulmonary fibrosis, his main interest was in cardiac radiology, and he left the Brompton in 1963 to become director of the department of radiology at the National Heart Hospital. He established there a world-wide reputation as a clinical radiologist and teacher. He travelled abroad on lecture tours, particularly to South America, attracting radiologists from many lands to come to study at the National Heart Hospital, where he held regular tutorials.

With Simon Rees he wrote a book on *Clinical Cardiac Radiology*, which has become a classic on the subject. A part of the book is devoted to skeletal changes in heart disease, which was the subject of the St Cyres lecture he was honoured to give in 1971.

He was a most kind and considerate man, having great patience in listening to others, and good sense in his advice. He was elected chairman of the medical committee of the National Heart Hospital for three years.

He was survived by his wife, Denys Marjorie, née Green, whom he had married in 1962. They had no children. IHK

[*Times*, 9 Nov 1977; *Brit. med. J.*, 1977, **2**, 1360; Photo]

JENKINS, Ritchie Teify *b*.8 Mar 1915 *d*.10 Oct 1982
BSc (1937) MB BCh Wales (1940) MRCS LRCP (1942)
MRCP (1947) DCH (1947) FRCP (1971)

Ritchie, the son of Daniel and Louisa Jenkins, was born in St Nicholas near Cardiff. He studied at the Welsh National School of Medicine, and served South Wales throughout his professional life. He qualified at the beginning of the war and undertook his initial house appointments at the Cardiff Royal Infirmary, where he became the RMO. Shortly afterwards he moved to the EMS Hospital at Morriston as a medical registrar, and subsequently consultant paediatrician. For many years he was the sole consultant paediatrician for Swansea and all points west. It was a daunting challenge which brought the best out of Ritchie. He rose to the occasion admirably and was constantly on hand to give advice or consultation, working through the day and frequently the night. Later, several others were able to share the burden and enable Ritchie to develop sub-regional specialties.

The son of a schoolmaster, it is hardly surprising that he gained a wide reputation as a teacher of both undergraduates and postgraduates. He enjoyed this side of his life enormously, and put much energy into conveying the principles of paediatrics and the logical steps required for diagnosis and investigation. Generations of doctors have avoided serious errors in the management of children thanks to Ritchie's aphorisms.

One of the highlights of the paediatric calendar in South Wales was the annual clinical meeting in Morriston Hospital. Series of children with rare and interesting diseases were presented on a summer's afternoon by Ritchie and his staff, all beautifully annotated and exhibited. It was an ideal occasion for the aspiring Membership candidate and a rapid up-date for more senior colleagues. The academic feast was followed by a first class meal and then the real business of the day began. This was to reveal another side of Ritchie's character—his enthusiasm for an excellent performance at cricket. The local Morriston team took on all-comers from Cardiff and elsewhere—and usually won. It gave Ritchie and his wife Joy considerable satisfaction when, in later years, their only son Huw, himself a budding paediatrician, captained Harrow School at cricket. It is natural that a born paediatrician like Ritchie Jenkins should be a family man. Their beautiful home was always open to others and the family bond of affection quickly extended to everyone. The family hospitality was proverbial.

Ritchie was able in later years to undertake considerable civic responsibilities, including that of becoming a Justice of the Peace with a special interest in the work of the Juvenile Courts.

He was survived by his wife Joy, a most loyal supporter, and herself a community paediatrician, and his son Huw, a paediatrician in training. OPG

[*Brit. med. J.*, 1982, **285**, 1435; *Lancet*, 1982, **2**, 941. Photo]

JESSOP, William John Edward *b*.30 July 1902 *d*.11 June 1980
BA (1925) MSc (1927) MB BCh BAO Dublin (1928) MD (1935)
DSc Ife Nigeria (1978) MRCPI (1940) FRCPI (1944)
MRCP (1964) FRCP (1968) Hon FACP (1972)

Born in Mullingar, Co. Westmeath, 'Jerry' Jessop was the eldest of the three sons of John Brabason Jessop, a farmer. His mother Mary Jane, was a daughter of William Anderson, another local farmer.

Jerry was educated at the Ranelagh School, Athlone and at Mountjoy School, Dublin. Entering Trinity College Dublin in 1920 he became a foundation scholar of the House, and graduated in 1925 with a first class moderatorship in experimental science. Two years later he completed his MSc in biochemistry, before graduating in medicine. In 1929, at the age of 27, he became professor of physiology in the schools of surgery in the Royal College of Surgeons in Ireland. He held this post until 1952, when he became the first professor of social medicine in the University of Dublin. He was the dean of the school of physic from 1959 until his compulsory retirement in 1972 on reaching the age of seventy. He then accepted an appointment as the first professor of chemical pathology in the new medical school at the Nigerian University of Ife. He was soon elected vice-dean of the Faculty of Health Sciences, and continued to be active in the development of the school until his final illness forced his second retirement in 1978.

A supreme joiner and organizer, Jerry Jessop joined so many scientific societies and bodies that the mere listing of them would be tedious. They included: the Physiological Society, the Biochemical Society, the Nutrition Society, the Society for Social Medicine, the Association for the Study of Medical Education, and the British Council for the Rehabilitation of the Disabled. Of all these he was an active member, often an office bearer.

A fellow of Trinity College Dublin, and a member of the Royal Irish Academy, in 1972 he was elected president of the Royal College of Physicians of Ireland. He was a member of the GMC and of the Irish Registration Council for many years.

An original member of the Irish Medical Research Council, founded in 1957, he was its honorary secretary (and chief executive, unpaid) from 1952 until his retirement in 1973.

His own scientific work related to nutrition in several aspects. In 1946 he organized a dietary survey which revealed the extent of calcium and iron depletion causing rickets and anaemia, due to the policy of using 100% extraction flour; also the dental caries survey, which led to the fluoridation of Irish water supplies in 1952. Again, the Boston-Ireland heart study was an innovation in its day.

His extra-medical activities included the councils of the Royal Zoological Society of Ireland and of the Statistical and Social Enquiry Society of Ireland.

Up to his last illness he was hyperkinetic in mind and body. Anxiety and insomnia seemed unknown to him. He loved company and was an inveterate luncheon host, when politics or fund raising could often be introduced into the social enjoyment.

He travelled widely and frequently, representing a remarkable variety of causes and institutions. In Dublin, and in Nigeria, he was an active and expert gardener. He collected glass and silver—and interesting people.

In 1930 he married Kathleen, daughter of Thomas Condell. They had three daughters and one son, John, a Fellow of the College. DMM

[*Brit. med. J.*, 1980, **281**, 316; *Lancet*, 1980, **2**, 46, 158; Photo]

JONES, Alan Trevor *b.*24 Feb 1901 *d.*10 June 1979
MB BS Lond (1924) MD (1927) MRCP (1927) DPH (1929)
FRCP (1953) Hon LLD Wales (1970)

Alan Trevor Jones was a man of outstanding breadth of vision and far-sightedness. Qualifying in London in the mid 1920's, and returning to Wales in 1929, he was struck by the low standards of health, and health care generally, in Wales in this period of poverty and unemployment. During his subsequent professional career he laboured unceasingly to attempt to correct this through the successive administrative appointments that he held in the health service and in the University of Wales.

A native of Glamorganshire, he was born and educated at Pengam, where his father was headmaster of Lewis School. Having completed his preclinical training at the University College of South Wales and Monmouthshire in Cardiff, he then proceeded to University College, London, for his clinical training, where he was fortunate in becoming houseman to Sir Thomas Lewis. From the outset of his career he began to develop an interest in administration and in public health. After being medical officer of health in Carmarthen he joined the staff of the Welsh Board of Health as medical officer. Two years later he was appointed hospital officer for Wales under the Emergency Medical Services scheme. After the war he helped to produce the hospital survey of South Wales and Monmouthshire [*Survey of Hospital Services of South Wales (1945)*] later becoming medical officer to the newly-established Welsh Hospital Board.

Recognising the vital importance for Wales of training more doctors, he became increasingly interested in the work of the medical school in Cardiff, and was appointed to the provostship of the school in 1955. His contribution to the administrative field of academic medicine in Wales was truly great, and his efforts were crowned with success in 1971 with the opening of the new medical teaching centre in Cardiff combining the Welsh National School of Medicine and the University Hospital of Wales on one site.

He had the ability immediately to make contact with new acquaintances, as a result of his sympathetic approach, his kindliness and his lively sense of humour. He was particularly good at encouraging the younger man entering medicine, both among undergraduates and postgraduates. He retired from the provostship and from the General Medical Council in 1969, but continued to serve as a member of the Board of Governors and later of the Hospital Management Committee for a number of years.

Alan was survived by his wife, Gwyn, a daughter who qualified as a nurse, a son who had become a consultant paediatrician, and a grandson also in medicine. JPDM

[*Brit. med. J.*, 1979, **1**, 1788; *Lancet*, 1979, **1**, 1358; Photo]

JONES, Arthur Morgan *b.*22 Nov 1910 *d.*3 Jan 1979
BSc Manch (1934) MSc (1935) MB ChB (1938) MRCP (1942) FRCP (1948)

Arthur Morgan Jones was a native of Glamorgan, the son of a Welsh schoolmaster. He was educated in Bangor, North Wales. Always attracted to the biological sciences he entered the Victoria University of Manchester, firstly as a Dalton scholar in physiology, but fairly quickly decided to turn to medicine.

His undergraduate career was distinguished by prizes and scholarships in physiology, medicine and pharmacology. After graduation he became house surgeon to Crichton Bramwell, and through him he was introduced to the specialty of cardiology, a specialty which became all absorbing to him, and to which he made great contributions.

Rejected for military service because of an attack of rheumatic pericarditis as a student, Morgan Jones spent part of the war in research at the University of Cambridge, returning to the Manchester Royal Infirmary as RMO in 1944. From 1946–1947 he worked in the United States, first of all as a holder of a Leverhulme research scholarship and later a Rockefeller travelling fellowship. Much of this time was spent in Harold Feil's department in Cleveland, and this was a period which he enjoyed very much, remaining thereafter a frequent visitor to the United States. He succeeded Crichton Bramwell as director of the department of cardiology at the Manchester Royal Infirmary on the latter's retirement in 1954, a post he held until his own retirement in 1971. His services to Manchester medicine were recognized by his election to the presidency of the Manchester Medical Society in 1969, and he also was a member and sometime councillor of the British Cardiac Society, a founder member of the Council of the British Heart Foundation, and a member of the Research Committee of the International Society of Cardiology.

The collaboration between Bramwell and Morgan Jones led to the founding of the university department of cardiology at Manchester Royal Infirmary, then the first University department in the country. He believed in the importance of clinical research and contributed to it throughout his life. From 1936 to 1947 he maintained a close working relationship with Walter Schlapp, professor of physiology in the University of Manchester. His clinical research interests were especially heart disease in pregnancy, a subject on which he wrote a classic book in 1951, and latterly, ischaemic heart disease. With Snow and Daber he was the first to show that sudden death was frequently not associated with demonstrable occlusion or infarction, and that fresh infarction was not always associated with a fresh occlusion, statements which then flouted current thinking but which are now accepted. His contributions to the field of coronary disease were recognized when he was invited to give the Strickland Goodall memorial lecture in 1969. He also edited *Progress in Cardiology* and *Modern Trends in Cardiology*.

The clear thinking of a medical scientist, combined with a warm hearted approach to his patients, made Morgan Jones an excellent teacher both at undergraduate and postgraduate level. He was an unpretentious and completely honest man, and these qualities were apparent in his dealings with students, staff and patients. Although he could be critical his comments were always well intentioned and invariably helpful.

Morgan Jones had two dominant interests outside medicine, golf and latterly music. After his retirement he developed rheumatoid arthritis, and golf became difficult for him. His interest in music deepened and he became particularly involved with the work and life of Haydn. In 1978 he developed symptoms of carcinoma of the bronchus, and although the lung was resected he died of secondary deposits. He left a brother, equally eminent in the field of education, and a sister. He was unmarried. EGW

[*Brit. med. J.*, 1979, **1**, 353; *Lancet*, 1979, **1**, 282.]

JONES, Ernest Grahame *b*.24 Mar 1910 *d*.10 Aug 1977
MRCS LRCP (1934) MB BS Lond (1934) MRCP (1943)
FRCP (1969)

Ernest Grahame Jones, the eldest son of Thomas Ernest Jones, a pharmacist, was born in Pontypridd, Glamorgan, in the Rhondda Valley. He was educated in Pontypridd, and from the Pontypridd Grammar School went to St Bartholomew's Hospital, where he obtained both the Conjoint qualification and also the London degree in 1934, the latter with a distinction in medicine.

He returned to Wales and worked as a resident first at St David's Hospital, Cardiff, then called the City Lodge, and later at Llandough Hospital, Penarth.

For the next three years, he was in general practice, first at Llanishen, and later in Lampeter in Cardiganshire. Grahame Jones volunteered for military service in 1939 and served with the RAMC, but was invalided out in 1941.

Following his discharge he studied for membership, which he obtained in 1943, and worked for a while as assistant lecturer in pathology at the Welsh National School of Medicine. In 1944 he was appointed as the first consultant physician at the Royal Gwent Hospital in Newport, at which time few of the visiting staff were engaged solely in specialist practice; the majority combined general practice and a surgical hospital practice. Other appointments followed, and at the time of the inception of the National Health Service he became consultant physician to the Newport and East Monmouthshire Hospital Management Committee, working both at the Royal Gwent Hospital and at the Griffithstown County Hospital.

His hospital duties were combined with a busy practice in which he was helped by his wife, Hilary Naunton Davies, whom he had married in 1939.

He was essentially a general physician whose main interest was in clinical bed-side medicine, but he had a special interest in cardiology and produced papers in 1957 and 1958 on hypercholesterolaemia and xanthomatosis.

He undertook committee work in the local hospitals; prior to the 1974 reorganization he had been a member of the hospital management committee and chairman of the hospital medical staff committee. Following reorganization he was both chairman of the medical division and of the medical executive committee. He looked upon hospital administration as part of his work in the interest of patients, but did not partake greatly in British Medical Association medico-political matters. He was also at one time chairman of the Society of Physicians of Wales and of the Gwent Medical Society.

His first wife died in 1964. He remarried in 1970 Dr Megan Richards, the widow of RD Richards FRCS, who had been a surgical colleague in Newport. He had two sons by the first marriage, the elder being an accountant practising in London, the younger being an administrator in the National Health Service.

Grahame Jones was one of that group of consultants who were responsible for the starting of consultant hospital medicine in the provinces, who adhered to a work ethos and set the high clinical standards to be found in today's National Health Service. JMS

[*Brit. med. J.*, 1977, **2**, 1485; *Lancet*, 1977, **2**, 1142; Photo]

JONES, Idris Griffiths *b.*27 Apr 1905 *d.*10 July 1976
BSc Wales (1926) MRCS LRCP (1930) MB BS Lond (1932)
MRCP (1934) MD (1935) FRCP (1968)

Although born in Birmingham, Idris Jones's family moved to Llanelli, South Wales, when he was six months old and he always considered himself a native of Llanelli, a town for which he maintained a very great affection all his life. His father, E Denbigh Jones, was the headmaster of Llanelli Grammar School and was held in great esteem locally.

Idris Jones attended Llanelli Grammar School before starting his medical career at University College, Cardiff, in 1924, where he obtained the BSc (Wales) in 1926. His clinical studies were at University College Hospital, London, where, after a long illness, he qualified MRCS in 1930 and in the same year obtained the BMA essay prize.

In 1930 he was house physician at Hampstead General Hospital, London, and then house surgeon at the ENT Hospital, London, following which he became RMO at Chester Hospital. In 1935 he was appointed RMO to the Royal Infirmary, Cardiff, then the main teaching hospital of the Welsh National School of Medicine, a post with considerable clinical and teaching responsibility.

Although in 1938 he became assistant registrar at the National Hospital for Nervous Diseases, Queen Square, London, he returned to Cardiff in 1939, when he was appointed honorary assistant physician to the Royal Infirmary, Cardiff, and clinical teacher to the Welsh National School of Medicine.

For eight years he was also senior assistant on the medical unit under AM Kennedy. With the inception of the National Health Service in 1948 he became consultant physician to the United Cardiff Hospitals and to the Welsh Regional Hospital Board. He was consultant physician to the Ministry of Pensions and a member of the Appeals Tribunal of the Department of Health and Social Security. A general physician, he took a special interest in rheumatology.

For many years he was internal examiner to the Welsh National School of Medicine and an examiner to the General Nursing Council.

He was chairman of the medical board of the United Cardiff Hospitals from 1966 to 1968. At this time the new medical and dental teaching centres were being established on the 53 acre site at Heath Park, Cardiff. The Dental School and Hospital were completed in 1965 and officially opened in 1966; the Medical School buildings opened in 1971. Idris Jones helped very considerably in ironing out difficulties in the initial working of the Dental Hospital. His help was much appreciated by the Dental Hospital authorities. He also played a very helpful and constructive part in the development of the Medical School in the new buildings at the Heath. His calm and unruffled temperament, his friendliness, his sincerity, his tactfulness and his wise counsel made him an admirable chairman. In addition he was always easily approachable; his willingness to help his colleagues at all times made him an exceptionally delightful colleague to work with.

At St Winifrede's Hospital, Cardiff, where he looked after his private patients, the nuns affectionately nicknamed him 'Nicodemus' (the wise and learned man, the kindly man, the generous man, the man who sought the truth, who spoke up against unfairness and the man who walked by night). This really summed up his character admirably. That he walked by night was because of his conscientiousness in his teaching and hospital work, and in a considerable private practice at his consulting rooms, which meant that at St Winifrede's Hospital he often visited his patients at night.

He married in 1943, Vera Harris, who had qualified medically at Cardiff two years previously. Idris and Vera Jones had one daughter, Celia Rhonwen, who entered the legal profession and married an accountant. Idris Jones died suddenly and peacefully at his home in Cardiff.

DAW

[*Brit. med. J.*, 1976, **2**, 1077]

JOULES, Horace *b*.21 Mar 1902 *d*.25 Jan 1977
MRCS LRCP (1924) MB BS Lond (1925) MD (1928) MRCP (1928) FRCP (1943)

Horace Joules graduated in 1925 from Middlesex Hospital, proceeding to his London MD with gold medal in 1928. After an appointment at Selly Oak Hospital in 1929, he came to the Central Middlesex in 1935 and for many years was its medical director.

The Times described him as one of the stormy petrels of the early days of the National Health Service. 'His pen and his voice, both of which he could use with facility and abrasiveness all too often did him and his cause a disservice.' Those who knew him better and worked with him were more generous in their appreciation. There was no doubt that he was a fighter. If he saw anything he considered wrong, either in the abuse of power or of vested interests he considered it a personal challenge. Frustration often made him angry but never led to despair. But fierce battle in committee never led to personal antagonism or rancour; many who disagreed with him publicly came to appreciate his warmth and friendship in private.

Horace was in every way a big man. By 1948 he had helped to raise the Central to a dominant place among the non-teaching hospitals of the country. Many will remember him striding down the main corridor at 9.00 a.m., pausing for a friendly word with painter or porter, houseman or cleaner. He took a personal interest in everyone who worked at the hospital. In his 1955 medical director's report he wrote 'Once again the staff, medical, nursing and lay have responded excellently despite inadequate salaries in many grades. Our thanks are due to domestic workers, porters, catering staff and other ancillary workers who do so much of the heavier work of the hospital'.

He will best be remembered as a physician with a passion for preventive medicine resulting from experience with his own patients: young women with tuberculosis, older men with chronic bronchitis or lung cancer, or miners crippled with dust disease. He was indignant when he saw his patients suffering needlessly from their environment or their own habits.

At the end of the war tuberculosis was a serious problem and 11,000 patients were awaiting admission to hospital. The high incidence of tuberculosis in nurses caused many general hospitals to refuse admission to these patients. In 1945 Joules opened two wards for tuberculosis at the Central, and took the greatest care to protect nurses from infection. As a result hardly a single nurse became infected, and their Mantoux conversion rate was much lower than nurses working in the old LCC or London teaching hospitals.

He had always been concerned about the tragedy of chronic bronchitis. The black smog of December 1952, when over 4,000 additional deaths occurred in London, resulted in his outspoken attacks on government and on medical inertia. As a member of the Central Health Services Council, he urged political action to control air pollution. The Beaver Committee was set up and later the Clean Air Act came into being. As a result the air of our major cities is much cleaner, and London smogs no longer occur. To the *BMJ* he wrote, 'I believe we shall not progress in the prevention of this and other chest diseases until we regard a persistent cough as seriously as persistent vomiting. The air we breathe is as important as the water we drink. It must be uninfected and unpolluted.'

He was particularly concerned with dust disease in miners, especially those who developed chronic bronchitis with no radiological evidence of pneumoconiosis. As a result they receive no compensation, an injustice which he fought hard to put right.

Following Doll and Hill's work in 1952 he campaigned strongly against cigarette smoking. He had been a heavy smoker for 30 years but managed to break his addiction. In the *Lancet* he wrote, 'Cancer of the lung continues to cause more and more deaths. It is in the approach to this grave national problem that the Ministry of Health has manifested its weakest aspect. We are witnessing an epidemic form of cancer which has been unknown in human society before. Unless trends are modified a million people in England and Wales will die of this cancer before the end of the century.' His prediction was more than justified, and at present rates the one million deaths he forecast will be reached well before the year 2000. He wrote, 'The Royal College of Physicians can re-enact history and help to revivify itself by giving advice comparable to that given in respect of alcohol 200 years ago.' Fortunately the College did take his advice, and six years later published its historical report on *Smoking and Health*.

Perhaps he will best be remembered for his Friday afternoon teaching rounds. He towered above all others in a characteristic pose, wagging his finger for emphasis. These occasions were immensely popular and 40 or 50 students would crowd round the beds. They were impressed by his gentleness, kindness to patients, his diagnostic skill, his fund of knowledge and his practical common sense. He thoroughly enjoyed the cut and thrust of teaching, and the students responded with fascination and delight. Since he was always interested in the social conditions of his patients, his teaching did not end in the wards. Once the round took place in the old Acton Power Station. After an hour at the furnaces, toasted in front and frozen from the wintery blast behind, and with soot dripping from their eyelashes, the students knew more about the causes of chronic bronchitis than they could ever have found out from a lecture.

In private life he was a keen gardener and took much interest in farming. He often enjoyed a few days on the Essex marshes bird watching, accompanied by a volume of John Clare, his favourite poet and natural philosopher. In 1962 the illness which had first shown itself during the war returned and forced an early retirement. Perhaps he had to pay for the constructive years and dynamic activity which had done so much for the Central, the profession and the Health Service. When manic depression was at last controlled he lived quietly at home in Colchester, cared for by his wife Mary, who survived him with one son and a daughter. KPB

[*Brit. med. J.*, 1977, **1**, 449; *Lancet*, 1977, **1**, 317; *Times*, 28 Jan 1977; Photo]

KARANI, Sorab Barjor *b.*21 Feb 1910 *d.*9 Aug 1980
MB BS Bombay (1934) MRCP (1937) DPH Eng (1939)
FRCP (1963)

Sorab Barjor Karani was the son of Barjor Phiroz Karani, a respected medical practitioner in Bombay, India, and the professor of biology at the Grant Medical College in that city. At the turn of the century, it was a tradition in the Parsi race – a tiny minority community, originating from the ancient Iranian empire – for sons to follow their medical fathers. Sorab Karani, not only inherited the compassion, wisdom and monitorial qualities of his father, but also, from his mother's side, inherited the supreme quality of a physician – charity. His mother was the grand-daughter of Sir Jamsetjee Jeejeebhoy, Bt (the first Indian to be made a baronet), who endowed and founded the Sir JJ Hospital in Bombay; which even today, 140 years later, reigns supreme as the premier teaching hospital of the Indian sub-continent.

He schooled at the famous St Xavier's High School in Bombay, and then graduated from the Grant Medical College. He completed his house posts at the hospital founded by his great-grandfather, the Sir JJ Hospital, from 1934 to 1935.

After two years at the Middlesex Hospital in London, he was admitted to the MRCP in 1937. He then joined the LCC as an assistant medical officer, having taken his DPH in 1939.

With the outbreak of war, he served with the RAMC as a specialist physician in Nigeria, Middle East and then in Europe, and was the first Indian to rise to the rank of lieutenant colonel in the RAMC.

In 1946, he was appointed senior resident physician at St Nicholas Hospital, London, and two years later was appointed consultant physician both at St Nicholas Hospital and also at Brook Green Hospital.

His breadth of interest in general medicine was expressed in the papers he wrote - hyperparathyroidism, Kartagener's syndrome, Behcet's disease, sarcoidosis, hypertension.

An ardent cricketer, he became in his later non-playing years a fount of wisdom on cricketing lore and knowledge. He was a keen stamp collector. From his forefathers and his Parsi origin, he had an innate love for horse racing, which he always treated as a great sport, and never as a 'gamble'.

In April 1943 he married Mary Brown Snow Macrae, daughter of Finlay Macrae, and he had two daughters and one son.

He gave his all to his practice of medicine, and became a highly sought after consultant by the local general practitioners. He used to love to teach and was proud of the young men and women who used to approach him for bedside training. There was rarely a Comitia at the College, when his old students and apprentices were to be admitted to the membership or the fellowship, when he would not be there, beaming his usual sunny and paternal smile. This was, probably, how he would have liked to be remembered -humility to the science and compassion in the art of medicine, charity to all, and a love for his students. RBK

[*Brit. med. J.*, 1980, **281**, 815, 1294; Photo]

KARAT, Aaron Benedict (Benty) Abiel *b.*2 June 1931
*d.*14 Mar 1982
BSc (1952) MB BS (1958) MRCP (1963) FRCPE (1972)
FRCP (1978)

Benty's father was headmaster and English teacher at the prestigious Christian High School at Udipe, Mangalore, South India. Benty's career was strongly to reflect this early influence. After qualifying in Madras (in 1958) and rotating internships in Vellore, he came to England to continue his training. His capacity for work seemed unlimited. Yet even as he studied he was putting his considerable talents, his insatiable thirst for knowledge and his enjoyment of life at the service of his patients. His own higher degrees came almost as a by-product.

In 1964 Benty Karat returned to India and became lecturer, senior lecturer and then consultant physician to the Christian Medical College, Vellore, and to the Schieffelin Leprosy Research Institute in nearby Karigiri. The next six years were probably the happiest of his life, and it was then that I really got to know him. In a remarkable relationship (both personal and professional) he and his wife Sakuntala (an orthopaedic surgeon) literally put Karigiri on the international leprosy map. Benty would spend his days in an intense and unique blend of basic research, clinical work in the wards, administration, and meticulous care of every aspect of his patients' needs. He and his team explored visceral disease in leprosy, patterns of neurological involvement in erythema nodosum leprosum, the use of new drugs and a wide variety of basic bacteriological and immunological problems. Their interests ranged from new epidemiological techniques to new methods for testing sweating under field conditions. Many important papers appeared in the *International Journal of Leprosy*. Somehow, Benty also found time for concern about the welfare of his steady stream of visitors. Although of diminutive stature, he was a dynamo of energy, and generated disciplined enthusiasm among all those he worked with.

I retain vivid memories of Benty's Karigiri days. It was a unique experience. His mind was always racing ahead, outlining his plans, as we set out over rough paths to the wards, to the sound of bird song in the translucent early Indian morning, right through to sundown when we would walk back as the sky above 'his' hospital took on, in quick succession, every colour of the rainbow. Here was a man at one with himself, his deep beliefs expressed naturally and without artifice in his every act.

After a short spell in Bangalore as consultant physician to the Church of South India and honorary professor of medicine to St John's Medical College, Benty returned to the United Kingdom in 1973. He was appointed consultant physician first in Birkenhead, and later in Sunderland. Here again, under darker skies, he threw himself generously and wholeheartedly into the care of his patients, without neglecting his many other interests. He tackled waiting lists without fuss or fury but with single-mindedness, solving – through quiet example – problems others had deemed insoluble. He continued to write, to teach, to comfort and to inspire – whether as a member of the editorial board of *Leprosy* in India, as honorary consultant to the Liverpool School of Tropical Medicine, as local organizer for the Geriatric Society, or as a member of the local area health care planning team for the elderly. His family and friends remained at the centre of his life and he found time to enjoy philately, table tennis and photography with them.

When a cruel illness took him, at the age of fifty, he had already given a great deal to many people, in various parts of the world. To those privileged to be with him during the last painful weeks, he gave even more: the rare and inspiring sight of an unshakeable faith, and the proof that the spirit of a good man fulfilled can put even death in its place. CP

[*Brit. med. J.*, 1982, **284**, 1203]

KEALL, Denis Dalmain *b.*2 Oct 1911 *d.*3 June 1983
MRCS LRCP (1936) MA MB BChir Cantab (1937) MRCS (1940)
FRCP (1968) FRACP (1973)

Denis Keall was associated with the Royal Perth Hospital, Western Australia, for a quarter of a century and he was both a witness to, and a participant in, many of the remarkable changes which took place in the hospital during that time. Tensions are inevitable when a variety of academic departments are grafted on to an administrative structure traditionally run by honorary consultants. With the establishment of the Western Australia Medical School in 1956, Keall found himself in the chair, mediating between the arguments of the left and the right in the policy-making advisory committees. By temperament he was conservative, and cautious when faced with new ideas and problems, but his probity and dedication were apparent to all. He quickly gained the respect of both sides, and the relative harmony between visiting staff and full time staff at the hospital in the late 1950s and 60s was clear proof of his influence as a wise moderator. In later years he displayed the same qualities when chairman of the Medical Board of Western Australia.

Keall was one of a handful of consultants who could truly be called general physicians. Like most general physicians he had his particular interests, notably in chest disease, and earlier in his career he had held an appointment at the Princess Margaret Hospital for Children, Perth. As a teacher he was admired by his students; as a physician he was as much, or more concerned with the emotional responses of his patients to physical illness as he was with the process of technical diagnosis. He was dedicated to his profession and his hospital, undemonstrative, and with the stoicism to accept with dignity whatever fate had in store for him.

Although born in Perth, a member of a distinguished legal family, he received his medical education at St Thomas's Hospital, London. His father was Harry Capel Fitzgerald Keall, a solicitor, and his mother, Elinor Louisa, was the daughter of John Henry Cooper, a bank manager. Educated at Hale School and the University of Western Australia, he came to England and took his MA MB BChir at the University of Cambridge in 1937, pursuing his clinical studies at St Thomas's. He took his MRCP shortly after graduating and served with distinction in the RAMC throughout the second world war. He returned to Perth in 1946, was appointed to the Royal Perth Hospital as physician, and practised in amicable partnership with Gordon Hislop. He married Patricia Badham (née Read) in 1940. There were two sons of the marriage, which was a very happy one.The last years of Keall's life were saddened by his wife's protracted illness. She died in 1980. GW/VL

[*Med. J. Aust.*, 1983, **2**, 152]

KEATES, Philip George *b.*1 Oct 1919 *d.*25 Oct 1981
MRCS LRCP (1943) MB BS Lond (1943) MD (1948) MRCP (1949) DMRD (1953) FRCP (1974)

Philip Keates, consultant radiologist to the United Leeds Hospitals, was educated at St Paul's School, London, and St Thomas's Hospital. He qualified in medicine in 1943 and, after house jobs, served with the RAMC in India and in the invasion of Europe. After demobilization, he first trained in general medicine and then in diagnostic radiology. Once qualified, he became the first research registrar in radiology to be appointed by the University of Leeds, and during this time did some early valuable work on intravenous urography, being responsible for the section on the renal tract in the then current edition of *A Textbook of Radiology by British Authors*.

Following appointment to the consultant staff of Leeds General Infirmary in 1957, he became one of the pioneers of cardiac radiology. Later he developed a particular interest in the technical side of X-ray equipment and was nationally recognized as an expert.

Philip Keates was a perfectionist. Anything he undertook was done with carefully thought out detail. He had a succession of hobbies ranging from horticulture to wireless telegraphy. At heart, he was an outdoor man, happiest trudging across the Dales or camping alone in the Highlands of Scotland. He was a well known nature and sports photographer, and in recent years much of his time was spent attending sporting occasions throughout Yorkshire with his camera. He left behind him a reputation as a first class radiologist, a man who could be relied upon to give a worthwhile opinion on most subjects, and many hundreds of beautiful and exciting photographs. KCS

KELLETT, Charles Ernest *b.*2 Mar 1903 *d.*20 Aug 1978
BA Cantab (1924) MB BChir (1927) MA (1928) MRCP (1928) MD (1931) FRCP (1949)

Charles Ernest Kellett was born at St Helen Auckland in Durham and died at Shotley Bridge, Durham. His father, Matthew Henry Kellett, a mining engineer who also owned several collieries, came from south Durham, where he was for many years colliery agent for the Peaces. His mother, Louise Jeanne Antoinette Montchal, was the daughter of Charles Abraham Montchal, a secondary schoolmaster in Geneva.

Kellett was educated at Bow Preparatory School in Durham, and from 1917 to 1920 at Rossall. In 1921 he was admitted to Sidney Sussex College, Cambridge, to begin the study of medicine. From there he entered University College Hospital medical school, where he qualified in 1927, gaining the degree of MD in 1931.

For family reasons he returned to Newcastle, where he did some fundamental research into immunological mechanisms and the role of complement. His interests were at first in paediatrics, and in 1930 he was awarded the Helen Hartley Jenkins Fellowship in paediatrics at the Johns Hopkins University. He had obtained, before this, a house appointment at the Hospital for Sick Children, Great Ormond Street, and later worked with James Spence at the Fleming Hospital for Sick Children at Newcastle. But, strongly influenced by Sir William Hume, a distinguished physician at Newcastle, he turned his attention to general medicine, and was elected to the staff of the General Hospital at Newcastle, where he became senior physician before retiring in 1967. He was also a senior consultant at Shotley Bridge Hospital, retiring in 1965. At the outbreak of war Shotley Bridge Hospital was made an emergency hospital, and Kellett was appointed medical director. He served on the staff of the Queen Elizabeth Hospital at Gateshead. He lectured, too, on the history of medicine, and was appointed to teach medicine to the dental students of Newcastle medical school, many of whom during the war came from Norway.

In 1932 he had married Elizabeth (Betty) Scott, the daughter of Frederick John Cleminson, FRCS, an ear, nose and throat surgeon at the Middlesex Hospital, and by her had a son and a daughter. Shortly after the end of the war, in 1947, he and his family moved into a delightful and interesting house at Shotley Bridge, where the large and productive garden was always a joy, and where he and his wife entertained a large circle of friends who could admire the magnificent views over the Durham hills. The death of his wife in 1975 was a blow from which he never really recovered, and Snow's Green House was never the same again.

He was an intelligent man and a good doctor: he had a keen, well stocked and sceptical mind, and, as a bibliophile, owned a large and fine collection of early medical and scientific books. His knowledge of his local countryside and what it contained was vast, and he was also the proud possessor of a vintage Rolls Royce car, which it gave him great pleasure to drive and to cherish. He contributed a number of articles to the medical historical press, which show considerable knowledge and learning.

Kellett was a person of high principles, who maintained the standards among which he had been brought up, in a changing world. One of his former colleagues remarked that he was the most cultured man in the Newcastle Medical School. He was also a very good friend and a delightful companion. A

[*Brit. med. J.*, 1978, **2**, 1234]

KEMP, Frederick Harold *b.*12 May 1912 *d.*2 Aug 1976
MB ChB Birm (1934) DMR (1938) FFR (1954) FRCP (1954)
MA Oxon (1960) MD Birm (1960)

Frederick Harold Kemp was born at Smethwick on the outskirts of Birmingham. His mother, who was a sister of the pioneer radiologist, James F Brailsford, died young, and Brailsford, who had no children, always took a great interest in his nephew. His influence undoubtedly inspired the boy to make his career in radiology. Kemp was brought up in the country in Shropshire, and always retained his affection for the countryside. He was educated at a private academy in Birmingham and from there went to Birmingham University as a medical student. While a student he received two years' preliminary training in radiology. JS Mitchell, who later became a leading radiotherapist and Regius Professor of medicine at Cambridge, was a fellow student. Kemp qualified in medicine with honours in 1934, having been awarded the Priestley Smith prize in ophthalmology, the Russell Memorial prize in neurology and a gold medal in surgery. After qualification he was house surgeon to W Gemmel, the professor of surgery at Birmingham, and house physician to L MacKay, the senior physician at the Queen's Hospital, Birmingham. In 1935 he was appointed clinical assistant, the equivalent of registrar, in the X-ray departments of the Sheffield Royal Infirmary and Royal Hospital.

In 1939 Kemp became assistant radiologist to the Radcliffe Infirmary, Oxford. The Infirmary was still reeling under the impact of the Nuffield benefaction, five new clinical professorial chairs having been established in 1937. Fortunately, AE Barclay was working as honorary radiologist to the Nuffield Institute of Medical Research, which had been opened in the old observatory on the Radcliffe site in 1935. Barclay was not only one of the most distinguished of the early radiologists but he was also a man of great personal charm; he was appointed consulting radiologist to the Radcliffe Infirmary and had a profound influence on Kemp. Unfortunately he developed a carcinoma of the stomach from which he died in 1949. I remember him holding up the X-ray film of his stomach, taken by Kemp, which he had asked to see and which showed an inoperable lesion. He turned to me, saying, 'A good radiologist, that boy, isn't he?'

Kemp was chairman of staff of the X-Ray department at the Radcliffe Infirmary from 1946 to 1973. He was radiologist to the Wingfield-Morris Hospital, later the Nuffield Orthopaedic Centre, from 1940 until his death. He raised the standard of radiology at both these hospitals to a high level. He also devoted a considerable fraction of his time to research in radiology in the Nuffield Institute, in collaboration with GM Ardran. They were pioneers in the use of cinéradiography and wrote many papers together, particularly on the pharynx, oesophagus and mechanism of swallowing. Kemp was writing a book with Ardran on the *Mouth and Pharynx* at the time of his death. In his clinical work and teaching he was much influenced by the Scandinavian school of radiologists, who had made radiology one of the primary clinical departments, serving as the ante-room to medicine and surgery. He was, indeed, a physician practising radiology, with an abiding interest in the physiology of the body. Students and staff were encouraged to see the X-ray examinations and films of their patients in the X-ray department, but he was at his best in the major case demonstrations, being dogmatic and provocative and loving the cut and thrust of an argument. Some of his radiological colleagues found him almost too rumbustious, and from time to time oil had to be poured on the troubled waters of the department.

Kemp married Amy Large of Swinton, Yorkshire, who had been a nurse. They had three children, a son who became a biochemist and a member of the staff of the Medical Research Council, and two daughters. They lived at Shipton under Wychwood on the edge of the Cotswolds and Kemp seemed tireless, starting work early and finishing late despite the long drive to work and back. He died suddenly and unexpectedly. He had always disapproved of memorial services, particularly in the event of his own death, but he was too forceful a personality for his passing to be left unnoticed and a well-attended memorial service was held at St Giles' Church, Oxford. LJW

[*Brit. med. J.*, 1976, **2**, 952; Photo]

KENDALL, Arthur Charles *b.*25 Apr 1920 *d.*9 May 1983
MB ChB Birm (1942) MRCP (1945) DCH (1949) FRCP (1969)

Arthur Kendall was born in Birmingham, and received his early education in his native city. He showed considerable academic ability during his studies at King Edward's School, Birmingham; where he was recognized as a hard working scholar with great enthusiasm.

After selecting medicine as his future career, he entered Birmingham University, and passed his M and ChB in 1943, gaining a distinction in medicine, and winning the senior medical prize.

Following early house appointments in Birmingham, he enlisted in the Army in South East Asia Command and served for three years as RMO. During the latter part of his army service, he was graded as a medical specialist.

While in India, he came into close contact with the general population, and was challenged by his experience with sick children. At this time, he decided that he would specialize in paediatrics. He returned to England, and during appointments to Birmingham Children's Hospital, quickly passed the examination MRCP in 1946. He then moved to the Radcliffe Infirmary, Oxford, where he served as registrar, and later senior registrar in the paediatric department. He was appointed consultant paediatrician to Coventry Management Team in 1950, and continued this work until his retirement in 1980. He was elected FRCP in 1969.

Throughout his hospital work Arthur Kendall demonstrated great diagnostic and therapeutic skills, which were devoted selflessly to the care of his patients and the comfort of anxious parents. A kind, sympathetic man, he was always able to find that little extra time for full discussion and explanation. These attributes made him a natural teacher. He played an active part in the instruction of undergraduate medical students from Birmingham University, many of whom were attached to his firm as clinical clerks. For the last five years he took a special interest in the training of community paediatricians, and he established a diploma course in community paediatrics at the

University of Warwick. He was chairman of the examiners for this diploma.

Arthur fully realized the need for close liaison between hospital and community care for children, and set up a child development unit in Coventry long before the advantages of such units were generally recognized. His frequent visits to special schools for physical and mental handicap were much appreciated and welcomed by medical colleagues and teachers alike. His interest in community care took him to (then) Rhodesia, where he served for one year as visiting professor of paediatrics in Salisbury. The special care baby unit at the Walsgrave Hospital was also his brainchild, and thrived on his constant interest and advice. From there he conducted careful research into the prognosis of various groups of at risk babies. Kendall's ability as a paediatrician was recognized by his colleagues when he was elected president of the Midlands Paediatric Association, and his interest in BMA affairs brought him the chairmanship of the local division. For relaxation Arthur liked to escape from city to country to follow his chief hobbies of gardening and fishing. He retired to his country cottage in mid-Wales to enjoy these pursuits further. He married Hilda Mary, daughter of David John Moran, a Congregational minister, in 1948. They had two sons, John and Charles. EEJ

[*Brit. med. J.*, 1983, **286**, 1989; Photo]

KERLEY, *Sir* **Peter (James)** *b.*27 Oct 1900 *d.*14 May 1979
KCVO (1972) CVO (1952) CBE (1951)
MB BCh BAO Dublin (1923) DMRE (1925) MD (1932)
FFR (1939) MRCP (1944) FRCP (1946) FRCR (1975)†

Peter Kerley was one of the most distinguished representatives of British radiology. He was born at Dundalk, Ireland, and qualified at the University of Dublin in 1923. In 1924 he went to study in Vienna, which was then the centre of the relatively new science of radiology. It was there that he first became interested in what was to be his principal professional preoccupation, the radiology of the heart and lungs. On returning to England he studied at Cambridge and passed the DMRE. He was awarded the MD University of Ireland in 1932. In 1939 he became a founder member of the Faculty of Radiologists. He was appointed radiologist at Westminster Hospital where he became associated with Sir Clement Price Thomas, an association which was to be of vital importance in later years. In 1933 he was invited by S Cochrane Shanks to collaborate with him in editing *A Textbook of X-ray Diagnosis by British Authors*, along with EW Twining. The first edition, in three volumes, has now been expanded to six volumes in its fourth edition, and the copyright has been assigned to the Royal College of Radiologists. He was editor of the *Journal of the Faculty of Radiologists* and author of many original papers the best known being the St Cyres lectures on the 'Radiology of the Pulmonary Circulation'.

Before the second world war Kerley was busily engaged in hospital and private practice, and shortly after the outbreak of hostilities he volunteered to join the RAMC as a specialist radiologist. He was sent to India and Singapore, where he contracted dysentery and was invalided home in 1944. On his return he was appointed to the Ministry of Health, to take charge of the mass radiography service then being established, for which – with his special knowledge of the radiology of the chest – he was particularly well fitted. In 1944 he was made MRCP without examination on presentation of his work in *British Authors*. Two years later he was elected to the Fellowship. In addition to his appointment at Westminster Hospital, he was radiologist to the National Heart Hospital and to King Edward VII Sanatorium, Midhurst. He was also consultant adviser in radiology to the Ministry of Health, an office which he held until he retired aged 70. Other appointments were as radiologist to Shell and Esso, both of which he held until shortly before his death, and he was adviser to the Ministry of Aviation.

In 1952 King George VI was taken ill at Balmoral and eventually came under the care of Sir Clement Price Thomas, who called in Peter Kerley. Together they diagnosed cancer of the lung, and from this initial introduction to the Royal Family ensued Peter Kerley's long association with Royalty. For these many services he was appointed CVO in 1952 and KCVO in 1972. He had already been appointed CBE in 1951.

Many honours were bestowed upon him in addition to his presidency of the Faculty (now the Royal College of Radiologists), of which he was awarded the gold medal in 1976. He was made an honorary fellow of the American College of Radiologists, the Australasian College of Radiology, the Faculty of Radiologists of Ireland and the Chicago Radiological Society. In 1944 he received the Röntgen award of the Toronto Radiological Society.

Of published works, in addition to the editorship of *British Authors* in which he was responsible for the sections on the chest (taking over from Twining, who died in 1940), he prepared the first two editions of *Recent Advances in Radiology*.

What of the man himself? Sir Peter had all the charm of the best of the Irish, and with it all an extraordinarily acute and intelligent mind. To be with him was always an exceptional treat, right up to his last days. His hobbies were golf, shooting and fishing, especially the latter. Each spring he would go north to the Dee to catch a salmon, and seldom would he fail to land several.

He married Olive MacNamee in 1929 and they had two daughters. His wife died in 1973. Both his daughters became doctors. SCS/GW

[*Brit. med. J.*, 1979, **1**, 959, 1095 & 1433; *Lancet*, 1979, **1**, 735; *Clinical Radiology*, **30**, No.3, p.359; Photo]

KEYNES, ***Sir*** **Geoffrey (Langdon)** *b.*25 Mar 1887 *d.*5 July 1983
Kt (1955) BA Cantab (1909) MB BChir (1913) MD (1918)
FRCS (1920) FRCOG (1950) FRCP (1953) Hon LLD Edin
Hon DLitt Oxon Cantab Birm Sheffield Reading

Geoffrey Keynes, the second of three children, was born into a comfortable middle class home in Cambridge. Though his father was registrary to the University and a fellow of Pembroke, it was hardly a highbrow family, but by the times Keynes died the name was a household one – principally, though not entirely, because of his elder brother's (Maynard) eminence as an economist, but also because it had become one of the great Cambridge intellectual dynasties, linked partly by marriage and partly by collaboration and friendship with the Darwins, the Adrians, the Huxleys, and the Wedgwoods. Geoffrey Keynes himself attained equal eminence in three separate spheres: as a surgeon and medical innovator; as a bibliophile, combining the roles of collector, writer, editor, and bibliographer; and as a public man, particularly his services as a trustee of the National Portrait Gallery from 1942 to 1966.

Educated at Rugby (where he was a contemporary of Rupert Brooke) and Pembroke College, Cambridge (where he was a foundation scholar and got a first in the Natural Sciences tripos), Keynes went to Bart's in 1909, winning the Brackenbury surgical scholarship and the Willett medal, and qualifying four years later. Deciding to devote himself to surgery – he was to taunt his uncle Sir Walter Langdon-Brown with the relative therapeutic impotence of the physician – he did house jobs at Bart's until he joined up at the outbreak of war. Before this, however, he had gained a certain eminence among his friends by saving Virginia Woolf's life when she attempted suicide with an overdose of drugs in 1913. He and Sir Henry Head washed out her stomach and spent the night by her bedside while she slowly recovered. Unlike his brother Maynard, Geoffrey Keynes was never a central member of the Bloomsbury group, although he knew many of the principal characters and shared their tastes for painting rather than architecture, ballet rather than opera, high thinking rather than good living; as a memento some years later Virginia Woolf gave him the manuscript of her essay 'On Being Ill' in gratitude for his professional care.

In the first world war Keynes served as a regimental medical officer in the trenches, as well as in military hospitals. At the latter he was able to introduce the new technique of blood transfusion, which, albeit primitive, was to save the lives of many soldiers. Despite this, however, the idea of transfusion provoked considerable opposition, something that Keynes was to encounter again in peace time when, having written the first textbook in Britain on transfusion (1922), he tried to introduce the technique on his return to Bart's. Thus, later in the 1930s, when he suggested and himself practised limited excision together with radium treatment for localized cancer of the breast, Keynes was fully experienced in coping with ill-based and obdurate professional argument. Likewise the third of his innovations, thymectomy for myasthenia gravis, also provoked much opposition when it was introduced during the second world war – yet again, like blood transfusion and 'lumpectomy', it is now a standard form of treatment.

All this, however, is to jump around a bit over the decades. Keynes returned from the first world war to obtain higher degrees and then to be appointed in 1920 as assistant to the newly formed medical unit at Bart's headed by George Gask. Thereafter he was appointed an assistant surgeon on the staff at Bart's, and also held specialist posts at Mount Vernon Hospital, the Radium Institute, the LCC Thyroid Clinic, and the City of London Truss Society. He also built up a large private practice, in particular acting as Lord Moynihan's assistant in London and specializing in the surgery of hernia, breast cancer, and thyroid disease. In the second world war he served in the Royal Air Force with the rank of acting air vice-marshal. He obtained numerous medical honours: the fellowship of two other Royal Colleges; at the Royal College of Surgeons three Hunterian professorships, (1923, 1929, 1945), as well as the Cecil Joll prize in 1953 and the Sir Arthur Sims Commonwealth travelling professorship in 1956; at the royal College of Physicians the Harveian oration in 1958 and the Fitzpatrick lecture in 1963; and at the Royal Society the Wilkins lecture in 1967. He was appointed Knight Bachelor in 1955.

Despite an energetic life in surgery, however, Keynes found the time for a totally different one outside the consulting room and operating theatre. He had started collecting books while an undergraduate at Cambridge and his first book, *A Bibliography of John Donne*, was published in 1914 just as he had arrived in the trenches. It was to be the first of many bibliographies of his many enthusiasms – particularly for seventeenth century authors such as Donne, Hooke, King, Evelyn, and Harvey – and, though his approach might be criticized by the stricter academic specialists, he contended, and most generalists agreed, that it was justified by the broader light that it shed on its subject. His skills were never put to better use than when he edited nine books – among them works by Harvey, Thomas Browne, and William Blake – for the Nonesuch Press, and he had a hand in at least six others. He had helped this from its early days together with its founders, (Sir) Francis and Vera Meynell and David Garnett. In 1975 he presented 250 volumes from his library by or about Sir Thomas Browne to the Royal College of Physicians but later suggested that these should be sold to Cambridge University and the money added to the College building appeal. His library from his beautiful house near Newmarket was also acquired by Cambridge University, after his death.

The rules of Bart's stipulated that consultants had to retire at 60, and Keynes had to leave in 1946, only a few months before the Health Service was introduced, under whose rules he would have been able to stay until 65. His colleagues at Bart's solved this dilemma by making him emeritus surgeon for five years, with few official duties entailed. But a man of Keynes's energies was hardly to remain underemployed either for this last five years or after he had completely 'retired'. He continued with some of his surgical interests, also travelling and lecturing, but threw himself into his other careers almost whole time. President of the Bibliographical Society in 1952–1954, he served as the chairman of the trustees of the National Portrait Gallery from 1955 to 1966; he wrote numerous articles and essays, and brought out new editions of some of his books; while his major biography of William Harvey was awarded the James Tait Black memorial prize in 1966. His last major work was his autobiography, *The Gates of Memory*, published in 1981, and he contributed to the introduction to John Dreyfus's *History of the Nonesuch Press*, published in 1982.

For most of his life Keynes was a trim upright man with a small moustache, who spoke with a rapid clipped voice that betokened an Edwardian upbringing. Latterly he became bent and walked with a stick, but he lost neither his good looks nor, despite a minor stroke, his sharpness or his intelligence. Reputedly arrogant and brusque in the '20s and '30s, little of this was apparent in his later years, and in any case these are not unusual attributes for a young man of high intelligence who is in a hurry. And in his life he had so much to do, for, besides the interests already mentioned, he was at times an enthusiastic rock climber, entomologist, camper, gardener, carpenter, and balletomane (devising the scheme for Ralph Vaughan Williams's *Job*). Almost certainly, part of the drive for all this came from his need to keep up with Maynard – though the latter had ignored him until his wife Lydia Lopokova (one of Diaghilev's ballerinas) drew his attention to Geoffrey's merits. But much also came from a need never to waste a minute and from the streak of puritanism that ran through him, as typified by his pride in never having been drunk in his life. He made friends easily and voraciously, had no snobbery in his make-up, and loved beauty in all its forms; he was an example that polymaths need not necessarily have feet of clay.

In 1917 Keynes married Margaret Darwin, who predeceased him in 1974. They had four sons, one of whom became a surgeon and another, who was elected FRS, professor of physiology at the University of Cambridge. SPL

[*The Gates of memory*, Oxford, OUP, 1981; *Times*, 6 July 1982; *Brit. med. J.*, 1982, **285**, 299, 384; *Lancet,* 1982, **2**, 168; *The Library: Transactions of the Bibliographical Society,* Vol.**4**, No.4, Dec 1982; Photo]

KIERNANDER, Frederick Basil *b.*29 Jan 1913 *d.*23 May 1982
MRCS LRCP (1936) MB BS Lond (1936) MRCP (1937)
DMRE Cantab (1938) FRCP (1972)

Basil Kiernander (he never used his first name) was born in Hertfordshire. His father was a banker in India and his mother the daughter of an Ayrshire physician. After attending a preparatory school in Surrey he was educated at Epsom College. Towards the end of his schooldays his family financial circumstances deteriorated, and there was some doubt whether he could proceed to university. However, he won the Jenks memorial scholarship at St Thomas's

Hospital, qualifying there in 1936. He had a brilliant undergraduate record winning many prizes, spurred on by the home difficulties, and he then achieved the rare distinction of passing the MRCP examination at the first attempt at the very early age of twenty three, within one year of qualification. After a house post and junior registrar post at St Thomas's he became assistant radiotherapist at University College Hospital, and clinical assistant to the physical medicine department at the Royal Free Hospital and Arthur Stanley Institute in 1938, becoming consultant in physical medicine to the Radcliffe Infirmary in 1939.

His progress was thus meteoric and he continued the rest of his career in physical medicine and rheumatology. He joined the Royal Air Force in 1942 when he was put in charge of the physical medicine department at the Royal Air Force Central Medical Establishment. At the end of the war he resigned his previous appointments and was appointed to the staff of the Hospital for Sick Children, Great Ormond Street, as consultant in physical medicine. His attitude towards disabled children was always practical and forward looking, and his constant aim was to minimize the effects of disability and to make the child as independent as possible both physically and emotionally. He always saw clinical problems from the viewpoint of the patient as a whole and not merely as an assortment of faulty limbs.

His expertise became recognized both at home and abroad and he was one of the few honorary members of both the British Orthopaedic Association and the American Academy of Physical Medicine and Rehabilitation. He maintained his links with the Royal Air Force as their civilian consultant in physical medicine.

He never married and took great delight in providing comfort for his parents who lived to a considerable age. He divided his spare time and energy between the Royal Society of Medicine, the Cheshire Foundation, and keeping in touch with his past registrars in whose careers he took great interest. At the Royal Society of Medicine for over twenty years he was a member of one or other of their major policy making committees as well as being president of his own section and the open section. He travelled overseas to advise the Cheshire Foundation on the setting up and management of their homes abroad and took a close personal interest in the one near his home in Angmering.

Unfortunately, in the last ten years of his life he suffered from angina and although he continued in active practice until his death, his activities necessarily became more limited as time went on.

He was a kindly man and an attentive host with a large circle of friends extending far outside medicine. He made few enemies but unfortunately those he had were in powerful positions, and many colleagues thought that the interval between the MRCP in 1937 and his fellowship in 1972 was unduly prolonged. EDRC

[*Daily Telegraph,* 28 May 1982; *Rheumatology and Rehab.,* 1982, **21**, 185; Photo]

KILOH, George Anderson *b*.30 May 1910 *d*.30 Mar 1981
MRCS LRCP (1934) MB BS Lond (1936) MD (1940)
MRCP (1941) FRCP (1962)

George Kiloh was born in London in 1910, the elder son of Ruxton Cuthbert Kiloh, an engineer, and Elizabeth Anderson, a farmer's daughter. He went to Battersea Grammar School, and from there to King's College Hospital where he qualified in 1934. After a succession of junior posts at King's, he was Crawfurd medical registrar there from 1939 to 1942, passing the London MD in 1940 and the MRCP in 1941. In 1942 he joined the RAMC, and was soon serving in India where he was lieutenant colonel in charge of a division from 1944 to 1946. After demobilization he was senior medical registrar at the National Heart Hospital for two years, until appointed consultant physician to the Chester Group of hospitals in 1948, a few months before the start of the National Health Service.

His appointment to this provincial hospital group was that of general physician, but his special interest in cardiology had been maturing during his period at the National Heart Hospital, and he immediately set about developing a unit for cardiac investigation in Chester. Cardiac surgery was about to become important, and Kiloh recognized the value of close association between physician and surgeon, arranging to hold joint clinics with Leslie Temple from the Liverpool cardiothoracic unit at Chester Royal Infirmary. Patients then met their physician and future surgeon, and treatment was discussed by all three. Out of this cooperation an outstandingly successful cardiac service became available to doctors and their patients in Chester and North Wales.

His interest in cardiology did not impair the service he provided in general medicine, and the old buildings at Chester City Hospital and Royal Infirmary were the scene of an enormous turnover of acute medical cases, providing excellent training for successive house physicians and registrars. The wide scope of the work, and the enthusiastic supervision and teaching they received from their physician, made the unit a popular training post. His association with his juniors seldom ended with their term of office, and he maintained contact with many in retirement. George Kiloh did not spare himself, and he expected the same industry from his juniors. It was quite usual for him to do his full ward round on a bank holiday, and he expected his team to be in attendance even when working hours for junior staff were much reduced.

He was an excellent lecturer. He took great pains to prepare his subject, so that he spoke fluently and with little reference to notes. Bad grammar and modern distortions of the English language were anathema to him. Pressure of work left little time for research, but he was a thoughtful physician, and occasional papers on his observations were an excellent example to his juniors, notably that on pure aortic stenosis, (*British Heart Journal,* 1950). He took much interest in the training of nurses, and examined regularly for the General Nursing Council in London as well as locally.

Starting his consultant career when the Health Service was about to begin, George Kiloh played a leading part in the organization of the hospital service in his area. He was always ready to take on more than his share of committee work. For long periods he was secretary of the local medical advisory committee, and of the Chester and North Wales Medical Society, chairman of the medical staff committee, and in his turn president of the Chester Medical Society. He founded the Chester branch of the British Heart Foundation, of which he was later made life president. He attended and contributed to meetings of the British Cardiac Society. He was a man of strong convictions, and a forthright speaker who would not hesitate to put forward unpopular views. His powers of argument and persuasion were vital to the development of the Health Service in a city whose hospitals in 1948 were antiquated and inadequate.

He played a full part in local life apart from his professional activities. He was a keen Mason, chairman of the Chester and District Marriage Guidance Council, president of the Free Church Council, and of the Rotary Club. He was vice-president of the Chester Football Club for over 20 years.

In 1939 he married Freda Heron, whom he had known as a nurse. They had one son and one daughter. On retirement in 1974 George and Freda went to live in the Isles of Scilly, where they had had a holiday home for some years. The last three years of his working life had been dogged by ill health due to aortic valve disease, a subject in which he had taken so much professional interest. He needed valve replacement twice, and installation of a pacemaker. Ill health eventually led George to decide on premature retirement, but after the second operation his health improved enough for him to enjoy six years of reasonable health in his island home.

He was survived by his widow, son and daughter. His younger brother (also FRCP) became professor of psychiatry in New South Wales.

ACCH

[*Brit. med. J.*, 1981, **282**, 1979; Photo]

KNIGHTS, Francis John Davison *b.*30 Dec 1911 *d.*27 Oct 1981
MRCS LRCP (1935) MB BS Lond (1936) MD (1939)
MRCP (1945) FRCP (1969)

Frank Knights, son of Edgar Robert Knights, master tailor, and Katherine Jane Davison, spent his early life in London. After attending Cheltonia College Preparatory School, he entered Dulwich College, leaving in 1929. He then went to Middlesex Hospital, qualifying in 1935. After house appointments at Middlesex, Miller, and London Chest Hospitals he married Kathleen Esther Murphy, daughter of a civil servant and a ward sister, and together they went, under the auspices of the Church Missionary Society, to West China, where their three sons were born.

Frank spent the war years as practitioner and teacher of medicine at the West China Union University in Chengtu, and ran a small tuberculosis sanatorium in an orchard during this time. He also spent a year up country, in a remote area, coping with both medical and surgical problems.

Returning to this country at the end of 1944, he obtained his MRCP, and in 1946 became assistant tuberculosis officer at the London Chest Hospital. In 1948, he was appointed consultant physician in diseases of the chest to Gloucester and Cheltenham Hospitals. Always immensely enthusiastic in everything he did, he quickly set about the organization of a chest service in Gloucestershire, and by the advent of the NHS had already paved the way for the ultimate control of tuberculosis in the county, then a major problem. He later developed the service to include non-tuberculous disease and especially allergic disease, in which he became extremely interested and an expert.

Apart from his enthusiasm and zest for life, he possessed an acute sense of humour and also an extraordinary clarity of thought, which made him a most valued member, and often chairman, of many committees, and his contribution in this direction was truly monumental, including membership of the council of St Paul's and St Mary's Teacher Training Colleges for nine years.

His interests apart from medicine were manifold. He maintained from boyhood a special interest in natural history, and he loved his garden and alpines especially. A highly intelligent man, he read widely all his life, especially philosophical and theological works, and he was a lay-reader for some years. He became an authority upon such diverse subjects as the life of Christina of Sweden, the eunuchs of Byzantium, Commedia del 'Arte, and Aesculapian medicine in Rome. In later life he became a true Italophile and learned to speak Italian fluently.

Ever young in mind and in heart, it was typical of him that before he retired from the NHS he had already made arrangements to take up an entirely different task in industrial medicine. His death was unexpected and premature. He was survived by his wife Kathleen and three sons, one of whom had qualified as a doctor. RHE

[*Brit. med. J.*, 1982, **284**, 59; Photo]

KREBS, *Sir* **Hans (Adolf)** *b.*25 Aug 1900 *d.*22 Nov 1981
Kt (1958) MD Hamburg (1925) MA Cantab (1934) FRS (1947) FRCP* (1958)†

Hans Krebs was born in Hildesheim, an old and beautiful town situated near Hannover. In his autobiography, which appeared about the time of his death, Krebs describes the town of his birth in some detail, and also mentions that it was almost completely destroyed during World War II. His father, Georg Krebs, was a surgeon who specialized in diseases of the ear, nose and throat, and his mother was Alma Davidson, the daughter of a banker.

Krebs received a humanistic education which put emphasis on Latin and Greek, with some mathematics and relatively little science. He appears to have enjoyed both his Latin and Greek, and in conversation he occasionally quoted Horace and the Iliad. Both his parents were Jewish but they had no religious association, and particularly his father was completely immersed in German culture. According to the autobiography already quoted, his father's heroes were Goethe, Bismarck, and Frederick the Great. The home background appears to have been fairly austere, indeed Spartan. High standards of behaviour were expected of the children, and according to Hans, demonstrations of emotion were frowned upon. There were 'no spontaneous hugs or goodnight kisses.' This upbringing left a permanent mark on him. He was reluctant to show emotion, and he remained essentially shy throughout his life.

The school career of Hans Krebs ended in 1918 with his conscription into the Army. He served for only a few months, but he wrote many years afterwards that some aspects of his Army service made a lasting impression, largely as a clear definition of responsibilities within a team, and the importance of 'self- and corporate-discipline.' After leaving the Army he went to Göttingen University, where he was much impressed by the lectures in chemistry of Adolf Windaus, the famous steroid chemist, and the professor in physics, Robert Pohl. Krebs then transferred to Freiburg, where he came under the influence of Möllendorf and particularly Knoop, whose work was of considerable importance to Krebs later in his career. After passing the Physikum (equivalent to the Second MB) he went to Munich, where the professor of medicine, Friedrich von Müller, who was also a good biochemist, greatly impressed him. This was the time when the German inflation reached horrendous proportions, and life for a university student must have been particularly difficult. After his finals, Krebs spent his pre-registration year in the Third Medical Clinic where he met David Nachmansohn and Bruno Mendel, who became life-long friends. In 1925 Krebs worked for a while in the department of Peter Rona, which was probably his first introduction into biochemistry, and his experience there may have decided him to concentrate on a clinical career with biochemistry as his major research interest. An opportunity offered itself soon, when he heard from Mendel that Otto Warburg was looking for a collaborator to work on cancer. Mendel suggested Krebs as a candidate, and he was duly appointed.

The four years which Krebs spent in the department of Otto Warburg were in many ways decisive for the future development of Krebs as a scientist. Krebs himself wrote a full appreciation of Otto Warburg in the *Memoirs of The Royal Society* (Vol. 18, 1972), of which Warburg was a foreign member, and also a full biography which appeared in German in 1979 and was translated into English in 1981. Warburg, who was one of the greatest biochemists of the last hundred years, was an unusual person. He was autocratic, and the extent of his autocracy was unusual even in pre-war Germany. He was touchy, full of prejudices, and by no means an easy colleague. However, his penetrating mind, his intellectual honesty, his imagination, and his singularity of purpose were equally outstanding. Krebs was conscious of the weaknesses of his teacher, but his admiration for the man prevailed, and Warburg's influence remained a dominant factor throughout the life and career of Krebs.

During the time that Krebs worked in Warburg's laboratory he was engaged mainly on problems set by his chief, such as the biological function and estimation of copper, the metabolism of tumours, and model experiments on catalysis by haem derivatives. But he learned a variety of methods which Krebs later used in his own work, and above all he acquired high and demanding standards of scientific work. Krebs left Warburg's laboratory in 1930 and joined the department of Lichtwitz, who was responsible for external medicine at the municipal hospital at Altona, now part of the city of Hamburg. During his time with Lichtwitz, who was a general physician with special interest in metabolism, Krebs acquired a very good training in clinical medicine. His clinical duties were quite heavy, but he managed to spend some time in the laboratory. Before long he was invited to join Tannhauser who, in addition to being a good clinician, was a widely-recognized expert on lipid metabolism and its disturbances. The university of Freiburg provided an excellent environment for Krebs. He was again responsible for a ward, he greatly enjoyed his clinical work, and his contact with patients. However, he had time for laboratory work, and it was here that he started to work completely on his own ideas, but using the techniques which he had learned in Warburg's laboratory.

In this work Krebs used the tissue slice technique which Warburg had extensively used in his studies of cell metabolism. A major advance in this technique was the introduction by Krebs of a new medium, which simulated blood plasma as closely as possible with respect to many of its constituents. This medium, which is an improvement on that of Ringer and that of Locke, has been widely used all over the world. Krebs found that liver slices could form urea from ammonia and carbon dioxide, but that the addition of the amino acid ornithine greatly stimulated this process. He showed that ornithine acted catalytically, as demonstrated by the fact that one mole of ornithine could promote the formation of something like 20 moles of urea. He further showed that the amino acid citrulline was the first product of the interaction of ornithine, carbon dioxide and ammonia, and that arginine was the next product which on interaction with the ènzyme arginase gave rise to ornithine and urea. This was the first demonstration of a metabolic cycle, and since the discovery of the mechanism of urea synthesis, a large number of cycles have been demonstrated. The detailed enzymatic mechanisms involved in these various reactions were largely discovered by other workers, but Kreb's work on urea synthesis must be considered one of the important milestones in modern biochemistry. This work earned Krebs almost immediately a great international reputation and led to his appointment as Privat Dozent in the University of Freiburg.

Within three months of Hitler's assumption of power all academic teachers who were of the Jewish race were either dismissed or placed on leave, and this meant that Krebs had to leave his laboratory in Freiburg in the middle of April 1933. Krebs had been working at that time on the biosynthesis, metabolism and function of glutamine, a topic which engaged his attention for many years. Krebs realized that he had to leave Germany if he wanted to continue with his scientific work and he decided to seek a position in England, a country which he had visited in 1928, and where he had some professional contacts. Sir Frederick Gowland Hopkins, who was head of the biochemistry laboratory at Cambridge, and at that time president of The Royal Society, invited Krebs to work in his laboratory. Throughout his life Krebs showed the utmost gratitude to Hopkins, and his feelings are well expressed in the third Hopkins Memorial lecture which he gave in 1961, and which is published in *The Biochemical Journal* (Vol. 80, p.225). In this lecture Krebs also relates in some detail how greatly impressed he was with the British way of life, and how he appreciated the friendly welcome he received from members of the Hopkins laboratory, and from the academic community generally in Cambridge.

During his Cambridge period he worked on topics which had already engaged his attention earlier, such as the synthesis and metabolism of uric acid, the biological function of glycarboxylic acids, and glutamine.

In 1935 Krebs was appointed lecturer in the department of pharmacology in the University of Sheffield. This department was headed by EJ Wayne, who was essentially a clinician trained by Sir Thomas Lewis, but who had taken a degree in chemistry. Krebs was able to transfer to Sheffield the equipment which he had originally brought from Freiburg. In time, a department of biochemistry was established in Sheffield, and ultimately Krebs was appointed professor of biochemistry. During the first few years in Sheffield Krebs did probably his most important piece of research, i.e., the discovery of the tricarboxylic acid cycle, or Krebs cycle. By 1932 it was known that glucose is not directly burnt or oxidised, but is first converted to lactic acid or pyruvic acid. It had also been shown by Albert Szent-Györgyi that the rate of oxidation in muscle preparations was greatly increased by adding succinic acid or related dicarboxylic acids: thus suggesting a catalytic effect of these compounds. The German chemists Knoop and Martius had shown that citric acid was converted by liver tissues to α-oxoglutaric acid. Krebs used these seminal findings and also some important new experiments of his own to suggest a cycle which starts with the condensation of oxaloacetate with acetic acid or acetyl-CoA to citrate, and then through α-oxoglutarate, succinate and fumarate back to oxaloacetate. One turn of the cycle brings about the production of two molecules of carbon dioxide associated with the consumption of two molecules of oxygen. This cycle is responsible for the oxidation of most of our food to carbon dioxide and water, and is the main oxidative pathway in most forms of life from bacteria to mammals. It is of some interest that a description of the essential facts about this cycle is contained in a letter to the editor of *Nature*, sent by

Krebs in June, 1937. The editor of *Nature* informed Krebs that, owing to congestion of papers, they could not publish his letter at the time, and advised him to submit his paper elsewhere. This paper, or a greatly expanded version of it, was in fact sent to the journal *Enzymologia*, which published it a few months after submission. It is no exaggeration to say that the formulation of the tricarboxylic acid cycle was one of the most important milestones in the development of biochemistry.

Krebs became a British citizen a few days after the outbreak of war in 1939, and a large part of his activities during the following years was connected with the war effort. Some of his work, which was carried out in association with Kenneth Mellanby, was concerned with the use of high extraction flour for human diets, particularly its digestibility, and the effect of the national wheatmeal on the absorption of calcium. Other work involved studying vitamin A deficiency, but his most important work during this period was concerned with vitamin C. By making use of conscientious objectors, he established quantitatively the minimum amounts of vitamin C required for the prevention of scurvy. The results of these experiments are still being quoted at the present time, especially the fact that 30 milligrams of vitamin C a day allow an ample margin of safety, and should be accepted as a reliable guide for formulating national policies.

In 1944 the Medical Research Council decided to set up a unit for research in cell metabolism at the University of Sheffield, with Krebs as its director. This unit, which was later transferred to Oxford, carried out research over a wide range of metabolism, such as gluconeogenesis, ketosis, energy changes in biological reactions, metabolism of purines, and related topics. The unit gave hospitality to many workers from overseas, particularly American scientists, and has been one of the focal points of biochemical research in the UK.

Krebs was very happy in Sheffield, and his outstanding contribution to science was becoming recognized to an increasing extent. In 1953 he received the Nobel Prize for physiology and medicine jointly with F Lipmann. In 1954 Krebs was invited to accept the chair of biochemistry in the University of Oxford, a chair which had been occupied by Sir Rudolph Peters for some years. Krebs was somewhat uncertain as to whether he should leave Sheffield and, before finally accepting the invitation, he consulted Peters. As Krebs reports in his autobiography, Peters thought that Krebs was not the ideal person for the post, and that only a scientist firmly based on a college could succeed in bringing experimental science into close contact with non-scientific academics. Krebs decided, however, to accept the post, and he was particularly attracted by the increasing possibilities which an Oxford chair would offer him both regarding teaching and research. Krebs probably found it not too easy to fit into Oxford, at least at first. He had relatively little small talk, and the weak position which professors in both Oxford and Cambridge occupy in relation to the colleges obviously disturbed him. He was fortunate in being able to transfer his unit from Sheffield to Oxford, and he was readily accepted by his academic colleagues. In time he became to an increasing extent part of Oxford life, and he greatly enjoyed being a member of Trinity College, of which he became an honorary fellow after his retirement.

A major scientific advance made during the Oxford period was the discovery of a new cycle, the glyoxylate cycle, which is a modification of the citric acid cycle, and which operates mainly in micro-organisms and in plants. This cycle represents the mechanism by which fat is converted into carbohydrate, a reaction which cannot be performed by higher animals. This work was done jointly with Sir Hans Kornberg.

Having reached the statutory age for retirement, Krebs relinquished his chair, but continued his research activities with the support of the MRC in a laboratory generously provided in the Radcliffe Infirmary by Paul Beeson, and this move was also supported by Sir George Pickering, the regius professor. A large number of the topics on which Hans Krebs and his co-workers were engaged were a continuation of their earlier activities. However, there was emphasis on problems which were related to medicine, and Krebs' intrinsic interest in clinical problems never left him. Krebs never did much work with isolated enzymes: his emphasis was either on the whole cell or on the whole organ, and thus work done with the perfused liver occupied much of his time. He also tried to integrate results obtained with systems such as tissue slices or perfused organs with what was happening in the whole organism. He made some progress with this work, but this was not completed by the time he died. Krebs remained in full possession of his physical and mental capacities until nearly the end of his life. He was much in demand at international meetings, and was a stimulus for others during the whole period of his retirement.

Although Krebs had some other interests, his devotion to science, and particularly the biochemistry of metabolism, dominated his life. He was delighted to have been able to train a large number of biochemists, and his influence on the development of biochemistry both nationally and internationally was profound. As already mentioned, he was a shy person, who had a very high standard of personal and professional integrity, and this was greatly appreciated by everybody who came into contact with him. His personal life was happy; he married Margaret Fieldhouse, and had two sons and a daughter.

AN

[*Brit. med. J.*, 1982, **284**, 59 & 517; *Lancet,* 1981, **2**, 1299; *Times,* 23 Nov 1981; *Clinical Science,* 1982, **63**, 225-30; Photo]

KUTUMBIAH, Pandipeddi *b*.22 Nov 1892 *d*.7 Feb 1976
BA Madras (1913) MB BS (1918) MRCP (1930) MD (1931)
FRCP (1958)

Pandipeddi Kutumbiah was the son of Pandipeddi Adinarayaniah, a lawyer, and Janikamma, the daughter of a *munsiff*. He was born in Kanigiri in Nellore Dt, Andhra Pradesh. After graduating from Madras Christian College, he had his medical training in Madras Medical College. On qualifying in 1918, he joined the Indian Medical Service, serving during the next five years in East Persia, Russian

Turkistan, Mesopotamia, Kurdistan, and the NW Frontier Province. He was demobilized in 1923 and joined the Madras Medical Service. During the next fifteen years he held successive lecturer appointments in medical subjects in both Andhra and Madras medical colleges. In 1938 he became professor of medicine in Andhra Medical College, Vizaghapatnam, and in 1945 professor of medicine and principal in Stanley Medical College, Madras. On retirement from government service in 1948 he became professor of medicine at the Christian Medical College, Vellore. Between 1950 and 1956 he was also principal of the College, and during 1956 to 1957 he acted as its director.

His interests in academic medicine were characterized by their breadth rather than originality. Acute rheumatism in childhood and adolescence was the subject of a number of papers and lectures, but his particular and continuing interest was the ancient systems of medicine, both Indian and of other countries. A number of short papers on ancient Hindu anatomy, physiology and medical theories were followed later in his life by larger works of considerable scholarship: *Ancient Indian medicine* (1962, revised 1969) and *Studies in Indian medicine* (1976). In 1947 he shared in the foundation of a society for the study of the history of medicine, now known as the Indian Association for the History of Medicine, of which he was at one time the president.

He was honorary physician to the viceroys of India, Lord Wavell and Lord Mountbatten. Between 1944 and 1956 he served on the Indian Council of Medical Research.

Kutumbiah was born into an influential Brahmin family. His life and character were profoundly influenced by his father's conversion to Christianity. The whole family, parents, five sons and four daughters, were baptized in 1901 when Kutumbiah was nine years old. This led to his attending a Christian school and college. At the latter, the guidance of a distinguished principal reinforced the formative example of his father and contributed to the integrity and almost ascetic simplicity which marked his whole life. He was a fluent and entertaining lecturer, and this with his natural and unassuming friendliness made him a popular teacher. He was a keen sportsman, with a particular enthusiasm for tennis. While on study leave in England, the day of his membership examination coincided with the Wimbledon finals. He unhesitatingly opted for Wimbledon, arguing that membership could be tackled in three months time but for Wimbledon he would have to wait a year. He continued to play tennis with students almost up to retirement, and understandably was held by successive generations in great affection.

He never married. His life in retirement was lonely but happy while filled with reading on ancient medicine. During his last years his sight failed, but this final burden he bore with his customary patience and fortitude. JKGW

[Photo]

LANGTON, Leonard *b*.2 May 1921 *d*.16 Nov 1981
MB ChB Leeds (1944) MD (1950) MRCP (1951) FRCP (1980) DMRD (1953) FFR (1967)

Leonard Langton was the son of Myer Leventhall, a wholesale grocer and provision merchant in Leeds. After schooling in Leeds at the Roundhay School, he entered the medical school in Leeds, qualifying in 1944 with a distinction in therapeutics. His early hospital appointments were in Leeds and Birmingham, but he then went back to Yorkshire for SHO and registrar posts in Halifax, where he had a considerable experience in general medicine and then passed the MRCP. At that stage in his career he turned to radiology, acquiring training in Sheffield and then Birmingham.

In 1960 he was appointed consultant radiologist, Dudley Road Hospital, Birmingham; and consultant neuroradiologist to the Midland Centre for Neurosurgery and Neurology; consultant radiologist to the Birmingham Eye Hospital; and honorary consultant neuroradiologist, Birmingham Children's Hospital. These posts he held till his sudden death at Dudley Road Hospital.

Leonard Langton was a quiet, soft spoken man with an easy friendly manner. In his early years he was athletic, playing rugby for Leeds Medicals and Leeds University. Latterly he became interested in gardening, largely through his wife Sheila (née Ryder); they both held office in the 'Friends of the Botanical Gardens' in Birmingham and lectured and worked organizing sales in support of the Gardens. Leonard's wife died tragically about a year before Leonard, and it was a blow his friends felt he superficially surmounted but never really recovered from. Throughout his professional career in Birmingham he was well known for the balanced authoritative opinion he gave on a variety of radiological problems, especially in the field of neuroradiology.

Quiet and self-effacing, his death in service saddened a wide circle of colleagues. He had a brother and sister but no children. BMcC

[*J. Fac. Radiol.*, 1959, **10**, 86-94; 1954, **6**, 134-138; Photo]

LEE, Julius *b*.17 June 1919 *d*.1 Nov 1977
MB BS Lond (1943) MRCP (1948) MD (1961) DSc (1969) FRCP (1973)

Julius Lee was born in the East End of London. His father's name was Nathan Lee, by occupation a company director. His mother was Gertrude, daughter of Joseph Goldstein, a minister of religion, who also lived in London.

Julius went to University College School and then studied medicine at Westminster Hospital Medical School, where he graduated in 1943. After qualification, he held resident appointments at the West Middlesex Hospital; subsequently he became medical registrar to JA Torrens at the same institution. In 1948, he took a lectureship in physiology at the Charing Cross Medical School, and he stayed at this

School for the rest of his career. He rose through senior lecturer to become reader in physiology in 1964, with an honorary consultant physician's appointment in 1967. In 1967, Julius Lee became professor of endocrine physiology, and in 1977 head of the department of physiology.

Lee was a superb teacher, much loved by his undergraduate students. He firmly believed that the teaching of clinical medicine must be very closely linked to that of basic sciences. Since he was a preclinical scientist who also practised clinical medicine – a rare combination – his teaching was very popular and respected by his students. His dual role conferred a special standing on him.

Julius Lee had a moving humility and modesty which came across to both his students and his colleagues. His observations in committees were penetrating, and he made his points with few words. His research work, focussing on the role of antidiuretic hormone in homeostasis, was of the highest order.

Stella Lee (*née* Cohen), whom he had married in 1945, survived him, with one daughter, Jennifer. AG(2)

[*Brit. med. J.*, 1977, **2**, 1293; Photo]

LEE LANDER, Frank Patrick *b.* – 1906 *d.* 12 Jan 1981
OBE MB BS Lond (1930) MRCP (1931) MD (1934) FRCP (1939)

Lee Lander was born at Morcombelake, Dorset, son of Edward Lee Lander and his wife Alice Mary. He was educated at Dover College and the Middlesex Hospital Medical School, qualifying in 1930. He became medical registrar at the Middlesex Hospital in 1931, and later combined this with a part-time registrarship at the Brompton Hospital, to which he was appointed in 1934. These appointments determined his future career as a physician specializing in pulmonary disease. In 1937, he was appointed physician to the Royal Free Hospital and to Putney Hospital, and in 1939 to the Brompton Hospital. While registrar at Brompton he undertook, with Maurice Davidson, clinical and experimental studies of the association between bronchiectasis and air-absorption collapse of the lung. From 1941 to 1945 he served in the RAMC, principally in North Africa, Sicily and Italy, as officer in charge of a medical division with the rank of lieutenant colonel, and was mentioned in despatches and appointed OBE.

On return to civilian life, he devoted himself to his hospital appointments and to consultant practice, and developed an additional interest in insurance medicine. In the College, he was Censor, 1952 – 1953, and Senior Censor, 1957. He gave the Mitchell lecture on 'Rest and Pulmonary Tuberculosis' in 1957. At various times he served as examiner in medicine at the Universities of London and Cambridge, and to the University College of the West Indies.

Under an easy and apparently casual manner, he had shrewd judgement, and the ability to come to acceptable decisions in confused situations where the opinions of others differed. Although his personal concerns were in clinical practice, rather than in research, he was sympathetic to the aspirations and needs of his more academic colleagues. These qualities made him a successful chairman of medical committees at both the Royal Free and Brompton Hospitals.

He married Dorothy Briggs in 1932 and they had two sons. Apart from his work and his family, he was an enthusiastic fisherman. JGS

[*Times,* 23 Jan 1981; *Lancet,* 1981, **1**, 397]

LEISHMAN, Austin William Drevar *b.*17 June 1907 *d.*17 Mar 1978
BA Oxon (1929) BM BCh (1932) MRCS LRCP (1932)
MRCP (1935) DM (1937) MA (1947) FRCP (1950)

William Leishman came from a distinguished medical family. His grandfather was regius professor of midwifery in the University of Glasgow. His father, Sir William Boog Leishman KCB, KCMG, CB was an FRS and FRCP and became director general of the Army Medical Service. His mother, Maud Elizabeth Gunter, was the daughter of a regular Army colonel who lived in Cardiff.

William Leishman was educated at Westminster School and University College Oxford, where he was a Theodore Williams scholar (physiology) and obtained a second class honours BA in 1929 in physiology. He trained in clinical medicine at St Bartholomew's Hospital, London and graduated in 1932. He was house physician to Lord Horder, and in 1935 resident physician at Ruthin Castle, North Wales. From 1935 to 1938 he was chief assistant at St Bartholomew's Hospital, working for Lord Horder and Geoffrey Evans. In 1938 he entered medical partnership in Stratford-on-Avon, and was honorary physician at Stratford-on-Avon General Hospital.

He was mobilized in 1939 in the Territorial Army, joined the 7th General Hospital as medical specialist and went to France with the British Expeditionary Force. In 1941 he was appointed to the Middle East Forces, where he served in Crete, from where he was one of the last to escape carrying his beloved flute and a photograph of his wife. He later served in Palestine, and in 1942 became officer in charge of a medical division in India. In 1944 he was appointed assistant consulting physician GHQ India and ADMS (clinical research), responsible for organization and coordination of research in India. He made a tour of German medical centres in 1945 on behalf of British Intelligence.

His service in the Army reawakened his interest in hospital medicine, and on demobilization in 1946 he was appointed first assistant to Edward (later Sir) Wayne at the Sheffield Royal Infirmary. In 1946 he was appointed honorary physician to the Sheffield Royal Infirmary and the Doncaster Gate Hospital, Rotherham. He became honorary clinical lecturer in medicine in the University of Sheffield, and he founded the first clinic in Sheffield for the study of hypertension, and was able to show that treatment of hypertension would prolong life and diminish the risk of strokes.

His publications consisted of an original paper on 'Clinical

Diagnosis of Polyarteritis Nodosa', in the *Lancet* 1937 and must have been one of the first ever published on this subject. He also published papers on his experiences of military medicine in India, *Lancet* 1944 and *Lancet* 1945.

His most important work however was a series of papers based on his meticulous note keeping and follow-up clinics for hypertension. These included: 'Hypertension treated and untreated' *BMJ* 1959, and 'Merits of reducing blood pressure' *Lancet* 1963, and numerous others which were recognized internationally.

Leishman was a physician of the old school, who combined personal charm and courteous manners with kindness and complete integrity. His upright military figure and careful dress set an example to his students, from whom he demanded a high standard. Despite suffering from angina for many years, he worked uncomplainingly until he retired in 1973 to his old Derbyshire farmhouse in the village of Hathersage.

He was a skilled musician who played the flute for many years with the Sheffield Philharmonic orchestra. When an anaesthetic lip prevented him from playing the flute it is characteristic of his personality that he learned to play the oboe, and continued to have lessons until his death.

In June 1938 he married Elizabeth Oldfield, the daughter of Carlton Oldfield a gynaecologist and the sister of an undergraduate friend who himself became a consultant surgeon in Leeds. Elizabeth and William were a perfect team. After his retirement they played golf and walked the Derbyshire moors in all weathers. He died suddenly when out shopping with her.

The years of his retirement were made pleasurable by watching the four children of his only daughter, Diana, grow up. William Leishman was a kind, gentle, humble man with style, an unforgettable figure almost of a bygone age. IBS

[*Brit. med. J.*, 1978, **1**, 926; *Lancet,* 1978, **1**, 782; Photo]

LEVITT, Walter Montague *b.* – 1900 *d.*25 Oct 1983
MB BCh Dubl (1923) DMRE Cantab (1924) MRCP (1931)
MD NUI (1933) FRCP (1940) FFR (1940)

Walter Levitt, honorary consultant radiotherapist at St Bartholomew's Hospital and barrister-at-law, was born at Rathmines, Co. Dublin, the eldest son of Lewis and Caroline Levitt. He was educated at Dublin High School and University College, Dublin, where he graduated in medicine in 1923. After serving in various resident hospital appointments he decided to devote himself to the newly emerging specialty of radiotherapy and obtained his DMRE (Cantab) in 1924. After a period of postgraduate work at Frankfurt-on-Main, he joined NS Finzi at Bart's as medical officer in charge of research into high voltage X-ray therapy, and lectured in X-ray therapy at the department of medical radiology in the University of Cambridge. At this time, radiotherapy was done mainly by radiologists occupied with diagnostic work, and radium therapy was the province of surgeons, gynaecologists and dermatologists. They combined to start radiotherapy in the 1930s, and the British Association of Radiologists was founded in 1934, followed by the Society of Radiotherapists in 1936. They were amalgamated as the Faculty of Radiologists in 1939.

Throughout the years prior to the outbreak of the second world war Levitt acquired great expertise in this rapidly developing specialty, and in 1939 he was appointed honorary physician in charge of radiotherapy at St George's Hospital. The total frustration of the hospital's building programme, owing to the war, led to the abandonment of projected new departments and he returned to Bart's as part-time honorary radiotherapist, combining this with the directorship of radiotherapy at the London Clinic. At Bart's he was closely associated with Sir Ronald Bodley Scott (*q.v.*) in the treatment of patients with leukaemia and reticulosarcoma. It was during this period that he made valuable contributions to the treatment of Hodgkin's disease, which is now generally curable as the result of advances in radiotherapy and chemotherapy. He also contributed to the understanding and treatment of spontaneous keloid. Together with Bodley Scott he contributed to the section on the reticuloses and reticulosarcoma in *British Practice of Radiotherapy*, 1965. He wrote many papers on radiotherapy during the '30s, and published his own *Handbook of Radiotherapy* in 1952. He was a founding fellow of the Faculty of Radiologists and, subsequently, a founding fellow of the Royal College of Radiologists. He was a one-time vice-president, then president, of the section of radiology of the Royal Society of Medicine, and chairman of the therapeutics committee of the Faculty of Radiologists. He served on the Ministry of Labour advisory panel in radiology, and was chairman of the research committee of the British Empire Cancer Campaign. In 1928 he was honorary secretary of the International Cancer Conference in London. At one time he was associate editor of the *British Journal of Radiology*, as well as honorary medical secretary of the British Institute of Radiology. He was a liveryman of the Society of Apothecaries.

In 1946 he was called to the Bar at Lincoln's Inn and withdrew from medicine, becoming especially interested in medico-legal matters on which he wrote several useful papers. He also published a *Short Encyclopaedia of Medicine for Lawyers*, 1966. But he soon decided that medicine was his first love and returned to radiotherapy in his honorary capacity at Bart's, and to his private practice, before his final retirement.

After retirement he served with the Metropolitan Traffic Commissioners from 1967 – 1973, and was deputy chairman for four years. He managed to keep busy with medico-legal interests up to the time of his death.

In 1929 he married Sonia Este Nirinsky, but they had no children. Shortly after her death in 1977 he married Violet Irene Hirschland. He was a charming and cultured man who was generous and considerate.

GW/VL

[*Times*, 31 Oct 1983; Photo]

LINDER, Geoffry Challen *b.*13 Dec 1892 *d.*3 Sept 1981
MRCS LRCP (1915) MB BS Lond (1915) MD (1920) MRCP (1921) FRCP (1946)

Geoffry Linder, emeritus professor of chemical pathology at the University of Cape Town, SA, was born at Croydon, England. His father, William Linder, was a clerk in business and his mother Margaret Maria (née Redgate) was the daughter of a merchant. Geoff was educated at Brighton Grammar School and St Bartholomew's Hospital, graduating in 1915. At the outbreak of the first world war he enlisted as a private in a field ambulance unit but was discharged under a War Office order to return to medical school and complete his studies. After qualifying he served as a medical officer RAMC in France, Egypt and Palestine, being wounded in the fighting near Arras. On demobilization he became house physician at Bart's, obtaining his MD and MRCP.

From 1922 to 1924 Geoff worked as assistant resident physician at the Rockefeller Institute for Medical Research, USA, in the laboratory of DD van Slyke, on the metabolism and blood chemistry of patients with nephritis. He also undertook various clinical duties. It was here that he met Ruby Marshall, a graduate of the Army School of Nursing, Walter Reed Hospital, who was then working in the diet kitchen of the Institute. They married in 1925 and had two children: a daughter who graduated MB ChB (Cape Town) and a son who is an advocate in South Africa.

Geoff worked in England from 1924 to 1929 as senior assistant in charge of chemical pathology in the pathological department of the University of Cape Town, under BJ Ryrie. He was honorary biochemist at the New Somerset Hospital and, subsequently, at the Groote Schuur. He also initiated the diabetic clinic at the Free Dispensary. During this period he ran the chemical laboratories with the aid of one assistant, EJ Duncan, and little other help. He also ran the diabetic clinic with one assistant – the dermatology house physician. To this day the staff of the diabetic clinic includes a member of the dermatology department. It is interesting to note that Linder's first insulin-taking patient was John D Rockefeller.

Before long Linder was joined by WPU Jackson (now professor of medicine, Cape Town) and Grayce: they were now a team of four. Jackson remembers how they were kept busy by an Italian gentleman named Toni, who had lost most of his small bowel. In those days little was known about the metabolic consequences of this. For a brief period Toni developed a hallucinatory psychosis which caused an uproar in the ward when everyone tried to locate Toni's two-dimensional dog – with Bill Hoffenberg (now PRCP) helping and attempting to placate Toni at the same time. The problem, of course, being that when a two-dimensional dog turns sideways it disappears! Toni's large bowel proved extremely adaptable – he often passed only a single motion a day, but that one stool had a volume of four litres or more. Geoff was constrained to remark that he worked in a laboratory and not a lavatory, and would they please take aliquots!

Linder was appointed the first professor of chemical pathology at the University in 1948, a post he held until he retired in 1957. In June 1958 he was elected emeritus professor. He contributed several papers to medical journals.

He was a quiet, unassuming, hardworking man with a splendidly dry sense of humour; a man who thought his job was to stay in Cape Town and run the laboratory rather than go gallivanting around the world attending meetings and raising money for projects. He was an outstanding gentleman of the old school, marvellous to work with, a good friend, and without great ambition in the usual sense. Having found his proper place he was content to fill it with distinction, backed by a firm family life and friends who genuinely loved him. Apart from his work and his family, his main interest was photography.

WPUJ/GW/VL

[Photo]

LISTER, William Alexander *b.*28 Jan 1897 *d.*21 Oct 1981
TD (1945) MRCS LRCP (1923) MRCP (1925)
MB BChir Cantab (1926) MD (1935) FRCP (1938)

William Lister was the son of Sir William Lister and a great nephew of Lord Lister. He was educated at Winchester College, leaving in 1915 to serve in the first world war. He was wounded in the trenches, losing an eye. On demobilization in 1919 he went to Trinity College, Cambridge, and the London Hospital, where he qualified in 1923. While holding resident appointments there he obtained the MRCP in 1925, and MB BChir in 1926. He was then appointed physician to the South Devon and East Cornwall Hospital, Plymouth.

Despite the loss of an eye, his deep sense of patriotism induced him to join the Territorial Army in 1930, until it was disbanded in 1939. He was awarded the Territorial Decoration.

In 1939 he formed, commanded and trained 129 Field Ambulance to a high degree of efficiency. On being posted overseas he commanded the medical division of No 6 General Hospital in Egypt and later he became commanding officer of I General Hospital at Secunderabad. He retired with the rank of honorary colonel.

He returned to a busy consultant practice in Plymouth, where he helped to initiate the NHS. For many years he was a member of the Hospital Management Committee. He was a magistrate from 1947. He was a founder member of the West Country Physicians Club.

'Billy' Lister was a man of great charm and character. He was an enthusiast, with catholic interests both within and outside medicine. His keen eye was first to note the natural history of the strawberry naevus and its tendency to spontaneous resolution. He was the embodiment of the wise and widely experienced consultant. He was disturbed by many aspects of the NHS, particularly the multiplication of consultants and consequent narrowing of his consultant field. He became greatly interested in chest diseases, especially the pathology of emphysema, publishing many articles on the subject until well after his retirement in 1962.

In retirement he became a painter, a gardener, a fisherman and a dog trainer. As churchwarden, he characteristically took over and transformed the churchyard of the village of his adoption. He kept his enthusiasm to the end.

In 1929 he married Esther Cecily Parsons of Bristol. They had two sons and two daughters. GRS

[*Brit. med. J.*, 1981, **283**, 1474; **284**, 62]

LITCHFIELD, John Alan *b.*20 Mar 1921 *d.*10 Apr 1980
MB ChB Birm (1944) MRCS LRCP (1944) MD (1956)
MRCP (1949) FRCP (1972)

John Litchfield was born in London and educated at Bablake School, Coventry, in which city his father, SE Litchfield, held a managerial post in industry. He proceeded to the University of Birmingham in 1939, graduating in medicine there five years later. After holding house officer appointments at the General Hospital, Birmingham, he served in the Royal Navy for two years, returning as resident medical officer to the Birmingham General Hospital in 1947. After election to the membership he became a senior registrar, and conducted some excellent research on electrolytes in skeletal muscle, with special reference to uncontrolled diabetes.

In 1956 Litchfield was appointed consultant physician to the Manor and General Hospitals in Walsall and the Bromsgrove General Hospital, to each of which he gave almost a quarter of a century of devoted service. Of handsome and distinguished appearance, with great kindness and personal charm, and a superb general physician, he inevitably had a very large practice, but despite this he accepted the appointment of the University of Birmingham's postgraduate clinical tutor at Walsall. His efforts were largely responsible for the building of a fine postgraduate centre there, and for establishing a thriving vocational training scheme and excellent facilities for the continued education of general practitioners. He served on the Walsall Area Health Authority and was chairman of the Walsall Division of the British Medical Association.

He suffered a long, complex and distressing final illness which he bore without complaint and with courage and cheerfulness. A staunch friend and a fine man, he made a valuable and unselfish contribution to medicine.

His wife, Patricia, and his son and daughter survived him, his son having graduated in medicine from the University of Birmingham in 1976. AGWW

[*Brit. med. J.*, 1980, **281**, 153; Photo]

LIVERSEDGE, Laurence Atkinson *b.*11 Apr 1914 *d.*1 Mar 1979
BA Manch (1938) BSc (1941) MB ChB (1944) MD Duke (1943)
MRCP (1946) FRCP (1962)

Laurence Liversedge was born in Middlesbrough, Yorkshire, the son of Thomas Atkinson Liversedge, sales manager of the Lancashire Steel Corporation, and Nellie Bendelow, daughter of Thomas Bendelow, a railway man. He was educated at Middlesbrough High School, Urmston Grammar School and Manchester University. At University he first read French, obtaining a BA degree with honours and then, after a short period in commerce, he returned to the University and entered medical school. He was awarded the BSc (Class 1) after second MB, and then received a Rockefeller Scholarship, and during its tenure undertook clinical studies at Duke University, USA, where he qualified MD in 1943 and did an internship in pathology in the same year. He returned to England and passed his final MB in 1944 with distinctions in medicine, surgery and pharmacology.

After qualification he was house physician to Crichton Bramwell and then chief assistant to Fergus Ferguson until February 1946. He served in the Middle East during the period 1947 – 1949, holding the rank of major, and was graded as a medical specialist and neurologist. On leaving the Army he resumed neurological training, when he worked as registrar in the pathology department in the National Hospital, Queen Square, under JT Greenfield. In 1950 he returned to Manchester Royal Infirmary and the University as lecturer in neurology, under Fergus Ferguson. In 1957 he was given an honorary consultant appointment to the Royal Infirmary and continued in this post until 1964. He was then appointed as neurologist to Crumpsall Hospital and the Royal Infirmary. Later his duties were confined to neurologist to the Manchester Royal Infirmary, and he retained this position until his death.

Liversedge's mark as a neurologist was the contribution he made to the art and science of clinical neurology. He wrote on many diverse subjects, including the management of myasthenia gravis, occupational cramp, the treatment of spasticity by phenol, and the use of ophthalmodynamometry in cerebral vascular disease. He was a clinician of outstanding ability, but his qualities as a teacher of undergraduates and young neurologists in training were unrivalled. His lectures were models of clarity, being laced with wit and humour, but always demonstrating the art of clinical medicine.

Laurie was a man of abundant energy, being a founder member of the North of England Neurological Association, and in later years devoted much time and energy to the promotion of the interests of the Multiple Sclerosis Society.

He had been a distinguished athlete in his youth, playing cricket, association and rugby football, and representing the University in all three sports. He was prominent in the affairs of the Students' Union, serving a term as president, and demonstrating an outstanding ability in public debates.

In 1941 he married Peggy Mason, a solicitor, who was to become a distinguished member of the legal professsion in Manchester. They had two sons and one daughter.

ECH

[*Brit. med. J.*, 1979, **1**, 827; *Lancet*, 1979, **1**, 624, 683]

Derek Gordon Abrahams

Douglas George Adamson

Lord Adrian

Janet Kerr Aitken

Richard Sydney Allison

Eric Newmarch Allot

Emmanuel Ciprian Amoroso

Lord Amulree

Edward William Anderson

Stephen Towers Anning

John Apley

Leonard John Henry Arthur

Sir Hedley Atkins

Joges Chandra Banerjea

Harry Barkley

Frederic Crosby Bartter

Lindsey Willet Batten

Cyril Carlyle Beatty

David Evan Bedford

Julia Bell

Major-General John Bennet

Francis Richard Berridge

Charles Herbert Best

Maneck Phiroshaw Bhagat

Sohan Lal Bhatia

Charles Allan Birch

Peter Maxwell Farrow Bishop

Anthony Charles Blandy

John Richard Bolton

Georgiana May Bonser

Richard Raymond Bomford

William Arthur Bourne

Sir John Boyd

William Boyd

Frances Braid

John Crighton Bramwell

Lord Brock of Wimbledon

John Fleming Brock

Edward Hilton Brown

George Malcolm Brown

Richard Charles Browne

Gladwin Albert Hurst Buttle

Rowland James Calvert

Alistair James Victor Cameron

Sir David Campbell

Marcolino Gomes Candau

William Howard Pinney Cant

Daniel Fowler Cappell

Edward Arnold Carmichael

James Carson

Frederick Stephen Carter

Sir Ernst Chain

Sir Clement Chesterman

Sir George Clark

Owen Clarke

Surgeon-Captain TL Cleave

Hugh Anthony Clegg

Baron Cohen of Birkenhead

Leslie Barrett Cole

Vernon Leslie Collins

Guy Malcolm Colson

Ernest Thomas Conybeare

Edward Derek Hurley Cowen

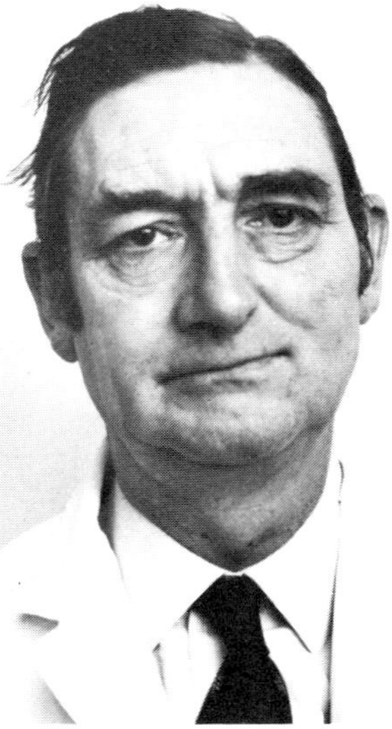

Robert Victor Coxon

William Hofmeyr Craib

William Alfred James Crane

Charles Richard Croft

James Crooks

Andrew Gordon Cudworth

Alphonso Liguori d'Abreu

Sir Weldon Dalrymple-Champneys

Samuel Whately Davidson

Sir Stanley Davidson

Charles Edwin Davies

David Lewis Davies

John Owen Fisher Davies

Leslie John Davis

George Davison

Derek Ernest Denny-Brown

Charles Enrique Dent

Dennis Charles Deuchar

Henry Victor Dicks

Richard Heyworth Dobbs

Pierre-Marie Dorolle

James Findlay Dow

Geoffrey Barrow Dowling

Ewen Thomas Taylor Downie

Sir Alan Drury

Sir Derrick Dunlop

Sir Stewart Duke-Elder

George Millar Edington

Alfred William Blair Edmunds

Ernest Hywell Evans

Keith Douglas Fairley

Geoffrey Ernest Ffrench

Harold Mason Foreman

Frank Forman

Alistair Douglas Forrest

Frank James Fowler

Frank Scott Fowweather

Thomas Neilson Fraser

Mohammad Mohammad Gaafar

Hugh Gainsborough

Harold Gardiner-Hill

Arthur Duncan Gardner

Gerald Garmany

Lawrence Paul Garrod

Oliver Garrod

Clarence John Gavey

Trevor Charles Noel Gibbens

James Edward McAlinney Glancy

Boris Golberg

Kenneth Leslie Grant Goldsmith

Neville Marriott Goodman

John Everett Gordon

Jethro Gough

Leon Julian Grant

George Stanley Graveson

Malcolm Kennedy Gray

Francis Henry Knethell Green

Sir Thomas Greenaway

Charles Raymond Greene

Christopher Gresson

Kenneth James Grice

Isidore Arthur Guest

Sir Ludwig Guttmann

Sir Alexander Haddow

Gilbert Steward Hall

Stephen Barton Hall

Charles Skinner Hallpike

Charles Keith Johnstone Hamilton

Patrick James Hare

Kenneth Edwin Harris

Ruth Freda Harris

Stanley Jack Hartfall

William Hartson

Thomas Bones Hamilton Haslett

Albert Joseph Hawe

Wilton Ernest Henley

Kenneth Stuart Hetzel

John Anthony Hickman

Thomas Cecil Highton

Sir Ian Hill

Leslie Charles Hill

James Clancey Hogarth

Portia Grenfell Holman

Aaron Holzel

Lt General Sir Alexander Hood

John Clifford Hoyle

Sir Douglas Hubble

Norman George Hulbert

Joseph Graeme Humble

Thomas Cecil Hunt

Donald Hunter

Mark Ian Alastair Hunter

Richard Alfred Hunter

Edward Weston Hurst

Herbert Hylton Hyland

Irwin Cole Isdale

Martin Cyril Gordon Israëls

John Harry Jacobs

Keith Edmund Jefferson

Ritchie Teify Jenkins

William John Edward Jessop

Alan Trevor Jones

Arthur Morgan Jones

Ernest Grahame Jones

Idris Griffths Jones

Horace Joules

Sorab Barjor Karani

Charles Ernest Kellett

Frederick Harold Kemp

Arthur Charles Kendall

Sir Peter Kerley

Sir Geoffrey Keynes

Frederick Basil Kiernander

George Anderson Kiloh

Francis John Davison Knights

Sir Hans Krebs

Pandipeddi Kutumbiah

Leonard Langton

Julius Lee

Austin William Drevar Leishman

Walter Montagu Levitt

Geoffrey Challen Linder

William Alexander Lister

John Alan Litchfield

Geoffrey Herbert Thornley Lloyd

L.J.A.Loewenthal

Samuel Lawrence Ludbrook

Frank Hirst Lumb

William MacAdam

Douglas McAlpine

Michael Blair Macaulay

Herbert Geoffrey McComas

Peter Knight McCowan

Walsh McDermott

James Peterson Ross MacFarlane

Ronald Charles MacKeith

James Robertson Monro Mackie

Arthur Ian Granville McLaughlin

Andrew Sinclair McLean

Sir Hector MacLennan

William Mathieson Macleod

William Henry McMenemey

Sir George McRobert

Montagu Maizels

Nicolas Borrell Malleson

Sher Mohd Kahn Mallick

Hugh Leslie Marriott

Sir Geoffrey Marshall

Laurence Cleveland Martin

Nicholas Henry Martin

Robert Benson Martin

Richard Michael Mason

Ronald Graeme May

Robert Woodside Meikle

Ambrose Neponucene Trelawney Meneces

Clarence Merskey

Henry Miller

Malcolm William Miller

Gordon Lewis Mills

John Alexander Milne

Thiri Pyanchi Min Sein

Natwar Jaisung Modi

Elio Federico Domenico Montuschi

Lord Moran, Baron Moran of Manton

Benjamin Branford Morgan

Edward Penistan Morley

Sir Arthur Morrow

Michael George Moshal

David Clark Muir

Sir Ellis Murphy

Sir Alexander Murphy

Nathan Mutch

Frederick John Nattrass

Walter Lindesay Neustatter

Samuel Nevin

Alexander Adam McIntosh Nicol

Patrick Henry O'Donovan

Alan Gordon Ogilvie

Gladstone Rule Osborn·

Alfred Patrick Menzies Page

Kenneth Nelson Veysey Palmer

Sir John Parkinson

John Scholes Parkinson

Sir Alan Parks

John Frederic Paterson

Brian Wilfrid Pay

Wilfred Walter Payne

Geoffrey David Pegrum

Wilder Graves Penfield

Richard Basil Perkins

Sir Rudolph Peters

Sir George Pickering

John Douglas Pickup

Bernard Laurence Pimstone

Charles Percy Pinckney

Lord Platt

Norman Swift Plummer

Keith Ridley Douglas Porter

Roy Kemball Price

Sir Eric Pridie

Francis Thomas Garnet Prunty

Robert Hector Quentin-Baxter

John Bulmer Randell

Sir Gordon Ransome

Thomas Glentworth Reah

William Esmond Rees

William Rees-Thomas

Tony Lothrop Reeves

Donald Darnley Reid

Frank Ridehalgh

Frank Lane Ritchie

Kenneth Moorhouse Robertson

Sir Hugh Robson

Sir Kenneth Robson

Cyril Max Ross

Stanley Graham Ross

Sir Alun Rowlands

Jack Rubie

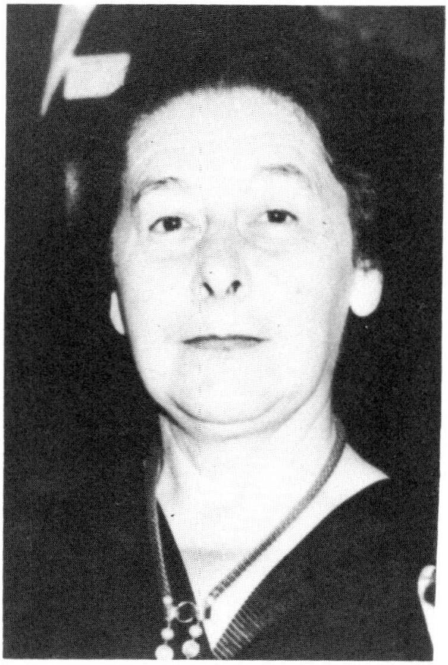

Dorothy Stuart Russell

William Ritchie Russell

Albert Sachs

Jack Sakula

Sir Ronald Bodley Scott

Sir Selwyn Selwyn-Clarke

Mazhar Hussain Shah

Seymour Cochrane Shanks

Alan Anderson Sharp

Sir Wilfrid Sheldon

Ian Alexander Short

John Charles Arthur Sibley

George Simon

Samuel Leonard Simpson

Robert Joseph Patrick Skelly

Eliot Trevor Oakeshott Slater

Joseph Smart

John Smith

Ronald Edward Smith

Walter Graham Spector

Ian Osborne Bradford Spencer

Baratham Ramaswamy Sreenivasan

Matthew Steel

Edward Samuel Stern

Aldwyn Brockway Stokes

Thomas Scott Stone

Thomas Copland Studdert

William Hedley John Summerskill

John Sutcliffe

Peter Neville Swift

Sir Charles Symonds

Victor Millington Synge

Sir Norman Talbot

Kenneth Harry Tallerman

Bernard Clive Tate

Peter Ewart Romney Tattersall

Robert Donald Teare

Otto Henry Johan Maxwell Telling

Sir Arthur Thomson

Sir Daniel Thomson

Gavin Leonard Bourdas Thurston

Henry Arthur Treble

Edmund Christopher Turton

Edgar Ashworth Underwood

Ramaier Viswanathan

William Victor Wadsworth

Joseph Walter

Anthony Peter Waterson

Joseph Aidney Weiner

Sir Ralph Whishaw

Stephen Robert Ferguson Whittaker

Sir Harold Whittingham

Alexander Solomon Wiener

Keith John Roy Wightman

Charles Wilcocks

Rupert Allan Willis

Donald Wilson

Isabel Grace Hood Wilson

Graham Malcolm Wilson

James Victor Wilson

Peter Andaer Overend Wilson

John Michael Winn

Francis Seaton Winton

Leslie John Witts

Sir Robert Wright

Arthur Gurney Yates

Eleanor Zaimis

Royal College of Physicians

LLOYD, Geoffrey Herbert Thornley *b.*6 May 1919 *d.*30 Sept 1981
MRCS LRCP (1942) MB BS Lond (1942) MRCP (1948) MD (1949) FRCP (1971)

Geoffrey Lloyd, consultant physician to the Clwyd North Hospitals, died prematurely after a very short illness.

He was born at Newport, Gwent, and educated at Bryntirion School, Bridgend, and later entered Wycliffe College, Gloucestershire, after gaining an entrance scholarship. His undergraduate medical training was at Guy's Hospital, and he qualified in 1942. His academic distinctions as a student included the Edgecombe prize in junior science, the Wooldridge prize in physiology, the Michael Harris prize in anatomy and the junior proficiency prize – all at Guy's hospital.

He held junior medical posts as house physician to Sir John Conybeare and to Sir Charles Symonds at Guy's, and he also worked in Sir John McNee's department in Glasgow. He was subsequently assistant registrar to the department of neurology at Guy's, and registrar at Queen Square and senior registrar in neurology in the Cardiff Royal Infirmary. He served in the RAMC from 1942 to 1946, and this included two years as regimental medical officer in North West Europe. He was appointed consultant physician to the then Clwyd and Deeside Hospitals in January 1953, and continued in this post until his death. He was also consultant neurologist to the Wrexham Group of Hospitals, and his opinion was widely sought on neurological problems throughout North Wales.

He had a particular interest in, and aptitude for, teaching and from the early days of the formation of the medical postgraduate centre at Rhyl he was one of the most enthusiastic and conscientious supporters of its activities. He took his full share of medical administrative duties, and had served in the past as chairman of the North Clwyd medical staff committee, and at the time of his death was the chairman of the medical division – a post which he held for several years. He also served as a member of the pre-registration committee of the Welsh National School of Medicine.

He was, in his limited leisure time, a keen gardener, hill-walker and car enthusiast. He was an excellent host, and he and his wife generously entertained a large circle of friends at their home in Colwyn Bay.

Geoffrey was essentially a kindly, gentle and courteous man – never ruffled in his dealings with patients, staff or colleagues. He was survived by his wife Isobel (who was a constant support and help to him in his chosen career), his daughter Jane, son Christopher and grand-daughter Katie. DEM

[*Brit. med. J.,* 1981, **284**, 1182; *Lancet,* 1981, **2**, 942; Photo]

LOEWENTHAL, Leonard Joseph Alphonse *b.*3 June 1903
*d.*18 Mar 1983
MB ChB Liverp (1925) DTM&H (1931) MD MRCP (1934)
FRCP (1968)

For forty years of his life Leonard Loewenthal devoted his energies to the furtherance of dermatology in Africa. No one else brought such dedication and intellectual brilliance to this field of African medicine. With no medical libraries, no expensive equipment, no academic associates and no comfortable appointments, he possessed both the gifts and the discipline to achieve a position at the forefront of his profession. Starting in 1931, in Uganda, with studies on tropical ulcer and vitamin A deficiency, he ended his career in Johannesburg forty years later with investigations on the skin of miners.

Loewenthal was both a retiring, asocial and industrious scholar-student and a dazzling entertainer in the social and medical limelight. He allowed his learning to find an outlet in writing, teaching and conversation. He had a fine natural wit which was guaranteed to enliven the dullest company, and a stylistic elegance in writing and speaking which was partly attributable to his aptitude for classical studies. His confident, authoritative style earned him the nickname of 'King Alphonse' for at times he reached the absurd majesty of a nobleman in comic opera. He had an avid grasp of facts, a clear understanding and excellent memory, which assured him a distinguished student career and a successful and multi-faceted life which falls naturally into five main phases: England and Europe until the age of 28; followed by ten years in the colonial medical service in Uganda; five years service in the Army during the second world war; twenty-five years in Johannesburg and, finally, eleven years in Spain.

Alphonse was born in Liverpool where his father, Max Sally Loewenthal, was a respected physician who had come from Europe and settled down in Princes Road. His mother, Amanda, was the daughter of Joseph Kehr, a banker. He was educated at St Christopher's Preparatory School and Malvern College, where he matriculated, passing all his subjects with distinction and being the first recipient of the Moore-Bayley prize for Greek, an award which still exists. He went on to study medicine at Liverpool University where he graduated with honours in July 1925. From 1926 to 1929 he acted as clinical assistant to the skin department at the Royal Infirmary, and as assistant dermatologist at the Liverpool Hospital for Cancer and Skin Diseases. During this period he also spent a year doing research in pathology, and visited Paul Gerson Unna in Hamburg where he spent some time cutting and staining skin sections. In 1930 he registered as a Colonial Office student, acquired the DTM&H, and was sent to Uganda. Those who knew how much work he accomplished during the next ten years in the tropics might not realize how broad and general were his duties at that time: clearing swamps, lecturing to orderlies, doing midwifery in the bush, making jail inspections, attending to hospital work, practising ophthalmology – all these tasks were part of the daily round but he never allowed them to interfere with his dermatological responsibility.

Within the first two years he had fully grasped the role that poor nutrition played in producing tropical ulcer, and he discovered that distinctive skin lesions result from vitamin A deficiency. By comparing different classes of negroes with different eating habits, he saw that the high incidence of tropical ulcer was confined to groups with poor nutrition. If infection was the precipitating cause, predisposition was even more necessary in allowing the disease to occur. Tropical ulcer continued to engage his attention until he produced his last and most comprehensive paper on the subject in 1968.

In 1933, in Kampala, he described the follicular signs of vitamin A deficiency. It was an original piece of research, independent of the two similar discoveries made by Lucius Nicholls in Ceylon and Chester Frazier in China. He submitted an MD thesis to Liverpool University, in 1934, on lymph stasis in the skin. It covered the role of onchocerciasis, Bancroftian filariasis, chromoblastomycosis, chronic ulcers and allied conditions in producing 'mossy foot'. That same year he passed the membership examination of the College. His pace did not slacken: between 1936 and 1939 he published in serial form a contribution in fifteen parts on diseases of the skin in negroes in the *Journal of Tropical Medicine and Hygiene*, and also placed Kaposi's sarcoma and xeroderma pigmentosum firmly on the African dermatological map. Ignorance, and the apparent rarity of these diseases, he rightly concluded, 'may be due to the lack of skilled dermatologists in the greater part of Africa'.

On the outbreak of war Alphonse wished to join the armed forces, but the Colonial Office refused to release him. So he released himself instead, went to South Africa, registered as a dermatologist with the Medical Council, and enlisted in the South African Medical Corps. He saw service in North Africa and Italy, rose to the rank of lieutenant colonel, became area dermatologist in Tripolitania, read Greek, learned Italian, sang operatic arias, wrote dermatological papers, and went escapading. While on active service he published three papers: one on the causation of lichenification in onchocerciasis, in which the microfilariae were held responsible and not the fly bites by *Simulium*; another dealt with the relationship between xanthism in Nigerian negroes and albinism; the last concerned the prophylactic antimalarial in the production of tropical lichenoid dermatitis, a relevant subject with troops in malarious areas.

The war over, Loewenthal set up as a dermatologist in Johannesburg. He was given a few sessions at the skin department of Johannesburg General Hospital where, as he was apt to say, the 'specialized equipment consisted of a piece of cotton wool and a bent pin'. His first appearance caused some astonishment: it was in 1945 and some colourless character was mumbling away about lupus erythematosus when suddenly this well-spoken, loud-voiced man swaggered in, slender, nattily dressed, bald, with an olive complexion and grey-blue eyes, a blue cloth suit and a gold cigarette case. He took over the discussion, digressing freely on HW Barber's views on the sulphonamides in lupus erythematosus at a time when no

Johannesburg dermatologist ever quoted articles or overseas experts. Forthwith, he began to drag dermatology in Johannesburg out of the shadows. In the outpatient department, in the wards, and at his house in Bergvlei, topics of current interest would come under discussion. The result was a significant heightening of general awareness; few of his enthusiasms were lasting but his latest ideas were most stimulating at the time. Awareness and current relevance – these were Loewenthal's great offerings. Falsehood, both popular and professional, he detested. If somebody claimed that acne was cured by marriage, he wanted to know if a civil or religious ceremony was better. 'Education', he once said, 'is impracticable if the charlatan is allowed to advertize'. During his Johannesburg period he made two substantial contributions: an account of itching purpura, and his treatment of eczemas resembling dermatitis herpetiformis with sulphones. Long drawn out struggles were not in his line though he was engaged on two battlefronts, concerning the respective places of skin radiotherapy and skin histopathology in dermatological practice. It was the old story of a claim over a method *v* ability to use it judiciously – a source of much fruitless argumentation.

Loewenthal was a prolific writer: the *Index Medicus* lists over one hundred of his papers, a mere fraction of what he wrote. Noteworthy among his medical publications are *The Eczemas* (1954), three chapters in Mitchell-Hegg's *Modern Practice in Dermatology* (1950), a WHO monograph on *Differential diagnosis of yaws* (1960) with CJ Hackett, and a massive chapter on ethnology and dermatology in *Jadassohn's Handbuch: Ergänzungsband 8*, ed. HA Gottron (1967).

Loewenthal was often humorously disrespectful; under cover of great mirth he could deliver some sharp truths. He was also capable of being unnecessarily harsh for the sake of a laugh. Not surprising, therefore, that his humour did not appeal to everybody. At a meeting where he had almost been pushed off the programme by other speakers exceeding their time, the chairman said: 'Now Dr Loewenthal will give you his address'. Alphonse stood up, said, '1 Smits Road, Dunkeld', and sat down again. Once, when meeting his cousin Harry at a medical meeting, Alphonse asked him: 'Want to hear a good lecture, Harry?' 'Well, it depends who's giving it'. 'I am, of course'. 'In that case I don't think I'll come'. Leaping back in mock horror Alphonse exclaimed 'Who would think that the blood of the Loewenthal's courses through *his* variocele'. Again, when chairing a discussion on the tuberculides, a Jewish dermatologist asked Alphonse: 'Why do we hear nothing these days about the rosacea-like tuberculide of Lewandowsky?' 'Pure anti-semitism,' he replied.

In the 1960s, during his last decade in Johannesburg, he was invited to study the skin rashes of miners in relation to acclimatization. This was perhaps the only piece of sponsored skin research he ever did. A number of studies appeared on the subject of sweat gland function and eczema, and he came up with some interesting answers.

His association with Spain began while he was still at school; during a summer vacation he tramped across the country with a friend and learned the language. It seems that he urgently needed to get away from both his father's anger and the Liverpool police: he had crashed his father's car (borrowed without permission) into a municipal bus. He survived in Spain by taking odd jobs, the most appealing being in a circus where he held the flaming hoop for a wild boar to jump through. He continued building his relationship with the country during each period of leave, and in 1970 he resigned from all his dermatological appointments and retired to Spain to write books. He dropped his titles, stopped practising medicine, and took up residence at San Pedro de Ribas (Barcelona) where he became known as a writer – Alfonso Lowe, correrspondent of the Royal Academy of Córdoba. A remarkable series of smoothly written and fastidiously prepared volumes on Spain and Italy marked the last decade of his life. These include *The Catalan Vengeance* (1972); *The Barrier and the Bridge*, an historical guidebook; *Companion Guide to Southern Spain* (1973), probably the best guidebook to date on this region of Spain; *La Serenissima: The Last Flowering of the Venetian Republic* (1974), and his last published book *The Culture and History of the Spanish* (1975).

Loewenthal's first wife, Kathleen Richardson, died in the 1940s and he married Stella Regina, daughter of William Herzfeld, in 1950. There were two sons and a daughter of the first marriage. In Spain, in the middle of 1981, Stella was killed in a motor accident and Alphonse was badly shaken and rapidly declined to become a near total invalid. He remained witty and uncomplaining, in spite of growing and embarrassing disability. Faltering as he was, he ensured that his companionship remained agreeable. He returned to Africa for the last months of his life and died in Cape Town. Towards the end, his son Richard asked him if he would have preferred another life or career. 'Never. I loved it all', was Alphonse's reply. GHF/CJH/GW/VL

[*SA med. J.*, 1983, **64**, 1064-1067; Photo]

LONGRIDGE, Robert George Mallory *b.*26 June 1911 *d.*28 Mar 1978
BA Cantab (1932) MB BCh (1935) MRCP (1938) FRCP (1963)

Robert Longridge was born in Mobberley, Cheshire, the son of Harry Morgan Longridge, an engineer, and of Annie Victoria, daughter of the Revd Herbert Leigh-Mallory. He was educated at Winchester College, Pembroke College, Cambridge, and St Thomas's Hospital. After qualifying in 1935 he became casualty officer and house physician at St Thomas's Hospital. He then worked for a year as RMO at the Maida Vale Hospital for Nervous Diseases, during which time he passed the MRCP. He returned to St Thomas's Hospital as medical registrar in 1939, but joined the RAMC at the outbreak of war and served as medical specialist. He rose to the rank of lieutenant colonel and was officer in charge of the medical division from 1943 until demobilization in 1945. He served with the British Expeditionary Force in France in the early days, and then, after a spell in the United Kingdom, went to North Africa and to the Far East.

He was appointed physician to Salisbury General Infirmary in 1948, at a time when most of his hospital colleagues were also in general practice. In 1948 he devoted himself enthusiastically to the development of the National Health Service, and played a large part in the establishment at Salisbury of a district hospital with a full complement of specialist services. He was one of the first practising physicians to recognize the importance of the involvement of clinicians in administration. He served on many advisory committees at district and regional level (and was often chairman), and was a member of the Wessex Regional Hospital Board.

Two years before retirement he gave up acute general medicine and took on the reorganization of geriatric services in Salisbury. Into this he put all his usual enthusiasm in spite of ill health, so that when he retired and a geriatrician was appointed there was an established and active department.

In 1939 he married Eleanor Margaret, daughter of John Thomas Mason. They had two sons.

Robert Longridge died at Salisbury after a long illness bravely borne. PMSG

[*Brit. med. J.*, 1978, **1**, 1219]

LUDBROOK, Samuel Lawrence *b.*31 Aug 1895 *d.*3 July 1976
CMG (1970) MB ChB Otago (1919) MRCP (1924) FRACP (1939) FRCP (1950)

Samuel Ludbrook was born at Ohaewai, Bay of Islands, North Auckland, the eldest of seven children. His father was a sheep farmer in the region. His mother was Hana Kinsella before marriage. Samuel was a great-grandson of Archdeacon Henry Williams, a very distinguished Anglican missionary whose daughter Caroline married his grandfather.

His primary education was at Takapuna and Huntly Schools, Marton, while his secondary education was at Wanganui Collegiate School, after which he proceeded to the Otago Medical School to qualify in 1919.

He was a house surgeon at the Auckland Hospital for two years and intended following a surgical career. The year 1922 was spent as a general practitioner locum at Tokomaru Bay on the east coast of the North Island, visiting patients on horseback or a model T Ford.

In 1923 he went to England where he obtained posts as house physician at the Royal Northern, and St George's Hospital under Sir Henry Letheby Tidy, who was responsible for his pursuing training in general medicine. At St George's Hospital he continued to play rugby but sustained a 4th nerve palsy with diplopia, resulting in a distinctive posture of the head which remained throughout life.

After obtaining his MRCP in 1925 he was RMO at the Shadwell Children's Hospital, where he remained for almost two years. On returning to Auckland in 1925 he became acting medical superintendent at the Auckland Hospital for six months. In 1926 he was appointed consultant physician to the Children's Hospital, and commenced practice as a consulting physician with a special interest in pediatrics.

He served as a captain and a major in the NZ Medical Corps, serving in the Pacific in 1945.

Samuel Ludbrook was a tall man of gentle manner and speech, with a warm, thoughtful personality which endeared him to child patients and their parents. His long experience and deep knowledge rendered him an excellent teacher and administrator, greatly respected by his contemporaries in the hospital service. He was the prime mover in establishing the Children's Hospital, and was the outstanding paediatrician of his time in Auckland and, indeed, New Zealand.

As a keen sportsman he pursued tennis, polo, horse racing and trout fishing.

In December 1927 he married Ailsa, daughter of Robert Burns, a merchant in Auckland. He had three sons who survived him, one of whom, John Ludbrook FRCS, became professor of surgery in Adelaide University. TGF

LUMB, Frank Hirst *b*.27 May 1926 *d*.4 Apr 1977
MB BS London (1948) MRCP (1954) FRCP (1973)

Frank Lumb was born at Slaithwaite, in Yorkshire, where his father was a company secretary. He received his scholastic education at Royds Hall Grammar School, Huddersfield, before proceeding to University College, London, and University College Hospital, where he graduated with honours in medicine in 1948.

At that time two years' national service was compulsory, and Lumb spent his as regimental medical officer to the 2nd Battalion of the Grenadier Guards. Thereafter he worked with two future College presidents, both with a special interest in hypertension and renal disease. He was senior house officer to Lord Platt in Manchester, and was with Lord Rosenheim at University College Hospital, publishing with him a British Council overseas booklet on the management of hypertension. In 1960 he was awarded the Edward Wilson memorial fellowship and spent the next two years at the Alfred Hospital in Melbourne. On his return to England in 1962 he was appointed physician to the Staffordshire General Infirmary, where he spent the rest of his life.

Frank was an excellent general physician, despite having devoted such a large part of his training to a relatively narrow area of research, and he quickly built up a large consulting practice and a considerable reputation. Unhappily, he died suddenly and unexpectedly when he was only 50. He was unmarried. AGWW

[*Brit. med. J.*, 1977, **1**, 1163; Photo]

MacADAM, William *b.*10 Dec 1885 *d.*19 May 1976
MA Glasg (1904) BSc (1907) MB ChB (1909) MD (1914)
MRCP (1916) FRCP (1932)

William MacAdam was born in Helensburgh, the son of a Glasgow business man. He was educated at Hermitage Grammar School, Helensburgh, and at Glasgow University. He graduated with honours in 1909 after winning the Brunton memorial prize. He proceeded to the MD, again with honours, in 1914, and in 1916 obtained the MRCP.

After resident appointments in Glasgow, he became a McCunn and Carnegie research scholar in pathological chemistry.

From 1915 to 1919 he served in the Army as a pathologist, first at Netley and later in India and Mesopotamia, and eventually as officer in charge of the pathological services to two military hospitals in Baghdad.

After the war he started his long association with the Leeds School of Medicine and University of Leeds, working with his fellow Scots, MJ Stewart and James MacLeod, at first from 1919 to 1922 as lecturer in pathology. However, his interest turned towards clinical medicine, and in 1922 he was appointed tutor in medicine. In 1925 he was appointed to the staff of the Leeds General Infirmary as assistant physician. He was also subsequently appointed to the Clayton Hospital, Wakefield, and to the General Hospital, Skipton, before being appointed to the full staff of the Infirmary as honorary physician. In 1932, he was also made part-time professor of clinical medicine, and subsequently professor of medicine, which post he held with distinction until 1945, when he was elected emeritus professor.

His move from pathology to clinical medicine occurred in the exciting years of the early 1920's when investigative procedures were developing fast, and his keen observation and early training enabled him to take full advantage of this period. He became especially interested in diabetes.

MacAdam was an astute and careful physician with exceptional learning, and a very hard worker who soon developed a large practice covering a very wide area. He never, however, allowed this to interfere with his hospital and university commitments, and particularly his teaching sessions in the Infirmary, which he regarded as his primary duty, and which he prepared with great care. These were much appreciated by his students, his residents and his registrars alike. To the former he was a somewhat awesome figure, but he gave much help and encouragement to the latter, who were devoted to him. He took a full part in the administration of the hospital and the University, especially in the critical days when the formation of the National Health Service was under consideration, and also as a member of the senate of the University. He was external examiner to a number of medical schools, including Newcastle and St Andrews.

He was an active member of the BMA, which he joined in 1913, subsequently becoming the president of the Yorkshire branch and twice chairman of the Leeds division. In 1959 his work for the BMA was recognized when he was made a fellow. He was also a founder member of the British Society of Gastroenterology, and for many years the driving force in the West Riding Medical Society.

Throughout his long life his work was always his main interest, an interest which never left him up to the time of his death, but he enjoyed golf, which he played at the weekends and occasionally on the summer evenings, and he was made an honorary member of the Alwoodley Golf Club.

In 1928 he married Irene Tincker, the daughter of a Congregational minister, and herself a doctor and a magistrate, from whom he received invaluable support throughout his married life. They had two sons and one daughter, all doctors, of whom they were justifiably proud. He died in Leeds. JRHT

[*Brit. med. J.*, 1976, **1**, 1537; *Lancet*, 1976, **1**, 1306; Photo]

McALPINE, Douglas *b.*19 Aug 1890 *d.*4 Feb 1981
MB ChB Glasg (1913) MRCP (1921) MD (1923) FRCP (1932)

Douglas McAlpine was a son of Sir Robert McAlpine. He was educated in Edinburgh and at Kirton College and was a medical student at Glasgow where he qualified with distinction in medicine and midwifery. In April 1914, he was house physician to WR Jack at the Royal Infirmary in Glasgow, and in August 1914 he enlisted as a temporary lieutenant in the RAMC. On his 24th birthday he was posted to the Cambridge Military Hospital at Aldershot, and shortly after this he embarked for France and, in September, joined the 13th Field Ambulance at Colomire and, in November, he became a regimental medical officer to the 2nd Battalion of the Queen's Own Scottish Borderers. At one stage in the battle at Ypres his unit was moved back behind the lines and a house taken over by fifteen medical officers in a row of houses which was called 'Harley Street'.

Early in 1915 he was posted to a hospital ship, and in August he resigned his army commission and transferred to the Royal Navy. He was posted to the 3rd Light Cruiser Squadron. He played rugger for the squadron and served in HMS *Falmouth* at the battle of Jutland in 1916. He was in the ship in August 1916 when she was sunk off Flamborough Head. He then served in Scapa Flow, where he boxed for the squadron and was knocked out in the second round by the chaplain (who later became the lightweight champion of the Mediterranean Fleet).

Douglas married in 1917 Meg Sidebottom, and in March 1918 he was posted to RN Sick Quarters in Plymouth, where he used hypnosis to cure nervous ailments and was mentioned in despatches for this work. He was demobilized in November 1918, and appointed as a clinical clerk to Archibald Garrod at Bart's. He then decided that neurology was his future career, and in 1920 and 1921 he worked with JG Greenfield at the National Hospital for Nervous Diseases, Queen Square, on post encephalitic parkinsonism. In 1921 he became assistant physician to the Belgrade Hospital for Children, and in 1923 he was attached for six months to Jean l'Hermitte at the Salpetrière in Paris, again working on post encephalitic pathology. In February 1924, he was appointed physician in charge of nervous diseases at the Middlesex Hospital and assistant physician and pathologist at the Maida Vale Hospital.

At the Middlesex he was an outpatient physician with no beds under his own care – not unusual for junior physicians in those hierarchical days. This meant that those referred for inpatient study or treatment were the responsibility of physicians who generally had no special interest in neurology, and it was not until a floor in the older part of the hospital became vacant that an inpatient neurological unit was created in 1930, a handsome gift from the family firm of Sir Robert McAlpine, which turned the deserted and barren group of little rooms into two handsome wards holding 24 patients.

At that time most teaching hospitals had neurology and neurologists as part of a general medical firm; only those students allotted to this firm could clerk inpatient neurological problems. The rest (about three quarters) had to be content with outpatient neurology. Douglas McAlpine arranged for his unit to have all the students in the second clinical year clerking in two months' groups in the wards, so that all undergraduates at the Middlesex Hospital were able to see neurological inpatients. When space became available neurosurgical beds were added to the unit. In this way he founded a tradition of teaching which has continued until the present day. Even now there are still teaching hospitals that have their neurological unit as part of a general medical firm and thus only a fraction of medical students see inpatient neurology and neurosurgery as a formal part of their teaching. Thus not only were his students given a reasonable exposure to the subject, but the junior hospital doctors, likewise, received a remarkable clinical education in neurology and neurosurgery. It is trite to say that a clinical unit takes its tone from the top; there is no doubt that Douglas kept the unit on its toes and, as his first house physician, I can vouch for the enthusiasm and gentle discipline that was exercised. It was this enthusiasm that ensured that so many of his juniors continued in neurology.

In the second world war Douglas was appointed adviser in neurology, first in the Middle East in 1941, and then to India Command, and finally to South East Asia, and it was here that he met Diana, his second wife. Although he was a brigadier he did not restrict himself to advising from a distance or visiting occasionally. During the El Alamein battle, when the first mobile neurosurgical team received over 200 head injuries in eight days, he joined in the examination, writing up notes and giving intravenous sulphadiazine to all penetrating head wounds. Together we learned how easy it could be for sulphadiazine to block the ureter if the urinary pH was not watched. When the rush of wounded was over he quietly disappeared to his advisory function, his parting words to me being 'It was nice to be your house physician for a week'.

The major work of Douglas McAlpine's life was the study of multiple sclerosis. He amassed a vast amount of clinical data and distilled it into his book *Multiple Sclerosis* first published in 1955. This book has gone through two reappraisals with co-authors, the last edition being in 1965. After retiring from the hospitals in 1955 Douglas continued to follow up his patients, and a new edition of his book was being prepared when he died.

It is wrong, however, to think that all his enthusiasms went into multiple sclerosis. Douglas was eclectic in his interests. When he worked in Japan for the World Health Organization, primarily on the study of demyelinating diseases, he was one of the first (if not *the* first) to distinguish the effects on man of eating fish that had been poisoned with mercury from industrial effluent. Even in his last years he led an enquiry into the proposal to build a high powered world broadcasting unit in his village, because he was concerned about the possible harmful effects that radiation from such a unit might have on the local community. Protection of the environment was always a major consideration of his.

It was Douglas McAlpine who, in 1951, sponsored the formation of the Multiple Sclerosis Society of Great Britain, and the Society was born in 1953. It was Douglas McAlpine who, at that time, had the vision to see that the medical profession and lay people could work in partnership. He formed the embryo society's medical panel and its medical advisory research committee, of which he was the first chairman. One of the first decisions this society had to make was whether it should be called the multiple sclerosis or the disseminated sclerosis society. The decision was for multiple sclerosis and it is interesting, and perhaps even entertaining, that this decision so dismayed a leading neurologist of the day that he withdrew from the Society's affairs.

Douglas was the first and, so far, the only recipient of the Charcot award given by the International Federation of Multiple Sclerosis Societies 'for significant contributions to and understanding of the cause, mechanisms, treatments and/or cure of multiple sclerosis'. The award was made in Washington in September 1969.

Douglas will always be remembered by his pupils and his patients. He was fundamentally a shy man, which at times made him appear a little brusque, but to get to know him was, indeed, to appreciate his genial and gentle humanity. MK

[*Brit. med. J.*, 1981, **282**, 827, 1244; Photo]

MACAULAY, Michael Blair *b.*14 June 1933 *d.*8 July 1983
BA Oxon (1954) BM BCh (1957) MA (1958) MRCP (1964)
FRCP (1976)

Michael Macaulay was the second son of distinguished Liverpool medical parents. His father, Blair Macaulay, who was originally a GP and took the MRCP rather later than usual, became Liverpool's first allergist. Michael's mother, Mary, pioneered birth control in the city and was renowned for her undergraduate lectures (complete with samples in a shopping bag) on what was then a rather recherché subject. Her lectures, books and television appearances were marvels of enlightenment but undoubtedly occasioned her student sons some embarrassing moments. An octogenarian uncle, Dr Blair, lived with the family for many years and had been a notable foreign traveller and author of anthropological works. Michael's elder brother John, while still an undergraduate, had the unfortunate experience of having his car break down in the university quadrangle during a Royal visit. He is now a successful pathologist in Canada.

Macaulay was educated at Leighton Park School before going up to Oxford and later to the Liverpool clinical school. He entered the Royal Army Medical Corps for his national service, taking a short-term commission and becoming a specialist in medicine with the rank of major before returning to Liverpool. He quickly became the sort of 'junior' doctor who, yeoman-like, are the backbone of a hospital, and in the Liverpool tradition of the day he remained a senior registrar long after he became a consultant in all but name. His ability and clinical flair led rapidly to his being regarded as a first rate opinion, prticularly for heart problems. When, at last, he was appointed consultant physician to Walton and Fazakerley hospitals his job was general medicine with responsibility for the diabetic clinic, and this soon became one of the largest and most efficient in Britain. Shortly after his appointment he began the battle to establish an intensive care unit which, thanks to him, became a model of its kind. He was also responsible for a large cardiac clinic and ECG service and although nominally part time, he devoted long hours to his hospital commitments. His opinions were widely sought, always carefully analyzed, and full of commonsense. His large private practice was run from his home and in this way he was ably assisted by his wife Doreen, herself a nurse. He gave the North Liverpool population a tremendous service both in the NHS and private practice, inheriting from his father the best qualities of both general physician and general practitioner.

Michael, despite many clinical commitments, showed that administration can be easy – providing one has an abundant supply of intellect, integrity, organization and fairness.He was a successful and popular bedside teacher with four 'firms' of students a year. He had an honorary lectureship in clinical medicine and published on a wide range of topics, including leucocyte antigens in pregnancy (his DM thesis), hospital listeriosis, cardiac pacing, hyperosmolar diabetes. But the most characteristic of his writing was his 'Virtuous Husband Syndrome' (*British Medical Journal*, 12 April 1975). He wrote '... for example ... a vicar who succours his parishioners day and night, or a doctor constantly attending his patients, or a businessman who by his skill and longworking hours has built up the wealth on which his family depends ... will be held in high esteem by all and his wife would herself be considered worthy of contempt were she to object to his activities. Yet she may be equally neglected and, without a reasonable outlet for her insecurity, may take refuge in ill-health'. Michael did not doubt '... that most practising clinicians will spot this syndrome from time to time ... in themselves'. Sadly, Michael could not write the sequel to his syndrome which eventually exacts its toll from the virtuous, too.

Michael Macaulay had a natural talent for friendship. This was partly due to his intellect; he was a charming, witty and well informed conversationalist, but also because he was naturally gregarious and compassionate. He excelled in the use of words, and I have rueful student memories of his beating all-comers in defining the most difficult words in the Oxford dictionary. However Michael's real relaxation was with his wife and their three daughters, Jane who works on the management side of Marks and Spencer, Catherine a St Thomas's nurse married to a stockbroker, and Anne currently still an undergraduate. Michael also loved to take his caravan to the remote hills where he walked at a prodigious pace to the most inaccessible places. He died, much as he would have wished, suddenly and unexpectedly in the hills of Scotland. Sadly, he was only 50. RH(1)

[*Brit. med. J.*, 1983, **287**, 505, 564; *Lancet*, 1983, **2**, 468; Photo]

McCOMAS, Herbert Geoffrey *b*.9 Feb 1907 *d*.9 Aug 1977
MRCS LRCP (1930) MB BS Lond (1932) MD (1935) MRCP (1932) FRCP (1971)

Geoffrey McComas was born in Coulsdon, Surrey, the son of Percy Herbert McComas, a shipping clerk. His mother was Norah (née Fawcus). He was educated at Lancing College and Guy's Hospital. After qualification in 1930 he became successively house physician and house surgeon at Queen Mary's Hospital, Stratford, London, and resident medical officer at the Children's Hospital, Sheffield. In 1932 he joined a general practice in Croydon, and in 1934 he was appointed physician to Croydon General Hospital, becoming consultant physician in 1948 at the inception of the NHS. He served on the staff of Croydon General Hospital for 38 years until he retired at the age limit in 1972. He was devoted to this hospital and gave his life to it.

At the outbreak of war in September 1939, he immediately joined the RAMC, and served in France with the British Expeditionary Force. After Dunkirk he served as a lieutenant colonel in charge of medical divisions of general military hospitals in West Africa, India and England. He was demobilized in November 1945.

He was a chief medical officer to the Prudential Assurance Company from 1946 to 1976, and life assurance medicine was always one of his major interests.

Geoffrey was utterly devoted to his patients and to his hospital. He arrived early in the morning and left late in the evening. He had a brusque manner and fools were not suffered, but his junior doctors were all very fond of him. He did not like social life and had few, if any, close friends. He preferred to take very long walks by himself, and he was a familiar figure on a Sunday in the countryside often many miles from Croydon. He was also interested in bird-watching and he was an avid reader of books, both medical and general. He took retirement badly, and he did as many locums as possible in the

Croydon Hospitals until he became progressively disabled by osteoarthritis of the hip. The operation he had for this was a disaster as it only greatly increased his immobility.

In 1931 he married Janet Mary Bruce SRN, the daughter of a director of a shipping company. They had three children, of whom two unfortunately died before he did. GPB

[*Brit. med. J.*, 1977, **2**, 646; Photo]

McCOWAN, Peter Knight *b*.3 Sept 1890 *d*.17 Mar 1979
MB ChB Edin (1912) DPM (1921) MD (1922) MRCP (1923)
FRCP (1934) Hon FRCPsych (1971) Barrister-at-law (1930) JP

After a brief illness, Peter McCowan died at the age of eighty-eight, a patient in a teaching hospital of his University. He was born in Perth, and after graduation he, like so many of his generation, spent some time in general practice, and then as a major in the RAMC, before he entered the specialty which he was to advance greatly.

His first eight years in psychiatry, from 1920, were spent with the LCC hospital service. His early achievement, and his promise, were recognized by his appointment in 1928 as physician superintendent of Cardiff City Mental Hospital and lecturer in the Welsh National School of Medicine. McCowan was no stranger to research – he was a Bronze Medallist of the Royal Medico-Psychological Association in 1926 – and in Wales his biochemical interests found considerable support.

It was however in clinical and administrative psychiatry that his talent was to find its most complete expression. In 1937 the directors of the Crichton Royal Hospital appointed him as their physician superintendent. At that time Crichton's wealthy endowment and clinical facilities could probably have attracted any candidate; McCowan's subsequent career showed the wisdom of his selection. His twenty years in Dumfries spanned a period of great expansion in active psychiatric treatment, and his creative energy and foresight exploited this to the full. The hospital's intake of patients from all over Britain and beyond expanded fivefold, and its reputation reached its zenith under his direction. In the second world war McCowan was again commissioned, in the rank of lieutenant colonel, and over two thousand officers were treated in the Crichton Military Hospital. He had a remarkable capacity to discern early, and to foster, every growing point in psychiatric practice, whether this were child psychiatry, clinical psychology, or whatever. The productive research departments he instituted, under W Mayer-Gross and J Raven, commanded at their peak resources not equalled by some university departments.

His contribution was not only parochial. He held important offices in the Royal Medico-Psychological Association, largely concerned with study and research, and his fostering of high professional standards played its distant part in the ultimate transformation of that body into the Royal College of Psychiatrists. His service to the RM-

PA was recognized in 1951 by his election to its presidency.

In former days, the position of physician superintendent of a good hospital was perhaps the peak of any psychiatric career. It lent itself, obviously, to accusations of autocracy and paternalism. McCowan was a curious autocrat; one who welcomed the collaboration, and indeed enjoyed the opposition, of figures of equal distinction; who gave his ambitious younger colleagues encouragement and freedom; who, when his power was trammelled by administrative and legal changes, still attained his objectives by subtle political judgement; and who liked nothing better than a game of bowls with his nurses and tradesmen. He was a masculine and gregarious man, and if his wit was often caustic it was usually tempered by a jovial chuckle.

He married Gladys Nunn in 1917, and had two daughters, one a doctor. After the death of his first wife, he married in 1933 Muriel Northcote, herself a distinguished psychiatrist, who also pre-deceased him.

ACT

[*Brit. med. J.*, 1979, **1**, 1026; *Bull. roy. Coll. Psychiat.*, July 1979; Photo]

McDERMOTT, Walsh *b*.24 Oct 1909 *d*.17 Oct 1981
BA Princeton (1930) MD Columbia (1934) FRCP* (1968)
Hon DSc Princeton (1974) Dartmouth (1976)

Son of a family doctor in New Haven, Connecticut, Walsh McDermott attended the public schools of that city. He did premedical work at Princeton University, and then studied for the MD degree at Columbia University Medical School. For intern and residency training he moved across Manhattan Island, to the New York Hospital, teaching hospital of the Cornell Medical College. This was the beginning of a lifelong association with Cornell.

During the early part of his medical career he was invalided repeatedly by flare-ups of pulmonary tuberculosis. For that he went through tedious periods of rest treatment at Saranac Lake, and later was given streptomycin therapy. In 1950, after partial pulmonary resection and isoniazid treatment, the disease was brought under control. Though handicapped afterwards by noticeable pulmonary insufficiency he was able to carry on a busy, rigorous life, involving much travel at home and abroad.

In the early phase of his academic career McDermott engaged in clinical academic medicine, with a special interest in the infectious diseases. He was soon given responsibility for the infectious disease division of the department of medicine at Cornell. Early on, syphilis was a major medical problem, and he made observations of arsenical therapy, then of penicillin when that became available. In 1948, after the discovery of chloramphenicol he went to Mexico, to conduct a study comparing three drugs: amphotericin B, tetracycline, and chloramphenicol; this gave a clearcut demonstration of the superiority of chloramphenicol. He was, of course, personally concerned about the chemotherapy of tuberculosis, and made some of the pioneer investigations of the pharmacodynamics of streptomycin in man. Later he was offered the opportunity to test the efficacy of the newly discovered isoniazid, in tuberculosis. For that work he shared the Lasker award with three colleagues (1955).

In his experimental laboratories McDermott worked in collaboration with a succession of able younger colleagues, among whom were two fellows of this College: John Batten and Harold Lambert. The central theme of their research was the phenomenon of microbial 'persistence', i.e., the capacity of some microorganisms to survive for weeks or months in cells or tissues of a host animal, in spite of continued treatment with an agent to which the organism retains *in vitro* sensitivity. This property is notable in *M. tuberculosis* and *T. pallidum*. For this work, as well as the early studies with chloramphenicol, streptomycin and isoniazid, he was elected to the US National Academy of Sciences (1967).

In the course of the isoniazid study McDermott encountered something that brought about a change in the character of his endeavours. To test the drug against severest forms of the disease he had gone to the southwest United States to try its effect in tuberculous meningitis and miliary tuberculosis. Those forms of tuberculosis were known to be common events among the Navajo Indians, in their reservations in Arizona and New Mexico. Indeed the drug proved able to save some lives, but in the course of the experience McDermott was appalled at health conditions in that disadvantaged ethnic group living within the continental United States.

He determined to find out what could be done by bringing modern methods of diagnosis and treatment to the Navajo population. He took over the chairmanship of Cornell's department of public health, and organized a programme to bring modern clinical medicine to the Navajo people. The experiment went on for six years. The result was enlightening though discouraging: it was clear that sophisticated medical care is not enough to improve the health of people who have insufficient food and drinking water, who live in extreme poverty, and who lack modern sanitary services.

McDermott's 'statistical compassion' – a phrase he frequently used – also found fulfilment near home. In New York's inner city areas, especially Brooklyn and Harlem, he and colleagues explored the subjects of drug addiction, air pollution, and health care delivery.

This broad range of interest and experience made him a much sought after adviser, to New York City, New York State, and to the federal government. He came to be thought of as one of his country's leading medical statesmen, and served on dozens of advisory committees. He wrote extensively on various aspects of health care, and was invited to give many named lectureships at home, as well as the Heath Clark lectures in London. For the federal government he led a task force which drew up a blueprint of a programme to improve living conditions of the American Indian. He served as chairman of the United States delegation, of more than 100 scientists, to a United Nations conference in Geneva on application of science and technology for underdeveloped countries. When Princeton University awarded him an honorary degree, the citation read, in part: 'As a pioneer in adapting modern medicine to primitive societies and as an innovator in the spread of the public health services of the nation, he has always kept as his goal the well-being of society as a necessary corollary of the health of the individual'.

Along with his other activities McDermott served for 25 years as editor of the *American review of respiratory diseases*, and for 20 years as co-editor of the *Cecil textbook of medicine*.

During the last nine years of his life he gradually shifted his base of operations from Cornell to Princeton, where he served as special adviser to the president of the Robert Wood Johnson Foundation. This gave him scope to study, and experiment with methods to improve systems of health care delivery in the United States.

At the same time he was serving as a trustee of Columbia University, and actively participating in the affairs of the Foreign Policy Association of New York.

One of his assets was facility in the use of words. As David Rogers put it: 'There are few individuals whose words can capture one's ear or mind in compelling ways, but Walsh was one of them. The turn of a phrase, an unusual or amusing analogy, a particularly noble ring to a sentence, a lucid rendering of a complex idea – such were the treats awaiting a listener or reader'.

He married Marian MacPhail while a resident at the New York Hospital. She followed a notable career in journalism, becoming a member of the editorial board of *Life* magazine. Their friends, in medicine, journalism, New York City politics, and in sports, made for them a full life. They shared a great affection for New York City with all its problems, and they worked to find solutions to some of those problems.

Walsh McDermott carried on actively and successfully, until the moment of his sudden death. PB

MacFARLANE, James Robertson Ross *b*.27 Jan 1926
d.10 Aug 1983
MB ChB Glasg (1948) MRCP (1952) FRCP (1982) FRCPG (1983)

James MacFarlane, consultant physician in geriatric medicine at the Victoria Infirmary, Glasgow, was born in that city and served it all his life. His father was a head teacher, John Campbell MacFarlane, and James was educated at Glasgow High School and the University of Glasgow, where he graduated in medicine. After house appointments in medicine and surgery at Glasgow Royal Infirmary, he entered the RAMC in 1949 on National Service, returning to the Infirmary in 1951 to complete his training as a physician. He continued his association with the Infirmary, as senior house officer and medical registrar, until 1958 when he was appointed senior registrar to Hairmyres Hospital, Lanarkshire. He remained on the staff, as assistant physician, until 1969, and then became consultant physician to the geriatric unit at the Victoria Infirmary.

MacFarlane was honorary clinical lecturer in geriatric medicine and wrote and gave many papers on the subject, being especially interested in the use and effect of diuretics and potassium sparing agents in elderly patients. This interest in the use of diuretics in the management of hypertension led to participation in the European Working Party on Hypertension in the Elderly. He organized the 14th workshop of the group in May 1982, which was notable for its quality and excellence. His clinical skills and genuine interest in his patients were greatly appreciated both by staff and students at the Infirmary.

MacFarlane was a member of his local Rotary Club, a trustee of the Scottish Trust for the Physically Disabled, an elder and former session clerk in his church, and chairman, secretary or committee member of many charitable groups – including the Pearce Institute in Govan and the Margaret Blackwood Housing Foundation for the Disabled.

He married Grace, daughter of Archibald Gibson, a master builder, in 1960, and they had a son John, and a daughter Mhairi. In his own family there was a long history of coronary disease and it caught up with him in 1974, but he refused to allow this to affect his work in the community or the hospital. He was a naturally courteous man, very hospitable, and travelled widely. His wife and children survived him.

GW/VL

[*Brit. med. J.*, 1983, **287**, 1313; Photo]

Mac KEITH, Ronald Charles *b.*23 Feb 1908 *d.*30 Oct 1977
BA Oxon (1930) MA BM BCh (1932) DCH Lond (1937) DM (1940) MRCP (1941) FRCP (1952)

Ronald Mac Keith was born in Southampton, he and his twin sister being 9th and 10th of a family of eleven children of a general practitioner, Alexander Arthur Mac Keith and his wife Alice, daughter of Henry Wipell Gadd, a pharmaceutical manufacturer of Exeter. Four of their sons took up medicine. Ronald went to King Edward VI School in Southampton, to Queen's College, Oxford (to which he was devoted), and to St Mary's Hospital, London. After qualifying in 1933 he was appointed house physician to the medical unit at his own hospital. He spent the following year, 1934–1935, as Radcliffe travelling fellow of the University of Oxford, in the pediatric department of Bellevue Hospital, New York, founding a fruitful and life-long friendship with Harry Bakwin. During a succession of junior hospital appointments he came to the favourable notice of Hector Charles Cameron at St James's Hospital, Balham, where he served during the London 'blitz'. War interrupted his hospital career. From 1942 to 1945 he was in the Royal Navy, emerging as a temporary acting surgeon lieutenant commander.

After the war Ronnie became a supernumerary registrar to AA (later Sir Alan) Moncrieff at the Hospital for Sick Children, Great Ormond Street, London. Moncrieff gave each supernumerary registrar a common paediatric problem, which most failed to solve. Mac Keith was told to investigate threadworm infestation, and his work on diagnosis and epidemiology is of permanent value. He also investigated and instigated trials of the new therapy with piperazine.

In 1947 he moved to Guy's Hospital, where two of his brothers had been trained. There he was elected consulting children's physician a few days before the National Health Service was instituted in 1948. At that time his special interests were in medical education, medical films – he became chairman of the medical committee of the Scientific Film Association – and improving the lot of children in hospital, especially by persuading Guy's to permit parental visiting every day instead of only twice a week. A persistent interest in handicapped children was indicated by his founding at Guy's the first cerebral palsy advice clinic, which was to become in 1964 the larger and more comprehensive Newcomen Centre for handicapped children. He was active in promoting understanding of psychosomatic medicine, and in 1950 he was appointed paediatrician to the Tavistock Clinic, and in 1960 to the Cassell Hospital; in 1961 – 1962 he was chairman of the Association of Child Psychology and Psychiatry. His advice led to the recognition of paediatric neurology in several European countries, about 80 years after its dawning emergence in the United States. He founded the British Paediatric Neurology Association.

In the 1950's Ronnie was associated with the National Spastics Society, and became director of its Medical Education and Information Unit, a position he held for the rest of his life. He founded the 'Cerebral Palsy Bulletin' which in 1962 became the *Journal of Developmental Medicine and Child Neurology*. Associated with it were monographs in a series of 'Clinics in Developmental Medicine' of which the 67th was a Festschrift for his seventieth birthday. The famous series of monographs was composed in part by recording conferences, especially the annual Oxford meetings of the International Study Group on Child Neurology which Mac Keith ran from 1958 to 1972. Each new participant was given a tie ornamented with red carnations, and this became a well known passport at international medical meetings. He also collaborated in writing books on infant feeding, the child and his symptoms, paediatric ophthalmology, and child health and developmental screening.

In 1972 he was awarded the James Spence gold medal of the British Paediatric Association, but in general he was more honoured abroad than at home, being awarded medals or honorary memberships in the United States, Sweden, West Germany, France etc. He spoke French with confidence.

In 1971 he succeeded to the directorship of the paediatric department at Guy's, where he laid a sound foundation for the future even though he himself had only two years to establish it. After retiring he continued to live in his London home and to work in the Hampstead office of the Medical Education and Information Unit. There he had a cerebrovascular accident nearly a year before his death, but he made a good recovery and was able to return to work and to the international scene. In his retirement he appeared happy and, at last, unhurried.

He was of medium height, strongly built, with aquiline features, their expression alternating between serious and quizzical. He was often untidily dressed but a touch of the dandy showed in his wearing a red carnation every day, and in the choice of shirts and ties. He was almost always busy, often appearing muddled, whereas in fact his mind was highly efficient as well as penetrating and original. He was sensitive, kind and unselfish but could be impatient with colleagues, never with patients. He was interested in the arts, especially painting. He was a good talker once he got going, and a stimulating teacher, although medical students could not always make out what he was getting at. Many came to value him the more highly the longer they had been in practice. His influence on the development of paediatrics was outstanding.

In 1943 he married Elizabeth Mary, daughter of Clement Osborne Bartrum of Hampstead, woollen manufacturer. She was an enthusiastic 'cellist and survived him with their two daughters and two sons.

His final illness was brief: he had been gardening on a Sunday morning, enjoyed lunch and then collapsed. He was taken to Westminster Hospital but was unconscious for the short time which remained to him. PRE

[*Brit. med. J.*, 1977, **2**, 1293 & 1361; *Lancet,* 1977, **2**, 1040; *Times,* 2 & 5 Nov 1977; *J. Audiov. Media Med.,* 1978, **1**, 39; *Guy's Hospital Gaz.,* 1977, **92**, 319-323; Photo]

MACKIE, Frederic Percival *b.*19 Feb 1875 *d.*15 July 1944
CSI (1932) OBE (1918) MRCS LRCP (1897) FRCS (1902)
MB BCh Bristol (1911) MRCP (1911) MD (1915) MSc (1916)
FRCP (1919) DPH (1925)

Mackie was one of the most distinguished medical scientists to serve in India during the days of Empire, and when he retired from the Indian Medical Service in 1932 he found that his services were as much in demand at home. His work on plague, relapsing fever, sleeping sicknesss, kala-azar, enteric dysentery, cholera, schistosomiasis, hydrophobia and sprue, was original and of first rate quality, but perhaps his administrative gifts and his overall contribution to tropical hygiene were of even greater value. He was a good speaker in debate; a dedicated professional who was also a witty and amusing man who enjoyed life.

Born at Bristol, the sixth son and ninth child of the Revd John Mackie, rector of Fylton, Gloucestershire, and his second wife Annie Bennett, he was educated at Dean Close School, Cheltenham, Bristol Medical School, and St Bartholomew's Hospital. He qualified in 1897, worked for some time at Netley under Sir Almroth Wright; gained the FRCS in 1902, and that same year won first place in the entrance examination for the Indian Medical Service. He began his service as medical officer to the Sir Francis Younghusband Mission to Tibet, in 1903. On his promotion to captain he was appointed assistant director to the newly established Plague Research Laboratory at Parel, Bombay, set up to combat an outbreak of plague which appeared in

Bombay in 1896 and spread north and east. Much of the research work he carried out in Bombay was on plague, but his most noteworthy discovery was the *spirillum* of relapsing fever, transmitted by bites of body lice. He was a member of the Uganda sleeping sickness commission in 1908, and special research officer on kala-azar in 1911. The Leishman-Donovan parasite had been discovered in 1903 as the causal organism of kala-azar, but it was Mackie who identified the sandfly as its mode of transmission; a finding authenticated fourteen years later by the Calcutta School of Tropical Medicine's team and the Government of India's special commission on the disease. Mackie was also associated with Hamilton Fairley on the dietetic treatment of sprue.

In 1914 he was promoted to major and during the 1914–1918 war he served in Baluchistan, Persia, Mesopotamia and France. Quickly and efficiently, he established a central bacteriological laboratory in Mesopotamia in 1916 after the breakdown of the original medical organization in that area, and succeeded in isolating a strain of cholera vibrio endemic to the region. He received the OBE for his services in 1918, and was twice mentioned in despatches. In 1920 he was appointed professor of pathology at Calcutta University, but was transferred to the post of director of the Pasteur Institute at Shillong in Assam. He was promoted to lieutenant colonel in 1922 and the following year returned, as director, to the Haffkine Institute for Medical Research in Bombay, where so much of his earlier work had been done. He remained at the Institute until he retired from the IMS in 1932. He was officiating public health commissioner, Government of India, from 1928 to 1932; served as chairman of the League of Nations expert committee on plague from 1928–1931; was president of the medical and veterinary section of the Indian Science Congress in 1925, and president of the tropical diseases section at the BMA centenary meeting in London. He held appointments as honorary surgeon to HM King George V and to the Viceroy of India. On retirement he was created CSI.

On his return to England Mackie became a lecturer at the London School of Hygiene and Tropical Medicine, and also served as pathologist at the Tropical Diseases Hospital, London, from 1933 to 1937. He was then appointed chief medical officer to British Overseas Airways Corporation, journeying by air to tropical colonies in Africa and Asia to supervise the sanitary requirements of the chain of airports then being established. His particular interest was in the prevention of the spread of yellow fever, and he introduced thorough fumigation of aircraft against all bloodsucking and disease carrying insects.

During this period, Mackie lived in his native Bristol at 3 Golding Avenue, and later at Pack Horse Farm, Mark, near Highbridge, Somerset. During the height of the air-raids on Bristol during the second world war he was an active warden and first-aid rescue worker in the streets. He married twice: in 1913 to Gladys May, daughter of WJ Ball. Their son and only child, Laurence Percival, entered medicine and served in the RNVR from 1944 to the close of the war.

His second wife, Mary Elizabeth Elwes, a widow and daughter of W Haddon Owen of Louth, Lincolnshire, survived him. They were married in 1926. GW/VL

[*Brit. med. J.*, 1944, **2**, 164-5; *Lives of the Fellows of the Royal College of Surgeons of England* 1930-1951, pp. 510-12; *Lancet*, 1944, **2**, 263; *Times*, 18 July, 1 & 19 Aug 1944; *Bristol Evening News*, 18 July 1944; *Nature*, 1944, **154**, 296; *Bristol med. -chir. J.*, 1944, **61**, 28]

MACKIE, James Robertson Monro *b.*21 Sept 1909 *d.*19 Dec 1982
MB ChB Aberd (1932) MD (1934) MRCP (1935) DPM (1949)

James Mackie graduated in medicine at the University of Aberdeen, the town in which he was born. He was the son of John Mackie (Mackie of Glenmillan), a mechanical engineer and director ofJohn M Henderson & Sons Limited, and his wife Isabella, daughter of James Munro of the Merchant Navy.

James Mackie's first postgraduate interest was in neurology, which was the subject of his MD thesis and won him the Fulton prize, but after various house posts at the Royal Sick Children's Hospital, Aberdeen, the West End Hospital for Nervous Diseases, London, the Maida Vale Hospital for Epilepsy and Paralysis and the King George Hospital, Ilford, he became senior registrar to the professor of psychiatry at Aberdeen Royal Infirmary in 1947, and switched his allegiance to this field of medicine. In 1949 he was appointed deputy medical superintendent at the Dundee and District Mental Hospital, becoming a consultant psychiatrist at High Royds Hospital, Menston in Wharfedale, in 1951, where he remained until his retirement. He encouraged the trend to unlocked doors in mental hospitals, and the return of patients to the community as soon as possible.

He was a frail man and slight of stature; a man of independent means who was, however, devoted to his work and with high ethical standards. Under a rather dour exterior there was a dry sense of humour and a real generosity towards friends and colleagues. He was also fond of animals, and devoted to his cat 'Tiberius'.

Outside medicine, his main interest lay in the study of medieval ecclesiastical architecture and Byzantine painting and sculpture. He also enjoyed Latin prose and verse of the post Augustine period.

In 1947 he married Elizabeth, daughter of John Noble Cruickshank, a master tailor; she was devoted to him. They had no children. PCR/GW/VL

[Photo]

McLAREN, John Watt *b.*26 Nov 1906 *d.*28 Oct 1982
MRCS LRCP (1931) MA Cantab (1932) DMRE (1935)
MRCP (1951) FFR (1951) MRCPE (1962) FRCP (1963)
FRCPE (1972)

John Watt McLaren was born in Essex to parents with engineering interests. He was educated at Cheltenham College, Caius College at Cambridge, and St Thomas's Hospital. He took up diagnostic radiology and became head of that department at St Thomas's Hospital, which he managed very successfully until his retirement in 1971. He moved in the higher reaches of his specialty, which earned him the College's recognition in an honorary MRCP in 1951 and a fellowship in 1963. He was a solitary bachelor with a somewhat discouraging and gloomy manner that prevented his talents from bearing the fruit that would have been expected. JBH

[*Brit. med. J.*, 1982, **285**, 1750]

McLAUGHLIN, Arthur Ivan Granville *b.*1 Jan 1896 *d.*23 Oct 1983
MB ChM Sydney (1920) MRCP (1932) MD (1950) FRCP (1950)

AIG McLaughlin ('Mac' to his many friends) was born in Sydney, New South Wales, the son of William Henry McLaughlin of the New South Wales Mounted Police. He went to school in Sydney and then joined the Australian Army, where he saw service in Egypt during World War I. Returning to university in Sydney he qualified in medicine (with honours) in 1920. After his house jobs he joined the RAAMC and served for a year with the army of occupation in New Guinea.

He came to the United Kingdom in 1922 and did house jobs at the Hampstead General Hospital and the Victoria Park Chest Hospital before joining the tuberculosis department at St Thomas's, where he worked until 1930, becoming chief assistant and submitting a series of articles on clinical and physiological aspects of chest disease. Having obtained the Dorothy Temple Cross research fellowship in 1930 he visited the United States where he met Leroy Gardner at Saranac Lake. This lit the fire of his enthusiasm for occupational chest diseases. He then spent some time at the Laënnec Hospital in Paris which gave him a familiarity with European medicine and a facility in French which he kept for the rest of his life. On his return he joined the medical unit at UCH until 1934.

This thorough grounding in chest medicine was an ideal preparation for his career in occupational medicine. He joined HM Medical Inspectorate of Factories in 1934 and was posted to Leeds. There two life long associations were made. He met his wife Rose, the daughter of BP Viret, the examining surgeon for Bradford. He also met the superintendent of Oakwood Sanatorium, AT Doig, who later joined him in the medical inspectorate. Individually and in partnership they added lustre to the study of occupational chest disease, particularly among welders and foundry workers.

There was no greater authority on occupational chest disease than Mac and it was a pleasure to sit at his feet and hear him deal with cases. His precision in taking an occupational history, his careful clinical examination of the chest and his skill at interpreting radiological signs were models of thoroughness and insight. There was no room for observer error when Mac looked at an X-ray.

He was superficially irascible and forthright in his criticisms. He had a slight impediment in his speech which became more pronounced when he was annoyed by shoddy work, unjustified criticism or just mere apathy. He did not get on well with his chief, ERA Merewether, who, I think, resented Mac's status in the professional world of occupational chest disease, in which Merewether thought himself to be the master.

Expert as he was in all forms of occupational chest disease, it was to foundry workers that he gave the best of himself. He was the principal author of the classic work on the subject *Industrial Lung Diseases of Iron and Steel Foundry Workers*. This and all his other publications are characterized by a rare clarity and lucidity. His competence as a writer as well as an expert in occupational disease was recognized by Sir Theodore Fox, editor of the *Lancet*, in which he wrote numerous editorials.

He never ceased to be an enthusiast, not only in his chosen profession, but in his hobbies such as antiques, ceramics, silver and wines. In these enthusiasms, as with all his other activities, he was staunchly supported by his wife Rose and by his family of two boys and two girls, of whom he was very proud.

He was equally proud of his membership and subsequently fellowship of the College, and was honoured by the newly created faculty of occupational medicine by being created a fellow by distinction.

Having left the Medical Inspectorate, he joined Donald Hunter's unit at the London Hospital where he had freedom to talk, investigate and teach. In his later years he became a formidable expert witness and was used by HM Treasury in all the cases of asbestos-related disease arising in the Royal Navy dockyards. As in everything else he was a stickler for the truth, even though he was naturally concerned to do the best he could for a sick worker. In pneumoconiosis he had no peer, but there were some who thought that his expertise in such matters as cancer of the bladder was of a lower order. It was his expert evidence which swung the judge in favour of Wright and Cassidy against Dunlop and ICI, a *cause celèbre* whose reverberations are still felt in the rubber and chemical industries.

As befits an Australian he had played tennis to a high standard and even got to Wimbledon in the 1920s. He was a member of the United Hospitals tennis team.

Above all he was a loving father and a true friend and his name will be remembered wherever pneumoconiosis, especially among foundrymen, is discussed. RM(2)

[*Brit. med. J.*, 1983, **286**, 485-486; *Lancet*, 1983, **2**, 1410; Photo]

McLEAN, Andrew Sinclair *b*.26 Mar 1919 *d*.27 July 1981
CBE (1975) MB ChB Edin (1943) DIH (1948) FRCP (1975)
FFOM (1979) Hon MD Edin (1981)

Andrew McLean was born in Edinburgh, his father, Andrew

McLean, having been a manager with the Bank of Scotland. He was educated at George Watson's College in Edinburgh and at the Forres Academy in Morayshire before entering Edinburgh University whence he graduated in medicine in 1943. He was house surgeon at the Royal Northern Infirmary, Inverness in that year, and then served as a captain RAMC from 1943 to 1946. After a year in general practice, he took his Diploma in Industrial Health and entered the field of occupational medicine and radiation protection, to which he was to contribute so much. He was appointed as medical officer to the Department of Atomic Energy of the Ministry of Supply at its Springfields works in Preston in 1948, and continued with that department, and with its successor in the United Kingdom Atomic Energy Authority, until 1971, becoming director of the Health and Safety Branch of its Industrial Group in 1957, and director of Health and Safety of the Authority itself in 1959.

This was a formative period in the development both of the theoretical and of the practical aspects of industrial radiation protection in this country. Andrew's breadth of scientific reading and interests, his feel for the essentials of occupational medicine, and his profound commonsense and wisdom enabled him to play an increasingly important part in establishing the principles and practice of this complex discipline. He collaborated easily and perceptively with colleagues in allied fields of work, developed strong teams of assistants, and was able to plan and supervise the safety of workers, in their varied and difficult workplaces, soundly and with foresight. At the time of the accidental release of radionuclides from an overheated Windscale reactor in 1957, his advice to the Authority and to Government ensured that appropriate actions could be taken on the basis of detailed and quantitative assessments of the environmental contamination, and of the most important effects of the accident and the counter measures available.

In 1971, the National Radiological Protection Board was set up, to keep the whole field of radiation exposure under review, and to advise government and industry generally on secure methods and criteria of radiation protection. As its first director, Andrew McLean had the qualities to ensure the Board's rapid development as a source of authoritative, objective and practical guidance on radiation protection in its various aspects; he had wide knowledge of the effects of ionising radiation, familiarity with new data and a sound assessment of their strength or weaknesses, and the capacity to foresee the needs for investigation or consideration of emerging problems. He had close contacts in the fields of radiation hygiene internationally, and his opinion was constantly valued in Europe and across the Atlantic. He was a member of the International Commission on Radiological Protection from 1969 to 1977, and of the World Health Organization's Expert Advisory Panel on Radiation. He worked on the Euratom Group of experts responsible for advising on basic safety standards; and on its Scientific and Technical Committee. At home he was a member of the Medical Research Council's Committee on Protection Against Ionising Radiation, and of the Radioactive

Substances Advisory Committee.

He was appointed CBE in 1975. His election to the fellowship of the College came in the same year, and to that of the Faculty of Occupational Medicine in 1979. The conferment of an honorary doctorate of medicine by his own University of Edinburgh in 1981 gave him great pleasure.

He married Christine, daughter of Colonel James Allen Mackintosh, TD FEIS, of Inverness in 1943, and they had two daughters. His home and his family meant a great deal to him and his warm and generous personality touched a wide circle of his friends and colleagues. EEP

[*Times,* 31 July 1981; *Brit. med. J.,* 1981, **283**, 624; *Lancet,* 1981, **2**, 376; Photo]

MacLENNAN, *Sir* **Hector (Ross)** *b.*1 Nov 1905 *d.*6 Jan 1978
Kt (1965) MB ChB Glasg (1928) MD (1932) FRFPS (1942)
FRCOG (1948) FRCPG (1964) FRCP* (1973) Hon FRCSE (1967)
Hon MMSA (1968) Hon FRCPS (1971) Hon LLD Glasg (1974)

Hector MacLennan was born in Glasgow. He was educated in that city, first at the High School and then at the University and, except for one year's residence at Chelsea Hospital for Women, he spent all his professional life there, becoming consultant obstetrician at the Glasgow Maternity Hospital and consultant gynaecologist at the Victoria Hospital.

Even as an undergraduate his qualities of leadership and his ability to impress his fellows were noted, when he was elected president of the University Union. He qualified at the age of 23, passed the MRCOG examination four years later, and only two years after that was appointed to the staff at the early age of 29. At this time he delivered the Blair Bell Lecture on the subject of contracted pelvis, a condition then often encountered in Glasgow.

He served as a representative of the members on the Council of the RCOG from 1941 to 1947, and was elected a fellow in 1948. His service on many College committees culminated in his election as president in 1963 – 1966. To this office he brought a fine presence and an excellent speaking manner, with a slight and pleasant Scottish accent. He was tall and broad, so that he seemed to stoop a little when speaking to anyone of less height, and a fine head of white hair set off his dark eyes and wide smiling mouth. His memory for faces and names was astonishing, and he was a shrewd judge of men and affairs. He was cautious in decision, and always courteous and persuasive in securing consensus. During his term of office as president he travelled widely, visiting nearly every country in the Commonwealth, and he gave the Joseph Price oration in the United States. Appropriately for a Scottish president, he delivered the JY Simpson oration in the RCOG.

He was a most skilful surgeon, and as an obstetrician he earned the complete confidence of his patients in a large practice. He taught his students and assistants by his example rather than any scientific originality, but many young men fell under his spell, and many

Scottish consultants owe their early training to him. As an external examiner he was much in demand, serving at Oxford, Cambridge, Newcastle, Edinburgh, Dundee and Aberdeen.

Hector, as he was universally and affectionately known, was knighted in 1965, and many other honours came to him, including honorary fellowships of the RCS Edinburgh, the RFPS Glasgow, and the American College of O and G, and he received the honorary degree of LLD from Glasgow University. But above all he took pride and pleasure in his appointment as High Commissioner to the Assembly of the Church of Scotland, when his fine bearing as the representative of the Queen was widely noted.

His service to medicine did not end with his presidency; he was a member of the GMC 1965–1969, president of the RSM 1967–1969, and he held the difficult post of chairman of the Advisory Committee on Distinction Awards 1971–1974, once again travelling much, but now through Britain. He served as chairman of an advisory committee on problems of tissue transplantation.

As a keen angler and shot he was an appropriate chairman of the Scottish Tourist Board 1969–1974, and in any Scottish hotel the deference with which he was received was almost as much on account of this office as of that of High Commissioner.

He married Isabel Adam, a Glasgow medical graduate, in 1933 and they had three sons and a daughter. After the death of Isabel in 1973, who herself became widely known in the gynaecological world, in 1976 he married Jean Leckie, who had been his personal assistant for 30 years. He spent his last years in Rogart in the Highlands, where he died. SC

[*Times*, 9 & 19 Jan 1978; *Brit. med. J.*, 1978, **1**, 181, 249; *Lancet*, 1978, **1**, 165; Photo]

MacLEOD, William Mathieson *b*.30 Sept 1911 *d*.21 Sept 1977
MBE (Mil) MRCS LRCP (1934) MB BS Lond (1934) MRCP (1937) FRCP (1962)

Bill MacLeod was honorary consultant general and thoracic physician at Southampton. He was born in London, the son of William MacLeod MC MD, a physician, and his wife Elizabeth, daughter of John Forbes, a general merchant. He was educated at Inverness Royal Academy, Merchant Taylor's School, and St Thomas's Hospital where he graduated in 1934. After house appointments at St Thomas's, the London Chest Hospital and Southend General Hospital, he was called up from the reserve to become medical specialist in the 13th casualty clearing station. He was captured in France in 1940 and for the next five years served as a medical officer in POW camps in Poland. He was very reticent about this period of his life, but for his outstanding services and inspiring example he was awarded the MBE.

On demobilization in 1945, he returned to medical posts at St Thomas's, the National Heart, and Brompton Hospitals. In 1946, illness, which had its origins in wartime hardships, forced him to rest but by 1947 he was back in harness, attaining consultant status at St Thomas's as tuberculosis officer, a post he held until September 1951. He was also medical assistant and registrar at the Brompton, with JG Scadding, until he was appointed consultant physician at the Southampton Chest (now Western) Hospital. Together with EF Chin, he developed a thoracic service in Southampton which rapidly became the centre of excellence of thoracic medicine in the Wessex region. He had the highest standards of clinical care; his wide experience and sound judgement made his opinion much sought after and his weekly clinical meetings became a great attraction. He initiated the annual clinical meetings at the Chest Hospital which are now a permanent feature of Wessex medical life, attended by many physicians and surgeons with wide specialist interests. He gave generous support to the new Southampton Medical School and cooperated in the integration of new academic interests and clinical services, taking on responsibility for a general medical firm, in addition to the thoracic service, to facilitate the process.

Bill MacLeod's published work exemplified the best in clinical research. His account of unilateral hypertransradiancy of the lungs – MacLeod's syndrome – will be remembered, but his later papers on alimentary tuberculosis and pulmonary fibrosis are equally authoritative. He became president of the Thoracic Society in 1975. In 1976 Southampton University bestowed on him its first honorary doctorate of medicine, an honour which gave him special pleasure.

In 1940 Bill married Margaret, daughter of Frederick Leonard Bell, a civil engineer. They had two children: a son and a daughter. Both his wife and children are doctors. Bill was very much a family man, and in recent years derived great pleasure from playing the 'cello as part of a family group. He spoke occasionally of the great happiness of his marriage and family life, but never of the five years of enforced separation. He delighted in his home, and the garden that he fashioned with such knowledge and hard work. He had a fine sense of humour, and pomposity did not survive long in his presence. GW/VL

[*Brit. med. J.*, 1977, **2**, 962; *Lancet,* 1977, **2**, 833; Photo]

McMENEMEY, William Henry *b.*16 May 1905 *d.*24 Nov 1977
MRCS LRCP (1929) BM BCh Oxon (1930) MA (1930)
MRCP (1932) DM (1933) DPM Eng (1935) FRCP (1948)
FRCPath (1964) FRCPsych (1971)

William McMenemey, the son of William Henry McMenemey and his wife, Frances Annie Rankin, was educated at Birkenhead School, Merton College, Oxford, and St Bartholomew's Hospital, where he graduated in 1929. He was house physician to Lord Horder, but already the example of AG Gibson (*Munk's Roll* IV p.530) had convinced McMenemey that pathology in a clinical atmosphere would be his bent. He held a junior demonstratorship in pathology at St Bartholomew's, and then for a short while was pathologist at the Napsbury and Shenley Psychiatric Hospital at St Albans; here it was he realized his particular interest was to be in neuropathology, and he maintained that he was the only pathologist with a DPM. Accordingly he held a clinical registrarship in neurology at the Maida Vale Hospital, and then was appointed assistant pathologist to that remarkable character WE Carnegie Dickson (1878 – 1954) at the West End Hospital for Nervous Diseases. It was from this hospital, in 1933, that McMenemey published his first paper, significantly on familial presenile dementia, for he was to become a leading authority on cerebral degenerative diseases; it was written jointly with Charles Worster-Drought (1888 – 1971), with whom he was to enjoy clinical collaboration over many years.

In 1937 McMenemey went to the Radcliffe Infirmary as assistant clinical pathologist to his Oxford teacher, Dr Gibson, and had the good fortune to learn something of Spanish neurohistological techniques, as del Rio Hortega, a refugee from the civil war, was neuropathologist to Sir Hugh Cairns. In 1940 McMenemey became pathologist to the Worcester Royal Infirmary and spent nine happy years transforming rather elementary laboratory facilities into a first-class pathology department, meeting the needs of general practitioners and hospitals, both civil and military; this was largely modelled on the transformation that had taken place in Oxford, where the laboratories of a provincial county hospital became a major university department, with regional integration under the aegis of the Nuffield Provincial Hospitals Trust. However, in the field of laboratory work, neuropathology was McMenemey's real love, and in 1949 he was invited to return to Maida Vale Hospital as pathologist. His contributions to the subject were recognized in 1965, with his appointment as professor of pathology at the Institute of Neurology. His particular interest continued to be the pathology of dementia, for which his laboratory became a reference centre for the South of England. It was characteristic of his encouraging enthusiasm that so many of his papers were written jointly, drawing in younger colleagues as well as his clinical associates, but in addition he contributed to Greenfield's *Neuropathology* (1959,1963) and the section on 'Diseases of the Nervous System' in Wright and Symmers *Systemic Pathology* (1960).

Though McMenemey's contributions to neuropathological knowledge were considerable, his greatest achievement was his ability to inspire his young trainees with a delight in the subject, and reveal to neurologists in training the value of an appreciation of the tissue changes in nervous disorders; certainly the weekly seminars he conducted at Maida Vale with his clinical colleagues were one of the most popular postgraduate exercises in the Institute of Neurology.

It was indeed his contributions in collegiation that have left their greatest mark on pathology. He had joined the Association of Clinical Pathologists in 1935, was soon serving on council, and was secretary from 1943 to 1957, a most significant period in the transformation of the Association into the scientific and educational body that it is today. The Association had been founded by Sidney Dyke, an exuberant Canadian in Wolverhampton who was always ready with a biblical quotation to confound his adversaries, yet on occasions his verbosity might engender disquiet, if not distrust; then it was that McMenemey with his gentle charm and wit, which concealed a singleness of purpose, would smooth any ruffled feelings and allow the major issues to be resolved.

It was also Dyke and McMenemey who were the leading spirits in efforts to help refugee pathologists from occupied Europe to find work in our laboratories; these men and women realized that clinical pathology 'à l'anglais' was a concept unknown outside the British Isles, but something that could with advantage be fostered elsewhere. Out of a desire to perpetuate this understanding arose the Association of Societies of Pathology, at first called 'European', then 'International' and now 'World'. McMenemey worked hard and enthusiastically at the administrative and integrative aspects of this idealistic body, often troubled with national differences as to the meaning of 'clinical pathology' and the purpose of their congresses; one of the last tasks on which he was engaged and which he finished just three weeks before his death, was a history of this association.

A less wayward body in whose genesis McMenemey played a large part was the International Society of Neuropathologists, which held its first congress in 1952, evolving from the neuropathology clubs established by Armando Ferraro in the USA in 1925 and JG Greenfield in this country in 1950.

It was natural that McMenemey's contributions in these fields were recognized by his election to the presidency and fellowship of numerous professional bodies at home and abroad, which he repaid by delivering masterly and thought provoking addresses, for his fondness for foreign travel, combined with his unassuming bonhomie and wit, rendered him an ever welcome delegate to pathological meetings.

When McMenemey left Oxford for Worcester in 1940, Gibson suggested that he should look into the life of John Wall (1708 – 1776), one time fellow of his own college of Merton and founder of the Worcester Porcelain Factory; from this arose McMenemey's considerable contributions to medical history, which latterly became his main interest.

In 1947 his authoritative *History of the Worcester Royal Infirmary* appeared, and consequent upon this were studies on Charles Hastings, Alexander Philip and the hospital movement of the 18th century. In his last years he was compiling a study of Worcestershire doctors and had completed a detailed account of Sir Charles Throckmorton, MD. However, McMenemey's historical interests were not restricted to the West Midlands; there was a volume commemorating the bicentenary of James Parkinson (1955), various studies of medicine in the 19th century, while his last published paper considered life and death in Shakespeare's London.

McMenemey was always immaculately dressed, favouring a bowtie, and his unassuming manner concealed a determination which could be quite immovable, for his standards were high, but it was his consideration for his junior colleagues and anyone in need of assistance and encouragement that was his outstanding characteristic.

Apart from literary and historic pursuits, he enjoyed gardening and music, being a pianist of some competence. Ill health caused his early retirement at the end of 1969 and his activities were restricted for the last seven years of his life, but he received wonderful support from his wife, Robina Inkster, also a physician, whose loyal affection and loving care continued to sustain him as they had done throughout his career. They had a son and a daughter. AHTR-S

[*Brit. med. J.*, 1977, **2**, 1551; *Lancet*, 1977, **2**, 1239; Photo]

McROBERT, *Sir* George (Reid) *b*.21 Jan 1895 *d*.6 June 1976
Kt (1947) CIE (1942) MB BCh Aber (1917) MD (1923)
MRCP (1923) DTM&H (1924) FRCP (1935) Hon FRCPE (1969)

George McRobert, son of Alexander Taylor McRobert, a company director, and his wife Isabella Ogilvie, daughter of James Reid, a bookseller, was born in Aberdeen. He was educated at Robert Gordon's College and the University of Aberdeen, where he graduated with honours in 1917. Immediately after qualifying he held a temporary commission in the RAMC, and saw active service in France and Mesopotamia. He was then granted a permanent commission in the Indian Medical Service, serving in the Waziristan campaign before transferring to the civil side in 1925. From 1922 to 1924 he was on study leave in England and during this time took the MRCP and the diploma in tropical medicine and hygiene, and also proceeded MD.

Returning to Burma in 1925, he was appointed professor of physiology and pharmacology to the newly founded University of Rangoon. The medical college was a residential establishment in which he held the additional post of medical warden. Although his duties left little time for research, he wrote on electrocardiographic changes during emetine therapy, on the pH of the alimentary tract in rats, and on the histology of the spleen in stress. For the last three years of this period he was secretary of the Burma branch of the BMA. In 1930 he reverted to clinical work as district medical officer in Maymyo, and in 1933 he returned to Europe to undertake further advanced medical studies. He was appointed professor of medicine at the medical college in Madras in 1934, and was also senior physician at Madras General Hospital, being elected a fellow of this College in 1935. During the ensuing nine years he established a reputation as an authority on tropical medicine and as a teacher of exceptional ability. He contributed valuable papers on smallpox and typhus, and on relapsing and cerebrospinal fevers. He also demonstrated the great value of iron in the treatment of the severe anaemia associated with hookworm disease, and participated in an important study of endemic fluorosis in South India. In recognition of his outstanding services in Madras he was appointed a CIE in 1942. During the second world war a proposal that he be appointed consultant physician to the Army in India was vetoed by the Madras Government, on the grounds of his indispensibility. He was promoted colonel on appointment as inspector general of civil hospitals in Bihar Province, a post which he held until he retired from India. He was knighted in 1947.

After his retirement from the IMS in 1951 he was appointed consultant physician to the Hospital for Tropical Diseases, London, a post he held until he retired in 1961. He was medical adviser to the Secretary of State for Commonwealth Relations from 1958–1962, and was previously consulting physician to the Colonial Office. For ten years he served on the governing body of University College Hospital, and was also a member of the governing council of Epsom College. From 1961 to 1963 he was president of the Royal Society of Tropical Medicine and Hygiene.

George McRobert was a man of absolute integrity who enjoyed the respect of all who knew him. He was unfailingly courteous, helpful, and loyal to his friends and colleagues, but never hesitated to express his firmly held convictions in forthright terms. He was famous for his outspoken book reviews, and also made valuable contributions to the *British Encyclopaedia of Surgical Practice* (1948) and to the 6th edition of Rogers' and Megaw's *Tropical Medicine* (1952).

He married Catherine Ellen, daughter of George Thomas Cooper Gregory, an engineer, in 1919. His wife died in 1969 and his son, Ronald, died in 1944 while a medical student. One of his two daughters is also a doctor. His leisure interests included golf, tennis and walking. GW/VL

[*Brit. med. J.,* 1976, **2**, 706 & 889; *Lancet,* 1976, **1**, 1420; *Times,* 10 June 1976; Photo]

MAIZELS, Montague *b*.30 Sept 1899 *d*.10 Feb 1976
MRCS LRCP (1920) MB BS Lond (1922) MD (1923) MRCP (1925) FRCP (1941) FRS (1961)

Montague Maizels, affectionately known as 'Monty', was the youngest of four children and the only boy. His father, Joseph Maizels, was a silversmith who had emigrated from Prague and settled in London, and his mother, Deborah, was one of the nine children of Rabbi Nakum Lipman, a distinguished Hebrew scholar and teacher. Monty was born in London and spent most of his childhood in Whitechapel, close to the very successful jewellery business established by his father and mother. He was a sensitive boy and hated the period he spent at a boarding school in Bedford between the ages of 7 and 9 years. The rest of his schooldays were spent at the Davenant Foundation School close to his home, where he made good progresss and formed stimulating friendships. Among his school friends was Samson Wright, who was destined to become not only a renowned professor of physiology at the Middlesex Hospital Medical School but also the husband of his sister Miriam. Two of his cousins, Walter Levitt and BS Nisse, were doctors.

Shortly after his seventeenth birthday he entered University College to study medicine, transferring to Guy's Hospital Medical School for his clinical training in 1917. He had a distinguished undergraduate career, being awarded the Beaney prize for pathology in 1919 and the

Treasurers' medal for medicine the following year. He qualified in 1920, and in 1922 graduated MB BS with a distinction in medicine. He became house surgeon, house physician and medical registrar at his teaching hospital, and obtained his MD in 1923.

His scientific inclinations led to his being drawn towards laboratory work, and while at Guy's he also held demonstratorships in the departments of pathology and physiology. It was during this period that he first embarked on studies of the chemical basis of the biophysical properties of the erythrocyte, which became his life-long research interest. In 1928 Monty was appointed clinical pathologist to the Infants' Hospital, Westminster, and there made detailed studies of the acid-base and electrolyte disturbances that accompany diarrhoea and vomiting in infancy; his findings led to considerable improvement in the management of infantile diarrhoea and congenital pyloric stenosis. In 1931 he was appointed clinical pathologist to University College Hospital where, in addition to responsibility for all routine laboratory investigations, he assumed a teaching commitment. He continued to make time for research, and carried out fundamental work on erythrocyte metabolism which had important implications for the development of techniques for the storage of blood for transfusion purposes. He was the first to show that a slightly acid medium favours red cell preservation, and he directed attention to the importance of glucose for the same purpose. He was also the first person to follow *in vivo* the chemical changes that take place in stored red cells after transfusion. Because of his expertise he was called upon to set up the Emergency Blood Transfusion Depot at Maidstone before the outbreak of hostilities in 1939. He directed all work there until 1945, and studied various practical problems that arose from the use of stored blood.

Monty's return to University College Hospital after the war coincided with an explosive growth in the demand for pathology investigations of all kinds, and he delegated responsibility for the day-to-day running of the routine microbiology and chemical pathology services, so that he could concentrate on haematology and maintain the impetus of his research. His experimental work on the transport of ions across the red cell membrane was prosecuted with the utmost vigour, in a tiny laboratory with most meagre resources. Throughout his career a steady stream of papers resulted from his investigative work, many being published in the *Biochemical Journal*, the *Lancet*, the *Quarterly Journal of Experimental Physiology* and the *Journal of Physiology*. In recognition of his contributions to the advancement of pathology he was appointed to a readership in clinical pathology in the medical school shortly after his return, after the war, and promotion to a professorship followed in 1951. He had been made FRCP in 1941 but what naturally gave him the greatest satisfaction was his election to the fellowship of the Royal Society in 1961.

As a researcher Monty was completely absorbed in his work, and when he retired in 1964 he managed to persuade his friend Sir Bernard Katz to provide him with a laboratory in the department of biophysics at University College, where he carried on working for another 10 years. Only those privileged to have been his research assistant know how hard he worked, and how able he was both intellectually and technically. His experiments were meticulously planned, and executed with remarkable precision, using the simplest of apparatus, often home-made. Results were always critically reviewed, and only when he was satisfied that they were completely reproducible would conclusions be drawn. His mind was always ahead of that of his young collaborators, and none could compete with him when it came to performing mental arithmetic.

Monty was an excellent and popular teacher. He prepared his lectures on his portable typewriter but when he delivered them they were enriched by never-to-be-forgotten stories. In the laboratory he gave demonstrations and tutorials to small groups of students, giving them an insight into what was involved when even a simple investigation was requested. His postgraduate trainees were encouraged to learn by practice rather than by reading, and were taught to become critical and self-reliant.

As a man Monty was modest and retiring. He despised lifemanship and unnecessary fuss and regarded administrative duties as a chore. Despite his friendly manner he shunned congresses and social occasions. He had a marvellous sense of humour but when roused could be formidable. He was widely read, enjoyed poetry, and got great pleasure from using an apt word or phrase. He had a wonderful memory which enabled him to quote long passages from the scriptures learnt in his childhood. He took a deep personal interest in his staff and acted as counsellor and friend to all of them. He had a great feeling of compassion towards the less fortunate members of society, and anyone who was a refugee or who had a physical handicap was sure of being given a helping hand. He had no real hobby but he enjoyed his pipe, classical music and English ballads and, in his younger days, walking in the Lake District and Wales.

He first met Dulcie, the daughter of John William Speight, a Yorkshire farmer, when on holiday in 1937 on the Sussex coast, only to discover later that she was a staff nurse at University College Hospital. They married the following year and lived in Hampstead. During the war Dulcie Maizels took an active part in the work at the Maidstone Blood Transfusion Depot, but on their return to London she devoted herself to providing Monty with a comfortable home, which meant a great deal to him. They had one daughter, Judith, who was born in 1947. FVF

[*Biogr. Mem. roy. Soc.*, 1977, **23**, 345-366; *Lancet*, 1976, **1**, 548; *Brit. med. J.*, 1976, **1**, 842; *Times*, 25 Feb 1976; Photo]

MALLESON, Nicolas Borrell *b.*30 Oct 1923 *d.*3 June 1976
MB BChir Cantab (1945) MA (1950) MRCP (1950) MD (1957) FRCP (1973)

Born in Surrey of the actor Miles Malleson and Joan, his doctor wife, Nic, as he was regularly called in adult life, savoured luxury and was exposed to severe privations from very early years. Indulgent nannies, boarding school by the age of three years, the recurrently agonizing sound of his father's retreating footsteps after leaving him at school; these belonged to the network of his experience. Henry Walton MD FRCPE FRCPsych writes movingly of Malleson's early life in *Students in Need: a collection of essays in memory of Nicolas Malleson* (1978). In the same book is a paper written by Malleson the medical student, more than thirty years earlier. His hopes for his future may well have seemed naive at the time but many of them came to pass: sophisticated group practices in general medicine, highly equipped health centres fully financed by the State.

He did not then foresee the growth of student health services, but it was as physician-in-charge of the Student Health Association of University College London, in 1949, that he began his life's work in that field, having previously been medical registrar at the Ipswich Group Hospitals, medical officer to RAFVR (UK and India), and house physician at the West Middlesex Hospital. In student health practice he proved himself a natural leader. Impulsive often to the point of rashness, he was nevertheless clear-sighted and far thinking, quickly earning for himself the respect, not only of leading administrators at UCH, but also of the University of London, of London medical schools, and of the vice-chancellor's committee, thereby extending his influence throughout the country. This culminated in his appointment to the Social and Preventive Medicine Committee of the Royal College of Physicians, on which he served from 1965–1970. As much as anyone, he was responsible for an ensuing report from a sub-committee on student health in 1966, which became something of a charter in the development of student health services in this country, and was complemented by Malleson's slim *Handbook of Student Health Services* (1965), which is a classic. In its 88 pages he succeeds in including sophisticated essays on the influence of emotional factors on achievement in university education, on the treatment of pre-examination strain, and on his ecological concept in student health practice in Britain. The latter was based on his work for his doctorate in 1957. Such was the range of the man.

By that year, 1965, he had already been five years in charge of another health centre, that of the Central Institutions of the University of London. This had freelance beginnings, having been built piecemeal by Malleson after his return from Australia in 1960. Very little is known about his venture into Australian University health practice. He was disappointed, both he and his wife seem to have been unhappy there, and it looks as if he was glad to accept support from university authorities there for the family's return to this country. He had left UCH in 1959 and was back in this country building another practice in 1960. By autumn that year he was covering the health of students at the School of Slavonic Studies, the School of African and Oriental Studies, and at Birkbeck College. He worked at an address on the west side of Woburn Square. These were difficult days, for he had to provide any medicines that he used out of his own funds, or by private prescription for which the patient paid, or by relying more than he liked on hospital casualty departments. Naturally, students who were already patients of other doctors could be counselled and referred back. But, as always, most of the needy ones were not registered under the NHS in London; any medical contact they had once had was far removed. Malleson, from the start, had a campaigning interest in catering for waifs and strays of this kind.

Matters improved when he succeeded to a NHS practice vacancy through death of a practitioner located at No 1 Woburn Square, on the east side. From then on he went from strength to strength. His detailed curriculum vitae, lodged at 20 Gower Street, lists seventeen sundry appointments, scholarships and fellowships in this country and in the USA. Few people knew of his work as Borough Councillor for St Pancras from 1946 – 1949, or of his Senior Fulbright scholarship in the department of mental hygiene at the University of Michigan in 1952. Much better known was his work as founder chairman of the Society for Research into Higher Education, now at the University of Surrey, and his membership of HM Government Standing Advisory Committee on Drug Dependence. He was a pioneer in the teaching of counselling. He was not schooled in psychoanalysis, but had had some personal experience of it, and consistently geared his short courses in counselling to analytic concepts and to human biological development.

Among his professional disappointments were the working parties which he convened from 1962 onwards for the promotion of a School of Medicine and Human Biology, which were abandoned after 1966; also Educational Redeployment Service Limited, which ceased functioning after a few years for lack of funds. His hope had been of a country-wide network of agencies interested in studying young people's difficulties.

Nicolas Malleson came of highly creative stock. His mother, Joan Graeme, was the daughter of James Bilson, a company director. She became a historic innovator in the field of gynaecological problem solutions, including her own teaching of contraceptive techniques. His father, Miles, was an actor and dramatist of considerable fame. Parents as eccentric as his were not easy to live with, and Nic seems rarely to have been at ease with them or within himself. At the same time he set himself parallel high standards for initiating change. Anyone who could tolerate his exasperating impatience and a degree of superficiality, which was the inevitable consequence of his having so many irons in the fire at one time, fell under the spell of his lovableness. He was easily hurt, not only by spitefulness but also by discovery of mistakes. Where others learned from mistakes, he tended to withdraw and work his way in a different direction. Sometimes he suffered acutely from finding himself thrust out of a concern which he had worked hard to establish. Malleson could be awkwardly rebellious and committees would be as relieved to see him go as they would be sad to miss the penetration of his thinking, the embrace of his warm-heartedness.

In the early 1950s he was in the vanguard of those who were prepared to educate young men and women in methods of contraception and made no secret of the fact. He was hurt by the obscurantism of some of his colleagues, and not easily able to allow for the genuine doubts of others. However, wounds heal and he would almost certainly have persisted had he not been smitten by the death of his elder daughter, Sarah; killed tragically as the carefree pillion passenger on a boyfriend's motor cycle. Those closest to him knew that he had never really recovered from depression following his mother's death by drowning at sea, some years previously. The blows were intolerable. Even so, his last message to his colleagues, over the telephone three days before he died was: 'Tell the Annual Conference that I am not sulking. I am tired. I hope to rejoin you all next year with my wife, for at least part of the conference then'.

His wife had been Jane Mary Owen, daughter of Colonel Owen Tucker OBE, an engineer. She met him first when she was a new girl at Dartington Hall Public School, where he was already a pupil. She survived him with three of their five children: Peter and Stephen had already become doctors, Kate was 13 when their father died. His body was found in his car in Gateforth Street, a little north of Marylebone railway station. At a subsequent inquest, Gavin Thurston FRCP declared an open verdict: death was said to be due to alcohol and barbiturates, self-administered, with insufficient evidence of motivation. AHW

[*Times*, 19 June 1976; *Brit. med. J.*, 1976, **2**, 50]

MALLEY, Brendan Joseph *b*.12 Mar 1912 *d*.23 Oct 1982
MBE (1945) MB BCh BAO NUI (1935) DPH (1940) MD (1940) MRCP (1939) FRCP (1972)

Brendan Malley was born in Dublin, the son of Luke and Marion Malley. He was educated at Belvedere College and University College, Dublin. His high academic promise as a schoolboy was maintained as a medical student and, having won most of the undergraduate prizes, he graduated with first class honours in all subjects. During his house physicianship at the Mater Hospital, Dublin, he became drawn to respiratory diseases and particularly to the challenges of the treatment of pulmonary tuberculosis. These interests were developed at the Grosvenor Sanatorium, Ashford, Kent, where he worked until the outbreak of war, cooperating enthusiastically with many leaders in the field of pulmonary tuberculosis. His association with Laurence O'Shaughnessy initiated his interest in surgical treatment and a friendship was kindled which lasted until O'Shaughnessy was killed in the early days of the war.

Malley was one of a family whose contribution to the Irish national cause in the 1920s had become legendary for feats of daring and valour. However, as a young man, his interests were intellectual and far removed from nationalism and politics. When the Anschluss in Austria was on everyone's lips and other rumblings of aggression grew louder, he insisted that war was a solution to nothing and another world conflagration an impossibility. He was daunted by the outbreak of war, yet felt his contribution was in service with the Royal Army

Medical Corps. Despite his family tradition of courage in battle, Malley was the least bellicose of men. Yet he served in the North African and Italian campaigns and set standards of competence and efficiency that were recognized by the award of the MBE.

On demobilization, he was appointed consultant physician in chest diseases at St Olave's Hospital, the Bermondsey Chest Clinic, and later to the Guy's group of hospitals. At that time, tuberculosis was rampant and as the chest clinic grew to vast proportions, Malley's unobstrusive yet incisive energy made the Bermondsey health centre a model of effective outpatient and domiciliary treatment.

Malley had a large circle of acquaintances and a select coterie of friends. With one of these, Raymond Bautock, he trod the Pilgrim's Way from Winchester to Canterbury. Between them they identified every furlong of the route, eagerly studied Erasmus's 1514 description of Becket's shrine and dutifully celebrated the two festivals of the pilgrimage, the day of the martyrdom and the day of the translation of Becket's body to the tomb beneath the shrine in the Trinity chapel.

Coupled with his literary interests, he was a cook of some ability, and his wide knowledge of French wines led to his election to the Saintsbury Club.

In his retirement he had the ill fortune of being struck by a hit and run driver and sustained injuries which eventually caused his death. He was unmarried. WS

[*Brit. med. J.*, 1982, **285**, 1752; 1983, **286**, 72]

MALLICK, Sher Mohammad Khan *b.*22 Jan 1900 *d.* – Apr 1979
MB BS Punjab (1924) MRCS LRCP (1926) MRCP (1927)
FRCP (1952) FCPS Pakistan (1964) Hon MD Punjab (1953)

Sher Mallick was born in Raiwind in Northern India, and his father was a land owner. He graduated from the King Edward Medical College in Lahore in 1924. After holding house posts at the Mayo Hospital, Lahore, he joined the Indian Medical Service in 1927. Having taken the MRCP, he was transferred to the medical research department of the Government of India in 1928, and soon became the assistant director of the Central Research Institute at Kasauli, where he was to work with Christopher and then with Sinton, particularly on the transmission and epidemiology of malaria. He assisted in uprating the new Glancy Medical College in Amritsar, and later became its principal and professor of medicine. Many of his students were to join the IMS and the IAMC as war-clouds gathered and then burst over India.

At the time of the partition of India, he opted for Pakistan, and soon became the principal and professor of medicine at the King Edward Medical College, Lahore. In 1952, he gained his FRCP, having the distinction of being the first Pakistani to be so elected. He had also helped in founding the new Fatima Jinnah Medical College for Women, in Lahore. He was then appointed principal and professor of medicine at the Dow Medical College in Karachi. During his term, a large number of new, young, highly trained consultants were appointed. In 1953, he was one of the speakers in a plenary session at the First World Congress of Medical Education. He became a member of the scientific advisory panel of the Ciba Foundation. In 1955, he went back to Lahore as principal of the King Edward Medical College, and in 1956 became the first director of medical services of the whole of West Pakistan. During his term in this office, he founded the Nishtar Medical College in Multan and the Liaqat Medical College in Hyderabad. In 1964, he was one of the founding fellows of the College of Physicians and Surgeons of Pakistan, and later became its senior vice-president. On retirement, he set up a medical research unit at the Sir Ganga Ram Hospital in Lahore, investigating the natural history of diabetes, hypertension and amoebiasis in West Pakistan, resulting in a number of published papers.

In spite of all these activities, he found time for cricket, shooting and gardening.

Sher Mallick had an amazing capacity for thinking big, and firing the imagination of all around him to greater deeds. There must be few fellows who have presided over the birth of four medical colleges and a research institute. He always had willing and devoted workers to help him; he asked for total loyalty, and he gave the same in return.

In 1927 he married Ivy Mary, daughter of Albert Taylor, and had a son and a daughter. RBK

[*Photo*]

MARRIOTT, Hugh Leslie *b.*6 Nov 1900 *d.*29 Jan 1983
CBE (1946) MRCS LRCP (1925) MB BS Lond (1927) MD (1929) MRCP (1930) FRCP (1938)

Hugh Marriott's life style was governed by certain distinctive qualities: he was a well coordinated driving force with a well organized mind; he was efficient and effective. He was also humorous and fairminded, with a humanity which made him a most likeable personality. His life's work revolved round the Middlesex Hospital and the Army; the Middlesex because he was educated there, qualifying in 1925 and becoming its most effective RMO and consultant physician; the Army because of an illustrious 1940 – 1945 war record.

Marriott was born in Durban, South Africa. He was the son of Samuel Augustus Marriott, a member of the firm of Russell & Marriott, accountants and notaries, and his wife, Ada Cording. He came to England and studied medicine at the Middlesex Hospital Medical School. After house appointments at St Charles Infirmary, he returned to the Middlesex as resident medical officer in 1928. This was a particularly significant time in the history of the hospital. The main block of the old hospital, which had been completed in 1848, was found to be unsafe and complete rebuilding became essential. Of the handful of people who had influence in the 1930s, Hugh Marriott contributed more than most to the rebuilding: the introduction of the unitary system of notes, the concept of placing the X-ray department at the heart of the building, the new relationships between school and hospital necessitated by the introduction of resident students, the reorganization of a central admissions systems, and many other features which are accepted as commonplace today were instituted by him in his early years of office. He succeeded Sir Robert Arthur Young as a consultant in 1936, and retired in 1966, having given his lifework to the welfare of the hospital. For a brief period he became the commandant of the Middlesex Hospital in order to put it on a wartime footing, leaving to join the RAMC in 1940 with the rank of captain, and serving with the Royal Army Medical Corps shock research unit under Colonel John Beattie in Bristol.

In 1941 he was appointed as a one man commission to report on the effects of heat stroke and sodium imbalance in the Western Desert – a report that had considerable effect on the medical care of troops fighting in tropical conditions. In his 1946 Croonian lecture on salt and water depletion he summarized the basic physiological principles on which the administration of the appropriate electrolyte fluid should be based; the lecture was published in the *BMJ*, and as a monograph in the series of *American lectures in physiology*, No 32, 1947. He also perfected the intravenous drip regulating apparatus, on which he had earlier worked with Alan Kekwick. The original equipment was complicated and cumbersome by modern standards, but it worked well and was a significant factor in facilitating the intravenous infusion of blood and other fluids. He took a leading part in performing the same service for oxygen therapy. In 1944 he was transferred as consultant physician to the Army in Burma. Again he left his mark, and many still remember not only his personal visits to their units but also his contribution in reducing the high sickness rate prevalent in the appalling conditions of the Burma jungle.

Marriott returned to the Middlesex in 1945 to put the hospital on a peacetime footing with the same superb organizing ability with which he had placed it on a wartime footing. At this stage of his life he had to choose between a university chair of medicine or a private consulting practice. He chose the later and remained at the Middlesex until his retirement. His teaching method was didactic and many generations of students will remember his ward rounds with pleasure. He would take a subject and explore it in a logical, sequential and systematic way. While he could be severe on sloppy thinking or work, he never demeaned his juniors by the use of ridicule. One might feel chastened, but not humbled. Few teachers can achieve this subtle distinction but to Marriott it came easily. It was an eloquent expression of the regard in which he was held by those who had worked for him that, upon his retirement, a large number of his former house physicians and registrars met at the Middlesex Hospital to dine and wine their former chief. His speech upon that occasion was in the true Marriott vein – short, pungent, humorous and non-pompous.

He married Alice Vida, daughter of William Cureton, veterinary surgeon, in 1930. They had no children. DGJ/RAW/GW

[*Brit. med. J.*, 1983, **286**, 811 & 1070; *Lancet*, 1983, **1**, 486-7; *Middx. Hosp. J.*, Aug 1966, **66**(4), 128-29; Photo]

MARSHALL, *Sir* **Geoffrey** *b*.23 Apr 1887 *d*.9 Aug 1982
KCVO (1951) CBE (1951) OBE (1917) MB BS Lond (1911) MD (1920) MRCP (1920) FRCP (1928) Hon FRCPI (1965)

Geoffrey Marshall died at the age of 95 years. He was physician to Guy's Hospital and the Brompton Hospital, as well as consulting physician to King Edward VII Hospital, Midhurst, and the Hospital of St John and Elizabeth.

The son of Henry Marshall of Bognor, he was educated at St Paul's School and Guy's Hospital, qualifying in 1911. He became a demonstrator in physiology and medical registrar at Guy's Hospital. When war broke out in 1914 he served in the RAMC as medical officer in France, and was in charge of the severely wounded transported by barge on the inland water transport unit. Thanks to his earlier specialization in physiology, he improvised means of administering gas and oxygen anaesthesia to these patients by a method which was the forerunner of Boyle's apparatus. For his services in France he was appointed OBE, and was twice mentioned in despatches. It was in hospital in France that he met Belle, a theatre sister, whom he married in 1918 a few days before the armistice. At the end of the war he was appointed physician to Guy's, with special interest in tuberculosis, and from then on he became one of the leading physicians in diseases of the chest.

At that time pulmonary tuberculosis was prevalent and required treatment by prolonged periods of bed rest. It was in caring for these patients that Geoffrey's outstanding qualities showed themselves. His personal interest and encouraging care helped many patients through this frustrating period. In 1934 he was invited to join the staff of the Brompton Hospital. He was quick to adopt new and more active forms of treatment such as artificial pneumothorax, and later furthered the introduction and use of streptomycin; he was appointed chairman of the clinical trials committee of the Medical Research Council. He early appreciated the value of thoracic surgery and worked closely with his surgical colleagues. He took a leading part in the formation of the Thoracic Society, which was formed to bring together all those concerned in the treatment of thoracic diseases.

During the second world war Geoffrey was physician in charge at the Brompton Hospital, sleeping either at the hospital or in the cellar of his house in Hampstead during the air raids. His unperturbed presence was a comfort to many at this time of uncertainty. It was then that he lost his son in Africa, a young officer in the Rifle Brigade. He was their only child, and Geoffrey and his wife Belle bore this tragedy with wonderful courage.

During the war he had the responsibility of looking after Winston Churchill, who had an attack of pneumonia and needed firm and urgent treatment at a critical stage of the war. Later, in 1951, Geoffrey was to have further heavy responsibility looking after King George VI when Clement Price Thomas operated on him for bronchial carcinoma. While staying in Buckingham Palace to supervise the King's recovery after the operation, he was knighted by the King. One of Geoffrey's treasured possessions was a letter from the King, written in his own hand, expressing his gratitude for all that Geoffrey had done for him.

In 1949 Geoffrey gave the Harveian oration, his title being 'Individuality in medicine'.

At Guy's Hospital his easy manner with the students resulted in many lasting friendships. He enjoyed their company and had many happy – and sometimes noisy – parties with them at restaurants in the evening, after his visits to the wards. He was naturally hospitable and he and his wife Belle made everyone welcome in their home. Their Christmas party at Hampstead was renowned; a fir tree growing in their front garden was decorated for all to enjoy.

Having spent part of his youth in the Sussex countryside he was always happy to spend holidays in the country. Cornwall was one of his favourite places, where he and Belle enjoyed golfing day after day on the course by the sea, and when seagulls flew off with his ball he only laughed. In London, he found great relaxation watching the ballet and he was a frequent visitor to art exhibitions.

His long and close partnership with his wife ended when Belle died in 1974. After this he was more retired, although still in touch with many friends.

In 1979 he married again, to Joan Wilson Brown. Once again more tragedy befell him; after two months of happy married life Joan became ill and died a few weeks later, early in 1980. Geoffrey was then becoming disabled with arthritis and increasing deafness, so he decided to give up his home. Shortly afterwards he was welcomed at King Edward VII Hospital at Midhurst, where he spent his last years in a flat in the hospital for which he had done so much. Up to the last he was mentally alert and enjoyed visits from many friends, and even visited Goodwood races a few weeks before his death.

All through his distinguished career, Geoffrey remained his unostentatious, courteous and kindly self. AMCM

[*Brit. med. J.*, 1982, **285**, 567 & 749; **285**, pp.1780-1783 'A doctor in the Great War – an interview with Sir Geoffrey Marshall', Dr Barbara Evans (cassette tape of full interview, No T70, 1966, in RCP Library); *Lancet,* 1982, **2**, 506; *Times,* 12 Aug 1982; Photo]

MARTIN, Laurence Cleveland *b.*24 May 1910 *d.*20 Oct 1981
MRCS LRCP (1934) MB BCh Cantab (1935) MRCP (1936)
MD (1939) FRCP (1946)

Laurence Martin was born in Southampton, the son of William Martin, a chemist. He was educated at Sherborne School, Caius

College, Cambridge, and the Middlesex Hospital. From Caius he obtained an exhibition to the Middlesex Hospital, coming back to Cambridge after qualification in 1934 as a house physician at Addenbrooke's Hospital. Subsequently he returned to the Middlesex Hospital to work in the Bland-Sutton Institute. While there he contracted tuberculosis and spent a year in his own hospital and at Midhurst, a period which gave him much time and food for thought.

In 1938 he became an Elmore research student, joining a team, formed by John Ryle in the department of medicine at Cambridge, all of whom achieved considerable distinction in later life. He continued to work in the same department after winning the Leverhulme scholarship in 1939; he resigned this scholarship at the outbreak of war. It was during this period that he started his researches on thyroid disease. He obtained his MD in 1939.

His previous health prevented him serving in the Forces, a matter which always seemed something of a disappointment to him. There is no doubt that his courage, temperament and personality would have made him an outstanding officer. During the war he remained in Cambridge, carrying a large workload in various hospitals in the area and becoming a specialist physician in the Emergency Medical Service. In 1946 he was appointed to the staff of Addenbrooke's Hospital.

His interests lay in general medicine and endocrinology, particularly thyroid disease. He was a founder member of the Thyroid Club. He wrote many papers, including his classic work on the hereditary and familial aspects of exophthalmic and nodular goitre in collaboration with RA (later Sir Ronald) Fisher. In 1948 *Clinical Endocrinology*, a model of its kind, appeared. It ran to five editions, the last in 1969; initially it was written in association with Martin Hynes, but Laurence Martin was the sole author of later editions. He subsequently contributed to the endocrinological section of Conybeare's *Textbook of Medicine*.

Martin was an individualist; a man of high ideals and strong personal views. A careful, indeed meticulous, clinician, nothing was too much trouble for him as far as his patients were concerned. He was a man of complete integrity and great kindness behind a somewhat formidable facade, to whom very many, not only the sick, turned for advice in their troubles. He had the ability to grasp the essentials of a problem – medical, social or administrative. He had a wide command of the English language and expressed himself, whether speaking or writing, with clarity and often with an unusual and trenchant phrase. He loathed all forms of pretentiousness and had no patience with committee men, career mongers and rulebound functionaries. His sense of humour, although sometimes caustic, was seldom exhausted.

Inevitably in the period in which he served he was involved in the development of the Health Service in East Anglia, and of Addenbrooke's Hospital into a major teaching hospital, but his influence, which was considerable, was mainly behind the scenes. He served for many years on the Faculty Board of Medicine in the University, at a time when there was prolonged controversy regarding an undergraduate clinical school.

He was an associate lecturer in physic and served for some years as assessor to the regius professor of physic. He was an examiner in medicine in the University of Cambridge, for the University of London and for the Conjoint Board. He served as an examiner on the membership panel of the College and was a councillor from 1967 to 1970.

He had a particular interest in medical history and in old medical books, of which at one time he had a considerable collection. In his retirement he wrote the life of John Crane, the 17th century Cambridge apothecary, one of whose benefactions remains as Crane's Charity for 'poor sick scholars', of which Martin was a Distributor for 25 years until his retirement. His researches for this work, which appeared in 1977, led to a further publication about this unusual family. At the time of his death he had just completed papers on John Addenbrooke and on the Downing Professors of Medicine, in collaboration with Arthur Rook. He was an enthusiastic gardener and a keen shot; he was able to enjoy these hobbies to within a day or two of his death.

In 1939 he married Mary, daughter of David Ellis, a well known and much respected surgeon, of Aberystwyth. They had three daughters and a son.

Martin had two serious illnesses in the last ten years of his life. He made a good recovery from both, although very slowly on the second occasion. He never complained. He always remained the same, and he stood for the best in medicine. APD

[*Brit. med. J.*, 1981, **283**, 1269; *Lancet,* 1981, **2**, 1060; *Times,* 28 Oct 1981; Photo]

MARTIN, Nicholas Henry *b.*26 Oct 1906 *d.*13 Dec 1981
BSc Durh (1928) MRCS LRCP (1936) MB BCh Oxon (1937)
MA (1938) MRCP (1939) FRCP (1959)

Nicholas Henry Martin was born in Newcastle upon Tyne, the son of William Martin, also a physician, and his wife Ellen Renfree, daughter of Nicholas Henry Holman, a company director. He was educated at Sedbergh, going on to the University of Durham, where he graduated with honours in chemistry. As a Phillip Buckle travelling fellow he then went to Munich and Berlin for postgraduate studies. He was awarded the diploma of Imperial College and became a fellow of the Royal Institute of Chemistry in 1930. In 1931 he went up to Oxford to study medicine under Sherrington and Peters. He qualified with the Conjoint in 1936, taking his BM BCh Oxon in 1937. He took his membership of the College in 1939, and was appointed pathologist in the Bland-Sutton Institute that same year.

During the second world war he served as a major in the RAMC, seeing active service in France and Africa. He was assistant director of pathology to the 21st Army Group and was twice mentioned in despatches. On demobilization he returned to the Bland-Sutton Institute, but was released to UNRRA as deputy consultant in nutrition to the European Zone. He wrote numerous papers on protein structure and protein dyscrasias.

Awarded a Rockefeller fellowship, he studied at Harvard Medical School under Janeway and Cohn. Returning to England in 1947 he became head of the department of chemical pathology at St George's Hospital, London, and before long he had gathered round him a small but active group of young biochemists, working on the clinical applications of the rapidly developing technologies of ultracentrifugation and electrophoresis in the study of the plasma proteins. As the years passed he was faced with the problem of automation in the clinical laboratories, and this was something he found hard to contemplate, since he believed strongly that the technical staff should remain experts at the old manual procedures, and not become dependent on machines. He decided to implement the change to automation slowly, leaving the major changeover to his successor, and this probably led him to retire a little early. He devoted much of his time thereafter to his work for the Association of Clinical Pathologists, of which he became president, and for the newly founded College of Pathologists. He was a member of the original council of the latter, taking an active part in the construction of the examinations in chemical pathology. He was also a member of the Lister Institute.

Nick's striking appearance and lively personality, combined with a somewhat eccentric manner, soon made him one of the best known and most popular members of St George's staff. Everyone called him Nicky, except his old Oxford and Middlesex Hospital friends who persisted with his student nickname of Sharky. This rather uncomplimentary sobriquet presumably was owed to his flashing white teeth, in a dark countenance.

He married Ursula, daughter of William Brodie, in 1948, and they had two sons. In his leisure time he enjoyed the pleasures of his lovely house and garden, and his holidays in Cornwall, where he spent most of his time after his retirement. He was keen on sailing and climbing, so far as hip trouble allowed before successful operation, and devoted much time to growing azaleas. GW/VL

[*Lancet*, 1982, **1**, 118; Photo]

MARTIN, Robert Benson *b.*3 Jan 1914 *d.*16 Aug 1981
MB BS Durh (1936) MD (1938) MRCP (1946) FRCP (1974)

Bob Martin, the youngest of five children, was born in Newcastle upon Tyne where his father was a licensed victualler. He was educated at the Royal Grammar School in Newcastle upon Tyne, from which he moved to the medical school which was then part of the University of Durham. After posts as house surgeon to Hamilton Barclay and house physician to Horsley Drummond at the Royal Victoria Infirmary, he entered general practice in Newcastle in 1938. In February 1939 he joined the Territorial Army and in September that year began war service with a field ambulance of the British Expeditionary Force in

France and later in the Middle East, until 1944, during which he attained the rank of lieutenant colonel, and was mentioned in despatches. From 1944 he was with Army General Hospitals and ended his service career as a medical specialist with the rank of major.

On his return to civilian life he became senior medical registrar to CC Ungley at the Royal Victoria Infirmary in Newcastle, and a consultant to the Northern Counties Chest Hospital. He became MRCP in 1946, and returned to general practice in 1948, including part time factory appointments. In 1967 he contracted bladder cancer and had to have an ileal conduit. Largely because of this he left general practice altogether in 1970 to become a full time occupational medical adviser. The firm to which he was attached, Proctor and Gamble of Newcastle upon Tyne, had a serious medical problem of occupational asthma, related to the use of enzyme soap powders, and Martin played a prominent part in the investigations into this and in implementing the measures which were brought in to enable workers to handle enzyme materials safely. He was accredited as a specialist in occupational medicine in 1978.

Martin took a keen interest in other patients with ileal conduits and when John Swinney, who had operated on him, started a conduit association, Martin was unanimously elected president, and later when a national conduit association was formed became president of that also.

During his University life he was a keen sportsman and played rugby football for Durham University, as well as cricket for the College of Medicine, and later rugby football for the Northumberland County Club. He was also a keen member of Northumberland Golf Club and interested in gardening and bridge.

He married in 1938 Audrey Alexander Benson, a physical training teacher and physiotherapist, but had no children.

Bob Martin was a quiet and kind man, who was very highly esteemed as a family doctor and as a careful clinician who inspired confidence. It was significant that amongst his patients were members of the consulting staff of the teaching hospital.

He retired in 1979, and died in the Royal Victoria Infirmary from complications following surgical treatment of an aortic aneurysm.

RIMcC

[*Brit. med. J.*, 1981, **283**, 1474-5; Photo]

MASON, Richard Michael *b*.27 Sept 1917 *d*.30 June 1977
BM BCh Oxon (1942) MA (1943) MRCP (1948) DM (1953) FRCP (1962)

Michael Mason was born in London but spent the first five years of his life in India. He came of an old Suffolk family and his father, Sir Laurence Mason, CIE OBE MC, was Inspector General of Forests in India. His mother, Margaret Menella, was the daughter of the Revd HC Jollye, rector at Walton, Warwickshire. Michael was educated at Marlborough, Christ Church, Oxford, and St Bartholomew's

Hospital, where he qualified in 1942.

He trained as a pilot in the Oxford University Air Squadron and joined the RAF as a medical officer in 1943, serving in the first jet squadron in the Allied Air Forces. He saw active service in Germany and during the liberation of Denmark. In 1947, on demobilization, he became medical registrar at Bart's. He decided to specialize in rheumatology and worked for WSC Copeman and Oswald Savage at the West London Hospital. He was appointed consultant in the department of physical medicine, Chase Farm Hospital, Enfield, in 1951 and joined WS Tegner in 1955 as consultant to the London Hospital. He also held appointments as consultant to King Edward VII Hospital for Officers, Osborne House, and the Royal Masonic Hospital, and was particularly pleased to become civil consultant in rheumatology to the Royal Air Force in 1970.

From 1968 to 1971 he was president of the British Association of Physical Medicine and Rheumatology (later British Association for Rheumatology and Rehabilitation) and president of the Heberden Society in 1974. He was a leading influence on the emergence of the specialty of rheumatology from its origins in physical medicine. He was closely associated with the Arthritis and Rheumatism Council, becoming chairman of the executive committee in 1971 until his death. Under his chairmanship the income and work of this charity greatly expanded, laboratories being built for research into rheumatic diseases at the London. Happily, during his lifetime, the seminar room at the London was named the Michael Mason Room, and his portrait hangs there.

Although Michael had to pace himself for a number of years, for health reasons, he enjoyed the large amount of time he devoted to teaching. His teaching was colourful and practical and much sought after both at undergraduate and postgraduate levels, at home and abroad. In 1967 he was visiting professor at Sydney University. Michael was masterly as a chairman of symposia and he wrote fluently, contributing to many standard textbooks as well as being co-editor, with HLF Currey, of *An Introduction to Clinical Rheumatology*. He gave the Samuel Hyde memorial lecture 'Clinical Trials' at the Royal Society of Medicine in 1962 and was chosen to give the Heberden round in 1966 – a vivid demonstration of Behçet's syndrome. His own research interests were largely clinical and often linked associated specialties; for example, drug-trial techniques, orthopaedic surgery, and doctor-patient communication. As a clinician his talents had breadth and depth; not only was he an outstanding diagnostician and a master at eliciting physical signs but he had the remarkable ability of giving every patient his undivided attention and sympathy.

He married Heather, daughter of Lt Colonel Robert Johnston OBE, in 1943, and they had a son and a daughter. Michael had played squash for the RAF, and his hobbies included skiing and yachting.

GW/VL

[*Brit. med. J.*, 1977, **2**, 198; *Lancet*, 1977, **2**, 151; Photo]

MAWDSLEY, Clifford *b*.31 Oct 1929 *d*.9 Mar 1983
MRCS LRCP (1923) MB ChB Manch (1953) MRCP (1958)
MRCPE (1968) FRCPE (1969) MD (1972) FRCP (1972)

At the time of his sudden and unexpected death Clifford Mawdsley was secretary of the Royal College of Physicians of Edinburgh, consultant neurologist to the Royal Infirmary and Northern Hospital, and senior lecturer in charge of the University department of medical neurology in Edinburgh.

He was born in Bolton and lived there for a large part of his life. He was proud of his Lancastrian origin and retained a forthright manner. His father, Gilbert Mawdsley, was a pharmacist, and his mother, Betty (née Ainsworth) was the daughter of an engineer. Clifford was educated at St James, Bolton, and Canon Slade, and graduated in medicine at the University of Manchester, being awarded the Turner medical prize.

He was a quick thinker and an articulate speaker; in no doubt as to where he stood on many issues. Once he had made his mind up about anything his opinion was unshakable. He hated compromise and this sometimes disconcerted his coexaminers in the clinical section of the MRCP examination in the Royal Infirmary. He gave either very good or very bad marks, and this could lead to conflict and fierce argument: on one occasion he asked if it was to be swords or pistols! At other times his disagreement was concealed by an uncharacteristic silence. His dogmatic manner did not always endear him to his colleagues, and he was formidable in dispute. He was, however, always stimulating to be with, for he had a very quick and retentive brain and had a wide range of interests. He was remarkably good company and an excellent teacher, popular with students and postgraduates, and on the whole a tolerant man and loyal colleague.

His first medical appointment was house physician to the late Fergus Ferguson and George Smyth. Fergus became his mentor and his course was set on a career in neurology. After a period of national service in Cyprus he returned to the department of neurology at Manchester for further training. He then spent a year with the late Denny-Brown in Boston, returning to become a lecturer and consultant in Manchester, where he emerged as a highly successful teacher. It was at that time that he developed an interest in television epilepsy, and in the neurological effects of boxing.

In 1965 he was appointed senior lecturer in medical neurology at Edinburgh University, and succeeded JA Simpson. In addition to clinical work and teaching, he became increasingly involved in overseas travel, the membership examination, and other interests. After a period at Baroda, India, as WHO visiting professor, he made frequent visits to Basrah as teacher and examiner, and latterly to Libya. He was deeply involved with the three Royal Colleges, in the membership examination and arrangements both at home and overseas. His writing was notable for its clarity and coherence, and he contributed chapters to several textbooks.

In 1955 he married Eve Muriel Roper, a fellow graduate and

daughter of a shipping manager. They had a daughter and two sons. Clifford was a devoted family man and said that he relived his youth in the company of his sons. He derived great pleasure from their achievements.

Clifford Mawdsley was a good conversationalist, sometimes exhausting but never boring. He was quick to establish friendly relations with strangers, whether colleagues or casual acquaintances. Open and extremely extrovert, he professed no religious belief but lived in accordance with the Christian ethic. An eternal optimist, his impulsive, dynamic style will not be forgotten, and he showed a strong urge to win whether in conversation, playing squash, golf or chess. He was well informed about cricket which was a life-long interest, and also on many other subjects from Persian carpets to puzzles. An early interest in English literature gave way later to an enthusiasm for pictures and he became a member of the Scottish Arts Club. He also became increasingly involved in committee work, where he was quick to conduct business and able to reach decisions with dazzling speed. His energy seemed to be boundless and he participated with vigour in everything he undertook. BA/GW/VL

[*Brit. med. J.*, 1983, **286**, 1069, 1156, 1361; *Lancet*, 1983, **1**, 719]

MAY, Ronald Graeme *b*.29 June 1920 *d*.11 Mar 1982
MRCS LRCP (1943) MB BChir Cantab (1943) MRCP (1954) FRCP (1974)

Ronald May, who was consultant in chest medicine to the Tunbridge Wells and Hastings Districts was the son of a dentist, Walter John May and his wife, Violet Madge Littlejohn. He received his medical education at Clare College, Cambridge, and St Mary's Hospital, London, qualifying in 1943. Shortly after qualifying he joined the RAMC, subsequently serving in the Airborne Division with command of a field ambulance.

He commenced his training in chest medicine, after the war, at Harefield Hospital, and was subsequently senior registrar at Yardley Green Hospital, Birmingham. His arrival in Tunbridge Wells as consulting physician in chest medicine in 1955 brought the responsibility for providing chest consultative services in both Tunbridge Wells and Hastings, in addition to the post of medical superintendent of Darvill Hall Hospital, a sanatorium situated between the two towns. Following the death of his junior colleague in 1968 he continued to provide, single-handed, a superb chest service for Tunbridge Wells and East Grinstead, still maintaining an interest in Hastings, and holding clinics additionally in Tonbridge and more recently, since the retirement of another colleague, in Sevenoaks. During the whole of his time in Tunbridge Wells he cheerfully shouldered an incredible burden of clinical commitment, involving patients from wide areas of Kent and Sussex, usually with little in the way of supporting staff and with an ever decreasing number of hospital beds. Despite this workload he was always concerned, considerate, and completely unhurried. His patients were his friends, he treated them as such, and he was as much interested in them as individuals as in their particular medical problems.

His activities were not confined to clinical medicine, as evidenced by his chairmanship of the Hastings Branch, and presidency of the Sussex Division of the BMA. For ten years he was secretary of the South East Thames Thoracic Society and a council member of the British Thoracic Society. He was a member of the Joint Tuberculosis Council and also of the South East Thames Thoracic Research Committee, and was concerned in the organization of various research projects. At the time of his death Ronnie May was chairman of the Tunbridge Wells District Medical Executive Committee.

He will be remembered for his clinical excellence and love for his fellow men, but his other memorable characteristic was his quiet, chuckling sense of humour, which he never could suppress when in the company of his family, his friends and casual acquaintances. My favourite among his never ending supply of anecdotes related to his time as a unit medical officer when he had a sergeant who insisted on carrying out his own form of medical triage. According to Ronnie, the door of the MI room would be thrown open, a group of reluctant heroes would shamble in to the accompaniment (from the sergeant) of a click of the heels, a smart salute and 'Six cases of 'eadache, sir'. He was a great lover of sport, a keen golfer and cricketer, and was a member of both the Nevill and the Rye Golf Clubs. He played cricket for the Bluebottles at Robertsbridge, for the Bluemantles, the Jesters and the Martlets. He believed in making games more fun for both his partners and opponents, and one always felt better for having spent some time in his company. He had a deep affection for all things beautiful in nature and the arts, and his interest in birds and flowers would cause interruptions of games of cricket or golf whilst particular species were identified and followed. His theatrical talent was much in demand when he and his family lived in Robertsbridge. He was an accomplished pianist and guitarist and was delighted that one of his children decided to take up music as a full time career.

Despite his many skills and interests his greatest joy was in his family. In 1951 he married Isobel Lindsay Mackinlay and they had four children: two boys and two girls. He was essentially a family man who took tremendous pride in the achievements of his children, and also their growing independence. It was Hilaire Belloc who wrote in one of his sonnets 'From quiet homes and first beginning, out to the undiscovered ends, there's nothing worth the wear of winning but laughter and the love of friends'. These words could surely apply to no one more than Ronnie May. RCK

[*Brit. med. J.*, 1982, **285**, 300; Photo]

MEIKLE, Robert Woodside *b.*15 Sept 1920 *d.*27 Jan 1980
MB ChB Glasg (1944) MRCP (1949) FRCP (1972)

Robert Meikle, although of Scottish descent, was born in St Helens,

Lancashire, the son of James Meikle, an electrical engineer, and Elspeth Woodside. He was educated at Hill House, Doncaster, and Liverpool College before going to the University of Glasgow where he was president of Mackay Hall in 1942 and 1943. After qualification he was house physician to Sir John McNee and house surgeon to Walter Galbraith and Gavin Young at the Western Infirmary, Glasgow. He served as a surgeon lieutenant RNVR 1945 – 1947, mainly in the Far East, where he met his future wife, Joan, who was nursing there. After demobilization he returned to Sir John McNee as a registrar where he stayed until he became a senior registrar in medicine in the Sheffield Hospitals in 1954.

In 1959 he was appointed consultant physician to the hospitals in the Goole district, also with sessions in Wakefield, the latter being replaced in 1966 with sessions in Pontefract. He was the only physician responsible for that large area of Yorkshire between Hull in the east, Pontefract and Leeds in the west, York in the north and Doncaster in the south. Without any resident junior medical staff, this remained until the end of his life an extremely arduous post, but Robert never complained about the long hours or frequent night and weekend work – the harder the going, the happier he appeared to be. He also developed the geriatric service in the Goole area. He was regarded as a fine example of a dying breed, a truly general physician.

His services both as a doctor and in other fields were in great demand by the community he served, and for many years he was a member of the Hospital Management Committee, a governor of the Howden County Schools, a commissioner of Income Tax and chairman of the local committee of the Royal Society of Arts. In the little free time that he had, he was interested in gardening, beekeeping, trout fishing and medical history. His last year was dogged with ill health, which he bore with the cheerfulness and fortitude that one would have expected of him.

In 1951 he married Joan McGinley, who survived him together with two daughters and two sons, one of whom followed his father into the medical profession. JRBT

[*Brit. med. J.*, 1980, **280**, 597. Photo]

MENECES, *Maj. Gen.* **Ambrose Neponucene Trelawney**
*b.*19 Mar 1904 *d.*28 May 1979
CB (1963) CBE (1944) DSO (1945) MB BS Lond (1928)
MRCP (1946) DTM&H (1949) FRCP (1960) Fellow of UCL (1950)

Ambrose Meneces was born in London, the son of Joseph Meneces, a Portuguese teacher of languages, and his wife Amy Trelawney Tremayne. He graduated in 1928 at University College Hospital and began his career in the Royal Army Medical Corps in 1929.

His early years were spent in India. In 1936 he returned to study at the Royal Army Medical College, where he distinguished himself in clinical subjects and qualified as a specialist in medicine. After service as a physician at Shorncliffe, Captain Meneces was posted back to

India in March 1939.

He spent a short time as medical specialist in Poona, and then transferred to administrative duties, in which he rapidly earned recognition for his intellect and industry. As a staff officer at GHQ India in 1941 he was largely responsible for the complete reorganization of the military training of the Indian Hospital Corps.

In 1944 he was appointed deputy director of medical services of the 15th Indian Corps, which took part in the Arakan operations, the capture of Akyab, Ramree and Rangoon. He was twice mentioned in despatches, received the DSO and was made CBE. His experience in Burma led to his being regarded as a leading expert in the medical evacuation of war casualties.

Major (T/Brigadier) Meneces returned to England in 1945 and resumed the practice of medicine at the Cambridge Military Hospital, Aldershot. He became MRCP in 1946 and obtained his MD in 1947. The next four years were spent as reader in tropical medicine at the Royal Army Medical College. He delivered a paper at the 12th International Military Medical Congress in Mexico in 1949, and became staff examiner for MD London, and examiner for DTM&H.

After two years as officer commanding the British General Hospital in Japan, and one year as chief of plans and operations of the medical branch of SHAPE, he regained the rank of brigadier in 1957, when he was appointed deputy director of Medical Services of 1 British Corps in Germany. Promotion to major general followed in 1958 on appointment as DDMS Western Command, and then director of Medical Services, BAOR, in 1961. He completed his service as commandant of the Royal Army Medical College from 1963, and retired after more than 36 years in March 1966.

He was appointed honorary physician to the Queen in 1960 and was awarded the CB in 1963.

Ambrose Meneces was greatly respected throughout his career for his intellect and his unfailing courtesy and helpfulness. His interests extended beyond medicine and its administration in peace and war, and included a wide range in the arts.

In 1934 in Sialkot, Punjab, he married Elsie Gertrude, daughter of Revd Francis Hunt. She died in 1976, and he was survived by his second wife, Cecilia Ethel Parker. ATC

[*Photo*]

MERSKEY, Clarence *b.*20 July 1914 *d.*10 Nov 1982
MB ChB Cape Town (1937) MD (1947) MRCP (1949) FRCP (1978)

Clarence Merskey was born in Alberton, Transvaal, where his father, Bernard Merskey, was an accountant, and he was educated with his brother at Sea Point Boys' High School when the family settled in Cape Town. After graduating in medicine from the University of Cape Town in 1937, he served as house physician to JF Brock (*q.v.*) in the newly built Groote Schuur Hospital, and from 1940 to 1946 as a captain in the South African Medical Corps in the East and North African campaigns of World War II.

On demobilization he became first assistant in the University of Cape Town's medicine department under Frank Forman (*q.v.*). In addition to complementing the latter's renowned bedside and teaching skills, he immediately brought to the wards and the nascent clinical laboratory a lively dimension of active investigation and effervescent enquiry, which characterized his whole career. He proceeded MD in 1947 with his thesis *The Erythron in Polycythaemia Vera*, and the following year he was awarded the Cecil John Adams fellowship which brought him to London and the MRCP in 1949. He spent two rewarding years working with Rosemary Biggs and Gwyn Macfarlane at the Radcliffe Infirmary, Oxford, where he developed his coagulation expertise and made valuable contributions to the study of haemophilia.

He returned for most of the '50s to an intensely productive programme of clinical, teaching and laboratory activities at Groote Schuur Hospital, and was elected a fellow of the University in recognition of his researches in haemostasis. The winds of change in South Africa were already in evidence, and Clarence was steadily drawn to the intellectual stimulus and scientific opportunity of the great centres. In 1958 he lectured in the USA as a Rockefeller foundation travelling fellow, and was invited by Irving London to join the Albert Einstein College of Medicine in New York's Yeshiva University. He became associate professor of medicine in 1966 and full professor in 1972, with added recognition as professor of laboratory medicine in 1974. In 1982 he became emeritus professor, but continued to work full-time in the laboratory.

Clarence Merskey's considerable contributions to medicine and haemostasis were expressed with a sustained vitality on three continents. In the land of his birth and early medical training he explored the then prevalent hypothesis that arterial thrombotic disease was a consequence of a 'hypercoagulable' state, and concluded that there was inadequate evidence to support that view. In Oxford he systematized the laboratory diagnosis of haemophilia, published the first scientific account of its presence in the human female, and was co-author of the initial account of Christmas disease by Biggs and her colleagues in 1952.

At the Albert Einstein College of Medicine in New York he ran a small research laboratory from which significant findings flowed in a steady stream. These data were often the product of collaborative studies, particularly with Alan Johnson at the New York University College of Medicine, with whom in 1966 he devised the definitive test for measuring fibrin degradation products by a tanned red cell haemagglutination inhibition immunoassay. This technique and modifications of it gained him worldwide acceptance in the diagnosis of disseminated intravascular coagulation, and made Merskey's name a byword in that field.

He was an instinctively friendly man with an infectious sense of humour, totally lacking in pretentiousness. These qualities blended happily with an exceptionally critical approach to new data or clinical findings, leading his colleagues to recognize three levels of proof: one that satisfied the investigator himself; a second that was sufficient for reviewing editors; and finally the proof that Clarence Merskey accepted. For all his great authority and sharp intellect, he was often diffident in his opinions and might startle a newcomer slow to perceive his talents, by revealing his true stature in the appropriate forum. The circumstances of his life and work, in addition to his personal warmth, led him continually to make new and enduring friends. When he died, large numbers of them set about creating a memorial to his achievements in medicine and haemostasis by endowing a research appointment in his name.

In 1939 in South Africa he married Marie, daughter of Herman Fine of Dublin. She became a professional librarian and survived him with three married daughters and four grandchildren. RSM

[*Lancet,* 1983, **1**, 254; Photo]

MIDDLEMISS, *Sir* **(John) Howard** *b.*14 May 1916 *d.*27 Apr 1983
Kt (1981) CMG (1968) MB BS Dunelm (1940) MD (1947)
FFR (1948) MRCP (1964) FFR (RCSI) (1969) FRACR (1971)
FACR (1972) FRCP (1972) FRCS (1976) FRCR (1976)

The son of Thomas Middlemiss, a banker, and grandson of Robert Mason, a Member of Parliament, Howard Middlemiss was proud of his Northumbrian origins and of being an alumnus of the University of Durham. While he was an undergraduate he achieved much that was a clear intimation of his future life. He played cricket for the University, and there was hardly a club ground in the whole of Northumbria that was not familiar to him. He showed his enthusiasm for travel by crossing Europe as far as Salzburg to listen to the music of Mozart – on a bicycle that had been constructed specially for him. He was identified by his perceptive contemporaries as the one most likely to succeed in his year. Most important of all he met Mary Pirrie, also a medical undergraduate; they were married soon after he qualified and began a partnership that ensured their own success, and also support for those who needed their help, for more than 40 years.

Almost immediately after he qualified, Howard joined the RAMC and served in Normandy and in India. During this time he gained considerable experience of medicine and of travelling abroad, and realized that he had a flair for administration. After the war he returned to Newcastle and committed himself to a career in radiodiagnosis. Bristol had the foresight to invite him to take on the first major challenge of his professional career, when he was appointed director of radiology in 1949. His outstanding clinical ability, administrative flair, and striking personality were a unique combination that enabled him to attract able colleagues to Bristol, and to inspire them with his own enthusiasm. His department acquired a worldwide reputation for both its clinical work and its teaching. He went out of his way to contact doctors outside his own specialty, and the links that he pioneered with them have become the accepted practice not only in Bristol but universally. In 1966 he was appointed to a personal chair in the University of Bristol – and at that time there was only one other chair of radiodiagnosis in undergraduate teaching hospitals in the whole kingdom. At least six of his postgraduate students subsequently gained their own chairs in five different continents. His commitment to the University included three successful years as dean of the Faculty of Medicine from 1977 to 1980.

In 1953 Howard had been invited to visit Africa as adviser, and began an unrivalled and unambiguous commitment of heart and mind to the underprivileged in the developing countries. In addition to the clinical work involved, he enjoyed rolling up his sleeves and dismantling equipment in order to repair it; took hazardous journeys to remote outposts; and once flew by helicopter close to the frontline in Vietnam in order to visit a hospital and conduct a ward round in French. Above all he encouraged others to visit centres in East Africa, West Africa, the West Indies, Malaysia and Burma in order to create and sustain a high standard of radiography and radiology. Whole teams of radiographers and radiologists from these countries visited the United Kingdom, usually in Bristol, in order to learn new skills that they could practise in their own environment. He was in constant demand to travel widely, and made a host of friends wherever he went. Several years ago he received a large number of guests at a reception in London; he did not know in advance who would be there, but recognized each by his full name, and this was not only because he regarded each one as an individual but because he cared generously for the welfare of each one. Conversely, it is a remarkable tribute to his personality that throughout the English-speaking radiological world he could be referred to by his Christian name alone with instant recognition. Recently he found that one of his friends, a radiographer from Vietnam, had escaped and was in a transit camp with very little hope. He initiated an interest that culminated in the ultimate arrival of his friend in a free country. The delight that he displayed at that time was characteristic of the overt pleasure that he showed in the success of others. He was justifiably and immensely proud of the Companionship of the Order of St Michael and St George that was conferred upon him for his services overseas.

Howard and many of his contemporaries believed passionately in the establishment of a Royal College of Radiologists. He had been involved energetically with its predecessor, the Faculty of Radiologists, for nearly a quarter of a century, and when he became president of the faculty launched a final sustained and successful effort from the platform created by his predecessors. It was one of the happiest days of his life when the Privy Council granted a Supplemental Charter in 1975, and characteristically he was working in the West Indies when he heard the news. He became the first president of the Royal College of Radiologists and filled the office with his own style and dignity. When his turn of office was over he continued the energetic interest he had in international education, and in setting up an examination structure now used in all the European countries.

Hard work and success were their own rewards for Howard, but also he received numerous honours. Fellowships of colleges and international associations were showered upon him, and he was invited to give no less than nine named lectures in this country and abroad. A knighthood was conferred upon him in 1981 for services to radiology, and in 1982 he was awarded the gold medal of the Royal College of Radiologists. This is the highest honour the College can give and it is awarded for outstanding contribution to the development and teaching of radiology. It is given rarely and was richly deserved by this man of fine intellect and liberal outlook.

He travelled far, but always loved to return to his home in Bristol. He and Mary opened it generously to scores of students from the Commonwealth and beyond, and took delight and pleasure in their friendship and success. Even his relaxation was energetic, and in recent years he and Mary had tackled a small neglected woodland nestling in the Malverns. Their first move was to cut bold pathways through it. At this stage they invited their colleagues and their families to visit them there. Howard armed the children with whistles and instructions to blow if they were lost, and then allowed them to roam freely along the paths he had cut. When the deadwood had been cut and carried away, he began to replant it with oak trees, an act that was symbolic of his whole approach to life. His own life fulfilled all the promises that his coevals had predicted. He enriched the life of all who met him.

He died in Bristol and was survived by Lady Middlemiss and their son and two daughters. ERD

[*Brit. med. J.*, 1983, **286**, 1586; *Lancet*, 1983, **1**, 1115-1116; *Times*, 4 May 1983]

MILLER, Henry George *b.*13 Dec 1913 *d.*25 Aug 1976
MB BS Durh (1937) MD (1940) MRCP (1940) DPM Lond (1943) FRCP (1953)

Henry Miller was born in Chesterfield, Derbyshire, the son of John Miller an engineer and his wife Mabel Isobel Bainbridge. He attended the Grammar School at Stockton-on-Tees from 1924 to 1931, when he became a student at the University of Durham College of Medicine in Newcastle upon Tyne, qualifying with honours in 1937. During his undergraduate career he was president of the University Union. After resident appointments in the Royal Victoria Infirmary in Newcastle upon Tyne he became assistant resident pathologist at Johns Hopkins Hospital, Baltimore, USA, in 1938, and then undertook clinical appointments at the Hospital for Sick Children, Great Ormond Street, London in 1939.

He was a neuropsychiatric specialist with the rank of squadron leader in the RAF Medical Service from 1942 to 1946, and after demobilization worked in neurology as a post-service registrar at Hammersmith Hospital and at the National Hospital, Queen Square, from 1946 to 1947. He was appointed assistant physician to the Royal Victoria Infirmary in 1947 and served in that capacity until 1958, when he was appointed consultant neurologist to the Royal Victoria Infirmary, becoming reader in neurology in 1961 and professor of neurology in 1964. From 1966 to 1968 he was dean of medicine, and in 1968 was appointed vice-chancellor of the University of Newcastle upon Tyne, an appointment that he held until his death in 1976.

In 1963 Henry Miller visited Brisbane as the Sir Henry Tooth guest professor of medicine, and during that tour lectured in the universities of Sydney, Melbourne, Karachi, Lahore, Bangkok and Tokyo. He also held visiting professorships in Canada and in the University of California, San Francisco. From 1967 to 1971 he was director of the British Medical Association's Planning Unit, and from 1965 to 1973 he was secretary-general-treasurer of the World Federation of Neurology. He was from time to time external examiner in medicine to Queen's University, Belfast, and to the University of Liverpool. In 1961 he gave the Milroy lectures to the Royal College of Physicians. From 1974 to 1975 he was president of the Association of Physicians of Great Britain and Ireland. On two occasions he was president of the Students' Medical Society in Newcastle upon Tyne.

His major publications included the following books: *Early Diagnosis* (1960), *Modern Medical Treatment* (1962) and 2nd Edition, with R Hall (1975), and *Medicine and Society* (1973). He was joint editor of *Progress in Clinical Medicine* which went through eight editions between 1948 and 1971; and wrote *Diseases of the Nervous System* with WB Matthews, the first edition being published in 1972, the second in 1975. He wrote more than 200 scientific papers on internal medicine, neurology and psychiatry in many medical journals and was also a regular contributor to *The Listener*, to *Encounter*, and to *World Medicine*.

When first appointed as assistant physician at the Royal Victoria Infirmary in Newcastle he prospered for several years as a busy and much sought after consultant in part-time private practice. Generations of medical students and staff owed much to his inspired teaching and example. In 1958 he established a new department of neurology, firmly based on clinical work and research, and this department developed rapidly and acquired an international reputation. Henry Miller's research on multiple sclerosis, head injury, accident neurosis and many diverse neurological topics won him wide renown, and his review articles, many published in the *BMJ*, were widely read and quoted, as were his outspoken criticisms of the National Health Service.

His energy, his drive, his remarkable intuitive clinical ability, his abounding flow of language spiked with barbs of at times wounding wit, and above all, his unbounded generosity to friends, colleagues and junior staff, were extraordinary. If he was not always popular with his peers, who frequently misunderstood and more often misinterpreted his roguish wit, he was loved by his juniors and contemporaries, especially those who worked closely with him and knew him best and readily forgave his outrageous remarks. Always a bon viveur and lover of the arts, a man of wide culture despite his outward buffoonery, he loved a spirited riposte and was never reluctant to admit either that he was wrong or that he had been bested in an argument.

As vice-chancellor his skill in handling the student body was matchless. Whether with senior academics, students, porters, clerks or visitors, however distinguished, he was superbly unpredictable, original and always irreverently cheerful. His major interests were in opera, literature, and in good food and wine, and he was an enthusiastic member of the Athenaeum and of the Garrick Club.

He married in June 1942 Eileen Cathcart MRCOG, daughter of George Gibson Baird, an engineer of North Shields, Northumberland, and they had two sons and two daughters. JNW

[*Brit. med. J.*, 1976, **2**, 591, 648, 765; *Lancet*, 1976, **2**, 527; *Times*, 27 Aug 1976; Photo]

MILLER, Malcolm William *b*.18 Jan 1911 *d*.2 Sept 1981
MB BS Adelaide (1932) MRCP (1935) MRACP (1961)
FRCP (1966)

Malcolm Miller was born in Adelaide, Australia, the son of Henry William Adair Miller, a life assurance officer, and his wife Eliza Warden, daughter of a farmer. He was educated at Prince Alfred College and the University of Adelaide, where he graduated in 1932 with the Everard scholarship and prize in medicine.

After a short period as resident medical officer at the Royal Adelaide Hospital, he came to England in 1934 and spent a year as medical officer at the Netherne Mental Hospital, Coulsdon, Surrey. It was during this time that he took the membership examination of the College. He returned to Australia in 1936 and became honorary clinical assistant in medicine at the Royal Adelaide. He served this hospital until 1957, being appointed honorary assistant physician in 1951 and physician in 1957. When the new teaching hospital, the Queen Elizabeth Hospital, Woodville, was opened he was appointed the first senior honorary physician. Apart from his clinical work, he was chairman of the physicians committee, a member of the advisory committee of the University of Adelaide, and a member of the postgraduate committee in medicine.

During the second world war he served as a part-time officer in the Army, with the rank of captain, having been found medically unfit for full-time service.

Miller married Elizabeth, daughter of Major Henry Trotter, in 1937, and they had two daughters. His hobbies included all forms of sport and an abiding interest in motor racing. GW/VL

[Photo]

MILLS, Gordon Lewis *b*.18 Oct 1929 *d*.20 Feb 1983
BSc Liverp (1953) MB ChB (1957) MRCS LRCP (1958)
MRCPE (1964) MRCP (1967) FRCP (1978) FRCPE (1978)

Gordon Mills was head boy at the Grammar School in Machynlleth in Mid-Wales, an appointment which clearly presaged a distinguished career in medicine with particular emphasis on qualities of leadership in the care of the elderly. His father, William Gordon Mills, was a forestry worker.

After service as a nursing orderly in the RAMC during his national service, Mills entered Liverpool University, where he graduated BSc with honours in anatomy and subsequently MB ChB. He was student president of the Liverpool Medical Students Society and was made an honorary life member. A source of great recent satisfaction was his election to serve as honorary president of the same Society.

Subsequent phases in his postgraduate career included the usual house officer jobs and a spell in general practice, becoming subsequently a medical registrar. It was at this point that he developed the consuming interest in geriatric medicine which was to shape his future career. Senior registrarships in his chosen specialty at Manchester and Oxford then followed.

An opportunity to put this training into practice occurred in 1967 when Gordon Mills was appointed consultant physician in geriatric medicine at the Central Middlesex Group of Hospitals, London. This densely populated area had only a very thin provision of medical services to cater specifically for its elderly citizens. To build up an appropriate organization and ensure that it functioned properly was a great challenge. He met this challenge with notable success for seven years. In addition, some original observations on the aetiology and management of hypothermia, incontinence and anaemia in elderly persons gave a further creative flavour to the work of the unit.

After a brief stay in a rather more academic environment in Central London, Gordon Mills returned to Liverpool University in 1977 as a professor. He was appointed at a time of change. The proportion of persons aged 65 years in the UK was rising, and the proportion in central Liverpool rising even faster. The Medical School had expanded its intake of undergraduates. The resources of the University were already beginning to be curtailed.

Because of the way in which the chair was originally funded the professor of geriatric medicine continued to have a specific day-to-day responsibility for the functioning of the geriatric services for central and south Liverpool. In view of these background factors, the professor was a very busy man. During five years sojourn in the chair, Gordon Mills accomplished a great deal.

Within the University Faculty of Medicine, undergraduate teaching in geriatrics was improved and extended by Gordon Mills, so that it is now represented in each of the three clinical years of the undergraduate medical course. Particular emphasis was placed on both the community and hospital aspects of health and disease in the elderly.

Paralleling his strictly University commitments, Mills was active in postgraduate teaching. He was enthusiastic in lecturing to groups of general practitioners locally, throughout the UK and abroad, on various geriatric topics. Special symposia were arranged by him on topics such as 'Incontinence of urine in the elderly', and 'Caring for mentally infirm old people'. Weekly seminars were also held by Mills for family doctors on problems related to the elderly, and various educational exercises were also staged for community nurses and health visitors. He was an examiner for the Health Visitors Diploma, and also a member of the management committee of the Liverpool Institute of Human Ageing.

On a national level, he served on the committee for geriatric medicine of the Royal College of Physicians of London. All this work was, of course, in addition to being himself an active clinical consultant.

Under Gordon Mill's dynamic leadership the geriatricians of the Mersey region were welded into a cohesive body with a definite sense of purpose. This together with his enthusiasm for teaching his subject, made him an outstanding benefactor to the Mersey region's 'senior citizens'.

In 1956 he married Aileen, daughter of Gilbert William Brown, and they had five sons. They were a happy and devoted family, and Gordon listed 'do-it-yourself' as his major hobby. DAPE

[*Brit. med. J.*, 1983, **280**, 1450; *Times,* 4 Mar 1983; Photo]

MILNE, John Alexander *b.*19 Feb 1920 *d.*21 July 1977
MB ChB Glas (1944) MRCP (1947) MRCPE (1962) MRCPG (1962) FRCPE (1965) FRCPG (1965) MRCPath (1966) FRCP (1968)

John Milne was the son of Colin Milne, journalist and drama critic, and his wife Isabella Hunter. He was born in Gourock, Scotland, educated at Greenock Academy, and received his medical education at the University of Glasgow. His undergraduate career foretold the distinction to which he later rose, and he graduated in 1944.

His original intention was to be a physician and he held clinical posts with Sir John McNee and Laurance Scott, but in 1945 he joined the department of bacteriology at the Western Infirmary where, as a McCunn medical research scholar he came under the influence of Carl Browning. In 1946 he became lecturer in pathology under DF Cappell. These two men greatly influenced his life; beginning as his teachers, they later became his close friends. It was they who first demonstrated to him the delights and intellectual excitements of microscopy. From his earliest days in pathology he became interested in the skin and, realizing that expertise could only grow more effective in conjunction with the clinical examination of patients, obtained the membership of the Royal College of Physicians of London in 1947. In 1951 he was awarded a Carnegie travelling fellowship to the United States and during his time there he formed a life-long friendship with Hermann Pinkus and Hamilton Montgomery, two of the most distinguished dermatopathologists in the world. In 1953 he was appointed as consultant pathologist in charge of the Area Laboratory Service in Ayrshire. He accepted an invitation to return to the Western Infirmary and the University of Glasgow in 1960, as reader in dermatology, and became its first professor of dermatology in 1968.

At Anderson College (Glasgow University) he planned and

supervised the development of an ever-expanding department of diagnostic and research pathology in relation to dermatology; his laboratories gave opportunities to numerous men and women, many of whom have since become eminent in their own fields. He attracted trainees and specialists alike, from all over the world, who came for days, weeks or months, to benefit from study of the varied collection of a life's experience in the histopathology of the skin. Within the University of Glasgow he became known as a man whose counsel was valued highly by staff at all levels and in many faculties, extending far beyond medical advice, and he became acknowledged as one of the 'pillars of wisdom' of the campus. Nevertheless, he remained to the end a 'plain' man of many simple graces but no airs whatever, intolerant of pomposity and always made uncomfortable by the limelight which inevitably fell upon him. He never overcame his natural shyness, though this was never obvious, and indeed incomprehensible to those who knew his skill as a lecturer. He displayed great patience in his personal teaching at the microscope, and never felt any task too irksome or menial.

John Milne was past president of the Scottish Dermatological Society, had served a term as member of council of the British Association of Dermatologists, and for 14 years – with his secretary – discharged the task of indexing the British Journal of Dermatology. He was also a member of the MRC Dermatology Research Review Committee. In 1972 his book on the histopathology of the skin was published and is now accepted as a standard reference book used by trainees and consultants alike, whether dermatologists or pathologists. He received numerous invitations to teach abroad and during visits to Poland and Hungary had conferred upon him honorary membership of the Polish and Hungarian Dermatological Societies. At the time of his death he was looking forward to visiting Australia, with his wife Margaret, for a tour as Essex visiting professor.

He remained a Scot and it was in Scotland that he found his greatest joys. His humour was essentially that of a Scot, and his favourite pastimes were fishing in the lochs and rivers, and photography. He married Gertrude Margaret Cram in 1946 and his source of inspiration and refreshment was his home life. Hospitality at his home was invariably a pleasure both in anticipation and recollection. To say that conversation there was stimulating is an understatement; there was never animosity in argument and always a feeling of good fellowship. John enjoyed good food, good wine and good company. He was a man of amazing surprises and contradictions; deriving special pleasure from jazz music, in particular that of Duke Ellington, whose last concert in Glasgow he attended, and from his love of art, more especially that of Russell Flint.

Although a world expert on dermatology and much in demand as a speaker at international meetings, and as a lecturer at medical schools throughout the world, John Milne will be best remembered in Ayrshire and Glasgow for his kindliness, his keen sense of humour and wide range of interests. GW/VL

[*Brit. J. Derm.*, 1977, **97**, 577; *Times*, 29 July 1977; Photo]

MIN SEIN, Thiri Pyanchi *b*.26 Dec 1898 *d*.7 Nov 1978
OBE (1947) MB Calcutta (1925) MRCS LRCP (1928) MRCP (1929) FRCP (1959)

Min Sein was a distinguished Burmese physician and a keen sportsman, He was born in Pyapon, Burma, the son of U Sine Hu, a landowner, and his wife Daw Yin Cane, and educated at Rangoon High School and the University of Calcutta, where he graduated in 1925. After graduation he spent two years as assistant lecturer at the Government Medical School, Rangoon, before coming to England to undertake postgraduate studies. From 1927 to 1930 he studied at Guy's Hospital, London, becoming clinical assistant to Sir John Conybeare and Sir Charles Symonds. He took the Conjoint in 1928 and his membership of the College in 1929. In the Burma Rebellion of 1931 – 1932 he was a battalion medical officer with the British Forces. He remained in Burma at the close of the rebellion, and in 1938 was appointed senior physician and lecturer in medicine at Rangoon Medical College.

Min Sein married in 1936 Daw Yin May, herself a distinguished physician and surgeon, and they had two children: a son and a daughter.

During the second world war he served with the British Forces from 1942 to 1946 as ADMS and DDMS, Civil Service, 14th Army. He was awarded the OBE in 1947.

In 1946 he was appointed senior physician to the General Hospital, Rangoon, a post which he held until his retirement. He was also medical superintendent, Rangoon, from 1946 to 1948, and wrote many papers on various aspects of medicine in Burma.

He was a member of the Burma Medical Council, the National Health Council and the National Fitness Council; a member of the Opium Enquiry Commission and of the Racing Enquiry Commission. He led a special mission to the USSR in 1954 and was a member of special missions to the United States in 1952, and Japan in 1958. From 1956 to 1958 he was president of the Burma Medical Association; he was president of the Burma Britain Association, vice-president of the Burma Veterans League, and president of the Medical College Research Society. He was also a member of the Technical and Scientific committee, WHO. In 1959 he was elected a fellow of the College.

Outside of his profession and family, his interests lay in the field of sport. He was a Guy's Hospital tennis Blue; inter-collegiate long jump champion, Calcutta; president of the Burma Olympic Association, 1948, and captain of the Burma Golf Club. He was president of the Burma National Amateur Athletic Federation, and also of the Weight Lifting and Body Culture Federation, and director and steward of the Rangoon Turf Club. GW/VL

[*Photo*]

MODI, Natwar Jaising *b.*20 Mar 1901 *d.*6 Sept 1977
MB BS Bombay (1924) MRCP (1929) FRCP (1966)

Natwar J Modi was born in Ahmedabad (Gujarat), the son of JP Modi, who was an eminent jurist of his time.

Modi had his early education in Lucknow, and his medical course at Bombay University, in the Grant Medical College. After passing MB BS in 1924, he went to the UK and took his MRCP in 1929.

Soon after his return to India in 1932, Modi joined the GT Hospital, Bombay, as an honorary physician, and held that post till he retired in 1956. He also worked as honorary professor of medicine at the Grant Medical College, Bombay, and as honorary physician at Sir Harkissondas Hospital, Bombay.

Modi actively participated in all the activities of the Association of Physicians of India. He was a member of the governing body and was an able editor of the *Journal* of the Association, being elected president of the Association for the year 1966. Modi was 'Netaji' orator for the API in 1974.

After retirement, Modi revised his father's book on *Medical Jurisprudence and Toxicology* and brought it up to date and published it. This revised edition of the book still serves as a useful guide in the courts and classrooms.

Modi was examiner for undergraduate and postgraduate degrees in medicine for many universities and worked hard towards raising the standard of medical education in India.

Natwar Modi was straightforward and outspoken by nature, and always acted up to his convictions. In this process, he incurred the displeasure at times of some of his friends and colleagues, but they in turn loved him for his integrity and intellectual honesty.

When Natwar Modi died he left behind him his wife, two sons and many grandchildren to mourn his loss. RVS

[*Jr. Assoc. Phys. Ind.,* 1977, 25; Photo]

MOHAMED, Shans-ud Deen Bhanji *b.*24 June 1930 *d.*27 Sept 1981
MB ChB Glasg (1955) MRCP (1962) MRCPE (1962) FRCPE (1972) FRCP (1977)

Shans-ud Deen Mohamed was born in Kenya, the son of Bhanji Mohamed, a general merchant. He was educated in Nairobi and came to Scotland in 1949. He attended a technical college in Aberdeen for a year and then became a medical student at Glasgow University. He undertook his clinical studies at the Western Infirmary and graduated in 1955, gaining the Bruton memorial prize. In his pre-registration year he was appointed to both medical and surgical professorial units, and he stayed in Glasgow until 1959; first as Faulds research fellow and then as Hall tutorial fellow. He then spent a year as a medical registrar to the late A Brown at the University College Hospital, Ibadan, Nigeria, and this appointment clearly had a profound impact on his life. While in Ibadan he set up the first controlled trial of anti-tetanus serum and enjoyed working in an expanding and developing medical centre. At that time there were many active research programmes based in Ibadan and he participated in a number of these.

On his return to Scotland, which he regarded as his adopted mother country, he worked at the Royal Infirmary, Aberdeen, until 1969. During this period he was seconded to the gastrointestinal unit at the Western General Hospital, Edinburgh, for a six month period, working with W Sircus. He was a prolific research worker and developed an interest in therapeutics, as well as in haematology and gastroenterology. He published a number of papers covering his clinical interests and in 1980, although his health was already failing, he presented an important paper on carbenoxolone in gastric ulcer.

In 1969 he was appointed consultant physician and gastroenterologist to the Wythenshawe Hospital and was responsible for the establishment and development of a clinical and investigatory gastrointestinal service for his district, which also covered a wider area in south Manchester and north Cheshire. He became postgraduate tutor at the Wythenshawe at a time when the new hospital was being developed. Possibly his major contribution, for which he will be remembered, was the planning and establishment of a well equipped, modern postgraduate centre and library. In this he was greatly helped and supported by his wife, Jean, and together they devised a most imaginative centre from an unpromising collection of sitting rooms and small offices.

Deen had a brilliant brain and an incisive approach to his work and made a considerable impact at Wythenshawe. His clinical work at the hospital earned him great respect and his opinion was widely sought on difficult clinical problems, particularly those involving the gastrointestinal tract. He worked very closely not only with his physician colleagues but also with the department of surgery, and he arranged regular meetings between the medical, surgical, and radiological departments to discuss problems and for the further training of junior staff.

The sudden and unexpected death of his wife in 1977, from a catastrophic subarachnoid haemorrhage, caused him deep distress and his own failing health made life increasingly difficult for him. He continued to work prodigiously, however, and never spared himself, for he was a perfectionist. He continued his various clinical responsibilities until the time of his death. Towards the end he was less seen in the hospital but he kept in close contact with his junior staff and assumed very real responsibility for the care of his patients until the end.

Deen's wife, Jean Constance Mary, was the daughter of Robert Addison, a haulage contractor. They had three daughters. In his younger days Deen enjoyed playing squash and throughout his life he derived great pleasure from books. CLB/GW/VL

[*Brit. med. J.*, 1981, **283**, 1182]

MONRO, Alan Bentley *b*.6 Feb 1910 *d*.30 May 1978
MB ChB Edin (1932) DPM (1937) MD (1949) MRCPE (1966)
MRCP (1967) FRCPE (1969) FRCP (1973) Hon FRCPsych (1973)

Alan Bentley Monro was born in Calcutta, India, the son of Charles George Monro who was himself both a physician and a clerk in Holy Orders. His mother also came from a medical family, her father being Dr James Maxwell Rattray.

Monro was educated at a preparatory school in Aberdeen, then at Monkton Combe School. He read medicine at Edinburgh University and had his clinical training at Edinburgh Royal Infirmary, graduating in 1932.

After qualifying, he held house appointments from 1932 to 1933 at St Luke's Hospital, Bradford, followed by a period in general practice from 1933 to 1935.

In 1935 he decided on a career in psychiatry, and was appointed a clinical assistant at the Maudsley Hospital, London, where he worked from 1935 to 1936. Subsequently, he served on the staff of various mental hospitals. During the 1939–1945 war he was placed in joint charge of a psychiatric unit at Farnborough Hospital, Kent, which was at that time associated with the psychiatric department of Guy's Hospital. This unit had been set up to deal specifically with civilian psychiatric casualties.

After the war, from 1949 to 1951, he served as physician deputy superintendent at Carlton Hayes Hospital, Narborough, Leicestershire. In 1951 he was appointed physician superintendent at Long Grove Hospital, Epsom, Surrey, which post he held until his retirement from the National Health Service in 1973.

It was during his superintendency at Long Grove that Monro really exhibited his outstanding clinical qualities. The 'industrial therapy' he established there created great interest, as did the day hospital. When the adolescent unit was transferred from St Ebba's Hospital, Epsom, to Long Grove, Monro took charge, so leading to his involvement in adolescent psychiatry not only at Long Grove but also at Kingston Hospital in a new outpatient clinic.

He found time, too, during this period to act as consultant adviser in psychiatry to the Department of Health and Social Security, and as a member of the Advisory Committee on Drug Dependency.

After his retirement from Long Grove he was appointed Lord Chancellor's Medical Visitor, a post he held until his death.

'Ben', as he was known to his friends, was a big man. He was big physically and, as his impressive tally of academic honours testifies, he was also intellectually big. He was a born committee man. There can be few committees to do with psychiatric matters at a local or national level on which he had not sat. He had remarkable gifts of verbal composition, and either orally or in writing he could simplify problems, particularly of a procedural or political variety, and point the way towards their resolution.

But he will best be remembered for his outstanding services to the Royal Medico-Psychological Association. He was appointed general secretary in 1957. He played a vital part in preparing the ground for and taking part in the prolonged and delicate negotiations with the Privy Council leading to the translation of the Association into a Royal College. He served as the College's first registrar in 1971. In 1973 the College acknowledged their debt to him by electing him to the honorary fellowship.

In 1934 Monro married Elsie, daughter of Thomas Race Kidd, an engineer. They had four children, three sons and a daughter.

Monro had in his younger days been a keen and proficient oarsman and had rowed in the 1st VIII at school and the 1st IV at the University. He had been an enthusiastic mountaineer, but in later life golf, photography and gardening were his main hobbies.

In spite of his prestige and his manifold distinctions Ben was a shy and reserved man. In a social setting, however, he could be amusing and witty. Asked, for example, why it was that he had chosen to publish so little, relatively speaking, he replied: 'One should think of the librarians.' HRR

[*Times,* 10 June 1978; *Brit. med. J.,* **1**, 1631; *Lancet,* 1978, **1**, 1373]

MONTUSCHI, Elio Federico Domenico *b.*10 May 1913
*d.*11 Jan 1979
MD Florence (1936) MRCP (1949) FRCP (1969)

Elio Montuschi was born in London of Italian parents and was educated in Florence and Bologna, where he graduated in 1935. He soon decided to take advantage of his dual nationality and returned to this country, because he could not accept the political climate of Italy. His first house appointments were at the Italian Hospital, and during the war he worked in the Emergency Medical Service, first at the Park Hospital, London, and later at Queen Mary's, Sidcup, where he was in charge of a pleural effusion unit. In 1944 he entered the RAMC and served in India, Rangoon and Singapore. In 1948, he became the youngest of the medical staff in the newly re-opened Italian Hospital, and he retained sessions there until his retirement. In 1957 he was appointed to the Whittington Hospital, to which he devoted most of his professional energies up to his retirement through ill health in 1977.

Wherever he worked Monty established a tremendous reputation, which was based on his sincerity and dedication to the welfare of his patients. He commanded great trust and was regarded as a kind friend as well as a compassionate physician. His clinical acumen was unsurpassed and his opinion on heart cases was widely sought. Rotund, benign, the embodiment of good nature, his approach to the patient was friendly, reassuring and unhurried, his appraisal of the problem penetrating and authoritative. He was a delight on the staff rounds at Whittington, particularly when demonstrating a case; his enjoyment was so manifest and his good humour so infectious. Monty was a genial man, perpetually good natured, and intolerant only of cant or of injustice.

He made many contributions to the study of clinical cardiology, particularly in the field of hypertension. It is some measure of the international regard in which he was held that the Faculty of Medicine of Bologna instituted a scholarship in his name, for young Italian doctors specializing in cardiology.

In 1947 he married Dorothy Staines, and they had two daughters and a son. He obtained the MRCP in 1949 and the MD in 1936 *maxima cum laude*. He was awarded the Commendatore (for Civic Merit) by the Italian Republic in 1967.

Outside medicine his interests lay in his family, music and philosophy.

AB

[*Brit. med. J.,* 1970, **1**, 543; *Lancet,* 1979, **1**, 451; Photo]

MORAN, *Lord* **(Charles McMoran Wilson) Baron Moran of Manton**
b.10 Nov 1882 *d*.12 Apr 1977
Baron (1943) Kt (1938) MC (1916) MB BS Lond (1908) MD (1913) MRCP (1913) FRCP (1921) PRCP (1941-1950) Hon FRCPE Hon FFPSG Hon FRACP

Charles Wilson was born at Skipton-on-Craven, Yorkshire. His father was John Forsythe Wilson of County Derry, who was a general practitioner in Skipton from 1878 to 1886; owing to illness he moved to a smaller practice at Wolston, a village near Coventry, and later to Barrow-in-Furness. His mother was the daughter of John Hannah. His elder brother, Lorton Wilson, was a doctor of medicine, and worked as a general practitioner all his life.

Wilson was educated at Rocklington Grammar School in Yorkshire and made up his mind to become a doctor at the age of sixteen. He had wished to become a writer, but taking the advice of his father he went into medicine to give him a more secure future. He entered St Mary's Hospital, Paddington, in 1902 – the same year as Sir Alexander Fleming – and qualified in 1908. Whilst a student he was editor of the hospital *Gazette*, captain of the rugby football fifteen, and already showed that he had a decisive mind and exceptional determination.

Within a year of qualifying Charles Wilson became disillusioned with some of his teachers and went abroad to study art in Florence and Rome. In 1912 he took a post looking after an elderly American widow who was living at Aswan on the Upper Nile. Whilst in Egypt he became interested in the temples on the Nile and also won a camel race at the Aswan Sports Club. On his return in 1913 he took his MD, being awarded the gold medal in medicine. He was appointed medical registrar at St Mary's, but on the outbreak of war in 1914 he enlisted at once in the RAMC and was posted as medical officer to the 1st Battalion the Royal Fusiliers. He spent two years in the front line and had a long and hard experience of trench warfare. He was awarded the Military Cross in 1916 for bravery on the Somme, and was twice mentioned in despatches. From 1917 to the end of the war he was in charge of the medical division of the 7th Base Hospital at Boulogne.

Much later (1945), when he was Lord Moran, he published a small book of about 200 pages giving an account of his years in the army. This was entitled *The Anatomy of Courage*. It is written with remarkable sensitivity and dedicated 'To my father who was without fear, by his son who is less fortunate'. In this brilliantly told story of heroism and tragedy in war can be found the reason (as he writes) for the author's 'loss of faith in the infallibility of authority', a trait which shows steadily in his later life. It is a book which expresses Wilson's personality, and shows his skill in picking out the essentials in the characters of others, a skill which he showed increasingly throughout his long career. For many years he lectured on courage at the Staff College at Camberley.

Soon after his return from France, Wilson was appointed honorary assistant physician to St Mary's Hospital (1919) and in the following year was elected dean. At that time St Mary's Medical School, which had an entry of some 20 students with a budget of about £30,000 per year, was threatened with closure, and had been advised to become a postgraduate school.

During his time as dean (1920 to 1945) Wilson transformed the School, and its position at the time of his death is the finest memorial to his work that he could have wished. Although unpaid, Wilson gave his whole energy and much of his time to his work as dean, becoming an outstanding leader in matters of medical education. He emphasized the importance in the selection of medical students of a general assessment of personality, character, and ability, rather than of judging solely by academic achievements; he made awards of clinical scholarships on his personal judgment, not on examination results, in a way comparable to the method used in electing Rhodes Scholars. This led to heavy criticism, and was stigmatized by some as just a way of rewarding athletic prowess.

During the years at St Mary's, Wilson also pressed for the initiation of full-time professorial units at the hospital and for a great increase in the number of beds available for clinical teaching. This he did by linking St Mary's with the old Paddington Infirmary in the Harrow Road, being himself a visiting physician there on the London County Council staff. He took a large part in the heated discussions of that time, between those who resented paid appointments of clinical teachers at an LCC hospital, and those who defended the honorary system of the voluntary hospitals. Wilson firmly backed the co-operation of the two systems, long before the days of the National Health Service, with which he later became so deeply involved. It was Wilson's remarkable skill in presenting the case which largely persuaded Lord Revelstoke and Lord Beaverbrook to give donations to the rebuilding fund of the medical school large enough to enable the new buildings to be built, and opened by HM King George V in December 1933. At the same time Lord Beaverbrook gave the money to buy the fine athletic ground at Teddington for St Mary's.

Wilson was knighted in 1938 and in the same year was elected treasurer of the Royal College of Physicians. In 1940 he became personal physician (see also T C Hunt) to Sir Winston Churchill, and accompanied him to conferences at Casablanca, Cairo, Teheran, Yalta and on other wartime visits abroad. He became a well known public figure when he successfully treated Sir Winston – with D Evan Bedford – for pneumonia near Tunis at the end of 1943. It was in this year that he was created a peer – First Baron Moran of Manton in the County of Wiltshire.

In 1941 he was elected PRCP, being re-elected each year until 1950, when he was succeeded by W Russell (later Lord) Brain. Moran was the youngest president of the College for many years, and owed his election greatly to the support of a small group known as the Younger Fellows Club, who believed that the College urgently needed a new approach to medical affairs.

Moran was president of the College during the difficult years preceding the introduction of the National Health Service. Between 1946 and 1948 the terms of service of the new Health Service Act were debated and furiously contested, and Moran showed tenacity and much political skill in working for what he believed were the best terms that could be got. In his efforts to obtain these he met fierce opposition from some of his consultant colleagues, but it was certainly his powerful advocacy of the distinction awards for consultants that gave them advantages they would probably not otherwise have had. He was a member of the 1948 Spens Committee for Consultants and Specialists, and the profession owes much to his determination and diplomacy, during the long drawn out arguments between the supporters of a full-time medical service and those who saw this as a disaster. Moran was in the centre of the political conflict between consultants and general practitioners.

He did much to bring consultants together, and worked hard to unite the three Royal Colleges and to form a representative committee of all consultants, which could offer expert advice to the Government on matters of policy. For a time he supported a project for the formation of an academy of medicine and surgery, which would link the College of Physicians and the College of Surgeons in a joint precinct in Lincoln's Inn Fields. This idea, which was initially put forward by Sir Alfred (later Lord) Webb-Johnson, president of the Royal College of Surgeons, ultimately came to nothing, for a number of reasons, and caused disappointment to many and feelings of regret for a great opportunity lost.

Moran made no secret of his belief that the consultants were in a different class from the general practitioners, and in 1958 caused bitter resentment by his replies to questions put to him on this point at the Royal Commission on Doctors' and Dentists' Remuneration. Asked if he thought consultants and general practitioners were to be regarded as on a 'level', he replied: 'emphatically no – could anything be more absurd? A medical career was a ladder on which those of outstanding merit rose to be consultants and others fell off to be practitioners.'

During the 1939–1945 war Moran was in charge of a large sector of the Emergency Medical Service, but much of his energy and time were taken up with his duties as personal physician to Sir Winston Churchill. There is no doubt that his judgment and skill were important factors in maintaining Sir Winston's health through the long continuing strain of those arduous times. In his special position as doctor, Moran necessarily became involved in matters of national importance, and this gave him almost a feeling of possessive obsession about his patient and his work. He was in fact supremely fitted for his role, being not only a wise physician but having the courage both to take risks when needed, and to persuade his difficult patient to follow his advice. His skill in choosing the right specialist at the right moment and in giving guidance to them in the handling of a sick and often obstructive patient was evidence of his exceptional ability in the art of medicine. One of the precepts which he had early learnt was Pitcairn's well-known saying 'The last thing a physician learns in the course of his experience is to know when to do nothing.'

After his elevation to the Peerage in 1943 Moran spoke effectively in the House of Lords, and his close association with Aneurin Bevan, Minister of Health, and his intimate contacts with others concerned with the Health Service, gave him a powerful influence in shaping future standards of medical practice. Few would deny the lasting debt which the profession owes him, if only (as he said himself) by preventing medicine from degenerating into a trade. It is greatly owing to Moran's vision that British medicine stands in so high a position, and his period of office as president brought the Royal College of Physicians increasing authority, both academically and nationally. Indeed it seemed to some that his position amongst the leaders of the country lessened his capacity to deal happily with the rank and file of consultants and practitioners. Though not aloof, he was sometimes intolerant of the prejudices of his fellow doctors and did not always find that special facility which brings affection rather than admiration. In spite of his devastating power of criticism he could show great kindness and sensibility, and would concern himself with trivial matters if by so doing he could help those in trouble.

In 1957 Moran was appointed chairman of the Army Medical Advisory Board and was consultant adviser to the Ministry of Health. His interest in the College and indeed in public affairs continued into his old age, and whilst he lived in Bryanston Square he continued to attend College dinners until he was well over eighty. He died in 1977 after retirement to his son's home in Hampshire, at the age of ninety-four, and was survived by his wife and his two sons, one of whom was ambassador at Lisbon at the time of his death.

Lord Moran's achievements owed much to the help of his wife, Dorothy, who married him in 1919. She was the daughter of Dr SF Dufton, an Inspector of Schools in Yorkshire, and Moran's devotion, during a terrible period when for nearly a year she was unconscious in St Thomas's Hospital following a stroke, was rewarded by her almost miraculous recovery and return to fully active life. Dorothy had been a student of Joseph Barcroft, and her exceptional qualities of patience, tact and friendliness made her the ideal partner in Moran's long and courageous career. Her father had been the first Science Fellow of Trinity College, Cambridge, which gave her valuable experience in academic affairs.

Moran's career will be remembered best for the effect it had upon the formation and development of the National Health Service, but the public will always associate his name with that of Sir Winston Churchill. His achievements in medical education – not only in the transformation of St Mary's Hospital, but in his determination to establish careers in academic medicine and to develop clinical units – are lasting tributes. As a writer he had a style and force which was the product of a great love of literature and much hard work. His Harveian oration delivered in 1952 'On Credulity' is a fine example of the way in which he could express his ideas with the maximum effect and the minimum of unnecessary words. His absorption in the life of Sir Winston and his fascination for writing led to the publication in 1966 of his book *Winston Churchill: the Struggle for Survival 1940–1965*, which recorded from his diary events and impressions during the association between them from 1940 to 1960. The last five years of Sir Winston's life are not included since Moran 'saw no point in continuing the story beyond the time when it ceased to have any historical significance'. It is certainly a book of historical importance, of over 800 pages, and written in Moran's own direct and very readable manner. It describes not only incidents and conversations of major national importance but also gives many details about personal and medical matters which only a doctor could possibly know. In the preface Moran explained that, although reluctant to write about Winston while he was his doctor, he was persuaded to do so by GM Trevelyan, who told him it was his duty to make known to posterity facts which were not known to others. It was these disclosures which led to strong feelings that Moran had overstepped the accepted standards of the profession, by publishing intimate medical information which many thought should have been kept confidential until at least some years after Sir Winston's death. Many of his fellow doctors, including the General Ethical Committee of the British Medical Association, disapproved of the book, and the wishes of Sir Winston's family and some of those mentioned in the book were, it seemed, against him. Others spoke enthusiastically of Moran as Winston's Boswell, and although perhaps too long, no one can read the book without absorbing interest.

Moran's skill as an orator was exceptional, and his annual addresses to Comitia at the RCP, in which he commemorated Fellows of the College who had died during the preceding year, delivered with hardly a note, were superb examples of the speaker's art. In the House of Lords he always drew full and attentive audiences, and his speeches have been compared with those of William Pitt! He seemed to confirm Disraeli's observation (noted by Moran in one of his lectures) that 'with words we govern men'.

As a clinician he could have been amongst the ablest diagnosticians of his time, but his other interests made him almost abandon both private practice and student teaching. He did much for the College in his efforts to raise the standard of teaching, in the shaping of examinations, and in the field of vocational training both of students and postgraduates. His constant emphasis upon the training of the mind as against the mere accumulation of factual knowledge was matched by his contempt for those who took up medicine for gain. He saw the doctor as a humanist and accepted for himself – as well as for others – the old Greek dictum 'A doctor should end his life as a philosopher'. TCH

[*Times,* 13 Apr 1977; *Brit. med. J.,* 1977, **1**, 1088, 1289; *Lancet,* 1977, **1**, 915-916; *Canadian Doctor,* Feb 1978; *St Mary's Hosp. Gaz.,* 1973, **79** (1); Portrait; Photo]

MORGAN, Benjamin Branford *b.*22 Feb 1888 *d.*27 Feb 1980
MB ChB Edin (1910) MD (1913) MRCPE (1924) MRCP (1925) FRCP (1937) FRCPE (1951)

Benjamin Branford Morgan was born in Norwich where his father was a chartered surveyor; one of eleven children, he was educated at Norwich School (King Edward VI) and Edinburgh, where he represented the university at association football and qualified in 1910. After house appointments in Sheffield and London he proceeded MD at Edinburgh University and in 1914 joined a general practice in Norwich. Six months later he left to serve as a captain in the RAMC (TA), spent four years in France and was mentioned in despatches. During war service he developed an interest in anaesthetics, and after his return to general practice in Norwich was appointed a part-time assistant anaesthetist to the Norfolk and Norwich Hospital. After obtaining both the London and Edinburgh diplomas of MRCP, he forsook his anaesthetic appointment for that of assistant to the cardiac department at the Norfolk and Norwich Hospital under HJ Starling, became a founder member of the British Cardiac Society – then the Cardiac Club – and in the same year, 1925, was appointed physician to the Jenny Lind Hospital for Children. Three years later he retired from general practice on his appointment as physician to the Norfolk and Norwich Hospital. Whilst physician to Great Yarmouth, Lowestoft and Cromer and District Hospitals, Branford Morgan built up a large consultant medical practice with a special interest in cardiology, interrupted from 1939 to 1940 by a year's service with the RAMC as a lieutenant colonel in Iceland. He examined in medicine at Cambridge University, and served for many years on the medical committee of the Norwich Union Insurance Society.

Branford Morgan – 'Branny' to his friends – was the last Norfolk and Norwich Hospital physician to be appointed from a local general practice. Ability, hard work and meticulous attention to his professional duties were qualities that did not fail him throughout his long professional life – for many years after retirement he remained active in private and insurance medicine. A kind and understanding man, he was adept at handling his Norfolk patients. As a younger man he fished and kept a boat on the Norfolk Broads; in later years he enjoyed gardening and golf and was a captain of the Royal Norwich Golf Club. In 1917 he married Ethel Wilcock, a nursing sister; she predeceased him and he was survived by their two married daughters and grandchildren. ABS

[*Brit. med. J.,* 1980, **281**, 66; *Eastern Daily Press,* 28 Feb 1980; Photo]

MORLEY, Edward Penistan *b.*13 Aug 1912 *d.*19 Sept 1979
BA Cantab (1936) MRCS LRCP (1939) MB BChir (1939)
MRCP (1947) FRCP (1969)

Edward Morley was physician emeritus to the Lincoln Group of hospitals. He was born at Barton-on-Humber, Lincolnshire, the son of Edwin Bertram Morley, a medical practitioner, and his wife Ada Mary, daughter of Alfred Dixey, a tea importer. He was educated at Mill Hill School and Trinity Hall, Cambridge, and was the fourth generation of medical practitioners in his family; his great-grandfather, grandfather and father having all been in practice at Barton-on-Humber.

He qualified at the London Hospital in 1939 and after house appointments at Chase Farm Hospital, Enfield, joined the RAMC. From 1942 to 1945 he served in military hospitals in India. On his return home after demobilization he held junior posts as supernumerary registrar at the London Victoria Park, and National Hospital, Queen Square. At the latter he developed a special interest in neurology, and just before the introduction of the NHS he joined the consultant staff at Lincoln County Hospital and John Coupland Hospital, Gainsborough. His early days at Lincoln coincided with the period of annual poliomyelitis outbreaks, and he assumed responsibility for the organization and care of these patients. He was interested in the whole of general medicine as well as neurology, and it was largely due to his efforts that a coronary care unit was set up at Lincoln when this was something of an innovation in peripheral hospitals.

In 1947 he married Joyce Frances, daughter of Albert George Bower, an engineer. Their two children, a son and a daughter, were both adopted. Outside his profession his main interests, apart from his family, were sailing and rugby football; he played for the Old Millhillians, London Hospital and United Hospitals, and occasionally for Cambridge. He was president of Cambridge University Medical Society in 1936. His book *Pins and Needles* was published by Medical Press in 1956.

A kind and conscientious man, Edward Morley was known as 'the doctors' doctor' for he was the one to whom his colleagues turned for advice when they, or their families, were in trouble. During his last illness his main desire was to save his colleagues the embarrassment of their own helplessness. He derived much comfort from his family and from a renewal of an early interest in painting. GW/VL

[*Brit. med. J.*, 1979, **2**, 1592; Photo]

MORROW, *Sir* Arthur (William) *b.*12 July 1903 *d.*22 Aug 1977
Kt (1959) DSO (1942) MB BS Sydney (1927) MRCP (1933)
FRACP (1938) FRCP (1949) Hon FACP (1967)

Bill Morrow was born in Maitland, New South Wales, had a brilliant scholastic career at Newington College, Sydney, and graduated in medicine from the University of Sydney in 1927 with first class honours.

Bill immediately entered the Royal Prince Alfred Hospital as a junior resident, and he was actively associated with that great hospital for the rest of his life. He became deputy medical superintendent in 1932, honorary assistant physician in 1934, honorary physician in 1951 and honorary consultant physician in 1963.

Mastery of clinical judgement through experience at the bedside, and the teaching of the science and art of the subject, were the dominating forces in his highly successful professional career. His wide reading and regular attendance at a vast number of postgraduate teaching sessions at many hospitals, both at home and overseas, enabled him to speak with authority on all current subjects, to the great advantage of his patients, colleagues and students alike.

Bill was a gracious and courteous gentleman, a very popular consultant, an outstanding teacher and dedicated to the welfare of his chosen profession. He exerted a profound influence for the best in the practice of medicine in Australia through his quiet personal contact with all members of the profession, junior as well as senior; whether in wards, in committee or on the golf course.

It is not surprising that Bill played an important role in the life of the Royal Australasian College of Physicians – foundation fellow in 1938, censor (1952–1966) and censor-in-chief (1962–1966). He was elected to the council in 1957 and became president for the term 1966–1968. In recognition of his services the AW Morrow Room was dedicated to his memory in the College.

Apart from the Royal Prince Alfred Hospital, Bill held consultant physician posts at the Repatriation General Hospital, Concord, and many other suburban hospitals in Sydney. He was lecturer in therapeutics at the University of Sydney from 1935 to 1963, and lecturer and examiner in clinical medicine from 1946 to 1963.

He was also deeply involved in many professional organizations which included the Australian Medical Association, being a councillor and president (1958–1959) of the New South Wales branch, the postgraduate committee in medicine of the University of Sydney and a number of private foundations.

In 1950 he was appointed to the Commonwealth Formulary committee, which later became the Pharmaceutical Benefits Advisory committee, and he served as its chairman until 1973. He was also chairman of the Commonwealth Drug Evaluation committee.

Early in his career at Prince Alfred, Bill showed interest in gastric disorders and he eventually established a gastroenterology unit in 1950, which was named the AW Morrow Institute in 1961. Owing to his insistence on the highest standards of patient care and research, together with an aptitude for selecting bright young physicians, the Institute now enjoys a worldwide reputation of high standing.

Bill had a very distinguished record of war service. He enlisted at the outbreak of war in 1939 and was appointed officer commanding the medical division of the 2/5 Australian General Hospital. This hospital was sent to Greece in 1941 but was soon recalled. As a lieutenant colonel, Morrow took command in the retreat to Africa, the commanding officer having been killed at Piraeus. For his work during this action Bill was awarded the Distinguished Service Order. Later the unit returned to Australia and he was promoted to colonel. During the remainder of his Army career he held posts of commanding officer of the 119 and 121 Australian General Hospitals, and in 1943 became assistant director-general Medical Service Land HQ, and the next year consultant physician Advanced Land HQ. With Hamilton Fairley, Bill had the task of controlling malaria, typhus and other diseases in the Australian Army in New Guinea and the tropics and this was successfully achieved.

In 1937 Bill married Jane Brown and thus began a most happy and successful family and social life. They had three wonderful daughters, but Jane's death in 1971 was a bitter blow to them all. However, some years later he was to find another fine companion in Margaret Chauvel, whom he married in 1974.

In spite of his very busy and demanding professional life, he never omitted his regular visit to the golf course, where he found immense pleasure not only in the game but also in the company of a vast number of friends.

And so Bill achieved his many ambitions in life, at the same time making an outstanding contribution to medicine in Australia. HMR

MOSHAL, Michael George *b.*23 Oct 1935 *d.*14 Oct 1981
BSc Capetown (1956) MB ChB (1960) FCP SA (1966)
MRFP Lond (1967) FRCP (1979)

Michael George Moshal was born in Durban, South Africa, the son of Bernard Moshal, also a physician and a member of the Royal College of Physicians of London. Michael was educated at Durban High School and the University of Capetown, qualifying in 1960. He entered the Groote Schuur Hospital, Capetown, for postgraduate training in medicine and gastroenterology, and held house appointments from 1961 to 1967. He was awarded the Cecil John Adams travelling fellowship in 1967 and spent a period at Hammersmith Hospital, London. From 1968 to 1969 he was a fellow in gastroenterology at the Mallory and Thorndike Institute, Harvard Medical School and Boston City Hospital, USA, and on his return to Durban in 1969 he established a gastrointestinal unit, which soon achieved national and international status on account of its research.

Michael Moshal published over 130 papers and attended numerous congresses in South Africa, Europe and the Americas. From 1977 to 1981 he was president of the South African Gastroenterology Society and was later made life president. He was appointed professor and director of the Research Institute for Diseases in a Tropical Environment, South African Medical Research Council, Durban, an institute which deals mainly with research into amoebiasis, schistosomiasis and malaria. He was also appointed director of the South African Medical Research Group for duodenal ulceration.

Michael was active in local medical politics and took part in the fight against discrimination on a racial basis in relation to doctors' salaries. He was a member of the Natal Coast Branch of the Medical Association of South Africa.

He married Denise Margaret, daughter of Abraham Kaplan, an attorney, in 1960. They had four sons. Michael was a sincere, forthright man, with an obsession for work, having few interests outside his profession and his family, being dedicated to research. He accomplished a great deal within a very short period and his workaholic behaviour made one wonder whether he perhaps felt that his stay on earth was short, and that he had to complete his work within a given time. He took a great interest in the underprivileged population and never practised racial discrimination. The large multiracial crowd which attended his funeral was a testimony to the many friends he had. Throughout his brief life he showed great fortitude, and never more so than in his fight against his incurable illness.
GW/VL

[*Lancet,* 1981, **2**, 1060]

MUIR, David Clark *b*.15 Mar 1898 *d*.28 Nov 1983
MRCS LRCP (1922) MB BS Lond (1923) MRCP (1925)
FRCP (1935)

David Clark Muir was the son of a family physician in Wales. He attended Llandovery School where he developed a life long interest in the classics, particularly in Greek, and also in rugby football, a sport at which he was highly successful despite his small physical stature. Two of his brothers became physicians and David followed a tradition in a family which has produced physicians and surgeons in successive generations. He chose the Middlesex Hospital in London and completed his first year before leaving to join the other young men of that period in the trenches of Flanders. He spent two years as a rifleman in the Rifle Brigade but was sent back to complete his medical studies when the need for doctors became an overriding priority. He duly qualified MRCS LRCP in 1922, obtaining the MB BS in 1922 and in 1925 proceeded to MD and gained the MRCP. He was elected FRCP in 1935. He was appointed medical registrar at the Middlesex and established lasting friendships with the post war group of physicians qualifying at that time. He also worked for a period at St Johns Hospital for Diseases of the Skin.

In 1927 he was appointed honorary physician to Hull Royal Infirmary and moved to East Yorkshire with his wife Anne. He was a first rate clinician and teacher. He had little opportunity for research but had an intense interest in the individual patient and his opinion was widely sought. He had particular skill in cardiology and, with J Brown from Grimsby, established a clinic in Hull which developed into a referral centre for congenital heart disease. He became a member of the Cardiac Society and it was a matter of great pleasure and pride to him when members of that Society held one of their meetings in Hull and visited the clinic.

His practice was interrupted by a further period of war service in 1939. He served for three years as a lieutenant colonel in charge of a medical division in the Middle East. After the war he resumed his consulting practice in Hull. He was appointed a member of the regional hospital board and spent much time on the board; working during the introduction of the NHS. He foresaw all too well many of the structural problems in the proposed medical staffing system, the employment difficulties that would face the trained specialists and the particular difficulties of the non-teaching hospitals. It was a matter of great and lasting regret to him that he was not able to influence the system so that these could be avoided.

He made great efforts to encourage the careers of house physicians and registrars who worked with him over the years and he was always pleased to learn of their progress. His own preoccupation with a busy clinical practice left him little time to develop outside interests and retirement placed a great strain on him. He had suffered from diabetes mellitus for many years and his increasingly poor health caused him great distress. He died at the age of 85, within a few months of the death of his wife.

He was survived by a daughter and two sons, one of whom is a physician and fellow of the College. DCFM

[*Brit. med. J.*, 1984, **288**, 80; Photo]

MUNRO, Ian Bruce *b.*16 Nov 1921 *d.*14 Sept 1980
MB ChB Glasg (1946) FRFPSG (1955) MRCP (1957)
MRCPE (1957) FRCPG (1970) FRCPE (1973) FRCP (1974)

Bruce Munro, consultant physician to the Rochdale group of hospitals, earned a reputation for being a shrewd diagnostician. He had a large practice in general medicine, with a special interest in diabetes and a flair for neurology. Although a reluctant committee man, he took more than his share of medical administration, acting as secretary to the medical executive and medical staff committees. For a year he was also consultant member of the management team. He was a lifelong member of the BMA and a faithful supporter of the Association during the troubled times of 1974.

He was born in Edinburgh, where his father Donald Munro was a bank manager, and educated at Grantown Grammar School, Morayshire, and the University of Glasgow Medical School. On graduation, after house appointments at the Victoria Infirmary and Ruchill Hospital, Glasgow, he was appointed senior registrar in medicine at the Norfolk and Norwich Hospital — an appointment he looked back on with affection. He married Mary Hewitt, daughter of a farmer, and they had one daughter.

Bruce was a very experienced physician whose wisdom and sharp intelligence, together with his wide reading, made others value his advice in difficult cases. He never despised the benefits of high technology medicine, but always maintained that careful history taking and clinical observation were of paramount importance. He

was a gentle, self-deprecating man, with an absolute loyalty to his colleagues which was greatly appreciated, and a dry, astringent wit which made him an amusing companion. Unfortunately, his health deteriorated and he reluctantly decided on early retirement. He was a keen golfer and gardener, and it was in his garden that he suffered a fatal coronary thrombosis. He was survived by his wife Mary, and his daughter Catherine.
GW/VL

[*Brit. med. J.*, 1980, **281**, 1150]

MURPHY, *Sir* **Alexander (Paterson)** *b.*25 Oct 1892 *d.*1 Oct 1976
Kt (1954) MC (1918) MB ChM Syd (1916) FRACP (1938)
MD Syd (1947) FRCP* (1954) Hon MD Qld (1967) Hon DSc (1958)

Alexander Murphy was born, bred and educated in Brisbane, and graduated from the University of Sydney in 1916. During the first world war he served in the AIF and in 1918 was awarded the Military Cross for conspicuous gallantry and devotion to duty. He also served as a consultant physician during the second world war. He returned to practice in Brisbane in 1920, first as a general practitioner and then as a consultant physician. In 1921 he married Esme Hobson, by whom he had three daughters.

Murphy was visiting physician to the Brisbane General Hospital until his appointment as honorary consulting physician, and upon establishment of the Medical School in 1937 became the first professor of medicine at the University of Queensland, an appointment which he held until 1946, continuing to serve as part-time foundation professor of medicine until 1950. A foundation fellow of the Royal Australasian College of Physicians in 1938, he was elected president in 1954, having served on council continuously in the intervening years; at the time of his retirement he had completed 20 years of unbroken service. His membership of the BMA/AMA extended over 60 years, and during this time he served on many committees and council, being president of the 7th session of the Australasian Medical Congress in 1950, when he gave a brilliant presidential address. He was much sought after as a lecturer and orator, and other outstanding addresses included the Bancroft Oration in Brisbane in 1954, the Listerian Oration in Adelaide in 1955 and the Syme Oration in Sydney in 1959. His association with the Australian Postgraduate Federation in Medicine extended back to its formative days in the 1940s, and he served on the council for many years, becoming patron of the Federation in 1967, a position which he occupied with distinction until his death. He was also a director of the Queensland Division of the National Heart Foundation. He received his knighthood in 1954, and in the same year was elected a fellow of the Royal College of Physicians of London. Other honours included the fellowship of the Australian Medical Association in 1964.

His numerous services to Australian postgraduate medical education began about 1929; and in later life, as doyen of the medical profession in Queensland, he was not only greatly respected in his home State but had also achieved an honoured position in Australian medicine as a whole. He was a doctor of great learning, with a marvellous ability to teach others, and one who, by his example, set a standard of medical practice to be emulated. He had little leisure time, but when he did find time to relax there was nothing he liked better than a game of golf. GW/VL

[*Med. J. Aust.*, 1977, **1**, 263; *Aust. Postgrad. Fed. in Med. Report*, 1977; *Med. Directory of Aust.*, 1974; *RACP Newsletter*, **8**, No. 4, Dec. 1976; Photo]

MURPHY, *Sir* **(Oswald) Ellis (Joseph)** *b.*2 Apr 1895 *d.*- July 1980 Kt (1963) MB ChM Sydney (1918) MRCP (1928) FRACP (1938) FRCP (1954)

Ellis Murphy, the son of Miles Murphy, a wool broker, and his wife Mary Josephine, daughter of Ernest Grenenger, tanner, was born in Sydney and educated at Lewisham High School and Sydney University. He graduated in 1918, with first class honours, and almost immediately joined the Armed Forces. As a captain in the RAMC he served as RMO No 4 AG Hospital, Randwick, from 1919 to 1920. On demobilization he was appointed physician to outpatients at the Mater Misericordiae Public Hospital, Brisbane, where he served from 1923 to 1938. He joined the RAAMC during the second world war and saw service in the Middle East and Ceylon, being promoted to the rank of lieutenant colonel. On leaving the Army, after cessation of hostilities, he was made an honorary colonel. From 1944 to 1954 he served as physician to Brisbane General hospital, and was visiting physician to Greenslopes Repatriation Hospital and Kenmore Sanatorium. He was also lecturer in tropical diseases at Queensland University and acting professor of medicine from 1950 to 1954.

Murphy was a foundation fellow of the RACP; chairman of the Queensland Division of the Red Cross Blood Transfusion Service, and deputy chairman of the Queensland Division of the Australian Red Cross. He was honorary secretary to the Queensland Branch of the BMA in 1936, member of the council 1936 to 1937 and in 1939; member of the council of the RACP 1958 to 1964, a director of the National Heart Foundation of Australia (Queensland Division) and chairman of the Work Assessment Centre Committee. Between 1929 to 1939 he contributed several articles to the *Medical Journal of Australia*.

In 1924, Ellis Murphy married May, daughter of the Hon Thomas Charles Beirne, draper. They had two sons, one of whom predeceased him, and two daughters. His interests outside medicine lay in sheep and cattle breeding, and yachting. He took his sailing seriously and was winner of both Ocean and Bay races. GW/VL

[Photo]

MUTCH, Nathan *b.*- 1886 *d.*3 June 1982
MA MB BChir Cantab (1911) MRCP (1913) MD (1917)
FRCP (1920)

Nathan Mutch was educated at Manchester Grammar School and Emmanuel College, Cambridge, and completed his medical training at Guy's Hospital, London. He married the third daughter of Sir William Arbuthnot Lane.

My first impression of Nathan Mutch was as a student at Guy's before the war when, on going to the medical block (Hunts House) for my chief's rounds – which usually started on time – I passed, on my way up the wide staircase, a group of disconsolate students waiting for Nathan, for he was invariably late although he nevertheless managed to leave sharp on time. At that time, he seemed a rather distant figure to me, and there is undoubtedly truth in what is said of him in the obituary notice which appeared in the *Lancet*: to some extent he was overshadowed by his colleagues who were an outstandingly brilliant and forceful lot.

Nathan, on the other hand, was of a much more modest and retiring nature. In those days the resident medical staff would put on a play in which various members of the staff were portrayed, sometimes quite unkindly, and I recall one in which Nathan was caricatured and labelled as 'Dr Nothing Mutch'. Nothing, in fact, could have been further from the truth, for there was very much to Nathan and the more one knew him the more one grew to admire and respect him, and this is precisely what happened to me during the years 1941–1943, when I had the good fortune to work for him, first as house physician and later as registrar, at the Guy's Base Hospital, Farnborough, Kent. Nathan was then senior physician at Guy's but spent all his time at Farnborough, living near the hospital, undertaking teaching rounds, and having the care of half the medical beds as well as carrying on research in the pathology laboratory, in his well loved field of pharmacology.

Contact with him then was close, for he spent a lot of his time in the Mess and took his meals with students and staff. He proved to be very different from the distant character we had thought him to be before the war. He was a warm, affectionate, amusing person with a great sense of fun. The more one saw him at work in the wards, the more one realized his extraordinarily wide grasp of medicine and his tremendous ability as a general physician, although gastroenterology was undoubtedly his main interest. He had various well known 'quirks' which related in particular to the gastrointestinal tract. I well remember his teaching, and trying the effect of some alkali-gel that he fondly imagined could settle in the base of the gastric ulcer and so fill it. Also, in gastric and duodenal ulcers, he would frequently want a Curtiss belt fitted, so that this would 'raise the intra-abdominal pressure' and so lift the stomach and help the ulcer to heal. His other 'quirk' or 'kink' was focal sepsis. Anyone with a PUO would need to have been investigated for focal sepsis before being presented to Nathan. This involved a full jaw X-ray for apical abscess, a cholecystrogram for cholecystitis, and one other – which I have now forgotten, although I must have been asked for it not once but a hundred times. Another favourite was 'uplift therapy' – his own words. If someone presented with fatigue, and anaemia or other organic disease had been excluded, we would be told to give the 'uplift therapy'. This meant kaolin and paraffin emulsion three times a day before meals and large doses of every vitamin conceivable. Strangely, and heaven only knows why, a lot of people seemed to feel the better for this. The 'Master' himself took it, and his fantastic good health, youthful appearance and ultimate longevity may, in retrospect, bear witness to there being something in this much derided 'uplift therapy' after all.

His interest in pharmacology started in his days at Cambridge, and he was a founder member of the British Pharmacological Society, and on the editorial board of the *British Journal of Pharmacology and Therapeutics*. His main contribution to therapy was the introduction of magnesium trisilicate as an antacid for the treatment of peptic ulcers.

As I have said, he was an outstandingly good general physician and a lovable man. He treated the staff with affection, consideration and patience. It was a treat to watch him examine a chest and teach us how to do it. I well remember summoning him urgently to the ward, one day after tea, to see a man I thought had suddenly developed aortic incompetence. Nathan listened for two or three seconds, stood up, and gently pointed out to me that it was pericardial friction.

Unfortunately, I can speak of him only as I knew him during that short time between 1941 and 1943. I saw little of him after that, except for one brief encounter at the RSM around 1950 – when he looked as young and sprightly as ever. GT

[*Lancet*, 1982, **1**, 54; Photo]

NATTRASS, Frederick John *b*.6 Aug 1891 *d*.19 Jan 1979
MB BS Durh (1914) MRCS LRCP (1914) MD (1920)
MRCP (1920) FRCP (1931) Hon DCL Newcastle (1974)

Frederick Nattrass was born in West Bromwich in the Midlands, son of the Reverend J Conder Nattrass BA BD, a Methodist minister, and his wife Hannah Clark. He had no brothers and one sister Charlotte, his senior by seven years, who was a fine musician and ultimately became deputy headmistress of a senior girl's school. His father was well known in the Methodist Church and composed a hymn tune (Stainforth) which was included in the Old Methodist Hymn Book; he had three brothers who ran a miller's business in Stockton on Tees.

Frederick was educated at King Edward's School, Birmingham, where his scientific and academic abilities were recognized and nurtured. When the family moved to the north-east of England he entered the dental school in Newcastle upon Tyne in the University of Durham, but soon transferred to the medical faculty and became one of the outstanding students of his generation, gaining the Turnbull prize in anatomy, and the Gibson prize in midwifery and in gynaecology. He obtained distinctions in no fewer than eleven subjects in the professional examinations during the medical course, graduating with first class honours in 1914. He then spent a year as a house physician and house surgeon in the Royal Victoria Infirmary and during this time, in the course of an illness, he was nursed by Gladys Vickers, the daughter of Benjamin Vickers of Lincoln, whom he married in 1915.

Afterwards he joined the Royal Army Medical Corps and served at home and in France, was captured by the Germans in their 1918 offensive and remained a prisoner in their hands for nine months. On his return to civilian life he took an appointment in the department of pathology at the Royal Victoria Infirmary, and then became a medical registrar. During the tenure of the latter appointment he gained the degree of doctor of medicine with the gold medal, awarded for the most distinguished doctorate submitted in that year. The subject of his essay was 'The Diagnosis and Treatment of Injuries of the Peripheral Nerves', an indication of his interest in neurology which remained throughout the whole of his professional life.

In 1921 he was appointed honorary assistant physician to the Royal Victoria Infirmary, becoming honorary physician in 1935. He also held appointments in neighbouring hospitals and quickly built up a large consulting practice. In 1941, on being appointed to the first whole-time chair of medicine in Newcastle, he at first curtailed and soon gave up consulting practice in order to devote his whole time and energy to the development of an outstanding department of medicine at the medical school and infirmary. It was typical of his high purpose that he made a very substantial financial sacrifice in order to accept this appointment, and also lost one of his deep and abiding interests, namely, the continuing and fruitful association with practitioners and patients in their own homes.

During his professional career, first as a physician and later as professor of medicine, he was an external examiner in medicine in the Universities of Bristol, Manchester, Belfast, St Andrews, Dublin and the National University of Ireland. He became a censor of the Royal College of Physicians in 1950–1952 and was senior censor from 1955 to 1956. He was president of the Newcastle upon Tyne and Northern Counties Medical Society from 1948 to 1949, president of the Association of Physicians of Great Britain and Ireland from 1953 to 1954, president of the section of neurology of the Royal Society of Medicine from 1954 to 1955 and president of the Association of British Neurologists from 1957 to 1959.

After his retirement he was president of the 3rd International Congress on Muscle Diseases when this was held in Newcastle upon Tyne in 1974, and it was during that Congress that his old University conferred upon him an honorary doctorate in civil law.

After retiring from the chair of medicine in 1956 he served for a time as professor of medicine at the University of Lagos in Nigeria in 1962–1963.

When the Association of Physicians of the Northern Region was founded he was not only a founder member but also its first president, and he took a continuing interest in this Association until he eventually relinquished the presidency in 1976. Nattrass had a deep and continuing concern with the Medical Pilgrims, that small and select travelling club of physicians founded by Sir Arthur Hurst, of which he was a founder member and secretary for 25 years.

Early in his professional career, in 1931, he published a textbook entitled *The Commoner Nervous Diseases* and subsequently wrote the section on 'Diseases of the Nervous System' in Chamberlain's *Textbook of Medicine*, published in 1951. He also did some interesting work on epilepsy which was the topic of his Lumleian lecture to the Royal College of Physicians. Latterly he became increasingly interested in diseases of muscle, and it was upon this topic that he gave his presidential address to the section of neurology of the Royal Society of Medicine in 1954. Not surprisingly, therefore, he was chosen as the first chairman of the Muscular Dystrophy Group of Great Britain, and after his retirement devoted much of his substantial energy to furthering the interests of the Group and overseeing its administrative, research and financial affairs, with his customary combination of infinite tact, deep concern, rational judgement and fair-mindedness. When, at the age of 84, he felt he could no longer attend regularly management and research committee meetings of the Group, it came as an immense pleasure to him that he was appointed its life president; even in 1978, despite deteriorating eyesight, hearing and general health, he continued to enquire perspicaciously about the Group and its affairs, remaining as sharp intellectually as ever, with continuing insight into the wider field of medicine.

Frederick Nattrass made a continuing contribution to medicine in Newcastle after his retirement through his activities as Pastoral Visitor in Medicine to the Northern Region. His judicial turn of mind enabled him to weigh evidence, to reach logical conclusions and to present these with clarity and force; as a physician he was precise, astute and yet compassionate and caring and as a teacher pragmatic, straightforward, never flashy nor given to flights of fancy but at the same time never dull. It was at the bedside rather than in the formal lecture theatre that his clinical acumen and kindly nature stood out, and his ward rounds were very popular with students and postgraduates. He had a considerable ability to gather around him young men and women of merit, including Henry Miller and Sir George Smart.

In his personal life Frederick Nattrass suffered many sadnesses, as his only son died young of Hodgkin's disease; his first wife died in 1951, suddenly, while he was examining in the MRCP examination in London; and his sister Charlotte, the schoolmistress, with whom he later lived, died in 1961. He found great joy in the company of his two daughters Pamela and Anne, and their respective families, and after his retirement moved to the south of England to live near them. His second marriage in 1963 to the charming Helen Byrne Bryce, into whose beautiful home at Burford he then moved, greatly enriched his later years, though sadly she too died in 1971. But for eight years he was able to share with her his abiding interest in ornithology and in music and art. In his early days in Newcastle, Nattrass had been president of the ornithology section of the Natural History Society of Northumberland and loved to take visitors to see the birds on the Farne Islands. A life-long ambition was fulfilled when he managed with Helen a trip to the Galapagos Islands when they were both in their seventies. He also had a good singing voice and was for many years a member of the Bach Choir in Newcastle, and one of the foremost bases in the choir.

In his last few years, despite failing eyesight and general health he remained as bright, as cheerful, and as interested as ever, and when the writer called to see him at Little Cocklands in Burford only a few weeks before his death, he showed intense interest in Newcastle and its medical affairs. Generations of colleagues and students will miss this delightful man, small in stature but upright and kindly in character. Until a few weeks before he died he seemed ageless, wise and indestructible. He left a mark on Newcastle medicine which can never be erased. JNW

[*Brit. med. J.*, 1979, **1**, 353, 483, 903, 1027; *Lancet*, 1979, **1**, 225, 337; *J. Neurol. Sci.*, 1979, **42** (1) 169; Photo]

NAYLOR, Granville Rex Etchell *b*.24 May 1920 *d*.26 Aug 1983
MB BChir Cantab (1945) MD (1954) MRCP (1946) FRCP (1976)

Granville Naylor was the son of the headmaster of Rotherham Grammar School, at which school he received his early education before coming to Gonville and Caius College, Cambridge, as a scholar in 1939. After a distinguished academic career, in which he achieved a double first in the Natural Sciences Tripos, he was awarded a Rockefeller scholarship to enable him to do his clinical studies at Cornell Medical College, New York. He was a medical intern at the New York Hospital in 1944 before returning to England to the Middlesex Hospital, where he was a house physician and casualty officer before coming to Cambridge as a demonstrator in pathology, and being appointed an official fellow of his old College, taking over the supervision in pathology of the College medical students. At once he showed that he was a superb teacher and this, coupled with his charming personality and genuine interest in his pupils, made him many lifelong friends. In the laboratory he was an excellent and meticulous research worker, and in cooperation with Muriel Adair he did much original work on the precipitation reaction.

In 1950 he was called up for his military service, and as a major in the RAMC was sent to Fayid in Egypt as the enteric officer to the Middle East Land Forces. Rex Naylor, as he was known to his many army friends, soon made a great reputation both as a scientific investigator and particularly for his personal friendly qualities. There had been substantial outbreaks of typhoid and paratyphoid fever amongst the service personnel in the Suez Canal Zone which he traced to urinary carriers amongst food handlers, and — of great importance

– he was able to show a relationship between these carriers and schistosomiasis of the bladder. So started his lifelong interest in enteric fevers, on which his thesis for the Cambridge MD was based. On leaving the army in 1951 he returned to Cambridge as a lecturer in pathology.

In 1963 RM Fry retired as director of the Cambridge Public Health Laboratory and Granville Naylor was elected to follow him. A happy choice, for his outstanding capacity for making friends enabled him to continue the excellent relationship that Fry had established between the laboratory and the doctors in the area. He also had to organize the move of the laboratory from the University site to the new Addenbrooke's Hospital, and the development of a single laboratory with the hospital microbiology laboratory. It was greatly to Naylor's credit that difficulties which might have occurred were avoided.

In 1975 coeliac disease, from which he had suffered all his life, became very much worse, and after a year away from the laboratory he resigned the directorship on medical grounds, and returned as lecturer to the University department, but unfortunately only for a short period.

In spite of his deteriorating health he threw himself energetically into his many hobbies. He was a craftsman in wood-working and the repair of antique furniture. In retirement he started a collection of ancient tools, and went to classes to learn book-binding. He was meticulous in all he did, as was shown when shortly before his death he was asked to audit the College silver. He set himself the task of becoming an expert in old silver, and made a complete inventory of the precise details of all the silver.

He was survived by his wife Nathalie whom he met as a fellow student while doing his clinical work at Cornell; she was the daughter of a New York doctor. They had two daughters and a son. RING

[*Brit. med. J.,* 1983, **287**, 1230; *Lancet,* 1983, **2**, 862]

NELIGAN, Gerald Anthony *b*.3 Feb 1918 *d*.1 June 1976
BM BCh Oxon (1942) MRCP (1947) DM (1948) FRCP (1967)

Gerald Neligan, reader in child health in the University of Newcastle upon Tyne, was born in Teheran, Persia. His father, Anthony Richard Neligan, was doctor to the British Legation and his mother, Kate Mary Leigh, was the daughter of Gerald Leigh Spencer, a clerk in Holy Orders. Gerald was educated in England, at Hazelhurst, Marlborough, and St John's College, Oxford University, where he read medicine, having entered with a scholarship in classics. He was awarded the John Radcliffe prize for clinical studies, graduating in 1942. After serving as house physician at the Radcliffe Infirmary, he joined the RAMC and saw active service in Europe. On demobilization he returned to Oxford and worked first as house physician to LJ Witts and then as registrar to Victoria Smallpiece. In 1948 he was appointed first assistant to Sir James Spence, at Newcastle, where his abilities were soon recognized, and he was promoted to senior lecturer in the University. In 1967 he was awarded a personal readership in recognition of his important contributions to research and teaching. He remained at the University for the rest of his life.

Gerald Neligan's interests and expertise in paediatrics were wide, and his DM thesis on pyogenic osteitis in childhood was published as a chapter in *Recent Advances in Paediatrics*, second edition (1959). His paper on hypoglycaemia appeared in the same book, third edition (1965). He also wrote important papers on undergraduate and postgraduate training, including a study of the work of regional consultant paediatricians. He was, however, best known for neonatal medicine. He was involved in virtually all aspects of new born medicine which were important and progressive, but was devastatingly critical of anything that was trivial, illogical, or inhuman. To a series of clinical problems he brought the same approach: he saw their importance, worked out logical, simple, and new ways of recognizing and treating them, and then strove to devise practical ways of prevention. It was as a result of his efforts that the Newcastle Study of Child Development was carried out. Through it, in particular, he successfully sought to relate perinatal events to subsequent life and progress, and demonstrated the nature and importance of social disadvantage.

Gerald used every activity as an occasion for teaching – of students, midwives, residents, and distinguished visitors alike. To have been broken in at the Princess Mary Maternity Hospital by Gerald was a unique experience, when both his boyish enthusiasm and his fine techniques were shared. His abilities were recognized well beyond Newcastle. He was external examiner at several universities, was a visiting professor at Boston, Khartoum and Athens, and served on the council and academic board of the British Paediatric Association.

In 1942 he married Mary Constance Windsor, daughter of Hugh Windsor Bell, a medical practitioner. They had six children. His interests outside medicine were in gardening and birdwatching, and he was happiest when at home with his family and friends. GW/VL

[*Lancet*, 1976, **2**, 158]

NEUSTATTER, Walter Lindesay *b.*7 Dec 1903 *d.*6 July 1978
BSc (1924) MRCS LRCP (1929) MB BS Lond (1931) MRCP (1932) MD (1941) FRCP (1967) FRCPsych (1972)

Walter Lindesay Neustatter was born in Munich, the son of a German ophthalmic surgeon, and an Australian mother. His father and mother found their lives together to be incompatible and they were divorced early in Lindesay's life (he was known to many of his friends by his second name and to some as Wally). His father then emigrated to the USA and at the age of four Lindesay came with his mother to England. She was a highly intelligent, progressive young woman who met her second husband when they were together at King Alfred's School, Hampstead. Controversial characters as they were, they together founded an experimental co-educational boarding school in Suffolk, which became the world famous Summerhill School. His mother was an ardent supporter of women's suffrage, and with fellow suffragettes was on occasion imprisoned in HM Prison, Holloway, London. Lindesay was brought up in an erudite radical milieu which influenced his outlook on life and may to some extent have fostered in him, as he grew up, an interest in psychology.

He was educated from 1913 to 1921 at King Alfred's School, Hampstead, for the next three years at London University and then at University College Hospital Medical School, qualifying as a doctor in 1929. At school he excelled in both work and games. At University College London, he took a BSc degree in psychology and obtained a first class honours degree in 1924. He was an all round sportsman, keen in particular on fives, tennis and cricket. He was captain of the University fives team and later president of the London University fives club. Whilst at UCH he was captain of the cricket club and he always retained a special interest in this sport, duly becoming a member of the MCC. One of his favourite hobbies was to watch first class cricket (and especially test matches) at Lords. It is noteworthy that throughout his student days he resided with his aunt, who was an Australian and a prominent author (*nom de plume* Henry Handel Richardson).

At University College Hospital he held the posts of house physician in medicine and neurology in 1929 and in paediatrics in 1930. On leaving UCH he became psychotherapist to the Maudsley (1931 – 1936) and then Rockefeller and York Trust research assistant at Guy's Hospital (1936 – 1939). In 1938 he was appointed physician in psychological medicine at Queen Mary's Hospital for the East End, and in 1948 to a similar post at the Royal Northern Hospital, London, positions which he retained until his retirement from the National Health Service.

During the war (1939 – 1946) he served in the Emergency Medical Service from 1939 to 1941, then in the Army with the rank of major (1941 – 1946), being promoted to acting lieutenant colonel during his time in the Middle East.

In 1948 he was appointed 'Advisor in Psychiatry' to the LCC school health service, and in 1950 he became consultant psychiatrist to St Ebbea's Hospital, transferring, when that hospital was closed, to Horton Hospital in 1962.

Neustatter was a prolific writer and was author of the following books: *Modern Psychiatry in Practice* (Churchill, 1936 and 1946); *The Mind of the Murderer* (C Johnson 1956); *Psychological Disorder and Crime* (C Johnson 1957) and *Psychiatry in Medical Practice* (Staples 1958). In 1960 he wrote an article on 'Diminished Responsibility and Murder' in the *Medico-Legal Journal* and in 1965 one on 'The State of Mind in Murder' for the *Lancet*.

Whereas his interests in psychiatry were always broad and well balanced, in later years he devoted progressively more of his time to forensic psychiatric work. Because his reports were intelligently compiled in a manner that was readily comprehensible to members of the legal profession, his opinion was often sought, and he frequently gave expert evidence in criminal proceedings, especially those concerned with crimes of violence. He was a member of the Medico-Legal Society for many years and its vice-president in 1964, and he was a founder member of the British Academy of Forensic Sciences. He regularly attended the meetings of these societies until his terminal illness, and seldom failed to make an observation or raise a query when the subject under discussion was within his field of interest. His enthusiasm in this sphere was indicated by his membership of the Howard League for Penal Reform and his personal concern with the abortion and homosexual laws. The high reputation in which he was held in the Courts is indicated by the number of salient homicidal cases in which he gave evidence. Amongst others whom he examined was Ian Brady, the notorious Moors murderer.

Neustatter was a man of honour and dedication, but the exact calibre of his personality was not easy to assess, since although he had a pleasant, friendly disposition that ensured a good rapport with patients and colleagues alike, one gained the impression that in thought and meditation he was introverted and lonely.

During his service in the Emergency Medical Service he met Mary Clutton-Brock, who was at that time an ambulance driver with the American Ambulance Corps and whom he married in 1941. After the war they purchased a house in Ewell where their two children were born, Patrick (a medical practitioner) and Angela (a journalist). He was devoted to his wife and perhaps largely dependent on her. Her death in 1969 was a stunning blow to him, which affected him profoundly. Always prone to be somewhat eccentric, he became much more so in his attitudes, beliefs and sartorial appearance. He died in July 1978 following a long and distressing illness. DASB

[*Brit. med. J.*, 1979, **2**, 278; Photo]

NEVIN, Samuel *b*.8 Sept 1905 *d*.13 Sept 1979
MB BCh BAO Belf (1927) BSc (1929) MD (1930) MRCP (1934) FRCP (1941)

Sam Nevin was the son of an officer in the Royal Irish Constabulary. A true Ulsterman, he never lost his pronounced Northern Irish manner of speech. He studied medicine at Queen's University, Belfast, graduating with first class honours in 1927. Two years later he took the BSc with first class honours in pathology, bacteriology and biochemistry, proceeding to MD in 1930. After house appointments at the Royal Victoria Hospital and a period as demonstrator in physiology at Queen's University, Belfast, he studied at the London Hospital and at the National Hospital, Queen Square, where he later worked in the clinical research unit. He was appointed assistant physician and neuropathologist at Maida Vale Hospital and, on the death of Kinnier Wilson, became assistant neurologist at King's College Hospital in 1937. The following year he also became consultant neurologist to the transferred mental institutions of the London County Council.

Nevin was arguably the best equipped all-round British neurologist of his time, for he was an expert in neurophysiology and neuropathology, quite apart from his clinical knowledge, and discriminating colleagues knew his worth. He was elected FRCP in 1941 and, in addition to his appointments at Maida Vale Hospital and King's College Hospital, he became director of the research laboratory of the Institute of Psychiatry, Maudsley Hospital, and professor of mental pathology in the University of London. Late in his career he spent a year in the USA so that he might learn electron microscopy. In retrospect, his most important work concerned the presenile dementias, and his presidential address to the section of neurology of the Royal Society of Medicine was on this topic. He combined with DP Jones to describe sub-acute spongiform encephalopathy in 1954, an important contribution for which the authors seem to have received scant international credit, though admittedly their early conclusions favoured a vascular aetiology which later proved to be incorrect. Muscle disorders were also among his special interests. His unassuming, modest temperament was liable to lead young men into faulty estimations of his capacity. He had a habit of posing seemingly simple questions as though he did not know the answers and many a new house physician, or registrar, responded confidently – ignorant of the concealed depth of knowledge within the questioner.

Sam was a private, devout person, and few knew him well. He possessed a first class inquiring mind and, outwardly, he was serious, even puritanical. Yet he had a great sense of fun and was the kindest of men and most caring of physicians. He neither expected nor desired professional awards, and seemed surprised when recognition came his way. He was afflicted with serious illness throughout his retirement, yet he continued to travel and attend meetings. His pursuit of learning and technological advances remained undimmed, and his friends, colleagues, and former students will remember him as a wise and warmhearted man.

In 1950 he married Margaret Esch and they had two children, a son and a daughter. GW/VL

[*Brit. med. J.*, 1979, **2**, 1151; *Lancet*, 1979, **2**, 702; Photo]

NICOL, Alexander Adam McIntosh *b.*25 Apr 1900 *d.*26 Mar 1983
MB ChB Aberd (1922) MD (1926) MRCP (1928) FRCP (1947)

Sandy Nicol, as he was known to his very many friends professional and otherwise, was educated in his home town of Aberdeen at the Grammar School and University. After holding house surgeon and house physician appointments at the Royal Sick Children's Hospital in Aberdeen, he emigrated south like so many of his countrymen, to hold house surgeon and house physician appointments at the East Suffolk and Ipswich Hospital, at Great Ormond Street and, from 1925 to 1929, at Hackney Hospital, becoming resident physician and deputy superintendent.

He came to Sunderland in 1929, initially in private general practice, but his high qualities were rapidly recognized and he was appointed to the consultant staff of the Voluntary Royal Infirmary, Sunderland, and of the closely associated Children's Hospital, as assistant physician in 1930, and also dermatologist in 1931. In 1943 he was appointed physician, and in 1946 senior physician to these two hospitals, as colleagues retired.

During and after the war years, Sandy also held visiting appointments at the EMS hospitals at Ryhope and Sedgefield, and at the Sunderland General Hospital, and with the aid of three general practitioners continued these heavy responsibilities without consultant support until 1947, when further appointments began to be made. He carried this enormous load in a town which was heavily bombed, on occasions within yards of his home. Only those who knew him well, his enthusiasm for his work, his energy, his good cheer, and his excellent relationship with his patients, can understand how he did it all. A great love for the Royal Infirmary, a very happy place in which to work, must have helped him greatly.

He helped in setting up an arthritis clinic in 1947, a pioneering effort in those days ('Organization of an arthritis clinic', *Lancet,* 1948).

Sandy's enthusiasm became channelled about the time of his retirement in 1965 into campaigning for the opening of a renal dialysis unit at the hospital. Initial official resistance was eventually overcome, and the unit was, very appropriately, officially declared open by himself in 1970 and has fully proved how great his foresight was. This was one of the high points of his career; another being his election to the fellowship in 1947, when he was the first doctor practising solely in the then County of Durham to be so elected.

He was an adviser in medicine to the Newcastle Regional Hospital Board, an associate clinical teacher of Newcastle University, and member of the Sunderland Hospital management committee from 1948 to his retirement, and a prominent member of the BMA locally and centrally.

Despite his very busy professional life Sandy found time to pursue his outside interests. His greatest was trout fishing in the upper reaches of the Coquet, which he continued until a few years before his death; he enjoyed a game of golf in his younger days, and he was a prominent Freemason who attended his Lodge meetings regularly until his terminal illness. He kept going despite needing a cardiac pacemaker during the last seven or eight years. He died in the hospital to which he had given so much. He was survived by his wife Edna, who gave him unfailing support over the years, his medically qualified son, his daughter and six grandchildren. RHV

[*Brit. med. J.,* 1982, **286**, 1452; Photo]

NICHOLS, Philip John Russell *b.*23 Sept 1923 *d.*8 Sept 1979
BA Oxon (1945) BM BCh (1947) MA (1949) D Phys M Lond (1952) DM (1959) MRCP (1969) FRCP (1974)

The death of Philip Nichols at the Radcliffe Infirmary at the age of 55 after a brief illness came as a shock to a host of friends all over the world. He personified medical rehabilitation in this country. He was chairman of the Royal College of Physicians committee on rehabilitation, former president of the section of rheumatology and rehabilitation of the Royal Society of Medicine, adviser in rehabilitation to the chief medical officer of the Department of Health and Social Security, and president of the newly formed Society for Research in Rehabilitation. He had served the Council of the British Association for Rheumatology and Rehabilitation for ten years, held the office of honorary secretary between 1966 and 1970, and was consulted before any important step in rehabilitation was taken. He served on the National Advisory Council on Employment of Disabled People, the Advisory Panel to the Disabled Living Foundation, and the Council of the Institute for Consumer Ergonomics of Loughborough University.

The quality that stood out throughout his life was his essential goodness. His enthusiasm, commitment, leadership and ability to evoke the best from others made him popular throughout his life. He had gentle humour, generosity and time for everyone. In 1958 he married Dorothy Eileen, daughter of Robert Nelson Hickson, a naval officer, and they had four daughters and a son. He was devoted to his family and friends.

He excelled as a physician, giving unstinted attention and compassion to his patients, encouragement, opportunity and responsibility to the professions supplementary to medicine, and scrupulous guidance to his students in helping them to choose their programmes of study.

Philip was born in London. His father was Philip Edbrooke Nichols, a surveyor, and his mother, formerly Dorothy Lizzy Russell, was daughter of a printer. He was educated at Christ's Hospital, Horsham, won an entrance exhibition to Exeter College, Oxford, and the prize for medicine at the Radcliffe Infirmary. At Oxford he played regularly for the Greyhounds and came close to winning a Blue. With panache he wrote and produced the Tynchewyke pantomimes at the Radcliffe. He graduated in medicine in 1947. After six months as house physician at the Radcliffe Infirmary he entered the Royal Air Force, in which he served with distinction for sixteen years and developed his interest in rehabilitation. He gained the Diploma for Physical Medicine in 1952 and wrote an excellent thesis for his DM in 1959. He pioneered the use of technical workshops for the rehabilitation of skilled tradesmen, encouraged the new profession of remedial gymnasts, was first senior medical officer at the RAF rehabilitation centre at Headley Court, was at the front of a service that had an outstanding reputation for the quality of rehabilitation, and displayed then, as he did later, his exceptional administrative ability; he thought clearly, perceived what was relevant, mustered the arguments and, having the facility to extract what was pertinent, he became a natural chairman. On his retirement he held the rank of wing-commander.

In 1964 he was appointed director of Mary Marlborough Lodge, the disabled living research unit at the Nuffield Orthopaedic Centre at Oxford, from its incorporation into the National Health Service. Under his leadership the 'Lodge' steadily developed not only as a conventional rehabilitation unit but also as a national functional assessment centre for the severely disabled, from whatever cause; to this was added an association with the Regional Artificial Limb and Appliance Centre in 1968, and the Rehabilitation Research Unit where techniques were developed to assess and measure disability and evaluate different methods of treatment. Gardening was encouraged for the assessment, treatment and recreation of the disabled. Nichols and his staff were responsible for compiling the series of books *Equipment for the Disabled*. In 1973 the 'Lodge' was designated by the DHSS a National Rehabilitation Demonstration Centre, and to this came over a thousand visitors a year. He held editorial positions with several journals, most importantly as first editor of the *International Journal of Rehabilitation Medicine*. From his pen flowed one hundred excellent papers, beginning with 'Those who are constitutionally fat die more quickly than those who are thin' and four books: *Rehabilitation of the Severely Disabled; Management; Living with a Handicap,* and *Rehabilitation Medicine*. He was responsible for an extensive programme of courses for the remedial professions. As a teacher he was much in demand at home and overseas, and went frequently to Europe and was visiting lecturer in America, South Africa and Australia. He gave the Richard Kovac lecture to the Royal Society of Medicine in 1971 on 'Some Problems in Rehabilitation of the Severely Disabled'.

Philip Nichols influenced the course of British medicine in this century, and his loss to the developing specialty of rehabilitation medicine was incalculable. The service of thanksgiving for his life was held at St Clement Danes, Central Church of the Royal Air Force.

GMC

[*Brit. med. J.*, 1979, **2**, 944; *Lancet,* 1979, **2**, 806; *Ann. rheum. Dis.,* 1980, **39(3)**, 298-300]

NOALL, Edward William Paynter *b.*18 Jan 1918 *d.*12 Nov 1982
MB BS Lond (1952) DPM (1958) MRCP (1963) MRCPsych (1973) FRCP (1976)

Edward William Paynter Noall, or simply 'Bill' Noall as we all knew him, was born at Strensall, Yorkshire. He was the eldest of three children born to WP Noall MS FRCS, a Cornishman who practised as a surgeon in York, and his wife Ethel, daughter of Canon WH Carr. His early upbringing and schooling (eventually at Kingston upon Thames Grammar School) was interrupted by the early death of his father, and by a series of moves from one home and one school to another which were consequently forced upon his mother in order to make both ends meet; and on the other hand by mastoid troubles. He was considered academically bright, but modest and self-effacing.

After leaving school, he worked for a time in a stockbroker's office and in Jersey Airways. He was called up in World War II and served as captain in the Royal Marines from 1940–45 in Africa, India, Ceylon, in the Battle of Britain, and in France and Belgium. His younger brother was sadly reported missing, presumed dead, after being torpedoed in the Atlantic in December 1942.

His entry into medicine was therefore comparatively late. He trained at St Thomas's Hospital, qualified in 1952, took two appointments as medical casualty officer and as house surgeon at St Thomas's, and subsequently (after a brief spell in general practice) as a house physician in the department of psychological medicine at St Thomas's. Thus at an early stage of his career he acquired an interest in psychiatry. Russell Pargeter, now a psychiatrist in Tasmania, was a close friend of his at St Thomas's, and Bill himself worked for three years as senior house officer and, later, registrar in psychiatry at Runwell Hospital, where he met a Norwegian contemporary, Nil Retterstol (now professor of psychiatry in Oslo), who became his closest friend and was to have a profound influence on his life.

Bill decided, however, to return to general medicine and worked as registrar at St Andrew's Hospital, Billericay, and senior registrar, and later was acting consultant physician, at Southend General Hospital. He obtained his MRCP in 1963 and was appointed consultant physician to Queen Mary's Hospital for the East End, Stratford, and East Ham Memorial Hospital in 1966. He never, however, lost his interest in psychiatry. He took his DPM in 1958. He held a clinic in psychosomatic medicine at East Ham (and endeavoured to establish a psychosomatic section in the Royal Society of Medicine). He was elected MRCPsych in 1973. In his later years in Newham he undertook a regular session each week as visiting physician to Goodmayes Hospital. In his original application for his consultant post in Newham he stated 'My previous experience in psychiatry I have found of the greatest help, as a very large proportion of the cases referred to the general medical clinics have a psychiatric background, and the early recognition of this saves considerable delay and facilitates treatment, especially in cases with an organic basis in addition.'

In addition to his work as consultant physician in Newham, he was for many years clinical tutor and he became closely associated with the formation, in 1972, of the postgraduate medical centre at East Ham and the Newham Medical Society of which he was the first secretary. He devoted a great deal of time and energy to this work, especially on behalf of his GP colleagues, who were eternally grateful for his help and encouragement.

In his spare time he was a keen sailor (for some time he had a boat at Burnham-on-Crouch), skier, walker, beagler and player of water polo. His great friend Nil Netterstol invited him to Norway, where he stayed once or twice every year and enjoyed skiing and walking in the mountains. He last went there in the summer of 1982. He was a member of the ski club of London and also of the Norwegian ski club. His interest in Norway was not however confined to these pursuits. He became an active member of the Norwegian community in South East London, at whose church, St Olav's Kirche in Rotherhithe, he was a regular worshipper and participant in the social functions. He became a member of the Anglo-Norwegian Society. He even applied himself to mastering the Norwegian language, as well as learning French, and was considering taking up a hospital appointment in Norway after his retirement from Newham. All this was something of a surprise to colleagues in Newham, when they attended his funeral service at St Olave's Kirche and found themselves singing hymns in Norwegian in his memory.

Few of his colleagues, indeed, knew him well. To his family, and a few close friends, he was a 'very private person' from his childhood onwards. At first sight he was socially inclined and generally affable, and he was undoubtedly possessed of a strong sense of humour. He missed few social occasions, but his appearances were brief and he appeared always anxious not to become too deeply involved. He had little small talk.

He seemed to be driven by a restless nervous energy, which he canalized into forthright and forcibly expressed views at committee meetings (which he attended with the same meticulous regularity as he did his clinical sessions). He had a need to dissipate some of his surplus energy in his sporting and open-air pursuits, and in his nocturnal perambulations around the streets of London. His habits and mode of dress appeared at times casual. He strode around Essex in knickerbockers, often tied up with string, high woollen stockings and walking boots.

He was intensely loyal and a constant support to his family. He devoted a great deal of energy to helping his younger sister (herself a trained nurse) in caring for his mother in her final illness. He was modest to a degree. Even his sister did not know of his distinctions, such as his election to the fellowship in 1976. The courage with which he faced his last illness, with its dreadful treatment, was remarkable and he preserved his sense of humour to the end. Only ten days before his final admission to hospital, and knowing the nature of his illness, he went off on a cycling holiday along the Dutch canals.

Bill remained single but he was by no means immune to feminine charms. There is an eye witness account which it would not be proper to relate, of a bout of fisticuffs with a rival for the hand of one particular lady.

R de M.

NORTHFIELD, Douglas William Claridge *b.*17 Feb 1902
*d.*18 July 1976
LDS RCS (1923) MRCS LRCP (1925) FRCS (1928)
MB BS Lond (1930) MS (1931) FRCP* (1966)

Douglas Northfield was born in London, son of William Ebenezer

Northfield, who had a small umbrella business in Charing Cross Road, and Emily Sarah, daughter of Joseph Taylor, a butler. He was educated first at Haverstock Hill LCC Primary School and then at Haberdashers' Aske's. On leaving he went directly to Guy's Hospital, where he qualified in dentistry in 1923 and in medicine in 1925. He proceeded to his MB BS with gold medal in 1930 and followed this with the MS in 1931. Northfield had already become FRCS (Eng) in 1928. Apart from the rapidity and ease with which he obtained higher qualifications, he also won many prizes at Guy's, including the Treasurer's medals in medicine and surgery, the Arthur Durham travelling fellowship and the Will Edmonds clinical research fellowship. In 1936 he was elected a Hunterian professor of the Royal College of Surgeons.

Northfield was occupied in resident posts at Guy's from 1925 to 1927; he was surgical registrar from 1928 until 1931. In 1932 and 1933 he was demonstrator in anatomy in the medical school. His life's work, though conceived when dissecting the brain at Guy's, really began in 1934 when he joined Hugh Cairns as house surgeon at the London Hospital, a road then taken by many aspiring neurosurgeons from home and overseas. In 1937 he became assistant neurological surgeon at the London, with promotion to neurological surgeon the following year on Cairns' departure for Oxford. Thereafter he served the hospital until his retirement in 1967, though his surgical work was carried out at Chase Farm Hospital during the second world war.

Douglas Northfield was first secretary and later president of both the neurological section of the Royal Society of Medicine and the Society of British Neurological Surgeons. He was president of the EEG Society and of the British Branch of the International League against Epilepsy, and he served as secretary of the third International Congress of Neurosurgery (1965). He was elected to the fellowship of the College in 1966.

In his earlier days Northfield worked on the problems of headache, making original observations on the distribution of pain-bearing structures within the head, and also on the thalamus. Later he published important papers on angiomatous malformations of the brain, Rathke pouch tumours, and the surgery of temporal lobe epilepsy. However, his main contribution to the literature was *The Surgery of the Central Nervous System*, a remarkable work which provides a lasting memorial to his achievement.

Northfield was an excellent neurological physician, and a surgeon of the highest technical quality. His clinical work was characterized by unlimited patience; he had no time for persons who took short cuts and neglected full history-taking and examination. His professional and scientific capacity were recognized throughout the world; surgical skill, wide knowledge and fine judgment brought many visitors to his department at Whitechapel.

Like Hughlings Jackson, a medical neurological predecessor at the London, Northfield received no public acknowledgment of his service, and perhaps there was none which was suitable; nor was he elected to the council of the Royal College of Surgeons. He held no non-medical appointments. The answers to this apparent paradox may be found in the man, a private person whose qualities were only appreciated by his close colleagues and others who knew him well. His beginnings were humble, and his achievements were the fruit of his own ability, industry and dedication; yet he never showed envy of those whose path had been easier. Although a charming host and friend he was austere at heart and unyielding in his pursuit of what he thought to be right. He abhorred loose thinking and argument and was quite intolerant of anything less than dedication to the task at hand. The soul of integrity himself, he was impatient and irritable with those prepared to accept what he regarded as lower standards of behaviour. Compromise did not come easily to him. Indeed, while his integrity, determination and pursuit of truth were immense assets in surgical practice, they made him a rather solitary figure on the larger stage. In summary, his standards were too high and his attitudes too inflexible for his time.

Northfield was never granted the space nor staff to develop a large department, and it is probable that he was at his best in a small group or on his own with a patient and the X-ray films. The neurosurgeons he trained were his loyal and affectionate supporters. While he had several interests outside medicine he allowed himself little time for them, working far into the night and at week-ends. Nevertheless his artistic skills are preserved in his drawings of operations.

He married (Eva) Marjorie, daughter of Philemon Murgatroyd Slater, a Yorkshire hotel keeper, in 1932, and she died in 1974. They had a son, a fellow of the College, and a daughter. RAH(1)

[*Brit. med. J.*, 1976, **2**, 372, 536; *Lancet,*1976, **2**, 266; *Times,* 20 July 1976]

NOSSEL, Hymie Louis *b.*11 July 1930 *d.*9 Oct 1983
MB ChB Cape Town (1953) DPhil Oxon (1964) MRCP (1960)
FRCP (1980) FCPSA (1958)

A specialist in haemostasis and blood coagulation, at the time of his premature death Hymie Nossel was professor of medicine in the College of Physicians and Surgeons, Columbia University, USA, and an American citizen. He traced his roots back to the city of Kaunas, Lithuania, from which his ancestors had fled to England and South Africa during the pogroms at the turn of the century. He was proud of his Jewish heritage and devoted to his family, from whom he derived much joy.

Born in Cape Town, South Africa, the son of Joshua Nossel, a farmer, he was educated at Wynberg Boys' High School and the University of Cape Town, pursuing his clinical studies at the Groot Schuur Hospital and graduating with distinction. After completing his residency posts he was appointed registrar, in 1956, to the medical unit run by Frank Forman. It was during this time that his life-long interest in blood coagulation was kindled by Clarence Merskey (*q.v.*), with whom he retained an abiding and characteristically loyal friendship. In 1960 he came to England as research bursar of the South African

Council for Scientific and Industrial Research to continue his studies in Oxford under Rosemary Biggs and Gwyn Macfarlane at the MRC Blood Coagulation Research Unit. He obtained the DPhil Oxon in 1962 for his thesis *Observations on the early stages of blood coagulation*. He followed this with a year as research associate at Mount Sinai Hospital, New York, in the haematology department. He returned to Cape Town for a brief period but soon rejoined Mount Sinai as senior research associate, becoming assistant professor of medicine, and assistant attending physician in 1966, as well as consultant to the Elmhurst Hospital. Later that year he was appointed assistant professor of medicine at Columbia University where he remained for the rest of his life, becoming full professor in 1972. He was also attending physician to the Presbyterian Hospital, New York.

In Hymie Nossel clinical and laboratory skills were combined to an unusual degree, and he was a prolific author. In addition to more than 70 scientific papers, notable for their originality and clarity, he was the author of three books: *The contact phase of blood coagulation* (1964); *The fundamentals of haematology* (1976) in collaboration with Rifkind, Bank and Marks; and *Pathobiology of the endothelial cell* (1982) together with Vogel. He also contributed chapters to a number of major textbooks, including those on haemostasis and its disorders in Harrison's *Principles of Internal Medicine*.

Nossel's wide-ranging contributions to medicine encompassed fundamental work on the early phase of blood coagulation, platelet-collagen interaction and platelet secretory proteins, the kinetics of fibrinogen cleavage by thrombin and plasmin (for which he devised brilliant techniques) and the role of the endothelial cell and its receptors in haemostasis and thrombosis. He was a born investigator, universally respected for his carefully conceived ideas and methodology. There is no doubt that had his life not been cut short many more achievements would have followed. Clear proof of his scientific standing is that he continued to command strong support from the National Institutes of Health throughout the years of financial restraint. He served on a number of NIH study sections and as a consultant to the Clinical Center of the NIH from 1972 to 1976. From 1978 to 1982 he was a member of the International Committee on Thrombosis and Haemostasis; he served on the executive committee of the Council on Thrombosis of the American Heart Association during the same period, and on the council of the International Society on Thrombosis and Haemostasis, acting as secretary from 1981 to 1982 and being chairman-elect at the time of his death. He was also on the editorial board of several international journals, including the *Journal of Clinical Investigation, Thrombosis Research*, and *Blood*, of which he was an associate editor.

He married Renée Abt, a child psychiatrist, in 1965, and they had three children: a son, Neon, and two daughters, Suzanne and Ilana. They were a happy and close-knit family. As a physician, colleague, father and friend, Hymie Nossel was utterly loyal and sincere. Despite his strength of purpose and great authority, he was essentially a shy

and modest man of wide culture and with an endearingly gentle sense of humour.
GW/VL

[*Lancet,* 1983, **2**, 1317; Photo]

O'DONOVAN, Patrick Henry *b.*- 1900 *d.*28 Nov 1977
MRCS LRCP (1923) MB BS Lond (1924) MD (1928) MRCP (1928) FRCP (1944)

Patrick O'Donovan was proud to have been born in London within the sound of Bow bells. He was the son of Patrick O'Donovan, civil servant, and his wife, formerly Beatrice Gibson, daughter of an iron foundry owner. He was a brother of WJ O'Donovan who became consultant dermatologist to the London Hospital. He attended Cooper's School and the London Hospital Medical College. He came to Nottingham General Hospital as house physician in 1925. In 1928 he was given leave of absence to study for the MD and MRCP. He served as RMO in the National Heart Hospital during this time and was successful in both examinations. He was appointed honorary assistant physician to the Nottingham General Hospital in 1930, honorary physician in 1937 and when the Health Service started in 1948, consultant physician. He was honorary librarian of the Nottingham Medico-Chirurgical Society from 1934 to 1937, and in 1956 the Society (composed of members from all medical disciplines in the area) conferred upon him its highest honour by electing him president for the year. He was a member of the British Heart Society for many years.

He was appointed honorary assistant physician at a time when there were very few trained specialists available outside teaching centres. The Nottingham Medical School was not to be established for another thirty years. He quickly showed his special interest and skill in cardiology and it was not long before he was widely recognized as giving an outstanding opinion in the Midlands. His private practice therefore made increasing demands upon his time, but he never neglected his hospital patients and for many years did a regular ward round on Sunday mornings.

In 1932 he married Mary Dobson and they had two sons. He continued to live in Nottingham after his retirement.

Patrick O'Donovan was not an easy man to get to know and he had few close medical friends, although all his colleagues had the highest regard for his professional skill and personal integrity. He was a shy man of few words, quiet but firm. If he was convinced that a cause deserved his support this was given with vigour and determination. On the other hand if he felt that something was wrong he had no hesitation in opposing it, even though this could be unpopular and unfashionable.

He was never a great sportsman. In his earlier days he enjoyed a little golf and an occasional day's shooting but work claimed a great deal of his time. He enjoyed reading, and in his later years he took up bowls. One of his unique experiences was to receive a blank cheque from JD Player of the wealthy tobacco family; this he did not complete but had it framed, and showed it with pleasure to his visitors who thus gained an interesting insight into his character.

Throughout his life he was a committed Roman Catholic, and one of his great joys was the Papal Honour, *Bene Merenti*, bestowed on him a year or two before he died. JMM

[*Brit. med. J.*, 1977, **2**, 1599; Photo]

OGILVIE, Alan Gordon *b.*17 Mar 1900 *d.*26 Feb 1983
MB BS Dunelm (1924) MRCP (1929) MD (1939) FRCP (1945)

Alan Ogilvie was born in Newcastle upon Tyne. He was educated at Corchester preparatory school and St Bees, and he studied medicine at the College of Medicine in Newcastle, then a college of the University of Durham. He graduated in 1924 and was later awarded the Doctorate of Medicine with honours and a gold medal.

He was married and had one son and two daughters.

In his younger days he was a not inconsiderable athlete, being one and two miles champion of Northumberland and Durham, and winner of the one, two and three miles at the University of Durham in the years 1920 to 1924 inclusive.

After being house surgeon and house physician at the Royal Victoria Infirmary, Newcastle upon Tyne, he became house physician at the Children's Hospital at Birmingham, and then at the Hospital for Sick Children, Great Ormond Street, London. In 1933 he was appointed assistant honorary physician to the Royal Victoria Infirmary and he became an honorary physician there in 1941. He was also an honorary physician to the pioneering Babies' Hospital and Mothercraft Centre, the inspiration of James Spence, one of Alan Ogilvie's closest friends.

Ogilvie was one of the 'characters' at the Royal Victoria Infirmary. Affectionately called 'The Og', he was sometimes referred to by the more timorous students and nurses as 'The Red Terror'. This latter appellation was to a great extent, however, a misnomer. True, he had somewhat crinkly sandy red hair, on the ward a somewhat abrupt manner and speech containing stereotyped sentences some of which could only be translated by those who knew him well, and a determination that the standards on his ward should be of the highest. Beneath this, however, he was a kind, modest person with a nice wit and one who was as straight as a die. He was deeply concerned for the efficiency of his hospital and devoted to the efficient care and welfare of his patients. He did everything with vigour, and this was very apparent in the manner of his percussion for which he was notorious; there were very few Christmas house concerts which did not contain some reference to it!

In his senior years Ogilvie inevitably became increasingly involved in the committee work of his hospital, to which he gave unstintingly of his time, but this was never allowed to undermine his clinical work, his teaching or the time he spent in clinical investigation. His main interest was in diseases of the respiratory system and, in particular, chronic bronchitis – the subject of his MD thesis. The study which he carried out with DJ Newall into chronic bronchitis in Newcastle was a model of its kind and showed the very high incidence of this condition in the locality. In 1962 he was elected president of the Thoracic Society.

Ogilvie loved the country and particularly the striking beauty of central Northumberland. He retired there to his cottage where, with his wife, he spent many happy years of retirement. GS

[*Brit. med. J.*, 1983, **286**, 990, 1156; Photo]

OSBORN, Gladstone Rule *b.*21 Nov 1903 *d.*27 Mar 1983
MB BS Melb (1927) MRCP (1959) FRCPath (1964) FRCP (1967)

Gladstone Osborn, formerly director of pathology at Derby Royal Infirmary, was born in Launceston, Tasmania, the son of Andrew Rule Osborn MA ThD, a Presbyterian minister, and his wife Annie Delbridge, daughter of a mining engineer. He was educated at Wesley College, Melbourne, and the University of Melbourne, graduating with honours in medicine in 1927, and winning the Mollison prize in forensic medicine. He married Thelma Mavis, daughter of James Jamieson, an accountant, in 1929. They had four children: three sons and a daughter.

After house appointments from 1927 to 1929 at Melbourne Hospital, he was appointed pathologist to the Commonwealth Health Laboratories in 1930. In 1935 he moved to New York as surgical pathologist to the Presbyterian Hospital, and in 1936 he came to Derby to take up an appointment as pathologist in charge to the Derby Group of hospitals. He was also appointed honorary lecturer in pathology to Sheffield University. He was a member of the Home Office committee on death certification and coroners set up in 1965.

Osborn wrote several papers and books, including *Applied cytology* (1953); *Pathology of the lung in stillbirth and neonatal death* (1953); *The incubation period of coronary thrombosis* (1963), and *Current concepts of coronary disease* (1964).

He had many interests outside medicine, being an enthusiastic photographer and gardener. He also enjoyed drawing, and exercised his Dalmatian dog by riding a bicycle when he took the dog for 'a walk'. He was an all round sportsman, rowing and playing cricket in his early days, and later playing tennis for the first division of the Derby League. He was also a member of the Derby Scientific Club. In his latter years he developed an interest in Cornish archaeology, together with his wife and his friend RA Willis FRCP (*q.v.*). He died in Australia. GW/VL

[Photo]

PAGE, Alfred Patrick Menzies *b.*17 Mar 1907 *d.*7 Feb 1979
MRCS LRCP (1930) MB BS Lond (1931) MD (1933) MRCP (1933) DCH (1938) FRCP (1968) JP (1960)

Pat Page was paediatrician to the Nottingham hospitals. He was born in Plymouth, the son of Alfred Matthew Page, Fleet surgeon RN, and his wife Susan, daughter of John Thomas Menzies, a wine merchant and shipper. He was educated at Bedford School and St Bartholomew's Hospital, where his father had been before him. After house appointments at Bart's and elsewhere, he became resident medical officer at the Royal Masonic Hospital and in 1936 was appointed medical director and physician at the City General Hospital, Leicester. He became increasingly interested in paediatrics and took the DCH in 1938. In 1947 he was appointed consultant paediatrician to the Nottingham hospitals. He was to retain this appointment until he retired, building up an excellent paediatric service at Nottingham, and serving on the staff of the Children's, Women's, City, and Highbury hospitals. He retired in 1973 with emeritus appointment to the Nottingham hospitals. He was also paediatrician to the Spastics Society.

Pat Page's interest in children was reflected in his work for the juvenile courts; he was appointed a JP in 1960, and was vice-chairman of the Nottingham Juvenile Court. He built up a large private practice in and around Nottingham and after retirement from the NHS continued to see his patients in their own homes. He was chairman of the Nottingham Division of the BMA in 1961, and president of the Nottinghamshire Branch BMA in 1968. From 1956 to 1966 he was president of the Sheffield Regional Paediatric Society. He was also a Freemason of many years' standing with the Leicester and Nottingham lodges.

He was married twice: in 1937 to Olive Frances, who died; and in 1965 to Georgina, daughter of George Ward, a shoe manufacturer. He had a son and a stepdaughter. His hobbies included fly fishing and he was vice-president of the Nottingham Fly Fishing Club, and a member of the London Fly Fishers Club. He was a most amusing companion, full of wit and charm, and had a host of friends.

GW/VL

[*Brit. med. J.*, 1979, **1**, 763; Photo]

PALMER, Kenneth Nelson Vesey *b.*16 Mar 1920 *d.*11 Dec 1982
MB BChir Cantab (1944), MRCP (1945) MA MD Cantab (1952) FRCP (1966) MRCPE (1967) FRCPE (1970)

Ken Palmer was a general physician with a special interest in diseases of the chest. He was born at Dartmouth and educated at Kingswood School, Trinity Hall, Cambridge, and Middlesex Hospital, London. He served as a medical specialist in the RAF 1948–1950. He maintained his brilliant undergraduate promise with a similar postgraduate career as house physician and senior medical registrar at the Middlesex Hospital, house physician at Brompton Hospital and reader in medicine in the Unversity of Aberdeen. He achieved academic distinction because he was unrivalled as a clinical teacher and because he was a thoughtful research worker. His Cambridge MD thesis on post-operative pulmonary complications led to a wide and productive field of investigation on aerosols to reduce sputum viscosity, expectorants, mucolytics, the hazards of smoking, hypoxaemia, exercise-induced asthma, bronchodilators, rheology, and lung scanning. He made anaesthesia safer.

Ken Palmer developed the pulmonary function laboratory at the Aberdeen Royal Infirmary and its continuing academic productivity will be an honourable epitaph.

He was rightly proud of his membership of the Association of Physicians, Thoracic Society, European Society of Respiratory Physiology, and the Scottish Society of Physicians. These professional achievements do not highlight his zestful personality, his unquenchable curiosity beyond medicine, his love of Brahms, his pursuit of fishing, and, above all, his affectionate family life. He was survived by his wife, Rosemary, who was an accomplished artist, two daughters, and a doctor son, who had already achieved membership of the Royal College of Physicians.

'The names of those who in their lives fought for life,
Who wore at their hearts the fire's centre.
Born of the sun they travelled a short while towards the sun,
And left the vivid air signed with their honour.'
(Stephen Spender)

DGJ

[*Brit. med. J.*, 1983, **286**, 1070; Photo]

PARKINSON, John Scholes *b.*10 Nov 1907 *d.*27 Nov 1980
BSc Manch (1929) MRCS LRCP (1932) MB ChB (1932)
MRCP (1936) DPH (1938) FRCP (1971)

Known to close friends as 'Jack', Parkinson was a small, slight, fair man of considerable intellect, a ready wit and a 'puckish' sense of humour.

A foundation scholar of Manchester Grammar School, he won a scholarship to Manchester Medical School, where he had a distinguished career as a student, winning a series of prizes. He became house surgeon to Professor Telford, and went on to hold senior resident posts in both Ancoats and Withington Hospitals, later returning to Manchester Royal Infirmary in 1936 as chief assistant on the neurological unit to Fergus Ferguson. He held this post for some six years, and in 1942 jointed the RAMC and served as a specialist physician (graded neurologist). Much of his service was spent in Belfast, and he and his wife (he had married Margaret Bowyer in 1939) grew to love Ireland, and were later to come back frequently with their family of four boys for holidays.

After the war, in 1946, he returned to the Manchester district, and was appointed visiting physician to Salford Royal Hospital, and also to West Park Hospital (Macclesfield) 1946 – 1950. He was one of the last of the general physician/neurologists. With the coming of the Health Service he became consultant physician, with special experience in neurology, first at Salford Royal and Hope Hospitals; he later changed Hope for Withington (University Hospital, South Manchester) and Wythenshawe. He took his full part in teaching, and many of his senior registrars now hold consultant positions. He is remembered by colleagues and juniors for his shrewd clinical judgement and readiness to help.

He served for many years on the industrial injuries medical appeal tribunals. He was a popular member, always full of common sense in his decisions, and certain to ease along a session by his wit and good humour.

He did not shirk his duties on committees. From 1948 to retirement he served as a member of the Salford Hospital Management Committee, the largest such committee in the Manchester area, and for several years was its vice-chairman.

An accident in childhood prevented him from taking an active part in sport but he was, from his earliest days, a keen supporter of Bury Football Club. From an early age he became interested in music, and became a good pianist; he particularly enjoyed playing duets with colleagues. When no more than 12 years old, he started to collect gramophone records – a hobby which lasted all his life. He amassed a vast collection of 78s, which included many rare records, and became very knowledgeable on the whole subject, and of the various recordings available of most classical music.

A few years before retirement he found an attractive house in Wales. He escaped there with Margaret whenever possible, developed his garden and took particular pride in his fine collection of camellias.

REL

[*Brit. med. J.*, 1981, **282**, 1555; Photo]

PARKINSON, *Sir* **John,** *b.*10 Feb 1885 *d.*5 June 1976
Kt (1948) MRCS LRCP (1907) MB BS Lond (1908) MD (1910)
MRCP (1911) FRCP (1923) Hon LLD Glasg (1951)
Hon FACP (1951) Hon DSc NUI (1952) Hon FRCPE (1953)
Hon FRCPS Glasg (1962) Hon FRCPI (1962) Hon FRSM

John Parkinson was the son of John Parkinson JP, of Thornton-le-Fylde, Lancashire. He received his premedical education at Manchester Grammar School and University College, London. He trained in medicine at the University of Freiburg, and the London Hospital, which he joined in 1903, and later described it as his medical home. There he gained prizes in anatomy and physiology, and the Anderson prize in clinical medicine.

He graduated in 1907, became MD London in 1910, and was elected FRCP in 1923. In 1913 he was first assistant to Sir James Mackenzie in the cardiac department of the London Hospital, and assumed charge of the department in 1919 when Mackenzie moved to St Andrews in Scotland. Parkinson was appointed assistant physician to the London Hospital in 1920, physician in 1927, and physician to the cardiac department in 1933. He also became physician to the National Heart Hospital, and during the years 1931 to 1956 was consulting cardiologist to the Royal Air Force.

In the first world war he served as medical officer to a casualty clearing station in France from 1914 to 1916, divisional officer at the military hospital for research on heart cases at Hampstead in 1916, and as major RAMC in charge of the military heart centre in Rouen from 1917 to 1919.

The excellence and constancy of his work in and for cardiology gained for Parkinson recognition and distinctions from many lands. He was elected president of the association of physicians of Great Britain and Ireland in 1930, president of the British Cardiac Society, 1951 to 1955, and president of the European Society of Cardiology. He was created an honorary member of the Cardiac Societies of France, Italy, Switzerland, Portugal, India, Brazil, Australia and New Zealand.

The Royal College of Physicians appointed him Lumleian lecturer for 1936, and Harveian orator for 1945, and awarded him the Moxon medal in 1957. He received the Fothergill gold medal from the Medical Society of London in 1947, and the gold stethoscope award from the International Cardiology Foundation in 1966. In 1948 he was invested with a knighthood.

Throughout the whole of his professional life, John Parkinson worked untiringly to establish cardiology as an acknowledged specialty within medicine. A notable step towards this ambition took place when the Cardiac Club of 15 members was enlarged to admit 85 members in 1937, and renamed the British Cardiac Society. Parkinson became its first president. The society now has a thriving membership, while its monthly journal, the *British Heart Journal*, enjoys an international reputation. He had set his heart on achieving for cardiology a premier position in medicine, and before retiring from active practice he had the satisfaction of knowing that this had come to pass.

Parkinson wrote no textbook of cardiology, but he did more, he undertook personal research into most ailments to which the heart is heir, and he conveyed his findings through his many publications. His collected papers, which rest in the library of the College, are literature enough for cardiology. He was no copyist. He cut his lone furrow, and those of us who viewed it from the headlands saw it as a pattern which we wished to follow. In his researches he never allowed his gaze to stray from his avowed object, to improve the diagnosis of heart disease in order to bring it within the compass of practical therapy.

Dealing first with treatment, he and Sir Alun Rowlands tested the effects of strychnine in heart failure at a time when it was standard therapy in such patients. They found that it produced no benefit. They announced their findings at the 17th International Congress of

Medicine in London in 1913.

Parkinson was the first to introduce adrenaline in the treatment of Adams-Stokes attacks. In 1917 he wrote on the uselessness of digitalis in the so-called soldier's heart syndrome, pointing out that the complaint sprang from the nervous system and not the heart. In 1922 he confirmed the benefit produced by quinidine in certain patients with paroxysmal or established auricular arrhythmia. He highlighted the beneficial effect of a mercurial suppository in 1936, some years before the introduction of the modern oral diuretics. In 1939, along with Gavey, he showed that digitalis was always indicated in heart failure, irrespective of the rhythm of the heart. He warned not to accept readily statements on the superiority of new analgesics over morphine, a drug whose universal use through more than a century gave proof of its efficiency, and he told an audience of doctors that some of them were mean in their use of analgesics, adding that their attitude might change when they became ill themselves.

To Parkinson, unfamiliar medicines were suspect, so that when new house physicians reported to him for duty, he warned them not to prescribe any medicine to patients admitted to hospital under his care until he had seen and examined them. We interpreted this caution as an absence of confidence in a new house physician, but we were soon to notice how well patients reacted to rest only, in the absence of any medicinal therapy. From Parkinson we learnt that nature was itself a physician capable of curing illness, and that a knowledge of the natural history of disease along with its lesson of *vis medicatrix naturae* was being annihilated by overzealous therapeusis.

In 1925, Parkinson supervised a patient with mitral valve disease in whom Sir Henry Souttar undertook digital dilatation of the mitral ring. He had retired from active medical practice when surgical treatment of heart conditions was gaining notable success, a progress he warmly applauded.

In the diagnosis of heart disease Parkinson made significant advances in several sectors. He and Bedford were foremost in correlating the symptoms and electrocardiographic signs of cardiac infarction (coronary thrombosis), especially identifying the changes that take place during the weeks and months which follow the initial attack. With Campbell and Bedford he wrote extensively on the arrythmias, on the heart in emphysema with Clifford Hoyle, and with Harold Cookson on the heart in goitre.

In 1930, Parkinson along with Louis Wolff and Paul White in America, described bundle-branch block associated with a short P-R period in healthy young people prone to paroxysmal tachycardia (the WPW syndrome). The paper in which they described and discussed this anomaly has been quoted in cardiological journals with a frequency probably greater than any other affecting the heart.

Jointly with Bedford and Papp he wrote a comprehensive dissertation on atrial septal defect, which presently led to its more frequent surgical treatment.

Parkinson's greatest contribution to diagnosis came from his compulsive encouragement to view the heart radiologically. Extolling this method, he pointed out that no organ was so favourably placed for X-ray inspection as the heart, for it was surrounded by translucent lung, while rotation of the patient enabled the heart to be viewed in all its dimensions. In this way, he said, we look at individual chambers of the heart separately and not just its mass.

Parkinson's wise leadership in clinical cardiology will be remembered as long as hearts keep beating, and an age ahead will rediscover the truths he taught so convincingly at the bedside. He relied on facts. He was never given to imagination, for the truth to him was what he saw. Indeed, he was a tyrant for truth, and through his diligent search for it, he often presaged it.

By nature, John Parkinson was a shy man. He enjoyed the company of close friends, when he was a generous host, but unless obligatory, he preferred not to dwell long in the company of strangers, other than those with a common interest, and especially the young seeking his advice; to them he would devote unlimited time and help. Those whom he had befriended and trained carried a passport to the world's foremost cardiological centres. Parkinson could converse in both German and French.

His punctuality was proverbial; never late at a consultation, lecture, ward-round, or outpatients' session.

He did not decry a thorough investigation of a patient's illness, but he warned sternly against unneeded investigations in a stinging epigram, 'There is always a moment when curiosity is a sin'.

Parkinson was a plunderer for perfection. Should one of his assistants submit a film of his own recording, expecting to win high praise from the master, it was more likely to draw a terse remark, highlighting a tiny flaw in the far corner of the film. Censure would then carry the injunction that no such exhibit should leave his department for publication. The assistant would retire subdued, but having taken a decided step nearer perfection. Parkinson sought perfection too in the lay-out of his garden, addressing each shrub by its Latin name, and in the choice of furniture and paintings in his home and consulting-rooms; he himself was no mean painter in water-colour.

It is not only what John Parkinson did and said that has so materially benefited our knowlege of the heart in health and in disease, but also the way he said it. His writings and his lectures abound with examples of the apt and happy turns of phrase which fell so naturally from his pen, and so authoritatively from his lips.

In 1917 John Parkinson married Clara Elvina, daughter of Alfred Le Brocq of St Helier, who died in 1974. They had one son who was killed in air combat over the channel in 1942, and four daughters.

WE

[*Brit. med. J.*, 1976, **1**, 1536; *Lancet*, 1976, **1**, 1359; *Times*, 8 June 1976; Photo]

PARKS, *Sir* **Alan (Guyatt)** *b.*19 Dec 1920 *d.*3 Nov 1982
MA BM BCh Oxon (1947) MD J Hopkins USA (1947)
MRCP (1948) FRCS (1949) MCh Oxon (1954) FRCP (1976)

Alan Guyatt Parks was an only child who at an early age developed a wide interest in crafts and hobbies. Later, he championed surgery as a craft to which he devoted his intellect and manual dexterity. The notice of his death described him as 'Master Surgeon', and this description fitted him exactly.

After early education at Sutton High School he obtained a scholarship to Epsom College, where he subsequently became head boy. As an Exhibitioner to Brasenose College, Oxford, he distinguished himself by becoming president of the Oxford University Athletic Club and playing rugby for the university. After graduating BA in 1943, Parks was one of a small wartime group selected for further training in America, as a Rockefeller student at Johns Hopkins, Baltimore. He was medical intern there and graduated MD in 1947 before returning to Guy's to complete his BM BCh in the same year. During the next two years, in which he served as house physician and research assistant, he took his MRCP and final FRCS. There followed two years in the RAMC as a surgeon with service in Malaya, Japan and Korea. On returning home he was resident surgical officer at Putney Hospital, then registrar and senior registrar at Guy's, until in 1959 he was appointed as a consultant surgeon to the London and St Mark's Hospitals, appointments which he held until the time of his death.

As a clinician, his innovative mind was not bound by the constraints of orthodoxy and he approached each problem from first principles. Patients recognized his conscientious concern for their welfare, and he justly enjoyed their complete confidence and affection. His MCh thesis in 1954, on the surgical treatment of haemorrhoids, described a new submucous procedure which his students dubbed Parks' painless proctoplasty. Subsequently, a series of papers radically altered surgical practice in the treatment of anal incontinence, fistula-in-ano, the removal of rectal tumours by the anal route, techniques for colo-anal anastomosis, and finally a new operation designed to avoid a permanent ileostomy after proctocolectomy for ulcerative colitis. His understanding of the anatomy and physiology of the pelvic floor, combined with the craftsmanship of his dissection, led to recognition of his work as a surgical pioneer of the very highest scientific quality. As a result, his clinical opinion and practical expertise were greatly in demand, and to the end of his life he remained a busy and dedicated clinician.

For Parks, research was a natural outcome of his questioning approach to clinical problems. His early work was based on anatomical study of thick sections of the breast and, later, he used a similar technique to study the anatomy of the anal canal and pelvic floor. In collaboration with others, electrical and pressure recordings were used to gain knowledge of the reflexes controlling the smooth muscle of the internal anal sphincter and the striated muscle of the pelvic floor and external anal sphincter. Strips of human muscle obtained at operation were studied in an isolated organ bath to investigate neurotransmitters and the effect of drugs. His clinical research involved detailed study of patients whom he had treated personally with particular reference to the outcome of various operative procedures.

In 1971 Parks was persuaded to stand for election to the Council of the College of Surgeons. His talents as an administrator were quickly recognized and he was soon appointed chairman of the Joint Consultants' Committee. His integrity and sense of humour made him a popular and successful chairman, and his valuable contribution to this negotiating committee between the profession and the DHSS was recognized by the knighthood conferred in 1977. It was no surprise when he was elected president of the Royal College of Surgeons in 1980. His genial manner, supported by the charm of his wife, combined with his wise and firm leadership, contributed much to the College during his period of office.

A strong Christian faith, developed at school, remained a major force throughout his life. As a keen supporter of the Christian Medical Fellowship, Parks at one time led their study group on ethical problems and was president elect at the time of his death. He was a staunch member of his local church and honorary surgeon to St Luke's Hospital for the Clergy.

Tall in stature, and with broad shoulders, Alan Parks was a commanding figure who did not hesitate to speak his mind, though he was approachable and extremely loyal to his friends and students. In 1956 he married Caroline Jean, daughter of John Cranston, an engineer, and they had three sons and a daughter. His family life was happy and he loved nothing more than to join his wife and children at their country cottage in Suffolk. A keen observer of all aspects of natural history, he gained great refreshment from his times in the countryside. His Christian faith persuaded him not to look for perfection in men, but he accepted people as they are, recognized that motives can be unworthy, and aimed to bring out the best in everyone he met. As a committee member his thoughts sometimes appeared far away, when he would suddenly rouse himself and bring the matter under discussion into focus with a few penetrating remarks. As an after dinner speaker, he spurned stories or jokes, and spoke in a simple, unaffected and direct manner.

Besides those already mentioned, many honours came to him such as honorary fellowships of the Edinburgh, Australasian and American Colleges of Surgeons, the Royal Colleges of Physicians and Surgeons of Glasgow and Canada, and the Italian Surgical Society. He was consultant surgeon to the Army, examiner in Surgery for Cambridge university and chief medical adviser of BUPA. His presidential address to the section of proctology at the Royal Society of Medicine was characterized by his conceptual approach. In 1978, he gave the Howard M Frykman memorial lecture in Minnesota; in 1979, the Fleming lecture to the Royal College of Physicians and Surgeons of Glasgow; in 1980 the Arthur Hurst lecture to the British Society of

Gastroenterology; and in 1982, the Cecil Joll prize lecture to the Royal College of Surgeons. An ardent European, he received the German Ernst Jung prize in 1980 for his unique contributions to colo-rectal surgery, and the following year he was awarded the Nessim Hapif prize of the University of Geneva.

Alan Parks regarded himself as a physician who operates, and he was proud of his fellowship in this College. He will long be remembered as a surgical craftsman, a clinical scientist, a medical statesman, and as a man of great integrity and character. JEL-J

[*Brit. med. J.*, 1982, **285**, 1434, 1569; *Lancet*, 1982, **2**, 111; *Times*, 5 and 27 Nov 1982; *J. roy. Soc. Med.*, 1983, **76**, 91]

PARRY, David Jackson *b*.11 July 1929 *d*.30 Dec 1981
BSc Lond (1950) MRCS LRCP (1953) MB BS (1953) MRCP (1960) FRCP (1975)

David Parry was the elder son of Edward Parry, a clerk to the Bank of England, and Rita, daughter of Frank Jackson, an accountant. He was born and brought up in Hampstead Garden Suburb, a neighbourhood with which his family remains closely identified. His link with this part of London was later strengthened when he married Dinah, daughter of John Norman Jones, master builder, whose firm had constructed many of the houses in the locality.

He attended University College School, where he became headboy, before entering St Mary's Hospital Medical School. He was awarded several prizes, intercalated for BSc, and graduated MB BS with honours in pathology, in 1953. He was house physician on the medical unit under the direction of George Pickering, and later held posts at Edgware General Hospital and Hammersmith Hospital, before becoming senior medical registrar at St Mary's Hospital and the West Middlesex Hospital. He held a short service commission in the medical branch of the Royal Air Force, working mainly at the Institute of Aviation Medicine in Farnborough; he spent a year on a fellowship in gastroenterology, working in Boston, Massachusetts.

In 1967 he was appointed consultant in general medicine with special interest in gastroenterology at Good Hope General Hospital, Sutton Coldfield, a newly created district general hospital for the North Birmingham District, where he worked for 14 years until his sudden and unexpected death at the age of 52. The appointment was a new one to a district with an expanding and varied population in which the pattern of medical practice was rapidly changing. His talents and personality were well suited to the job. He combined an informal, cheerful and relaxed manner, with a strong commitment, not only to individual patients but to wider aspects of the organization and development of medical services. He acted as a catalyst and facilitator in such tasks as establishing a representative committee structure in the district, and in providing an occupational health service. Because of his diplomatic skills, sense of fairness and practical idealism he was persuaded to hold office in all the important local committees. While serving on the Standing Committee of Members of the College he became increasingly convinced that, for many districts, the separation of geriatric medicine from the main stream of general medicine, was illogical and could have detrimental consequences. It was typical that he should act on his convictions, rather than propose them as policies for future practice by others. For several years he voluntarily added to his busy life as general physician and gastroenterologist, the clinical care and administrative responsibility for a large population of old people in North Birmingham.

David Parry possessed a gift for making friends and maintaining old friendships, particularly those established during his student days and in his early professional life. In his work he had an unusual ability for unobtrusively influencing and inspiring people; rigid posturing and circumscribed patterns of behaviour usually crumbled under his influence. He was an expert and energetic gardener; even when holding busy junior posts in London he made time to tend an allotment. Listening to music provided another enjoyment; he was a devotee of Benjamin Britten, and a few days spent at the Aldeburgh Festival each year provided particular pleasure for him and his wife.

He was known locally for his clinical ability and humanity; for his cheerful, friendly and modest manner, which overlay a sense of dedication and seriousness towards his professional life; and for the pioneering and selfless decision he made to embrace geriatrics, while retaining responsibilities in the full range of general medicine, which he had accepted at the time of his appointment. DDG

[*Brit. med. J.*, 1982, **284**, 231, 278]

PATERSON, John Frederic *b.*11 Apr 1911 *d.*6 June 1979
BA Cantab (1932) MB BChir (1936) MD (1938) FRCP C (1950) FRCP* (1969)

John Frederic Paterson was born in London and educated at Felsted School and Emmanuel College, Cambridge. He pursued his clinical studies at St Bartholomew's Hospital, London. His father was a manufacturer, Herbert May Paterson, and his mother, Catherine Ethel, was the daughter of John Parsons, also a manufacturer.

After moving to Canada, he served in the Royal Canadian Army Medical Corps throughout the second world war, both in Canada, England and NW Europe, and retired with the rank of major, medical specialist. On demobilization he was appointed director of medicine at the department of Veterans' Affairs Hospital in Kingston, Ontario. In 1948 he became director of the chest clinic, Christie Street and Sunnybrook Hospitals, Toronto; he was attending physician at Toronto Western Hospital, was appointed consultant to the Princess Margaret Hospital, Toronto, in 1959 and was head of the department of medicine, Sunnybrook Medical Centre, University of Toronto, from 1966 to 1974.

His many students will remember his devotion to education since starting, in 1949, as a clinical teacher, then assistant professor, and later associate professor of medicine at the University; finally being appointed coordinator of continuing medical education for the nine departments of medicine in Toronto teaching hospitals in 1974, when he also became professor and head of the department of medicine in the University. He was deeply involved in establishing Sunnybrook as an academic teaching centre; he recruited many of the staff and set a pattern for cooperation between departments which the staff were glad to follow.

In 1937 he married Trude Anna, daughter of Friedrich Rehm, a manufacturer, and they had four children: two sons and two daughters. He listed his hobbies as collecting Canadian furniture and growing trees.

John Paterson was a modest man who would seldom talk about his achievements, but his reputation as an expert in the field of industrial lung injury was worldwide, and during his distinguished career he received many honours and awards. Those who knew and worked with him remember a true gentleman, to whom courtesy and consideration for others were as natural as breathing; he preferred to instruct by example, and his students and staff learned many a lesson in care and compassion. GMD/GW

[*Lancet*, 1979, **2**, 374; Photo]

PAY, Brian Wilfrid *b*.25 Sept 1921 *d*.28 May 1983
BA Cantab (1942) MB BChir (1945) MA (1947) MRCP (1955) FRCP (1976)

Brian Pay was the son of a housemaster at Pocklington School, Yorkshire, and received his schooling there before reading natural sciences at St John's College, Cambridge, where he was an exhibitioner. He pursued his clinical studies at St Thomas's Hospital, graduating in 1945. Called up for national service in the RAMC, he served in Singapore and Malaya from 1947 to 1949. In 1955 he was appointed senior registrar to Viscount Waverley at the Royal Berkshire Hospital, Reading. He was appointed consultant physician to the Reading hospitals in 1965, and worked at Prospect Park Hospital until the Abbey unit at Battle was opened in 1972. He was responsible for planning the medical department at Abbey and, despite considerable resistance, succeeded in the construction of a modern unit.

In 1956 Brian Pay married Nina Emily, daughter of Edward James H Norman, an engineer. There were no children of the marriage.

He was a man with few enemies, a softly disposed Yorkshireman who practised medicine in the old way. He was quiet, deliberate and unhasty; a man who earned the profound respect of his patients and who will be remembered by his colleagues with great affection. His quiet manner concealed a fine sense of humour; for those who knew, as he dissected the esoteric but poorly founded diagnoses of others, his quiet chuckle expressed more scorn than words.

His last few years were marred by illness which he endured with characteristic bravery, and his interest in medicine and his concern for his patients and junior staff kept him at work until a month before his death. In his earlier years he rowed for Lady Margaret Boat Club, Cambridge, and was a keen swimmer and bridge player. GW/VL

[*Brit. med. J.*, 1983, **286**, 2066-7]

PAYNE, Donald James Harwood *b.*26 Oct 1917 *d.*2 June 1982
MRCS LRCP (1942) MB BS Lond (1943) Dip Bact (1953)
MRCP (1972) FRCPath (1963) FRCP (1979)

Donald Payne was born in London. His father, James Alfred Payne, was an architect and, although his immediate family circle had no medical connections, his great uncle, Sir David Wire, was a Lord Mayor of London from 1854 to 1855, and was one of the founder members of the National Hospital for Nervous Diseases, Queen Square, London.

He was educated at Brentwood School, Queen Mary College London, and the London Hospital, and qualified in 1942 before undertaking house appointments at London Hospital Annexe, Brentwood.

It was at the London Hospital in 1942 that he met and married his wife, Patricia Margaret , a nursing sister and the daughter of Commander Patrick Joseph McKenna RN.

On completion of his house appointment in 1942, he joined the RAMC as a captain, and was posted to North Africa, subsequently taking part in the landing at Sicily and the advance through Italy. In 1944 he was posted home to take part in the Normandy landings and the invasion of Northern Europe. In 1946 he returned to the London Hospital as a registrar in pathology, in particular to the study of microbiology. In 1949 he joined the Public Health Laboratory Service and was appointed as a director of the laboratory at Northallerton and honorary consultant microbiologist to the hospital, where he established his reputation in the control of brucellosis which was prevalent in the area. His work on salmonellosis and brucellosis gained him an international reputation. In 1979 he was invited by the New Zealand government to tour that country and to advise on the protection of veterinary surgeons against brucellosis.

In 1964, he was appointed director to the PHLS Laboratory at Portsmouth, and honorary consultant bacteriologist to the Portsmouth and Isle of Wight Area Pathology Service.

A few years after his appointment the laboratory was designated as Regional Laboratory, not only for identification and control of brucellosis but also for the serological typing of *Salmonella*, and the control of hospital infection. At the same time he also became a member of the Parliamentary Working Party on the disposal of sewage. In 1972 he obtained his MRCP as a result of his published work, and was elected a fellow in 1979.

His publications were numerous and his department was run competently and successfully. Individual members were always encouraged to do their own research and develop their own ideas, and as such his department established an outstanding reputation both in the public health field and the hospital fraternity.

Donald was never a keen committee man; he preferred to settle any problems after prolonged individual discussion, preferably over a pint of beer.

During the early part of his life he was a keen and gifted yachtsman, and but for the 1939 war would almost certainly have been selected for the Olympic trials of 1940, although he was runner up to the bronze medallist in the Olympic trials for Melbourne in 1953. He was also keenly interested in ocean cruising, and was invited to take part in a number of international ocean races. In view of his navigating skills he was elected a member of the Royal Ocean Club, of which he was justly proud.

The last few years of his life were marred by his wife's prolonged illness, whilst he himself developed both diabetes and arthritis, which necessitated a bilateral hip replacement. Both disabilities were borne without complaint whilst he continued his medical duties.

His final illness proved to be short and distressing, which he bore with considerable fortitude.

He was survived by his wife Pat, and three daughters; two were associated with medicine before marriage: his second daughter was a hospital administrator, the youngest a nurse. EMD

[*Brit. med. J.,* 1982, **285**, 384; *Lancet,* 1982, **2**, 168-9]

PAYNE, Wilfrid Walter *b.*25 Mar 1894 *d.*28 Dec 1978
MRCS LRCP (1919) MB BS Lond (1920) MRCP (1938)
FRCP (1951)

Wilfrid Payne was born at Brighton, the son of William Henry Payne, an accountant with the London, Brighton and South Coast railway, and his wife, Alice Flora Smith. He was educated at Brighton Grammar School and Guy's Hospital, his undergraduate career being interrupted by two years' service as a sub-lieutenant RNVR, 1917–1918, in destroyers. He qualified from Guy's in 1920 and was assistant house surgeon, outpatient officer and house physician successively, then demonstrator of physiology, pathology, and clinical chemistry; and lastly medical assistant.

In 1926 Payne transferred to the Hospital for Sick Children, Great Ormond Street, as chemist, his title changing through the years through biochemist to chemical pathologist. Although retiring from the National Health Service in 1959, his love of his work led him to Queen Charlotte's Hospital for three years, followed by seven years with the Neonatal Unit at Hammersmith Hospital. Moving to Bristol in 1969 he worked in the Child Health Unit until 1973, when he retired finally.

A man of prodigious work output but little writing, his major papers were on 'Visceral pain in Upper Tract', 'Dextrose tolerance curve in health', Infantile renal acidosis', 'Renal tubular defects in childhood, 'Familial hypoglycaemia precipitated by amino acid, 'Free diet in the treatment of diabetes mellitus', and 'Forty years of nephrosis in childhood'; and it should be noted that all but the third paper were written jointly. Payne also founded and edited the *Great Ormond Street Journal* throughout its short life.

He came to paediatrics at a time fortunate for him, when paediatric chemistry was growing up. During his long service he saw and helped to develop flame photometry and chromatography, enzymology, fat balances and chylomicron counting, and a host of other methods and techniques. He enlightened the treatment of gastroenteritis, did pioneer work on calcium and phosphorus metabolism, and much of the work leading to the understanding of coeliac and fibrocystic disease.

Two special interests must be mentioned. Firstly, the interest in diabetes which he brought from Guy's, resulted in the founding of a diabetic clinic at Great Ormond Street. This became such an institution that the hospital's charter permitting the treatment of children up to the age of 12 had to be reconsidered, so that Payne's diabetics could continue to be looked after when over that age. Secondly, the development of chemical micro-techniques, using finger or heel-prick blood, saved many children much suffering. Among the many honours Payne received were the Dawson Williams prize in 1959 and the James Spence medal in 1971; he also gave the second Blackfan lecture in Boston.

Payne was an avuncular and benevolent figure. Retaining his Sussex intonation and genuine courtesy, he was a much loved colleague and companion. Nothing was too much trouble for him in helping his junior (and senior) fellows, at any time of day or night, with advice or technical demonstration, and he was in much demand for the help so freely given.

His hobbies were gardening and walking. He so enjoyed the latter that in the days when he lived in Brighton he walked from Victoria Station to Bloomsbury and back for the pleasure the exercise gave him.

In 1921 Payne married Winifred Grace, daughter of William Scott, stores manager, and they had a son and a daughter. His first wife died in 1968, and in 1971 he married Anne King, who survived him, with his children.

IABC

[*Brit. med. J.*, 1979, **1**, 132, 483, 829; Photo]

PEGRUM, Geoffrey David *b.*16 Feb 1931 *d.*25 Dec 1980
MRCS LRCP (1955) MB BS Lond (1955) MRCP (1961)
MRCPath (1963) MD (1965) FRCPath (1978) FRCP (1978)

Geoffrey Pegrum was born in Surrey and educated at Raynes Park County Grammar School. His father, Ronald Frederick, was a retailer. Geoffrey qualified at Charing Cross Hospital Medical School where he met and married his fellow student Doreen Rothman. There followed house posts and then service in the RAF, where he began his training as a pathologist. After leaving the services he returned to

Charing Cross Hospital, holding various posts in the pathology department, and attaining the MRCP in 1961. The same year he was appointed senior lecturer and honorary consultant in haematology.

During the next decade he contributed much to the expansion of his chosen specialty, haematology. Latterly during this period he was heavily involved in the planning of the department of haematology for the new hospital, which was to open in 1973, at which time he was appointed reader. Throughout these years he took an active part in many aspects of the life of the hospital and the medical school, playing hockey, rugby, squash and tennis. He was a man of enthusiasm and energy who endeared himself to the students as a sympathetic and energetic teacher.

The period between 1973–1978 was a time of hectic activity, organizing the clinical and research work of the greatly expanded department. He established a loyal and happy group of clinical and laboratory researchers with many interests but with special expertise in chromosome studies and tissue typing. He published extensively and presented many papers at national and international meetings. Although an energetic research worker, he never allowed himself to be cloistered in the laboratory, but was in his element working and teaching at the bedside. Geoffrey worked equally hard in many administrative roles; perhaps the most taxing and vital for the smooth running of the new hospital was that of medical representative on the first District management team.

A founder member of the Royal College of Pathologists, he was elected to the fellowship of that College and of the Royal College of Physicians in 1978.

That year proved to be the pinnacle of his career, as he was then appointed to the chair of haematology at Westminster Hospital. Tragically at this time of great achievement malignant disease was detected, which was to cause his death. Geoffrey decided not to move to the post at Westminster but chose to stay at Charing Cross Hospital Medical School, and was appointed to take charge of the department of haematology with the title of professor. Over the next two years his true emotional strength and courage shone out as an example to all those who knew him. With the loving support of his wife and children he determined to fight the disease and continue an active professional life, even at times directing his clinical and research work from his hospital bed. Steadily the illness eroded his health, but not his determination to live his life at full strength – 'the only way I know how'. Eventually he died on Christmas Day 1980, lovingly cared for by his wife Doreen, his daughter Helen and son Anthony. RAP

[*Brit. med. J.*, 1981, **282**, 158; *Lancet*, 1981, **1**, 287; Photo]

PELLEW, Richard Alfred Amyas *b.*9 June 1911 *d.*28 Mar 1976
MB BS Adelaide (1934) MRCP (1937) MRACP (1939)
FRACP (1957) FRCP (1970)

Richard Pellew was born at Balaklava, South Australia, the second son of Leonard James Pellew, a surgeon, and of Hirell Alice Ternouth, both of Adelaide. He was educated at St Peter's College and Adelaide University, graduating in 1934.

He was junior resident medical officer at the Royal Adelaide Hospital in 1935, and senior RMO in 1936. He went to London and took the MRCP in 1937. In 1938 he was medical registrar at the Westminster Hospital, and then returned to Australia to become medical superintendent of the Adelaide Children's Hospital in 1939.

Early in 1940 Pellew volunteered for the Royal Australian Army Medical Corps, and embarked for the Middle East theatre in April 1941 with the rank of captain, as regimental medical officer of the 2/3rd Machine Gun Battalion, Australian Imperial Force. The unit saw action principally in Syria. In January 1942 he was promoted to major and was posted as a specialist physician to the 2/1st Australian General Hospital. The hospital soon returned to Australia, with many other Australian units, in response to the Japanese advance, and was stationed in Western Australia. From there, Pellew was transferred to No 105 Australian Military Hospital, Adelaide, was promoted to lieutenant colonel, and was invalided from the service in 1944.

On his return to civilian life he entered private practice in partnership with his elder brother Leonard, a surgeon. He also resumed his association with the Royal Adelaide Hospital, and this continued until his death. He was successively: honorary clinical assistant in general medicine, honorary assistant physician, honorary physician, and senior visiting physician until his tragic death in an accident in his home, in March 1976, which occurred only a few months before he was due to retire from the hospital on reaching the age limit.

For many years, between 1948 and 1955, he was actively involved as visiting medical officer in the infectious diseases wing of the hospital. In 1950–1951 a large epidemic of poliomyelitis occurred, causing scores of admissions and many deaths. At that time he became interested in the illnesses which could simulate non-paralytic or mild poliomyelitis. This led to a pioneering paper: 'A clinical description of a disease resembling Poliomyelitis seen in Adelaide 1949–51' (*Med. J. Aust.,* 30 June 1951, p. 944-46). He carefully followed the progress of the patients with this, at that time, puzzling illness, and with a virologist colleague later described some further, inconclusive attempts to isolate and define the causal agents: 'Further investigations on a disease resembling Poliomyelitis seen in Adelaide', (RAA Pellew & JAR Miles, *Med. J. Aust.,* 24 September 1955, p 480-82). Adequate virological techniques for these agents had not at that time been developed. In 1958 he was co-author of a further clinical report on cases of Bornholm Disease in Adelaide: 'Bornholm disease in an Adelaide suburban area' (L Kaupmees and RAA Pellew, *Med. J. Aust.,* Vol. 1, 1958, p 517-18).

He was basically a general physician with a liking for neurology and a strong bent toward bedside work, an attitude he tried to impart to his students. He was not much given to elaborate laboratory work-ups or biochemical profiles, but he was a strong advocate of the value of pathology as a basis for clinical medicine. He was generous, impulsive and warm-hearted, and also irascible and impatient in a good-natured way, and there was no trace of pomp in the way he ran his ward. He liked to teach, he was good at it, and his down-to-earth practical bedside approach made him very popular with the undergraduates. For many years he held an informal crowded weekly ward round, at which there were nearly always some senior visitors, who had come to contribute in a relaxed and friendly fashion in which 'one-upmanship' was out of place.

He had many loyal friends both within and outside the profession, and many supporters among South Australian general practitioners, especially from country districts. He was always interested in and well informed about rural affairs and about sport and outdoor pursuits. As a young man he represented his university and the State of South Australia at baseball. Later in life he was an expert cricket watcher, and at home worked energetically in his large rambling garden.

He married Winifred Ruth, daughter of Frank Sandland Hone, a physician, of Adelaide, in 1938. She survived him, with their only child Richard, a graduate in agricultural science at the University of Adelaide.

JSR

[*Med. J. Aust.*, 8 May 1976, **1(19)** 718-9]

PENFIELD, Wilder Graves *b*.26 Jan 1891 *d*.5 Apr 1976
OM (1953) CC (1967) CMG (1943) MD J Hopkins USA (1918) MA Oxon (1920) FRCSC (1929) DSc (1935) PRCSC (1939-41) FRS (1943) Hon FRCS Hon FRSM Hon FRCP (1955)†

Wilder Graves Penfield was born at Spokane, Washington, USA, the son of Charles Samuel Penfield, a surgeon, and Jean Jefferson, daughter of a banker. He was educated at Princeton and awarded a Rhodes Scholarship to Oxford in 1913, but before taking it up spent a year as full-time coach to the Princeton football team. In 1914 he went to Oxford to study medicine as a pupil of Sir William Osler; the first world war intervened and Penfield served with an American Red Cross Hospital in France. In 1916 he was severely wounded and returned to America to study at Johns Hopkins Medical School, Baltimore, where he graduated in 1918. He then returned to Oxford, completing his degree in 1920. From 1921-28 he was junior attending surgeon at the Presbyterian Hospital, New York, and also assistant professor of surgery at Columbia University. In 1924, on the suggestion of William Clarke, the surgical pathologist, Penfield began to study the process of healing of experimental wounds in the brain. Disappointed with his histological techniques, he recalled that Sherrington had advised him to try the methods of Ramon y Cajal, and from March to September 1924 he worked in Madrid with Pio del Rio-Hortega, Cajal's brilliant pupil. This short period was of great importance in his future career. As he wrote later, 'With the anatomical skills I had learned in Madrid, I could now make my own fundamental scientific approach to problems in neurosurgery. And I longed to apply it to the whole field of clinical neurology.'

In 1928 Penfield moved to Montreal, Canada, as neurosurgeon to the Royal Victoria and Montreal General Hospital, and remained there for the rest of his life. He became a naturalized Canadian citizen in 1934, the year in which he was elected professor of neurology at McGill University and director of the Montreal Neurological Institute (endowed by the Rockefeller Foundation), which he founded. He resigned his professorship at McGill University in 1954 but remained a director of the Institute until 1960, when he retired.

Penfield was one of the great neurosurgeons of his day, and the Montreal Neurological Institute soon became the Mecca for neurosurgeons and neurologists from all over the world. He based his brilliant surgery on a sound and deep knowledge of the working of the brain which, inspired by the teachings of Sir Charles Sherrington during his studies at Oxford, excelled that of any of his contemporaries. Penfield's studies in epilepsy were classics of accurate observation and documentation and the Institute had an international reputation in this special field. In collaboration with HH Jasper he had the support of the new science of electroencephalography. His operations on conscious patients carried him into the study of the localization of cerebral function, and thus into the deeper realm of philosophy concerning language function and the relation of brain, mind and spirit, subjects which absorbed more of his thoughts in his later years. He wrote well and clearly, and had the gift of making abstruse concepts intelligible to the average reader. Together with Herbert Jasper he wrote *Epilepsy and the Functional Anatomy of the Brain* (1954). His last book was entitled *The Mystery of the Mind* (1975). In 1958 he delivered the Sherrington Lecture at Liverpool University on 'The excitable cortex in conscious man'.

Wilder Penfield was president of the Royal College of Physicians and Surgeons of Canada from 1939 to 1941. In Britain his standing was recognized by his election, in 1943, to the fellowship of the Royal Society, and by his appointment to the Order of Merit in 1953. In 1967 he was appointed Companion of the Order of Canada. He was an honorary fellow of the Royal College of Surgeons of England, and Edinburgh, and of the Royal College of Physicians of London, and Edinburgh. He was an honorary Doctor of Civil Law at Oxford University and held several other honorary doctorates from Canada, USA and Europe. A man of outstanding intellect, which he applied with insight and compassion to a diversity of subjects, he was not only a fine surgeon and a great scientist, he was an even greater human being. He was infinitely concerned about his profession and the whole human race, and there was nothing he would not do to help wherever he could.

In 1917 he married Helen Kermott, daughter of Edward Kermott a physician, and they had two sons and two daughters. They were deeply in love with one another and it was an extremely happy marriage.

Penfield held that it was in the power of most people to adopt a second career after retirement from their first. He himself exemplified this by writing a number of enchanting novels and biographies. He was engaged in writing his own autobiography when he died, and this was published in 1977, *No man alone: a neurosurgeon's life,* Boston/Toronto, Little Brown and Company, with a foreword by Lord Adrian. He was a gentle, charming, erudite, and very approachable man, a great organizer, administrator, surgeon and teacher, devoted to research and the advancement of knowledge, a prolific writer and a fine citizen. The Montreal Institute was founded on the concept of a multidisciplinary approach, and he left behind him many pupils throughout the world trained in various neurological disciplines, and themselves making advances to knowledge. GW/VL

[*Biogr. Mem. roy. Soc.,* 1978, **24**, 473-513; *Brit. med. J.,* 1976, **1**, 1079; *Lancet,* 1976, **1**, 868; *Times,* 7 & 17 Apr 1976; *Osler Library Newsletter,* June 1976, No. 22; *Osler Club Newsletter,* June 1976; *Canadian Med. Assoc. J.,* 1976; Photo]

PERKINS, Richard Basil *b.*9 Feb 1910 *d.*19 Dec 1980
BSc (1933) MB BS Sydney (1936), MRCP (1939) MRACP (1945) FRACP (1956) FRCP (1965)

Richard Basil Perkins, the only son of Dr Richard Perkins and his wife Helen Philipps, was born at Morpeth, New South Wales, in a house which has been the site of a medical practice for over a hundred years. His father was a general practitioner there, and his grandfather, AE Perkins, was also a doctor who had practised in Sydney.

Richard was educated at St Aloysius' College, Sydney, of which he became *dux* before entering the faculty of medicine at the University of Sydney in 1929. He interrupted his medical course for a year to do an honours BSc in physiology and graduated in medicine in 1936, also with honours. He then became a resident medical officer at the Royal Prince Alfred Hospital for two years, proceeding to London in 1938, where he obtained his MRCP the following year. Having gained an appointment to the staff of the St John's Hospital for Diseases of the Skin, he was awarded the Chesterfield medal for 1939.

At the outbreak of World War II, Perkins returned to Australia to enlist in the RAAMC and was given command of a field ambulance. However, he expressed a firm preference for clinical rather than administrative work, and was appointed dermatologist to the 2/7 Australian General Hospital at Lae, New Guinea, where at the request of the Army Directorate he wrote a booklet on *Tropical Diseases of the Skin* for the guidance of medical officers. After the war he was appointed honorary assistant dermatologist to the Royal Prince Alfred Hospital, eventually becoming head of the department of dermatology. He was the first Australian dermatologist to be trained in the English tradition of first qualifying in internal medicine before taking up the specialty of dermatology.

In 1956 he was elected president of the Dermatological Association of Australia, and was a foundation fellow of the Australasian College of Dermatologists, to which he made significant contributions. Perkins was meticulous in all he did, and his opinion was eagerly sought in difficult dermatological problems because of his widespread experience and his detailed knowledge of the literature. He was also widely informed on a variety of non-medical subjects and this, together with his unobtrusive sense of humour, made him a most convivial companion for his large circle of friends.

In 1960 he was stricken by cancer of the lung which was successfully treated by surgery and radiotherapy, although this involved the sacrifice of his superior vena cava. He faced these trials with remarkable faith and courage, and after recovery returned to his duties at the Royal Prince Alfred Hospital and at the School of Tropical Medicine as lecturer in tropical dermatology.

In 1940 Richard married Katherine Bull who had been a theatre sister at the Royal Prince Alfred Hospital. This happy union gave them three sons and two daughters. MRJ

[*RACP Newsletter,* Aug 1981, **13**, No. 2; Photo]

PETERS, *Sir* **Rudolph (Albert)** *b.*13 Apr 1889 *d.*29 Jan 1982
Kt (1952) MC (1917) MA Cantab (1914) MB BChir (1915)
MD (1919) FRS (1935) FRCP* (1952)†

Rudolph Peters was born in Kensington, the son of Albert Edward Duncan Ralph Peters, a general practitioner in Midhurst, and later in Petersfield. His grandfather, Ralph Benjamin Peters, had been born in Denmark, the son of Rudolph Peters (1781 – 1861), a captain in the Danish Army who had been appointed, by King Christian VIII, a Knight of the Order of Dannebrog for his part in the defence of Altona against the French.

His mother, Agnes Watts, was the granddaughter of Commander CN Watts, RN, whose father, Admiral George Watts CB, had been engaged in many naval actions in the time of Napoleon. Another Watts ancestor fell while serving under the Duke of Kent in Martinique in 1794, and yet another had fought under the Duke of Cumberland at the Battle of Culloden.

He was educated first at Warden House, Deal, where he became head boy, and later at Wellington, where he entered as a classical scholar and was at first put onto the classical side, which the Headmaster assured him would provide a most suitable background for medicine. He had no formal teaching in science until his last year at Wellington, although by the age of 17 he had become interested in it as a hobby.

On leaving Wellington, and while waiting for a vacancy for admission to Cambridge, he spent a year in London at King's College. In 1908 he entered Gonville and Caius College, and in 1910 obtained first class honours in Part I of the Natural Sciences Tripos. While working for his Part II in physiology he embarked on his first research problem. This was to determine the relationship between iron and oxygen in haemoglobin. The results he obtained were of fundamental importance in showing that they exist in stoichiometric proportions, and that although the oxygen is dissociable it is present in true chemical combination with the iron.

He was, unfortunately, unable to sit for his Part II examination because in the early summer of 1912 he developed typhoid fever, and was forced to spend five weeks in a nursing home in London.

On returning to Cambridge in the autumn of 1912 he worked with AV Hill on the relation between heat production and lactic acid formation in muscle following stimulation through the nerve.

In 1914 he was awarded a fellowship at Caius, but on the outbreak of World War I he left Cambridge for London to complete his medical education at his father's old hospital, St Bartholomew's Hospital. He was evidently very happy at Bart's as he has recorded that 'it was a very warm cosy place. The old ladies used to call you "dearie", and you really got some sense of what clinical medicine meant in the Bart's surgery. It was a very splendid place.'

After qualifying in the summer of 1915 he joined the Royal Army Medical Corps, and in November of that year was sent to France. He served for six months with a field ambulance and at advanced dressing stations around Béthune, and was then posted to the 1st Battalion of the 60th Rifles as their medical officer. He was with them throughout the Delville Wood, Vimy Ridge and Beaumont Hamel battles, being awarded the Military Cross and Bar, and was also mentioned in despatches.

Early in 1917 he was recalled to England to carry out research on the medical aspects of chemical warfare in the experimental station which had been set up at Porton on Salisbury Plain in 1916, and which later became the Chemical Defence Establishment of the Ministry of Defence. Initially the working conditions at Porton were cramped and primitive, and for some months Peters lived in the hut which was used as the physiological laboratory, and had his bath, which was of the round tin type, in the post-mortem room. He spent the rest of the war at Porton working on phosgene, arsenical smokes and mustard gas, and he has said that the experience which he gained there, and the horrifying impact that the advent of 'gas' warfare had on him, orientated much of his later work.

In 1918 he returned to his fellowship at Caius where, together with H Hartridge, he studied the effect of pH on interfaces between oil and water. His interest in cell surfaces had been stimulated by his observations while at Porton on changes in the lung alveolar epithelium induced by phosgene and other respiratory irritant gases, and in his Harben lectures in 1929 he put forward some highly original ideas concerning the internal organization of cells which, as is now evident, clearly anticipated the modern concept of the ultrastructure of the cell.

In 1923 he left Cambridge, having been invited to accept the Whitley chair of biochemistry at Oxford. The facilities for biochemistry in Oxford at that time were poor, but in 1925 he obtained a grant from the Rockefeller Foundation and in 1926 he and his staff moved into a new and attractive biochemistry laboratory.

Peters next embarked on the research for which he will be best remembered, a study of the 'anti-neuritic' vitamin which is capable of curing beri-beri and which was known at that time as vitamin B_1. Together with his colleagues he carried out the large scale preparation of active fractions from baker's yeast, and by 1932 crystalline preparations of high vitamin B_1 activity had been obtained.

With the help of these highly purified concentrates he went on to investigate the nature of the underlying damage in the nervous system of the vitamin deficient pigeon, and in 1936, in a lecture that he gave at the National Hospital for Nervous Diseases in London, he concluded that vitamin B_1 (thiamine) acts as a co-enzyme for the oxidative removal of pyruvate, one of the degradation products of glucose metabolism, and that, in the absence of the vitamin, pyruvate accumulates in the tissues and in the blood. He had therefore, for the first time, described the way in which a vitamin acts inside the body, and also for the first time the 'biochemical lesion' that exists in the tissues of a vitamin deficient animal.

With the outbreak of the second world war Peters was asked to return to chemical warfare problems, and by September 1939 he had recruited an extra-mural team for the Ministry of Supply to work under his direction on the mode of action of vesicant gases (in particular mustard gas and lewisite), with a view to devising specific antidotes to them capable of being used therapeutically. In the case of lewisite this objective was achieved, a highly effective antidote, 2:3-dimercaptopropanol (British Anti-lewisite or BAL) being developed. Peters was at first somewhat sceptical of the 'dithiol theory' underlying this discovery which had been put forward by members of his team, but he later took an active part in establishing the value of BAL in the treatment of post-arsphenamine dermatitis and of certain other metal intoxications. He was also at that time engaged in research for the Medical Research Council on the biochemical changes, both local and general, occurring in thermal burns.

Throughout the war, and indeed from 1930 on, Peters was much involved in the work of the Accessory Food Factors Committee of the MRC, and was chairman of this committee, and of a number of its sub-committees, from 1943 to 1954.

After the war he turned his attention to a different toxicological problem, and in a series of elegant and imaginative studies he succeeded in unravelling the mechanism underlying the toxic action of fluoroacetate. This compound, which was known to be highly toxic particularly to the nervous system and the heart, had been shown to be the toxic principle of a South African plant *(Dichapetalum cymosum)*. Peters' contribution was to show that its toxic action depends on its metabolic conversion inside the body into another compound, fluorocitrate, which then competitively blocks one of the enzymes of the tricarboxylic acid cycle. This is an example of what Peters called a 'lethal synthesis' in contrast to the protective syntheses used in many detoxification processes.

In 1954 Peters retired from his chair at Oxford, having been invited by the Agricultural Research Council to become head of the biochemistry department at the ARC Institute of Animal Physiology at Babraham, near Cambridge. Here he continued his work on the toxic action of various fluorine-containing compounds, becoming particularly interested in those plants containing compounds of this type that present a threat to livestock.

When, at the age of 70, Peters finally retired from his post at Babraham, Sir Frank Young FRS at once invited him to join the University department of biochemistry at Cambridge. Here for many years he arrived daily on his bicycle, and carried on an active programme of research supported by grants from a number of sources, particularly the Wellcome Trust. Among other problems he studied, with JM Walshe, the toxicity of copper to brain tissue, and concluded that the toxic action is in part due to reaction of the copper ions with membrane-bound ATPase.

Rudolph Peters was a very distinguished figure in biochemistry and medicine, not only in this country but throughout the world. He was also a man of great personal charm, an inspiring leader and a warm and generous friend. He had a quick, enquiring mind, and a friendly and confiding way with all his colleagues. Under his guidance the biochemistry department at Oxford was a very happy place, and he himself attached much importance to keeping it so. His lectures were exciting and delivered with an enthusiasm which carried his audience with him, and gave them a sense of participating in whatever he was describing.

In addition to his enthusiasm for science, he had from very early years a love for music. He was an accomplished violinist, and throughout his life he found much enjoyment in playing chamber music with his friends, including two of his scientific colleagues, Malcolm Dixon FRS, and Sir Ernst Chain FRS.

He was elected a fellow of the Royal Society in 1935, and was awarded the Royal Medal of the Society in 1949. A knighthood was conferred on him in 1952 in recognition of his many services to science. He was made an honorary fellow of Gonville and Caius College, Cambridge, and of Trinity College, Oxford. He was invited to give many special lectures, including the Croonian lecture of the Royal Society and the Louis Abrahams lecture of the College (1952). The honorary degrees and other honours awarded to him by many universities, colleges and societies both in Britain and overseas reflect the interest which he took in the international aspects of science. He played a central part in bringing into existence the International Union of Biochemistry, he was a founder member of the International Brain Research Organisation, and from 1958 to 1961 he was president of the International Council for Scientific Unions, a post which he filled with great distinction.

In 1917 he married Frances Vérel, who had been at school with his sister and who survived him. They had two sons, the elder of whom is a doctor in Canada and the younger a business man living in Italy.

RHST

[*Brit. med. J.*, 1982, **284**, 589; *Lancet*, 1982, **1**, 635-6; *Times*, 2 Feb 1982; *Biogr. Mem. roy. Soc.*, 1983, **29**, 495-523; Photo]

PICKERING, *Sir* **George (White)** *b.*26 June 1904 *d.*3 Sept 1980
Kt (1957) FRS (1960) MRCS LRCP (1928) MA MB Cantab (1930) MRCP (1930) FRCP (1938) MD (1955) Hon FACP (1955) Hon FRCPI (1965) FRCPE (1967) Hon MD Ghent (1948) Siena (1965) Univ W. Austral (1965) Hon DSc Durh (1957) Dubl (1962) Hon LLD Manch (1964)†

George Pickering was born in Whalton, Northumberland, into a family with very strong farming traditions. He was always proud of his Northumbrian origins and liked to return to those wide rolling landscapes with broad horizons that reminded him of his youth. His father was a schoolteacher, who unfortunately died at an early age, and George was brought up, together with his sister, by his mother, who was responsible for their early education up to the age of seven. They lived in Newcastle and while George could not claim to be a true Geordie, he certainly had a wide range of Tyneside songs which were produced at suitable times, and often enlivened the somewhat staid proceedings of international conferences. He attended the Newcastle Grammar School from the age of nine and he soon showed his independence of spirit as well as his assessment of what was best for him by persuading his mother to send him far away to school at Dulwich College, where he was an exceptional student. At Cambridge he sat an examination for a scholarship in science, intending to do a degree in agriculture. With that good fortune that often seems to favour the exceptionally talented, he met Rudolph Peters, who persuaded him to change his aim to biochemistry or physiology. He was subsequently awarded a scholarship at Pembroke College. At Cambridge his mind turned to physiology, where he was obviously stimulated by the research and views of, among others, Barcroft, Rideal and Adrian. The step from physiology to medicine seemed natural and he was given an entrance scholarship to St Thomas's. He qualified in 1928 and became house physician to Sir Maurice Cassidy, a cardiologist of originality and who was the first to associate carcinoid tumours with valvular lesions on the right side of the heart. By a fortunate chance, which owed a lot to Pickering's friendship with Henry Barcroft, who was together with him at Cambridge, his wish to pursue clinical science was met when Sir Joseph Barcroft suggested he tried to work with Sir Thomas Lewis at UCH. Good fortune once more favoured him and a vacancy which had arisen by what would be delicately called temperamental incompatibility, was offered to Pickering, and here began perhaps the most important formative period in his life in clinical science. A different sort of union also occurred at this time, since he then married Dr Carola Seward, daughter of the professor of botany and master of Downing College, Cambridge, and this was one of the best decisions he ever made in his life. There were a son and three daughters of the marriage.

At University College he entered what was the leading medical centre for the pursuit of scientific knowledge, and there was a collection of original minds which has not been equalled since. In Lewis's department there were Wayne and Grant, and a succession of eminent overseas research fellows. The department of medicine, directed by TR Elliott, who was the original proponent of the 'adrenaline hypothesis of sympathetic nerve action' when working with Langley in Cambridge, contained Himsworth, Smirk and McMichael, and all the other departments had their luminaries. One whose company Pickering particularly enjoyed was Wilfred Trotter, a neurosurgeon, whose philosophical approach he admired and whose essays he often quoted. Pickering was with Lewis for eight years, and during this time his interest in the control of the circulation was firmly established. It was there that he did his early studies on blood flow, and finally in 1938, together with Prinzmetal, he re-discovered renin, which had been patiently waiting since its original discovery in 1898 by Tigerstedt and Bergman. His period of apprenticeship was now over. He owed a great deal to the example of Lewis, who had the same critical spirit of enquiry that he himself always showed. His move to St Mary's Hospital Medical School in October 1939 was the beginning of his most important contributions to medical research. He was brought there through the clear appreciation of his merit by Sir Charles Wilson, later to be Lord Moran, who achieved great fame, firstly by rescuing the medical school in the early 1930s when it was threatened by closure, and secondly as Churchill's doctor. It was no surprise, except perhaps to the more traditionally minded members of the medical staff of St Mary's, when he chose the youngest star in an intellectual firmament to direct the medical unit. This coincided with the outbreak of the war, and while Pickering made extremely important contributions in a wide variety of clinical fields, such as constrictive pericarditis and the cause of pain in peptic ulcer, it was not until the medical school, which had been evacuated largely to Harefield Hospital among other country sites, returned to London that his research blossomed fully. By example in the laboratory and at the bedside he created an atmosphere of excitement and critical enquiry which spread to everyone. Even those who were frightened of his trenchant criticisms respected him, and his influence was instrumental in gradually making St Mary's the place that people wanted to get to, both from abroad and at home, to work with George Pickering. He touched on many fields apart from hypertension, and so his interest in the pain of peptic ulcer led to a demonstration that it was the pH of the stomach contents that mattered rather than spasm of the stomach or duodenal wall. He took a keen interest in fever, so that work developed in search of the pyrogen that caused it in many clinical disorders as well as experimentally. This led to the setting up by the MRC of a body temperature research unit within the medical unit. However, his enduring fame will be in relation to hypertension. His initial work on renin led to further experiments which defined the role of the kidney in experimental renal clipping hypertension in the rabbit, and it was out of this interest that work on angiotensin, which led to its isolation and amino acid analysis, developed. Perhaps the most widely known work came when he decided to look at genetic and environmental factors and their part in blood pressure distribution in populations. He showed, together with his colleagues, that the sharp differentiation between normotension and hypertension was an artificial division and that blood pressure, like many other qualities, was distributed as a continuous variable. This led to the famous Platt/Pickering controversy, since Robert Platt believed that 'hypertension' was inherited as a dominant characteristic in families, and that the distribution of pressures within populations could be seen to be biphasic due to the occurrence of a truly hypertensive group that could be distinguished from the normotensive remainder. Since then all the evidence relating blood pressure to morbidity and mortality supports Pickering, since there is no obvious cut-off point, even though clearly at the very high levels of pressure morbidity and mortality increase markedly. The series of papers on this subject can be said to form the basis of the epidemiological approach to the study of blood pressure in populations, and to have brought numeracy into clinical thinking, since these considerations have had considerable impact on clinical practice.

Pickering was always more interested in causes and mechanisms of hypertension than in treatment. In fact he had stronger views on the treatment of bleeding peptic ulcer than on hypertension. His house physicians, who had to keep patients with bleeding peptic ulcers alive while up to forty pints of blood were transfused, sometimes wished that he had had less definite views on the place of surgery in these conditions. In the treatment of hypertension he was more content to watch the efforts of his young colleagues on the medical unit as they tried to master the art of giving ganglion blockers to patients with severe hypertension, to enable them to spend more time on their feet and less being picked up off the floor, to which the resultant hypotension had consigned them.

In 1956 he moved to Oxford as regius professor, where his task was to revive clinical research in a new department created for this special task. He threw himself into this with evident enjoyment and enormous energy, despite the fact that osteoarthritis of his hips, which was to cloud much of his activity with continuous pain, grew in severity. Once more he attracted young people to his cause and his two main interests at this stage led to fresh developments. The first was a reinvestigation of baroreceptor mechanisms, particularly the carotid sinus, a subject he had investigated in his youth; and the second, the general subject of vascular wall disease, in which he was attracted by the old ideas of Virchow, and the similar and somewhat later ones of Duguid. They both believed that fibrin deposition on the vessel wall led to its incorporation and appearance subsequently as plaques. He further believed that they were the source of platelet emboli, and their direct demonstration in retinal vessels always delighted him. This led him to disbelieve any hypothesis of transient loss of vision or of cerebral function based on vascular spasm, since he was so impressed by observations, both in patients and experimentally in animals, which showed how platelet thrombi and emboli could be formed and swept away with only temporary blockage of small vessels.

In 1960 his contributions to the scientific basis of medicine were recognized appropriately when he was elected a fellow of the Royal Society.

The busiest of men are always given the greatest and most numerous tasks, and his clarity of mind, his great energy, and his width of knowledge, led to him being asked to perform on a larger stage. He was a member of the Medical Research Council, and chaired the MRC working party which conducted one of the first large scale trials of anticoagulant treatment in coronary thrombosis. He was a member of the Council for Scientific Policy, which was the precursor of the present Advisory Board to the Research Councils. A task which he clearly enjoyed was chairing the committee which saw the new Medical School at Nottingham University through from its first consideration to its final accomplishment.

His greatest contribution has to be the influence he had on all those who came into intimate contact with him. Despite the temperamental differences, one could feel that the flame that was kindled for British medicine by Thomas Lewis was given perhaps extra power by Pickering's patent enthusiasm, allied to his considerable intellect and his gusty sense of humour. This attracted young men from all parts of the world, who carried the same light with them, so that his influence was spread to countless others. He was not only a clinical scientist of the highest order but he was also a physician of great understanding, who taught everyone never to spare themselves either in the pursuit of knowledge or the care of their patients. WSP

[*Brit. med. J.*, 1980, **281**, 752, 878, 952, 1224, 1365; *Lancet*, 1980, **2**, 599, 655; *Times*, 5 Sept 1980; *Biog. Mem. roy. Soc.*, 1982, **28**, pp. 431-449; *St Mary's Hosp. Gaz.*, 1971, 77; Photo]

PICKUP, John Douglas *b.*31 May 1915 *d.*27 Aug 1977
MB ChB Leeds (1939) MD (1945) DCH Lond (1945) MRCP (1975) FRCP (1976)

Douglas Pickup was the only son of the Reverend Holden Pickup, a distinguished minister of the Methodist Church, who had roots going back to the beginnings of Methodism in North East Lancashire. Great firmness of principle, fearlessness in witness, joy in natural things and love of walking were common to father and son. His mother also was a child of the Manse and had grown up in the Isle of Man in an atmosphere of 'plain living and high thinking'. Their influence upon their son determined his later unselfish involvement in pastoral concerns, through the Pontefract Micklegate Church and the considerable honour of circuit stewardship. Characteristically, Douglas Pickup then out-distanced his associates in unsuccessful attempts at Anglican/Methodist conciliation, and was in even greater isolation in advocating an amalgamation between his own and the rival Methodist Church in Pontefract! Like the puritan General Waller, he might well have said of himself 'Where my conscience is interested all other obligations are swallowed up'.

Douglas Pickup went from Bradford Grammar School to study medicine at Leeds University, qualifying shortly before the second world war and soon volunteering for service with the RAF, mostly in the Middle East. Returning to his parents' home in Silsden he married Mary Fletcher, from a distinguished local family of manufacturers, and vigorously resumed his career in paediatrics, firstly at the end of a long, rich clinical era with Wilfred Vining, and then as lecturer, from 1946 for five years, helping WS Craig create a University department and introduce into Leeds the wider concept of paediatrics and child health.

An appointment to become the first district paediatrician responsible for a wide area centred upon Wakefield, Pontefract and Dewsbury came in 1951, and called for remarkable powers of organization in addition to a clinical load which would seem unbelievable a generation later. Gradually, with new consultant appointments, his paediatric work concentrated upon Pontefract, where he was chairman of the Medical Advisory Committee and postgraduate tutor. In this role he promoted a splendid postgraduate centre (1970), which now bears his name.

An indifferent letter writer and uncommonly slow to put pen to paper, Douglas Pickup was a talker of Johnsonian dimensions, equally at ease in general conversation, in committee or on the lecture platform. At times he appeared to have a relative by marriage or best friend in the chair of every relevant administrative body around Leeds, and even in death he shared a single page of obituary in the *BMJ* with his life-long friend, AA (Joe) Driver, formerly SAMO to the then Leeds Regional Hospital Board. An authoritative chairman, totally lacking in pretension, he was genial but business-like, combining trenchant views with a refusal to compromise on issues of principle.

Few contemporary physicians can have had lives which overflowed more extensively into other fields. A naturalist, he was president of the Yorkshire Naturalist Trust, past president Yorkshire Naturalists Union, founder member and at one time president of the Castleford Naturalist Society and, what was particularly dear to his heart, chairman of the advisory committee to Fairburn Ings Royal Society for the Protection of Birds reserve. Douglas Pickup was a dedicated bird-watcher and was elected to the Council of the RSPB in 1976 to represent Yorkshire interests. He paralleled his church activities by being an enthusiastic Rotarian, serving as president of the Pontefract Club 1973/74 and delighting meetings with ornithological slide displays, made possible by anticipating nearly every conceivable local difficulty in projection. When elected to membership of the British Paediatric Association in 1959, Douglas knew few colleagues outside the Leeds region, but was quickly a familiar figure with close friends via fly fishing, hill climbing, watching marshland birds or the nocturnal activity of badgers. A member of BPA Council 1972–75, he was predictably co-opted to the executive committee to provide an authoritative peripheral viewpoint. Retiring prematurely in 1976 to allow more opportunity for non-medical activities, he was faced almost at once with an oesophageal malignancy and began a protracted defiance. His wife, Mary, the sister of Richard Fletcher FRCP, survived him with their son and daughter, and they respectively provide links with natural history and medicine.

His memorial must surely be the Fairburn Ings bird sanctuary. There during twenty years of wardenship, either en route for his next hospital or domiciliary visit or at the end of the day, Douglas might be found welcoming visitors, reporting intruders, protecting and shaping for the future. Who else but he could have successfully established natural beauty alongside pit heads, giant chimneys and the Great North Road? RJP

[*Brit. med. J.*, 1977, **2**, 898; *Lancet*, 1977, **2**, 619; Photo]

PIMSTONE, Bernard Laurence *b*.30 May 1933 *d*.15 Jan 1979
MB ChB Cape Town (1955) MD (1962) MRCP (1963) FRCP (1974)

Bernard Laurence Pimstone, son of Dr Mark Pimstone and his wife Gertrude, of Cape Town, died at the age of 45, but already with an international reputation in endocrinology. He had been educated at the SA College High School, University of Cape Town and Groote Schuur Hospital. His student career was distinguished by the award of first class honours in surgery (1955) and the gold medal in medicine (1953). Later he was awarded a Cecil John Adams travelling fellowship, and Eli Lilly and the Ernst Oppenheimer overseas advanced study grants. With the benefit of these valuable and well deserved awards, he earned for himself a reputation as an authority in several adjacent fields of endocrinology.

When appointed to the joint staff of the University of Cape Town and Groote Schuur Hospital, he became head of the thyroid clinic and director of the isotope and immunoassay laboratories of the department of medicine. His record of some sixty scientific publications and contributions to international congresses and study groups led to his becoming an international authority in his field, which included endocrine disturbances in malnutrition. His own university elected him to a permanent research fellowship and later to a personal chair. He carried out the other parts of his joint responsibility to the University and the hospital with enthusiasm and expertise, and in spite of his rather shy manner was popular with patients, students and staff. He was an excellent clinician.

Bernard had a very happy home, a devoted wife and three children. Shortly before his final illness he had been invited to attend a Kroc Foundation symposium on 'Hormones of the Gut and Brain', and had been invited as a guest speaker to the International Diabetes Federation Congress to be held in Vienna in 1979. Sadly he died of a slowly fatal disease, which he bore with courage and fortitude. JFB

[*Lancet*, 1979, **1**, 451; Photo]

PINCKNEY, Charles Percy *b*.28 Apr 1901 *d*.20 Feb 1982
MRCS LRCP (1925) MA MB BChir Cantab (1928) MRCP (1929) FRCP (1941)

Charlie P, as he was affectionately known by colleagues and friends, began his medical career as RMO at St George's Hospital and he worked his way up eventually to be appointed to the staff, firstly as a physician and then as the first full-time paediatrician to the hospital. He built up the children's department at Hyde Park Corner and subsequently at Tite Street, Chelsea, when the Victoria Hospital there came under St George's wing. He later took the unit down to its new home at Tooting Broadway. He was also paediatrician to the Windsor Group of hospitals and to the Chailey Heritage Hospital for handicapped children.

As a schoolboy he had a fine athletic career and he loved sport, especially swimming, skiing and tennis. He took an extremely keen interest in student activities and enjoyed leading the annual staff *v* students tennis match for many years.

Charlie P was an excellent committee man, courteous, tolerant, and above all fair and firm in his decisions. His quickness of grasp of situations, based on detailed analysis, was an impressive part of his chairmanship of committees and this ability was always being called into action. Above all he was a clinician. He loved to unravel a difficult clinical problem, but in chasing the clues for diagnosis he never for one moment forgot the patient. He sought no advancement or honours for himself but was elected president of the paediatric section of the Royal Society of Medicine. When he retired at the age of sixty-five he was asked to stay on at St George's to look after the staff, and this he did for a further four years. The honour that gave him the greatest pleasure was the naming after him of a ward at St George's Hospital, Tooting, and in 1980 he took part in this ceremony and celebration with the keenest enjoyment.

Pinckney had a most receptive mind and an enviable intellectual humility. He was always eager to learn and avidly embraced new knowledge and ideas from his specialist colleagues, whom he admired and valued. He was a humble and modest man whose quick insight into the value of change produced many revolutionary practices at St George's, including the admission of mothers with their children at Tite Street well before the country had accepted this philosophy. He was always a popular figure at the Chailey Heritage Hospital where the staff welcomed him with open arms and where he knew each patient and how they had changed since his previous visit. He made his patients, his staff and all who met him feel valued and worthwhile. He was unfailingly even tempered and never showed impatience however much the provocation. He loved his family and his work, he loved life, and all of us at the hospital loved him. His passing reflected the loss of an era which is unlikely to return.

SMT

[Photo]

PLATT, *Lord* **(Robert), Baron Platt of Grindleford** *b.*16 Apr 1900 *d.*30 June 1978
Life Peer (1967) Bart (1959) MB ChB Sheff (1921) MD (1923)
MRCP (1925) FRCP (1935) MSc Manch (1949)
PRCP (1957 – 1962)†

As the man mainly responsible for the move of the College house from Pall Mall East to Regent's Park, Robert Platt has an assured place as one of the College's great presidents. He was also the first wholetime professor to hold the office; the first president to live and work outside London, and the man mainly responsible for the College's renewed and greatly increased interest in postgraduate education and in preventive medicine in the second half of the twentieth century.

He was born in the parish of St Marylebone, the second son in a family unconnected hitherto with science or medicine, but infected as he himself said, with 'music, the stage and the wanderlust'. His father, William Platt, worked for some time in the family wholesale woollen business (though probably more interested in music and other pursuits) but later with his wife Susan Jane, née Willis (daughter of William Willis, a much travelled Scot who eventually settled in Forfar), founded a co-educational boarding school in Grindleford, Derbyshire. Susan Willis was the first woman to become one of HM Inspectors of Schools. An uncle was a close friend of Keir Hardie, and Robert was a cousin, through his father's mother's family, of Portia Holman FRCP (q.v.), who was involved in the Spanish Civil War.

Robert was educated at King Alfred's School, Hampstead; at his parents' school at Grindleford and at Sheffield University, where he qualfied MB BCh (with two gold medals) in 1921 and became an MD in 1923. He took the MRCP in 1925 and was elected FRCP in 1935. In later years he received many honorary degrees including Hon LLD Sheffield 1959, Belfast 1959, Manchester, 1969, and Hon MD Bristol 1959. He was created Baronet in 1959 and became a Life Peer as Baron Platt of Grindleford in 1967.

He was appointed assistant physician to the Royal Infirmary Sheffield in 1931 (at the age of 31) and full physician in 1934, rapidly acquiring a considerable private practice. He was later to describe this as 'professionally the most satisfactory period of life'.

Platt served in the RAMC as a lieutenant colonel, OC Medical Division, from 1941 to 1944 in Britain, North Africa and Italy, and records that his promotion to brigadier consultant physician, Southern Command India, did not greatly please him, for after his experiences in North Africa and Italy he found the quasi-peacetime atmosphere of Indian clubs and messes to be distasteful. Others who served in India remember him as an energetic and dedicated consultant physician, if a somewhat bedraggled brigadier.

Wartime service seemed to have converted Platt the successful consultant physician, to Platt the socialist and enthusiastic supporter of the NHS (who resigned from the BMA in 1947 and never rejoined), Platt the humanist and, after much heart searching, Platt the wholetime professor of medicine. He once said that he thought he was awarded the chair of medicine at Manchester in 1946 because he told the appointments committee that he was not sure whether he really wanted it.

When he arrived in Manchester the space allotted for his department contained only an ancient device for wet-cupping. He left behind a flourishing department respected by both clinicians and medical scientists, with a record of first class work in many fields. Platt himself will be remembered as the man who first proposed the 'intact nephron hypothesis' of the mechanism of chronic renal failure in his Lumleian lectures in 1952 (thus anticipating Bricker, to whom this is usually attributed); as the doughty contestant of his friend, Sir George Pickering, in their long controversy over the nature of benign hypertension, and as a pioneer in the application of genetics to medical problems.

Outside clinical medicine he was a man of wide and varied activities. Among other appointments he was a member of the Medical Research Council and later chairman of its Clinical Research Board; a member of the Royal Commission on Medical Education, about some of whose recommendations he had serious reservations; chairman of the first joint working party of the profession and the health departments, set up to review the medical staffing of hospitals; chairman of the Merit Awards Committee, and at different times president of the Eugenics Society, the Family Planning Association, ASH (Action on Smoking and Health) and the National Society for the Abolition of Cruel Sports. Apart from some ninety papers, he wrote *Nephritis and Allied Diseases* (1934); *Doctor and Patient* (the Rock Carling Fellowship 1963), and a somewhat picaresque autobiography *Private and Controversial* (1972). This revealed him as a very human person – a man of wide interests and strong opinions, some of them distinctly controversial. His views on the value of exposing undergraduate medical students to general practice were well ahead of his time, as was his support for women in medicine.

Platt succeeded Russell Brain as PRCP in 1957, at a time when plans were in existence for an unsatisfactory extension upwards of the Pall Mall building. Almost immediately there occurred the first of three pieces of good fortune which, as he himself said, aided him in achieving the move to Regent's Park. The Hon George Drew, High Commissioner for Canada, came to reopen the question of Canada acquiring the RCP building. The College was promised a considerable sum for surrendering its Crown lease, but more money was needed. Horace Evans (Lord Evans of Merthyr Tydfil) came to suggest an approach to the Wolfson Foundation, which eventually gave a further near half million pounds. No site in Regent's Park could be found, and most prestigious estate agents strongly recommended a site in the Harley Street area. Comitia voted by a small majority to accept the advice and move to that site. It was perhaps Platt's greatest contribution in this matter that he said that he accepted the vote as a decision to move, but not necessarily to that particular site. Not much later – the third piece of good fortune – the late Edward Cullinan FRCP came to say that the Someries House site in Regent's Park was available if the College wanted it, and this was, of course, exactly what the College did want.

Platt consulted Sir John Somerson whose advice, that a new RCP in Regent's Park must be an uncompromisingly contemporary building, caused him some dismay, but he followed it. He chaired the small committee which chose Denys Lasdun (now Sir Denys Lasdun) as architect; presided over all the planning and eventually steered the controversial plan and model of the proposed building through Comitia with a *nem con* vote. In spite of some good fortune, there is no doubt that it was Platt's enthusiasm and leadership that gave the College its new building. He had retired by 1964 when it was at length opened by Her Majesty Queen Elizabeth II. His other main contributions to the College were the postgraduate conferences, which he inaugurated in Pall Mall and which were to flourish exceedingly in the new building, and his encouragement of the Smoking and Health Report (1971) which led to the campaign against smoking and other developments in the field of preventive medicine. Quite as important as the new building was the new direction and impetus which he provided.

In 1967 he became a life peer and attended regularly and enthusiastically in the House of Lords for the next eleven years. He sat on the cross benches, in order, as he said, to be able to speak for medicine rather than to represent a party point of view. After a slow start he spoke effectively and often on many subjects, including the National Health Service, health education, divorce, pornography, and voluntary euthanasia. Latterly he displayed what many thought to be some less progressive concerns, notably in his support for the preservation of the Elizabeth Garrett Anderson Hospital, and in his opposition to a bill for the compulsory wearing of seat belts in cars.

Outside medicine his greatest interest was music, and in particular playing the cello in string quartets. Coming of a musical family he developed as a child a quite precocious expertise in tonic solfa, learned to play the piano and started lessons in cello playing from the age of nine. He practised the cello, on most days, to the end of his life, and reached a standard respected by professional players. There is said to have been a cello-playing president of the College in the eighteenth century, but it is likely that Platt was the only president ever to practise alone at night, and then to play in string quartets in the Censors' room. He served on the Committee of the Hallé Concert Society from 1947 to 1953, and was a member of the council of the Royal Manchester College of Music. From 1952 to 1965 he was chairman of the Manchester Chamber Concerts Society.

Platt was something of an enigma to some of his contemporaries – a successful consultant who became a distinguished wholetime professor, but who turned severely to criticize some aspects of wholetime medicine and professorial units in his Harveian oration in 1967; a humanist and outspoken critic of revealed religion, who showed selfless dedication to his patients and to the many causes that he espoused, and a socialist who defended hereditary representation in the House of Lords: yet in spite of these apparent inconsistencies it was rightly said at the time of his death:-

'he has been one of the great personalities of British Medicine during the past half century and still a human, approachable and friendly man. He could show firm authority, yet he never failed to give full weight to, and ensure a just hearing for the views of others. He thought it right to state the strong beliefs he held on some controversial subjects, but he never sought to force them on others. He became a widely respected public figure. In any medical generation there are a few who are recognized by a wider public not merely as great figures in their profession but as men or women of stature in the world beyond it, and able to take the broader view. Robert was such a one...'

One could ask how did a man with such a background and such ideas come to exert the influence he did on a traditionally conservative body like the RCP? But perhaps equally, could a man of more traditional type have had his vision of the future of the College?

His first marriage in 1922 to Margaret Irene Cannon MB BCh DPM produced a son and two daughters. The marriage was dissolved in 1974 and he married secondly Sylvia Jean Haggard (née Cavely) ARCM (viola). His son, Sir Peter Platt, Bart, became professor of music at the University of Sydney.

Robert Platt died in University College Hospital some weeks after sustaining a fracture of the femur in a fall on the steps of the College. At his express wish there was no memorial service, but on 22 November 1978, the Lydian String Quartet gave a concert in his memory in the College library, concluding with Beethoven's last important composition, the Quartet in F major, Op. 135.

An admirable portrait by Merlyn Evans hangs in the College, and a tape 'Talking with Robert' is preserved in the library. RRB

[*Brit. med. J.*, 1978, **2**, 211, 440; *Lancet,* 1978, **2**, 114, 275, 384; *Times,* 1 July 1978; *Med. Today,* 1969, **3**, 1-5; Photo]

PLUMMER, Norman Swift *b.*10 June 1907 *d.*3 April 1978
MRCS LRCP (1930) MB BS Lond (1931) MRCP (1932) MD (1933) FRCP (1941)

Norman Plummer was born in Butterworth, South Africa. His father Walter James Plummer was a bank manager. His mother was Marianne Eveline Clarence. He was educated in South Africa before training at Guy's Hospital, where he had a brilliant student career, obtaining a gold medal in medicine. After house appointments at Guy's Hospital and a year's postgraduate work in Amsterdam, he was appointed in 1933 medical registrar at Charing Cross Hospital. Two years later he was appointed physician to the Hospital, a post he held until his retirement in 1973.

He was fully engaged in hospital work at Charing Cross Hospital and in teaching, research, and private practice when the 1939–1945 war started. He served with great distinction, enjoying his arduous army service acting as consultant physician to the army in the Middle East with the rank of brigadier. He returned after the war to Charing Cross and the London Chest Hospitals. He was also consultant physician to Bromley and Edenbridge Hospitals. He served in these smaller hospitals as a consultant physician in the true sense of the word; though not concerned with day to day management, he showed his superb skill and judgement, spending endless time on a difficult problem.

Plummer was the ideal physician to successions of senior registrars at Charing Cross, London Chest and Bromley Hospitals, and many considered him the finest physician they had known. He did an immense amount of clinical work, despite the fact that he was responsible for a large number of beds with rapid turnover in different hospitals. He never shed this heavy load during the time when the trend was for consultants to have fewer patients all confined to one hospital. Much of his postgraduate teaching and research were carried out at the London Chest Hospital; his special interest in later years was a study of aspergillosis, on which he did much original work. He made pioneer contributions in the field of fungal chest infections. He acted as senior vice-president and senior censor to the College in 1970.

Plummer was modest and unassuming but could be very outspoken when the occasion arose. He would have found particularly irksome concepts mostly introduced since he retired, such as consensus decisions made by health teams in the management of patients. He hated the proliferation of committees, especially when these encroached on the working day. His quiet self-confidence was a comfort to the patients. He had a peculiar quality of unassailable integrity, difficult to describe but obvious to those who knew him. He was intolerant of shoddy behaviour, and would go to any lengths to help not just his friends but anyone he felt had been unfairly treated. He worked in an era when the part-time London teaching hospitals physicians had the greatest influence on British medicine, and when the autocratic attitude of this group caused some resentment. However, he was always as critical of his part-time colleagues who failed to pull their weight, as of the full-time staff who did not meet their commitments.

His recreations included tennis and golf, but he also played cricket against the Charing Cross students for many years. He was especially kind to junior colleagues whom he entertained in the happy atmosphere of his home. He had a fine sense of humour, and showed characteristic courage in his terminal illness. He left a wife, Helen, the daughter of Tom Kenneth Wilson, a businessman, three daughters, and a son who also became a doctor. PBSF

[*Brit. med. J.,* 1978, **2**, 284; *Lancet,* 1978, **1**, 946; *Times,* 13 Apr 1978]

PORTER, Keith Ridley Douglas *b.*27 Mar 1913 *d.*5 Dec 1977
MBE (1943) MRCS LRCP (1938) LDS RCS (1939) DPH (1947)
MRCP (1968) FRCP (1972) FFCM (1972) QHP (1977)

Keith Porter, regional medical officer of the South East Thames Regional Health Authority and honorary physician to HM The Queen, was born in Ismailia, Egypt. His father, Douglas David Porter, was a quantity surveyor, and his mother, Olive Lucia, was the daughter of John Deck, a medical practitioner. He was educated at Monkton Combe School, Bath, and qualified in medicine and dentistry at Guy's Hospital, London, just prior to the second world war.

He had a distinguished war record, serving in the Middle East and Europe. He was promoted to lieutenant colonel and appointed MBE in 1943. On demobilization he spent a number of years in East Africa with the Overseas Food Corporation, before returning to a short but valuable period in general practice in England.

His administrative career began with the regional hospital boards of the Oxford and Birmingham regions. In 1964 he was appointed senior administrative medical officer to the Northern Ireland Hospitals Authority and for the next five years he worked unstintingly in a very difficult environment to create an efficient hospital organization in the province of Northern Ireland. He won great respect for his work and many friends, and the organization he helped to create still benefits from the contribution he made in the 1960s. In 1969 he returned to England; first as senior administrative medical officer of the South East Metropolitan Regional Hospital Board and then, after the reorganization of the National Health Service, as regional medical officer of the new South East Thames Regional Health Authority.

Keith Porter was grossly overworked, yet he never complained, and despite his many commitments he found time to serve on the council of the London School of Hygiene and on the school council of his own alma mater. From 1971 to 1977 he also served on the council of Professions Supplementary to Medicine. He was elected a fellow of WHO in 1963, a fellow of the College in 1972, and was appointed a member of the Court of the University of Kent in 1977. He was a very distinguished figure in the emerging specialty of community medicine and had the highest possible reputation in this field. He was a leader who inspired the confidence and loyalty of his staff, and his wide preparation and training gave him a profound knowledge of medical administration and the practice of medicine in all its many facets. He was an indefatigable worker who took the minimum of holidays, and during the last two years of his life the pressures on him increased enormously, for he was fighting to make sure that the current financial stringencies should not be allowed to reduce the quality of service in the South East Thames region.

Many honours and distinctions came his way, and he was especially pleased by his appointment as honorary physician to the Queen, which came shortly before his death.

As a man, Keith Porter was a gentle and compassionate friend whose ability and devotion to service were a natural result of his personality, In 1939 he married Elsie Grace, daughter of Hartley Holmes, a Royal Artillery Officer, and they had three children: two sons and a daughter. His married life was extremely happy, and he had many interests outside his work. He loved music and was an accomplished organist. He also enjoyed golf, gardening and sailing.

GW/VL

[*Brit. med. J.*, 1977, **2**, 1676; *Lancet,* 1977, **2**, 1371; *Times,* 10 Dec 1977; Photo]

PRATT, Richard Thomas Charles *b*.24 Oct 1917 *d*.20 Mar 1983
BA Oxon (1939) BM BCh (1943) MA (1944) MRCP (1944)
DPM (1948) DM (1950) FRCP (1962) FRCPsych (1972)

Educated at Cheltenham College, Dick Pratt studied medicine at Trinity College, Oxford, where he gained a first in physiology, and at the Middlesex Hospital Medical School. After qualification he became house physician at the Middlesex Hospital to T Izod Bennet, who had earlier encouraged him to study medicine. From student days he had been interested in neurology and psychiatry, and following appointments with Barham Carter at Ashford and at Shenley Hospital he was appointed Comyns Berkeley research fellow, and later senior registrar in the neurology department at the Middlesex Hospital. In these posts he worked closely with Douglas McAlpine (*q.v.*) and Nigel Compston in studies on multiple sclerosis, undertaking a study of the genetic aspects of the disease which formed the basis of his DM thesis, and of his life-long interest in the genetic aspects of neurological and psychiatric disorders.

In 1952 Dick became senior registrar to Eliot Slater (*q.v.*) in the department of psychiatry at Queen Square. This appointment ideally suited his interests and talents, and he was greatly influenced by Eliot Slater, whom he held in great respect and affection. In 1953 he was awarded the Gaskell gold medal in psychiatry, and in the following year he was appointed consultant in psychological medicine to the National Hospitals for Nervous Diseases, working initially at Maida Vale, but after the retirement of Eliot Slater moving to Queen Square, where he was a greatly valued member of the staff until his retirement in 1982.

Throughout his career Dick was deeply interested in the interrelationships between psychiatry and organic neurology, and he was particularly interested in depression, becoming highly skilled in the management of patients with this condition. He was a strong advocate of the use of unilateral ECT as being important in minimizing the damaging effect of therapy. He related its effects to cerebral dominance and towards the end of his career became interested in its effects on cerebral evoked potentials. His continuing interest in genetics led to a series of important papers, and culminated in the publication, in 1967, of his monograph on *The genetics of neurological disorders*, an outstanding work which assembled in a masterly fashion a mass of important data not previously assimilated in a single work.

A skilled, concerned clinician of outstanding integrity, Dick's help and advice were greatly sought after and valued by his colleagues and patients. Gentle and unassuming to a degree, but at the same time firm in his opinions, a true scholar and scientist, he was generous in his help with ideas and advice to his colleagues and above all his juniors, and his considerable contributions to psychiatry tended to be masked by his modesty and generosity in ascribing credit to his collaborators.

Never fond of large professional gatherings, and as a teacher at his best in seminars and smaller gatherings, Dick was not a zealous member of national and international gatherings and travelled little. In part this was due to his nature, and in part to the fact that he suffered since adolescence from diabetes. From student days onwards he concealed to a remarkable degree the impact of this condition on his life, and in his later years when he developed painful and disabling complications of the disease he hid his suffering and, with great courage, did not allow it to interfere with his work. With his wide range of interests and his keen mind, Dick was a delightful, gay, slightly whimsical companion, unstinting in his kindness and loyalty to his friends. Singularly happy in his marriage, he was devoted to his wife Eileen (née Holgate) and two sons, and delighted in the privacy of his home where, untroubled by any ambitions of office, he could enjoy his family life and indulge his interests in reading, in medical history, and in later life in sundials, which he studied with characteristic thoroughness. PM/LP Le Q

[*Brit. med. J.*, 1983, **286**, 1659; *Lancet*, 1983, **1**, 999; *Times*, 9 Apr 1983]

PRICE, Roy Kemball *b.*15 June 1905 *d.*27 Apr 1979
MRCS LRCP (1929) MB BS Lond (1930) MD (1932) MRCP (1932) FRCP (1950)

Roy Price was one of four sons of Charles Royale Price, a building contractor, and his wife Beatrice Angela French, both of Crouch End, London.

Price was educated at Highgate School and at St Bartholomew's Hospital, where he qualified in 1929 and obtained the MD and the MRCP in 1932. He was house physician to Dr, afterwards Sir, Francis Fraser on the medical unit at Bart's, and later to Charles Harris in the Children's Department. He then became RSO at the Royal Manchester Children's Hospital, where he met and afterwards married the senior resident medical officer, Mary Campbell Clark, daughter of James Graham Clark, a clergyman in Renfrewshire. There were two children of the marriage, a boy and a girl, but it ended in divorce. In 1948 he remarried.

In 1934 he entered general practice in Brighton and in 1936 was appointed physician to the Hove Hospital. In 1937 he became assistant physician to the Royal Sussex County Hospital and in 1938 physician to the Royal Alexandra Hospital for Sick Children in Brighton. From 1942 to 1946 he served with the RAMC in UK, West Africa and India, attaining the rank of lieutenant colonel.

After his return to Brighton he became full physician to the RSC Hospital and, on the retirement of Donald Hall, took charge of the department of cardiology there. In 1947 he relinquished his appointment as physician to the RA Hospital for Sick Children, in order to become the cardiologist there. During those early post-war years he also worked as registrar to Samuel Oram in the department of cardiology at King's College Hospital, and his cardiological practice in Brighton and district increased steadily. He became president of the Brighton and Sussex Medico-Chirurgical Society in 1960.

Roy Price was a kind and friendly man, a sound physician, and a good cardiologist who organized and greatly improved cardiological facilities in Brighton and Hove. His contributions to medical literature were small but his skill and knowledge were ever available to his colleagues, and his sympathy and consideration always a source of comfort to his many private and hospital patients. As a young man he was a keen tennis player, but as he grew older gardening occupied most of his scant leisure. CBP

[*Brit. med. J.*, 1979, **1**, 1575; *Lancet*, 1979, **1**, 1253; Photo]

PRIDIE, *Sir* **Eric (Denholm)** *b.*10 Jan 1896 *d.*3 Sept 1978
KCMG (1953) CMG (1941) DSO (1918) OBE (1931)
MRCS LRCP (1922) MB BS Lond (1923) FRCP* (1958)†

Eric Pridie was born at Chingford, Essex, the son of John Francis Pridie and of Florence (née Gilbertson). His father was then in medical practice there, though not long afterwards he moved to a practice in Liverpool. Eric Pridie went to Holmwood Preparatory School, Formby, and then to St Bees School, Cumberland. The first world war broke out shortly after he had begun his medical training. He volunteered for service and was very soon commissioned in the 6th and 7th Battalion of the King's Own Royal Lancaster Regiment, in which he reached the rank of captain. He served in the front line in France in 1915–1916 and was wounded at Loos. He was later invalided to England with severe pneumonia. After recovery he was trained as a bombing officer and, in 1917, went out to Mesopotamia. In the Mediterranean the ship on which he was travelling was torpedoed and sunk, but after a time in the water he was rescued. To the end of his life he kept the watch he had then been wearing, and which had stopped just after his entry into the water. Although he had already distinguished himself in action by being mentioned in despatches, it was in Mesopotamia that his greatest war time activities took place. In the fierce fighting at the Battle of Kut, he led a party attacking the enemy lines and at close quarters killed with his revolver some six of the enemy. For his part in this action he was awarded the DSO in 1918.

He was demobilized in 1919 and resumed his medical studies at Liverpool. He qualified first with the conjoint diploma and then MB, BS of the University of London. After house appointments at the Liverpool Royal Infirmary, he joined the Sudan Medical Service in 1924. He worked, first, as a medical officer in the Kassala and Blue Nile Provinces, but in 1930 was promoted to be assistant director of medical services. In 1933, at the early age of 37, he became director of the Service and remained so until 1945.

Pridie's 12 years as director of the Sudan Medical Service are remembered particularly for the increasing Sudanization which he encouraged, often in the face of considerable resistance. In peace, as in war, he was a fearless fighter for what he thought to be right. Very many Sudanese were to become grateful to him for his support and help in their careers. The Kitchener School of Medicine, Khartoum, had only been in existence for nine years when Pridie became director and by virtue of his office he became chairman of the School Council. He took a very active interest in its affairs and fostered its growth at every opportunity. He was also particularly keen that the standards of training there should be comparable with those in Britain, and in 1938, largely through his efforts, the qualifying examination of the school was approved by the Conjoint Board, England. Since that time a senior examiner from the Board has regularly participated in the final examination at Khartoum, and the high standard of Khartoum graduates has been testified by their innumerable successes in postgraduate examinations. In 1934 he became a member of the Council which advised the Governor-General on all aspects of government in the Sudan. Pridie's influence on the Council was great and was not limited to medical matters. He foresaw that war was likely to break out in 1939, and ensured that all preparations possible in the Sudan were made; in particular he made certain that large stocks of medical and other supplies were built up, and these proved to be invaluable when war was declared.

Throughout his period as director he made frequent visits to peripheral hospitals and units. He enjoyed being with his staff and his visits were greatly appreciated. These visits were not without their humourous incidents and the story is told by a reliable informant that on one occasion when Pridie went by river steamer to visit a hospital he was disappointed on disembarking to find that there was no one to meet him. His wait at the jetty however was made interesting by the sight of a chimpanzee riding a bicycle. His astonishment was increased when the chimpanzee approached him and gave him a letter. The letter was from the local medical officer and explained that he was unable to be present because he had been called upon to perform an emergency operation. The next day, Pridie on his tour of the hospital noticed a bed in which there seemed to be two occupants, but the bedclothes were covering their heads. Attempts to get him to walk past this bed were unavailing. The story then came out that the medical officer who had trained the chimpanzee to perform a variety of useful tasks rewarded the animal and its mate with alcoholic beverages, and the effects of this reward were now being slept off.

During the 1939–1945 war Pridie became DDMS of the military command in the Sudan and held the rank of brigadier. The degree of integration of the civil and military medical services which he was able to bring about in the East African campaign was of great value in the conduct of the war. Pridie was himself present at the battle of Karen and was twice mentioned in despatches. His knowledge of the region and of its diseases was the basis of much insistent advice which he gave concerning the conduct of the campaign, advice which fortunately was heeded, with the saving of many lives.

In 1945 he was appointed health councillor at the British Embassy in Cairo, and had an important part to play in the many discussions concerning reorganization in the Middle East following the war. This post he retained until 1949 when he was appointed chief medical officer at the Colonial Office. His selection to this post was a remarkable tribute to him, for he had never been a member of the Colonial Medical Service; the Sudan Medical Service, like the Indian Medical Service, was quite outside the Colonial Medical Service.

In the wake of the second world war, morale in the Colonial Medical Service was low. Pridie, very soon, was able to visit the larger territories and to meet their medical officers, and he later managed to visit most territories within the Service. He made a point of trying to rectify grievances and he established himself firmly in the confidence of his staff. His memoranda, like his conversation, were incisive and effective, and some of those on housing in colonial territories, on hospital development and on the preventive aspects of medicine in the Colonies have come to be known as model documents of great value.

After his retirement from the Colonial Office he undertook for the World Health Organization a number of short term consultancies in Turkey, Taiwan, the Philippines and Afghanistan. For a while too he was an adviser to the Government of Bahrein.

For the remaining 15 years or so of his life he was a well known, much loved, cheerful companion to members of the Athanaeum and to his numerous friends in many parts of the word. His travels became legendary; he occupied the greater part of each year with them and took delight in reaching the most remote parts of the world. Just before his eightieth birthday he announced with pride that he had then visited every country in the world; he had set foot on the Antarctic Continent and on the Arctic ice and such remoter places as Tierra del Fuego, Outer Mongolia, Red China, the Falkland Islands and the smallest countries in Central America and Africa. Nearer home he spent much time in Scotland and in Ireland.

During his latter years he was much incapacitated by Parkinson's disease, but even this did not prevent him from travelling. Six months before his death, I found on arriving at the Sudan Hotel, Khartoum, that he was there making his annual visit to his friends in the Sudan. Most evenings I had a whisky with him sitting on the verandah of the hotel; he always limited himself to one large whisky before dinner,and after dinner would go straight to bed. He spent the morning reading, mostly *The Times* which he would go to considerable trouble to obtain. I particularly recall visiting the home of his old driver, Taha, then the prosperous owner of a taxi business in Khartoum. There were about ten present and a great spread of delicacies was put before us; the regard in which he was held was manifest in the eyes of all, and as the warm sunlight turned quickly into a starlit Khartoum night there was obvious emotion as he said his farewells, though he himself, with his speedy manner, was able to disguise his feelings.

He will be remembered particularly for his ability as an administrator, his farsightedness, his kindness, his modesty and his regard for his fellow men. Above all, as architect of the modern Sudanese medical service, and as the mentor of innumerable Sudanese physicians, his work will have continuing and far reaching results.

AWW

[*Brit. med. J.*, 1978, **2**, 839, 1156; *Lancet*, 1978, **2**, 641; *Times*, 7 Sept 1978]

PRUNTY, Francis Thomas Garnet *b*.5 Jan 1910 *d*.24 Sept 1979
BA Cantab (1932) MA (1935) MRCS LRCP (1941)
MB BChir (1941) MRCP (1941) MD (1944) FRCP (1950)

Garnet Prunty was born in Hampstead, the son of Frank Hugh Prunty, an Australian, and Una Elizabeth Newnham (née Marsden). After his father's death in 1919 he went with his mother to Australia, and his education began in Sydney. It continued, after return to England in 1921, at St Paul's School and after graduating BA with first class honours in Natural Sciences from Trinity College, Cambridge, where he became a Senior Scholar, he worked at the Lister Institute as a research biochemist, and later as a government chemist. Realizing that his true bent lay in the medical field, he became a student at St Thomas's Hospital Medical School, from which he qualified in 1941 and, in the same year, he became a member of the College. Also in that year he was appointed demonstrator in chemical pathology at St Thomas's, which enabled him to bring his scientific tranining into medical service.

In 1944 he proceeded MD and was awarded the Raymond Horton-Smith prize at Cambridge; he was then promoted to a lectureship. Later, with the award of a Rockefeller travelling fellowship, he went to the United States, and from 1945–47 was a research fellow in medicine at Harvard University and assistant in medicine at Peter Bent Brigham Hospital, Boston. Here he developed his lifelong interest in metabolic and endocrine disorders. Returning to St Thomas's, he set up a routine chemical pathology laboratory, and began the researches which continued throughout the rest of his professional life and established his international reputation. In 1947 he became reader, and his clinical skill was recognized by his appointment two years later, in 1949, as honorary physician to St Thomas's Hospital. A personal professorship was awarded in 1952, and he became the first incumbent of the chair of chemical pathology, which was established in 1963. He was Humphrey Rolleston lecturer in 1956. He retired in 1975.

Prunty, despite his quiet, somewhat austere manner, played a deceptively important part in the development of clinical chemistry in general and endocrinology in particular. At the time he started, chemical pathology was barely recognized but, along with other pioneers, he established its validity both as a scientific discipline and as a clinical service of real value to patients. Through his persuasion, the University of London accepted it as a distinct subspecialty of pathology. The importance of his department is reflected by the growth in the numbers of its staff engaged in routine analyses, treatment of patients, and research, from two to eighty. Among those who underwent a substantial part of their training in his department, nine later became professors, ten consultant chemical pathologists and three consultant endocrinologists, an eloquent testimonial to his teaching qualities. His own contributions, characterized by their scientific scrupulousness and integrity, include two books and nearly 100 original papers and chapters in books.

Prunty's reputation as an endocrinologist received its recognition, not only by his election as president of the section of endocrinology of the Royal Society of Medicine but, in the international field, by his becoming the first secretary and later chairman, of the International Society of Endocrinology, in the foundation of which he played a leading part. He was life governor of the Imperial Cancer Research Fund, having served as a member of Council; an emeritus member of the Biochemical Society; and an honorary member of the Society for Endocrinology, the British Nuclear Medicine Society, the Sociedad Medica de Occidente (Guatemala) and the Romanian Society of Endocrinology.

He married Rita Hepburn Stobbs in 1933, by whom he had a son and daughter. The marriage was dissolved in 1971, and in 1972 he married Jean Margaret Maxwell-Moore.

Garnet Prunty's sporting interests were considerable. In the 1930s he won several cups for rifle shooting, and took part in the Monte Carlo rally during the pre-war days, before the professionals took over. After the war, having learned to sail, this became his abiding interest, and he was elected to membership of the Royal Thames Yacht Club; centred on Itchenor, he won many cups and prizes and was a regular attender at Cowes Week. GIMS

[*Brit. med. J.*, 1979, **2**, 944; *Lancet*, 1979, **2**, 805; *Daily Telegraph*, 25 Sept 1979; Photo]

QUENTIN-BAXTER, Robert Hector *b*.- 1891 *d*.30 Aug 1979
MC (1917) MB BCh NZ (1916) MRCP (1925) FRACP (1938)
FRCP (1952)

Robert Quentin-Baxter was educated at Otago Boys' High School and the Otago Medical School. Graduating in 1916, he was a house surgeon at Wellington Hospital and then joined the New Zealand Medical Corps, in which he served until 1920. He saw much heavy fighting on the western front, and at the Battle of Passchendaele received the immediate award of the Military Cross for attending the wounded under fire.

On leaving the Army Quentin-Baxter had a short period of postgraduate study at St George's Hospital and at the West End Hospital for Nervous Diseases, London, where he developed an interest in neurology and came for a brief time under the influence of Sir James Collier. While at St George's he played rugby for his hospital – he had already excelled at this sport both at school and at Otago University.

He gained the MRCP in 1925 and later was elected a fellow of the Royal College. He was an original member of the Australasian Association of Physicians, soon to become The Royal Australasian College of Physicians, of which he was a foundation fellow in 1938 and New Zealand vice-president in 1951–1952.

He returned to New Zealand in 1925 and after a short period as medical officer at Hanmer Hospital, where he undertook the care of war-neurosis patients, was appointed to the honorary staff of Christchurch Hospital as assistant physician. Commencing private practice when specialization in the various disciplines was just developing, he became one of the first to do so in medicine, and soon acquired a large consulting practice. His interest was primarily in diseases of the nervous system, and after World War II he became a close colleague and friend of Murray Falconer FRCS, who had established the first neurosurgical unit at Otago. Quentin-Baxter retired from his hospital post in 1952 when he was elected to the honorary consulting staff. For a number of years he continued with his consulting work in neurology but also turned some of his attention to geriatric medicine, at a time when this special field of medicine was in its infancy. He joined the honorary staff of the Mary Potter Hospital for the Aged Sick, a project of the Roman Catholic church.

Quentin-Baxter was more than a competent physician with a great love and concern for his patients; he was tolerant, just, and had a strong sense of fair play. His early sporting achievements in both cricket and rugby, and his later abiding interest in trout fishing influenced his outlook. His mischievous sense of humour enlivened many occasions.

While in England after the first world war he married another New Zealander, Dorothy Barclay of Waimate, New Zealand. He was devoted to his talented family of one daughter and three sons. His family and wife survived him. A son, Quentin, became professor of International Law at Victoria University, Wellington; Kimball farms near Christchurch; Graham is in business and his daughter Gillian married Jonathan Bennett, professor of philosophy at Syracuse University, USA and son of FO Bennet FRACP.

During Quentin-Baxter's later years, when the specialty of neurology was beginning to grow in New Zealand, he took an active part in forming a New Zealand Neurological Association, and it was therefore natural that he should have been elected its first president in 1957.

Quentin-Baxter was the kind of person whose influence lives after them. Stories will continue to be told of his ward rounds, and yet he was not an outstanding clinical teacher. He will be remembered as a kindly gentleman. CGR

[*Brit. med. J.*, 1979, **2**, 1230; Photo]

RANDELL, John Bulmer *b.*25 Aug 1918 *d.*30 Apr 1982
BSc Wales (1938) MB BCh (1941) DPM (1945) MRCP (1947)
MD (1961) FRCP (1964) FRCPsych (1971)

John Randall studied medicine at the Welsh National School of Medicine, graduating in 1941, and after house appointments in Wales he joined the RNVR. From 1942 to 1946 he served, as a surgeon lieutenant, first in a destroyer and then at Cholmondeley Castle – then known as HMS *Standard*. On demobilization he became registrar at St Ebba's Hospital, Epsom, and first assistant at Guy's Hospital. He was appointed assistant psychiatrist at St Thomas's Hospital in 1949, becoming physician for psychological medicine at Charing Cross

Hospital in 1950. He was a founder fellow of the Royal College of Psychiatrists (1971) and a fellow of the Royal Society of Medicine.

It was while working at the Charing Cross Hospital that his interest in the adrenogenital syndrome gained him international recognition for his work on gender identity, transvestism and transexuality. He founded the psychiatric unit at Temple Hill, Hampstead, which he ran successfully and which proved of inestimable value to patients from all over the world. Apart from conventional treatment, deconditioning therapy was used in cases of phobias, addiction, and sexual deviation. He had a deep understanding of affective disorders, a considered approach to treatment, and always remained an astute clinician. His book *Sexual Deviations* appeared in 1973 and he also published several papers on addiction.

Born in Penarth, Glamorgan, the son of Percy George Randell, an ophthalmic optician, and his wife Katie Esther, née Bulmer, daughter of a master mariner, he was educated at The College, Penarth, and the University of Wales, pursuing postgraduate studies at Guy's Hospital. In 1944 he married Margaret Davies MB BCh DRCOG, and they had one daughter who also qualified in medicine.

John Randell was an expert gardener, enjoyed playing golf, and took a special interest in quality vintage cars. He loved France, which he knew well, and fully appreciated its gourmet delights. He was himself an excellent host and often entertained members of his 'firm' at home. He was saddened by the transfer of Charing Cross Hospital, and the closure of his unit in 1981. He died from a myocardial infarction and was survived by his wife and daughter. GW/VL

[*Brit. med. J.*, 1982, **284**, 1703; Photo]

RANSOME, *Sir* Gordon (Arthur) *b.*6 May 1910 *d.*18 June 1978
KBE (1972) CBE (1962) MRCS LRCP (1933) MRCP (1935)
PJG Singapore (1967) DTMH (1969) DJMK Datuk (1969)
Hon MD Singapore (1969)

Gordon Ransome was professor of medicine at the University of Singapore, and a pioneer of modern medicine in Singapore and the territories of Malaysia. He was born in Salop, England, the son of Maurice John Ransome, rector of Pulverbatch, and was educated at Dauntsey's School and London University. He qualified in medicine from St Bartholomew's Hospital in 1933, subsequently holding house appointments in several London hospitals and obtaining his MRCP in 1935. During this time he also attended courses at the London School of Hygiene and Tropical Medicine. After six years of postgraduate training he left England for Singapore in 1938, on his appointment to King Edward VII College of Medicine as associate professor. Together with RB Hawes, then head of the department of medicine, he established a clinical laboratory at Tay Tock Seng Hospital and there, with the help of other outstanding physicians, turned out many well trained doctors with the LMS diploma. They formed the nucleus of those men and women who cared for the sick and wounded in

Singapore during the second world war and the Japanese occupation. Today, the standing of the medical graduates of the University of Singapore is second to none in Asia, and much of the credit for this must go to Gordon Ransome. An able clinician and administrator who never allowed his outlook to be blinkered by specialization, he set a high standard and fine example.

After the capitulation of Singapore to the Japanese, Gordon Ransome was the subject of some criticism because of his decision to escape to India to carry on his work. To do this, he deliberately faced great dangers and his later work in India and Burma fully justified his decision. He investigated the problems of salt and water balance, pioneered the management of unconscious patients, dealt with cholera epidemics and established specific methods of treatment for cerebral malaria. He held the rank of major in the 12th Army, was twice mentioned in despatches, and ended the war as a lieutenant colonel. He was elected a fellow in 1947.

On demobilization he returned to Singapore as acting head of the department of medicine at the General Hospital, and in 1948 he was appointed professor of medicine at King Edward VII College of Medicine. Among his many professional appointments he was honorary consultant to the Sultan of Kelantan, who bestowed the Datoship (DJMK) on him in 1969; the same year in which he was awarded an honorary doctorate of medicine by the University of Singapore. In 1967 he received the Meritorious Service Medal (PJG) in Singapore's National Day Awards. He was appointed a CBE in 1962, and a KBE in 1972. He was the first master of the Academy of Physicians and Surgeons in Singapore, which he had been instrumental in founding, and which later became the Academy of Medicine, Singapore. He was a member of the Singapore Medical Council, and ex-president of the Association of Physicians, Malaya. He contributed some 22 papers to scientific journals, both in Singapore and abroad. Although an excellent general physician and outstanding administrator, his greatest interest was in neurology. His name is perpetuated in Singapore by such foundations as the Academy of Medicine and by the biennial Gordon Arthur Ransome oration.

Gordon married twice. In 1940 his wife was Eryl Arundel and they had a daughter. In 1955 he married Daphne Mary, daughter of Colonel Lawrence George Beach RE, and they had three children: two sons and a daughter.

As a man Gordon Ransome was kind and softly spoken. He had the serenity to accept what could not be changed, the courage to change what could be changed, and the wisdom to know the difference. He was always ready to answer any cry for help from patients, staff or colleagues. He had a reputation for being absentminded, but time was of no consequence to him if someone needed him. He would sometimes wax philosophical and regarded worry as a destroyer of clear thinking. Although a prominent figure in Singapore society, his life style was simple. He enjoyed hunting, shooting and fishing, and read military and medical history. He had many devoted friends and his influence on the multiracial culture of Singapore was unique. He can be said to have served Singapore and medicine to the utmost of his ability. GW/VL

[*The Telegram,* Singapore, 21 June 1978; *Brit. med. J.,* 1978, **2**, 508, 644 and 1440; *Ann. Acad. Med. Singapore,* 1 Jan 1972; 6 Oct 1977; Farewell Address, July 1975; Mem. Service, St Andrew's Cathedral, Singapore, 20 July 1978; Photo]

REAH, Thomas Glentworth *b.*20 May 1905 *d.*11 Feb 1977
MRCS LRCP (1929) MA MB BChir Cantab (1931) MD (1934)
MRCP (1932) FRCP (1969)

Thomas Reah was born in Stockton-on-Tees. His father, James Carter Reah, was a grocer; his mother was Elizabeth Harriet Cooper prior to her marriage.

Reah was educated at Middlesbrough High School and then went to Downing College, Cambridge, and later embarked on his clinical studies at the London Hospital. He was awarded the Anderson prize for medicine in 1927 and the Treves prize for clinical surgery and the prize for surgery in 1929. He qualified, passing the Conjoint in 1929, before taking his degree in 1931.

From 1930 to 1932 he held several junior posts at the London Hospital, including house physician to the medical unit, receiving room officer, and later assistant in the department of pathology. Between 1932 and 1934 he was resident medical officer at Maida Vale Hospital and then at Selly Oak Hospital, Birmingham. In 1935 he moved to general practice in Harrogate, and within a very short time was appointed to the consulting staff at the Harrogate General Hospital, Royal Bath Hospital and Ripon Hospital.

In Harrogate he took a special interest in neurology within his general medical practice and, in addition, developed an increasing interest in rheumatology. From 1944 to 1946 he served in the RAMC, spending a greater part of the time abroad, and in 1945 he attained the rank of lieutenant colonel in charge of the medical division of a general hospital in West Africa. In 1946 he returned to Harrogate where he continued to work as a consultant physician.

At the London Hospital he had been fortunate in having outstanding teachers and throughout his career he continued to apply their high standards uncompromisingly. His clinical judgement was extremely sound and he relied very much on this rather than on laboratory and radiological investigations. If one of his residents asked for what he considered to be unnecessary investigations he was careful to make sure that the resident knew why he had requested them. He kept his own personal detailed records of the diagnosis and duration of inpatient stay of all his patients admitted to hospital, and could always be relied upon to produce accurate statistics when necessary.

Reah was a long standing member of the British Medical Association, the Heberden Society and the Royal Society of Medicine, in which he served as president of the section of physical medicine in 1962. He was chairman of the Harrogate Division of the British Medical Association when they held their Annual Meeting in Harrogate in 1970, and he discharged his duties with a tact and organizing ability which helped to make it a most successful meeting. He was president of the local branch of the British Diabetic Association for many years.

Thomas Reah was a modest, quietly devout man who was a sidesman at his church. He was a man of great integrity in all aspects of his life. He was a member of the Yorkshire County Cricket Club and enjoyed nothing better than a day at Headingley. He was also an enthusiastic gardener.

It was a great loss to him when his wife Ruth, who trained as a nurse at the London and Middlesex Hospitals, died in 1971 after a long battle with crippling rheumatoid arthritis, and throughout their marriage he was a most devoted husband. His own last years were marred by a progressive disabling illness, whose inexorable advance he recognized and bore with stoicism and rare courage. He had two sons, both of whom have studied Law. WSS

[*Brit. med. J.*, 1977, **1**, 654; Photo]

REDDISH, *Sir* Halford *b*.15 Aug 1898 *d*.12 Oct 1978
Kt (1958) FCA (1921) Hon FRCP (1977)

Halford Walter Lupton Reddish was the embodiment of the bold, if autocratic, entrepreneur who preached and practised in industry the principles of free enterprise. He was educated at Rugby School and served in the Army during the first world war. On demobilization he was articled to accountancy. By 1920 he had become gold medallist and institute prizeman of the Institute of Chartered Accountants, of which he eventually became a Fellow. He made a special study of insurance, which led him into the service of the Scottish Union and National Insurance Company and subsequently to its board in London. He was also an underwriting member of Lloyd's. Besides an early association with the cement industry, he was interested in engineering and metallurgy. He became chairman of the Trussed Concrete Steel Company and Charles Nelson and Company, and director of the Meldrum Investment Trust and of Granada Theatres. He was a valued member of the Dollar Exports Council and led a mission to Canada in 1957. He was knighted in 1958.

As chairman and chief executive of the Rugby Portland Cement Company and its subsidiary companies, from 1933 to 1976, he became a spokesman for his chosen industry, especially in the Midlands, but in a wider sense for the industry of the country as a whole, which he vigorously defended against growing nationalization.

Halford Reddish married Valerie, elder daughter of Dr Arthur Grosart Lehman Smith. She died in 1971, a year after he had presented £5 million to establish a medical research trust in his name at the King Edward VII Hospital, Midhurst, for research on diseases of the heart and lungs.

For all his short stature (5′3″) he gave the impression of being a big man, with strong features and heavy reinforced spectacles. It was once written of him that his passionate defence of free enterprise made the

Institute of Directors – on whose Council he had sat since 1948 – 'look like the Left Book Club'. He had his foibles: the Churchillian rate of cigar-smoking, the booked double seat in the aircraft, and the splendidly groomed appearance of the traditional professional man. He was known to a wide circle of friends as a man of culture, with a lively appreciation of art, and he was an accomplished chess player.

GW/VL

[*Times*, 14 Oct 1978]

REES, William Esmond *b.*28 Nov 1900 *d.*7 Aug 1977
MRCS LRCP (1924) MB BS Lond (1925) MRCP (1927) MD (1928) FRCP (1944)

William Esmond Rees was born in Abergavenny, Monmouthshire, where his father, Gwilym Rees, was in the steel industry and became a tinplate works manager. His mother, Margaret, was born in Llansamlet, Swansea, and her father was also called William Rees. He was a mill foreman. Amongst his friends, WE Rees was always referred to as 'Esmond'.

Esmond Rees was educated at Gowerton County School and at Clifton College. He proceeded to the Welsh National School of Medicine in Cardiff, and subsequently to St Thomas's Hospital Medical School. He married Marion Balmforth of Bradford. They had a son and a daughter; the son became a consultant neurologist, John E Rees MD FRCP, of Brighton, Hove and Mid-Sussex Health Districts.

From 1924 to 1926 WE Rees was clinical assistant to the skin department and ante-natal department, casualty officer, and then house physician, St Thomas's Hospital, to Sir Farquhar Buzzard. This was followed, between 1926 and 1929 with posts as resident house physician and resident medical officer, at the National Hospital, Queen Square, and from 1930 to 1933 as clinical assistant in out-patients at the Cardiff Royal Infirmary; combined with an appointment as demonstrator in anatomy at the Welsh National School of Medicine. In 1933 he became assistant physician, Cardiff Royal Infirmary. Meanwhile, from 1930 to 1948 he was honorary consulting physician to the Swansea General and Eye Hospital, physician in charge of the diabetic department, and honorary consultant neurologist at the Swansea and West Wales Hospitals. For 19 years, until his retirement in 1967, Rees was senior consultant physician to the Swansea General and Eye Hospital, consultant in charge of the diabetic department, and consultant neurologist to the Swansea General Hospital; Morriston Hospital, Swansea; Neath General Hospital, and Caernarvon and West Wales Hospitals.

Rees was greatly sought after as a neurologist and had a special interest also in diabetes. A good number of his medical beds were always occupied by diabetic patients whose complications he most assiduously and skilfully managed. He showed endless patience in the care of such patients. He engaged in private consultant practice both as a general physician and as a neurologist.

Small of stature, he was a extremely energetic man both in his professional capacity and in other more general activities. He had a highly critical mind and would not be put off by irrelevancies or untidy presentations of problems. He was therefore a valuable committee member. He was impatient of illogical thinking processes and was always highly aware of the legalistic aspects of administrative measures and suggestions. In all these fields of his work, both his hospital clinical and committee work, he proved himself a medical man of the highest integrity and considerable intellectual powers. He was elected chairman of the Swansea Division of the BMA, an office which he filled with distinction, and was also highly regarded as a Welsh member of the Central Committee for Hospital Medical Services of the BMA.

In a more direct professional capacity, he was a founder member of the Association of British Neurologists and a founder member of the Society of Physicians in Wales. This latter was particularly his brain child. Its success was to a large degree due to Esmond Rees's efforts and he remained the Society's treasurer for many years, guiding its affairs skilfully. His clear mind made him an invaluable medical worker in the field of medico-legal work, in which he became very experienced. He was a meticulous and accurate performer of any task he set himself. Nothing was done casually. When he supervised any project it had to be done with an aim to perfection, a situation which some collaborators and subordinates sometimes found irksome and excessively demanding. Among other things, he was a keen and successful gardener. EAD

[*Brit. med. J.*, 1977, **2**, 837; Photo]

REES-THOMAS, William *b.*15 June 1887 *d.*-1978
CB (1950) MB BS Lond (1909) MD (1910) MRCS LRCP (1912)
DPM (1914) MRCP (1913) FRCP (1933) FRCPsych (1971)

William Rees-Thomas was born in 1887 of a Welsh farming family, at Bailea, near Senny Bridge in Breconshire, the youngest child and only son of his parents. He was educated at the County School at Brecon; his abilities won him scholarships and he entered on the study of medicine at University College, Cardiff, and afterwards at Charing Cross Hospital. More prizes came his way, and he graduated with honours in 1909, proceeding to the London MD in the following year. In 1912 he was awarded a Murchison scholarship of the Royal College of Physicians of London. By this time his interest had turned to psychiatry, his first substantive appointment being that of medical officer and pathologist at the East Sussex County Mental Hospital, Hellingly. Besides the recently instituted DPM of Cambridge University, he acquired the older certificate of the Medico-Psychological Association (MPC), and won the Gaskell gold medal of that Association; moreover under the existing regulations he won honours in psychological medicine at the MRCP examinations. He was elected FRCP in 1933.

In the absence of a special institution for mental defectives in Sussex, Hellingly Hospital cared for many such patients, and Rees-Thomas's first published article was on 'Syphilis among mental defectives'. He soon took this branch of psychiatry as his specialty. In 1914 Moss Side Hospital at Maghull, near Liverpool, opened as a state institution for 'criminal and violent' mental defectives, and Rees-Thomas was appointed its first medical superintendent; but within a few months the buildings were taken over for use as a war hospital, mainly for the treatment of neurosis and 'shell shock', and Rees-Thomas left for active service in the RAMC. He was in action in Gallipoli, and afterwards served in Mesopotamia and India.

He returned to Moss Side in 1919, but again within a short time the use of the hospital was changed, and he was transferred with his patients to Rampton Hospital in Nottinghamshire which, having been built as a second Broadmoor, was now allocated to mental defectives needing special security. In the next twelve years Rees-Thomas developed the hospital on progressive lines, with full occupational and recreational facilities, so that its reputation stood as high as that of any psychiatric hospital in the country.

In 1932 Rees-Thomas was appointed one of the two medical senior commissioners of the Board of Control, which at that time supervised the welfare of mental patients, inspected the mental hospitals and was directly responsible for the state institutions (later called 'special hospitals'). His older colleague was Sir Hubert Bond, and together they encouraged the developments made possible by the Mental Treatment Act of 1930, such as the opening of psychiatric clinics and cooperation with local authority services, as well as the new physical methods of treatment. After the disruption of the second war years (during which the Board's headquarters were at St Anne's-on-sea, Lancashire) Rees-Thomas was concerned with the changes connected with the inclusion of psychiatry in the National Health Service, and then with progressive developments such as community care and the informal admission of patients, foreshadowing the provisions of the 1959 Mental Health Act.

By this time the Commissioners also held office in the Ministry of Health, and Rees-Thomas, like his colleagues, felt that there was no longer a need for an independent Board of Control. The Royal (Percy) Commission agreed with this, and the Board's existence came to an end in 1960, when Rees-Thomas retired – long after the usual age. He had been made a CB in 1950.

He had throughout taken an active part in the affairs of the Royal Medico-Psychological Association, and after serving as vice-chairman of its Mental Deficiency and Educational Committees, occupied the presidential chair in 1949–1950. He inaugural address, entitled 'What the patient thinks', was essentially a plea for congenial conditions in mental hospitals, with emphasis on the prevention of boredom and deterioration. He served also, for several years, as the RMPA's representative on the General Nursing Council. He was made an honorary member in 1955.

Rees-Thomas was generally regarded by his psychiatrist colleagues as a man of progressive ideas tempered with caution, relying much on tact and diplomacy to achieve the results he sought. In his private life he exemplified his own gospel of occupation and his leisure activities, though given in *Who's Who* as photography and golf, in fact ranged widely from bird-watching to knitting and sewing.

He married in 1917 – presumably while on leave from army service – Muriel Hodgson Jones, a clergyman's daughter, whom he had met while at Moss Side. By her he had a son and daughter; the latter married DWT Roberts, obstetrician and gynaecologist to St George's Hospital. His first wife died in 1935, and in 1948 he married Ruth Darwin, a granddaughter of Charles Darwin who, like himself, was a senior commissioner of the Board of Control, having previously for many years been actively engaged in promoting the welfare of the mentally defective. After their retirement they lived at High Hackhurst, near Abinger Hammer in Surrey, where they devoted themselves to the beautifying of their garden, which was regularly open to the public. Mrs Rees-Thomas died in 1972 but her husband lived for another six years, dying in 1978 at the age of 91.

AW

[Sources: personal recollections and communications; Board of Control Reports]

REEVES, Tony Lothrop *b*.5 Jan 1919 *d*.11 Oct 1977
MRCS LRCP (1943) MB BS Lond (1943) MRCP (1946) MD (1948) FRCP (1970)

Tony Reeves was born in Westminster, London, the son of Gilbert Nelson Reeves, a company director, and his wife Ruth Doris, daughter of Sir Arthur Mudge Branfoot KCIE, surgeon-general in the Indian Medical Service. He was educated at Tonbridge School and Guy's Hospital, London, where he graduated in 1943. He married twice: in 1943 to Geraldine Margaret Campbell, and in 1959 to Anita Edith Cole, and had four children, a daughter and three sons.

After house appointments at Guy's, he was appointed EMS B1 Grade physician and deputy superintendent to Queen Mary's Hospital, Sidcup, in 1945, where he was to spend the remainder of his life. He was appointed consultant physician in 1960. In the 1940s the hospital consisted of a conglomeration of huts which had been built during the first world war as a military hospital for plastic surgery. Tony Reeves spent much of his life planning the new hospital that was to replace the makeshift original, and had great influence in moulding the new district hospital to the needs of the local community. The new hospital was opened in 1974 and Tony's pride in the new was only limited by a vague nostalgia for the passing of the old, smaller, and more intimate community to which he had become accustomed.

His career was essentially one of service to his patients, but also to his colleagues. He was chairman of the staff committee at the hospital, served for two years with the Central Hospital Services, and was a member of various Whitley committees. He was vice-president of Sidcup Rotary Club, previously the Sidcup and Chislehurst Round

Table. He also acted as director and company secretary to his family firm of GN Reeves Limited. He had integrity, fairness, and an unusual grasp of detail, which made him sought after for administrative duties.

As a physician he was respected by his peers, and as a man he was loved by a wider community. Basically placid and calm, he could be roused to passion by any threat to the integrity of his profession, of which he was very proud. He was distressed when the profession became involved in industrial action.

Outside his work, his interests lay in rifle shooting, ciné and still photography, and travelling. He won the King's Prize at Bisley in 1937.

GW/VL

[*Lancet,* 1977, **2**; *Guy's Hosp. Gazette,* 1977, **92**; Photo]

REID, Donald Darnley *b*.6 May 1914 *d*.26 Mar 1977
MB ChB Aberd (1937) MD (1946) PhD Lond (1949) MRCP (1958) DSc Lond (1959) FRCP (1965)†

Donald Reid was born at Buckie, a small fishing village on the coast of Banffshire, a few miles from Lossiemouth. His father was an engineering inspector in the service of the General Post Office. Reid took his second name from his mother, Mary Darnley, the daughter of a railway contractor. Her father, John Darnley, had lost money constructing a railway line to Lossiemouth and her early years were thereby impoverished. Donald was an only child, had great affection for both his parents and was considerably influenced by his mother's strong character and great integrity. When he was about six years old the family removed to Inverness, and here he passed the rest of his childhood, being a pupil of the Inverness Royal Academy. He studied medicine at the medical school of the University of Aberdeen, serving on qualification as house physician and house surgeon at the Royal Northern Infirmary (1937–1938). Having joined the Volunteer Reserve of the Royal Air Force he was called up in September 1939 and posted to Bomber Command.

As a station medical officer he was in close contact with the aircrews, for whose courage and endurance he had a profound admiration. In such circumstances, not conducive to research, he set about trying to measure objectively their physical and mental reactions to the tremendous stresses to which they were exposed, and to assess what might be done medically to alleviate them. This original work brought him to the attention of Sir Harold Whittingham (*q.v.*), the Royal Air Force Director-General of Medical Services, and Reid was posted to the research section of the medical directorate. Here he continued his studies with statistical epidemiological guidance from Dr (later Sir Austin) Bradford Hill, who was attached to the section. He was demobilized in 1946 having risen to the rank of squadron leader, and returned to civil life as a lecturer in the department of medical statistics at the London School of Hygiene and Tropical Medicine. Here his own war experiences and contacts made him a very successful teacher of the mature medically qualified students who were returning from the war to take up careers in public health. Developing his own career at the London School he was appointed reader in epidemiology and vital statistics in 1950; in 1959 the title of professor of epidemiology was conferred upon him and in 1961 he succeeded Sir Austin Bradford Hill as director of the department of medical statistics and epidemiology.

During these years he was awarded the degree of MD (with commendation) of the University of Aberdeen, and the PhD and DSc of the University of London. In 1948 he spent a period as visiting associate professor of biostatistics at the University of California.

After a brief excursion into the field of mental disorders, an interest which he never wholly lost, (WHO *Report on Epidemiological Methods in the Study of Mental Disorders,* 1960), Reid's main research interest lay in the influence of the environment upon the spread and incidence of respiratory diseases. His early work and assessment of the relevant literature were summed up in the Kilroy lectures of the Royal College of Physicians (*Environmental Factors in Respiratory Disease,* 1958), and later in life he returned to one special section of the field, bronchitis, in the College's Marc Daniels memorial lectures (*The Social Background of Bronchitis,* 1976). In between these dates he published many papers, alone or with colleagues, on the epidemiology of cardiovascular and respiratory diseases. In particular, in the early part of the period, he promoted international studies of migrants who had moved from the UK or Norway to the USA, and whose mortality in the new environment could be contrasted with that prevailing in their native countries. As a result of this work he became a great traveller, which he greatly enjoyed, for he was a good 'mixer', and made a host of friends in many parts of Europe and the USA.

Another major research undertaking was the medical examination of nearly 20,000 UK male civil servants, and a long-term follow-up to measure their subsequent mortality from chest and heart diseases, and the relative importance of the possible causes (see e.g., *Myocardial ischaemia, risk factors and death from coronary heart-disease,* 1977).

His work in the cardiovascular field, jointly in the UK and USA, led to an honorary fellowship of the American College of Cardiology. Reid was chairman of the medical section of the Royal Statistical Society in 1956–1958, and president of the section of epidemiology and community medicine of the Royal Society of Medicine in 1960–1968. He served as consultant in epidemiology to the Royal Air Force, on the Clinical Research Board of the Medical Research Council, as chairman of the Epidemiology Panel of the National Coal Board, and on the Royal College of Physicians' sub-committee on cardiac rehabilitation. To these and many similar bodies, he brought clear thinking and, sometimes, forthright views – though under his apparent self-confidence lay (to those who knew him well) a modest diffidence, and even doubt regarding his own powers. Nevertheless he built up and administered with success a large department of medical statistics and epidemiology at the London School of Hygiene and Tropical Medicine, and thus made a notable contribution to the development of the subject in Great Britain. The School has instituted a medal and cash prize to be given in his memory for work in epidemiology. This is awarded trienially in association with the Royal College of Physicians.

Outside his professional life his main interests were music and photography. In 1939 he married Christine Macleod who had been with him at the Inverness Royal Academy, and who was the daughter of Donald James Macleod OBE DLitt, HM Chief Inspector of Schools and a noted Gaelic scholar. She bore him two daughters, one of whom took a medical qualification at the University of Edinburgh.

In his later years Reid had been under treatment for hypertension. He died suddenly and without warning at his home in Hampton-on-Thames. ABH

[*Brit. med. J.*, 1977, **1**, 981; *Lancet*, 1977, **1**, 763; *Times*, 30 Mar 1977; Photo]

RIDEHALGH, Frank *b*.4 June 1907 *d*.7 Jan 1977
BA Cantab (1929) MRCS LRCP (1932) MA MB BChir (1935)
MD (1948) DM Oxon (1962) MRCP (1943) FRCP (1950)

Frank Ridehalgh was born at Rishton, Blackburn; his father was Fred Ridehalgh, a furniture dealer, who married Bertha Ann Greenwood, daughter of a shopkeeper. He attended local schools, including the Queen Elizabeth Grammar School, Blackburn, from which he obtained Tattersall and Irvine scholarships to take him to King's College, Cambridge. He obtained an open scholarship to Charing Cross Hospital Medical School, where he was Travers prizeman in practical midwifery, and he obtained class prizes in several other subjects.

After house jobs at Charing Cross he took a post at Frimley Sanatorium, and this led to his appointment as the first Prophit Scholar of the College, an appointment made possible by a legacy from the late JMG Prophit for research in tuberculosis. Frank Ridehalgh readily grasped the opportunity for research on a group basis into the disease which at that time was a major cause of death and disability in young adults. The concept of multi-centre studies then hardly existed, but he obtained cooperation from many hospitals, medical schools, tuberculosis clinics and industrial firms, to establish the work of the survey amongst different population groups. His natural courtesy, and ability to get on with people from all walks of life, undoubtedly contributed to the success of this project, which required a great deal of organization and careful tuberculin testing. It was on the firm foundations laid by Frank Ridehalgh that the scholars who followed him were able to build, and ultimately to produce the report of which he was co-author.

A short period as tuberculosis officer in Staffordshire followed, and then some ten years in the Leeds Chest Service, where from 1943 he was senior chest physician during the difficult war years and the reorganization of the tuberculosis service subsequently. A colleague of those days recalls particularly the clinical discussions that he organized with the involvement of thoracic surgeons as well as physicians. In

1951 he was appointed to Oxford, where he took over from William Stobie, who had been appointed by Sir William Osler to be in charge of tuberculous patients some 40 years previously. Ridehalgh retired in December 1970. During that period he supervised the development of the Oxford Chest Services to include all aspects of modern respiratory medicine. In spite of a period of ill health, which caused him a great deal of physical discomfort at the time of his arrival in Oxford, he took over his new job with enthusiasm and his warm and friendly personality soon made him many friends in Oxford. The University, recognizing his efforts in the teaching sphere, made him a lecturer and he later served on the Board of Governors of the Radcliffe Infirmary.

His qualities as a clinician were reflected in the esteem in which he was held by his patients, colleagues and staff. He showed a genuine concern for those in his care or service, and was a keen member of Oxford City Care Committee and president of the Berkshire Care Committee. He was an able committee man, and in addition to serving as chairman of the local medical staff council, he was for many years active in the British Thoracic and Tuberculosis Association, of which he became president. He was for some years after 1954 a member of the Ministry of Health Standing Advisory Committee on Tuberculosis.

His interest in the specialty of chest medicine is shown by his membership of the committee of the Tuberculosis and Chest Diseases Group of the BMA and by the work he continued to do after his retirement, indeed until shortly before his death, in monitoring the posts advertised in the specialty and the problems in filling them. He was among the first to foresee the need to expand the training grades in respiratory medicine, and to include a proper base of general medicine. Both locally and nationally he worked quietly and effectively to achieve these objectives. He work was the subject of a paper in the *British Medical Journal,* and was of great value to the Joint Tuberculosis Committee of the British Thoracic and Tuberculosis Association and the Thoracic Medicine Committee of the College.

Frank Ridehalgh was a generous host whose many interests outside medicine, which included music, antique furniture, gardening and the photography of alpine plants in their natural surroundings, always made visits to his home a noteworthy occasion. His wife Mollie (born Vera Mary Jones, daughter of a bank manager; they were married in 1936) contributed much to these occasions and was always a great source of strength to him, especially during the final six months of an illness which he knew to be fatal, and which he bore with characteristic fortitude and cheerfulness. He was survived by his wife and their three children, two sons and a daughter. VHS

[*Brit. med. J.,* 1977, **1**, 1035; *Lancet,* 1977, **1**, 867; Photo]

RITCHIE, Frank Lane *b*.6 Dec 1918 *d*.14 Jan 1982
CBE (1974) MB BS Sydney (1943) MRCP (1948) FRCPE (1957) FRACP (1969) FRCP (1974)

Frank Ritchie was born in Sydney, Australia, the only son of Harold John Ritchie, also a doctor, and his wife Elizabeth Jane, daughter of Hugh Swift, an engineer. His early education was at Tudor House and Geelong Grammar School. He studied medicine at Sydney University, pursuing his clinical studies at Sydney Hospital, and graduated in 1943. After a short period as a resident medical officer at Sydney Hospital, he enlisted in the Army Medical Corps of the Australian Imperial Forces, serving as medical officer to the 2/12th Field Ambulance, regimental medical officer to the 2/17th Australian Infantry Battalion, and physician to the 113th Australian General Hospital. On demobilization he undertook postgraduate studies at Johns Hopkins Hospital, USA, having been awarded a Nuffield travelling fellowship.

On his return to Australia he practised as a consultant physician in Macquarie Street, Sydney, for many years. He was also lecturer in therapeutics at Sydney University, senior physician at St Luke's Hospital and Sydney Hospital, vice-president of the board of Sydney Hospital 1962–1968, and president of the board from 1968 until his death. He was a fellow of the Royal College of Physicians of Edinburgh, a fellow of the Royal Australasian College of Physicians, and was elected a fellow of the Royal College of Physicians of London in 1974. Outside the field of medicine he held appointments as chairman of the board of the National Mutual Life Association of Australia, and chairman of Intercommercial Properties Pty. He was awarded the CBE in 1974.

In 1947 he married Mary Elizabeth, daughter of Faunce Blair Tainton, a grazier, and they had one son and two daughters. The marriage was dissolved in 1972.

Frank Ritchie was an outstanding administrator as well as a good physician. He applied himself with dedication and skill to serving the needs of worthy causes, and in this respect the survival and advancement of Sydney Hospital as a teaching and general hospital on the Macquarie Street site became a matter of great importance and interest to him. He worked tirelessly for the institution with which he had a lifelong association, as student, intern, resident, teacher, vice-president and, finally, as chief executive. During his 14 years as president of the board he successfully steered the hospital through some of the most difficult times in its long and remarkable history. He had a strong belief in a role for Sydney Hospital as a centre for medical research, and was instrumental in establishing a research foundation which was inaugurated in 1978. He possessed the rare quality of being able to reduce complex issues to simple terms, and was thorough and resourceful in everything he did. Expecting high standards, he knew how to inspire and bring forth the best in others. He had a keen sense of history, an excellent understanding of politics, and a strong feeling of pride in Australian achievements.

Frank was a reserved man, given to philosophical thought, and with a quiet but well developed sense of humour. He enjoyed life and worked and played with enthusiasm. His leisure time, like his work time, was given to a wide range of activities. He was an adventurer, navigator, sportsman and electronics technician. In the later years of his life he made an annual sailing pilgrimage over the same route taken by Captain Cook when he travelled from Botany Bay to Cape York. Such journeys tested his skills, which included game fishing. They also provided release for his restless and adventurous spirit. He was a good physician, a good administrator, a good friend – and an outstanding Australian. JJW/GW

[Eulogy, Sydney Hospital, 1982; Photo]

ROBERTSON, Kenneth Moorhouse *b.*20 Jan 1907 *d.*11 Apr 1981
MB BS Lond (1930) MRCP (1935) FRCP (1947) MRCPE (1958) FRCPE (1963)

Kenneth Robertson was a son of a missionary working in Rhodesia. He was educated at Eltham School and went with a scholarship to St Thomas's Hospital. His student career was distinguished and he won the William Tite and Musgrove scholarships, William Dunn prize, Mead medal, Bristow medal, Wainwright prize and Beaney scholarship. He qualified in 1929, and he gained the MB BS London with honours in 1930. Despite the hope that he would stay at St Thomas's he went straight into general practice in Winchester, where besides practising in the town he was one of the doctors to Winchester College.

Even before he had a hospital appointment his colleagues in practice were asking his advice about their more difficult problems. He shared the Murchison scholarship with J St C Elkington in 1930, and gained the MRCP in 1935. He was appointed consultant physician in 1936, continuing also with his practice. In 1947 he was elected FRCP, and he then gave up his general practice, shortly afterwards becoming consultant physician at the Royal South Hants Hospital, Southampton. He also consulted at Lord Mayor Treloar's Hospital, and at Lymington and Romsey Hospitals.

Kenneth Robertson devoted very nearly all of his efforts to medicine and his capacity for hard work was legendary. He built up a very large practice, both inside and outside hospital, and was in great demand to visit patients in their homes, which he often did in the evenings. Patients were often surprised by the late hour at which he would come to make a consultation. For many years he had a photographic recording electrocardiograph, and his juniors would often find him in the hospital around midnight developing the tracings he had made during the visits of the evening. His kindness and humanity and his touch in dealing with patients, perhaps strengthened by his years in general practice, endeared him to all and he was held in universal love and admiration.

Despite his busy life with the patients, he was up to date with publications over a wide range of journals to a quite astounding degree. He managed this by reading into the small hours, and it was said that if he took a holiday (which he rarely did) his luggage consisted of a spare shirt packed between journals and textbooks. Though not a prolific publisher, he had important papers on temporal arteritis, on hepatitis in Hamburg after the war, and on Weil's disease of which there was an outbreak in Winchester.

He was an excellent teacher, and held an open round for general practitioners and hospital staff one afternoon a week. A large number of doctors, seldom less than 20, would sit on chairs in the ward, with the patients in their beds, and the cases were discussed openly but tactfully before everybody. Such was his skill in handling the teaching that this never gave rise to any difficulties, and these sessions were invariably interesting and informative. Senior registrars would come in rotation, year after year, from St Thomas's and never failed to return without being deeply impressed. He was a founder member and moving spirit in the Wessex Physicians Club, whose meetings are attended twice annually by physicians from Bath to Worthing. A Kenneth Robertson memorial lecture has been endowed by this club and a distinguished lecturer is soon to give the first presentation in his honour.

Kenneth became the first postgraduate clinical teacher in Southampton in 1963 and together with his colleagues set up the postgraduate centre, started the library, and arranged for the appointment of a secretary; in this and other ways he was a key figure during the period when the medical school in Southampton was planned.

His ward rounds were always long, as there were so many interesting patients, but they were never tedious. Coffee and sandwiches would be taken in the Sister's room and often at these times Kenneth would recall events during his life as a doctor. Some of these stories, such as that of a man who had three consultants down from London in one day; or of the warden of the College who insisted on having his operation in the school sanatorium and bought an operating table for the purpose, gave insight into medicine as it used to be, while other stories had a more clinical message. All were fascinating.

At a late stage in his career Kenneth thought that he was in need of refreshment and decided to take the Edinburgh MRCP course. He sat through the lectures and clinicals, and it was a surprise to a recent senior registrar at Southampton, who had been appointed to a post in Edinburgh, to find the roles were reversed and he was expected to teach his former mentor! At the end of the course he insisted on taking the examination, and passed to become MRCP Edinburgh in 1958. Later he was elected FRCP Edinburgh in 1963.

Patients would visit Kenneth from all over Hampshire. He was always very modest about his success and when once asked if his patients visited him at his house he replied 'Yes, both of them'. His commitment to medicine left little time for outside pursuits but one abiding interest, apart from his family, was rugby football. At Eltham he had played for Kent Schoolboys, and he later played for Scottish Schoolboys. At St Thomas's Kenneth played in the famous cup winning side of 1926, and he later became a referee. In later years he would seldom miss an important match on television.

Kenneth Robertson was greatly admired by his many registrars and housemen who benefited much from his wisdom and teaching, and nearly all of them returned to Southampton to honour him at a dinner when he retired. For several years after retirement he worked in general practice with his son-in-law in Surrey.

In 1930 he married Eleanor Margaret Greening, whose loving support made possible his remarkable achievements. They had five children, of whom three are doctors. JB

[*Brit. med. J.*, 1981, **282**, 2064; **283**, 239; Photo]

ROBSON, *Sir* **Hugh (Norwood)** *b*.18 Oct 1917 *d*.11 Dec 1977
Kt (1974) MB ChB Edin (1941) MRCPE (1947) FRCPE (1952) FRACP (1954) MRCP (1961) FRCP (1966) FRSE (1975)†

Some men are born leaders and Norrie Robson was of their company. He was an outstanding administrator in both university and medical affairs. A Scot, he was a Borderer from Langholm, Dumfriesshire, where his father, Hugh Robson, was a civil servant with the Inland Revenue. His mother, Elizabeth Warnock, was a farmer's daughter. Norrie was educated at Langholm and Dumfries academies and then studied medicine at the University of Edinburgh. As a student he evinced a rare combination of *gravitas* and high good humour which earned him both affection and respect. It was during his undergraduate days that he met Alice Livingstone, a fellow medical student, whom he married in 1942, a year after he graduated. The second world war separated them soon after their marriage when Norrie served as a surgeon lieutenant in the RNVR. His war service took him widely all over the world, from the Western Approaches to Singapore.

Norrie found ample outlet for his youthful enterprise and exuberance in Singapore when he found himself, soon after VJ Day, among a small group of doctors billeted in the bridal suite of the Adelphi Hotel, because it had a telephone in it. Their job was to provide a medical service for the ships of all nations, which filled the harbour. Norrie Robson was instrumental in acquiring the transport essential for the job; it consisted of two scruffy and ancient launches which he christened HMS *Cyanosis* and HMS *Dementia*, and from them the Malay skippers proudly flew white ensigns of uncertain provenance. If ever there was a time when enterprise was needed to do work which occupied the best part of twenty four hours this was it, and Norrie had enterprise in abundance.

On demobilization he resumed his academic career, being appointed to a lectureship in medicine in Edinburgh in 1947, to a senior lectureship in medicine in Aberdeen in 1950, and to the Mortlock chair of medicine in the University of Adelaide in 1953. He was thirty five years old at the time and it was the first full-time professorship in medicine in Adelaide – indeed, only the second in all Australia. Norrie had to face the task of developing a department of medicine with full-time staff, instead of the older and well established system of part-time clinical teachers. Recognition of his success and brilliant administrative gifts was clearly evidenced by the list of appointments to which his colleagues elected him; many were professional, but others were non-clinical or advisory. He took great pride in one in particular – that of consultant physician to the Royal Australian Navy. He was also honorary physician to a number of Adelaide hospitals and a member of many bodies, including the National Health and Medical Research Council of Australia, the Australian Drug Evaluation Committee, and the Papua and New Guinea Medical Research and Advisory Committee. He was president of the Australian Society of Haematology and councillor for Australia of the International Society of Haematology. He was dean of the faculty of medicine 1959 – 1961, chairman of the professorial board 1961 – 1963, and member of council 1964 – 1965; and he acted as external examiner for a number of universities. The twelve years of his stay at the University of Adelaide were to see his flowering as a teacher and clinical practitioner of medicine, as well as service to the University as a whole. His public service within Australia would itself merit a full tribute.

All this experience in Australia stood Norrie Robson in good stead when he returned to Britain in 1966 to become vice-chancellor of the University of Sheffield. Invaluable also were the three years he had spent as a senior lecturer in Aberdeen under RS Aitken, later to be vice-chancellor of Birmingham University. Both men had a high intellectual capacity and remarkable scientific insight, combined with kindliness of spirit and determination of purpose. Robson's arrival at Sheffield was timely, for at that time Aitken was the only other medical vice-chancellor in the United Kingdom, and it was clear that the universities were to be faced with many problems of medical policy and medical education. They were to be years of student unrest and student change, of necessary internal reorganization and development; a time of rapid expansion with the doubling of student numbers after the Robbins report, and it was the confidence and trust which Norrie Robson inspired in the whole community which carried the University through the turbulence of the next few years, without the stresses experienced in many other universities.

One of his favourite stories concerned a distinguished foreign visitor whom he had to entertain soon after his own arrival at the University. Over lunch, as vice-chancellor, he sang the praises of the University library, to which the guest was to make a gift of books. Once lunch was over, he led his guest at a brisk pace across the campus, coming to a sudden halt to ask his registrar, 'Where is the damned library, anyway?'

From the beginning an important part of his role was to add lustre to the University by making his mark in national affairs, and he found the way open in his own field. His years in Adelaide had provided considerable experience in medical politics, not just on local, but on an international scale, and he was now able to put it to good use. Within three years he became chairman of the Central Committee for Postgraduate Medical Education (Great Britain), and then of the Council for Postgraduate Medical Education in England and Wales, newly formed in 1970. He was vice-chairman of the committee of vice-chancellors and principals, being elected chairman in 1972, when he succeeded Sir Fraser Noble. In 1971 he had also become chairman of the Advisory Council on the Misuse of Drugs. They were hectic and difficult years in which to combine such varied responsibilities. Everything began to go wrong with the world's economic system, and in Britain the zeal for reform produced endless complexities for every institution. There was an obsession with the machinery of government and administration, so that the design was constantly changed instead of being efficiently improved. Nobody was more impatient with this than Norrie, yet he endured the wasteful calls on his energy with patience and goodwill. His health sometimes caused anxiety, and he suffered pain from arthritis, but although he was never a compliant patient he came through these strenuous years resiliently. When his *alma mater* called him to return in 1974, as principal and vice-chancellor, he responded with the enthusiastic pride of a young Scot picked for his first international at Murrayfield.

He was clearly elated by the prospect of a return to his native land, and to the city and university where he had begun his service in medicine, and where he had met and courted Alice Livingstone, the constant source of so much of his strength. He was also keenly aware of the growing calls for devolution in Scotland and their implications for the universities, in which he had been rallying opinion against the hints of regionalization of higher education, which Sir William Pile had first cast around at a meeting of the CVCP held in Sheffield in 1972. He was therefore prepared for one aspect of his new role, but nothing in his Sheffield experience paralleled the internal constitutional horrors which confronted him in his first year in Edinburgh. He had to rally all his personal resources and draw on reserves of tact and acumen. In this he was greatly helped by the election of a new rector with whom he formed a determined and skilful alliance. He was also supported by the wisdom and experience of senior colleagues on senate and court, and he set himself to resolve the problems and strengthen the University to enable it to meet the challenge of hard times. Within two years he had won the affection and respect of the whole University, restoring its pride in the greatness of the past and its confidence in the future.

Norrie Robson was a man of courage and determination who liked to think things through for himself. He had a gift of lucid, uncomplicated exposition and his straightforward honesty and directness earned him credit and sympathy in many a difficult debate. There was also something of a stubborn streak in him which refused to give way before the best intentioned argument, and sometimes he appeared to overlook the subtle complexities of certain problems, seeing things in black and white. It is however a measure of his sincerity and strength of purpose, and of his ability as an administrator, that his friends and colleagues were not only saddened by his untimely death but also felt they had been deprived of a unique store of wisdom and experience.

Robson was knighted in 1974; he held the title of emeritus professor in the University of Adelaide, an honorary LLD of the University of Sheffield, and an honorary DSc of the University of Pennsylvania. He also acted as external examiner in medicine in the universities of Sydney, Melbourne, Western Australia and Otago, and held visiting professorships or guest lectureships at the universities of Sheffield, New York, Chicago, St Louis, Salt Lake City, Sydney, Melbourne, Brisbane, Perth, Christchurch and Dunedin. He served as Honeyman-Gillespie lecturer in Edinburgh 1949–1959; as Listerian lecturer in Adelaide in 1954; as Bancroft lecturer in Queensland in 1965, and as Keith Inglis memorial lecturer in Sydney in 1968.

Norrie was a man who believed in the concept of community; a man who succeeded in fostering cooperative working relationships in all parts of a university, and who was successful in bringing about easier interaction and communication between university, city and region.

He was survived by his wife, two daughters, one of whom is a doctor, and a son. FN/GW/VL

[*Brit. med. J.*, 1977, **2**, 1676; 1978, **1**, 249, 375; *Lancet*, 1977, **2**, 1370; 1978, **1**, 166; *Times*, 12 Dec 1977; *Times Higher Ed. Supplement*, 16 Dec 1977; *Year Book RSE*, 1979, pp.58-63; Photo]

ROBSON, *Sir* **Kenneth** *b*.5 Mar 1909 *d*.7 Dec 1978
Kt (1968) CBE (1959) MRCS LRCP (1933)
MB BChir Cantab (1934) MA (1934) MRCP (1935) MD (1944)
FRCP (1943) FRCPE (1975)†

Kenneth Robson was the 39th registrar since 1579, and succeeded Sir Harold Boldero in 1961 at a critical time for the College, for the new building was about to begin. His greatest service was to ensure with exemplary tact that the outburst of new ideas and activities which followed the move to Regent's Park did not obscure the historic mission and traditions of the College, the preservation of which he felt to be the particular responsibility of his office.

Ken, or KR as he was widely known, came from a Scottish Presbyterian family, his grandfather and great grandfather having been ministers of that church, as is one brother. He was born in London, the youngest of eight children of John Ajmer Robson, a stockjobber, and Katherine, the daughter of Samuel Osborn, a steelmaster. His nephew Angus Osborn Robson was elected FRCP in 1973. Ken's qualities of kindness, patience, diligence and inflexible integrity may well have owed much to his upbringing in this closely knit religious family.

He was educated at Bradfield and Christ's College, Cambridge, before entering the Middlesex Hospital, where he had a distinguished undergraduate career and became the second Broderip scholar. After qualifying he held appointments at the Middlesex Hospital and at the Brompton Hospital, where he soon developed his lasting interest in thoracic medicine. He was appointed to the staff of both St George's and the Brompton Hospitals and continued to serve them until his retirement in 1975. He was also on the staff of King Edward VII Hospital for Officers in Beaumont Street (Sister Agnes's) and King Edward VII Hospital, Midhurst, and was chief medical referee for the Confederation Life Insurance Company. He was awarded the CBE in 1959 and received a knighthood in 1968. He became a fellow of the Edinburgh College of Physicians in 1975 and was also an honorary fellow of the Royal Australian College of Physicians, the Royal College of Physicians of Ireland, the American College of Physicians and the South African College of Physicians.

In 1938 he joined the medical branch of the Royal Air Force Volunteer Reserve, and spent his wartime service mainly as medical specialist at RAF Hospital Cosford, near Wolverhampton, and No 9 RAF Hospital, India, before becoming RAF consultant physician in India and the Far East, until he was demobilized in 1946 with the rank of air commodore. In 1949 he succeeded Sir John Conybeare as civilian consultant to the Royal Air Force, and in 1977 was appointed honorary air commodore to the RAF Central Medical Establishment, an honour only once bestowed before. 'He was', wrote two Air Force colleagues, 'a good friend of generations of RAF physicians and he made it his business to know them all personally ...'.

Of the many societies and clubs to which he belonged he was happiest in the Thoracic Society, of which he was secretary from 1947 to 1960, president in 1965 and thereafter an honorary member; and in the Wilks Club, of which he was the indefatigable secretary and epicurean caterer till the time of his death.

Sir Kenneth's long association with the College began when he took the MRCP in 1935. He was elected to the fellowship in 1943 and in 1944 gave the Goulstonian lectures. He was an examiner from 1949 to 1957 and a censor in 1959–1960. When Sir Harold Boldero died suddenly in 1961 there was an hiatus in the College. Who could be found to succeed this man who had become almost a college institution? Discussion soon centred on one name and, as it turned out, Ken Robson was a happy choice. He served as adjutant and confidential adviser to five presidents. At different times each paid tribute to the help that they had received from this quiet, conservative and old-fashioned (in the best English sense), but very efficient and effective man, and to his wisdom and firmness when firmness was required. He made no secret, for instance, of his strong disapproval of any kind of industrial action by doctors. He could be tough, particularly in matters affecting the interests of the College. There is a well-authenticated story of a fellow who arrived for a council of obligation announcing that he must leave by 4.0 pm. He was told that he must see the registrar. The registrar's reply was terse: 'Show Dr So-and-so to the telephone so that he can cancel his next engagement'.

The two important and long-term changes in the College in his time, namely the controlled expansion of the fellowship to make the College less an élitist body and more representative of consultants as a whole, and the establishment of the common membership UK, which brought the Scottish and London colleges closer than they had ever been before, did not originate with Ken. But once convinced of the need for such changes, he supported them loyally and applied his undoubted administrative talents to ensuring their successful implementation. Nor did he neglect overseas relationships, for he travelled widely on behalf of the College, and his four honorary fellowships from overseas colleges show how much his interest in them was appreciated.

In his own College his extraordinary memory for detail, including the deeds and misdeeds of individual fellows, was proverbial, as was his meticulous keeping of College records, and his detailed preparation for all meetings, particularly those concerned with elections to the fellowship. Outside his own College the respect with which he came to be regarded was shown by his election from 1972 to 1974 as chairman of the joint consultants committee. He retired from the staff of his hospitals and the registrarship in 1975, but continued private practice from his house in Sydney Street, Chelsea, till he died.

Ken had countless friends and few enemies, for it would have been difficult for even the most rabid radical to become seriously angry with someone of such patent integrity, profound knowledge of the facts of any case he argued, and quiet modest manner. Further, his slow but genial smile was irresistible. His capacity for friendship was shown by the great popularity of his 'firm' at St George's Hospital, the very large number of his house physicians and registrars who came from far and wide to a farewell dinner on his retirement, and by the esteem in which he was held in all the clubs, societies and institutions with which he was connected. A member of the portering staff of the College recalls that, on passing through the front hall on his way out, he always raised his hat (or strictly slid his hat down onto his chest) and bade them each goodnight by name. He was a generous and skilled host and a good raconteur. His great interest outside medicine was association football and in particular the fortunes of Wolverhampton Wanderers ('The Wolves'), with whom his association started during his RAF service and continued till he died.

He remained unmarried. He died unexpectedly of cardiac infarction in Sister Agnes's Hospital, while awaiting an operation for a different complaint. As was said at the time, 'the end was characteristic of the man and was, like everything else he put his hand to, precisely and tidily accomplished'. A large congregation attended a memorial service in the Chapel of St Clement Dane (the RAF church) on 13 February 1979, when the address was given by Sir Cyril Clarke FRS. His portrait by Walter Woodington hangs in the College. RRB

[*Brit. med. J.*, 1978, **2**, 1720, & 1979, **1**, 61, 134; *Lancet,* 1978, **2**, 1320, & 1979, **1**, 58; *Times,* 17 Dec 1979; Photo]

ROSS, Cyril Max *b.*26 Feb 1922 *d.*15 Apr 1980
MB ChB Glasg (1944) MRCP (1949) FRFPS (1949) FRCPG (1971) FRCP (1979)

Cyril Ross was born in Glasgow. His father was Harry Louis Ross, a businessman, and his mother Gertie was the daughter of Morris Sagman. He was educated at Albert Road Academy and the University of Glasgow, his clinical studies being undertaken at the Glasgow Royal Infirmary. He married Hannah Braverman in 1945 and they had three children: two sons and a daughter. After house appointments at the Royal Infirmary, he joined the RAF with the rank of squadron leader and was appointed officer in charge of infectious diseases and dermatology at Princess Mary's RAF Hospital, Halton. On demobilization he was appointed to the skin department of the Victoria Infirmary, Glasgow, in 1948, and was subsequently senior registrar at the Sunderland Royal Infirmary.

He emigrated to South Africa in 1954, being appointed dermatologist to the Far East Rand Hospital and the Springs Mine Hospital. He was also appointed as a consultant to the SA Iron and Steel Industrial Corporation. From 1957 to 1969 he was dermatologist at Boksburg-Benoni Hospital, and also dermatologist at No 1 Military Hospital, Voortrekkerhoogte, from 1957 to 1961. In 1969 he was appointed dermatologist to the Hendrik Verwoerd Hospital, Pretoria, a post he held until his death.

Ross was an associate founder of the College of Physicians, Surgeons and Gynaecologists of South Africa, and a committee member of the dermatological faculty committee. He was active in Jewish affairs in South Africa, being chairman of the friends of the Hebrew University, Pretoria, and of the Jewish ex-servicemen's league. He published many papers in various medical journals.

Outside his professional and family life, his interests lay in bowls and golf, and he was an enthusiastic collector of modern South African paintings. GW/VL

[Photo]

ROSS, Stanley Graham *b.*29 Apr 1888 *d.*26 Mar 1980
DSO MC MD CM McGill (1913) FRCP (1938) FRCP(C) (1949)

Stanley Graham Ross died in Montreal, Canada, in his ninety-second year. He had been associated with the Montreal Children's Hospital since 1919.

Graham Ross was born in Dundas, Ontario, the son of Dr James Ross, a member of a pioneer Quebec family and a graduate of the McGill Medical School. Graham too came to McGill, graduating in arts in 1910 and in medicine in 1913. Postgraduate training at the Royal Victoria Hospital was interrupted in 1914 by the outbreak of World War I. As an officer in the Sixth Field Ambulance, Canadian Army Medical Corps, he served with great distinction on active service from the autumn of 1914 until the war's end in 1918. He was awarded both a DSO and an MC for 'bravery in the field'.

Following discharge from the army, he spent a year at the Hospital for Sick Children, Great Ormond Street, London. On his return to Canada in 1919, he was appointed assistant physician to the Montreal Children's Hospital – at that time the Children's Memorial Hospital – and to the staff of the Royal Victoria Hospital. He decided to pursue further study at Johns Hopkins Hospital, Baltimore, where, in Dr Howland's department, he had two research years in the laboratory with James Gamble and Frederick Tisdale. Their memorable pioneer work, published in a classic paper in 1923 in the *Journal of Biological Chemistry*, did much to clarify the problems of electrolyte metabolism in sick babies. These three young investigators were among the first to see the importance of electrolyte balance, and their research helped set the stage for all that has gone on since.

In 1922 he resumed his hospital responsibilities in Montreal and soon was recognized as a sound clinician, a gifted teacher and a critical scientist. At the Royal Victoria Montreal Maternity Hospital it is recalled that he was responsible for the introduction of newborn care under paediatric responsibility. To his patients he was their beloved physician; to house physicians he was their model of the doctor who gave unstintingly of his skill, time and energy for the benefit of others; to his professional colleagues abroad he was that highly respected Canadian paediatrician.

Graham Ross was a gracious host, an avid reader, keenly interested in world events. In his younger years he had studied Greek and on retirement from practice, he returned to the University, to refresh his skill so that he might enjoy to the full his reading in the original Greek.

While still active he had been an ardent fisherman, usually accompanied by enthusiastic friends. His interest in nature was evident both in his gardening and his development of a successful tree farm near his lake in the Laurentians.

His general influence in the profession can be seen by his election to the presidency of the Montreal Medical-Chirurgical Society and of the Association of Paediatricians of the Province of Quebec, of which he was a founding member. He was a former president of the Canadian Pediatric Society, and vice-president of the prestigious American Pediatric Society, at a time when few Canadian paediatricians were recognized outside their own country. GW/VL

[Compiled from Minutes of the Council of Physicians and Dentists, Montreal Children's Hospital, Canada; Photo]

ROWLANDS, *Sir* **(Richard) Alun** *b.*12 Sept 1885 *d.*1 Mar 1977
KBE (1946) CBE (1944) OBE (1920) BSc Wales (1906)
MRCS LRCP (1911) MB BS Lond (1914) MD (1916) MRCP (1916)
FRCP (1924) Hon LLD Wales (1946)

Alun Rowlands was born in the Bryngwran Valley in Anglesey, the son of Richard Rowlands, a master tailor and draper, and of Anne, daughter of Owen Griffith, a farmer. He never lost the manner of speech nor the warmth of heart of his native island.

Educated at the Beaumaris Grammar School and the University College of North Wales, he obtained a BSc before entering the London Hospital Medical College in 1907 with a science scholarship. He qualified with the conjoint diploma in 1911 and took the MB BS with honours and distinction in medicine in 1914, the MD and the MRCP in 1916, and was elected FRCP in 1924.

After qualification he spent two years as demonstrator and lecturer in physiology, and as assistant to the lecturer in cardiac research, James (later Sir James) Mackenzie, followed by appointments at the London Hospital as house physician and house surgeon. In 1914 he volunteered for the RAMC, but was seconded to become medical registrar at the London Hospital from 1914 to 1920, in which year he received the OBE. He became physician to Poplar Hospital for Accidents in 1919, medical tutor at the London in 1920, and assistant physician to the London Hospital in 1934. He was also at different times a member of council of the College, president of the section of medicine of the RSM, and an examiner for the conjoint board and the Universities of London and Liverpool. In 1950 he published *A study of psittacosis* jointly with Robert (later Sir Robert) Hutchison and SL Simpson.

In 1939 Rowlands, having never before shown nautical leanings, surprised even some of his closest friends by blossoming as a temporary surgeon rear-admiral RN (though he had in fact been civilian consultant to the Royal Navy since 1937). In this capacity he served mostly at RN Hospital Haslar till 1946, when he was awarded the KBE and made honorary LLD by the University of Wales. He then returned to civilian life and to the London Hospital, until he retired in 1951. Thereafter he continued for some years to live and practise in Harley Street.

Despite the fact that generations of students and junior staff made fun of 'Daddy' Rowlands' accent and mannerisms, he was a considerable figure in the London Hospital. He was a first class clinician, and at his own pace, which sometimes seemed painfully slow, he solved problems which had defeated his faster working colleagues. His thoroughness was proverbial, as was the seeming prolixity of his clinical notes all written in a fine round hand. It was a great tragedy to him that his voluminous notes of many years' work were destroyed by enemy action. As a teacher he was painstaking in the extreme, if hardly dynamic.

In the Royal Navy he was much appreciated for his evident clinical skill and for his fight to retain the keeping of naval health statistics. Throughout the war he combined his naval duties with those of president of the Anglesey Agricultural Society; it was no surprise, therefore, that in his years at Haslar and purely by his own physical efforts he kept the officers' mess supplied with fresh vegetables – delighting, it is said, in being mistaken for the regular gardener.

Rowlands was a man held in genial affection by patients, hospital and private, students and colleagues. Above all, he was a son of Wales who is said never to have missed his daily reading from the Welsh Bible given him by his mother.

In 1962 he sprang a second surprise. Apparently a confirmed bachelor till the age of 77, he announced his marriage to Lucienne Delva, widow of JP Delva and daughter of Albert Hauchamps, a solicitor. Though increasing deafness limited his social life in later years, he enjoyed the companionship of Lucienne till he died in the Westminster Hospital at the age of 91. RRB

[*Brit. med. J.*, 1977, **1**, 719, 981, 1165; *Times*, 2 Mar 1977; Photo]

RUBIE, Jack *b.*10 Nov 1914 *d.*2 May 1983
MRCS LRCP (1939) MB BS Lond (1939) MD (1948) MRCP (1948) FRCP (1971)

Jack Rubie was an undergraduate at King's College Hospital and qualified in 1939. He worked as a house physician at Paddington Hospital, London, and Queen Alexandra Hospital, Portsmouth, before joining the Royal Air Force Volunteer Reserve in December 1940. He served as a medical officer in the Royal Air Force until 1946.

After the war he started his career in paediatrics. He was a senior registrar at Highgate Hospital, working with the MRC streptomycin unit treating tuberculous meningitis with intrathecal streptomycin. He then worked as a senior casualty physician at Great Ormond Street, and first assistant to the paediatric department of St George's Hospital, before being appointed assistant to the Nuffield professor of child health at the Hospital for Sick Children, Great Ormond Street, and Queen Elizabeth Hospital, Hackney in 1953 – 1954.

In 1954 he was appointed consultant paediatrician to King Edward VII Hospital, Windsor, Upton Hospital, Slough, and Heatherwood Hospital, Ascot. With his energy, encyclopaedic knowledge and sensitivity he soon built up a busy, efficient department. He was involved in the design and development of Wexham Park Hospital, and insisted on excellent facilities for the mothers to live in with their children, and plenty of play facilities for the children. Very soon most of the children on the ward had their parents with them. His ward rounds were always informative and enjoyable, with his great sense of humour and fund of stories enlightening the procedure, but his alert mind never missed any detail. He had a phenomenal memory for written articles and could usually quote references with amazing accuracy.

Jack had a great interest in cerebral palsy and was appointed to the Spastic Society almost at its inception in 1955. He established a system whereby patients with cerebral palsy were assessed by a paediatrician, clinical psychologist and social worker with a view to the best possible placement, whether in a school, residential institution, sheltered workshop, etc., before the concept of assessment had been established. He travelled a great deal visiting spastic patients in their homes when they were unable to travel to assessment panels, and visiting schools throughout the British Isles and Channel Islands. He developed a tremendous feeling for their problems and always approached them with great commonsense.

He left behind an assessment panel system which was well established, and which was much appreciated by patients and by referring doctors.

Jack also travelled widely, lecturing on cerebral palsy in the Far East and America, as well as Europe. His lectures were always prepared with great care and good humour and were often provocative.

Jack's other main interest was the mentally retarded child. He was appointed consultant paediatrician to the Ravenswood Foundation and Village Settlement, and with his advice and energy he helped to develop this unit into one of the most outstanding residential centres for the mentally handicapped in this country. In his last five years Jack developed a relationship between Ravenswood and King's College Hospital, and was appointed honorary senior lecturer in King's College Medical School, and thus became involved in the teaching of mental handicap to the medical students.

After Jack retired from the health service in 1980 he continued his work with the Spastics Society, and at Ravenswood and King's College Hospital. He was also appointed a member of the commission to investigate the vaccine damaged children, and was appointed paediatric advisor to the Thalidamide Trust.

Jack's life was devoted to his work and family. He was very fond of both his parents and contacted his mother almost daily. His father, who died in his late 80s, had the same dynamic personality and showed a similar energy and love of work.

Jack and his wife Hilda (née Cadle), who were married in 1941, were a devoted couple. They supported and complemented each other throughout their married life and had one son, David, who became a solicitor.

ABD

[*Brit. med. J.*, 1983, **286**, 1907; Photo]

RUSSELL, Dorothy Stuart *b.*27 June 1895 *d.*19 Oct 1983
MB BS Lond (1923) MD (1930) MA Oxon (1942)
ScD Cantab (1943) MRCP (1943) FRCP (1948)
Hon LLD Glasg (1951) Hon DSc McGill (1959)

Born in Sydney and orphaned at the age of eight, Dorothy Russell was educated in England at the Perse School for Girls in Cambridge and at Girton College, from where she graduated in 1918 with a first in the Natural Sciences Tripos. The first world war determined her choice of medicine as a career, at a time when women were encouraged to join the profession. She entered the London Hospital Medical College in 1919, where she was attracted to pathology by the prestige and influence of Hubert M Turnbull, who then occupied the chair of morbid anatomy. She was awarded the Sutton prize in pathology and after obtaining her medical degree in 1923 was appointed assistant in the Bernhard Baron Institute of Pathology under Turnbull. She first devoted her main research efforts to a systematic study of renal disease, which was published in 1929 as a special report of the Medical

Research Council (*A Classification of Bright's Disease*). This work formed the basis of the thesis that she submitted for her MD degree in 1930 and for which she was awarded the University medal.

Her interest in neuropathology, a territory then almost uncharted in Britain, was encouraged by Hugh Cairns, who had recently returned to the London after training with Harvey Cushing at the Peter Bent Brigham in Boston. As a Rockefeller medical fellow, Dorothy Russell first went to work with Frank Mallory in Boston in 1928 and, the following year, joined Wilder Penfield at the Montreal Neurological Institute, where she rapidly gained masterly expertise in the use and knowledge of metallic techniques of the Spanish school and their application to the study of the central nervous system and its tumours.

She returned to the London in 1930 where she established a tradition of neuropathology which, as the result of her work and the respect that it commanded, was to gain increasing renown. In 1933 she was appointed to the scientific staff of the Medical Research Council at the London Hospital. In 1939 she decided to join Cairns, who had been appointed Nuffield professor of surgery in Oxford, and one year later succeeded Rio-Hortega as the neuropathologist at the Radcliffe Infirmary. She held that position until 1944, when she was invited by Turnbull to return to the London. In 1946, she succeeded Turnbull as professor of morbid anatomy and head of the Bernhard Baron Institute of Pathology. She was appointed emeritus professor in 1960, having over the preceding three decades made a series of outstanding original contributions that encompassed almost every facet of neuropathology.

Dorothy Russell was one of the pioneers in the application of tissue culture techniques to the study of cerebral tumours, and it is in the field of human neuro-oncology, in which she became the unquestioned leading world authority, that she left her deepest mark. She displayed uncanny diagnostic skills that were widely recognized and sought after, as evidenced by the innumerable cases that were sent to her for consultation ('no post is complete without its little cylinder', she was wont to say). Among her many contributions to the understanding of human cerebral tumours should be quoted her identification of the so-called 'pinealoma' as a form of teratomatous neoplasm unrelated to the structure of the pineal gland; her recognition of primary lymphomas of the central nervous system as a group that was distinct from malignant gliomas and which she termed microgliomatosis; her studies on the spread and metastases of gliomas in the cerebrospinal pathways, and the application of the wet film, or brain smear, technique for the rapid neurosurgical diagnosis of cerebral tumours. Her profound comprehension of the subject and her unparalleled experience culminated in the publication, in 1959, of her book on *Pathology of Tumours of the Nervous System* (on which she co-opted LJ Rubinstein as the junior author). That text was widely acclaimed and its successive editions have continued to record her vast experience in neoplasia of the central and peripheral nervous systems.

Neuro-oncology, however, was not the only field in which she made far reaching contributions. Her monograph entitled *Observations on the Pathology of Hydrocephalus*, published in 1949 and reprinted in 1967, is still regarded today as the definitive treatise on the subject. Other areas in descriptive neuropathology in which she was a pioneer include the pathology of radiation changes in the brain; neurotoxicology, in which she first threw light on the pathogenesis of cerebellar atrophy following organic mercury poisoning; the experimental production of cerebral abscesses and their response to chemotherapy and antibiotics; the pathology of subacute sclerosing panencephalitis; and the nosological relationship of acute haemorrhagic leucoencephalitis to disseminated encephalomyelitis. She thus played a major role in the foundation and growth of British neuropathology.

Numerous honours recognized her accomplishments. She was an honorary fellow of Girton College, of the Royal Microscopical Society and of the Royal Society of Medicine. She was president of the Association of Clinical Pathologists and an honorary member of the Pathological Society of Great Britain and Ireland. She was awarded honorary doctorates by the University of Glasgow and by McGill University, the John Hunter medal and triennial prize of the Royal College of Surgeons in 1934, and the Oliver-Sharpey prize of the Royal College of Physicians in 1968. She delivered the Bryce memorial lecture at Somerville College, Oxford, in 1961, the foundation lecture of the Association of Clinical Pathologists in 1961, the second Hugh Cairns memorial lecture at the London Hospital in 1962, and the Schorstein lecture at the London Hospital again in 1971. Her achievements contributed greatly to the advancement of the position of women in British medicine. She was the first woman to become head of a department of pathology in a London medical school, or indeed anywhere in the Western world, and she was the first woman member of the Medical Research Society.

She wielded a profound influence as a teacher. One of her main sources of pride was the fact that so many of those whom she had attracted to her department subsequently came to occupy chairs in pathology, neuropathology or medicine. These included CWM Adams (pathology), A Bignami (neuropathology), JB Cavanagh (neuropathology), PM Daniel (neuropathology), LJ Rubinstein (neuropathology), JP Shillingford (medicine), JC Sloper (pathology), JF Smith (pathology), H Urich (neuropathology), J Vallance-Owen (medicine), HK Weinbren (pathology) and ED Williams (pathology).

Dorothy Russell was a woman of stately dignity. Few knew her really well, and many were awe-struck by the ascendancy of her personality, in which a penetrating intellect, uncompromising honesty and gravity of demeanour were combined with a felicity and clarity of expression, both verbal and written, that were almost legendary. At the London, she was known as 'The Lady', a description that sums up the mixture of affection and respect which her towering formality and her distinction inspired. Her somewhat reserved and apparently lofty public persona concealed a sensitive and receptive nature, and in particular a warm sympathy for her junior colleagues, whom she not only protected and encouraged in their academic and research careers, but in whose personal problems she was genuinely, even touchingly, concerned. She was truly unselfish and, despite (or because of) the eminence she had achieved, even inclined to moments of self-doubt. Her complex personality and her qualities are faithfully reflected in the correspondence exchanged over a span of almost twenty-five years with the writer, who, in that period of time, was the privileged recipient of almost three hundred of her letters. These letters, free of erasures and written in a firm and exquisitely legible hand, not only mirror the qualities of conciseness and clarity that were so evident to those who first met her, but also spontaneously express the kindness, the generosity and the modesty that were revealed only to her closest friends. Her genuine humility is apparent from remarks such as these: 'I believe, of course, that we are right when we differ from others, but I am always terrified lest we should be hoodwinked by ourselves' (7 February 1962). 'I have always found it difficult to accept praise, and often wish I could enjoy it but my inner knowledge of shortcomings always casts its own particular shadow' (25 February 1962). 'Today I heard formally that I am now an honorary member of the Pathological Society and am very pleased about this, though I cannot think why they picked on me for this very considerable honour. I suppose most of us are painfully aware of our own limitations but if these are not too obvious to others it is perhaps of some comfort' (22 July 1963). On the other hand, her spirit and combativeness are exemplified in the following comment on a controversial issue: 'A certain amount of passion is demanded by a situation of this kind: a need to hit hard and leave no doubt of the stand taken. People have become too tepid in their polemics. You would have to go back to the last century, and further, for the real battles' (30 July 1963). As to the gift for the apt phrase, for the concluding comment that could sometimes be so devastating at scientific meetings, these letters abound in such touches. Referring to the long delay in the reprinting of one of her monographs by HM Stationery Office, 'stationary', she remarked dryly, 'would be more appropriate'. The technique of the light aside is practised in a masterly way. 'AB is to get the FRCP this month', she wrote in May, 'very suitably on Ascension Day'. Her reply on being told a few years ago that a tribute was being prepared in her honour in a neurosurgical journal is also worth recording: 'The obituary is somewhat premature, and although I may have one foot in the grave, the other one is lagging far behind'.

She was indeed fortunate, after her retirement in 1960, to enjoy many years of happiness in Westcott, near Dorking, maintaining a vigorous interest in her field, helping and counselling her colleagues and friends, while her scientific contributions continued to be authoritatively quoted throughout the world. In the surroundings of her simple but comfortable house, with its lofty view of the Surrey hills, she was able to satisfy her long interest in gardening and botany. Numerous friends visited her. She loved music and made a regular yearly pilgrimage to Glyndebourne. She long maintained a spirit of indomitable energy, which made her willing to undertake distant travels to Puerto Rico, Yucatan and Ethiopia in her late seventies. Her mind stayed active and its acuity unimpaired till almost the very end. She died at the age of 88, after a brief illness and a life filled with impressive achievements. With her passing, a truly extraordinary person went, leaving to us an imposing body of scientific work that continues to stand the test of time, a model to others in the setting of intellectual standards and of meticulous performance that few are able to match, and the memory of a scholar and teacher whose influence and example immeasurably enriched those who were fortunate to have known her. LJR

[*Surgical Neurology*, 1976, **5**, 267-268; *Times*, 20 Oct 1983; *Lancet*, 1983, **2**, 1039; *Brit. med. J.*, 1983, **287**, 1477-1478; Photo]

RUSSELL, William Ritchie *b.*7 Feb 1903 *d.*8 Dec 1980
CBE (1952) MB ChB Edin (1926) MD (1932) FRCPE (1933)
FRCP (1943) DSc Oxon (1955)

Ritchie Russell was born and bred in Edinburgh, son of William Russell, professor of medicine there. His mother was Beatrice, daughter of James Ritchie, a civil engineer. He was educated at Edinburgh Academy and University and qualified in 1926. He was house physician and house surgeon at the Royal Infirmary, Edinburgh, and in 1928 became resident medical officer at the National Hospital, Queen Square, London. In 1930 he returned to Edinburgh as clinical tutor and received a Medical Research Council grant at the same time. In 1934 he became assistant physician at Edinburgh Royal Infirmary. His work was particularly neurological and in 1938 he was made lecturer in that subject.

From 1940 to 1945 he was in the Royal Army Medical Corps, becoming officer in charge of the medical division of the Military Hospital for Head Injuries in Oxford, and consultant neurologist to Middle East Forces with the rank of brigadier. A pre-war interest in head injuries found ample scope during the war. His personal card index of patients in the Hospital for Head Injuries, described by a colleague at the time as Russell's Folly, formed the basis for many excellent papers by himself and colleagues then and in the post-war years. The detailed records, especially of penetrating gunshot wounds, permitted more accurate comparisons than ever before between the site of brain injury and functional defect. His work in the Hospital for Head Injuries brought him into close touch with Sir Hugh Cairns, the neurosurgeon who was responsible for the establishment of that hospital, and in 1945 Cairns arranged his appointment as consultant neurologist in Oxford.

In Oxford his office at first was a table and chair in a corridor, and other facilities in proportion, though he had the benefit of association with a thriving neurosurgical service run by Cairns and, later, Joe Pennybacker. He built his department up over the years to give a neurological service to the Oxford region, and to have a substantial influence beyond that. While continuing his work on head injuries he turned to a neurological problem, new to this country after the war, that of epidemic poliomyelitis. He tackled all aspects of treatment of the acute disease, and he got together a team who became efficient – rare in those days – at long term artificial respiration, and were pioneers in introducing intermittent positive pressure respiration to this country, after its emergency use in Denmark in 1952. Other problems studied included pain, especially in phantom limbs, multiple sclerosis, and the management of those with chronic neurological disability. In 1966 he became the first professor of clinical neurology in Oxford, and he retired in 1970. His chair enabled him to meet what was something of a family challenge, for his father had been professor of medicine in Edinburgh and his brother, Scott Russell, professor of obstetrics and gynaecology in Sheffield. From 1948 to 1969 he was editor, to its great benefit, of the *Journal of Neurology, Neurosurgery and Psychiatry*. His books included *Poliomyelitis*, *Brain Memory and Learning* and (jointly) *Traumatic Aphasia*.

Clinical research was his great interest. He knew that this depended on a clinical department which gave good service, and he gave the necessary time to administration to create it. In committee his advocacy might seem disastrous, but in the corridors of power he could make the strength of his case so clear that he often got his way against strong competition. To graduates his teaching and discussion were stimulating, though undergraduates could find that he talked of problems of current interest rather than the established facts which they had to learn.

After retirement his interest in neurology continued. He also played an important part in the building of a block of flats expressly designed for the elderly. It was called Ritchie Court after him, and he lived there when not in his house in the south of France. He became a keen member of Exit, the euthanasia society, the advocacy of which he applied to his own end.

In 1932 he married Jean Stuart Low and they had one son, who became a doctor, and one daughter. JMKS

[*Brit. med. J.*, 1981, **282**, 78; *Lancet*, 1980, **2**, 1385, & 1981, **1**, 57, 228; *Lancet*, 1970, **2**, 141; *Times*, 11 Dec 1980; *Glasgow Herald*, 28 Mar 1966; *Oxford Mail*, 5 June 1952; Photo]

SACHS, *Major-General* **Albert** *b.*18 May 1904 *d.*23 Jan 1976
CB (1955) CBE (1952) BA Dubl (1926) MB ChB BAO (1926)
MSc (1935) MRCP (1953) FRCP (1964) FRCPath (1964)

Albert Sachs was born in Pretoria, South Africa. His father was John Sachs JP, a chemist, and his mother Dorothy was the daughter of Samuel Kantor, a business director.

He was educated at Pretoria High School and Trinity College, Dublin, where he graduated in medicine in 1926. He joined the Royal Army Medical Corps in 1927, and the following year was posted to India, where he continued to serve, with brief interludes in the United Kingdom, until 1941. During this time he served as pathologist to military hospitals at Bannu (1928), Jubbulpore (1929–1930), Nasirabad (1930), Bareilly (1931), Peshawar (1932–1934) and Quetta (1936–1941), being promoted captain in 1930 and major in 1937.

From the outset, Sachs eagerly grasped the numerous opportunities that tropical service provided. He investigated an outbreak of meningitis among Indian recruits at Nasirabad in Rajputana, and reported his findings to the War Office. He collaborated with Major (later Major-General) LT Poole in a study of the aetiology of sandfly fever. He saw active service on the North West Frontier in the Mohmand operations in 1933, and was awarded the medal and clasp. Returning to the UK in 1934 he published observations on relapsing fever and passed the specialist course in pathology at the Royal Army Medical College with distinction. Back in India as deputy assistant director of pathology at Quetta, Sachs energetically followed up the work pioneered by Large on the antigenic structure of the non-mannite fermenting dysentery organisms, with which their names are now associated.

After the outbreak of the second world war, Sachs served in India and the UK until appointed assistant director of pathology to the 10th Army in 1942, when he proceeded to the Middle East, serving in Africa, Italy and Iraq. He studied typhus fever which was then endemic in Iran, and later published observations on some three thousand cases. He was appointed assistant director of pathology, Central Mediterranean Force, in the rank of colonel, in 1945.

After serving again in India during partition, Sachs returned to the UK and, after a brief spell as reader, was appointed professor of pathology at the Royal Army Medical College in 1949. At that time this was a conjoint appointment with that of consultant pathologist to the Army and director of Army pathology. He was promoted brigadier and his responsibilities, besides those of clinical pathology and transfusion, embraced the medical aspects of atomic, bacteriological and chemical warfare, then in their infancy, and immunology, to which he made substantial contributions. He directed the field trial to assess the relative merits of phenolized and alcoholized TAB vaccines and, in collaboration with Mollie Bar, investigated methods for the prevention of tetanus in the wounded, as a result of which Army policy was revised.

In 1953 Sachs was promoted major-general and appointed deputy director of medical services, Eastern Command. He retired from the Army after three years in this appointment in 1956, and was appointed consultant pathologist to the Queen Victoria Hospital, East Grinstead, Sussex.

Having been away from the bench for some years, the numerous practical problems now confronting him as a single handed clinical pathologist made considerable demands, which he met with all his characteristic energy. He took a leading role in the development of the new burns unit and pioneered the production of a *Pseudomonas pyocyanea* vaccine for the prophylaxis of infection. He published several papers on the pathological aspects of tissue transplants and on the immunoprophylaxis of infection in burns. His colleagues at East

Grinstead soon realized, as one wrote, that they 'had acquired a man of rare character with immense charm and wide experience ... who radiated good cheer which illuminated the lives of all who worked with him'.

Known to three generations with affection as 'Bertie', Sachs was devoted to the Corps with which he maintained the closest contact all his life. He was honorary colonel 44 (Home Counties) Infantry Division RAMC (TA) (1956–1961) and colonel commandant RAMC (1964–1969). He was also much in demand as a speaker on its history and outstanding personalities, of which he was one of the most colourful. He had many interests: he was a Freeman of the City of London, a patternmaker and a fine swimmer, while tennis, gardening and philately were other favourite preoccupations.

He married Olga, daughter of Winter John Le Chasseur, a business director of Jersey, on 18 December 1930, at Jubbulpore. She was awarded the Kaisir I Hind medal in 1948 for services to the WVS in India. They had no children. MHPS

[*Brit. med. J.,* 1976, **1**, 404; *Lancet,* 1976, **1**, 374; Photo]

SAKULA, Jack *b.*26 Feb 1908 *d.*31 Jan 1982
MRCS LRCP (1930) MB BS Lond (1932) MD (1936) MRCP (1936) DCH (1937) FRCP (1968)

Jack Sakula was consultant paediatrician at the Central Middlesex Hospital. He was born in London and won an entrance scholarship to the Middlesex Hospital Medical School in 1926, qualifying with the conjoint diploma in 1930, followed by the MB BS in 1932. After several junior appointments at the Middlesex, including house physician to Evan Bedford and Harold Boldero, he held a junior residency at Acton Hospital.

In 1933, Jack was appointed as a medical officer at the Park Royal Hospital, which was later to become the 'Central Middlesex'. When he joined the Park Royal, the old infirmary was being updated, and he was fortunate to join a team of remarkable men, of the calibre of Illtyd James and Norman Matheson; and later, when Horace Joules and Avery Jones arrived, the scene was set for the creation of a superb modern hospital, which was to become internationally famous.

His duties at first were general, but he soon decided to specialize and he took charge of medical cases in the children's ward. It was here that he was to perform his great work for sick children for the next forty years, building up a paediatric department of international stature. In the early, pre-antibiotic days, he battled with innumerable cases of gastroenteritis and bronchopneumonia. Jack was also responsible for a further 200 children in the children's homes and another 50 in the babies' block. All this he initially coped with virtually alone, without the assistance of one house physician. He was also clinical assistant at the Children's Hospital, Vincent Square.

In 1940, Jack was promoted to consultant paediatrician at the Central Middlesex, and also at Neasden Hospital, Acton Hospital,

Willesden General Hospital and Haperbury Hospital for the mentally retarded. He developed a close liaison with the local authority children's clinics, so that he was virtually supervising all the paediatrics in the group. In 1955, he produced a six page illustrated booklet for parents of children admitted to hospital, which proved such a success that it was copied around the world.

In 1937, the new maternity department at the Central Middlesex opened, averaging 2000 births per annum. Jack became the first physician to take charge of all newborn infants, and was recognized by the Central Midwives Board as a lecturer on the care of the newborn. In 1951, he planned, and had built, the special nursery for intensive care of premature babies which was named 'The Jack Sakula Unit'.

At the end of the second world war, Jack was a major in the RAMC, serving as medical specialist in a Northern Ireland military hospital, but in the earlier days of the war, Middlesex Hospital undergraduates began to receive part of their clinical training at the Central Middlesex. Jack's teaching rounds and lectures in paediatrics were extremely popular, and he was later recognized by the University of London as a teacher of paediatrics at the Middlesex Hospital. Moreover, his postgraduate teaching attracted large numbers of students from home and abroad. His advice on paediatric problems was widely sought. He served on the council of the section of paediatrics, Royal Society of Medicine, and on the paediatrics committee of the Royal College of Physicians, and became chairman of the board of examiners for the DCH. He was a senior member of the British Paediatrics Association, and for five years was chairman of the North West Metropolitan Regional Paediatrics Society.

Meanwhile, his academic work flourished. Important papers were published on infantile pleural effusions, on meningitis (research in which he engaged with the late Lady Florey) and on coeliac disease — the last mentioned with Margot Shiner in 1957, when they reported the first intestinal biopsy in that condition. The Middlesex County Medical Society had been formed in 1934, and Jack was its first secretary as well as secretary of its research committee for many years.

Jack was a natural bon viveur, fond of good food and wine, a connoisseur of the arts, keen on travel, and he enjoyed his golf and growing choice vegetables on his allotment, but probably his chief pastime was his painting. He had a very special talent in oils and he often exhibited at the Society of Medical Artists. He was also a keen Freemason and was past master of St Martin's Lodge and Grosvenor Mark Lodge. Following his retirement in 1973, these pleasures were unfortunately cut short when he developed his final prolonged illness, which he bore with courage. He was survived by his wife, Denise, whom he married in 1941. AS

[*Brit. med. J.,* 1982, **284**, 673; *Lancet,* 1982, **1**, 406; Photo]

SANDERS, Elias *b.*28 May 1916 *d.* – June 1979
MB ChB SAfr (1939) DCH Eng (1947) MRCP (1948) FRCP (1973)

Elias Sanders, better known as Alec, was the first paediatrician in Zimbabwe. He gained a fine reputation in his field of medicine. It needed courage to set up his specialist practice amongst a relatively small and limited population upon whom to depend for a livelihood. But his judgement was correct, and his success encouraged others to follow him. The Government appointed its first paediatrician a few years after Sanders had started, by which time the value of his specialty to the public was recognized and he was appointed honorary consulting paediatrician to the Salisbury Group of Hospitals. A few years later, the Government appointed a full time paediatrician to Harare African Hospital. With the establishment of the Medical School in Salisbury, Sanders was appointed part-time lecturer in paediatrics and an examiner in the final MB ChB for five years.

He recorded several interesting observations, and was one of the 'first' to show that the early phase of bilharziasis (the Katayama syndrome) might be serious, with possible cerebral and cardiac effects.

Sanders took a most active interest in medical association affairs in what was formerly Rhodesia. In 1956 he was elected to the Mashonaland branch of the BMA and served as president of its council in 1963 and 1964. When Rhodesia declared itself independent in 1968, he continued as chairman of the reconstructed Rhodesian Medical Association. He also served on the medical advisory board to the Ministry of Health.

Alec Sanders married Joy Black, and they had three children, a son who also became a paediatrician, and two daughters. MG

[*Brit. med. J.*, 1979, **1**, 1573]

SCOTT, Peter Duncan *b.*13 June 1914 *d.*6 Aug 1977
CBE (1974) MRCS LRCP (1939) MB BChir Cantab (1939)
DPM (1944) MD (1947) MRCP (1965) FRCP (1971)
FRCPsych (1971)

Peter Scott was the second son of Walter and Jennie Scott. His father was the owner of Ansell's brewery near Hereford, and his older brother John subsequently managed the business. Peter was born in Birmingham, educated at St Cuthbert's preparatory school in Malvern, at Bromsgrove School and at St Catharine's College, Cambridge, taking his clinical training at the London Hospital.

At the outbreak of war in 1939 he joined the Navy and served in destroyers. He had originally intended to become a surgeon, but on becoming shore based, it is said as the result of unmanageable seasickness, he joined the naval psychiatric service, where his great talents emerged. After the war he became registrar at the Maudsley Hospital, and after a period at Runwell Hospital, joined the staff of the Maudsley, where he stayed until his death after a short illness at the age of 63.

For some fifteen years he was psychiatrist to the London remand home for boys, and treated young delinquents in the children's department. During this time he wrote hundreds of reports to court, and developed his pithy, penetrating style of description and his reluctance to use technical terms. When dealing with adult offenders exclusively in later life, he always saw the child and adolescent which the adult had once been, and developed his outstanding talent for analysing the forces which led to personality development and were accessible to treatment.

He was first and last a clinician, tirelessly devoted to the needs of the individual patient. Although he read widely and was always interested in theories and classifications, he never allied himself with any particular school. This no doubt explained his great pleasure and skill in teaching from the individual case, in which the unique and the general could be discussed and analysed. His clinics were always very popular and the students fully involved.

His own diagnostic categories, painfully evolved from his experience of the young, and applied to homosexual offenders, murderers, shoplifters and the like, were highly original, realistic, and expressed in non-technical language. He wrote relatively little but his publications were models of compression, originality, and penetrating observation, and were very influential.

Scott did nothing to promote his own reputation, which built up in ever widening circles of colleagues, administrators, and judges. His advice was sought on many commissions and government working parties – the Ingleby committee on the law relating to young offenders, on the special hospitals, on the organization of the prison medical service, the advisory council on the penal system, the Aarvold subcommittee on dangerous offenders, and many others. On such occasions he offered his advice frankly, in a quiet and unassuming manner, and left it to others to accept or reject it. He never campaigned publicly or privately to get his views accepted more widely. He was, for example, passionately convinced that the National Health Service should take over the work of the prison medical service. When this was rejected by the Government and a compromise plan evolved to set up 'joint appointments' to the health service and to the prison service, he accepted the first of these between the Maudsley Hospital and Brixton prison, and did his loyal best to make it work satisfactorily, though it ultimately failed.

His advice was sought in many controversial situations, of which the best known was his advice on the conduct of the Spaghetti House and Balcombe Street hostage-taking sieges. His advice to temporize and restrain those who believed in an immediate use of force was successful, and earned the gratitude of the Commissioner. The technique of managing such incidents, here and abroad, owes much to his influence.

Personally, he was quiet and reserved and permitted few to become intimate. He was devoted to his wife, Lilian, and two daughters. He was deeply interested and expert in bird-watching, in carpentry, brick-laying and other 'do-it-yourself' activities. Beneath his modest manner he had great decisiveness and self-confidence. He listened carefully to the views of social workers and psychologists, but rarely needed advice, and once he had made up his mind about an offender or a policy kept to it with great determination. Apart from his evident compassion for offenders and endless work on their behalf, his most endearing quality was loyalty. He never criticized a colleague, and without ever being fulsome or insincere would say nothing unless it was a favourable comment. As one of the editors of the *British Journal of Criminology* he tended in the same way to point out the virtues of papers submitted, even when they were inadequate for publication. He was equally loyal to society in believing firmly that compassion did not mean sentimentality, and that the psychiatrist's role was to help the offender to come to terms with society as it is, and not as it should be.

He will be remembered chiefly as a brilliant teacher who left his mark on a whole generation of post-war consultants. At the time of his premature death, from an extremely rapidly growing glioma, he was acknowledged as the foremost forensic psychiatrist of his time.

TCNG

[*Brit. med. J.*, 1977, **2**, 646, 777; *Lancet*, 1977, **2**, 415; *Times*, 12 Aug 1977]

SCOTT, *Sir* **Ronald Bodley** *b.*10 Sept 1906 *d.*12 May 1982
GCVO (1973) KCVO (1964) BA Oxon (1928) BM BCh (1931)
DM (1937) MRCP (1933) FRCP (1943)

Ronald Bodley Scott was born into a medical family. His father, Maitland Bodley Scott OBE FRCSE, was a distinguished general practitioner in Bournemouth. His mother was Alice Hilda Durance George. He was the only son to enter medicine and was educated at Marlborough College and Brasenose College, Oxford, where he obtained a BA in Natural Sciences in 1928. He entered St Bartholomew's Hospital Medical College, and came under the influence of such men as Walter Langdon-Brown, Thomas Horder and Francis Fraser, teachers who dominated the scene and provided the intellectual stimulus. Bodley later ackowledged how much they had influenced him. Shortly after qualification in 1931 he returned to Bournemouth to join the family practice. He had evidently made such an impression as a student and house physician that he was invited to return to St Bartholomew's Hospital, first as chief assistant to Dr Gow, and then as first assistant on the medical professorial unit. He obtained the diploma of membership of the Royal College of Physicians in 1933. It is evident from his published papers (now held in the Contemporary Medical Centre at the Wellcome Institute) that his interests in haematology began about that time, with papers on the reticuloses and haemorrhagic states. He learned the newly developed technique of bone marrow aspiration; an account of its use formed the basis of his thesis for a doctorate of medicine at Oxford University in 1937. His interests naturally led him to haematological malignancy, and in collaboration with AHT Robb Smith he described the clinical entity of histiocytic medullary reticulosis in the *Lancet* in 1939.

Within a short time of obtaining his first consultant appointment at the Woolwich Hospital the second world war started. He joined the very distinguished group of medical men who were brought together in the Royal Army Medical Corps in the Middle East, a theatre of war which was to assume great importance and where he remained for four years, gaining promotion to lieutenant colonel in charge of medicine in the 63rd and 43rd General Hospitals. Busy as he was with wartime duties, he found time to lecture for the British Council and to examine in medicine at the Fouad el Awal University of Cairo. He was elected a fellow of the Royal College of Physicians in 1943.

In 1946 he was elected physician to St Bartholomew's Hospital, where his clinical skills were soon appreciated and his ability in the field of leukaemia and lymphoma recognized internationally. His penetrating intelligence, great clinical skill and inordinate capacity for hard work rapidly made him pre-eminent among the physicians of his generation. His appreciation of the value of pathology and clinical science made him sympathetic to the efforts then being made to bring laboratory and clinical medicine together. Those who worked for him remember how generous and forthright he was with his support for research.

In 1949 he was appointed physician to the Household of King George VI. In 1952 he became physician to Queen Elizabeth II, receiving a KCVO in 1964, and had the singular honour of being advanced to GCVO some nine years later. He held many appointments including consultant physician to British Railways from 1957, honorary consultant in haematology to the Army from 1957, consultant physician to the Florence Nightingale Hospital in 1958, consultant physician to the King Edward VII Hospital for Officers in 1963, honorary consultant to the Ministry of Defence in 1965. The number of these appointments gives a measure of his capacity for hard work and the value placed on his judgement.

He was a dutiful undergraduate teacher, but excelled in a postgraduate setting. His lectures on haematology and chemotherapy, the Lettsomian lectures to the Medical Society of London in 1957, the Langdon-Brown lecture in 1957, the Croonian lecture of 1970 and the Harveian oration of 1976 will long serve as well-researched sources on these subjects. He was interested in literature, contributing an article to the *Lancet* on 'The doctor in contemporary literature' – an amusing look at doctors in the detective novels he enjoyed. He also wrote a little on the history of medicine, contributing a perceptive history of medicine at his own hospital in the first part of the twentieth century to the anniversary commemoration volume produced in 1973.

At the Royal College of Physicians he was successively councillor (1963 – 1966), censor (1970) and vice-president (1972). He was president of the Medical Society of London (1965 – 1966), president of the British Society of Haematology (1966 – 1967), and the section of medicine of the Royal Society of Medicine (1967 – 1968). he was master of the Apothecaries (1974), and served as a member of the council of the Imperial Cancer Research Fund (1968) and the British

Heart Foundation (1975), eventually becoming chairman of the latter. A chair in cardiology tenable at St Bartholomew's Hospital has been named after him.

His extensive knowledge of medicine and his felicitous use of English were undoubtedly the basis for the success of his edition of Price's *Textbook of Medicine* and the *Medical Annuals*. His last book, *Cancer: the facts*, was published in 1979.

He was a complex man: an eminently successful physician in the most conservative of professions, he had a deep understanding of clinical science and the need for innovation and experiment. Apparently reserved, almost shy, he had a considerable interest in his fellow men, and an acute appreciation of their foibles. He had an astringent wit that could be used with devastating effect if he detected humbug, deceit or injustice. A rich vein of kindness and humility ran through his character, inspiring love and loyalty in all those who worked for him. Those who were privileged to enjoy his friendship counted themselves most fortunate.

Bodley was married in 1931 to Edith Daphne, daughter of Lieutenant Colonel E McCarthy RMA. They had two daughters. Daphne died in 1977. In 1980 he married Mrs Jessie Gaston, the widow of Dr Alex Gaston of Sevenoaks. JSM(1)

[*Brit. med. J.*, 1982, **284**, 1567, 1779; *Lancet*, 1982, **1**, 1195; *Times*, 13 May 1982; Photo]

SELWYN-CLARKE, *Sir* **Selwyn** *b.*17 Dec 1893 *d.*12 Mar 1976
KBE (1951) CMG (1945) MC (1918) MRCS LRCP (1916)
BS Lond (1919) MD (1921) DPH Cantab (1921) DTM&H (1923)
MRCP (1926) FRCP (1937)

Selwyn Selwyn-Clarke, formerly Governor of the Seychelles (1947–1951), was educated at Bedales and St Bartholomew's Hospital, London University, and after a brief spell as RMO and assistant anaesthetist at Bart's joined the RAMC as medical officer in charge to 285 Brigade RFA, and later to HM Queen Victoria Rifles. He was promoted to captain in 1918 and received the MC. On demobilization he began what was to be a long and distinguished career in the colonial medical service, and the year 1919 found him on the Gold Coast. He was called to the Bar by Gray's Inn in 1929.

His services in East Africa were interrupted by a period in Malaya at the height of the depression. He advised his seniors on health services despite the prevailing financial gloom. Returning to the Gold Coast he became ADMS in 1932, deputy director of health services, Gold Coast, in 1933, and the Gold Coast delegate to the Pan-African Health Conference in Johannesburg in 1935. He was appointed director of medical services, Colonial Medical Services, in 1937, and was elected a fellow of the College. That same year he became civil DMS, Hong Kong.

In 1935 he married Hilda Alice, daughter of Harry Browning of Horsham, Sussex, and they had one daughter. His wife, known as

'Red Hilda', was an ardent left-winger with political ambitions, and she played an important part in his history. Throughout his service Selwyn-Clarke never hesitated to go over the heads of his superiors and at times tried their patience sorely.

Selwyn-Clarke had been director of medical services (civil) in Hong Kong for nearly four years before war began in the Far East in 1941. He moulded the existing services to his design, and provided emergency services for thousands of mainland Chinese who fled into the colony illegally before the Japanese invaders. His wife and child did not accompany the families of the armed and government services when they were evacuated to Australia; Selwyn-Clarke, with the support of his wife, considered that if citizens of Chinese or mixed races were not to be moved from an area in which hostilities seemed imminent, his own family should remain and share whatever fate lay in store. He was courteous in his dealings, he was more often than not right in his judgements, he did not drink or smoke, and he and his dynamic wife found little of interest in much of the social life of Hong Kong at that time. These characteristics earned him respect from many and a degree of envious criticism from others, which left him unmoved.

When Hong Kong was surrendered to the Japanese in December 1941 Selwyn-Clarke, with his wife and child, and with a small staff from his medical department, was not at first interned. He was allowed a very restricted degree of liberty to try to restore the health services shattered during the fighting. He used part of this time to acquire small quantities of special food and drugs which he foresaw would be essential for the treatment of the deficiency diseases which would soon appear in the colony. These stores were carried laboriously, but openly, to their destinations by bands of women organized by his wife. All allied wounded were concentrated in the British Military Hospital and it also received sick from the prisoner of war camps. Advice on the prevention and treatment of the deficiencies was conveyed secretly to the doctors in the hospital, and this service helped morale at a time when the outlook was grim. Supplies were also sent to prisoner of war and internment camps, and the system, which began before stocks from the International Red Cross became available, continued after his arrest until the end of the war.

During this period of restricted freedom he had passed, he thought secretly, two messages to the neighbouring Portuguese colony of Macao. In one he tried to hasten the arrival of Red Cross help for Hong Kong; in the other his aim was to warn the American Command in the Pacific that large numbers of allied prisoners, mostly British, were about to be shipped to Japan. The latter message failed in its purpose, for the *Lisbon Maru* was torpedoed in October 1942 by an American submarine with very heavy loss of life.

In May 1943 he was arrested by the Japanese gendarmerie, the *Kempeitai* of evil repute. Among the many charges brought against him was one of communicating Japanese naval and troop movements to the British Embassy in Lisbon. He denied all. For the next ten months he was kept in solitary confinement in a tiny cell with no window and only a faint glimmer of indirect lighting. He was clad only in unwashed shirt and trousers, with the floor for his bed and a latrine bucket and a mug of water for furnishing. He was interrogated almost constantly, beaten frequently, suspended by the wrists, and given the water treatment in an attempt to get him to incriminate himself and others. He was in sight and hearing of fellow prisoners beaten senseless by their questioners. After a short time he underwent what passed for a trial and was condemned to death, but even then questioning, beatings and similar persuasive measures continued. At one time he reached the stage when he told his captors, not begged or even asked them it should be noted, to get on and carry out the sentence. He would not give way, but ten months after his arrest he was transferred to another prison, still in solitary confinement but in a slightly bigger cell, with a small window which gave a glimpse of the sky. Towards the end of 1944 he was tried again; there may have been local influences at work, for the death sentence was replaced by a three year prison sentence. After just under two years in prison he was released to join his wife and child in a small internment camp. He carried a severe physical disability until his death, but when the Japanese surrendered in August 1945 he could not be dissuaded from working to set up the medical department again, his first thought being, as always, for the benefit of the remaining citizens of Hong Kong. A British fellow prisoner saw him at that time as a gaunt, bent and disabled man, whose mental powers and resolution remained undimmed. He did not go on leave for another two months and later he returned to Hong Kong, again as director of medical services, before he took up his appointment as Governor and Commander in Chief, Seychelles, in July 1947.

Selwyn-Clarke was brought up in a Christian household, but in adult life he was not a religious man. He drew for support only on his own concept of what is good and what is not. He was an extremely stubborn man and would never compromise on any matter of principle. He could be hard on people who had strayed from the path along which he considered duty lay, but after the Japanese surrender he never blamed any of his staff who had broken under pressure. He, better than anyone else, knew what they had had to endure. He refused to give evidence against Japanese accused of war crimes 'because the victors could not properly be judges in their own cause', and he helped certain Japanese who had shown him small kindnesses, in secret, in prison. He dedicated his memoirs, *Footprints*, to a Japanese interpreter, a Christian minister of religion in civil life in Japan, who had risked his own life to help many in Hong Kong who were victims of the war, even though they were officially enemies of his own country. He was also the author of numerous books, reports and articles, ranging from practical medicine, through travel, to sociological subjects.

At the end of his long service overseas, Selwyn was still an alert and able man with a drive towards public service. Although over the normal age limit for recruitment, he sought and obtained a principal medical officer post at the Ministry of Health. He was a firm believer in the NHS and anxious to help it in any way he could, even though the new post meant a different outlook from the authoritarian direction of colonial services with which he was familiar. For five years he applied his great energy to the problems of medical manpower in the hospitals, and to liaison work in the regions. Although he made new friends, the work was not congenial and at 60 he turned to work for the Society of Medical Officers of Health, where he hoped to further the development of community medicine in which he so strongly believed.

Selwyn made no major contribution to knowledge or to thinking, but he was – and remained – a good physician. He was a meticulous and tireless administrator; he was also single-minded, and favoured his own ideas and plans. He argued in their support politely, but strongly and persistently, and often sought to proceed further and faster along his own lines than others thought wise. As might be expected, he ruffled the feelings of many people in the process. He was a very brave man; few could have approached the level of courage with which he endured imprisonment. He was also an obstinate man; it must have given him satisfaction to reflect that, in the end, his will did not give way. DCB/GEG/GW

[*Brit. med. J.*, 1976, **1**, 775, 968; *Times*, 15 & 19 Mar 1976; Photo]

SHAH, Mazhar Hussain *b.*3 June 1902 *d.*21 Feb 1979
MB Punj (1926) MRCS LRCP (1930) MRCP (1932) DPM (1938) FCPS Pak (1964) FPAS (1973)

Mazhar Shah was the son of Mahbub Shah, a civil servant of the Government of India. Born in Gujrat in the Punjab, he graduated in medicine in 1926 at Lahore from the King Edward Medical College, winning a gold and silver medal for being first in medicine. The usual house posts followed at the Mayo Hospital in Lahore, and in 1930 he passed the conjoint diploma.

In 1931, he was commissioned in the Indian Medical Service, and in 1932 he was admitted an MRCP. He transferred to the civil side of the Indian Medical Service and soon became interested in psychiatry. He returned to England and passed the DPM. He was later physician in charge of the Irwin Hospital, Delhi, and civil surgeon for Delhi, and also lecturer in medicine at the Lady Reading Medical College. During the second world war, he served as consultant in medicine at various hospitals in SE Asia Command.

With the partitioning of India in 1947, Shah moved to Karachi and founded the Jinnah Central Hospital (today the postgraduate medical centre of Pakistan). He was also civil surgeon and the chief medical officer of Karachi. In addition, he was honorary professor of medicine at the Dow Medical College, Karachi.

In 1951, he was awarded a Fulbright fellowship and spent a sabbatical year studying cardiology at the Massachusetts General Hospital in Boston. On his return to Pakistan, he founded the 'Heart Clinic'. He was also personal physician to the governor general of

Pakistan from 1949 to 1957.

Shah finally retired in 1957, but his insatiable interests led him to found the Naveed Clinic for group practice. He was also the first president of the Pakistan Cardiac Society, and the first president of the Pakistan Academy of Medicine.

He wrote on various aspects of medicine, but his main interest was in Avicenna, and his desire was to integrate ancient systems of medicine with modern theory and practice. He was tireless in his pursuit of medical advances, always concerned with the mind and the mental state in systemic disease, and he brought a humanity both to students and patients which was unequalled.

In 1934, he married Suraiya, daughter of Mian Afzal Husain. They had two sons, the elder of whom became a surgeon. RBK

[*Brit. med. J.*, 1979, **1**, 1349; Photo]

SHANKS, Seymour Cochrane *b.*9 Apr 1893 *d.*14 May 1980
CBE (1958) MB ChB Glasg (1915) MD (1932) MRCP (1938)
FFR (1939) FRCP (1942)

Cochrane Shanks was born in Barrhead, Renfrewshire, the son of William Shanks and Catherine (née Cook McCallum). He was educated at the Glasgow Academy, and qualified from the University of Glasgow, where he subsequently obtained his MD degree. He was barely qualified as a doctor when he joined the RAMC and served in Egypt and France in the first world war.

It was fortunate for the medical discipline of radiology that he decided on that branch of medicine as a career. He became radiologist at the Prince of Wales General Hospital in 1920, and an assistant radiologist at Charing Cross Hospital in 1923. He was appointed to be director of the X-ray department at University College Hospital in 1939, and he retired from this post in 1958.

Shanks was a man of considerable intellectual capacity which, allied to his Scottish characteristics of hard work, tenacity and shrewdness, ensured his success in his chosen vocation. Appreciating that there was no published textbook in his own subject and recalling his own lack of formal training in his specialty, he enlisted the help of two of his senior colleagues in the subject and in 1938 published the well known *Textbook of X-ray Diagnosis by British Authors*. This had an immediate and continued success.

In like manner he saw the need for an association of medically qualified radiologists to promote the science in its several aspects, particularly the clinical and educational. With others he formed the British Association of Radiologists, of which he became the first secretary, and saw this body blossom into the Faculty, now the Royal College of Radiologists. Over a period of 19 years he played a vital part in the formative phases of these organizations. As warden he ensured the status of the fellowship and he initiated the training programme for young radiologists; he was president of the faculty from 1940 to 1943.

University College Hospital benefited considerably from his wise guidance when he was both dean of its medical school and chairman of its medical committee. He was allotted the task of reconditioning the old St Pancras Hospital and was also energetic in reviving the then declining dental school.

It was not surprising that he was one of the five doctors chosen from the profession to serve on the important Spens committee, which determined the remuneration of consultants when the National Health Service was instituted. The BMA valued his medico-legal interest, made him chairman of its medico-legal committee, and in this capacity he served for 21 years; he was also one of the outstanding presidents of the Medical Defence Union.

He was senior vice-president of the 6th International Congress of Radiology in 1950 and greatly helped in securing the overwhelming success of this function. The Minister of Health used his skills to good advantage as consultant adviser for nearly twenty years, and some acknowledgement of his service to medicine was seen in the award in 1958 of the CBE.

In his commitment to patient care he was equally active. He organized and administered a very efficient X-ray department at University College Hospital, and published many scientific papers, mostly on gastro-intestinal diseases. He built up a highly successful private practice, where he continued his work until well over 80, and once said to a younger colleague who was retiring 'Don't give up practice, let it give you up'.

His leisure was pursued and enjoyed with the same intensity as his medical life; motoring was a pastime from the age of 16, he thoroughly enjoyed world wide travel, he played a sound game of golf, and delighted in tennis at Wimbledon and opera at Glyndebourne and Covent Garden. He lived his life to the full with the devoted support of his first wife Edith (née Govan), and from 1956 of her younger sister Chrisma; there were no children. RES

[*Brit. med. J.*, 1980, **280**, 1380; *Lancet,* 1980, **1**, 1151; *Times,* 17 May 1980; Photo]

SHARP, Alan Anderson *b.*19 Aug 1925 *d.*18 Oct 1983
BSc Edin (1946) MB ChB (1947) MD (1957) MA Oxon (1963)
MRCP (1969) FRCPath (1971) FRCP (1975)

Alan Sharp was born and brought up in Edinburgh. He was educated at George Watson's College and entered the medical school in Edinburgh at the age of sixteen, graduating BSc in 1946 and qualifying in medicine the next year. Like many Scotsmen, he spent all his professional life outside Scotland, but retained his accent and an abiding affection for his beautiful native city.

His interest in haematology was kindled while clerking in Stanley (later Sir) Davidson's wards at the Royal Infirmary in Edinburgh and he began his training in clinical pathology in Carlisle and Newcastle. In 1955 he moved to Oxford as lecturer in haematology and was immediately enveloped in the exciting environment created by Gwyn Macfarlane and Rosemary Biggs. He became deeply and enthusiastically involved in their work on coagulation and fibrinolysis, and in 1957 the University of Edinburgh awarded him a gold medal for his MD thesis on platelet physiology and antigenicity. Two years later he became consultant haematologist to the Radcliffe Infirmary and established for himself an international reputation as an authority on disorders of blood coagulation.

He was a founder member of the Royal College of Pathologists, was a member of council and elected vice-president in 1978. He had a special interest in the training of pathologists, not only in the committee-based planning of a curriculum, but he also set an example in his own laboratory, with his flair for exciting the enthusiasm of his colleagues and his ability to create the happy atmosphere in which cooperation between the laboratory and the bedside became indissoluble.

Alan Sharp was a big man who believed in living on a large scale. He liked to drive fast cars fast, he loved flying and he was an expert and fearless sailor. He combined a natural gift for leadership with a warmth of character which created a feeling of good fellowship, whether in the laboratory, the classroom or in a committee, and he liked to finish the day with a group of colleagues in a nearby hostelry, recounting the day's events with good humour and much wit. His accounts of some of his friends' actions were sometimes acerbic, but never hurtful and resolved before the day was out in an atmosphere of good humoured tolerance; at the beginning and at the end of the day everyone was his friend.

He was an excellent committee man because he always did his homework, was totally straightforward, and maintained a friendly informality which helped a hung committee to get off the hook and co-operate again in a positive fashion. He made a vital contribution to the planning and opening of the John Radcliffe Hospital in Oxford and such was his integrity that whenever difficult decisions about services or staff had to be made, his help was always sought.

Alan Sharp had a large circle of friends. He and his charming wife Joy were always the most generous of hosts in their home at Woodstock, where they had brought up their family of two sons and a daughter in that friendly and welcoming atmosphere that turned every acquaintance into a friend.

It was sad that he died after a long, distressing illness in the year in which he was president elect of the British Society for Haematology, to which he had contributed so much. RFM

[*Brit. med. J.*, 1983, **287**, 1557; *Lancet,* 1983, **2**, 1095; Photo]

SHAW, Maurice Elgie *b.*1 July 1894 *d.*30 Oct 1977
MA Oxon (1921) BM BCh (1921) MRCP (1923) FRCP (1934)

Maurice Shaw was born at the dean's residence at Guy's Hospital. His father, Lauriston Shaw FRCP, was physician to the hospital and dean of the medical school. His mother was born Mary Spalding, the daughter of Howard Spalding, director of Spalding and Hodge, stationers. John Spalding FRCP, consultant neurologist to the Oxford United Hospitals, was a cousin.

Maurice Shaw was educated at Bradfield College and at New College, Oxford, before 1914. His studies were interrupted by the war in which he served as a combatant in France and in the Dardanelles, attaining the rank of captain in the Gloucestershire Regiment. In 1917 he was demobilized through ill health and resumed his studies at Oxford, and later at Guy's. His MA dates from 1921 and in the same year he qualified BM BCh (Oxon). In 1923 he became a member of the Royal College of Physicians and in 1934 was elected to the fellowship. He was an examiner in medicine to the College and Oxford University.

After qualifying, he was house physician at Guy's and later medical registrar. With a Radcliffe travelling fellowship he studied abroad in the USA and in Paris. In 1927 he was appointed assistant physician to the West London Hospital and shortly afterwards joined the staff of East Ham Memorial and other small hospitals. He also became chief medical officer to the Canada Life Assurance company, succeeding his father. He worked in the emergency medical service from 1939 to 1945 at Upton Hospital, Slough, and at Maidenhead and Windsor Hospitals.

Maurice Shaw was a general physician, but gastroenterology was his main interest and he belonged to the British Society of Gastroenterology. He was highly esteemed as a teacher. His students learnt from him the importance of taking a careful history, and his evident concern for his patients as individuals set an example. One of his registrars recalls how his teaching rounds were often interrupted if a patient's unusual occupation or hobby fascinated him.

The West London Hospital had held a postgraduate college since the end of the last century. In 1937 this was closed and an undergraduate school for women begun, as there were so few places open to them in the old medical schools. Maurice Shaw was made dean of the new school, and this post, which he held until his retirement in 1959, gave him the opportunity of making his greatest contribution.

He was not only their teacher, but also the adviser and friend of his students, always available to them. Many who are now consultants owe him the chance of continuing their education after being rejected by some other medical school, after failing an early examination. Later, the West London school accepted numbers of students from the Commonwealth, particularly Nigeria and Malaysia. Maurice Shaw kept in touch with them after their return home, and they often called on him when visiting London.

For many years he was a faithful member of the West London Medico-Chirurgical Society, and he was at one time its president.

His main hobby was music, especially part-singing and the piano. He was a keen gardener and many of his colleagues recall the delightful summer evenings when he entertained old students at his lovely home, Morton House, in Chiswick Mall, where he lived from

1952 until his death in 1977.

In 1927 Shaw married Christine Beck, the daughter of Conrad Beck, managing director of R & J Beck, manufacturers of precision optical instruments. The Shaws had four children, two daughters and two sons, one of whom, Jonathan, became a fellow of the Royal College of Physicians and consultant neonatal paediatrician to University College Hospital. LPEL

[*Brit. med. J.*, 1977, **2**, 1360; *Lancet*, 1977, **2**, 1041]

SHELDON, *Sir* **Wilfrid (Percy Henry)** *b*.23 Nov 1901
d.9 Sept 1983
KCVO (1959) CVO (1954) MRCS LRCP (1923)
MB BS Lond (1924) MRCP (1925) FRCP (1933) MMSA (1972)
Hon FRCOG (1972)

Sir Wilfrid Sheldon was an outstanding personality in the history of paediatrics in this country. In many ways he represented a link between the beginnings of paediatrics as a branch of medicine and the modern era of paediatrics which really began in the late 1960s.

He succeeded, at King's College Hospital, Sir George Frederic Still, who was the first professor of child health in Britain. Still gave up his chair in 1916 when London University 'took over' the London medical schools. At that time Still was offered retention of his chair but as this involved relinquishing the right to private practice Still, who had no private income, was forced to abandon his professorship.

Sheldon, who had qualified at King's College Hospital in 1924, was appointed consultant at King's College Hospital in 1926. Even in those days, this was a very young age to be appointed consultant and a few years later Sir Wilfrid was appointed as consultant physician to the Hospital for Sick Children, Great Ormond Street.

Wilfrid Sheldon's early life was complicated by the death of his parents when he was quite a young boy and he was supported through school and his medical education by an elder brother (J Harold Sheldon FRCP) who, it is fair to say, was worshipped by the younger Wilfrid. He quickly showed himself to be an outstanding clinician and produced one of the first major textbooks of paediatrics entitled *Diseases of Children* which was based, in the early editions, very largely on his own wide clinical experience.

He became the outstanding young physician at the Hospital for Sick Children, Great Ormond Street, and on the retirement of Still he took over the directorship of the department of child health at King's.

Sheldon was a tall, slim, aristocratic looking figure. A pleasant face when smiling, he could look extremely stern when displeased. When in critical mood, his eyes had the appearance almost of being 'hooded' and gave him a 'hawk-like' appearance which disappeared as soon as his sense of humour, which could be ebullient, forced its way into the situation. He was a very handsome man and was a great socialite, having a fund of stories and a great ability as a conversationalist.

During the second world war, he was largely responsible for

organizing the care of sick children transferred from Great Ormond Street to the country branch at Tadworth.

His research interest in medicine was very largely devoted to coeliac disease, in which his powers of clinical observation were responsible for him being one of the first paediatricians to realize that coeliac disease was due to an intolerance of wheat products. His interest in coeliac diseae brought him international fame but he was also famed in his own country for his teaching ability to students in general, and by his ability to impart to his assistants the clinical acumen that he had collected over the years.

He became paediatrician to Her Majesty The Queen at a time when she first became a young mother and was very personally known to the Queen Mother, as well as to the Queen herself. He became a 'father figure' in British paediatrics and was a very popular president of the British Paediatric Association.

His two great hobbies were gardening and golf. In the first he was a great expert and created a wonderful garden around his home on Kingston Hill. At golf he was less of an expert but was a great humourist who enjoyed not only the game, but the companions with whom he played it.

Right to the end he retained his great critical faculties and his deep love of his family was accompanied by a very deep affection for his friends. He ultimately died due to secondary carcinoma in the liver from a primary in the colon. It was typical of him that he himself made the clinical diagnosis of both his primary carcinoma and the occurrence of the secondary deposits, many years later, in the liver. In the six weeks or so before his death he visited all his friends to say 'goodbye' to them and at that time he said that he felt that he had been blessed with a very happy life and happy family, and his only regret was that he was unable to look after his wife, Maithe, who herself was ill, and that his death would leave her without him. Above all, he will be remembered as a kind, gentle man, with an ability to be critical and forceful, a great teacher, and a man who loved his family and his friends.

CES

[*Brit. med. J.*, 1983, **287**, 918, 992, 1146; *Lancet*, 1983, **2**, 749; *Times*, 14 & 21 Sept 1983; Photo]

SHEPPARD, Philip Macdonald *b.*27 July 1921 *d.*17 Oct 1976
FRS (1970) Hon FRCP (1975)

Philip Sheppard died from acute leukaemia at the age of 55. In 1956 he came from Oxford to the University of Liverpool and was head of the department of genetics from 1959. He was particularly distinguished for contributions to ecological genetics, his central interest being how natural selection works and its effect on the genetic constitution of organisms. His genius lay in the experimental approach, whether it was with butterflies, moths, snails or man. He was elected FRS in 1970. He was awarded the Darwin medal of the Society in 1974 and in the same year received the gold medal of the Linnaean society. In 1975 he was elected an honorary fellow of the

Royal College of Physicians of London.

Philip was born at Marlborough, the only child of George Sheppard, the mathematics master at Bradfield College, and Alison, born Macdonald. His father had been a ward of the Harmsworths (Lady Harmsworth was Philip's godmother), and his mother was related to the Cornfords and consequently, by marriage, to the Darwins. However, Philip had no Darwin genes, and it is of interest that his Darwinian outlook was entirely the result of environmental factors – his upbringing, his teachers and his training; a phenocopy if ever there was one.

He went to school at Marlborough College, and is best remembered there for making the natural history society one of the best in the country. At the age of eighteen he joined the RAFVR and after training in the USA and Canada, he became a navigator and was on the first 1000 bomber raid on Cologne. He was taken prisoner of war on his sixteenth operational flight on 27 July, his twenty-first birthday. He was rescued by an enemy minesweeper; the Germans treated him well and Philip was taken on the bridge to be shown where they were. Being a navigator he realized that they were in the centre of the area where they had been dropping mines a few nights previously.

After the war he read honours zoology at Oxford and came under the influence of EB Ford, who introduced him to the science of ecological genetics. It was this discipline that was to be his great strength. He was an excellent naturalist and a genuine biologist as well as a geneticist, and this led to his interests becoming extremely wide. A colleague writes that his comments on cherished ideas were sometimes blunt to the point of pain, but they were always given with good humour and never tinged with malice. His friends said that he reversed the normal academic procedure; he stabbed you in the front, and did you favours by stealth.

I persuaded him to come to Liverpool in 1956 by the simple method of telling him that I did not think the post would suit him. It worked! and we had a very happy association for more than 20 years, working initially on the genetics of hybrid butterflies and then extending into a study of evolution of mimicry.

During the early days it seemed to me that we should begin applying Philip's knowledge to medicine. One day, motoring to the Norfolk Broads, I asked him his views. 'Blood groups' he said, and blood groups it was, for he had been well trained in the EB Ford school, and Ford himself in 1945 had suggested that factors such as disease might be responsible for the maintenance of the polymorphism in the ABO and other blood groups. We started with group O and duodenal ulcer and then, much more importantly, became interested in the Rhesus complex and so into the prevention of Rhesus haemolytic disease of the newborn. This led to the Liverpool team developing a safe and reliable method for the prophylaxis of Rhesus immunization, which has been standard practice by the NHS since 1968. Philip's expertise as a statistician and geneticist was of fundamental value in this very interesting piece of work. During these early years the Nuffield Foundation, impressed I think by the clinical enthusiasm of the

Liverpool physicians together with Philip's professional abilities, set up the Nuffield Unit of Medical Genetics, and Philip remained a key member of the unit from its inauguration (in 1963) until the time of his death.

It was said of Philip that he disliked committees, but if he gave his mind to a topic he could be of great value, and I had no hesitation in appointing him to the RCP fluoride committee to assess the value and safety of the fluoridation of water supplies in the prevention of dental caries. It was evident to both of us that the evidence was overwhelmingly in favour of the prophylaxis, yet at one stage we had some difficulty in obtaining complete unanimity among our members. Philip and I therefore one weekend wrote a 'mock up' for the committee, advocating fluoridation of milk rather than water. This had an immediate effect, the committee turned and rent us, the cuckoos being delighted at the opportunity of having a go at the president. Gradually Philip and I gave way and in the end we had an unanimous verdict for the water.

As PRCP I had the pleasure of admitting him to the fellowship and of pronouncing the formula 'I wish you all happiness'. Knowing the state of his health at the time, this could have been ironical, but in fact he was entirely conditioned to his illness and carried on his work exactly as if nothing were wrong. We had an inviolable weekend programme – 4.30 to 7 pm on Saturday evening and 9.30 to 1 on Sundays. During these periods Philip would dictate drafts of papers at incredible speed, my wife acting as a secretary. It is of interest that in the last three years, when we were both working against the clock – he against his illness and I against presidential duties – we did more research and published more than at any other time.

I was with him a few hours before he died. He lucidly discussed the state of our various current research projects, and as we chatted I thought what an immense contribution he had made to medicine. Though doctors at first maddened him, he was so fascinated by our problems that he threw himself into medical research and showed us how to design experiments which would give an early answer, with the minimum risk to volunteers. In his last illness, although he was still critical of doctors as pure scientists, I know that secretly he was full of admiration for the way he was looked after, and for the Hippocratic tradition in action. CAC

[*Brit. med. J.*, 1976, **2**, 1140; *Lancet,* 1976, **2**, 977; *Times,* 19 Oct 1976; *Biogr. mem. roy. Soc.*, 1977, **23**, 465-500]

SHORT, Ian Alexander *b.*19 May 1921 *d.*15 Oct 1976
MB ChB Glasg (1944) FRFPS (1949) MRCP Lond (1949)
MRCPG (1962) FRCPG (1964) MRCPE (1972) FRCP (1974)

Ian Short was consultant physician to the Western Infirmary and Gartnavel General Hospital. He was born at Saltcoats, Ayrshire, where his father John McGibbon Short was a headmaster. His mother was Florence Mary, daughter of John Grant Kennedy, a postmaster.

He was educated at Ardrossan Academy, where he was dux medallist in 1939, and Glasgow University, where he graduated in 1944. During the second world war he served as general duties officer in the RAMC, returning to the Western Infirmary, Glasgow, on demobilization. He was registrar from 1948 to 1952, took his MRCP in 1949, and was appointed senior registrar in Manchester in 1952. In 1958 he was appointed consultant physician at the Western Infirmary and assumed responsibility for the first haemodialysis unit for kidney disease in the west of Scotland. He also devoted special study to diabetes and sarcoidosis.

In 1948 he married Margaret Albertha Elder, daughter of Andrew Wauchope Smith, a medical practitioner, and herself a doctor. They had four children: three sons and a daughter. One son is also a doctor.

Ian Short was a general physician in the Oslerian tradition. His clinical acumen was remarkable and his integrity absolute. The best testimony to his abilities was the number of medical colleagues who sought his advice when ill, and whom he attended with a devotion far beyond the call of duty. He was a man of high intellect and culture, and particularly devoted to music. He played the piano and the clarinet. He also greatly enjoyed a game of golf, and walking. GW/VL

[*Brit. med. J.*, 1976, **2**, 1329; Photo]

SIBLEY, John Charles Arthur *b.*30 May 1923 *d.*—Aug 1981
MD CM Queen's (1947) MRCP (1952) FRCP(C) (1952)
FACC (1959) FACP (1963) FRCP (1974)

John Sibley was born in Mazenod, Saskatchewan, Canada, son of a minister of the United Church of Canada, and received his medical training at Queen's University, graduating MD in 1947. He obtained his postgraduate training in Hamilton, Ontario, and then came to Britain to continue his studies at King's College Hospital, Hammersmith Hospital and Newcastle General Hospital, obtaining his membership of the College in 1952. He was elected to the fellowship in 1974. He was also a fellow of the American College.

In 1954 John Sibley entered private practice in Hamilton, and became head of the department of internal medicine of the Joseph Brant Hospital in Burlington in 1959. In 1967 he joined McMaster University as associate professor, with particular responsibility to the vice-president of the division of health sciences for coordinating education in the allied health professions. He was therefore one of the initial group who founded the Medical School at McMaster. He was appointed associate dean (education) in 1979, a post he held at the time of his death.

Sibley was a very successful internist with particular interest in cardiology. Under his leadership the Joseph Brant Hospital in Burlington became one of the most highly regarded community hospitals in Canada, and he was a pioneer in the application of intensive care and coronary care. He was also deeply interested in rehabilitation and was a member of the Ontario, Canadian and

American committees on this subject. He wrote more than thirty papers covering various aspects of rehabilitation and medical education.

John Sibley was a dynamic man, greatly in demand as a clinician and administrator and also in community affairs. He left nobody in any doubt about what he thought about any particular issue, and any committee chaired by him reflected this decisiveness.

His main interest outside his professional duties at McMaster was in the development of the Third World. He had a longstanding interest in Africa and was a member of the board of directors of Operations Crossroads Africa in New York, and chairman of Canadian Crossroads International. He was active in promoting medical education, medical services and missionary programmes, and made numerous visits to African countries as part of his commitment to this work. He received the Canadian Centennial medal in 1967 and the Queen Elizabeth Silver Jubilee medal in 1978.

In 1944, John Sibley married Laura Jean MacIntosh and they had four children: two sons and two daughters. One of his sons predeceased him. Outside his work, his main relaxation was boating with his family in the Thousand Islands region of Lake Ontario.

EJMC

[Photo]

SIMON, George *b*.4 Sept 1902 *d*.30 Sept 1977
MRCS LRCP (1925) MB BChir Cantab (1927) DMRE (1927)
MD (1938) FFR (1947) MRCP (1958) FRCP (1964)

George Simon was born at Sale, Cheshire, the son of Louis Simon, cotton shipper, and his wife Louisa, daughter of Moritz Rothenstein, wool merchant, and sister of the artists William Rothenstein and Albert Rutherston.

He was educated at Charterhouse, Emmanuel College, Cambridge, and St Bartholomew's Hospital, qualifying with the conjoint diploma in 1925, and graduating MB BChir in 1927. The early onset of deafness, which rapidly became severe, led to his decision to take up dianostic radiology rather than clinical medicine. In the 1930s he was chief assistant in radiology at Bart's, and was working as part time radiologist at a number of peripheral hospitals. At the beginning of the second world war, he was posted in the emergency medical service to the sector hospital at Hill End, St Albans, where one of his clinical colleagues recalls that 'he did a superb job – nothing was too much trouble and he worked incredibly long hours'. He was appointed consultant radiologist to Bart's in 1945, and to the Brompton Hospital in 1948; it was at these two hospitals that he built up a world wide reputation as a clinical radiologist and, above all, as a teacher of radiology to both undergraduates and postgraduate students.

He wrote textbooks on *X-ray Diagnosis* (1949, 3rd edition 1975), *Principles of Bone X-ray Diagnosis* (1960, 3rd edition 1973), *Principles of Chest X-ray Diagnosis* (1965, 4th edition 1978, translated into Spanish 1965) and, jointly, on *Surface and Radiological Anatomy* (4th edition 1958) and *X-ray Anatomy* (1978). He also wrote more than 100 papers in journals. He had a remarkable capacity for concentrated work, and a special aptitude for collaborative studies with clinicians, pathologists, physiologists and anatomists. His principal original contributions were to chest radiology, especially in relation to chronic bronchitis and emphysema. He insisted upon the importance of description of radiological appearances as shadows before interpretation of them, and upon obtaining the maximum of information from simple methods. He gave the Marc Daniels lecture in 1966 on 'Radiology in epidemiological studies and some therapeutic trials'. The Thoracic Society acknowledged his outstanding contribution to respiratory medicine by electing him its president in 1967. His activities for the Royal College of Radiologists were recognized by the establishment of a George Simon lecture, the first of which he gave in 1974. He was a founder member of the Fleischner Society, and was a regular contributor to its meetings in the United States and Canada; this society initiated in his memory an award for the best paper by a junior at its annual meeting.

He was at his best in informal teaching, to which he devoted much time and effort. For many years, he conducted at Brompton Hospital a weekly evening seminar on chest radiology, which, though unadvertised and not part of any official course, was enthusiastically attended. Another important part of his teaching activities was the creation of radiological film libraries at Bart's and the Brompton, and for the Royal College of Radiologists.

George Simon was of somewhat below average height. His short figure hurrying in to sit in the front row of the lecture theatre, usually with a bundle of X-rays under his arm; his hearing aid operating at such power that those sitting near him could hear it blasting into his ear, so that he never missed a point in discussion; and the distinctive voice occasioned by his deafness, but nevertheless so well articulated as to be notably clear, were recognized with affection and respect for many years by his colleagues and by students at Bart's and Brompton. After his official retirement in 1967 they became well known also at Hammersmith, the National Heart, University College, King's College and Northwick Park Hospitals, where he undertook further teaching activities. In his limited leisure, he maintained a well informed interest in art, and, in spite of his deafness, in music; and played tennis. He enjoyed travel, regarding his visits to meetings abroad as in part recreation.

By his first marriage, he had one daughter. In 1945 he married Joanna Mary, daughter of John Shuckburgh, civil servant, and they had two daughters and a son. He died suddenly at home in London, after a few months of failing health. JGS

[*Times,* 30 Sept 1977; *Brit. med. J.,* 1977, **2**, 1031, 1094; *Lancet,* 1977, **2**, 776; *Brit. J. Radiol.,* **51** (602); 159, Feb 1978; Photo]

SIMPSON, Samuel Leonard *b*.8 Oct 1900 *d*.3 Aug 1983
MRCS Eng LRCP Lond (1925) MB BChir Cantab (1926)
MRCP (1928) MA MD (1930) FRCP Lond (1940)

Sam, as he was affectionately known by his family and close friends, but Leonard was used on more formal occasions, was a most unusual man of many talents and endearing qualities. He was born in London, educated at Westminster School, and at Cambridge, where he was a boxing Blue and captain of boxing. He did his clinical course at the London Hospital and after graduation held a number of positions there, finally being first assistant to Sir Robert Hutchison. He must have been an able and hard working individual, because within four years of qualifying he wrote an extensive treatise on carcinoma of the lung, in which he clearly drew attention to the probable aetiological link with inhaled pollutants, including cigarette smoking. One sees this work referred to even today in the pathological literature dealing with lung cancer. He wrote several other important papers at this time, including an excellent account of Raynaud's disease, and methods for investigating peripheral vascular disease. He was also closely associated with the first account of the viral origin of psittacosis in man. In 1930 he spent a year at the Mayo Clinic, a leading centre for endocrine investigation and research, and he was greatly influenced by this experience. He returned to London determined on a career in clinical endocrinology, and joined the staff of the Lister Institute, where he remained for four years. He worked closely with V Korenchevsky and Marjorie Dennison and did a great deal of work with rats, studying the metabolic and endocrine effects of gonadectomy, adrenalectomy and substitution therapy with testosterone, progesterone, oestrogen and adrenal cortical extract. He became a consultant on the staff of the Princess Louise Hospital for Children, and the Willesden General Hospital, specializing in endocrinology. He obtained wide experience in the use of adrenal cortical extract, and the newly discovered and synthesized adrenal hormone, desoxycorticosterone (DOC). He was well aware of the limitations of the treatment of Addison's disease (because cortisol was not then available) and wrote several perceptive papers dealing with the hypokalaemia and hypertension which could arise from over-treatment with DOC. He wrote papers on endocrine aspects of childhood, especially obesity, and introduced the concept of adipose gynism and gynandrism to explain much of obesity in children, especially the constitutional aspect. He was indefatigable in the pursuit of more and more scientific information about his endocrine patients, and collaborated with many groups undertaking quite difficult assessments, including looking for the excessive androgen secretion in the urine in cases of female virilism and hirsutism. He was, of course, greatly hampered by the lack of precise methodology and this situation existed until the 1950s. The introduction of steroid chromatography, and later radio-immunoassay, transformed the scientific aspects of endocrinology. In 1938 Simpson published his textbook *Major endocrine disorders* which gave a very good and concise clinical description of the endocrinopathies as they were understood at that time. The book enjoyed quite a vogue and went to three editions. During the war, Simpson's endocrine work was set to one side while he worked with the emergency medical services, especially in the transfusion branch. After the war he was appointed to St Mary's Hospital, W2, and for the next twenty years he was the consultant endocrinologist at this hospital.

A great burden which Simpson took on his shoulders with apparent ease was to play an active part in running the firm of clothiers, S Simpson Ltd. This had come about by the unfortunate early death of his brother, Alexander, in 1937, leaving Simpson with the responsibility of looking after the family's interests in this firm. In 1957 he became chairman, and he continued in this task until he died. Under his chairmanship the firm prospered and despite all the economic difficulties of the 1970s, Simpson's of Piccadilly flourished, both as a merchandizing and manufacturing operation, with world wide business connections. Apart from his medical and business activities, Simpson had many interests throughout the community. He was a keen horseman, particularly interested in all equestrian activities. He supported golf and tennis, providing sponsorship for both through his firm. He was an able painter and exhibited at the Royal Academy. He had extensive farming interests and entertained a wide circle of friends, both at his country home, Grouselands, in Sussex, and also at Hyde Park Gate (Winston Churchill's last residence). Simpson was a member of many academic, business and sporting associations and clubs, both in the UK and abroad. In 1940 he married Heddy Monique, Baroness de Podmaniczky, and they had one daughter, Georgina. She married the actor, Anthony Andrews, and they have two children, Jonathan and Jessica. It was a delight to watch Sam playing cricket with his grandchildren on the lawns at Grouselands, and he did this until a day or so before his death. He was a happy man, endowed with many excellent human qualities. An enduring memorial is the Alexander Simpson Laboratory for metabolic research at St Mary's, which Simpson endowed in 1965 and named after his brother. VW

[*Brit. med. J.*, 1983, **287**, 564; *Lancet*, 1983, **2**, 526; *Times*, 6 Aug 1983; Photo]

SKELLY, Robert Joseph Patrick *b.*12 Mar 1925 *d.*7 Nov 1981
MB BCh BAO UC Dubl (1949) MD NUI (1955) MRCPI (1957) MRCP (1962) FRCPI (1971) FRCP (1974)

Robert Skelly, consultant physician to Whiteabbey Hospital and the Royal Victoria Hospital, Belfast, lecturer in medicine to the dental faculty of Queen's University, Belfast, died suddenly and unexpectedly at the age of 56.

Bob Skelly was born in Dublin and received his early education at O'Connel's School, Dublin. He entered University College Dublin by scholarship and graduated in medicine in 1949. After early junior appointments in Dublin, London and Oxford, he served for some years as a senior registrar in medicine at the Belfast City Hospital and the Royal Victoria Hospital, Belfast. In 1963 he was appointed consultant physician to Whiteabbey Hospital.

Skelly was, above all, a man of vision. His appointment to Whiteabbey Hospital seemed to his contemporaries an inauspicious start to a consultant career for a young man of his promise and ambition. The hospital had enjoyed a high local reputation as the leading tuberculosis sanatorium in Northern Ireland and was in the process of conversion to a small district hospital. Skelly, as its first general physician, was alone in recognizing that the hospital had the potential to be, irrespective of size, a centre of excellence. His life's work was to make the dream a reality, and in this he succeeded. He established links with the Royal Victoria Hospital and in due course became a member of its staff. Eventually he built up a department of medicine which embraced general medicine, respiratory medicine, cardiology, gastroenterology and geriatrics, an enterprise in which he was joined by three other consultant colleagues. Although he would have described himself as a general physician his main interest was in diabetes. Realizing that high quality junior medical staff were crucial to the success of the unit, he set about recruiting them, largely by the excellence of his postgraduate and undergraduate teaching and by the high success rate achieved by his pupils in the membership examination. There was no lack of applicants for his junior posts and in time he got the best.

He was a naturally gifted teacher, widely read not only in medicine but in the English classics. Fluent both with tongue and pen, he used the English language as only one who loves it can. His simplicity of address and his logical approach to every clinical problem impressed itself on a whole generation of Belfast medical students and graduates. In due course he was appointed lecturer in medicine to the dental faculty of Queen's University, a post which gave him more pleasure than any other which he held. He took a deep personal interest in all his students and in turn he earned both their respect and affection.

Bob Skelly was a friendly man. He had a cheerful word for everyone whom he met, and in this he recognized no distinction of rank or status. Even in Northern Ireland he was totally incapable of grasping the distinctions which other men make in respect of nationality, race or creed. It was therefore completely natural for him to extend the right hand of fellowship to all the overseas graduates who came to the hospital. He was like a father to them, celebrating with them in the good times, supporting them in the bad times and furthering their careers in every way he could. Junior medical staff are always perceptive, often harsh but usually correct in the judgements which they pass on their seniors. His junior staff pronounced judgement shortly and succinctly in one simple inscription on his wreath – 'To a Great Physician'.

Honours deservedly came his way. He was for a time chairman of his area medical advisory committee, and as such had a seat on the area health and social services board and formed part of its area executive team. Distance prevented his achieving the prominence in

College affairs which might have been his lot had he been resident in mainland Britain. For all that, he maintained a keen interest in College affairs and in its personalities, and he served as a regional specialty adviser in Northern Ireland.

Outwardly a gregarious person, exuding gaiety, charm and wit, he was beneath it all a sensitive and deeply reflective man who, whilst enjoying the company of others, could be equally content with his own. In truth, he was a sincerely religious man. His faith was deep rooted but he was the most tolerant of men and stoutly upheld the right of others to differ. It has been said that the difference between a religious and an irreligious man is that the religious man knows that he is making a journey whereas the irreligious man denies that there is any journey to be made. Robert Skelly knew with certainty that he was making a journey. Both for him and for those fortunate enough to be tramping along at his side it was a happy, carefree one. WHM

[*Brit. med. J.*, 1982, **284**, 1339]

SLATER, Eliot Trevor Oakeshott *b.*28 Aug 1904 *d.*15 May 1983
CBE (1966) MRCS LRCP (1927) MRCP (1930) MB Cantab (1931)
DPM (1934) MA MD (1940) FRCP (1945) FRCPsych (1971)

Eliot Slater's idealism and compassion originated in part from his family background. His father, Gilbert Slater, was a Fabian, a principal of Ruskin College in Oxford, socialist mayor of Woolwich and at one time professor of economics in Madras. His mother, Violet Oakeshott, was a Quaker. But the originality and intellectual passion with which he pursued his manifold medical, scientific and artistic interests were his own. He was educated at Leighton Park School, Cambridge University, and St George's Hospital, London. Early in his career modesty and a distaste for any form of display or self glorification were to obscure his talents. There was some truth in the entertaining account he gave in an autobiographical note of his ineptitudes as a young doctor. But independent accounts show this to have been something of a parody. Those who were to attend his clinical rounds and conferences at the National Hospital at the Maudsley in later years were to have the rare experience of observing one of the best endowed and sharpest intellects in psychiatry, drawing freely upon insight and intuition as well as first hand observation in reaching a diagnosis. They were also taught a lesson in how to conduct an interview in the presence of others without encroaching on the dignity or integrity of patients. Even in the peak years of the scientific work which he pursued with a rare intellectual fervour, he put his duties as a doctor first.

In 1931 he joined the staff of the Maudsley Hospital where he was soon to be profoundly influenced by a group of eminent psychiatrists who had fled from Nazi Germany. Alfred Meyer, Willy Mayer-Gross and Eric Guttmann brought with them an empirical scientific approach towards the problems of psychiatry. Reared in the tradition of Meyerian psychobiology which was humane and many-sided, but loosely knit and scientifically sterile, Slater found the approach of Mayer-Gross in particular like 'a view of a new world'. The influence of RA Fisher and later training in psychiatric genetics in Munich provided a powerful impetus for a man with Slater's natural mathematical gifts. It was to genetics that he attributed the combination of self-esteem and humility, that placed an unmistakable imprint upon the entire corpus of his scientific contributions. He was the first English psychiatrist to have matured into a clinical scientist in the modern sense of the term.

The Socratic method he would use in testing the soundness and clarity of reasoning of his clinical and research students was not very different from that he employed in dialogues with his children, who were treated from an early age as intellectual adults. One of them tells of discussions they would have on the topic of the weekly essay in the course of Sunday walks. One week it was, 'Which would you rather be? A jack-of-all-trades or a master of one?' He would carefully elicit all the arguments in favour of one position, and as soon as he was convinced that it was correct, turn around and view the question from the opposite camp. She would be irritated by his refusal to give a straight answer for he would either straddle two camps or, in the case of a particularly clear-cut alternative, adopt the unconventional view until the very end.

He could have had chairs, including the highest in the land, but he preferred working on his own or with a very few chosen colleagues. The wide sweep of his interests is reflected in the range of subjects in which his investigations have become internationally renowned. They include the neurotic constitution, hysteria, schizophrenia, the inheritance of many forms of mental disorder, the methodology or genetical research in psychiatry, the pathography of musicians of genius, and the judicial process, all of which were to engage his unflagging curiosity. The agility and ruthless self criticism with which he handled the data, and the incisiveness and elegance he displayed in their analysis and interpretation, have probably not been equalled by any other psychiatric investigator of his generation. He was a genuine intellectual, pursuing any problem with a detached interest, arguing it with a cerebral fervour devoid of acrimony. Pedantry and pretence were alien to his nature. Despite his reticence and modesty, he was tremendous fun to be with, a brilliant conversationalist and appreciative listener who retained the gift for irrepressible, loud laughter into old age. His sensitive, compassionate nature led him to detest prejudice and snobbery. The writer once heard him in debate with a colleague of great eminence who reasoned that snobbery was an estimable and under-rated character trait. He was reduced with the aid of a few swift parries to concede that if he had that day been placed at lunch, next to a noble earl who happened to suffer from severe mental subnormality, he would have good reason to take pride in the experience.

In his professional and public life, he was unworldly, above ambition or desire for material success. This was manifest in his style of life. He was content with his small house, his garden and the birds welcomed in it, his scholarship and his painting.

After retirement, he devoted himself seriously to Shakespearian scholarship, in which he had dabbled early in his career. His doctoral thesis on *'The Problem of "The Reign of King Edward III (1596)": A Statistical Approach'* had already exerted considerable influence on the use of vocabulary tests in Shakespearian studies, even prior to the forthcoming publication of the thesis by the Cambridge University Press. Frequent reference is made to his techniques and the findings from the tests he has conducted on the entire Shakespearian canon. It was wholly characteristic of him that he should take up an unusual and perhaps even somewhat discredited line, devise his own rigorous application of it, give the technique a scholarly respectability and make significant influential findings with it. His own method had been developed from one devised by Udney Yule which had received little attention for some decades. Yule was an erstwhile fellow of St John's, Eliot's old College in Cambridge, which elected him to an honorary fellowship a few years before he died.

The generosity with which he gave of his time and energy to others, and young investigators in particular, even near the end of his life, was exemplary and little known. His own contributions in a number of important enquiries are to be found in the form of a brief acknowledgement of his help at the end of papers that embodied the findings. He devoted several weeks to the translation of a number of papers from the German for one of his registrars engaged in the investigation of the 'organic' schizophrenias.

The eleven years he served as the editor of the *British Journal of Psychiatry* served to transform it into one of the world's most influential journals. Letters to authors from his pen in this period served as a kind of sustained master class in psychiatric reasoning and methodology. His correspondence merits a publication to itself. An editorial letter about a genetical paper began as follows: 'I hope you will not take me amiss if I liken your work to a magnificent ruin; one could not stand on it without risk of breaking an ankle. But it was a splendid enterprise and has many lessons for clinicians, psychologists and geneticists. Its weaknesses are nearly all due to the difficulties of the terrain on which you are building. Let us now come to practicalities. The work clearly must be published; but I should like you to reconsider ...'.

At one time he took up weaving, mastered it, and made two very attractive chair seats, one with a fine Douanier Rousseau-esque design of his own of an owl in a leafy setting – and having succeeded so well, gave it up. There was something delightful in the way he uninhibitedly took up in succession artistic pastimes for the sheer unalloyed pleasure they gave him.

It was perhaps in his pathographic writings, as in his studies of the sonnets of Shakespeare and the identity of William of Stratford, that his psychodynamic insights, his compassion and his disciplined clinical imagination were most clearly displayed. In the last few years much of his writing was devoted to medical ethics, euthanasia, and nature conservation. He challenged the arrogant presumption that man was lord and master rather than merely an integral part of nature, and his gentle, compassionate spirit had been deeply stirred by the threat of pollution, over-population and the destruction of mankind which he saw looming ever larger.

His post on the day he died included circulars from the many charities he supported. Most of his estate was made over to ecological charities – the Royal Society for the Preservation of Birds, and organizations working for the protection of endangered species among them.

Many of his publications and each of his textbooks were widely influential in the improvement of clinical practice and the advancement of scientific knowledge in psychiatry. *Physical Methods of Treatment* with William Sargant and *Clinical Psychiatry* with W Mayer-Gross and Martin Roth were, between them, to be translated into ten languages. *The Genetics of Mental Disorders* with Valerie Cowie (1971) remains the standard book on the subject.

Eliot Slater had four children by his marriage to Lydia Pasternak, sister of the poet and novelist whom he met while working in Rudin's Institute in Munich. They have inherited and acquired equal, but overlapping, proportions of his manifold gifts. His elder daughter is a clinical psychiatrist and the younger a Shakespearian scholar and author. One son is a well known medical scientist and the other a university lecturer in mathematics. He was survived also by his devoted second wife, Jean, who shared his enthusiasm for art and is a talented painter in her own right. MR

[*Brit. med. J.*, 1983, **286**, 1906; **287**, 67; *Lancet*, 1983, **1**, 1231-2; *Times*, 21 May 1983; *Brit. J. Psychiat.*, 1973, **122**, 621-3; Photo]

SMART, Joseph *b.*14 Feb 1909 *d.*22 Oct 1982
BA Cantab (1930) MRCS LRCP (1932) MB BChir (1933)
MA MD (1938) MRCP (1937) FRCP (1953)

Joseph Smart was born in Cambridge, the son of Frederick Smart, a corn and seed merchant, and his wife, Margaret Ruth Pask, a schoolteacher. From the Perse School, he entered Emmanuel College, Cambridge, where he graduated in natural sciences before proceeding to St Bartholomew's Hospital, London, for clinical studies.

At Bart's he was house physician to FG Chandler and the children's department before applying, at Chandler's instigation, for a house physicianship at the London Chest Hospital, a move which decided his choice of specialty. A Dorothy Temple Cross travelling fellowship took him to Sweden where he studied the treatment of pulmonary tuberculosis by artificial pneumothorax and obtained material for his MD thesis. After holding the posts of RMO and registrar at the London Chest Hospital, he was elected to the consultant staff in 1938. At the outbreak of the second world war he was pronounced unfit for military service by reason of bronchial asthma, and was enrolled in the emergency medical service at Friern Hospital, acting as chief assistant to George Graham. He was appointed physician to the Connaught

Hospital, Walthamstow, in 1948, and until 1951 was visiting physician to King Edward VII Sanatorium, Warwick. He was physician to the Midland Bank; was elected FRCP in 1953 and, after serving as secretary of the Medical Society of London, he became president in 1969, an office which gave him much pleasure.

After the war, Smart was quick to appreciate the growing importance of physiological methods in the investigation of respiratory disease, and he started the clinical physiology department at the London Chest Hospital, where he and his colleagues undertook studies on the relationship between effort tolerance, spirometry, and blood gas analysis in bronchitic and emphysematous patients. He was not, however, greatly attracted to academic medicine; the clinical field held more appeal and gave full scope for his skill as a physician.

Joseph Smart was a man who held strong opinions. But this is not to say he was unresponsive to the opinions of others, for he was, by temperament, honest and fairminded. He accepted a heavy burden of committee work on behalf of the chest hospitals and it was in large measure due to his exertions that the London Chest Hospital, which had suffered severe damage from enemy action in 1941, survived and expanded. He was chairman of the medical committee of the LCH for many years, and a member of the board of governors of the chest hospitals for twenty-five years. At the time of the closure of the country branch of the LCH at Anglesey the Brompton Hospital offered sessions to those consultants affected. Smart thus became associated with the Brompton, and from 1969 until his retirement in 1973 he held the post of dean of the Institute, a period coinciding with the merger of the institutes of the chest and heart hospitals which added responsibility to the office.

In his younger days Joe was a keen tennis player and athlete. He excelled at the high jump, winning several cups and representing Bart's and the United Hospitals Athletics Club; more recently he sought relaxation in sailing and painting. In 1938 he married Phyllis Mary, daughter of Albert Frampton, a property company director, and they had two sons and two daughters. Joe was a deeply religious man. In 1962 he, with his wife and family, turned to the Baptist Church, and he was a deacon of the church in Swanage, near his home, at the time of his death. NLR

[*Brit. med. J.*, 1982, **285**, 1499; Photo]

SMITH, John *b.*24 July 1892 *d.*19 June 1976
MB ChB Aberd (1915) DPH (1919) MD (1922) DSc (1927)
MRCP (1930) FRCP (1937) FRCPath (1964) LLD Aberd (1965)

John Smith, son of a Banffshire farmer Alexander Smith and his wife Louisa (née Smith), was born at Bogs of Enzie and graduated at Aberdeen University in 1915. He served in France as a regimental medical officer from 1915 to 1918 and was invalided from the Medical Corps. He obtained the diploma in public health at Aberdeen and in 1920 he was appointed assistant medical officer of health, with special duties in connection with the clinical and laboratory diagnosis of infectious diseases at the City Hospital, Aberdeen, where a new laboratory was just being established. The laboratory services developed rapidly and the post became a full time laboratory commitment with John Smith as director. In this laboratory, firstly under the local authority and latterly, from 1948, as part of the National Health Service, he spent the entirety of his working life, during which he accomplished much that was worthy of note in the fields of clinical bacteriology and infectious diseases. Specimens were submitted to the laboratory at the City Hospital not only for bacteriological examination, but also for biochemical, haematological or pathological examination. Such specimens came from the general practitioners in Aberdeen and the surrounding counties as well as from the City Hospital and other hospitals in the area, and from the different public health authorities.

Thus, in the north east of Scotland at an early stage, the needs of the general practitioners were met and their use of laboratory facilities was encouraged by the provision of pre-paid postal specimen outfits. This development was well ahead of its time and much of the credit for the establishment of a laboratory service for general practitioners must go to John Smith. Once the service was functioning in a satisfactory manner he felt that it would be unacceptable for him to devote his time only to the supervision of the various procedures for the diagnosis of disease, although that must always remain the prime function. As a result a rich harvest of research work emanated from the laboratory, made possible by the abundant supply of material on which extended investigations could be conducted. Thus the bacteriological and serological characteristics of organisms isolated from cases of disease occurring in a particular outbreak were correlated with the epidemiology of the outbreak. The results of such investigations were published in many papers, sometimes as purely personal contributions by himself and frequently in conjunction with colleagues engaged in administrative and clinical aspects of public health. In all he published more than eighty scientific papers, many of great importance, contributing much to our understanding of disease and enhancing his reputation both nationally and internationally.

Of particular significance was his work on the causation and source of infection in puerperal fever for which he was awarded the Nichols prize of the Royal Society of Medicine in 1931, and again in 1934. He also received the Katherine Bishop Harman prize of the British Medical Association in 1932 for his work on the prevention of puerperal fever. A further award came to him in 1954 from the Royal College of Physicians, Edinburgh, in the form of a Lister fellowship for his bacteriological researches into infantile gastroenteritis and the association of serological types of *Bact. coli* with that disease. His contributions to our understanding of Weil's disease and undulant fever, and the demonstration of new types of salmonellae, are worthy of note.

John Smith retired in 1957, and in the years that followed he read much and pursued his horticultural interests, including the growing of orchids. He met his old friends regularly and kept up his expertise on the billiards table, a skill which he had possessed from his student days. He died while on holiday in England visiting his son, a consultant obstetrician.

IAP

[Photo]

SMITH, Ronald Edward *b.*18 Jan 1901 *d.*18 Oct 1983
MRCS LRCP (1925) MB BChir Cantab (1927) MRCP (1927) FRCP (1939)

Ronald Smith was born at Swaffham, in Norfolk, where his father Walter Smith was a farmer. His mother was Eleanor, the daughter of John Bloom who was also a farmer in East Anglia. 'RE', as he was always affectionately known, was at Swaffham Grammar School before going to King Edward VI School at Norwich. He won a Matthew Parker exhibition to Corpus Christi College, Cambridge, and from there he went to Guy's Hospital, qualifying with the conjoint in 1925 and obtaining his Cambridge medical degree and his membership of the College two years later. For a year he held a visiting fellowship at the Henry Phipps Institute, a part of the University of Pennsylvania in Philadelphia. At Guy's he was medical registrar and tutor, and chief clinical assistant to the children's department. There he met Maud Campbell, a beautiful Guy's nurse and the daughter of Douglas Campbell, a merchant, and they were married in 1931. RE's old tutor at Corpus, Sir Will Spens, who was by then master of the College, suggested that he should apply for the post of physician to Rugby School. He was appointed by Sir Austen Chamberlain, chairman of the governors, in the cabinet room in Downing Street and took up his duties and that of physician to the Hospital of St Cross in Rugby the same year. While at Rugby his interest in the infectious diseases of childhood led to the revolutionizing of the practice of quarantine and isolation, and he published excellent papers in the *Quarterly Journal of Medicine* and *Lancet* as well as making it the subject of his Milroy lecture at the College in 1940. He also studied the implications and natural history of undescended testicle, and in 1941 used this experience for his Hunterian professorship at the Royal College of Surgeons. It resulted in royalty and nobility from all over the world seeking his advice over their heirs. In 1947 the epidemic of poliomyelitis involved four boys at Rugby, which greatly worried and upset RE. He had already contributed two papers on the disease, and a third, 'All about polio', was of the greatest value. He became president of the Medical Officers of Schools Association, and health adviser to the National Association of Boy's Clubs. Another of his splendid papers on the physicians to Christ's Hospital reflected his deep interest in adolescent medicine. His skill and kindness are remembered with affection and gratitude by many old Rugbeians who were his patients at school and have become pillars of the state.

RE already had a great reputation and a large consulting practice in the Midlands when the National Health Service was established in

1947, but then he also accepted the appointment of physician to Gulson Hospital at Coventry, resigning his post at Rugby School and being appointed consulting physician to the school two years later. At Gulson, RE's advent had a dramatic effect; the excellence of his own work and the impact on other members of the staff impressed everyone. His practice was enormous and he worked unceasingly until he reached retiring age.

In 1961 he accepted the appointment of the University of Birmingham's area director of postgraduate medical education for Coventry and Warwickshire. He had always been intensely anxious to further the careers of his juniors and this new work gave him enormous happiness; after his retirement from clinical practice in 1966 he devoted his whole time to postgraduate medical education. He was the driving force behind the building and successful establishment of the Warwickshire Postgraduate Medical Centre and he was also, with John Lister, responsible for the foundation of the National Association of Clinical Tutors.

RE was of course firstly a superb physician, with a special interest in adolescent medicine and postgraduate medical education, but he was also a great scholar. His papers on Lord Randolph Churchill, George Eliot and George Henry Lewes bore the stamp of historical distinction, and only an hour or so after giving a magnificent paper on Joseph Chamberlain before the West Midlands Physicians Association, of which he was a past president, he collapsed with a stroke from which he did not recover.

RE's achievements were prodigious, his friends and his disciples were legion, his contribution to the welfare of his medical colleagues and his fellow men was enormous; yet he was always modest in the extreme and ever anxious to do more. A magnificent portrait by GR Corbett captures the warmth, the distinction and the selflessness of the man.

His intense loyalty to Corpus, to Guy's, to the hospitals at Rugby, Coventry and Nuneaton, to the Royal College of Physicians, the Association of Physicians, the universities of Birmingham and Warwick and everything else with which he was associated was remarkable. In the College he rarely missed Comitia and served as a councillor from 1954 to 1956; no institution could have had a more loyal and unselfish servant.

In his early years RE was keen on shooting; later he became a keen gardener and was a formidable bridge player. His home always bore the hallmark of his kindness, his hospitality, his generosity, his scholarship and his loyalty. His wife, and one son and two daughters, survived him.

AGWW

[*Lancet,* 1983, **2**, 1040; *Times,* 24 Oct 1983; *Brit. med. J.,* 1983, **287**, 1386-87; Photo]

SMITH, Walter Thomas *b.*30 Sept 1923 *d.*23 Dec 1982
MB ChB Birm (1947) MD (1957) MRCPath (1964) MRCP (1969) FRCPath (1969) FRCP (1975)

Walter Smith was born in Worcestershire and was educated at Halesowen Grammar School, where he got his colours for rugby and cricket, and the University of Birmingham, where he graduated in medicine in 1947. For a time he thought seriously of a career in clinical neurology and he served for a year as a neurological registrar, an appointment of the greatest value in his ultimate specialty choice of neuropathology. He became a lecturer in pathology in the University of Birmingham in 1949 and two years later he went to the Institute of Neurology, where he worked under William McMenemey, and saw much of JG Greenfield and Dorothy Russell. He returned to Birmingham in 1952 and did valuable research on the malignant neuropathies and the presenile dementias. At the same time he established a superb neuropathological diagnostic service in the Birmingham region and became the valued friend and adviser of all the neurosurgeons and neurologists in the West Midlands. He arranged regular meetings with his clinical colleagues which were of great academic value and did much to enhance the standard of clinical practice. In 1961 the University of Birmingham elected him a reader in neuropathology and in 1970 he was given a personal chair.

Walter Smith's contributions to the neuropathological literature were immense; he was assistant editor of the *Journal of Pathology*, joint editor of *Recent Advances in Neuropathology*, editorial adviser to *Neuropathology* and *Applied Neurobiology*, and published papers on the neurological complications of coeliac disease and the experimental induction of cerebral tumours. Many honours marked his later years. He was president of the British Neuropathological Society 1973–1975 and of the Midland Neurological Society 1981–1982, and was a member of the working party on training in neuropathology and of the WHO panel on neurosciences. All this was achieved despite illness throughout his adult life, with innumerable perilous abdominal operations for Crohn's disease, and for long periods physical frailty and malnutrition, which greatly distressed his many friends. Walter, however, ill as he was, was never deterred from his academic, research and service responsibilities, or from his many leisure interests – music, gardening, the Warwickshire County Cricket Club and the Coventry Rugby Football Club. In addition he contributed much to his University in return for the honours they gave him. He was a most successful editor of its *Faculty of Medicine Bulletin* and served for many years on the committee of the *University Gazette*. Outside the university he was governor of the Coventry Schools Foundation and a member of the Solihull Education Committee and of the Solihull Health Authority.

Always impeccably dressed, ever courteous and ever anxious to be of help to his colleagues, Walter inspired the affection of all who knew him; their admiration for his courage and achievements despite his chronic ill health was boundless.

In youth he was a promising pianist and organist, and although he largely gave up playing himself, he amassed a vast collection of classical records, focussing towards the end of his life on Bartok, Mahler and Beethoven's last quartets. In gardening his green fingers enabled him to sport a buttonhole almost as a trademark, exotic blooms often betraying a dandyism at odds with his austere personality.

He married Beryl, a fellow medical student of great beauty, who supported him magnificently in all his endeavours. There were two sons of the marriage, one of whom qualified in medicine.

AGWW/JMJ

[*Brit. med. J.*, 1983, **286**, 403; *Lancet,* 1983, **1**, 370]

SPECTOR, Walter Graham *b.*20 Dec 1924 *d.*7 Jan 1982
MRCS LRCP (1947) MB BChir Cantab (1947) MRCP (1948)
FRCP (1966) FRCPath (1972)

Walter Spector, the only son of Henry and Sarah, was educated at the City of London School and at Queen's College, Cambridge, where he did his pre-clinical studies. He came to University College Hospital Medical School for his clinical years, and qualified in 1947. He served as house physician to the paediatric unit at UCH, where he acquired an interest in childhood disease which never left him, but his career truly began when he joined Professor (later Sir Roy) Cameron in 1949 as Graham scholar in pathology. It was then that he learned his skill as an experimental pathologist, and began the work on mediators of the inflammatory response which he continued for the rest of his life. He remained in Sir Roy's department until 1962, becoming Beit memorial fellow (1951–1953), lecturer (1953–1960) and senior lecturer (1960–1962). He had an outstandingly successful career as research worker and teacher in these years. In 1956–1957 he was awarded a Rockefeller travelling fellowship, which took him to the Walter and Eliza Hall Institute in Melbourne. It was no surprise when he was appointed to the chair in pathology at St Bartholomew's Hospital in 1962, at the early age of 38.

After his appointment to the chair, he was called upon to serve on many advisory bodies. He served the Medical Research Council, he was secretary to the Beit memorial advisory board, he was a member of the Council of the Imperial Cancer Research Fund and of the Cancer Research Campaign. He became treasurer of the Society of Pathologists and editor-in-chief of the *Journal of Pathology*. He was a member of the scientific board of the Foundation for the Study of Infant Death, and a governor of St Bartholomew's Hospital.

There was more to Wally Spector than this conventional account of a successful career shows. His slight figure and apparently diffident manner concealed a firm mind and a strong temperament. His friendships lasted for life, and to his friends he never changed. He had a dry sense of humour and was the author of many *bon mots* which are remembered and quoted by his old colleagues. We remember him with affection and with gratitude for the many joyous times that we had together. Amongst them were the journeys we made as young men to look at English churches and old country houses. One also recalls a memorable visit to the chateaux of the Loire when, apart from enjoying the houses, it was also possible to follow his taste in wine, of which he had a considerable knowledge. In 1957 he married June Routley of Melbourne. There were two sons of this marriage, which was dissolved in 1977.

His death at such an early age was a terrible blow to his friends, who remember him daily with sorrow for his loss, and with pride and affection for the gift of his friendship. JDJ

[*Brit. med. J.*, 1982, **284**, 429; *Lancet,* 1982, **1**, 233-4; Photo]

SPENCER, Ian Osborne Bradford *b.*29 Mar 1914 *d.*–Jan 1978
MB BS Durh (1932) MRCP (1948) FRCP (1967)

Ian Spencer was the son of George Herbert Spencer, a well known general practitioner on Tyneside. He was educated at Newcastle Preparatory School and later at Sedbergh School, becoming an undergraduate in the medical school at Newcastle in the University of Durham in 1932, and graduating in 1937. After graduating he held various junior hospital posts in his teaching hospital, and in the Newcastle area, and in 1939 joined the RAMC, becoming medical officer to the 2nd Battalion of the Gloucester Regiment. He was captured at Dunkirk and was a prisoner of war in German hands from 1940 to 1945, being mentioned in despatches for his distinguished services during the campaign which led to the evacuation from Dunkirk.

After his release from captivity, he returned to Newcastle, becoming a post-service medical registrar at the Royal Victoria Infirmary, where he worked with AG Ogilvie and his assistant physician, Henry Miller. At the inception of the National Health Service, Spencer was appointed senior registrar, and continued to work in that capacity in general medicine until 1950, when he spent a year as senior registrar in paediatrics with Sir James Spence. Late in 1950 he was appointed physician in general medicine to the Tynemouth Victoria Jubilee Infirmary and the Preston Hospital, where he served until his untimely death in 1979.

As a senior registrar, he was a popular and enthusiastic teacher, and when he moved to Tynemouth he continued to invite students from the medical school to be attached to his clinic because of his interest in undergraduate teaching, even though in the 1950s it was not conventional for students to spend time in regional hospitals. He was a compassionate, thoughtful and caring physician, who continued to contribute to the medical literature on various topics in general medicine after his appointment to his consultant post, despite carrying a very heavy burden of clinical responsibility and a thriving part-time private practice. Several of his papers on factors associated with perforation in peptic ulcer, on haematemesis and melaena, and on ferrous sulphate poisoning in children, each published in the *British Medical Journal*, attracted considerable attention.

Ian was a popular consultant with local general practitioners, and was frequently called upon by colleagues whenever members of their own families required medical attention. He was a faithful member of the Newcastle upon Tyne and Northern Counties medical society, a regular attender at scientific meetings locally, and frequently, even in his later years of practice, presented papers to the Regional Association of Physicians. Outside his work, his principal interest was in golf, and he was for many years a member of the Northumberland Golf Club, where at one time he held a handicap in single figures. He also played at Bamburgh on the north east coast where he spent many family holidays with his wife, Elspeth Catto, née Strang, and their two daughters. JNW

[Photo]

SREENIVASAN, Baratham Ramaswamy *b.*14 June 1909 *d.*23 May 1977
LMS Singapore (1931) MRCGP (1952) MRCP (1953)
Hon LLD Malaya (1954) FRCP (1966) FRCGP (1973)

Sreeni, as he was known to his friends and colleagues, was born in Gemas, Malaya, the son of Baratham Sreenivasan Ramaswamy, a cashier, and his wife Runmani, daughter of Screebivasa Acharyan, a landowner. He was educated at St John's Institute and qualified in medicine in 1931 at the King Edward VII College of Medicine, Singapore. He obtained his MRCP in 1953 and was elected a fellow in 1966. In 1934 he married Elizabeth Jeeraratnam Heynes, daughter of a medical practitioner. They had two children: a son and a daughter.

Sreeni was a true scholar as well as a physician, but despite his academic background it was as an ordinary family physician that he liked to be known. He was principal of the Singapore division of the University of Malaya in 1961; vice-chancellor of the University of Singapore 1962–1963; a founder member of the Royal College of General Practitioners; a past president of the Malaya branch of the BMA, and president of the Singapore Medical Association. From 1954 to 1957 he was president of the medical council of Singapore. He served the people well, spending countless hours with the Singapore Antituberculosis Association, chairing many government commissions on Malayanization schemes, and was a member of the inquiry into government expenditure and efficiency. During the second world war he served as a medical officer at the civil General Hospital during the Japanese occupation.

He was a gentle, humble man, with a deep love of the classics and a knowledge of Shakespeare which would put many Shakespearian scholars to shame. A conversation with Sreeni was always interesting, and often an educational experience as well. Despite his wide academic interests, on his personal CV he listed his favourite hobby as 'walking'. GW/VL

[*Brit. med. J.,* 1977, **2**, 131; Photo]

STEEL, Matthew *b*.15 Mar 1916 *d*.5 Aug 1980
MRCS LRCP (1940) MB BS Lond (1940) MRCP (1942) MD (1949) FRCP (1965)

Matthew Steel was born in Berkshire, son of James Steel, farmer, and his wife Annie Love (née Kirkwood), who also came from a family of farmers. Matthew was educated at Reading School and University College Hospital, London, where he graduated in 1940 having obtained the Fellowes gold medal and the Butterworth prize. Following resident appointments in University College Hospital, he served in the RAMC until 1947.

On leaving the Army, Matthew Steel returned to UCH and served as resident assistant physician prior to his appointment as consultant physician in Grimsby in 1951. He was subsequently responsible for the development of the medical services in Grimsby, and was appointed clinical tutor following the introduction of postgraduate medical education. He was largely responsible for the building of the existing postgraduate medical centre. He devoted much of his time to tutorials for the junior staff for many years, providing two sessions a week of preparation for the MRCP.

In 1942 he married Margaret Harriet, daughter of Robert Leslie Ridge, a medical practitioner, and they had two sons.

Matthew Steel was a warmhearted and generous man whose whole life was based upon firmly held Christian principles. He was a staunch supporter of his local church. He remained a country man, loving country life, and was a keen salmon fisherman. He was also interested in history, and vice president of the local Rotary Club. He died six months before his retirement as consultant physician at Scarthos Road Hospital, Grimsby, and his fortitude and acceptance of the inevitable in his final illness gave a fine example to all. DBC/GW

[*Brit. med. J.*, 1980, **281**, 876; Photo]

STERN, Edward Samuel *b*.10 Mar 1905 *d*.15 July 1976
MB BChir Cantab (1931) MRCP (1931) DPM (1932) MD (1936) FRSS (1962) FRCP (1964) FRCPsych (1971)

Edward Stern was born at Burton on Trent where his father, Arthur Landauer Stern was head brewer and biochemist at Bass's brewery. His mother, Grace Madeleine (née Falk) was the daughter of a merchant, Ernest Falk.

He was educated at Clifton College and received his medical education at Cambridge and at University College Hospital, London, qualifying in 1931 and proceeding MD in 1936.

After he had completed his appointment as house physician at University College Hospital, he decided on a career in psychological medicine. He was appointed assistant medical officer at Napsbury Hospital in 1931, from where he took his DPM the following year. He became deputy medical superintendent at the Towers Hospital, Leicester, in 1937, and was appointed medical superintendent at the Central Hospital, Warwick, in 1942 where he remained until his retirement in 1971. He was appointed a founder fellow of the Royal College of Psychiatrists in the same year.

He held his post as medical superintendent at Warwick with the greatest sense of responsibility and clinical enthusiasm. His quiet dignity, his warmth of personality, and his sense of duty earned him the lasting respect of his medical and nursing colleagues. The care and consideration he showed to his patients was also characteristic. He made a point of visiting the wards daily, would see every new admission as soon as possible, and knew every patient by name, being on personal and friendly terms with each one of them.

Stern was an excellent committee man, who could be persistent and even formidable if the interests of the patients were in any way threatened. He was active in promoting realistic rehabilitation facilities, and pioneered the resettlement of patients in supervised accommodation within the local community. He would encourage every new treatment approach in the care of the mentally ill, yet would never interfere at the clinical level, not even with the most junior colleague. Moreover, he encouraged his juniors to take advantage of training schemes at other centres, although an inspiring and gifted clinical teacher himself.

He was also concerned that the patients under his administrative care should have every possible social amenity. He saw to it that they had an extensive and comfortable library, and he would arrange classical musical concerts for their entertainment and education. He was persistent in his appeals to lay committees to visit the wards to observe conditions for themselves. Needless to say, he was an enthusiastic advocate of the principles of 'the therapeutic community' and 'the open door'.

Stern became concerned with the cost of medical care, and published jointly with his sister Babette E Stern, a statistician, an article on 'Efficiency in mental hospitals' in the *British Journal of Preventive and Social Medicine*, **17**, No 3, July 1963. Using a similar theme he published 'A statistical study of departures from a mental hospital' in the *British Journal of Psychiatry*, **116**, No 530, January 1970.

He travelled widely and visited many psychiatric centres in other countries. He wrote an article on 'Psychiatry in Israel' in the *Middlesex Review*, **2**, 323, 1963. He published an article on one of his wife's ancestors entitled 'Dr Hodgkin's relationship with his distinguished friend and patient Sir Moses Montefiore Bt. FRS' in *Medical History*, XI, No 2, April 1967, describing their visits together to the Holy Land in the year 1827 and subsequently.

He was appointed to the council for music in hospitals in 1947, and had been a committee member of the Mental After Care Association since 1965. He was chairman of the child psychiatry section of the Royal Medico-Pyschological Association in 1946, and was later secretary, then chairman of the Study Tours sub-committee. He had been an examiner in psychological medicine at Birmingham University. In 1962 he was elected a fellow of the Royal Statistical Society. He was also president of the Leamington Medical Society.

Stern was a witty after dinner speaker, with unusual verbal facility and a ready memory, so that he would often surprise his audience by off the cuff quotations from English and even Greek literature. In his spare moments he would busy himself with amateur carpentry, and after his retirement to a beautiful country house on Edge Hill, which he had himself designed, he became a keen and enthusiastic gardener. He was an active member of his masonic lodge and would often be called on to propose the visitor's toast.

He married Alice Daisy, daughter of Nathaniel Sampson Lucas, a pathologist, in 1933, and had two daughters; Valerie who married a lecturer in social anthropology, and Julia who married a doctor who became a consultant in nuclear medicine at Edinburgh.

His wife died tragically in May 1975. Subsequently he married Christine Orton who had been closely associated with his work at the Central Hospital in her capacity as chairman of the house committee there. CT

[*Brit. med. J.*, 1976, **2**, 535; Photo]

STOKES, Aldwyn Brockway *b.*23 Feb 1906 *d.*3 May 1978
CBE (1947) BA Oxon (1927) MRCS LRCP (1931) MRCP (1932) MA BM BCh (1934) DCH (1935) DPM (1936) FRCP(C) (1947) FRCP (1957)

Aldwyn Stokes was born in Newport, Monmouthshire, the son of Reginald George Briant Stokes, comptroller to a firm of solicitors in the town. His mother was Mary Price, daughter of William Price, a farmer from Penycaemawr, Monmouthshire. He attended Newport High School for Boys, and went up to Jesus College, Oxford, where he read physiology in the school of natural sciences, gaining an honours BA in 1927. He had won a state scholarship while at school, and was an exhibitioner in natural sciences and later a scholar in anatomy at Oxford in 1928. He did his clinical work at King's College Hospital, London, during his tenure of a Burney Yeo scholarship. An early interest in psychiatry found him the recipient of the class prize in psychological medicine at King's in 1929. He graduated in medicine in 1931 with an Oxford degree and took his London MRCP a year later. After internship he undertook residency training in paediatrics and internal medicine, before finally turning to psychiatry.

In 1935 he was appointed to a staff position at the Maudsley Hospital, London, where he was awarded a Rockefeller travelling fellowship in 1937. He had been intrigued by the work of Rolf Gjessing on metabolic psychiatry in Norway, and he elected to use his fellowship further to pursue this interest. He joined Gjessing at the Dikemark Mental Hospital near Oslo, and spent a fruitful year in studying his methods and contributing to his research. In 1938 he returned to London and was appointed assistant medical superintendent to the Maudsley Hospital. When war came in 1939 he joined that part of the Maudsley Hospital which had been evacuated to Mill Hill, and continued as medical superintendent until 1945 when the hospital returned to London. He continued as medical superintendent for the following two years and was decorated for his services to the EMS.

In 1947 he was invited to Canada and was appointed director of Toronto Psychiatric Hospital and professor and head of the department of psychiatry of the University of Toronto, succeeding CB Farrar. Despite the widely acclaimed scholarship of his predecessor, Stokes quickly established his own reputation as a teacher of psychiatry broadly based in biology and medicine, psychology and sociology. For him patients suffered from a breakdown in living. His students quickly came to recognize his excellence as a teacher, while his colleagues in Toronto appreciated his wise decisions and organizational ability. He actively promoted research enquiries in many fields.

In Toronto Psychiatric Hospital he invited Gjessing to spend a year as a visiting professor and encouraged him to establish a metabolic unit for the investigation of periodic catatonia. He also sponsored a team of social psychologists to investigate a community living in metropolitan Toronto; the report of this enquiry was published as a book entitled *Crestwood Heights*.

Toronto Psychiatric Hospital possessed only 72 beds and its small building was inadequate to support the facilities Stokes envisaged. For much of his tenure in Toronto he struggled to remedy this. He brought together influential people from university and business interests, and allying these with a provincial government he set in motion those forces which ultimately resulted in the 1966 opening of the Clarke Institute of Psychiatry (*Psychiatry in Transition 1966 – 1967*. Edited by Aldwyn B Stokes. Published by University of Toronto Press 1967). He became its first psychiatrist-in-chief prior to his retirement, and his portrait has hung in the auditorium of the Institute since then. Following his death the auditorium was named after him.

Aldwyn Stokes was the recipient of many honours. He served on national and international scientific committees and was instrumental in founding the Canadian Psychiatric Association, of which he became president in 1970. He was elected vice-president of the American Psychiatric Association in 1964, and in 1978 was made a life fellow and awarded its gold medal.

Stokes's psychiatric interests ranged widely over all aspects of his specialty and were reflected in his lectures and publications. His early interest in metabolic psychiatry was evidenced in a number of studies on periodic catatonia which he undertook following his return from Norway. His contributions included those on geriatric psychiatry, forensic psychiatry and many others. In addition to his popular lectures, which he regularly gave to undergraduate medical students and residents in psychiatry, he was in great demand as a speaker to non-medical groups.

Aldwyn Stokes was a genial soul. He was ever ready to share his counsel and his scholarship with his students and his colleagues, whether these observations were culled from his professional experience or from his wide knowledge of the sports and the geography of his adopted country. He was an eclectic psychiatrist, always pursuing a rational interpretation of his specialty and preferring that aspect of it which was firmly rooted in medicine and the basic sciences. Each summer when he was not attending a convention he would take his annual vacation as a crew member of a craft sailing on Lake Superior. Here he delighted in running the ship's galley. Later on as he grew older he would spend his vacation with his family at Burnegie Bay on Lake Joseph, and relax amidst the resin scented pine forests of Muskoka district.

In 1935 Stokes married a King's nurse, Margaret Agnes FitzGerald, daughter of Major Leo FitzGerald, Indian Army. The couple had two sons and two daughters, but none followed him into medicine.

Aldwyn Stokes retired prematurely and was honoured with the title of professor emeritus. Ingravescent Parkinson's disease brought about a progressive disability, which ultimately led to his death. JWLD

[Photo]

STONE, Thomas Scott *b.*20 July 1908 *d.*25 June 1982
MRCS LRCP (1930) MB BS Lond (1930) MRCP (1933) MD (1934) FRCP (1970)

Scott Stone was educated at Sedbergh School and qualified from the London Hospital in 1930. He became a member of the Royal College of Physicians in 1933 and MD (London) in 1934 – later joining a partnership in general practice in Cliftonville. During the 1939–1945 war he served with the Eighth Army as a lieutenant colonel RAMC in charge of a medical division.

In his early forties he paid little regard to illnesses, requiring a partial gastrectomy and thoracoplasty, and continued his very active way of life. At the start of the National Health Service he was appointed consultant physician to the Kent and Canterbury and Isle of Thanet District Hospitals and, while remaining in every sense a general physician, he developed a special interest in cardiology and diabetes. He was elected FRCP in 1970 and retired in 1973.

He had an active retirement. As a keen gardener he specialized in growing alpine plants and had an international reputation in this field. Natural history, photography and music were also absorbing interests and his love of fast cars remained throughout his life. Even after knowing him for years one could still be surprised by stories of his earlier achievements. He had apparently raced a motorcycle (a Scott) on the Isle of Man TT course, and he never quite gave up the thought of motorcycling again in his seventies. He had also been in demand as an expert ballroom dancer. Scott was regarded with affection by all who knew him and will be remembered as a modest and retiring man, always gentle and kindly. He was a true physician.

His early years of retirement were marred by the death of his first wife Christine, in 1975; but he married again, to Phyllis Milligan, in January 1981. He had a son and a daughter of his first marriage. RHA

[*Brit. med. J.*, 1982, **285**, 382; Photo]

STOTE, Cuthbert Lawson *b.*1 July 1903 *d.*19 Oct 1978
BA Cantab (1924) MRCS LRCP (1926) MB BChir (1929)
MRCP (1929) MA MD (1940) FRCP (1954)

Cuthbert Stote was born in Swindon. His father was headmaster of the local Church of England school, and his mother was descended from the Quaker family of Hardman in Liverpool. He was educated at Swindon Secondary School and won an open scholarship to Gonville and Caius College, Cambridge, where he was a prizeman in natural sciences and gained an honours BA. His clinical undergraduate years were at the London, where he was awarded the Andrew Clark, Treves, Anderson and other prizes. After graduation in 1926 he was house physician to Sir Robert Hutchison and was elected to membership of the College in 1929. On New Year's Day 1930 he joined LJ Godson in general practice in Shrewsbury, and within two years he was elected to the consultant staff of the Royal Salop Infirmary as physician in charge of the electrocardiographic department. The following year he became a full physician on the retirement of Willoughby Gardner, and he developed a deep affection for the hospital and a profound interest in its history. The advent of the National Health Service enabled him to devote himself wholly to hospital and consultant practice and he was elected a fellow of the College in 1954.

His great ability as a physician, his tall handsome figure, his courtesy, his charm and his kindness brought heavy professional demands, but he was a man of wide interests and culture. He was keenly interested in archaeology and especially that of the beautiful town of his adoption, which he loved and whose citizens took him to their hearts. He was a founder member, chairman and vice-president of the Shrewsbury civic society, and one of the only two honorary members of the Salop society of architects. His own home, Swan Hill Court House, built in 1761 – 1762 and previously the home of the Earl of Bath, was one of the most beautiful houses imaginable and when, in 1966, he was president of the West Midlands Physicians Association he entertained its members there in magnificent style. He was a talented painter, a connoisseur of antique furniture, a capable cabinet maker and a first class photographer. He had a wonderful, but never unkind, sense of humour, and was a brilliant after dinner speaker. After retirement he enjoyed doing pensions appeal tribunals all over the country. Though plagued for many years by renal calculi, he lived to the age of 75, dying from cardiac failure. He married Sheila Davis, the daughter of a London civil servant in 1930. They adopted a son and a daughter.

AGWW

[*Brit. med. J.*, 1978, **2**, 1567]

STUDDERT, Thomas Copeland *b.*13 Nov 1918 *d.*1 May 1982
MB BS Durh (1941) MRCP (1943) MD (1945) FRCP (1959)

Tom Studdert was born in Wylam upon Tyne. His father, Thomas George Studdert, was an optician practising in Newcastle. His mother was Eleanor, daughter of James Gibson, a corn merchant. He was married in 1945 to Mary Felicia, daughter of Major The Hon. Wellesley Fitzroy Somerset. They had three sons. Tom Studdert went to preparatory school in Newcastle and then to Sedbergh, where one of his most valued achievements was a prize for bird photography, an interest which he resumed in his retirement. He went to medical school in Newcastle and qualified in 1941, with first class honours. He attained distinction in medicine, surgery and midwifery. He worked as house physician and medical registrar in the Royal Victoria Infirmary, Newcastle, until he joined the Royal Air Force in 1943. Until 1945 he served as squadron medical officer in coastal and bomber commands and was posted to West Africa. There he enjoyed his work and took the opportunity to study tropical medicine, developing an interest in infectious diseases and gathering material that formed the basis of his MD thesis. He completed his service career with a year as squadron leader (medical specialist) in the RAF hospital in Ranceby.

On return to civilian life, Tom Studdert spent a short time in Newcastle and was then appointed medical registrar to the Cumberland Infirmary, Carlisle, where he worked till he retired. In 1948 he became a consultant physician to the East Cumberland group of hospitals and set about developing two small wards into a first class medical unit, which soon attracted final year students from Newcastle to work as clinical clerks, and often to return as house physicians. These young colleagues were quick to recognize Tommy's superlative gifts as a teacher of clinical medicine, a role in which he was always happy. His interests in medicine were wide but in his early years in Carlisle he developed his expertise in treating cases of meningitis and poliomyelitis. He was kept very busy by his general practitioner colleagues who valued his help in domiciliary consultations. In this work he travelled all over Cumberland and north Westmorland and became specially interested in rural medicine. This led to his original contributions on the subject of 'farmer's lung', and to a study of zoonoses in which he collaborated with veterinary colleagues. His medical school asked him to lecture on both these subjects, and also invited him to examine in the final MB examination. Although he was no great enthusiast for administrative work he served for a while as a member of the East Cumberland Hospital Management Committee, and in 1957 he was chairman of the medical staff in Cumberland. He had a very successful spell as postgraduate clinical tutor, and acted as deputy representative for the College in the northern region. He was also a committee member of the Regional Association of Physicians, and served for a year as president of the Carlisle Medical Society.

In 1967 he had a myocardial infarct. From this he made a good recovery and characteristically developed an interest in cardiology, which inspired him to establish and administer the coronary care unit and cardiac arrest teams in the Cumberland Infirmary. In 1975 while returning from a College dinner he was involved in a major train crash at Nuneaton. He was trapped in the wreckage and lost the fore part of one foot. This, together with osteoarthritis of his hips and angina, made life difficult, but he continued to work, cheerful, uncomplaining, and always ready to take a humorous view of his disabilities. He retired from his consultant appointment in 1979 but continued to see patients at his home until the day before he died. His retirement enabled him to spend time in his garden of which he was justly proud. He also developed his old interest in ornithology. His death came suddenly in the garden of his home on the outskirts of Carlisle.

Tommy was a general physician in the best tradition, much loved by his patients, who appreciated the broad and human interest which he showed in them, as well as the skill with which he helped them. His colleagues valued him greatly for his wisdom, courage, friendship and good humour, but perhaps most of all for the splendid memory with which he enhanced his professional skills and enlivened many a meeting. He was a devoted husband and father, and a generous, cheerful and understanding friend and colleague. CFR

[*Brit. med. J.*, 1982, **284**, 1778, 1943; **285**, 221; Photo]

SUMMERSKILL, William Hedley John *b*.8 Jan 1926 *d*.9 Mar 1977 BA Oxon (1947) MRCS LRCP (1949) BM BCh (1949) MA (1951) MRCP (1953) DM (1955) FACP (1966) FRCP (1967)

It is perhaps paradoxical that one so remarkably English should have made his greatest mark in the midwest of the United States. For at the time of his sudden death, at the early age of 51, Bill Summerskill was director of the gastroenterology unit and professor of medicine, Mayo Medical School, University of Minnesota.

William Summerskill was born in London of a medical family. His father was William Hedley Summerskill, an ophthalmologist in Portsmouth, and his aunt was Baroness Summerskill of Kenwood. He was educated at Harrow, where he became head boy, and went on to Oxford with an Evelyn Rothschild scholarship, gaining a rugby Blue, and later entering St Mary's Hospital Medical School with a university fellowship. After house appointments and service with the RAMC he became a registrar in 1953 at the Royal Postgraduate Medical School, London, where he worked with Dr (later Dame) Sheila Sherlock. It was during this period that he did the scrupulous and original work on hepatic coma and the pathogenesis of portal-systemic encephalopathy which established his reputation as a clinical research worker. None who heard them will ever forget the brilliance of his staff round presentations at that time. His gilded sophistication was hardly in the Hammersmith tradition of that era, and he was the only registrar in living memory who appeared at work in black coat and striped trousers on the day of the Eton and Harrow game at Lord's. But his hardworking efficiency, his literary skill, his uncompromising dedication to research, and his sheer clinical ability marked him out as one destined for the highest success.

He was a man of wide interests and culture. Readers of the *Lancet* will remember his crediting Shakespeare with the first description of hepatic encephalopathy in the alcoholic Sir Andrew Aguecheek, who believed that his wits were harmed by eating too much beef.

In 1955 a Rockefeller travelling scholarship of the Medical Research Council enabled him to spend a period with CS Davidson in the Thorndike Laboratories of the Harvard Medical School, where he made a lasting impression. Returning home in 1957, he became senior registrar to Sir Francis Avery Jones at the Central Middlesex Hospital, and there he expanded his interests into the wider field of gastroenterology. During this time he was secretary and vice-president of the Harveian Society of London, and played an important part in organizing the Harvey Tercentenary Commemoration.

In 1959 he was invited to develop a new gastroenterology unit at the Mayo Clinic. His outstanding talents were now given full rein, and he built up one of the best gastroenterology departments in the world. His enormous capacity for hard work, his administrative ability, and his enthusiastic encouragement of the highest standards of clinical reearch combined to create a unique group of gastroenterologists, who have attracted as research fellows some of the most brilliant young men in both Europe and the United States. He continued in active research, particularly on chronic hepatitis and the treatment of cirrhosis, and he was the author of some 130 original papers and many chapters in monographs and textbooks. In 1966 he became full professor in the University of Minnesota and, at the time of his death, he was also vice-chairman of the department of medicine at the Mayo Clinic. He was a past president of the American Association for the Study of the Liver, and on the governing board of the International Association for the Study of the Liver. He also served on numerous United States Government committees, particularly on those concerning food and drug administration and on the organization of gastroenterology.

He served his adopted country well, but remained essentially English. He never had a trace of an American accent. He kept up his links with England, being elected to the Association of Physicians of Great Britain and Ireland in 1966 and becoming a fellow of the Royal College of Physicians of London in 1967. In 1967 he was also visiting professor at the Royal Free Hospital, and had been invited to give the Lilly lecture at the RCP in 1978.

He married Elizabeth (Betsy) Sheppard in 1950, by whom he had one son. She died in 1965, and in 1969 he married Barbara Ehmcke.

He was a keen sportsman, maintaining his interest in both rugby and American football. He was a generous and genial host and a stream of international visitors were welcomed to his department, to his home, and to his boat on the Mississippi. Cruising the inland waterways of the USA was one of his favourite hobbies.

As the years went by and his hair turned to a distinguished silver his reputation became legendary. He stood for excellence and retained throughout his life the ideals and fearless convictions of his earlier years. His candour was unflinching, sometimes provocative, occasionally abrasive, but beneath the exterior there was a remarkable human being who commanded the intense loyalty of his colleagues and who had a Churchillian capacity for generosity and magnanimity.

The warmth of his personality will be remembered by all who knew him. GW/VL

[*Brit. med. J.*, 1977, **1**, 913; *Times*, 18 Mar 1977; *Lancet*, 1977, **1**, 710; *Gastroenterology*, 1977, **73**, 435-7; *Am. J. Dig. Dis.*, 1977, **22**, 934-5; Photo]

SUTCLIFFE, John *b*.27 June 1913 *d*.15 Oct 1980
MA MB BChir Cantab (1938) MRCP (1947) DMRD (1949) FFR (1953) FRCP (1969) FRCR (1975)

John Sutcliffe was a paediatric radiologist of international repute. He was a founder member of the European Society of Paediatric Radiology and president in 1966, when the society held its London meeting. He was born in Hyde, Cheshire, the son of James Sutcliffe, a wholesale supplier, and his wife Frances, daughter of Richard Burrows Smith, a rope manufacturer. In 1966 he married Maureen Grace, daughter of Malcolm Henry Harper, an insurance official. They had no children.

He was educated at Hyde Grammar School and read medicine at Cambridge and St Thomas's Hospital, London, graduating in 1938. After house appointments at St Thomas's, he joined the RAFVR in 1939 and served throughout the second world war, being stationed for some time in India. On demobilization, he returned to St Thomas's and was appointed consultant radiologist in 1953. His interest in paediatric radiology covered a wide field and he took his role as a teacher seriously, expecting a high standard from his students. He had earlier spent some time in postgraduate study in America at the Children's Hospital Medical Center in Boston, returning to become the first fully trained paediatric radiologist in Britain.

Apart from his professional work, he had a strong sense of altruism and responsibility towards his fellow men, finding time to give help and advice to the National Society for the Prevention of Cruelty to Children over the vexed issue of non-accidental injury.

Outside his work he was an enthusiastic sportsman. In his younger days he was a brilliant athlete and was a member of Britain's Olympic soccer team in 1936. To watch any sport in his company, be it football, tennis or cricket, was a stimulating experience because of his deep knowledge of the game. He also enjoyed good food and international travel. GW/VL

[*Lancet*, 1980, **2**, 928; Photo]

SWIFT, Peter Neville *b*.6 Jan 1917 *d*.22 June 1977
MRCS LRCP (1941) MRCP (1948) FRCP (1970)

Peter Swift was consultant paediatrician to the Bromley Area Health Authority. He was educated at Malvern College and Guy's Hospital, London, where he qualified with the conjoint in 1941, having previously spent some time in veterinary studies. He subsequently joined the Indian Medical Service, transferring to the Indian Army Medical Corps and seeing service in the Mediterranean, where he lost a leg during the Allied landings in southern Italy. He obtained the MRCP in 1948 and was elected a fellow in 1970.

Peter was born in Eccleshall, Staffordshire, the son of a retired farmer, Henry Swift, and his wife Alice, daughter of Thomas Hallam, a mill owner. In 1945 he married Barbara Grace Margaret, daughter of Thomas William Minchin, a corn merchant. They had three children: two daughters and a son. All his life Peter remained a lover of the country, and his interests included riding, beagling and tennis. He was also a talented artist. In 1969 he went to Mbale, Uganda, to set up a regional paediatric department, and during this time he made an exquisite collection of paintings of the wild flowers of that country. He had great talent as an administrator and the excellent records he kept during his stay in Uganda have formed the basis for further research work in the planning of health centres in developing countries.

He was appointed consultant paediatrician at Farnborough Hospital, in the Bromley group, in January 1950, and was consultant to the children's department at Sevenoaks Hospital, and to the general practitioner maternity unit when this was opened. During his early years he also provided consultant cover over a wide area of Kent. His interest in paediatrics covered a broad field, including mental subnormality. He carried out a research project on the genetic aspect of this disorder and was paediatrician in charge of Cheyne Hospital, West Wickham, a long-stay hospital for handicapped children. He initiated a comprehensive perinatal survey of all the babies born in the Bromley area, extending it to cover hospitals in the Cray Valley and Sevenoaks group. He also obtained approval for a computerized project, which has been continued. He wrote a considerable number of articles, despite his heavy clinical load, and was interested in antibiotics and their correct use. His book *The Physician's Guide to Chemotherapy* was published in 1952, and an article on antibiotics and host resistance appeared in the *British Medical Journal* in 1957.

On his retirement he moved to Dorset, where he maintained his interest in medicine and acted temporarily as consultant paediatrician at Dorchester. He was much in demand on working parties of the Conference of Missionary Societies, the British Paediatric Association, and WHO. He also spent a happy year making a survey of those trees in the district which he thought worthy of a preservation order; a list which was accepted in full by the authorities. GW/VL

[*Brit. med. J.,* 1977, **2**, 711; *Lancet,* 1977, **2**, 259; Photo]

SYMONDS, *Sir* **Charles Putnam** *b.*11 Apr 1890 *d.*7 Dec 1978
KBE (1946) CB (1944) MRCS LRCP (1915) MRCP (1916)
BM BCh Oxon (1919) DM (1919) FRCP (1924)

Charles Symonds, son of Sir Charters Symonds MS FRCS, surgeon to Guy's Hospital, was educated at Rugby, New College, Oxford, and Guy's Hospital, where he qualified in 1915. His medical training was interrupted by the first world war during which he saw service in France in the RAMC, was wounded, and awarded the Médaille

Militaire. On demobilization he served as house physician at the National Hospital, Queen Square, and medical registrar at Guy's. He graduated BM BCh in 1919, taking his DM in the same year, and then studied at Johns Hopkins Hospital, Baltimore, USA, with a Radcliffe travelling fellowship. In 1920 he was appointed neurologist to Guy's Hospital, shortly after Arthur Hurst had started a neurological clinic there. Symonds soon attracted the attention and respect of other neurologists by his exposition of the complex picture of encephalitis lethargica, and this was followed by an increasing flow of original work and critical reviews. Accepting and treating the psychoneuroses as part of his duties, he always maintained that a neurologist should be able and willing to do this.

He became honorary consultant neurologist to the Royal Air Force in 1934, and during the 1939–1945 war he gave up his large private practice and devoted his skill and experience to service in the RAF, conducting investigations into stress among bomber crews. He rose to the rank of air vice-marshal, was appointed CB in 1944 and received his knighthood two years later. On his return to civilian life he resumed his work as consultant physician in nervous diseases at Guy's, and the National Hospital, Queen Square. He was also honorary visiting neurologist to Johns Hopkins Hospital. In 1953 he toured Australia and New Zealand as Sims Commonwealth travelling professor in neurology, and gave the Harveian oration at the College in 1954. Elected an honorary fellow of the Royal Society of Medicine in 1964, he was an ex-president of the sections of psychiatry and neurology. He was also secretary of the section of neurological and psychological medicine of the BMA at the annual meeting in 1923, and president of the section in 1939. He was an honorary member of many societies, including the American Neurological Association and the New York Neurology Society.

A prolific writer, the publication of a selection of his papers, *Studies in Neurology* (1970), was received with acclaim. It was one of the few medical works to receive an extensive review in the *Times Literary Supplement*. He wrote the section on nervous diseases in Taylor's *Handbook of Medicine*, and acted as joint editor of later editions.

Charles Symonds was undoubtedly the most distinguished neurologist in Britain in his day. When he retired from the active staff at Guy's in 1955 he had been neurologist to the hospital for thirty-five years and had secured an enduring reputation by establishing the neurological department as it is known today. He will probably be best remembered for his skill in clinical diagnosis and his abilities as a teacher. The whole thinking about clinical neurology was immensely influenced by his example. His superb diagnostic powers were due to his high intellectual ability, deep learning, and rigorously logical appraisal of clinical evidence. He continued as mentor and teacher to his students even when they had already reached their 'clinical maturity'. He was rarely mistaken in his opinions, but when events proved him wrong there was never any cover up of evidence. No one was more anxious than he to go over everything again and pinpoint the error, and to ensure that the lessons learned would not be lost. He was a clinical observer in the tradition of Hughlings Jackson and Gowers, and will be remembered for the contributions he made to the study of head injuries, epilepsy, the psychiatric aspect of neurology, and the neurological aspects of psychiatry. He was above all the neurologist's neurologist, and in this role stepped into the position which Sir Gordon Holmes had formerly occupied. Charles Symonds' scientific integrity was absolute, and no man was less a slave of his hypothesis. He remained a perpetual student and well into his eighties he would surprise his younger colleagues by his knowledge of the current literature on his specialty and his extraordinary capacity for relating the observations of others to his own clinical experience. His mind was always open and receptive, and he never assumed that fixity which often comes with advancing years.

In 1915 he married Janet Palmer Poulton, who died four years later. In 1920 he married Edythe Dorton, and they had four sons. His favourite relaxation was fly fishing, although in later years his activities were limited by a vascular accident which left him somewhat unsteady, and he suffered from progressive deafness. However, the vigour of his conversation was unimpaired, although he said that his memory was not as good as it was – his own estimate was a reduction of 30% – yet not long before he died he was in correspondence with one of his most distinguished 'senior pupils' about some very new ideas and experimental findings related to the physiology of sensation.

GW/VL

[*Brit. med. J.*, 1978, **2**, 1793; 1979, **1**, 134, 483; *Lancet*, 1978, **2**, 1389; *Guy's Hosp. Gaz.*, 1979, **94**; *Times*, 19 Nov 1978; *Daily Telegraph*, 12 Dec 1978; Photo]

SYNGE, Victor Millington *b.*5 Sept 1893 *d.*25 Feb 1976
BA Dubl (1916) MB BCh BAO (1918) DPH (1919) MD (1919)
MRCPI (1919) FRCPI (1921) FRCP* (1962)

Victor Synge was born in Dublin, a son of Edward Hatch Synge, a land agent. His mother, Ellen Frances Price, was the daughter of James Price, a civil engineer. His uncle, John Millington Synge, was the well known Irish playwright, and his brother John Lighton Synge FRS, was a theoretical physicist of international reputation.

Synge was educated at St Andrews College, Dublin, from which he entered Trinity College, Dublin. He won many prizes as an undergraduate and was elected to a foundation scholarship of the College in experimental science. After graduating BA in 1916 he volunteered and served as a surgeon probationer, RNVR. On qualifying in medicine he was at once appointed assistant to the professor of pathology. He resigned the post three years later on being elected visiting physician to the Royal City of Dublin Hospital, an appointment which he held until his retirement in 1972.

In academic medicine he held most of the posts available to him in turn. First at the Royal College of Surgeons in Ireland, he was successively professor of preventive medicine and medical jurisprudence and then professor of medicine. He resigned the latter appointment in 1934 when he was elected King's professor of the practice of medicine at Dublin University. This chair he held until its abolition in 1962. He had already become the first full time professor of clinical medicine in 1955, and the next year was elected regius professor of physic. He was a past president and honorary member of the Association of Physicians of Great Britain and Ireland.

Synge was essentially a scholar. His friends regretted that he read so much but wrote so little. His contributions to local meetings always attracted an appreciative audience, combining his very personal wit with often iconoclastic findings on some fashionable test or therapy. His formidable intelligence was more often used critically than constructively. A conscientious general physician of authority and wide range, he was popular with students as a logical, lucid and entertaining clinical teacher. He was not successful in directing the energies of his juniors, for he had little inclination to delegate clinical responsibility or to encourage research. Although he enjoyed travel and had a useful knowledge of European languages, he seemed to have few interests outside his work. He could be found in his wards seven days a week until his eightieth year. He then retired to his cottage in the Dublin hills, where he cultivated his forestry plantation until his death in 1976.

In 1919 he married Mary Edith, daughter of John Allen, farmer, of Dunlavin, Co. Wicklow. She died in 1973. They had two sons. DMM

[*Brit. med. J.*, 1976, **2**, 118; Photo]

TALBOT, *Lt. Gen. Sir* **Norman (Graham Guy)**
*b.*16 Feb 1914 *d.*27 Feb 1979
KBE (1966) OBE (1945) TD (1950) O St J (1966)
MRCS LRCP (1937) MB BS Lond (1938) MRCOG (1951)
MD (1953) FRCOG (1960) FRCP* (1973)

Born in Hastings, the second son of the Reverend Richard Talbot MA, and his wife Ethel Stuart, Normal Talbot was educated at Great Yarmouth Grammar School and Reigate Grammar School. From there he proceeded to King's College, London, and King's College Hospital, during 1932 – 1937, for his undergraduate medical training, qualifying in 1938. Posts as house physician, house anaesthetist and house surgeon (obstetrics and gynaecology) at King's College Hospital, during 1937 – 1939, followed, and until the outbreak of war he was RMO in the private maternity wing of King's, relinquishing the post of junior obstetric registrar in 1939 to commence his war service.

His first RAMC appointment was regimental medical officer to the 12th Light Anti-Aircraft Regiment, Royal Artillery, and in 1940, as an anaesthetist with No 5 General Hospital, he went to France with the British Expeditionary Force. He subsequently served in the Middle East as an anaesthetist and second in command of a mobile casualty clearing station. From 1943 to 1944 he was commandant of the British Medical Mission to the National Army of Liberation of Yugoslavia and commanded the Grumo Military Hospital, Italy, transferring in

1945 to the 45th General Hospital, Taranto. From 1946 to 1947 he was assistant director of medical services at general headquarters with the Central Mediterranean Forces.

After the war, Talbot obtained the following appointments: adviser in obstetrics and gynaecology to the War Office, 1951 – 1958; adviser in obstetrics and gynaecology to the Ministry of Defence, 1963 – 1966; OC Cambridge Military Hospital, Aldershot, 1966 – 1967; deputy director of medical services HQ 1 (Br) Corps, 1967 – 1968; commandant and director of studies, Royal Army Medical College, Millbank, 1968 – 1969; director general Army Medical Services, 1969 – 1973; and honorary surgeon to Her Majesty the Queen, 1968 – 1973.

His qualities as a leader were strong and became obvious from his last two posts: as director of studies at the Royal Army Medical College and as director general of the Army Medical Services, when he had to apply the very difficult requirements of the Todd report to the Army Medical Services.

Norman Talbot married Winifred, the daughter of William Kilby of Donnington, Lincolnshire, in 1939 and they had two sons and a daughter. He enjoyed the constant love and support of his wife for some 42 years. He was a deeply religious man and a staunch supporter of his local church. Subsequent to his retirement from the Army, with the rank of lieutenant general, he became medical director of the Margaret Pyke Centre in London. JPB

[*Brit. med. J.*, 1979, **1**, 960; Photo]

TALLERMAN, Kenneth Harry *b.*3 Nov 1894 *d.*25 Oct 1981
MC (1917) MRCS LRCP (1921) MB BChir Cantab (1922)
MRCP (1923) MA MD (1925) FRCP (1936)

Kenneth Tallerman was educated at Charterhouse School and commenced his medical studies at Cambridge and St Thomas's Hospital Medical School. With the outbreak of the first world war, his medical studies were interrupted and he joined the Friends' Ambulance Unit, in which he served until September 1915. He was then commissioned in the Royal Artillery and was awarded the Military Cross in 1917.

After the war he resumed his medical studies, qualifying with the conjoint diploma in 1921 and graduated MB BChir the following year. He held several junior appointments at St Thomas's Hospital and obtained the MRCP in 1923. He then embarked on a career in paediatrics, spending two years at the Institute of Paediatrics in Washington and six months as a house physician at the Hospital for Sick Children, Great Ormond Street. His association with the London Hospital started with a registrarship in 1926, followed by his appointment to the consultant staff in 1931. He held other consultant appointments at Paddington Green Children's Hospital, the Westminster Children's Hospital, Harrow Hospital and St Margaret's Hospital, Epping, over the years, but his first love and his greatest interest was the London. He was elected to the fellowship in 1936.

He served his country for a second time, in the RAMC as a medical specialist from 1941 to 1944, and returned to the London as head of the children's department, from which he retired in 1959.

Kenneth Tallerman was an eminent figure in British paediatrics. He was president of the section of paediatrics of the Royal Society of Medicine in 1950–1951, and was elected president of the British Paediatric Association in 1957. His special interest was infant nutrition, and he published several articles on this subject.

He was very happily married and his wife, Alice (née Rose), was a successful consultant anaesthetist. It was sad that in the year of his retirement she was stricken with a fatal disease. However, a few years later he married Mrs Florence Keeble, and was able to enjoy a long and peaceful retirement in his charming old house in the depths of the Essex countryside. Kenneth never had children of his own but in a long career in paediatrics, lasting thirty three years, he had very many children as his patients and he was always proud of the fact that many of these patients brought their own children to him as the years went by.

Those who worked with and for Kenneth Tallerman at the London were always impressed by his consideration for his juniors. He had a love of dogs, gardening, good food and good wine. He used to bring his dog to the London in his car, and at the end of his ward rounds the whole firm would proceed with Kenneth to the car park where the said dog was released for a few minutes, before its master returned to the staff room for tea.

ADMJ

[*Brit. med. J.*, 1981, **283**, 1269; *London Hosp. Gazette,* Dec 1959, 62(5); Photo]

TATE, Bernard Clive *b.*1 Sept 1901 *d.*31 Jan 1979
MBE (1942) BA Cantab (1923) MRCS LRCP (1926) BChir (1926) MB (1930) MA (1933) MD (1934)

Bernard Tate was born at Handsworth, Birmingham, where his father was a schoolmaster. He was educated at King Edward VI School, Birmingham, and Gonville and Caius College, Cambridge, and his high intellectual ability was soon demonstrated by the award of numerous scholarships, exhibitions and prizes. Although he rowed in his College boat he missed a Blue. After graduating in medicine in 1926 he held numerous junior hospital posts including that of resident medical officer at the General Hospital, Birmingham, thus obtaining a wide knowledge and experience of general medicine, and becoming a member of the College in 1928. Thereafter he turned to dermatology and after junior appointments at the West London Hospital, Great Ormond Street and St John's Hospital, was elected consultant dermatologist to the Children's Hospital and the General Hospital in Birmingham. He made a number of valuable contributions to the dermatological literature, and his opinion was so greatly valued that he always had an enormous practice.

He was a lecturer in dermatology in the University of Birmingham, president of the British Association of Dermatology and of the section of dermatology of both the Royal Society of Medicine and the British Medical Association. During the 1939–1945 war he served for six years as a consultant dermatologist, with the rank of lieutenant colonel, in the Middle East and in Southern Command, and his outstanding contribution was recognized by the award of the MBE. After retiring from his hospital appointments in Birmingham in 1966, he went to live at Findon in Sussex and soon after his arrival there the Worthing General Hospital persuaded him to hold regular dermatological clinics for them. In 1975 he moved back to the Midlands and died suddenly at his home at Little Aston.

In 1935 he married Millicent Moseley who was also medically qualified. She died in 1975. There was one son of the marriage, who achieved distinction in the British Broadcasting Corporation.

Tate was a handsome, courteous, kindly man, who though quiet had a great gift for friendship, particularly towards his junior colleagues, whom he constantly strove to help. AGWW

[*Brit. med. J.*, 1979, **1**, 483; Photo]

TATTERSALL, Peter Ewart Romney *b.*1 May 1915
*d.*20 May 1982
MB ChB Leeds (1939) MD (1946) MRCP (1946) FRCP (1968)

Born in Neath, South Wales, Peter Tattersall followed his father and elder brother Rex (see Vol.VI) in taking up medicine. Educated at Epsom College, where he showed no special aptitudes and did not shine at games, he graduated from the University of Leeds in 1939 with first class honours and was awarded the William Hey gold medal. At the outbreak of the second world war he joined the RAMC and saw service in France with the 51st Highland Division. During the evacuation of the BEF a medical officer was needed to stay with a large group of wounded men – Peter lost the toss and spent the rest of the war as a POW in various camps, looking after prisoners of many nationalities and enduring great hardship and semi-starvation. On 22 January 1945 he, with some 6000 other prisoners, left Stalag 344 at Lamsdorf in Silesia, close to the Polish border, on a forced march of some 600 miles in bitterly cold conditions. Hitler apparently thought that Allied POWs might be useful as hostages and ordered them back towards Berlin in front of the advancing Russian armies. During the following three months Peter kept a daily diary until he, with the 2000 others who survived, were liberated by the Americans in West Germany on 12 April. This diary, along with others he kept, is in the Imperial War Museum. It is a fascinating factual account of this incredible journey done on starvation rations in often freezing conditions; marching 20–30 kilometers a day with inadequate boots and clothes, and with many of the men sleeping in barns with a little straw, or even outside in the snow. Dysentery, pneumonia, starvation, multiple vitamin deficiencies, diphtheria and sheer exhaustion caused most of the deaths. Peter himself suffered a very severe febrile throat infection with membrane formation which he thought was diphtheria, although it may have been Vincent's angina. He only survived by hanging onto a horse drawn cart for several days. Never, during those three months, however ill or exhausted he was himself, did he fail to attend the sick in his care. He was sometimes able to get a few of the worst cases into a civilian hospital and to arrange rough transport for some of the others. His supplies of drugs were pitiable. There is, however, no hint of despair in his writing, although he was clearly obsessed by hunger and detailed the meagre ration with meticulous care. When the sun shone he recorded it with thankfulness – when the diet was supplemented in any way he rejoiced.

He clearly not only lived up to the highest standards of the medical profession, but was also a man of great personal courage and endurance. He was just seven stones when liberated.

I have dwelt at some length on his wartime experiences as they epitomized Peter's character. Although small he was tough; he was also cheerful, tolerant, shrewd, highly intelligent and a very kind and good doctor. He had great insight into human character, and his patients and many friends found themselves talking freely to him in an unusual way. He had great charm of manner and was as popular with men as he was with women, who found him very attractive.

Medically, he had a clinical flair for diagnosis and an ability to integrate modern investigations and treatment methods with the best traditional medicine. He avoided administration – outside that of his own department – if he could, and was sometimes very brusque to those administrators whom he considered had failed him.

When he arrived at the County Hospital, Omagh, Co. Tyrone, in 1949 much was needed in the way of beds, staff and equipment to bring it up to modern standards. While Peter's main love was his own department and his hobby was cardiology, he did much to help the needs of the other consultants and pulled his weight as a medical staff member.

At this time the fishing in the rivers and lakes of Northern Ireland was excellent and Peter was an expert fisherman – both for trout and salmon. Deep wading in fast rivers with many stones, boulders and rocky ledges is hazardous, but Peter throve on it and his rewards were rich. In his later years when the dredging of rivers, silage effluent, over-netting in the sea and estuaries and poaching had done much to ruin the fishing, he still had the knack of knowing where to go and when.

Grouse also were plentiful in the area in the 1950s (now virtually extinct) and Peter enjoyed many a day walking up behind setters and pointers. He kept setters himself for many years – if they were not perfectly disciplined one sensed that he himself had had his fill of discipline and privation and that he wanted to fill his remaining years with enjoyment, subject only to this not interfering with medical responsibility. Rough shooting, open air skating and cricket he enjoyed. He was also a good golfer and bridge player, but Peter did not neglect his creature comforts. He lived well, liked good food, good wine and good company and he found plenty of the latter in Ulster. The Northern Irish hospitality is world famous and Peter used to love telling how a domiciliary visit in the country might end up with the GP driving him home.

He was himself, with Helen his wife, an excellent host and was particularly good to his junior staff, whom he entertained regularly, and he was renowned for his bedside and outpatient teaching. He was an early authority on sarcoidosis and a very keen cardiologist, although he was general physician, paediatrician and geriatrician for many years. He had studied cardiology at the Middlesex Hospital after his repatriation, and while working for his MD and MRCP, and always acknowledged his lifelong debt to Evan Bedford.

If Peter had a fault it was a reluctance to put pen to paper. There was a wealth of clinical material in his area upon which he taught with great ability and authority, but the task of disease indexing and publishing did not appeal to him.

There is no doubt that this area of Northern Ireland was extremely fortunate in having as its very first physician such a good all rounder as Peter Tattersall. He was in great demand by his colleagues and the general practitioners; was worshipped by the nursing staff, and loved by his patients. In all his work and other activities he was most ably helped and supported by his wife Helen (née Kilburn) who waited five long years for him to come back from the war, who bore him three children, and who lovingly nursed and supported him during his last years when crippled by severe drug-resistant Parkinson's disease. TJW

[*Brit. med. J.*, 1982, **285**, 68; Photo]

TEARE, Robert Donald *b*.1 July 1911 *d*.17 Jan 1979
MRCS LRCP (1936) MRCP (1937) MB BChir Cantab (1938)
MD (1948) DMJ (1962) FRCP (1962) FRCPath (1962)
Hon LLD Sheffield (1978)

Donald Teare was born in the Isle of Man, the son of a newspaper proprietor, Albert Hugh Teare, a Manxman of note who became a member of the House of Keys, and his wife who was the daughter of a Manx farmer. Schooled at King William's College, Isle of Man, where he became head scholar, Donald prepared for a medical career at Gonville and Caius College, Cambridge, and entered St George's Hospital, from where he qualified in 1938, proceeding to MD in 1948. He became a member of the Royal College (by examination) in 1937, and was elected a fellow in 1962. He was a founder fellow of the Royal College of Pathologists, serving on its council from 1964 to 1967, and being treasurer from 1968 to 1973.

Donald married Kathleen Gracey, daughter of Lieutenant Colonel Thomas Gracey of Northcote Manor, Umberleigh in Devon, in 1937, and his family life, enriched by three sons and a daughter, was plainly a vital pivot for his professional life. His charming, warm hearted wife was a constant support to him in his private life. She shared his interest in public service and was a magistrate in London. Donald Teare was elected master of the Society of Apothecaries in 1977, where his comfortable authority and equable character emerged repeatedly in his many easy and humorous speeches.

His early steps in pathology were largely guided by another 'character' at St George's, John Taylor, a large avuncular man of means, to whom over the years Teare bore an increasing resemblance. Amiable and tolerant, they both commanded a natural respect from students and had no need to impose discipline, but acquired affection and respect for their sincerity and 'plain man's teaching' of the basic principles of pathology. Both were plainly authorities in their specialties, and both earned the gratitude of 35 years of students at St George's and at St Bartholomew's Hospitals for their sound practical teaching in forensic medicine. Of the two men, Donald Teare emerged as much the more prepared to take the responsibilities of public office, becoming president of the Association of Forensic Pathologists (1961 – 1962) and president of the Medico-Legal Society (1965 – 1966). He was appointed to a personal chair in the University of London in 1968, and in 1978, in consequence of his many contributions to society, association and conference affairs and his undoubted authority in this field, the University of Sheffield honoured him with the degree of LLD.

His contributions to the literature of his chosen specialty were few. His forte was his power of speech, of constructive comment, of communication with his fellows at meetings, rather than of lengthy textual writing. Comments such as 'there are quite enough books on the subject', and 'especially your own, my dear chap', 'there are too many journals', 'a good thing if they were all suppressed for a while', may well explain his relatively few contributions to the literature. After dinner speaking came naturally, almost always without notes. His sense of humour served him well and anything he had to say was couched in the relaxed effortless style that so became his character.

Donald Teare's contributions to pathology, mainly in the field of medico-legal practice, included recognition in 1958 of that curious hypertrophy of the left ventricular muscle which for a time, with Russell Brock's surgical interest, became known as 'Teare's asymmetrical hypertrophy', following Teare's initial description of it in the *British Heart Journal*. Although he wrote little, he lectured widely and well, being best remembered for his pithy contributions to English and international congresses – in Paris, Budapest, Scandinavia and the United States in particular. He was motivated by a desire to inject his practical experience into the records. He plainly set out to promote a clearer understanding of the safe legal inferences to be drawn from observations, so as to ensure an informed balance between prosecution and defence views. He was above all a reasonable man, placid under work pressure, and imperturbable in the witness box under cross examination, being prepared to accept an alternative proposition if it had substance, and to resist it firmly when it appeared to him to have bias. Lawyers and juries both felt a sense of justice being 'seen to be done' when he gave his experienced views. He never sought publicity and shunned the press, referring journalists to the 'officer in charge of enquiries' with a courtesy that made his refusals to accede to pressure from the press to reveal crime details easily acceptable. His best known crime cases were those of Timothy Evans, the 'cleft chin' murder (Martirosoff), the Camb 'porthole' case, and the Podola murder which challenged the 'McNaughten rules' in a novel manner.

Donald Teare relaxed in his native Castletown, where he could indulge in golfing companionship and feel his basic Manx independence. An active retirement was, alas, denied him by a succession of minor strokes which fortunately for him ran a short course, eroding only his memory until just before his death. The oft-repeated phrase 'he will be sadly missed' is, in Donald Teare's case, only too true. He was much respected and loved – a combination not always achieved by men of distinction in medicine. CKS

[*Brit. med. J.*, 1979, **1**, 354, 483; *Lancet*, 1979, **1**, 225; *Daily Telegraph*, 19 Jan 1979; *Brit. med. J.*, 1967, **4**, 812; Photo]

TELLING, Otto Henry Johann Maxwell *b*.5 Mar 1911 *d*.2 Nov 1980
BA Oxon (1933) BM BCh (1936) MRCS LRCP (1936)
MRCP (1938) MA DM (1942) FRCP (1946)

Max Telling was born at Leeds, the son of Maxwell Telling, consulting physician to the General Infirmary at Leeds, and Ingeborg Aagaard of Denmark. From Shrewsbury he won a classical scholarship to University College, Oxford, but he returned to Leeds for his clinical training. After house appointments at Leeds he became first assistant to George Graham at Bart's. He then went to the London Chest Hospital as house physician, later becoming medical registrar.

Soon after the outbreak of war he was seconded to the Emergency Medical Service and later became assistant physician at Goodmayes Hospital, Ilford. In 1942 he joined the RAMC and served in North Africa and Italy as a medical specialist, eventually becoming lieutenant colonel i/c a medical division.

After the war he spent a short time as physician to Clare Hall Co. Hospital before being appointed assistant physician to the General Infirmary at Leeds in 1948, eventually retiring in 1976 as senior physician. He was also senior clinical lecturer in medicine to the University of Leeds and for some years was consulting physician to St James's Hospital and the Leeds Public Dispensary and Hospital.

Telling was a general physician in the orthodox mould with a special interest in chest diseases. He was a most careful and conscientious physician with a strong sense of duty to his patients, colleagues and students. He examined in medicine at Leeds and for the Royal College of Physicians. The style of his publications reflected his classical education, which was also the basis of his skill as a precise, effective teacher and lecturer.

His powerful physique was an asset for the football and cricket he greatly enjoyed as a young man, and contributed to his skill as an expert carpenter in later life. As a senior Freemason he had a very wide circle of friends in many walks of life. He spent many of his vacations in a caravan in Scotland and was a dedicated bird watcher. He was an expert on port, a gourmet and a devoted Savoyard.

His last ten years were marred by a severe, disabling illness which he bore with great fortitude, supported by his devoted wife. In 1940 he married Dorothy (Jerry), daughter of Valentine Henry Gordon, a Glasgow graduate who practised in Australia, where she was born, and later in England. They had one daughter. DT

[*Brit. med. J.*, 1981, **282**, 79; *Lancet,* 1981, **1**, 57; Photo]

THOMAS, Edward Gwynne *b.*6 Apr 1907 *d.*21 May 1976
OBE (1946) VRD (1943) BSc Wales (1927) MRCS LRCP (1929)
MB BS Lond (1930) MD (1933) MRCP (1933) FRCP (1971)

Edward Thomas started his medical studies in the Welsh National Medical School, Cardiff, and graduated BSc in pre-clinical studies in 1927. Owing to a temporary interruption of clinical teaching in Cardiff he, with many of his fellow students, completed his clinical training at University College Hospital, London, where he qualified with the conjoint in 1929 and MB BS in 1930. He passed the MD London in 1933 and was admitted to the membership of the College in the same year.

He early showed an interest in dermatology and became senior registrar at St John's Hospital for Diseases of the Skin, and was also assistant in the skin department of the Hospital for Sick Children, Great Ormond Street. He was awarded the Chesterfield medal in 1933, an award made annually by examination at St John's Hospital.

At that time dermatology and venereology were not completely separate disciplines and Thomas's interest and activities covered both, leaning more in the direction of the latter. He was for many years head of the department of venereology at UCH, and lectured in that subject in the medical school, but regularly deputized for the dermatologist when necessary, and was appointed consultant dermatologist to the Whittington, New End, and French Hospitals. After his retirement he was honorary consultant dermatologist and venereologist to UCH.

Thomas joined the RNVR as a surgeon sub-lieutenant in 1928 and served throughout the 1939 – 1945 war as a specialist in naval hospitals in the UK and Australia. He was demobilized with the rank of surgeon commander and awarded the OBE in 1946.

Gwynne Thomas contributed the chapter on venereology in Garland and Phillips' *Textbook of Medicine* (1953).

In 1936 he married Lisbeth Helen Mair, daughter of Griffith Thomas, general manager of the British Linen Bank, and they had one son. Sadly, his wife died in 1950.

Thomas was a quiet, amiable man who shunned the limelight and personal advancement. He enjoyed playing golf. FRB/GW

THOMSON, ***Sir*** **Arthur Peregrine** *b.* – 1890 *d.*15 July 1977
Kt (1959) MC MB ChB Birm (1915) MRCP (1920) MD (1923) FRCP (1930)

Arthur Thomson was born in British Guiana where his father, Arthur Henry Thomson, was a colonial civil servant. He was educated at Dulwich College and the University of Birmingham, and to both he retained lifelong allegiance and showed profound gratitude. His high intelligence and abundant energy were soon evident, and at Birmingham he was Queen's scholar, Ingleby scholar, Russell memorial prizeman and achieved first class honours in medicine, surgery, obstetrics and gynaecology. He graduated in 1915 and immediately thereafter joined the RAMC serving in the trenches in France as a regimental medical officer with the Guards until he was, somewhat against his will, promoted to command a field ambulance. He was awarded the Military Cross, the Croix de Guerre with Star and was twice mentioned in British and once in French despatches. On demobilization he was invited to join the consultant staff of the General Hospital in Birmingham and despite having no higher qualification he was appointed assistant physician in 1919. The following year he was elected a member of the College and in 1923 he obtained his MD.

A long career of success and service as a consultant physician and academician followed, which few in the twentieth century have equalled. Small in stature, he had the appearance, the manner, and always the behaviour of a gentleman. To everyone he was courteous, charming and generous whatever their station, and even to those who wounded him he was incapable of bearing a grudge. No man had greater consideration for the feelings and welfare of his colleagues or fellow men.

As a physician he was one of the giants of his generation. His reputation and his practice embraced the length and breadth of the land, for he had a diagnostic flair that enabled him to solve problems which had defeated all others, and a capacity always to say – in a few words – exactly what was appropriate and kind to every patient and to every colleague in every situation.

'AP', as he was always affectionately called, had an enormous capacity for work, the ability to deal with patients and their relatives quickly and yet to leave their anxieties solved, and the knack of brevity and clarity in his letters; thus despite an enormous practice and heavy academic commitments he had time to read, and enjoy country pursuits, and was such a cultured and knowledgeable man that his company at lunch or dinner was always exciting, full of interest, wit and friendship.

Essentially a general physician, he ran the diabetic clinic in Birmingham for many years, and published a number of important papers on diabetes at a time when treatment first became possible for its victims. He also contributed to the epidemiology of rheumatic fever and was instrumental in establishing the Baskerville School for rheumatic children. An outbreak of psittacosis in Birmingham led to a series of publications about a disease until then unrecognized, and later, appreciating the implications of increasing life expectation, he devoted much research to the 'Problems of ageing and chronic sickness' which was the subject of his Lumleian lecture in 1949. In 1930 he had been elected a fellow, and in 1962 received the high honour of being Harveian orator.

In 1947 he was appointed part-time professor of therapeutics in the University of Birmingham. In 1951 he became dean of the faculty of medicine and the following year vice-principal of the University. He was a member of the General Medical Council 1951 – 1965, of the governing body of the University College, Ibadan, and of the Inter-University Council for Higher Education Overseas. He also served on the Hinchcliffe and McNair committees, and on the council to advise the Minister of Health on the efficiency of hospitals. He was president of the British Medical Association 1958 – 1959, and chairman of the Birmingham regional hospital board, to which he gave magnificent service over many years, 1962 – 1963. He was knighted in 1959 and received honorary degrees from the Universities of Edinburgh and Birmingham. In 1959 he was Linacre lecturer at St John's College, Cambridge.

'AP' was one of the original members of that most exclusive club, the Medical Pilgrims, and a prominent and popular member of the Association of Physicians of Great Britain and Ireland. He was chairman of the Union Club in Birmingham and also of the Buckland Club. The evening of his long life was marred by heart block, Stokes-Adams attacks and a pacemaker, but he refused to be daunted and continued to play bridge every afternoon at the Edgbaston Golf Club, to read, to walk and to enjoy talking to and dining with his countless friends, until very shortly before his death.

A fine bust of him by Franta Belsky is in the medical school of the University of Birmingham, where the great assembly hall bears his name. The building of the West Midlands regional health authority is 'Arthur Thomson House'. However, there was never a man less in need of such reminders of his great contribution to medicine. He will ever be remembered for his distinction as a physician, for his kindness and generosity – he gave almost all his material possessions to the University of Birmingham – and for his unswerving devotion to Birmingham Medical School and its teaching hospitals. Unlike so many of subsequent generations he resisted all temptations to diversify his energies and efforts outside the city he loved, and this was one of the secrets of his greatness.

He married Minnie Scott Lindsley with whom he was supremely happy. They had one adopted daughter. Lady Thomson died in 1960.

AGWW

[*Brit. med. J.*, 1977, **2**, 395; *Lancet*, 1977, **2**, 311; *Times*, 27 July 1977; Photo]

THOMSON, ***Sir*** **Daniel** *b.*30 May 1912 *d.*29 Oct 1976
Kt (1975) CB (1963) MB ChB St And (1935) DPH (1946)
MD (1948) MRCP (1965) FRCP (1970)

Daniel Thomson, the son of a journalist, John Duncan Thomson, and his wife Janet Simpson McFadyen, daughter of Lachlan McFadyen, a master mason, was born at Dundee, and went to school at Downfield and subsequently at the Dundee High School. He was a medical student at St Andrews University and the Dundee Royal Infirmary, and qualified in 1935. He did various house jobs at his teaching hospital and at the Radcliffe Infirmary (1937) and the North Middlesex Hospital (1938) and he went into the RAMC in 1940. He saw action in the desert with a field ambulance, and was DADMS in Palestine and the Middle East Headquarters. Later he commanded a hospital in Scottish Command at Fort George.

Thomson entered the service of the Surrey County Council in 1947 and joined the Ministry of Health in 1950. He was attached to the epidemiology division with WH Bradley, where he worked on many infectious disease problems, including whooping cough, tuberculosis and poliomyelitis, and he contributed largely to departmental policy in these fields, with his historical background and incisive understanding of communicable disease. He was very concerned that medical objectives to improve the standard of life should not be superseded by technical advances, and that hospitals should not improve at the expense of general practice. In 1958 he became deputy chief medical officer with responsibility for local government medical matters, including epidemiology, civil defence (where he contributed much good sense to what others were apt to regard as tiresome distraction) and medical education. He also made several exhausting but important trips to the Middle East for the Foreign Office. He fulfilled these duties with much distinction, was made Queen's honorary physician (1962 – 1965) and delivered the Milroy lecture to the College in 1966 on 'Mass immunization in the control of infectious diseases' which was published in the *British Medical Journal* the same year. He was president of the section of epidemiology at the Royal Society of Medicine in 1964. Other publications during this period include 'The ebb and flow of infections' (1955); 'The changing pattern of disease' (1957); 'Whooping cough, a review' (1953); 'Non-paralytic poliomyelitis' (1954); 'Poliomyelitis in the neonatal period' (1954), and 'Changes in epidemiology and preventive medicine' (1965).

It was with great regret, tinged with pride, that the Ministry of Health lost him when he became the Treasury medical adviser. This switch might be regarded by some as a step down – the DCMO post had great implications for the National Health Service – but the TMA post meant an independent command and had enormous possibilities too, of which he took full advantage. The post became that of medical adviser to the Civil Service in 1968; he was still occupying it at the time of his sudden death. He took with him his old interest in epidemiology and seized the marvellous opportunities of the captive Civil Service population, publishing 'Sickness absence in the

Civil Service' in 1970. He had many epidemiological projects in progress or in the pipeline when he died, particularly in the field of cardiovascular disease, work done with DD Reid. But the Civil and Foreign Service will not only remember him as an epidemiologist. He was above all a doctor, concerned as much with the mind as with the body, and many people can testify to the infinite trouble he took with individuals in medical need. Ambassadors, permanent secretaries, principals, executive officers, clerical officers, messengers – no one looked in vain for help; and the most careful medical examination, diagnosis, treatment and aftercare was insisted upon.

His hobbies included walking and travelling, especially with his wife and two sons, and he was always curious about different ways of life and in the continuum of life, which was reflected in his keen interest in his own background; he ancestors came from the Hebrides and Argyllshire and he was a real Highland Scot. He always spent a part of the holidays in Argyllshire with his family. But his work was also his relaxation and he gave his undivided enthusiasm to everything he did.

Tommy (no one ever called him Daniel) was a very rare person whose death shocked everyone. He was very Scottish, with his forthright expression of opinion and his highly developed and sometimes mischievous sense of humour. He was a loyal and good friend and a man of great integrity and honesty, who never said what he did not believe, or said behind anyone's back what he was not prepared to say to their faces. A first rate doctor, an admirable administrator and an outstandingly lovable person – that was Tommy.

He married in 1946 Dorothy Violet Coles, the daughter of Arthur Coles, a solicitor, and they had two sons. He died at home in Worplesdon, Surrey, very suddenly. ALW

[*Brit. med. J.*, 1976, **2**, 1204; *Lancet*, 1976, **2**, 1094; *Times*, 30 Oct 1976; Photo]

THURSTON, Gavin Leonard Bourdas *b.*26 Mar 1911 *d.*15 June 1980
CBE (1966) MRCS LRCP (1933) MRCP (1937) DCH (1937)
FRCP (1969) FRCGP (1969) Hon DMJ Soc Apoth Lond (1963)

Gavin Thurston was the fourth son of John Bourdas Thurston of London. He was educated at Dulwich College, London, and entered Guys's Hospital Medical School in 1928, qualifying MRCS LRCP in 1933. After completing house appointments at Pembury and the Belgrave Hospital he went into general practice in Brentwood, Essex, being admitted MRCP in 1937 and obtaining a DCH in the same year. He served in the RAMC from 1939 to 1945 as a medical specialist in India and NW Europe, obtaining the rank of lieutenant colonel and upon cessation of hostilities returned to practice.

He shortly after came under the influence of an older Guy's man, Percy Barnard Skeels, a solicitor of the City firm of Hoddinott & Skeels, then HM coroner to metropolitan Essex, and was appointed his deputy in 1949, intending to turn to coronership. Few deputy coroners at that time achieved London appointments without the patronage of William (later Sir William) Bentley Purchase, so he attended the coroner's court at St Pancras from 1952 to 1956, eventually achieving appointment at Westminster (Inner West London district) in 1956, a post he occupied until his death in 1980. He served both as treasurer and as secretary to the Coroner's Society and in due course became president for a year. His wide experience of coronership resulted in his views and advice in this field being sought from all quarters.

He took further interest in medico-legal affairs by joining the Medico-Legal Society, becoming editor of its journal in 1958, and president in 1969. He was also a member of the British Academy of Forensic Sciences and lecturer for a short period at the West London Medical School until its closure. He sat on the council of the Medical Defence Union from 1960 to 1980.

He had, in order to achieve his London coronership, read for the Bar, being admitted from the Inner Temple in 1952, but never practising as a barrister.

Gavin Thurston had always expressed his views crisply and in a few well chosen words. He joined the Authors' Club, becoming its chairman for 1967 – 1969, wrote a standard work on *Coroners' Practice* in 1958, and contributed sections on the same subject to Atkin's Court Forms and to Halsbury's Laws of England. He was examiner for the DMJ of the Apothecaries Hall. He also found time to write two further books with a medico-legal flavour – *The Great Thames Disaster* (1965) and *The Clerkenwell Riot* (1967) and articles, editorials, etc. in the *Medico-legal Journal*.

Thurston spent his first few years as a doctor in medical practice in Brentwood, and in later years this experience was invaluable to his understanding of doctors' problems in general practice. He was particularly proud of his election to the fellowship of the College in 1969. The Royal College of General Practitioners also paid him the same compliment shortly after their inception – the only coroner to receive this mark of esteem. He was made CBE in 1966.

Gavin Thurston was twice married, firstly in 1935 to Ione Witham, daughter of JT Barber. They had a son and a daughter. His first wife died tragically in an accident. In 1939 he married Janet Hazell MB ChB LRAM, a talented administrative medical practitioner.

Thurston was imbued with a natural humanity. He lived a long life of public duty, more than twenty-five years of which was spent in the responsible position of HM coroner. He never used his position to impose authority and anyone who appeared before him in court was handled with a quiet, patient courtesy and understanding. His fellows referred to him as 'a splendid chap', his officers, who both liked and respected him, referred to him as 'The Guv'nor', and relatives were often heard to speak of him as 'that nice man' – all words which reflected his very likeable, but very upright character so well. He had a clear sympathy with, and a discerning understanding of, his fellow men which gave his enquiries so much more than mere factual accuracy and justice. He was, indeed, a man who brought much credit to the ancient office of coroner in this country; a distinguished doctor who practised the art of healing in the London courts. CKS/GW

[*Brit. med. J.*, 1980, **280**, 1623; *Lancet*, 1980, **1**, 1427; *Times*, 17 June 1980; Address, Memorial Service, Guy's Hospital Chapel; Photo]

TREBLE, Henry Arthur *b*.8 Dec 1907 *d*.21 June 1981
BM BCh Oxon (1932) MRCP (1935) FRCP (1955)

Henry Treble was born in Croydon, Surrey, the only child of Henry Arthur Treble MA, and Sarah Robson, daughter of Robert Bewick Toplady, a schoolmaster. HA Treble senior taught classics at Selhurst Grammar School, Croydon, and was the author or co-author of several successful books on classical subjects, notably *Everyday Life in Rome* with KM King for the Oxford University Press, and *A Classical and Biblical Reference Book* for John Murray. He was a scholarly and precise man – his brother, Treble's uncle, was a mathematics teacher – and this critical and scholastic background was strongly inherited from both sides of the family.

Treble was educated at Whitgift School, Croydon, from 1916 to 1926; he distinguished himself on the science side but was no athlete. He entered Magdalen College, Oxford, as a Demy (foundation scholar) and took second class honours in animal physiology in 1929; from Oxford he won the senior science War Memorial scholarship to Guy's Hospital Medical School, worth £100 per annum. At Guy's he qualified MRCS LRCP in July 1932, adding the Oxford BM BCh in December, having served his apprenticeship under Douthwaite, Murch, Fagge and Davies-Colley; the MRCP followed in 1935, and a medical registrarship. During his postgraduate years at Guy's he contributed a paper to *Brain* (1938, LXI, p.116) with S de Navasquez on 'A case of primary generalized amyloid disease with involvement of the nerves', and might have been in the running for a consultant appointment, but Norman Ashton, formerly director of pathology at Canterbury and Treble's contemporary and close friend, recalls that 'his outspoken and even acerbic comments counted against him'.

Instead he joined the general practice of the Wachers, a Canterbury dynasty, in 1939 and was appointed honorary assistant physician to the Kent and Canterbury Hospital; it was then normal for general practice and hospital appointments to be combined, although there were already a few full time specialists on the staff. The building was brand new, opened in 1937, and the prospects for a well qualified physician excellent. Then came the war and disruption. Treble, who remained in civilian practice for the duration, lodged in a Canterbury hotel and nearly lost his life when it suffered a direct hit from a bomb – he was cut about and his spectacles broken. After the war, his father having retired, he set up house for his parents near the hospital, a matriarchy based on Mrs Treble and their old family retainers. Ashton, a frequent visitor, remembers 'watching with admiration their swift disposal of *The Times* crossword'. Treble remained unmarried.

Treble's practice of medicine was refined into an efficient machine;

he thought and acted quickly; his intellectual grasp of a subject was illustrated by his self-taught mastery of dermatology, when a gap in this subject needed to be filled following the premature death of a colleague. At the bedside and in the clinic he was brisk, even brusque, with no time wasted, no small talk, recognized by some as the performance of a shy man who found difficulty in making human relationships; others, made of tenderer stuff, were frightened or repelled. His neighbours remember his kindness, often obscured by the abruptness of insecurity; thus he never quite came into the 'beloved physician' category although he was a much respected doctor. At the hospital he undertook more than his share of committee work and was a superb performer, as member or chairman. In 1947 he was an early member of the South East Metropolitan Regional Hospital Board and he influenced the development of hospital services in the region. In 1955 he was elected fellow of the Royal College of Physicians and took great pleasure in this at a time when it was relatively rare for a provincial physician to be thus honoured. He retired from clinical practice in 1972, aged 65 and in indifferent health. A newly commissioned medical ward was named after him, which gave him some wry pleasure.

There was another HA Treble. Quite separate from his medical life, he developed an amazing range of 'cultural' interests, to each of which he applied his perfectionism, and each of which he shared with a group of like-minded friends. In 1942 while the war was still in progress he joined with the cathedral organist and other enlightened persons to found the Canterbury Music Club, a concert society now (1982) in its 39th season, and he remained a guiding committee member for many years; he was not a practising musician but a keen music lover with refined and specialized tastes – only the best record playing equipment was good enough for him. He was an authority on oriental ceramics and his collection of Celadon ware from the Han and Sung periods was well known. He was a passionate lover of Italy and all things Italian, a great traveller, especially to Italy, and a master of the Italian Renaissance. He was an expert gardener and an epicure. He was also a stoic who faced the problems of deteriorating health and the difficulties of a bachelor life with masterly objectivity. He was a many sided man; in the words of a professorial friend, 'a true eccentric'.

He died at home in Canterbury. He left his residual estate to Magdalen College, Oxford, 'for travel grants or other forms of scholarship which will encourage and enable undergraduates to travel abroad, particularly scientific undergraduates wishing to visit Italy'. A typical act.

JML

[*Brit. med. J.*, 1981, **283**, 626; Photo]

TURNER, John William Aldren *b*.13 Feb 1911 *d*.12 Oct 1980
BA Oxon (1932) BM BCh (1935) MA (1937) MRCP (1937)
DM (1940) FRCP (1946)

John Turner was born in Harley Street where his father practised as a neurologist and was physician on the staff of King's College Hospital and the National Hospital, Queen Square. His mother Helen was a daughter of Dr John Macdougall, himself the son of a general practitioner in Galashiels; John Macdougall FRCS practised during the season in Cannes. His paternal grandfather, Sir William Turner KCB FRS, was the son of a carpenter in Cheshire; he won a scholarship to St Bartholomew's Hospital where he qualified; he became a demonstrator in anatomy at the University of Edinburgh and subsequently professor of anatomy and later principal and vice-chancellor.

John was educated at Clifton and New College, where he gained first class honours in natural sciences and the Theodore Williams scholarship in anatomy. He spent his undergraduate clinical years at Bart's where he gained the Walshian prize in pathology and the Brackenbury scholarship in medicine.

He graduated in 1935 and was house physician to Hinds Howell. He became house physician, then RMO at the National Hospital, Queen Square. When war came in 1939 the hospital temporarily closed, and he was sent to an EMS hospital for functional nervous disorders in Kent under TA Ross. After a short time he moved to Hurstwood Park Hospital, Haywards Heath, where the medical and surgical work of the National Hospital continued under Arnold Carmichael, Julian Taylor and Harvey Jackson, with regular visits from Gordon Holmes. In January 1942, he joined the RAMC. At St Hugh's Hospital, Oxford, he became command neurologist to the very busy Northern Command at York and later to Western Command at Chester, then adviser in neurology to Southern Command, India, with the rank of lieutenant colonel. On demobilization he was elected to the staff of St Bartholomew's Hospital.

As may be inferred from his distinguished early academic accomplishments, John had academic ambitions, but lost them after a serious illness which required a partial gastrectomy, followed by a number of complications which necessitated a stay of ten months in the London Clinic, ending with a neuralgic amyotrophy, a disorder which he named and on which he published a number of papers. He bore this long illness with courage and patience. He made a satisfactory recovery and, until his last short illness, enjoyed good food and wine with a special liking for dry martinis, in spite of what he called the remnant of his stomach.

The writer and his family were privileged to enjoy a close friendship, and for thirty-five years he spent a week at Easter with us at our home in Derbyshire. He stayed with us for the main York race meetings in May and August. He spent many holidays with us in Scotland and abroad, the last in Cyprus which he enjoyed, although he was weak and knew he was dying. He died a few days after returning home.

His hobbies were a study of the behaviour of racehorses (mainly at York, Doncaster, Sandown and on television. He kept careful accounts of his small bets and one year announced with pride that he had lost only forty pounds); stately homes and antiquities, described by his friend Brodie Hughes as old ruins.

He had a pleasant sense of humour and a placid temperament, only roused to anger when a fancied horse was narrowly beaten. JC

[*Brit. med. J.,* 1980, **281**, 1222, 1294, 1435, 6252; *Lancet,* 1980, **2**, 8200; *Times,* 15 Oct 1980; *St Bartholomew's Hosp. Journal,* Winter 1980, **50**]

TURTON, Edmund Christopher *b.*24 July 1915 *d.*4 Aug 1983
MRCS LRCP (1944) MB BCh Oxon (1944) MA (1945)
MRCP(1945) MSc Lond (1947) DPM Brist (1950) MD (1954)
FRCPsych (1971) FRCP (1971)

The son of a barrister who was killed in the first world war, Christopher Turton was born in London. He was educated at Eton and Balliol College, Oxford, before going on to St Bartholomew's Medical School in London where he qualified in 1944, obtaining the MRCP the following year. After a post as house physician on the medical professorial unit at St Bartholomew's, he worked as a registrar in the Radcliffe penicillin unit of the MRC, before becoming senior lecturer in physiology at St Bartholomew's. During this time he published a number of papers concerned both with the use of penicillin, then very new, and various physiological subjects. He obtained the London MSc in physiology in 1947. His increasing interest in neurophysiology led him to the field of psychiatry and the study of electroencephalography. In 1949 he became registrar in psychiatry at the Barrow Hospital in Bristol, obtaining the Bristol DPM in 1950, in which year he also moved on to become a senior registrar, and thence to consultant status in 1951. Thereafter he continued his research work in electroencephalography, obtaining the London MD in this field in 1954. He took over and built up the small EEG department at the Barrow Hospital and was also much involved in the teaching of medical students. In 1958 he took the unusual step for that time of moving from the University setting to Park Prewett Hospital in Basingstoke. There were strong family reasons for this move but prior to his early retirement in December 1973, the contribution he made to the advancement of the care and treatment of patients at that hospital was inestimable. His work as a member of the management committee of the hospital achieved much. In 1971 he was elected fellow of the Royal College of Physicians and the Royal College of Psychiatrists. Despite his high academic attainments, Christopher was an extremely modest, unassuming individual with an excellent sense of humour. Never a man to push himself forward, he nevertheless gave unstintingly of his time and great experience to all who asked of him, and his quiet, friendly charm and obvious ability won the affectionate respect of patients and colleagues alike.

He was a man of culture, education and refinement, a good teacher, of clear judgement. His ability to work smoothly in even the most difficult situations was considerable. A keen yachtsman and a skilled fly fisherman, he was never happier than when out on a day's fishing with his wife. Sadly, the last few years of his retirement were marred by progressive ill health which he bore with philosophic resignation. He was survived by his wife, Jean (née Martin), whose care and devotion did so much to make his last years as happy as his declining health would permit, and by the two children of a former marriage.

JSL

[*Brit. med. J.*, 1983, **287**, 697; Photo]

UNDERWOOD, Edgar Ashworth *b.*9 Mar 1899 *d.*6 Mar 1980
Chevalier de la Légion d'Honneur (1947) BSc Glasg (1924)
MA MB ChB (1924) DPH (1926) MD (1936) MRCP (1959)
FRCP (1965) Hon DLitt Glasg (1970)

Edgar Underwood, son of David Underwood, a bus driver in Dumfries, and his wife Janet Grierson, a descendant of Sir Robert Grierson of Lag (the Sir Robert Redgauntlet in Walter Scott's novel *Redgauntlet*) was born in Dumfries. At the Academy in Dumfries he received his early schooling, obtaining the Boya bursary to Glasgow University in 1917. His university career was notable for the breadth of his scholastic accomplishments, as exemplified by degrees obtained in philosophy (MA), science (BSc) and medicine (MD). He was awarded the Cullen medal and Hunter medals in midwifery and clinical medicine. His proclivity within the subject of medicine was reflected by his obtaining the DPH in 1926, and his appointment in 1927 as assistant medical officer of health, County of Lanark. During his next appointment at Rotherham, which included that of tuberculosis officer and medical superintendent at Oakwood Sanatorium, Underwood produced his *Manual of Tuberculosis, Clinical and Administrative* (1931). This ran into three editions by 1945. Later, in 1932, he moved to Leeds, where he was honorary lecturer in public health at the University, and in 1937 he went to West Ham as medical officer of health – where he stayed through the war years until 1945. Later in life he would often refer to his experiences during this period, and his epidemiological anxieties. But about this time the focus of Underwood's medical interests changed dramatically.

In 1946 Underwood became director of the Wellcome Institute for the history of medicine, an appointment he held until 1964. In 1947 he became a member of the British Society of the History of Science, of which he was president from 1957 to 1962. He had become a fellow of the Royal Society of Medicine in 1933, and was secretary of both the section of epidemiology and the section of the history of medicine between 1942 and 1947, becoming president of the section of the history of medicine in 1948 – 1950. He remained an active member of the council of that section until his death.

For some years his activity in the field of medical history had coincided with his friendship with the distinguished medical historian, Charles Singer, and in 1949 Underwood married Singer's daughter, Nancy Waley Singer.

As the director of the WIHM, Underwood was strongly influenced by his sense of the overwhelming richness of Sir Henry Wellcome's collection. He was well aware of the extent to which this remained unexplored, perhaps most acutely so when he supervised its removal from Portman Square to Euston Road. His reaction to this state of affairs was one of tenacious preservation, whilst he slowly and meticulously evaluated and organized the collection. These methods characterized not only his attitude towards the Wellcome collection, but towards medical history in general. Underwood was a perfectionist, a trait which manifested itself in his numerous lectures. He delivered the Vicary lecture in 1946 at the Royal College of Surgeons, the Garrison lecture to the American Association for the History of Medicine in 1947, the Fitzpatrick lectures at the Royal College of Physicians, London, 1971 – 1972, and a number of papers to the Royal Society of Medicine between 1935 and 1962.

Underwood's best known work was a revised edition of his father-in-law's *Short History of Medicine* (1962); and the two volumes of *Science, Medicine and History: Essays in honour of Charles Singer* (1953) exhibit his skilful choice of authors and his editorial capacities and organization. It is significant that he played no part in revising the later editions of Singer's *Short History of Scientific Ideas*, for Underwood was not so interested in ideas as in the history of epidemiological diseases and the lives of doctors.

Tenacious, meticulous perfectionism Underwood applied to his own work, as doggedly and conscientiously as to that of others. It led him to a passion for collecting facts; it underlay his collection of a library of some 15,000 books relevant to his work, which occupied every nook and cranny of his home. It led him, also, to refuse to publish his own works if he considered them unsatisfactory. His unpublished *Life of Edward Jenner* may well come into this category.

Though not an easy man to know intimately, Underwood was generous with his help to those who passed the acid test of his criticism. His personal interest in his staff, his practical help to them in an hour of need, were known to them alone. This concern for people was coupled with a deep knowledge and reverence for books. Perhaps less well known were his twin loves of music and mountain climbing – he learned the art of 'scree-skiing' at the age of 65. A tragedy of the final years was failing eyesight, forcing him to leave incomplete a second volume of the history of the Society of Apothecaries, a history of urology, the papers of Edward Jenner and other writings. Music, the company of his dogs, visits from his two daughters and grandchildren, were his solace until he died at his home at Walton-on-Thames three days before his 81st birthday. KDK/MER

[*Brit. med. J.*, 1980, **1**, 948; *Times*, 8 Mar 1980; Obituary in *Medical History*, 1980, **24**, 349-352; Photo]

VISWANATHAN, Raman *b.*8 Oct 1899 *d.*14 July 1982
BA Madras (1926) MD (1931) MRCP (1932) FRCP (1980)

Raman Viswanathan was a leading figure on the Indian medical scene for over half a century. Graduating from the University of Madras in 1926, he obtained his MD in 1931 and MRCP (Lond) in 1932. Returning to India he worked as assistant professor of medicine at the Madras Medical College and later as professor of medicine and therapeutics, Andhra Medical College, Vishakhapatnam. He served in the second world war as colonel in the Indian Medical Service and officer in charge medical division. After 1945 he was adviser in tuberculosis and subsequently deputy director general of health services to the Government of India. He was founder director of the Vallabhai Patel Chest Institute, University of Delhi, where he worked from 1957 till his retirement in 1969, and continued to work as professor emeritus at the same Institute until his death. He was dean, Faculty of Medical Sciences, University of Delhi from 1947 to 1974.

His life long interests were in pulmonary tuberculosis and diseases of the chest. He contributed much new knowledge in both these fields and published over 100 papers in Indian and foreign journals. He also published seven books, including an autobiography. Original papers included those on tropical eosinophilia, oedema of high altitude, acute massive collapse of the lung, bronchiectasis and chronic bronchitis. A new species of *Candida* was named after him. He was closely associated with the Tuberculosis Association of India for many years and was a member of all its important committees. He was a founder fellow of the National Academy of Medical Sciences. He was the president of the Association of Chest Physicians of India from its foundation until 1981, when it became the National College of Chest Physicians. He was the founder president of the Asthma and Bronchitis Foundation of India. He presided over the 8th National Congress of Diseases of the Chest in 1963, the Conference of the Association of Physicians of India in 1968, the National Tuberculosis Conference in 1968 and the World Congress on Asthma, Bronchitis and Allied conditions in 1974.

Raman Viswanathan was the recipient of many national and international honours. He was awarded the Padma Bhushan, and was honorary physician to the President of India. He also received the gold medal of the Tuberculosis Association of India and the Dhanwantri prize of the National Sciences Academy. The Eugino Morelli prize and Forlanini medal of Italy were awarded to him for his work on pulmonary tuberculosis.

Viswanathan distinguished himself as a teacher, and was responsible for the guiding of many a thesis on chest diseases of postgraduate students at the University of Delhi.

He was a legend in his life time. His passion for work made him stay at his desk and laboratory from 9 to 5 every day until a month before his death in spite of two heart attacks. A tall, erect and slim figure, he was easy of approach to young and old alike and the picture of equanimity on all occasions. He was widely travelled in India, Europe

and in the United States. He represented a generation that had seen the best of British medicine in India, and was a pioneer in the development of new traditions and educational methods in the post independence era.
SP

[Photo]

WADSWORTH, William Victor *b*.4 Apr 1920 *d*.4 Sept 1983
BSc Manch (1941) MB ChB (1944) DPM (1948) MRCP (1960) FRCP (1965) FRCPsych (1971)

William Wadsworth was born in Urmston, an outer suburb of Manchester, and was educated at the William Hulme Grammar School, Manchester, where he had a distinguished career, captaining both cricket and rugby and finishing up head boy. He elected to follow in the footsteps of his uncle, Tom Wadsworth, who practised medicine in Rodney Street, Liverpool, and he qualified in Manchester in 1944.

In his first year at medical school he obtained his rugby colours and in 1942 represented the Northern Universities; and he also found time from his studies to be treasurer and later secretary of the University Rugby Club. Bill was not, however, a typical college rugger player, being a serious student and appearing more mature than many of his year. He married while still a student, unusual in those days, but unhappily this marriage only lasted a few years.

He decided soon after qualification to go into psychiatry and mapped out his career in a way unusual for young medical students, starting with a post as house surgeon to the illustrious neurosurgeon Sir Geoffrey Jefferson. He was then called up for military service and served as general duties officer at the head injuries unit in St Hughes Hospital, Oxford, and later went to India with a mobile neurosurgical unit.

On returning to civilian life in 1947 he became medical registrar to the Manchester neurologist Fergus Ferguson. He then moved to Cheadle Royal Hospital as a psychiatric registrar. Cheadle Royal had been closely associated with Manchester Royal Infirmary until the NHS started in 1948, and Fergus Ferguson still had close links with Cheadle. Bill was promoted to deputy medical superintendent in 1951 and on the retirement of Dr Roy, who had held the post since 1922, he was appointed superintendent at the early age of thirty-three. This gave him the opportunity of carrying on the Cheadle Royal tradition of lavish entertainment, thus effectively cutting him off from most of his contemporaries who were still struggling to make ends meet as registrars. Many people in Manchester, both lay and medical, remember with nostalgia the Cheadle Royal parties of those days.

He steered the hospital through the early difficult years when it had to change from virtually being the psychiatric department of Manchester Royal Infirmary (which in the early days in Piccadilly Gardens it had literally been) to becoming a private hospital independent of the National Health Service, although always retaining links with it. He also steered it through the changes which occurred in psychiatry in this period, discarding locks on doors and using drugs, ECT and insulin coma therapy, but later more and more discarding the physical treatments for psychotherapeutic ones. He was a pioneer in two developments: industrial therapy and day hospitals, helping to build up the very successful industrial unit Cheadle Royal Industries, which virtually became a paper hat making factory, selling to firms such as Woolworths. At this time he wrote a number of papers on the rehabilitation of schizophrenic patients by industrial therapy.

In 1959 he invited Gordon Cross to come from the Bristol Day Hospital to open a similar one at Cheadle. This developed as a therapeutic community and in association with the industrial unit helped in the rehabilitation of both neurotic and psychotic patients.

Later he was influenced by Franz Greenbaum, a Jungian analyst, and his interest changed to psychotherapy, at first with a Jungian bias, but later moving to a very original method using abreactive techniques, which did not entirely find favour with either local psychiatric establishments or even his own lay committee. Finally, in 1971, he left Cheadle Royal to establish a private clinic at Toft Hall in Knutsford where he started a charity, 'The Society for the Investigation of Human Values'.

His later years were unhappy. He split up with his second wife, Barbara, who had helped him in the work at Toft Hall, and because of financial problems had to give up this venture to establish a smaller but similar one at Alderley Edge. He had several heart attacks during these last years and perhaps the best way to illustrate his energy and enthusiasm is to relate a story about one of these. A colleague went to see him in the intensive care unit at Manchester Royal Infirmary, the day after a severe attack, to find him propped up in bed dictating to his secretary. He explained that he had to carry on as all those working at Toft Hall depended on him. In fact he appeared to have no hobbies apart from his work.

He was survived by Barbara and four children, Victoria, Anna, Clare and Andrew, none of whom have gone into the medical profession. CMD

[*Brit. med. J.*, 1983, **287**, 992; Photo]

WALTER, Joseph *b*17 Dec 1910 *d*.6 Feb 1979
BA Oxon (1933) MA BM BCh (1936) MRCP (1939) DMRE (1940) FFR (1952) FRCP (1973) DHMSA (1974)

The son of Abraham Walter, cap manufacturer of Salford, Lancashire, and of Fanny Green, whose father, Joseph, came from Jassy in Romania, Joseph Walter was born in Salford and had an outstanding scholastic career at Manchester Grammar School, topping the classical forms for six years before gaining a state scholarship, as well as the open scholarship, to Oriel College, Oxford, where he was senior classical scholar. However, medicine attracted him and he began his medical studies, responding to the inspiration of KJ Franklin, his tutor. Graduating first BA (honours school of animal physiology), Walter proceeded as Burney Yeo scholar to King's College Hospital, qualifying in 1936. He gained clinical and pathological experience in King's and Dulwich (1936 – 1939) before his appointment as assistant medical officer to the Sheffield Radium Centre in 1940, the year after taking the MRCP and DMRE.

The rest of his life was to be spent in Sheffield, mainly as deputy director of the Sheffield National Centre for Radiotherapy (from 1943), but he served his adopted city in many other ways, not least as a Rotarian and member of the council of social service, and in establishing with his wife, Marianne, a chartered architect, and others, the 'Dronfield Pioneer Health Centre', on the lines of Scott-Williamson's Peckham project. His concern for the welfare of others thus extended beyond the boundaries of medicine. Once involved in radiotherapy, he gave himself wholeheartedly to the care of patients and to the improvement of cancer treatment, not alone by radiation but also by chemotherapy, becoming one of the first true oncologists.

Patients found him compassionate and understanding, and colleagues valued his opinion. He was quick to appreciate the value of radioactive isotopes when they became available, using radio-gold in treating malignant effusions, and in 1960 wrote the first report of its replacement by yttrium. Earlier work on the spontaneous regression of cavernous haemangioma prompted the discontinuance of its treatment by radiation, and it was his advocacy that initiated the use of cytotoxic drugs in the Sheffield Centre, after he had, with habitual thoroughness, proved their safety and efficacy in preliminary trials. This work developed to embrace intra-arterial therapy, plus various combinations with surgery and radiation.

Joseph Walter's interests were clinically determined rather than research orientated and, just as he responded to patients' problems and needs, he understood the learning requirements of students at all levels of the caring professions. *A Short Textbook of Radiotherapy*, written with his physicist colleague Harold Miller, was an instant success on its first appearance in 1950, reaching a fourth edition just before his death; whilst his *Cancer and Radiotherapy* (1971 and 1977), intended as a short guide for nurses and medical students, attracted both commendatory reviews and appreciative letters from nursing tutors, and has gone into French, Italian and Spanish translations. He was widely read, with a positive hunger for knowledge in a variety of academic disciplines; was competent in three modern languages, and read the Greek classics in the original. He wrote two plays, one of which anticipated by two decades the Harrisburg nuclear accident. The University of Sheffield enjoyed his services as honorary clinical lecturer in radiotherapy for over thirty-six years, and later as honorary lecturer in the sub-department of the history of medicine; he served the cause of radiological education as a member of the fellowship board of the Faculty of Radiologists and had been an examiner both for that body and for the Society of Radiographers.

Joseph Walter was by nature a retiring man, but his enthusiasms were no less intense for being muted, and a gently ironic wit lent point to many of his debunking criticisms, and to his skilful pricking of the bubble of pretension. Though neither an organizer nor a committee man by inclination, he played a leading role in those causes which he espoused, such as the Wholetime Consultants Association of which he was honorary secretary, and Rotary, and he took his share in the planning of the Weston Park Hospital, a radiotherapy and oncology hospital wherein were concentrated the previously disparate provisions for radiotherapy services in the Sheffield area.

In July 1941, he married Marianne, daughter of Dr Emil Löhnberg of Hamm, Westphalia, a well known ENT specialist. There were two children, a boy and a girl, neither entering medicine.

The humility of the scholar characterized this gentle, compassionate doctor, who served his fellows well. TL

[*Brit. med. J.*, 1979, **1**, 1157; Photo]

WATERSON, Anthony Peter *b*.23 Dec 1923 *d*.17 Oct 1983
MB BChir Cantab (1947) MRCP (1950) MD (1954) FRCP (1970) FRCPath (1973)

Tony Waterson died at the age of 59, having recently retired as professor of virology at the Royal Postgraduate Medical School, London. Academically his record was quite outstanding. He was an open entrance scholar at Epsom College and gained an open scholarship in classics at Emmanuel College, Cambridge, where he obtained a double first in Natural Sciences. He carried out his clinical studies at the London Hospital Medical College, qualifying in 1947.

After house appointments at the London, Waterson served as medical officer in the RAF in Germany. He then returned to Cambridge, first as a house physician at Addenbrooke's Hospital to Sir Lionel Whitby and Lawrence Martin, followed by an appointment as assistant pathologist in the clinical laboratories. In 1952, Waterson transferred to the University, first as Elmore research student in the department of medicine and then as university demonstrator and later lecturer in the department of pathology, where he stayed until his appointment to St Thomas's Hospital in 1964. During this period, Waterson was able to combine and achieve distinction in his College and departmental activities. Thus, after being elected to a fellowship of Emmanuel College in 1954, he successfully became director of studies in medicine and assistant tutor and college lecturer in pathology. He was a member of the governing body of Emmanuel College and also served on the College council and tutorial committee. In the department of pathology, Waterson was involved in important discoveries, most of which were related to the fine structure of viruses in which the then newly recognized technique of negative contrast staining was used. His book, *Introduction to Animal Virology*, was designed specifically for students studying pathology for part II of the Natural Sciences Tripos in Cambridge; it was widely popular, not only in Cambridge but wherever basic virology was being taught.

However, unlike most academic virologists during this time, he realized the potential of the clinical applications of virology, and actively encouraged research into the clinical aspects of virus diseases. When he moved to St Thomas's Hospital in 1964, after a year's sabbatical in the Max Planck Institute for Virus Research, Tübingen, he was amongst the foremost to develop clinical services and research into clinical virology. After three years Waterson moved to the Royal Postgraduate Medical School, where he also developed clinical services and continued to supervise research both in basic and clinical virology. His interests and activities covered a wide field and included viral hepatitis, slow virus infections, as well as various aspects of the fine structure, taxonomy and evolution of viruses. He threw himself with enthusiasm into a study of viral infection and cardiomyopathy. At Hammersmith, Tony Waterson was respected and admired for his distinctive approach to clinical virology. His clear, forthright, but unassuming contributions to staff rounds were always received with attention and remembered for their value.

Like many people of high intellectual achievement he was reserved, and despite the breadth of scholarship, truly modest. He never thrust his opinions and views upon others, and was an admirable and imaginative collaborator in research. Those who worked with him appreciated his style, knowledge and competence as well as his capacity for tolerance and understanding.

One of his major achievements was his bringing together of clinical virologists at first in small, but later in much larger groups for meetings at a time when there was no forum available. The large and flourishing clinical virology group, now incorporated into the Society for General Microbiology, provides a tribute to Waterson's foresight and enthusiasm. Shortly after his retirement, a 'Festschrift' was arranged on his behalf at the Royal Postgraduate Medical School. Despite this coinciding with both a complete rail and London Transport strike, it was a measure of the high esteem in which Tony Waterson was held that a large number of his friends and former colleagues still managed to come, not only from the UK but also from abroad.

Tony was a scholar in every sense of the word; he had a considerable knowledge of history, both ancient and modern, and the book he wrote with Lise Wilkinson on the *History of Virology* is a classic. Unknown, even to many of his closer friends, Waterson was a biblical scholar of some repute and had read the Bible in the original Greek. Those who came to know him well found him kind and considerate, and his behaviour that of a true gentleman; he was also a man of deep religious conviction. He was devoted to and obtained great pleasure from his family; he was survived by his wife, two daughters and a son. JFG

[*Brit. med. J.*, 1983, **287**, 1386 & 2559; *Lancet,* 1983, **2**, 1040; *Times,* 4 Nov 1983; Photo]

WEINER, Joseph Sidney *b.*29 June 1915 *d.*13 June 1982
BSc Wits (1934) MSc (1936) PhD Lond (1946) MRCS LRCP (1947)
DSc MA Oxon (1971) MRCP (1973) FRCP (1978)

Joe Weiner, environmental physiologist and physical anthropologist, was founder of the Society for the Study of Human Biology and a prime mover in the creation of the *Annals of Human Biology*. He was born in South Africa, the son of Robert Weiner, a timber and builders' merchant, and was the second child in a family of seven. He obtained his early schooling at the Boys High School, Pretoria, and later entered the University of Witwatersrand in Johannesburg, where he read physiology, anatomy and anthropology. He graduated BSc in 1934, and proceeded MSc in physiology in 1936. In 1937 he migrated to Britain and, though he frequently returned to South Africa for short periods, Britain became his home and his country. From 1940 to 1941 he was a demonstrator in the department of applied physiology in the London School of Hygiene and Tropical Medicine, and from 1942 to 1946 scientific member of the MRC unit in Queen Square. He was awarded his PhD London in 1946 and qualified MRCS LRCP from St George's Hospital, London, in 1947. Around this time WE Le Gros Clark, professor of human anatomy at Oxford, was looking for someone to fill the vacant readership in physical anthropology in his department, and chose Weiner for the job, partly because of his former training with Raymond Dart in Johannesburg but also because Le Gros Clark recognized that physical anthropology needed a totally new orientation, especially in the direction of human physiology. Weiner was to hold this readership for seventeen years, throughout most of which Le Gros Clark continued as professor of human anatomy. In 1963 Joe Weiner moved back to the London School of Hygiene and Tropical Medicine as director of the MRC environmental physiology unit. He had been honorary deputy director of the MRC Climatic and Working Efficiency Unit since 1955, which had been set up by Le Gros Clark in 1948. When Le Gros Clark was succeeded, at Oxford, by GW Harris, who had his own MRC unit, there was not sufficient space in the Oxford anatomy department to continue to accommodate the Climatic Unit. Weiner had to decide whether to remain with the unit and take it to London, or continue in the readership. Though he always cherished his Oxford connections he chose the first course of action and, in 1965, became professor of environmental physiology in the University of London, a post which he held until his retirement in 1980. He took his MRCP in 1973 and was elected a fellow of the College in 1978. After retirement he lived at Oxford, for the most part, but continued to spend much time working at the London School of Hygiene and Tropical Medicine, as well as taking on various teaching and examining roles in the department of biological anthropology at Oxford.

From 1962 to 1974 Weiner played a critically important part as convenor of the human adaptability section in the International Biological Programme (IBP), which took him all over the world promoting human biological research. He was also active in the affairs of many learned societies and organizations including the Ergonomics Research Society, the Physiological Society of Great Britain, the Royal Society, the Royal Society of Medicine, and the Scientific Committee for Problems of the Environment. He was president of the Royal Anthropological Institute from 1963 to 1964, honorary secretary of the Society for the Study of Human Biology from 1958 to 1963, and chairman from 1968 to 1973. He authored and co-authored over three hundred scientific papers and books, and was awarded a number of honours and distinctions including the Vernon medal, the Rivers memorial medal and the Darwin and Huxley lectureships.

Weiner gave outstanding leadership to the MRC research teams whch he directed. Of his many lasting contributions to human physiology and biological anthropology, perhaps the most important of all was his firm guidance towards the integration of physiology, genetics, ecology and evolutionary theory in the analysis of human population biology. To understand fully his achievements one needs to remember the quite dreadful state of physical anthropology prior to the war. With a few exceptions, it was practically a dead subject, preoccupied with trivial issues and lacking direction, ideas and purpose. Worldwide its exponents were almost exclusively concerned with creating racial typologies, and attempting to reconstruct racial affinities, mainly from endless measurements of the body, particularly of the head and skull. They had totally failed to grasp the significance of the neo-Darwinian revolution that was under way in general biology and, particularly in theoretical population genetics. The dynamic changes which occurred in the subject, following the second world war, are more due to the influence of JS Weiner than to any other single individual. At University College, London, with the help of Nigel Barnicot, he gradually and persistently transformed the subject in Britain, and his ideas, directly and indirectly, slowly spread worldwide, particularly through IBP. One of us can recall spending some hours with him, waiting at a London airport on a foggy day, listening to his visions and plans for the rebirth of physical anthropology. This was in the 1950s, and he achieved them all. Sadly, they have not yet been properly recognized. Too often the microscope, rather than the telescope, is used to evaluate scientific contributions.

Weiner's work covered a broad canvas, but he also made some very specific discoveries. One which particularly pleased him was the exposure of the Piltdown forgery. This 'fossil' had been a central issue in discussion of human evolution for almost fifty years. It is indicative of Weiner's imagination that he was the one who first seriously thought of it as a fraud and took steps to uncover it. It might seem 'obvious' with hindsight, but it had baffled a generation of anatomists and palaeontologists. The exposure of the forgery cleared the way to making sense of the palaeontological record of human evolution. Other important contributions included investigating affinities of peoples in Southern Africa, analysing the components of adaptability to environmental temperature variation, and unravelling the physiology of the human sweating mechanism. Weiner was much involved in the establishment of the science of ergonomics. One of his last ventures was to collaborate in producing a 'cooling bed' treatment for heat stroke victims, particularly Mecca pilgrims, and his advice was sought by the British Coal and Steel boards. He also assisted the EEC commission in regard to these industries. His authoritative book *Principles and Practice of Human Physiology*, edited with his close colleague Otto Edholm, embodies much of the substance of his longstanding physiological interests.

In 1943 he married Marjorie Winifred, daughter of Frederick Edward Daw, a station master, and they had two children, Julia and Edmund. Joe was a delightful companion with a rich fund of anecdotes and a great sense of humour; this endearing characteristic complemented the warmth and generosity of his nature. His interests outside his work also covered a broad field: music, English literature, history, theatre and gardening. GAH/KC/GW

[*Brit. med. J.*, 1982, **285**, 982-3; *Times,* 16 June 1982; *Lancet,* 1982, **1**, 1477; Photo]

WHISHAW, *Sir* **Ralph** *b.*29 Mar 1895 *d.*13 July 1976
Kt (1958) CBE (1957) MB ChM Sydney (1918) MRCP Lond (1935) FRACP (1938) FRCP (1954)

Ralph Whishaw was born in Croydon, England, the son of Reginald Robert Wishaw FRCS and his wife Isabel Rhoda. His family can trace its lineage back to the 15th century. After the early death of his wife, his father emigrated to Tasmania in 1904, when Ralph was nine years old, and practised medicine in Macquarie Street, Hobart. Ralph was educated at the Friends' School, Hobart, and at the University of Sydney, NSW. At the outbreak of the first world war he was a third year student at Sydney University Medical School. He enlisted in the Army in 1915 and became a staff sergeant (pharmaceutical duties) in C Section of the 7th Field Ambulance, AIF, and served at Gallipoli. Later he took up an option to return to Sydney and complete his medical studies, with a view to rejoining the AIF.

After graduation he became an assistant to Bettingham-Moore, and was later associated with Hamish Scott Reid. At the close of the war he commenced practice in Hobart, where he soon became recognized as one of the most outstanding men in his profession. He became consultant physician to the Royal Hobart Hospital, and visiting consultant in medicine to the Repatriation General Hospital, Tasmania. He was also consultant medical officer for the Tasmanian branch of the Australian Mutual Provident Society. On return to Tasmania from postgraduate studies in London, he brought with him the first electrocardiograph machine to be used in the island. He achieved eminence as a cardiologist and was chairman of the Australian Cardiac Society in 1954. He had already been elected a fellow of the Royal Australasian College of Physicians in 1938, and became vice-president of the College in 1954.

In 1955 he retired prematurely from the Royal Hobart Hospital which he had served loyally and faithfully, and with such distinction, for many years. He received the CBE in 1957 and became a Knight Bachelor in 1958, honours which were richly deserved.

During World War II he served with the Australian Army Medical Corps in the Middle East, returning to Hobart at a time when Australia was exposed to invasion by the Japanese armed forces. He did invaluable work among returned servicemen, especially among the shell shocked and psychotic patients, and would differ profoundly with a decision to send back to duty any man whom he considered should have further treatment. His own family were deeply involved in war service, and he was profoundly affected by the deaths of many of his relatives.

In 1921 he married Violet Beckley, by whom he had a daughter, named Dat. Violet Beckley had come across to Tasmania from Victoria with her father who had been appointed general manager to the Cascade Brewery. In 1938 the Whishaw family settled down in a delightful old rambling house, 'Sentosa', which overlooked the beautiful Derwent Estuary. The word *sentosa* is Malayan and means, aptly enough, 'house of peace and contentment'. It became a happy and popular rendezvous for many members of the RACP, and several prominent physicians in Australia owe their success to its tranquil and inspiring atmosphere – for they sat there for their written paper for the membership. His married life with Violet was a long and happy one.

His leisure activities included cabinet making, of which he was a master, and photography. After the end of the second world war he acquired some American blueprints for a first class cruising yacht, and he built his own 38ft 15 ton yacht which he christened *Fortuna*, and later sailed her in the Sydney–Hobart race in 1947, coming home in fifth place.

His quiet, determined character made him an excellent leader, and he had a profound influence on all who were associated with him. His legacies to his residents at the Royal Hobart Hospital were a passion for meticulous detail in history taking and records, a sense of humour, and a balanced viewpoint. GW/VL

[*Med. J. Aust.*, 1976, **2**, 657; *Med. Directory of Aust.*, 1974; *Who's Who in Aust.*, 1974; Photo]

WHITTAKER, Stephen Robert Ferguson *b*26 Dec 1909
d.1 Nov 1979
CBE (1971) MRCS LRCP (1935) MA Cantab (1935)
MB BChir (1937) MRCP (1938) MD (1946) FRCP (1947)

Stephen Whittaker was born in Dublin. His father, Sir Edmund Whittaker FRS, was then Astronomer Royal of Ireland, and later professor of mathematics at the University of Edinburgh, whither the family moved in 1912. His mother, Mary, was the daughter of Thomas Boyd, a Presbyterian minister in Liverpool, and her grandfather had been Lord Provost of Edinburgh. Stephen was the fourth of five children. One of these, a mathematician like his father, was JM Whittaker FRS, vice-chancellor of Sheffield University 1953–1965, while the third boy, Edmund, became vice-president of the Prudential Insurance Company in USA. Stephen was educated at Edinburgh Academy, and having already determined upon medicine as his future career, he spent a year at Edinburgh University taking the first MB. Then he went to Trinity College, Cambridge, where he became a scholar and in due course gained a first in physiology in the Natural Sciences tripos; taking his clinical training at University College Hospital in 1932 and qualifying in 1935. For the next three years he was successively resident medical officer and resident assistant physician at his teaching hospital, and obtained the MRCP.

At the outbreak of war, Whittaker became a physician to the Emergency Medical Service, then joined the Army in 1940 as a medical specialist, spending the next five years in the RAMC in the Middle East and Italy, with an eventual rank of lieutenant colonel, commanding the medical division of the 48th General Hospital. His natural authority and sociability made army life congenial to him, and its hierarchical orientation towards a common purpose influenced him strongly in his later adherence to the National Health Service. On leaving the Army in 1945 he spent two years as senior registrar at the postgraduate school of medicine in Hammersmith, and was elected a fellow of this College in 1947, aged 38.

Unsuccessful in his bid for a physician post at University College Hospital, Whittaker decided to be of that band of talented crusaders who merged their personal ambitions with one of the goals of the new Health Service, that of creating centres of excellence away from those traditional in capital cities. Accordingly, after prospecting some provincial centres, he was appointed in February 1947 consulting physician to the Warwickshire County Council, at hospitals in Warwick, Stratford, Nuneaton, Rugby and Solihull. He was drawn to Warwick by Wilfrid Gaisford, who was vacating this post which he had inaugurated, turning himself to paediatrics. The two men were colleagues in Warwick until Gaisford's assumption of a chair in paediatrics later in 1947. To start with, Stephen's was a fragmented job, entailing a radial itinerary to all segments of a large county, with voluntary hospitals standing everywhere watchful on the limits of their territory like invaded robins, and the instant amalgamations of the Health Service did nothing to dissolve rivalries. Upon this disintegrated foundation Whittaker began at once to build. He had clear ideas of what he wished to achieve in a provincial medical centre. His priorities were to concentrate his hospitals and to attract to them a first class senior staff, to deflect influential local interests towards the welfare of the hospitals, and to establish a collegiate atmosphere within his own unit, bringing young people of high quality to work with him.

In realizing these aims, Whittaker was greatly aided by a local physician of shrewdness and foresight, Alexander Cheyne. Whittaker's pre-eminence in the administrative fields was at once recognized and, after serving on the local hospital management committee, he was appointed to the Birmingham Regional Hospital

Board in 1958, on which he served as chairman of the consultant services committee, and subsequently 1974–1978 on the West Midlands Regional Health Authority, with special responsibility for medical staffing. An outstanding man of affairs, his public advocacy marvellously combined intellectual force, mercurial repartee and singleness of aim. Other bodies on which he later served were the Pharmaceutical Whitley council, the Medical Whitley council, the Distinction Awards committee, and the Salmon committee on senior nursing staff structure. In 1968 he was elected a councillor of the Royal College of Physicians, and in the same year was appointed as a College examiner. He was also an examiner for the Cambridge MB. In 1971 he became a member of the council of the University of Warwick.

Warwick became a centre for postgraduate education in medicine soon after Whittaker's arrival, and it was perhaps on this achievement that he most prided himself. He encouraged undergraduate attachments from teaching hospitals long before they became fashionable, and many of these people returned later to take local house posts at a time when a general shortage of juniors in hospital was embarrassing many provincial hospitals. The figure for successes in the MRCP since 1948 among his pupils is illustrative, being no fewer than eighty.

Though he lived alone and never married, Stephen Whittaker was hospitable and gregarious, and had a great gift for friendship; he was zealous to retain friendships that he had made at every stage of his career. He was a familiar and popular figure at the College and at the Association of Physicians. He was proud of the achievements of his colleagues, and of the later careers of those who had worked for him. At the time of his retirement most of these returned to Warwick to do him honour.

Whittaker sought and enjoyed authority and influence, and could be ruthless towards those he did not respect. He was pleased to become a deputy lieutenant of Warwickshire in 1962. He was realistic in self-evaluation and recognized not only his gifts of appraisal and advocacy, but also that he was not scientifically creative, though a clinician and teacher of the first rank. Shining intelligence irradiated his personality, which was spiced by his enjoyment of the small change of human relationships, and by a rather naughty sense of humour. He was a rapacious smoker, and the manipulation of a cigarette became a part of his charisma.

In 1962 he was awarded a CBE for services to medicine, and in 1975 he retired from clinical work. He had always relished his fine house and garden close to Warwick Castle. After retirement he began to suffer from his heart. He faced the likelihood of his death with clear-sighted stoicism, and succeeded in living his last years to the full. His death in November 1979 was sudden, after a day filled with the sort of activities that he loved.

MMacG

[*Brit. med. J.*, 1979, **4**, 1302; *Lancet*, 1979, **2**, 1088; *Times*, 16 Nov 1979]

WHITTINGHAM, *Air Marshall Sir* **Harold (Edward)**
*b.*3 Oct 1887 *d.*16 July 1983
KCB (1944) KBE (1941) CBE (1930) MB ChB Glasg (1910)
DPH (1919) DTM&H (1920) FRFPSG (1926) MRCP (1927)
FRCPE (1945) FRCP (1946) Hon LLD Glasg (1943)
Hon FRCSE (1945)†

Harold Whittingham, known to his friends as George, had a long and distinguished career in the medical service of the Royal Air Force and was its director general from 1941 to 1946. He was a legendary figure in aviation medicine and in 1973 the professorship of aviation medicine, RCP, was renamed the Whittingham professorship in recognition of his outstanding leadership in this field. After he retired from the RAF he worked as a medical adviser to the British Red Cross, 1946–1948, and from then until 1956 he was director of medical services to the British Overseas Airways Corporation. He maintained close links with military aviation medicine as chairman of the Flying Personnel Research Committee from 1949 to 1967.

Harold was the second son of Engineer Rear Admiral William Whittingham CB, and his wife Elizabeth Annie, née Crowley. He was educated at Christ's Hospital and Glasgow University, where he graduated MB ChB in 1910. From 1910 to 1914 he was pathologist and assistant director of research at the Royal Cancer Hospital, Glasgow. At the outbreak of the war he worked first for the Scottish National Red Cross and then joined the RAMC, serving in India and Mesopotamia and being mentioned in despatches. In 1919 he transferred to the medical branch of the RAF (then the Royal Flying Corps) as pathologist and was granted a permanent commission. Promotion was rapid: he was air commodore in 1936, air vice marshal in 1940 and air marshal in 1941. In the years between the wars he was director of pathology to the RAF, 1925–1930, and for the greater part of the same period he was also a lecturer in biochemistry at the London School of Hygiene and Tropical Medicine.

During the influenza epidemic of 1918 Harold Whittingham did pioneering work on the production of a vaccine against the commoner secondary invaders, although he was unable to isolate the causative organism. After the war, when the Air Council recognized the burden of sandfly (phlebotomus) fever affecting forces in the Mediterranean area, Whittingham was appointed to head a commission of inquiry, and he and his team worked at the RAF seaplane base at Kalafrana, Malta, from 1921 to 1923. He studied the habits and life cycle of the sandfly and was the first to breed it in captivity. As a result of his recommendations, sandfly fever became a rarity in the RAF. This research was accompanied by his beautiful and detailed pen and ink drawings of every stage in the life history of the insects.

While serving as a consultant at Princess Mary's RAF Hospital, Halton, Whittingham founded the RAF Institute of Pathology and Tropical medicine; finding time to plant and tend the flower beds around the building. He was also largely responsible for sowing the seed which flowered into his second institute, the RAF Institute of

Aviation Medicine, Farnborough. It was then called the RAF Physiological Laboratory and Harold took the closest possible interest in it, staffing it with doctors of his own choice, directing its research and formulating plans to establish it permanently. At the beginning of the second world war he was director of hygiene at the Air Ministry as well as chief executive officer of the Flying Personnel Research Committee, and recognized as an authority on the medical problems of aviation as they affected fighter and bomber air crews and other flying peronnel. In 1941 he was appointed KBE and Glasgow University conferred on him an honorary LLD. That same year he became director general of the RAF medical services, a post he held until 1946. Although he retired in 1946 he continued to keep himself informed not only in the general medical progress but in the policies, performance and personalities of the medical branch, which owed so much to his wise and able administration. During the war, and after, he fashioned the organization and the means to give the fullest physiological and psychological support to the air crews, but he did not allow the men and women who, directly or indirectly, kept the aircraft flying, to be neglected. By force of personality he was able to persuade the Air Council to provide the resources he needed. He also attracted from the university research departments, and the great hospitals, the talent to exploit them.

When he joined British Overseas Airways in 1948 as director of medical services Harold Whittingham, together with his counterparts in other pioneering transglobal airlines, led the way in safeguarding the health of passengers, aircrew and airline staff, around the world. In the early days hygiene and sanitary arrangements on the ground and in aircraft were primitive. Safe water supplies had to be ensured, and arrangements had to be made for the supply of safe meals to passengers and aircrew along the routes, and for their medical care if necessary. Whittingham and his team regularly visited each station used by BOAC to ascertain the best medical facilities available locally, and maintain links with the doctors and hospitals concerned. He also regularly inspected accommodation for aircrew stopping to rest. Close contact was also maintained with WHO and IATA to ensure that the medical requirements for airlines were kept as up to date as possible. In addition, Whittingham was one of the first to arrive at the scene of an aircraft crash in which there was injury or death; not only to care for the injured but also, in his capacity as a member of BOAC's air safety committee, to help in establishing whether the cause of the accident was human error or technical failure. All who now travel round the world with such apparent ease and immunity owe much to his pioneering work and that of his colleagues.

In 1912 Harold Whittingham married Agnes Kerr Seright, the daughter of a medical practitioner, and they had a son and a daughter. His wife died in 1966, and he later married Rita, daughter of W Harold White.

GW/VL

[*Brit. med. J.*, 1983, **287**, 369, 698, 919; *Lancet*, 1983, **2**, 410; *Times*, 20 & 28 July 1983; Photo]

WIENER, Alexander Solomon *b.*16 Mar 1907 *d.*6 Nov 1976
AB Cornell (1926) MD New York (1930) FRCP* (1974)

Alexander Wiener died from leukaemia in New York, USA, aged seventy years. Wiener graduated from Boys High School, studied at Cornell University and received his medical degree from the State University of New York in 1930. He was an intern at the Jewish Hospital of Brooklyn and subsequently went into private practice in Brooklyn and the Jewish Hospital made him head of its blood transfusion division. He joined the department of forensic medicine at the New York University Medical School in 1938 and was appointed full professor of forensic medicine in 1968. In 1938 he became serologist for the chief medical examiner of the City of New York. Throughout his life Wiener remained in private practice in Brooklyn and was very highly regarded by his patients. His forensic medicine laboratory was universally recognized as the most reliable in the world and although he is best known for his blood group discoveries, his work in the field of forensic serology should be more universally recognized. He was instrumental in the passage of bills in New York State upholding the validity of blood tests in disputed paternity in 1935 and, again, in 1952, compelling such tests in assault and homicide cases. He was, on many occasions, an expert witness on these subjects.

Early in his career, he began working with Landsteiner and it was at this time that he began his contributions to the study of the Rh factor. Wiener was one of those who worked out the serology and complexities of the system and he devised his own Rh-Hr nomenclature for these blood types. It is for his work and his discoveries in connection with the Rh blood group system that he will always be remembered, but he discovered other blood group factors, including U and I, and others within the Rh system itself. He made significant contributions to the technology and to the theory of blood groups. In the field of forensic medicine, he devised methods for grouping secretions and dried blood stains and developed a general formula for the chances of excluding paternity. He was an expert mathematician and an avid research worker, and became a leader in the new field of immuno-haematology. He contributed 700 scientific papers and twelve books to the literature.

During his career, he was awarded the Ward Burdick award (1946), Lasker award (1947), Passano Foundation award (1951), the Karl Landsteiner award (1956), and the Kennedy Foundation award (1966).

Al, as he was always known, was an engaging and fluent speaker and argued cogently for his views, which were always supported by strong experimental evidence. He was a good teacher and contributed enormously to the field of immuno-haematology. He was a kind and generous man, an excellent host and a colleague whom it was a privilege to know. He was always strongly supported by his family and left a wife, Gertrude Rhoda (née Rodman), and two daughters. FS

[*New York Times,* 7 Nov 1976; *Time,* 22 Nov 1976, **108**, 62; *Current topics in immunohematology and immunogenetics, AS Wiener Festschrift, Budapest 1972, ed. SR Hollán; Photo*]

WIGHTMAN, Keith John Roy *b.*12 May 1914 *d.*10 Mar 1978
MD Toronto (1937) FRCPC (1942) FRCP* (1974)
Hon DSc Newfound (1974) Hon LLD Toronto (1976)

Keith Wightman, 'Kajer' as he was generally known, was born in Sandwich, Ontario, grew up in Peterborough, and lived most of his adult life in Toronto. His father, Keith St Clair Wightman, son of a sea captain of the Great Lakes, was a teacher and a distinguished educator who became director of education for the city of Peterborough. His mother Mary Elizabeth Stinson, who descended from the Earl of Warwick, wrote for the Atlantic Monthly Magazine; she died while Kajer was overseas. Kajer was a sensitive boy; when he cut his hand rather badly while playing, he waited for his father and mother to waken from their afternoon sleep before asking their help in stopping the blood and bandaging his hand.

In high school he was a brilliant student and was editor of the school paper. He graduated at the age of 15 and so had to wait for a year before going to university. He took his Bachelor of Education degree from Queen's University, Kingston, and then went into medicine at the University of Toronto, graduating in 1937 with a gold medal, Ellen Mickle fellowship, and the admiration of all his classmates. He was a member of the Alpha Omega Alpha, Honour Medical Society, and years later was its counsellor. The Ellen Mickle fellowship gave him a year of study with Sir Alan Drury in Cambridge, and throughout his life he visited Cambridge and Sir Alan as frequently as he could. He returned to the Toronto General Hospital and served as junior intern and then as senior intern and fellow. He finished his postgraduate training in 1942, enlisted in the army and served with No 12 Canadian General Hospital. In 1946 he was recalled from the casualty clearing station at Bruges by the University, and discharged from the army with the rank of major.

Wightman had passed his examination for fellowship in the Royal College of Physicians of Canada in 1942 and was elected a fellow of the Royal College of Physicians of London in 1974. He joined the faculty of medicine at the University of Toronto in 1946, and over the next 25 years occupied a series of increasingly important positions in the department of medicine. In 1953 he was named head of the department of therapeutics and in 1960 became the Sir John and Lady Eaton professor of medicine, a position he held until 1970. During this period he was very active not only in undergraduate teaching but also in graduate teaching, and had the fun of working with a large number of residents and fellows who formed the Wightman Club. Most of them have continued in the academic field. This was a period of great expansion of the University. There was money, there was consistent enthusiastic support from the deans, John Hamilton and Lawrie Chute. Three hospitals were added to the group of University hospitals, Women's College Hospital, Mount Sinai, and Sunnybrook. As head of the University department of medicine, Wightman felt responsible for building up the staffs and facilities in all the teaching hospitals. His support was greatly appreciated by the chiefs of the various units, and there was a great feeling of unity within the department of medicine. During his period as professor of medicine he was also physician-in-chief of the Toronto General Hospital, where he helped it to understand its role as a University teaching hospital. Upon completion of his term as department chairman, Wightman became associate dean and director of the division of postgraduate medical education of the faculty of medicine. In 1974 Wightman took on his final responsibility, that of medical director of the Ontario Cancer Treatment and Research Foundation, a position which he held until his death.

From the time Kajer was a student, his life and contributions were intimately associated with the life of the University of Toronto. The University recognized this in 1976 by conferring on him the honorary degree of LLD.

In addition to his responsibilities at the University of Toronto, Wightman was a major force in Canadian medicine. He played a key role in the development of the Canadian Association of Gastroenterology, the Canadian Association for the Advancement of Therapeutics, the Canadian Society for Chemotherapy and the Hepatic Foundation of Canada. In fact there were few organizations in the health field in Canada during this period which did not benefit from his support and encouragement.

For many years Wightman was active in the affairs of the Royal College of Physicians and Surgeons of Canada and served on several committees. He was a member of council, and on the executive and finally president 1974 – 1976. He played an important part in building up the Royal College and setting up the subdivisions of medicine within the College.

One of his special interests was the Gairdner Foundation. He was chairman of the medical advisory committee and president of the board for many years, and was instrumental in developing the Gairdner awards, which are now so highly prized among medical scientists around the world. In 1976 the Gairdner Foundation set up a special award for the Canadian who had made the greatest contribution to medical science; it is called the Wightman award and it was appropriate that Kajer should be the first recipient.

Among all his accomplishments perhaps none was greater than the impact he made upon his students and his house staff officers. He was the perfect teacher. He did not goad them with sarcasm nor embarrass them with his brilliance, but he challenged them with his example, supported them with understanding and encouraged them with consistent interest and friendship. One reason why Kajer was such an excellent medical teacher was because he was a superb physician. At the bedside he demonstrated repeatedly the excellence of his clinical skills, and showed an intuitive awareness of the importance of psychological factors in illness.

Kajer enjoyed life, he was happy to see so many of the projects he was working with grow and make significant contributions to Canadian medicine. He was slow to take credit for himself, quick to praise, and quick to encourage.

Kajer recognized that one cannot keep up one's own resources and enthusiasm unless one takes time away from responsibility to think and study. It was because of his philosophy of sabbatical leave, shared with his colleagues, that when he retired as professor of medicine, the Wightman fund was established for the support of staff who might feel the need of sabbatical leave. Although the fund was to honour Kajer, he himself supported it generously and it became the Lois and Kajer fund. It was chosen by his family as one of his interests that could be supported by his friends to honour him.

In August 1941, while still a medical resident, Kajer married Lois, whose father, Albert Francis Hawke, a Grimsby merchant, was the son of a Methodist minister who came from England. It was Lois and the three children, Carolyn, Pamela and Peter, who provided the answer to the question of how one person was able to have so many interests and be involved in so many activities, all at the same time. Lois was his manager, accountant, social secretary and charming companion, active in the hospital Women's Auxiliary, and she shared most of his interests and activities and provided some of his brightest ideas.

By all their friends they were recognized as the Lois and Kajer team, reflecting how closely they worked together. She also shared his non-medical interests, music, their cabin in the country, and their church. Kajer was consultant to the Diocese of the Arctic. 'His life was gentle; and the elements so mixed in him, that nature might stand up and say to all the world, "This was a man"'. IMH

WILCOCKS, Charles *b.*10 Apr 1896 *d.*6 Mar 1977
CMG (1952) MB ChB Manch (1924) MD (1932) DTM&H (1941) MRCP (1943) FRCP (1950)

Charles Wilcocks was born in 1896, and started a course in English at the Manchester University just as war began. He was then 18 years old. He immediately volunteered and was posted to an officers training corps. When commissioned in 1915 he was posted to the forces guarding the Suez Canal. He recalled the disastrous attack by the British forces at Gaza in 1917, across an open plain against Turkish troops well dug in on low hills. He was one of the two out of twenty officers who survived, saved, he said, by a bullet through a shoulder. Half the other ranks were lost. Immediately a number of the senior staff were posted out of the command.

On demobilization in 1919, he returned to Manchester but now had little taste for English, and transferred to medicine. He graduated in 1924.

He married Frances Gertrude Bullough in 1921, who also graduated in medicine. She died in February 1976, after some months of failing health through which Charles devotedly attended her.

After graduation he went into general practice. Some time later a visit by an old friend of student days, on leave from the Colonial medical service in Tanganyika, opened for them the attractive opportunities for work and life there. Soon after they were in Tanganyika (1927).

His career began much like that of any new arrival, relief duties at out-stations, field team work, and infectious diseases hospitals. In the last in Dar-es-Salaam he became interested in the amount of tuberculosis among Africans.

Some time later, while recovering from paratyphoid at a hill station, he heard that the director of medical services had proposed the establishment of a centre for the study of tuberculosis in the rural population. Charles indicated to the DMS his interest in this work. He was advised to call upon HH Scott of the Bureau of Hygiene and Tropical Diseases during his approaching leave in London. If he satisfied Scott the post was his. Scott approved, and he was appointed tuberculosis research officer in 1930. His leave was extended for him to widen his experience in all aspects of tuberculosis. This he did with S Lyle Cummins and bacteriologist WH Tytler at the King Edward VII Welsh National Memorial Association (prevention, treatment and abolition of tuberculosis) in Cardiff. He often said how much he owed to those devoted workers. He returned to East Africa with a portable radiographic set, and a generator that was driven from the back wheel of a motor car.

In Tanganyika he was based in Moshi, a delightful hill station, in the high country against Mount Kilimanjaro. As accommodation for his unit was not ready his work commenced under canvas. He led an active life with heavy field work. Much pulmonary tuberculosis in the Africans was found. He recalled how he found some acid-fast bacilli which he thought were not pathogenic, but he had neither the time nor facilities to follow this up.

On leave in the UK after his third tour (1934 – 1937) in Tanganyika, a pulmonary tubercular focus was found in a radiograph taken for a 'normal' control. He wondered if this was a laboratory or a field infection. He was invalided out of the service in 1937. After three months in Switzerland he returned to London to begin a new life.

Charles was appointed Scott's assistant in the Bureau in 1938, and upon Sir Harold Scott's retirement in 1942 he became acting director; he was made director in 1946. He was well equipped by his field work in East Africa to meet the many calls made on the Bureau in the service of the medical officers of the armed forces of the Allies during the war. This was specially met by the *Bulletin of War Medicine* (1942 – 1946).

With the end of the war he recommended that the Bureau expand its activities to embrace the whole field of medicine. This was vetoed by some timid but powerful members of his governing body. Such a broad approach was soon after undertaken by the BMA and the Dutch.

Under Charles's capable guidance the *Bulletin of Hygiene* and the *Tropical Diseases Bulletin* developed with the times, and continued to be essential tools for workers in these fields.

He retired from the Bureau in 1961, but maintained his interest in his past activities and life by accepting a consultantship to the Counties

Public Health Laboratories, London, 1962–1975. His broad and up to date acquaintance with public health problems in the tropics and their solution made his advice very useful. He also devoted much care to writing an autobiography based on his diaries.

In 1960 he gave the Heath Clark lectures of London University on *Aspects of medical investigation in Africa* which were published in 1962. He was co-author of the 17th edition of *Manson's tropical diseases* (1972). Among other publications were *Tuberculosis in Tanganyika* (1938), *Health and disease in the tropics* (1950), and *Medical advance, public health and social evolution* (1965).

Charles sometimes wondered if he made the right decision when he joined the Bureau. He had a feeling that he might not have used his qualities there as fully as he might perhaps have done had he followed a more active career in research. Those who had time out with pulmonary tuberculosis 30–40 years ago will recall the initial weakening of self-confidence as a new life is started, and the uncertainty of finding the restricted employment imposed by the then lack of chemotherapy. Charles did in fact have a slight relapse of his infection in 1946. All who benefited from the work of Charles and his staff at the Bureau would assure him of the importance of their contribution to the health of populations in all continents.

He was a member of the court of governors of the London School of Hygiene and Tropical Medicine from 1963 to 1971, and also a member of the board of governors of University College Hospital from 1953 to 1956.

He was a loyal fellow of the Royal Society of Tropical Medicine and Hygiene. He joined the Society in 1938, was a member of council 1943–1963, honorary secretary 1951–1963, president 1963–1965 and editor of the *Transactions* 1964–1970.

Charles was a gentle but strong, helpful person, never complaining. He had wide general interests; there was music in his family and he painted for pleasure. He was one of that band of colonial medical service officers who after devoted service loved Africa and its people for ever afterwards. Tropical service in Africa in Charles's time was not a life of power and luxury or domesticity; the suppression of malaria, and the chemotherapy of the prevalent bowel infections were then not known. Nowadays air travel has made possible a quality of family life that was not imagined in the 'bad old days'. CJH

[*Brit. med. J.*, 1977, **1**, 847; *Trop. Med. Hyg. News,* June 1977; Photo]

WILLIAMS, Harold Parry *b*.25 Apr 1903 *d*.14 May 1978
MRCS LRCP (1926) MRCP (1945) FRCP (1955)

Harold Williams was born in Merthyr, Glamorgan, where his father, William Parry Williams, was a pharmaceutical chemist. At school in West Monmouth, Pontypool, he became head boy and played in the First XI. He went on to study medicine at King's College Hospital, London. After obtaining the conjoint diploma in 1926, he joined the Royal Navy on a three year commission and, in 1932, entered general practice in Ansty, Leicestershire. His developing interest in paediatrics led him to spend most of his available spare time at the Leicester Royal Infirmary, in the company of Vernon Braithwaite. In 1938 he moved to general practice in Portsmouth, where he had heard that a paediatric appointment was a possibility. The following year he was called up to the Army. An operation for the relief of intestinal obstruction, the sequel to appendicitis in childhood, prevented his serving abroad and, until his discharge from the Army in 1946, he served in base hospitals. He then returned to Leicester and worked for Vernon Braithwaite as an ex-service registrar. In 1947 he was appointed to Coventry as its first paediatrician.

In Coventry he established a children's unit from scratch. As the sole paediatrician, his commitments were heavy, but matched by his energy and enthusiasm. Apart from his annual holiday, which was never longer than two weeks, and occasional visits to paediatric meetings outside Coventry, he worked a seven day week and was on call constantly. He was particularly interested in teaching. Any junior doctor who showed interest would be invited home for tuition. His remarking at a medical meeting that Coventry was in need of a postgraduate institute eventually led to the postgraduate centre, of which he was the first treasurer. He was senior clinical tutor and external examiner to the University of Birmingham. He retained, until his retirement at the end of 1968, his enthusiasm, spare figure, dark auburn hair, sense of humour and characteristic laugh. The respect in which he was held by his hospital colleagues was matched by the general practitioners, who, at their own farewell dinner in his honour, presented him with an illuminated address. As one of them said, 'He always gives the person he is talking to the feeling that they are the one person he was hoping to meet'. In 1970, he was presented with the Coventry award of merit and gold medal for his services to children.

Parry Williams moved to Oxford where for the next three and a half years, he was first locum paediatrician and then honorary associate paediatrician. He did outpatient work for three sessions a week, continued teaching, and interested himself particularly in a hearing assessment clinic. Another of his interests, spina bifida, resulted in the publication of his last paper. In 1972 he went to live in Minehead, from where he was able to visit Taunton. There he assisted the librarian in the postgraduate centre, and played an important part in establishing and running the audiology assessment clinic. In 1977 he moved to Lymington, and in the following year died of mesothelioma of the pleura.

Apart from paediatrics, which was his abiding interest, he was fond of gardening and he was an avid reader of biographies. His first wife died six months after marriage. He subsequently married Winifred Hurlstone of Brighton, by whom he had a son who died aged 14 years, and a daughter, who died in 1975. ACK/GW

[*Brit. med. J.*, 1978, **1**, 1630]

WILLIAMS, Morvyn *b*.29 Jan 1910 *d*.15 Apr 1979
MA MB BChir Cantab (1934) MRCP (1935) FRCP (1959)
FRACP (1938) Hon FACP (1966) Hon FRANZCP (1966)

Notwithstanding Tim Williams' distinction as a physician, it is as a man and a companion that he will be remembered by a greater host of friends than most people have the good fortune to claim.

He was born in Masterton, New Zealand, the second son of HG Williams of Lansdowne and a great-grandson of the pioneer missionary Henry Williams. His mother, Helen Jones, had come from Wales to settle in the new country, and one of his grandmothers was a Beetham. Tim's descent from two of the more prominent colonist families led naturally to his great interest in and love of early New Zealand history, its places and personalities.

In pre-war days it was not unusual for young New Zealanders to be sent to university in Britain and, after school at Christ's College, Tim entered Jesus College, Cambridge, where he captained the rugby side and won an honours degree. Thereafter he qualified in medicine from St George's Hospital, London, and before long had become in 1935 one of the youngest successful MRCP candidates. In 1937 he returned to an appointment as visiting physician to Wellington Hospital, a post he held until his retirement in 1975. During the war he served in the New Zealand Medical Corps in the Middle East and the Pacific and he remained in the Medical Corps for some years afterwards, retiring with the rank of lieutenant colonel. He was a member of the War Pensions Appeal Board until the time of his death. In due course he had become senior physician to Wellington Hospital and chairman of its medical staff, serving in these capacities on many hospital, health department and other official committees. From 1969 he was the nominee of the Royal Australasian College to the New Zealand Medical Council.

Although the London College retained his loyalty to the end, in 1938 Tim became a foundation fellow of the newly formed Australasian College of Physicians, and thereafter worked unsparingly to increase its stature and scope. He was appointed to the New Zealand board of censors and later, between 1962 and 1968, served twice as chairman of the New Zealand committee. He was elected to council in 1956 and in 1964 became the second New Zealander to be elected president. During his term of office he travelled widely, and his massive and friendly presence was a familiar one in many parts of Australasia, Britain and North America.

Beyond the confines of medicine Tim's interests were far-reaching. Continuing a family interest, he was chairman of Independent Newspapers Ltd and a member of the Historic Places Trust. He had a great love for his farm at Kumu Kumu in the Wairarapa, and a range of enthusiasms which included music, vintage cars and fishing. His knowledge of rugby and cricket made it a delight to have him as a companion at a big match. He was big in stature and big of heart, a great conversationalist, a mimic and wonderful company.

In 1938 Tim married Philippa, daughter of DHS Riddiford of Longwood, Wairarapa, and he was happiest of all in the company of his wife and four daughters, whose keen minds and high spirits so well complemented his own. JMT

[*The Dominion,* Wellington NZ, April 1979; Eulogy Funeral Service, St Paul's Cathedral, Wellington, 19 Apr 1979]

WILLIS, Rupert Allan *b.*24 Dec 1898 *d.*26 Mar 1980
MB BS Melb (1922) MD DSc (1930) FRCP* (1942) FRACP (1961) FRCS (1961) LLD Glasg (1962) Hon FRCPath (1970) Hon MD Perugia

Rupert Willis was born of English stock and reared in Yarram, Victoria, a village about one hundred and forty miles from Melbourne. He received his early schooling from his father and this had a great influence in moulding his attitudes to life and work; he did not attend a school until the age of ten. In 1922 he graduated in medicine from Melbourne University – in the same class as Roy Cameron and Macfarlane Burnet – and spent several years in general practice in Tasmania before returning in 1927 to Melbourne as the medical superintendent of the Austin Hospital. It was there that Willis, who had no formal training in pathology, developed his interests in the morphology and behaviour of tumours in man. In 1930 he was appointed pathologist to the Alfred Hospital in Melbourne and lecturer in pathology at Melbourne University. He was awarded a Rockefeller fellowship in 1933–1934 and worked with Sir Arthur Keith in the Royal College of Surgeons in London; this experience stimulated his interest in the embryological aspects of pathology and influenced much of his subsequent investigative work. In 1945 he returned to London as the Sir William H Collins professor of pathology at the Royal College of Surgeons and three years later became pathologist to the Royal Cancer Hospital. In 1950 he accepted the invitation to the chair of pathology in Leeds in succession to Matthew J Stewart but ill-health forced him to retire prematurely in 1955.

Freed of administrative chores, which he did not enjoy, Willis had a new lease of life in his 'retirement' at Nancledra in Cornwall. In the Riverside Laboratory – in the back garden of his cottage – he continued to do experimental work in association with JW Cook, who was then vice-chancellor of Exeter University. His writing of books and papers was prolific and he received a steady flow of tissue sections of many problem cases for his opinion from all over the world. In 1959 he was appointed as honorary consultant pathologist to the Imperial Cancer Research Fund where he set up a tumour reference collection which now consists of over eight thousand documented specimens of a wide variety of human and animal tumours and is appropriately housed in the University department of pathology in Leeds. In 1963–1964 he was the first occupant of the Macfarlane chair of experimental medicine at Glasgow Royal Infirmary.

Willis published about one hundred and forty papers which reflect the breadth of his interests: infectious diseases, disorders of growth, experimental carcinogenesis, the comparative pathology of neoplastic and non-neoplastic diseases, and the transplantation of tissues in rodents. However, his main and abiding interest was tumour pathology and his major contributions were published in textbooks. *The Spread of Tumours in the Human Body* (1934, third edition 1973) was based entirely on personal observations made through autopsy dissections. *The Pathology of Tumours* (1948, fourth edition 1967) has been translated into a number of languages and was a major reference text for practising histopathologists throughout the world. *The Borderland of Embryology and Pathology* (1958, second edition 1963) was Willis' own favourite work, and he was actively engaged with IMP Dawson in writing a new edition at the time of his death. *The Pathology of the Tumours of Children* was published in 1962, and the third edition of *The Principles of Pathology and Bacteriology*, a textbook for undergraduates written in collaboration with his son Trevor, in 1972.

Rupert Willis made an immense contribution to human tumour pathology; his clearly expressed views, always concise, sometimes dogmatic and uncompromising, provoked his readers to think more deeply about their day-to-day diagnostic problems. He had a profound influence on a generation of histopathologists. His work helped much to formulate the modern approach to tumour classification and histogenesis.

Many organizations and institutions recognized his achievements: his honours included an MD of the University of Perugia, an LLD of the University of Glasgow and the fellowship of the Royal College of Pathologists.

Willis lived a very full life and he had many extra-professional interests, including music, botany, petrology, pottery, photography and philately. His enthusiasm for his hobbies was highly infectious and he loved to share them with many friends of all ages. Great personal charm and an open, frank, warm and unassuming manner, endeared him to all who knew him and he had a very special way with children and young people; sons and daughters of his friends and colleagues have lasting happy memories of times spent with him.

Willis became a legend in his own lifetime to thousands of pathologists and clinicians but those who were privileged to know him remember with great affection a thoughtful, kind, compassionate and loyal friend. During his last few years, which were spent in his daughter's house in the Wirral in Cheshire, he again endured with courage and stoicism a chonic and at times severely debilitating illness. An obituary of Rupert Willis would be incomplete without a reference to his wife, Margaret, who was his constant and devoted companion and partner until her death in 1962. ARC

[*Brit. med. J.*, 1980, **280**, 1150 & 1191; *Lancet*, 1980, **1**, 940; Photo]

WILSON, Donald *b.*13 Apr 1908 *d.*20 Oct 1978
MRCS LRCP (1931) MB BS Lond (1936) MRCP (1941)
FRCP (1970)

Donald Wilson was consultant in rheumatology and rehabilitation at the Royal West Sussex Hospital (St Richard's), Chichester. He was born at Colchester, the son of Harry Percy Wilson, a headmaster, and his wife Clara Margaret, daughter of John Rogers Bradley, a farmer. He was educated at the Royal Grammar School, Colchester, and qualified in medicine from St Mary's Hospital, London, in 1931. Throughout the second world war he served as a medical specialist in the RAFVR. He married Kathleen Tephi, daughter of Edward Geddes Redman, a fish exporter, in 1941. She died in 1962, and in 1965 he married Asenath Olga (Zene), daughter of George Jackson, an antique dealer. He had two children: a son and a daughter.

Immediately after the war he was appointed honorary physician in charge of physical medicine at the Royal United Hospital, Bath. With the commencement of the NHS he was appointed to the Chichester group of hospitals as consultant in physical medicine and rheumatology. He remained in this post until his retirement in 1973. He was president of the section of physical medicine, Royal Society of Medicine, in 1953; and president of the section of physical medicine, British Medical Association, from 1955 to 1956. He was honorary secretary to the Regional Hospital and Specialist Association for ten years and a member of the central consultants committee for five. From 1956 to 1959 he was honorary treasurer of the British Association of Physical Medicine and Rheumatology, and he was also a member of the Heberden Society.

Donald contributed much to the medical scene and social life of Chichester. He built up a very large and efficient department of physical medicine (as it was then called) and was loved and respected by generations of physiotherapists and by his many patients. He was a shrewd clinician and took a special interest in the young disabled. It was fitting that the new department for their treatment was named Donald Wilson House. He was a superb medical administrator in the best sense of the word: many were grateful to him for advice and counsel on medico-political matters. He was a first class chairman of committees, and had a great ability to cut through red tape.

Donald had a delicious sense of humour, gently cynical but never hurtful. Beneath his somewhat stern exterior he was a gentle, sensitive person, and a man of great courage. He rose above much familial and personal illness. He had many interests outside medicine, being a prominent Freemason, an ardent fly-fisherman, and an enthusiastic sportsman. While at St Mary's he represented the hospital at rugby, cricket, golf and hockey. In later life he took an interest in photography. GW/VL

[*Brit. med. J.*, 1978, **2**, 1376; Photo]

WILSON, Isabel Grace Hood *b*.16 Sept 1895 *d*.8 Dec 1982
CBE (1961) MB ChB Edin (1921) DPM (1924) MD (1926)
MRCP (1937) FRCP (1947)

Isabel Wilson was born in Lasswade, Scotland, the daughter of George Robert Wilson, who was a physician and psychiatrist. Her mother was Susan Charlotte Sandeman, the daughter of Frederick Stewart Sandeman, a clergyman. She was educated at a small school with only about ten other children and by governesses, and went to Edinburgh University, qualifying in 1921. After various house physician posts, including some at the Children's Hospital, Myrtle Street, Liverpool, she became assistant medical officer in 1922 to Severalls Mental Hospital, Colchester, where she remained until 1926, and then became pathologist on the psychiatric staff of the Tavistock Clinic until 1930. At various times and for different periods, to gain experience, she did locums or part-time work at Bethlem Royal Hospital, the Lady Chichester Hospital, the Prince of Wales Hospital, Tottenham, and Bowden House, Harrow.

In 1931, having by now acquired a wide and varied knowledge of psychiatry, she became a commissioner of the Board of Control, which post she held from 1931 to 1948, becoming a senior commissioner from 1949 to 1960, after which time the Board was abolished and her post was called that of principal medical officer, Ministry of Health. She was a member of the panel of medical members of the North West Metropolitan Mental Health Appeals Tribunal from July 1961.

She wrote sparingly, and her work included *Home from Work*, a physiology for children, (1931); *Psychology for Nurses* (1934); *A Study of Hypoglycaemic Shock Treatment in Schizophrenia* (1936); *Cardiazol Treatment in Schizophrenia* (1938), and *Mental Deficiency: What it Means* (1954), the last three published by Her Majesty's Stationery Office.

Her colleagues recognized her distinction by making her president of the Royal Medico-Psychological Association in 1962–1963. She was also a member of the executive committee of the Mental Health Research Fund in 1961, an associate of the World Federation for Mental Health, and an associate of the College of General Practitioners.

Isabel Wilson was a quiet but clearcut and decisive personality. She was an active and devout member of the Society of Friends, to which she had been converted fairly early in life and which meant a great deal to her. Her professionalism was immaculate – she was kind, generous, but highly principled, and never lost sight of what she felt were the purpose and duties of psychiatry. She had a nice sense of humour and was very good company. Her main hobby was painting, especially in watercolours, and she was a member of the Medical Art Society, the Ridley Art Club, and the club of the Royal Watercolour Society. As one might expect, her watercolours were gentle in colour, highly accomplished, and most pleasant to look upon.

She was a good friend, and those who had the privilege of her friendship valued it very much. Her life was deeply imbued with her religious beliefs and she could be serious-minded and conscientious, but the fun was never far below the surface and kept peeping out.

Her contribution to psychiatry as a commissioner and later a senior commissioner of the Board of Control was very great, and as principal medical officer to the then Ministry of Health she contributed a great deal to her non-psychiatric as well as to her psychiatric colleagues. She was a dear and most lovable person, and when she retired she went on coming to College functions for a considerable time, but in the end a stroke prevented her from doing so. ALW

[*Bull. Roy. Coll. Psychiatrists,* May 1983, **7**, 98; Photo]

WILSON, Graham Malcolm *b.*16 Apr 1917 *d.*15 Apr 1977
MB ChB Edin (1940) MRCPE (1942) MRCP (1946) BSc (1947) FRCPE (1947) MD (1950) FRCP (1956) DSc (1964) FRCPG (1967) FRSE (1969)

Graham Wilson, regius professor of medicine in the University of Glasgow, died at the untimely age of 59. He was a remarkable man.

Born at Cheam in Surrey, the son of an Edinburgh botanist, Dr Malcolm Wilson, he married Elizabeth Bell Nicoll, also a doctor and the daughter of a doctor. They had six children, two of whom are now doctors. His brother, Cedric, was professor of pharmacology at Trinity College, Dublin. Graham Wilson was educated in Edinburgh, first at the Academy and later with exceptional distinction at the University, where he gained the Ettles scholarship, a BSc with first class honours, an MB with honours and the Leslie gold medal, an MD, also with gold medal and later a DSc. In 1946 he became a member of the London College of Physicians, in 1956 a fellow. He was Bradshaw lecturer at the College in 1962. In 1969 he was made fellow of the Royal Society of Edinburgh.

After qualification he became house surgeon and house physician at the Edinburgh Royal Infirmary, joining the RAF medical service in 1941. He was in North Africa at the height of the campaign in 1943. On discharge in 1946 he worked with Professor Drennan in Edinburgh for a while, and later went south to London, joining GW Pickering in the medical unit at St Mary's Hospital. He then moved to Sheffield where in quick succession he was promoted lecturer (1950), senior lecturer (1951) and professor of pharmacology and therapeutics (1954). In 1967 he made his final move to Glasgow as regius professor of medicine, continuing the Sheffield tradition as a training school for Glasgow professors, Sir Edward Wayne and Sir Andrew Watt-Kay having moved before him from Sheffield to regius chairs in Glasgow.

Graham Wilson had a very wide range of interests. His research began after demobilization with Drennan in Edinburgh, and then with GW Pickering in London, working on the physiology and pathology of the peripheral circulation. He collaborated with Bradford Hill in an early trial of drugs acting on the peripheral circulation. Later he became more interested in research on endocrine disease. The period

1952–1953 was spent at Harvard with Francis Moore, developing new methods for the measurement of body electrolytes and body water. He was a prolific scientific writer.

Some of his interests were unusual in a professor of medicine, many showing the spirit of a reformer. He was an active member of the Todd Royal Commission on medical education, whose influence in reforming the teaching of medical students is still with us. Within his own department he stimulated a lot of research into medical education: new techniques for audio visual aids were developed, and methods of examining medical students were compared and tested. He also believed that research into the operation and efficiency of the health service was neglected compared with the efforts spent on research into causation of disease. A health service research unit was set up at the Western Infirmary with the aid of the Nuffield Provincial Hospital Trust and the Scottish Home and Health Department, and Graham Wilson was its honorary director.

The proportion of women training in medicine increased markedly during the 1960s. Graham Wilson saw little point in this increase if the newly qualified woman could not reconcile marriage and child-bearing with medical practice. He created part-time medical posts specifically for women. It was a successful move.

Perhaps his most important contributions were in clinical pharmacology. He was one of the founders of the subject, recognizing earlier than others that a specialist discipline was needed to deal with the increasing use of drugs and their actions, interactions and idiosyncrasies. He encouraged the formation of new departments of clinical pharmacology. He did a lot to bridge the uneasy gap between the pharmaceutical industry and clinicians. Clinicians, he felt, needed to know more of the problems of industry, and industry needed better methods of assessing the safety and efficacy of drugs. With support from GD Searle Ltd he created a new post in his department for a clinician working part-time in industry and part-time in academic medicine. It is sad that he did not fulfil completely one of his most enduring ambitions: to reform and reset the standards by which the safety of medicines are judged. He felt that too much reliance was placed on toxicological studies in animals, too little on monitoring the long term effects of new drugs in man. He became chairman of the Safety of Medicines Committee in 1976 but within only three months developed the first symptoms of his final illness.

He was a lively friendly man, enormously hardworking. Six active children, a busy successful wife, elderly relatives and frequent visitors made their house in Westbourne Gardens seem like an elegant railway station. He enjoyed the activity. Their cottage on the shore of Loch Sunart was typical of the family. Graham built it himself from sections transported with great difficulty from Sheffield, and on a site which was completely inaccessible except by Land Rover or boat. He was also a fine fisherman and keen gardener.

As a personality he was an unusual mixture: bold and cheerful with professional contacts and with friends, he was an obvious leader at scientific meetings, in committees and with his family. But he was also shy and reserved personally. He was less good at social gatherings, and clearly he did not like cocktail parties. He was an interesting man to be with, widely read and a good and animated talker. He died a few hours short of his 60th birthday, after a long and painful illness which he diagnosed correctly and then bore with a mixture of curiosity and extreme fortitude. AFL

[*Brit. med. J.*, 1977, **1**, 1363; *Lancet*, 1977, **1**, 1017; *Times*, 19 Apr 1977; Photo]

WILSON, James Victor *b.*14 Nov 1909 *d.*9 May 1982
TD (1948) MB ChB BAO Belf (1933) MD (1937) MRCP (1944) FRCP (1962) FRCPath (1964)

Jim Wilson was a twin son of Samuel Wilson, a headmaster, and Sarah Margaret (née Thompson). He was educated at the Royal School, Dungannon, Co. Tyrone, where he played rugby for the school and was also in the athletics team. He proceeded to Queen's University, Belfast, to read medicine, and while there he was awarded a university Blue for athletics, and was captain of the athletics club.

After qualification, he held the posts of resident house physician and resident house surgeon at the Royal Victoria Hospital, Belfast. He then became house physician at the Northern Hospital, Liverpool. It was at this stage that he developed an interest in pathology and became resident biochemist and later assistant pathologist at the Royal Victoria Hospital, Belfast. In 1937 he joined Sinclair Miller at the Yorkshire Clinical Laboratories in Harrogate; this was a private pathological service which covered a very large area of Yorkshire, and here he extended his particular interests in haematology and diabetes as well as in genetics.

At the outbreak of the second world war he was medical officer to the West Yorkshire Regiment, but in December 1939 he was posted to Malta where he developed a blood transfusion service on the island, as well as being DADP until 1942. From 1942 to 1944 he was pathologist to the Palestine Command, holding the rank of major, and from 1944 to 1946 he was associate professor of pathology at the University of Alexandria in Egypt. It was while he was in the Middle East that he wrote a book, as well as several articles, on the pathology of traumatic injury and also on blast injuries.

On his return to England in 1946 he was appointed consultant pathologist to the Harrogate General Hospital, where he developed a first class department with an excellent reputation for its up-to-date facilities.

Jim Wilson was a forward looking man of considerable ability and energy. He was a founder member of the College of Pathologists and he was the medical representative on the planning committee for the building of the new District Hospital in Harrogate. He served on many hospital committees in Harrogate, being chairman of the Medical Advisory Committee as well as a member of the Hospital Management Committee and the Harrogate Hospital House Committee. He was a prime mover in the planning of the Nuffield

Nursing Home in Harrogate in 1960, and was a president of the Harrogate Medical Society.

He was a man of many interests outside medicine; he read widely and this was reflected in the extensive library which he had in his own home. He had a profound knowledge of poetry, literature and history, and his ability to quote from these sources often surprised people who did not know him well. He had an active mind and to be in his company was a stimulating experience, and his keen sense of humour was always refreshing. Jim Wilson was an active worker in Christ Church, Harrogate, where he was churchwarden and for many years served on the parochial church council; he also took an active interest in the care of the elderly in Harrogate and helped to form the '61 Club'. He was president of the Harrogate Rotary Club and a past master of Doric Lodge in Harrogate, and also reached provincial rank. He was an enthusiastic golfer and served on the Harrogate Golf Club committee but would, however, never play golf on Sundays, which he felt was a day which should be spent with his family and in his church activities. 'JV' was a friendly and warm, but in many ways, a shy man. On his retirement from hospital practice in 1975 he went to live in Malta, and he was greatly missed by his friends and colleagues in Harrogate, but he and his wife did later return to live in this country in Berkshire, for the last few years of his life.

In 1944 he married Barbara Elizabeth, the daughter of Thomas Alborn Clapham of Keighley, herself a doctor and graduate of Leeds University, and they had three sons and one daughter, all of whom survived him.

WSS

[Photo]

WILSON, Peter Audaer Overend *b.*18 July 1918 *d.*11 Dec 1981
CBE (1981) MB BChir Cantab (1943) MA (1944) MRCP (1948) FRCP (1969)

Peter Wilson was born in Leeds, the son of Walter Audaer Wilson, a gas engineer, and his wife Gertrude Mary Sinclair. He was educated at Clifton College and St John's, Cambridge, graduating from the London Hospital in 1943. After holding house appointments at the London, he joined the RAMC, serving in Europe and the Far East until demobilization in 1946. From 1948 to 1950 he was registrar at the Leeds General Infirmary, and registrar and senior registrar, 1950 – 1952, at the National Heart Hospital, London. In 1952 he was appointed consultant cardiologist to the Government of Iraq, later being appointed consultant physician to the Kuwait Government in 1953, where he remained for the rest of his life.

For some years he was senior physician at the Amiri Hospital, Kuwait, and in 1959 he was instrumental in the formation of the department of medicine at the newly built Sabah Hospital, where he was also senior physician and director of the department. He was personal physician to the Emir, and adviser to the State on all health matters. The Kuwaitis regarded him as the father of modern medicine in their country; he trained most of their physicians and also arranged postgraduate training for them in the United Kingdom. He played a major part in forming the Kuwait Medical Association and was on the editorial board of its journal, to which he contributed many scientific papers. He was also the local representative of the British Medical Association. He officially retired in June 1981, but was persuaded by the Kuwait Government to remain with them in order to give advice on the design and equipment of new hospitals. He was awarded the CBE in the 1982 Honours List but, sadly, died before the official press announcement.

His main interest was in cardiology, and the Cardiac Society meeting was a yearly event for him, but he was also an all-round physician whose skill, competence and modesty were admired by all who came in close contact with him. He enjoyed people, and had a natural charm. He was a friendly person and a generous host, both in Kuwait and at his villa in Italy. He was an enthusiastic sportsman but, being a Yorkshireman, cricket took pride of place, and his visits to this country usually coincided with a test match at Lords. He was a member of the Kuwait Cricket and Golf Clubs, and chairman of his church. He also had a wide knowledge of music and gardening. He never married.

GW/VL

[*Brit. med. J.*, 1982, **284**, 757; Photo]

WINN, John Michael *b*.15 Nov 1917 *d*.16 June 1982
BA Cantab (1939) MRCS LRCP (1942) MRCP (1950)
DMRD (1951) FRCP (1969)

Michael Winn's final years were marred by a succession of devastating illnesses that would have defeated a lesser man, but almost to the end he continued to work and take a lively interest in the General Infirmary, Leeds. He had returned to Leeds in 1950 to study radiodiagnosis at the Infirmary, and soon distinguished himself as an extremely able radiologist. In 1954 he was appointed consultant radiologist and found his main interest in neuroradiology. He set out to develop a first rate neuroradiology service in Yorkshire, extending it to cover the neurological units at Chapel Allerton Hospital, Leeds, and Pinderfields General Hospital, Wakefield. He proved himself to be an excellent organizer and administrator, encouraging the appointment of able younger consultants and cooperating with them and his colleages at St James's Hospital and Bradford Royal Infirmary in setting up an excellent postgraduate training scheme.

During his period as chairman of the department of radiodiagnosis he gave all his energy, and much of his spare time, to replanning, extending, and re-equipping the department with great success. In 1974, with the reorganization of the Health Service, he became consultant member of the district management team. No better man could have been appointed: he had a gift for grasping essentials, for deflating pomposity and pretension – whether medical or administrative – a wide experience of people and many personal contacts. He made an immense contribution to the development of the health service in Leeds at a very critical period.

Winn was born in Helston, Cornwall, the son of Frederick Arnold Winn and his wife Winifred Jane (née Hall) whose father was a headmaster. He was educated at Leighton Park School, Reading, Queen's College, Cambridge, and Leeds University Medical School, qualifying in 1942. He was appointed casualty officer at Birmingham Accident Hospital, where he met his wife Cecilia Neville-Jones, widow of a physician and daughter of Joseph Rath. They married in 1944; there was a son, John, of the marriage and a stepdaughter, Pauline.

From 1944 to 1946 Winn saw service with the RAMC, first with No 6 Light Field Ambulance in Italy, and then in India, being promoted to the rank of major. On demobilization he returned to the Midlands and to registrar posts at the General Hospital, Birmingham, and the Coventry and Warwickshire Hospital. In 1949 he was appointed house physician to St James's Hospital, Balham, before returning to Leeds in 1950.

Mike Winn was a brilliant raconteur and had a wonderful sense of fun. He enjoyed mimicry and had a lifelong interest in accents and languages. He was also a warmhearted man with a great gift for friendship; approachable and courteous, he was always ready to help with personal or professional problems. Both he and his wife Cecilia were very hospitable and he found much happiness in his home, in his family life, and in his grandchildren. He was survived by his wife and children. GW/VL

[*Brit. med. J.*, 1982, **285**, 982; Photo]

WINTON, Francis Seaton *b.*26 Apr 1906 *d.*25 July 1982
MRCS LRCP (1930) MRCP (1932) FRCP (1968)

Seaton Winton was a gifted and unusual man. The study of public transport was for him an absorbing hobby and while resident assistant physician at St George's Hospital, London, he would sit in a window overlooking Hyde Park Corner, noting the passing buses. He could tell the type, the number of that type in each garage, and such mundane details as their routes and timetables.

He was born in Wimbledon, London SW19, where he spent the greater part of his life. His father, William Balcombe Winton FRCP, also practised in Wimbledon and married Maria Elizabeth Bentley-Taylor, the daughter of a clergyman. Seaton was educated at the Cottesmore School, Hove, Gresham's and the University of Cambridge, pursuing his clinical studies at St George's. He never married.

After a period at St George's he returned to Wimbledon and entered general practice, like his father before him. Asked why he made this choice instead of waiting for an appointment as physician at St George's he said that he would have found such a post uncongenial. In practice, he was courteous and able. He never summoned a patient from the waiting room by sounding a bell but preferred to greet each one personally and conduct them to his consulting room. A spontaneous pneumothorax prevented him from entering military service during the second world war and he became, first a senior resident medical officer at the Nelson Hospital, and then consultant in the NHS to the Nelson and Wimbledon hospitals. All his life he endeavoured to work to the highest medical standards, yet he showed little interest in any further reading of medicine, although he was an omnivorous reader of detective novels.

Seaton played golf, snooker and bridge: after winning the spring meeting at the Royal Wimbledon Golf Club he gave up the game in favour of snooker; after winning the challenge cup for snooker he stopped playing, but until ill health prevented him he continued to play bridge with players of near international standard, such as Rodney Smith (Lord Smith of Marlow). He also enjoyed walking and gardening, characteristically only using the Latin names of his many flowers and shrubs.

He retired from medicine after suffering a partial left hemiplegia, but continued to live in his house which contained 'the surgery'. He succumbed to a second stroke and died in St George's Hospital. He expressly forbade a funeral service. He was survived by his sister, Joan.

AJWB/GW/VL

[Photo]

WITTS, Leslie John *b.*21 Apr 1898 *d.*19 Nov 1982
MB ChB Manch (1923) MD (1926) MRCP (1926) FRCP (1931)
DSc Dublin (1955) MD Bristol (1961) Hon DM (1938)

Leslie Witts was both an early and a late developer, having a brilliant career in medical school at Manchester, and in junior research appointments in Cambridge, in the USA and at Guy's Hospital, and yet to the end of his days maintaining great breadth of interest, and revealing new talents of self-expression in the series of 'Personal Views' whch he contributed to the *British Medical Journal*. His early distinction as a clinical investigator and an outstanding teacher led to his appointment while still in his thirties to the chair of medicine at St Bartholomew's Hospital Medical School. The four years which he spent at Bart's were important, and marked by his studies on iron-deficiency anaemia, on the treatment of haematemesis, and on the dangers of ritual purgation, a contribution which deserves to be ranked with Richard Asher's later questioning of the value of arbitrary periods of rest in bed. While at Bart's, Leslie Witts developed a close collaboration with the surgical unit, directed by Paterson Ross. These years at Bart's were happy ones, but he was not the man to refuse a challenge, and he accepted the invitation to become the first Nuffield professor of clinical medicine, and to set up a full-time medical unit in the Radcliffe Infirmary, Oxford.

Although he must in 1938 have foreseen the possibility of war, he could not have expected its duration, nor the additional burdens which would be laid on his infant department by the development of an undergraduate clinical school at Oxford, and by the increase in national advisory commitments which naturally came the way of a physician of his wide knowledge and clearly expressed wisdom. He was already a member of the Medical Research Council when war broke out, and he served a second term from 1943 to 1947. These must have been difficult years, with both the pressure of external commitments, and the continued need to press for the replacement of makeshift accommodation by a building worthy to house a major clinical and research department; yet he was always accessible to his junior colleagues, and he maintained a considerable practice, particularly but by no means exclusively in clinical haematology. As his Harveian oration of 1971 clearly shows, he took a broad view of the responsibilities of a professor of medicine. He believed that in the clinical sphere these involved competence in general medicine as well as in a specialty, and the competence to evaluate the psychological and social aspects of illness, as well as its organic aspects. Modern medicine is quite often criticized for being long on science and technology, and short on compassion. Leslie Witts both preached and practised a different outlook, saying 'One of the lessons the clinical student and the young doctor has to learn is how to gain both the respect and the affection of their patients'.

The early struggles to attain adequate accommodation were belatedly successful in the post-war years, and allowed the growth of an internationally renowned department, attracting a stream of graduates from home and overseas, and ultimately successors of the calibre of Paul Beeson and David Weatherall. In these same years, Leslie Witts was quick to see the importance of the developing subject of clinical pharmacology – had not the first therapeutic administration of penicillin been carried out in his wards? He was a member of the Committee on Safety of Drugs, and he took a particular interest in clinical trials, editing a book on that topic. Through more than a quarter of a century in a leading chair of medicine, he set an example of well-informed and broadly based medical practice, and provided research opportunities and leadership for numbers of people. In his later years, he no doubt sacrificed his personal research to creating opportunity for others; and he summed up his own particular skill better than anyone else could have done, when he said 'My scientific leanings are those of a student, with emphasis on the synthesis and application of knowledge rather than on discovery'. What he did not say was that in these particular areas, and in his exposition of them, he was beyond all praise. Not only did he do the office of his vocation sincerely – he also helped the commonalty of physicians in two notable ways: he was a very popular secretary, and later president, of the Association of Physicians; and in the Royal College of Physicians he gave Goulstonian and Lumleian lectures, and he was Harveian orator and vice-president.

Leslie Witts was characteristically helpful to his memorialist by revealing a good deal of his own view of himself, both in the *Lancet*, as 'Doctor Don', in 1939, and later on in the 'Personal Views' series in the *BMJ*. In these papers, he tells of his religious upbringing – 'Strict upbringing as a Congregationalist has left me with an indelible imprint of Christian morality'. Like so many doctors he could appreciate and express both the fascination and the fulfilment of medicine, yet remain aware of the frequent tragedies inherent in the human condition. Having said that 'such poetry as medicine brings is in the elegiac vein' – and he quotes particular instances of sorrow – he goes on to say, 'For all that, there can be no life with greater opportunities for delight in work than medicine'. I think he was exaggerating in both directions when he claimed in 1939 to have exhibited 'my particular blend of evangelism and hellenism, of St Anthony and Dionysus' – for like the rest of us, he was neither saint nor libertine, but a man who recognized clearly that, in his words, 'It is not given to mortal men to be the arbiters of life and death, or to solve the riddles of the Universe. We must constantly remind ourselves of the dangers of arrogance and cherish the virtue of humility'. And it was not a Dionysus who said 'Libertarianism and permissiveness finally destroy true freedom'.

As a mentor of a fledgling research worker and physician, he was quite ideal – his vast store of erudition was open to a questioner, he took infinite pains over the presentation of papers, and he gave patient and strong support in those inevitable periods when the research is going badly. I first knew him in a time of national danger, and of endless local frustrations, which must have worried any man as sensitive as Leslie; but he was selfish only in this, that he kept these worries to himself, and did not share them with his colleagues – though he may have done with his family. He could at times be preoccupied – who would not, in such circumstances? But those of us who were privileged to see him at home could be in no doubt of the essential warmth of his character.

In 1929 he married Nancy Grace, younger daughter of LF Salzman, the historian. They had one son and three daughters, and at the time of his death there were ten grandchildren. It was a long and very happy marriage. Nancy sustained him through his professional life, and her unfailing support proved invaluable during the last years, when he was somewhat frail. DAKB

[*Brit. med. J.*, 1982, **285**, 1667-8; *Times,* 23 Nov 1982; Photo]

WRIGHT, *Sir* **Robert (Brash)** *b.*1 Mar 1915 *d.*4 Dec 1981
OBE (1945) DSO (1946) BSc Glasg (1934) MB ChB (1937)
FRCSE (1947) FRFPS (1948) ChM (1952) FRCSG (1962)
FRCP* (1971) Hon FRACS (1968) Hon FRCS (1975)
LLD Glasg (1981)

The small community of Overtown, near Wishaw in Lanarkshire, lies on the border of the coalmines and steelworks of the industrialized lower Clyde Valley to the west and north, and the rolling slopes of the famous Clyde orchard area with its fruit, vegetable and flower farms to the south and east. Further south still, is the attractive town of Lanark and beyond that the high moors which stretch almost to the borders of Scotland and England. In this setting Hugh Wright and Janet Brash settled down to spend a lifetime as local practitioner and wife. They had three sons and a daughter. Robert Brash Wright was their second son.

Life and practice in Overtown, then as now, are divided between the urban and rural aspects of the community, and to this background Robert Wright often referred in later years. He clearly enjoyed the life it offered, first in the local school and later at the more prestigious Hamilton Academy, an excellent secondary modern school in the county town some five miles away. He was a good pupil and a keen cricketer and rugby football player. As in later life, he had a sturdy stocky build, which must have been useful on the sportsfield.

At the relatively young age of seventeen he was accepted into the medical faculty as an undergraduate in the University of Glasgow in September 1932. He travelled from home by train and bus daily and although taking some interest in University life he was much attached to home affairs. He qualified in 1937 with honours. It might have been expected that he would find an opening as a house officer in a University unit, but his independence of spirit was already well developed and he took a post as a house surgeon in Burnley, where a friend of his father's had offered him good experience; thereafter he remained in Burnley for a further six months as a house physician in the same Victoria Hospital. By now he knew he wanted to be a surgeon and he obtained a post in a surgical unit in Plymouth in September 1938. Fate stepped in after a very short time when his father had a severe stroke and young Robert was summoned home to hold the family practice together. His knowledge of the district and practice personalities must have been a great support to him in what would nowadays be regarded as an almost impossible burden for so inexperienced a graduate. But other events were soon to take over as 1939 wore on. By September, Robert was in the RAMC, commissioned as a lieutenant and posted to No 10 Field Ambulance which proceeded to embark for France later in the month. He remained there until May 1940, transferring to No 159 (Welsh) Field Ambulance, and then in August of that year returning to UK where he remained until February 1942, latterly in 219 Field Ambulance. He then embarked for India with No 158 and in July 1942, served three months with the India Military Hospital before rejoining No 158 Field Ambulance, now in the Middle East. He later transferred to No 33(1) Field Ambulance with which he remained until December 1942. He was then appointed as commanding officer to a series of field ambulances, Nos 31 and 10 in the Middle East, and finally until his demobilization in December 1945, he was serving with No 4 Casualty Clearing Station as its CO with the rank of lieutenant colonel.

During 1944 his unit, like many others, was drafted to Italy and took part in the fighting there. On 24 September 1944 he received wounds in his foot and hands from an exploding mine and was for a time in hospital. He used to say that he had parts of Italy under his skin for evermore, which was as close as he ever got to discussing the episode.

His was a distinguished war service, earning him the DSO and military OBE, but he never discussed the details with his colleagues or family. The DSO was awarded for his service with the Indian division in Italy; the military OBE was awarded for his enormous administrative contribution.

The war over, RB, like so many other hopeful young doctors discharged from the services, realized that however great his wartime experience there was much of his chosen specialty yet to be learned. He availed himself of the clinical refresher scheme designed for ex-service men for one year and spent the time in the professorial unit of CFW Illingworth at the Western Infirmary in Glasgow. He took his FRFPS (Glasgow) and FRCS (Edinburgh) in 1948. In Illingworth's department he came into contact with many wartime colleagues and friends, among them William Sillar, a fellow pupil from Hamilton Academy with a distinguished war record like his own, and later to be a lifetime colleague at the Southern General Hospital. After a year, however, they split up and RB went to work as a junior 'extra-dispensary' surgeon with Murray Newton, an excellent teacher and distinguished thyroid surgeon. Later he climbed the promotion tree to work with AB Kerr, like himself a war veteran although older in years and, also like Bob, a future president of the Glasgow College. RB's drive, surgical skill and ability quickly gained him promotion, and his research work led to a ChM with honours. His experience was general, with particular interests in vascular surgery, and in thoracic and thyroid surgery, reflecting the interests of the units in which he worked. His ChM thesis was on the subject of varicose veins and gravitational ulcer. This was his most productive period of original research.

In 1948, with the advent of the NHS, he had been graded as consultant surgeon and shortly thereafter he was given some surgical sessions in a small but prestigious hospital in Govan, founded by the famous Govan shipbuilder William Elder, and called the Elder Cottage Hospital. These sessions were much sought after and usually held by young surgeons thought to have a good future. Normally the tenure was relatively brief and relinquished on obtaining a charge appointment in the parent hospital. As will be related, RB was associated with the Elder Cottage for the rest of his professional life.

In 1946, on his return home, Robert married Helen Tait, a school-time friend whom he originally met on a summer holiday at North Berwick. North Berwick was a favourite holidaying place for the Wright family and many others from the Hamilton and Wishaw areas, where Helen also came from. Indeed, Dr Wright senior used to refer to one spot on the beach as 'Wishaw Cross'. Their marriage was an entirely happy one, each setting the other off in excellent harmony and yet in many ways being quite different in interest and attitudes. Their family consisted of a son, Hugo, and daughters Margaret and Patricia, and their life was spent in several houses in the village of Bearsden in Dunbartonshire, west of Glasgow. Bob, a lifelong non-smoker and teetotaller, was a most excellent host as was Helen a delightful hostess. They kept up their attachment to North Berwick by acquiring a holiday house there and for many years that was their main holiday spot, until in his last ten years or so of active professional life Helen and Margaret persuaded him to take his vacations in a series of Mediterranean countries.

His outside activities were gardening, walking, and, for a time, golfing. He played cricket at school and later in life it became an absorbing hobby. He would be off on his own to spend days at Lords and Headingly watching Test matches whenever his busy life allowed it. He took a great interest in Rotary, being a member of the Glasgow Rotary Club through which he met a number of non-medical acquaintances and friends. His church, New Kilpatrick in Bearsden, was important to him and he became an elder and took his duties seriously. His was a simple uncomplicated faith and fitted in well with his lifestyle, which was upright, honest and kindly. He was a forthright sort of man whom some thought too dogmatic, but his essential honesty also compelled him to see the point of view opposite to his own. Those who knew him well valued his straightforward approach and kindness.

The remaining loves of RB's life were his hospital, his college activities and his contribution to medical affairs at all levels.

In the years immediately following the second world war the College (or Faculty as it then was) in Glasgow was seeking a new status and a new role. It was slow to rise to the immediate demands for postgraduate education which the returning service doctors found so necessary for their progress. This vacuum was filled in part by the Medico-Chirurgical Society, an old-standing group representing all disciplines in medicine. Its meetings were popular and well attended and it clearly filled a much felt need. In 1949 RB was appointed honorary secretary and he remained actively associated with the Society throughout his life, becoming president in 1966. His influence was immediately felt and continued when in later years other postgraduate activities, including those of the College, began to compete with the Society. Among other changes, he introduced research reports to the Society in 1962. He remained very attached to the 'Medico-Chirurg' and indeed the Society owed much to his efforts and continuing interest. In 1981 he was created an honorary member. It was a major interest in his medical life in the post war years and through it he became known to the Glasgow medical world.

During this time it became obvious that RB Wright was to be one of the significant future figures in Scottish surgery. Some assumed that he would follow an academic career and although his record to date would have made that possible, research did not hold special attractions for him. Teaching, on the other hand, did appeal to him, and he was a superb lecturer and clinical instructor in clear simple language, using every day similes which appealed to his students. He opted for a teaching hospital role, outside the major teaching hospitals as it happened. His remaining hospital work was to be carried out in an ex-poor law institution in Govan, the centre of the then thriving shipbuilding industry.

Robert Wright came to the Southern General Hospital (SGH) in

1954 to replace W Arthur Mackey. The hospital, an ex-local authority building dating from 1870, had been acquired by the NHS in 1948. Before the war, the MOH of Glasgow, Sir Alexander MacGregor, decided to upgrade its medical and surgical services, and Arthur Mackey continued this and developed the number of specialties by encouraging James Levack, who had been the resident surgeon in post since 1936, apart from war service, to enlarge his interests in genito-urinary surgery, and by importing another Illingworth protégé, William Sillar, to start an accident and orthopaedic service. At the same time, about 1950, surgical undergraduates began to attend the unit regularly for daily teaching. This then was to be Bob's inheritance – a thriving, developing surgical unit with keen and energetic staff, all about his own age.

It was an appointment half-expected and yet to some surprising. He was only thirty eight and there were other more senior surgeons who might have reasonably expected to get this much sought after post. There were acid remarks from some of Bob's contemporaries and more especially from those who had suffered slightly – or imagined they had – from his direct and critical method of comment. To some he was 'opinionated', which is not easily tolerated by Scots in Scotland, but in the end most had to admit that he was practical, fair and usually correct. Everyone felt he had taken on a large task. It was therefore somewhat surprising when he sought to enlarge it even further.

Near the Southern General Hospital lay the Elder Cottage Hospital, a small but active establishment much loved by the Govan folk who were in the main honest hard workers in shipbuilding or in jobs associated with the shipyards. Elder himself had been a shipbuilder and had shown great kindness to the parish which had made his wealth. The 'Cottage', as it was known, had medical and surgical beds and it was a great honour to be appointed either visiting physician or visiting surgeon to ECH. This was reserved for the two most promising young men at the Western and Royal Infirmaries. Alex Imrie (FRCP) had been appointed physician and he was based at the Royal Infirmary. RB Wright had been appointed surgeon in 1948, as has already been recorded. Here he ran the surgical wards and a weekly operating session and clinic. The Cottage had come under the new board of management of Glasgow SW Hospitals, which included the Southern and another of Elder's beneficences, the David Elder Infirmary. But the Cottage continued its way of life with its own matron and staff as if the NHS had never been born. To RBW it was an ideal place, entirely his own, the medical beds having recently been given over to surgery. Here he could work as long and as hard as he pleased. To his practical mind the sensible thing was to combine this appointment with his new job. This was more easily said than done and to begin with his plan met with opposition. Probably the general practitioners of Govan had some influence in the eventual decision, which was to let Bob keep both appointments. So the Cottage continued to provide patients and doctors with a magnificent service, based almost solely on RBW, until his retirement, having withstood several attempts at closure or change of use. Many a junior surgeon paled at the thought of doing the chief's enormous clinic when he was absent. Bob merely asked for another cup of tea and got on with the work in his characteristic fashion.

In the Southern the impact of the new man was quickly felt. Robert Wright was somewhat appalled at the bread-and-butter surgical waiting list, and set out to overcome that in his first year. Although he had trained himself to perform mitral valvotomies, it was typical of him that he said quite firmly that he would accept none in his first year until he had established himself with his staff, and in his job, and overcome the list of hernias and varicose veins. It was also typical of him that in a year he was ready to start valvotomies again, and characteristic of his attitude that when open-heart surgery came along he was the first to say that he would not enter that field in his type of unit with its heavy routine load, and that he would therefore abandon cardiac surgery in favour of the big centres.

The unit at the SGH had always been popular with undergraduates; under the new chief its reputation for excellent teaching grew, students being much attracted to RB's form of instruction. It was simple, crisp and practical, full of homely phrases and analogies, interspersed with flashes of real humour and all delivered in Bob's direct fashion and Lanarkshire tongue. For some it was too blunt and too direct and penetrating, but students and junior staff loved it. There was no 'humbug' about Bob. As a result, there was fierce competition to join his unit as students, house officers, or junior trainees. In a short time he was a member of the board of management. His approach appealed to the lay members if not always to all of his medical colleagues, but his contribution was considerable and he remained a member until the board disappeared in 1974.

Another activity was in postgraduate education. As the first specialty adviser in surgery of the newly formed West of Scotland postgraduate committee, RB set up a scheme of rotation between the city and district hospitals for surgical trainees. This was an immediate and continuing success. Only one of Bob's determination, however, could have ensured that such an arrangement would survive the built-in prejudice of the central hospital teaching units to become a reality.

This then was the background to his professional life at the time when he became involved in the work of the Royal College of Physicians and Surgeons of Glasgow, an association which was to lead to his becoming successively treasurer, president and representative on the General Medical Council, and to his being known throughout the world of surgical Colleges. Soon he had persuaded the Colleges to reconsider their examination methods and to permit Glasgow to experiment, monitor and report on new examination techniques, with such success that others have followed this example. In later years there were repercussions and RB was accused of 'going it alone' in Glasgow. In fact, of course, he acted strictly according to his remit and, when published data showed that the Glasgow examination was performing its function as well as the older systems but even more objectively, he encouraged the College to retain the new system.

Others have now copied the Glasgow system either completely or in part.

During his time as president (1968 – 1970) in Glasgow, the College, which combines physicians and surgeons, was in close debate and negotiation with the London and Edinburgh Colleges of Physicians and exploring the possibilities of a unified examination. Although the MRCP (UK) was to appear in his successor's period of office, Bob and the president of the Royal College of Physicians of London, Lord Rosenheim, had an immediate understanding of each other's point of view. This was to develop into a considerable degree of respect and friendship and must have been most helpful in the talks which led to the development of a common MRCP Part 1. Largely because of this, he was elected a fellow, under Bye-law 39(b), of the Royal College of Physicians of London in 1970 and this was, perhaps, the most prized of his many honours.

At home, his presidency was also distinguished by his wish to make the College more widely known to his fellow citizens of Glasgow. With his many connexions, particularly through his membership of Rotary, he set up the friends of the College group and established regular luncheons for distinguished Scottish laymen. He also encouraged local groups to visit the College, entertaining them with interesting and amusing anecdotes about the individuals whose portraits grace the College walls, about the buildings themselves and items of College history.

In 1971 after retiring as president, he was elected as the College representative on the General Medical Council. This also meant that he retained a seat on the College council, so that he was a member of that council from 1966 until his death in 1981. RB took immediately to the General Medical Council. His impact was quickly seen and 'his interventions in debate were always well timed and carefully assessed and cogently argued' as Sir John Walton has said, and as one can imagine. What also quickly became clear was his personal integrity, his kindliness and intellectual honesty, not to mention considerable personal energy. He quickly became involved in the work of the overseas committee and, as its first chairman in 1972, he headed visiting deputations to Malta, to South Africa, to Australia and New Zealand. During this time he made many overseas friends and learned much about the educational problems of students in less privileged countries. He became interested in disciplinary matters and was elected deputy chairman of the disciplinary committee under Lord Richardson in 1974. There too he made a strong impression. In this work he realized the importance of health questions in disciplinary cases and was thus well placed to offer good advice in the formation of the new health committee in the restructured Council. Rapidly, Robert Wright became one of the most respected members of Council and it was no surprise when he was knighted in 1976 and in due course succeeded Lord Richardson as president in 1980. He immediately launched into a series of programmes on the registration and training of overseas doctors in the UK; on reviewing the role of the register; and on the Council's new tasks in relation to postgraduate education.

There can be no doubt that he would have had much to offer in his role, so soon and so tragically to be terminated.

RB's health had always seemed robust. He had occasionally minor problems with his old wounds and an early brush with coronary disease which did not trouble him again until one cold evening walking from Victoria to his favourite Caledonian Club, carrying a suitcase heavy with Council papers, he suddenly experienced angina. Although no infarct was found, he had continuing discomfort. Over a Christmas break he had bypass surgery with immediate success and he seemed well set for the future. But within a year a new and sinister ailment had affected him and he knew exactly what it was. He attended his last Council meeting in that shadow, returning home to have his fears confirmed. Like the courageous fellow he was, he sat down and wrote his letter of resignation to the College. Within six weeks he was no more.

He was a man of medicine, which was his life. Awards of all kinds came his way: honorary fellowships of the English and Australasian surgical colleges and of the London College of Physicians; and the honorary degree of LLD of his own University of Glasgow in 1981. But these told little of the man who was a distinguished surgeon and, more than that, one of the great statesmen of medicine. GBS

[*Brit. med. J.*, 1982, **283**, 1616; **284**, 131, 211; *Lancet*, 1982, **1**, 117; *Times*, 12 Dec 1981; Photo]

YATES, Arthur Gurney *b*.19 Nov 1881 *d*.26 Jan 1977
MA MB ChB Edin (1908) MD (1910) MRCP (1911) FRCP (1929)

When Arthur Yates died, at the age of 95, he had been retired for about thirty years. Those who live so long have lost most of their contemporaries, most of their erstwhile colleagues, and many of their former students, but Yates had interests and friends until the end of his life.

His father was a Congregational minister in Spalding, where Yates was born; his mother had been a missionary. He was educated privately and later at Spalding Grammar School, after which he was for a time apprenticed to a pharmacist in Sheffield. He left Sheffield to take a medical degree at the Edinburgh Medical School, after which he returned to Sheffield to take up junior hospital appointments at the Sheffield Royal Infirmary. This was in 1908. In 1910 he was medical registrar, and from 1912 to 1948 honorary physician to the Royal Infirmary. During part of this time he was also consulting physician to the City General Hospital, Sheffield, and during the 1914–1918 war he was registrar to the 3rd Northern General Hospital in Sheffield. He was a lecturer in medicine at Sheffield University.

After retiring age he stayed on for some years as physician in charge of the neurological department, Sheffield United Hospitals, and was president of the Association of Physicians at their meeting in Sheffield in 1952.

In his early years, Yates published papers on the relation of streptococcal disease to rheumatism, and later wrote an account for the Medical Research Council on the clinical aspects of the Sheffield outbreaks of epidemic encephalitis. His main interests were in neurology, and in the psychological aspects of illness, but medicine was not so specialized in his time, and psychiatry had only begun to invade the general hospitals.

Yates was a somewhat retiring person, but a very good scholar and, in consequence, a good speaker and a good teacher, but he had some of the absent-mindedness which is said to go with such personalities. For instance, he would walk down from his consulting rooms to the Royal Infirmary and only later in the day remember that his car was a mile away uphill where he had left it in the morning. He would teach with meticulous care on his student round, sometimes never getting beyond the first bed. His house physician would then have to rearrange the beds so that Yates did not teach again on the same patient on his next visit. He was an inventor, in the sense of taking up new techniques, and was the first in Sheffield to introduce bronchography and ventriculography.

One final, if intimate, story should be told. It must have been in the 1930s that he noticed a lump in his abdomen while he was having a bath. He consulted a colleague and they agreed that he had cancer of the pancreas. Time was to prove that they were wrong, but during the time of suspense there was no noticeable change in Yates's demeanour, or his attitude to life. His daily work continued exactly as before.

He reached high office in Freemasonry and was noted for his speeches. He made an excellent speech to friends who had gathered to celebrate his 90th birthday. His main hobbies during his long retirement were photography and cabinet-making.

He was married twice: first to Dorothy, daughter of Arthur Neal, solicitor; secondly to Doris Hope Duplock, daughter of a tea planter. By his first marriage he had two daughters. P

[*Brit. med. J.*, 1977, **1**, 654; Photo]

ZAIMIS, Eleanor *b.*16 June 1915 *d.*3 Oct 1982
MB Athens (1938) MD (1941) BSc (1947) MRCP (1968)
FRCP (1974)

Eleanor Christides – Nora to her many British friends – was educated at the Greek Gymnasium and graduated in medicine at the University of Athens. She then spent nine years as assistant to Professor Joachimoglu, professor of pharmacology at the University. During this time she gained an MD, pursued studies in chemistry leading to a BSc, was a member of the committee set up in Greece to evaluate the new antibiotics, penicillin and streptomycin, and gave valuable service to the youth centre run by the municipal department of health in Athens. She came to England in 1947 as a British Council scholar and, after working briefly as a research assistant in the department of pharmacology at Bristol University and later at the National Institute for Medical Research (then at Hampstead), she moved to the department of pharmacology at the school of pharmacy, London University, in 1948, being appointed lecturer in pharmacology in 1950. That same year she was elected associate to the Physiological Society, becoming a full member in 1951 and serving on the committee from 1967 to 1971. In 1954 she was appointed head of the department of pharmacology at the Royal Free Hospital Medical School, becoming professor in 1958. She shared the Cameron prize (1956) and the Gairdner Foundation international award (1958) with William (now Sir William) Paton, and in 1979 was made honorary FFA RCS. She was an honorary member of the Rome Academy of Medicine and a corresponding member of the Academy of Athens. She was awarded the Cross of Commander of the Greek Order of Benevolence in 1962, and in 1968 the NP Kravkov pharmacology medal of the USSR Academy of Medical Sciences.

Nora wrote many papers and her *Textbook on Hygiene* (1948) won the Greek Academy's prize. She also edited *Nerve Growth Factor and its Antiserum* (1972), and 'Neuromuscular Junction', volume 42 of *Heffter's Handbook of Experimental Pharmacology* (1976).

Throughout her career, Nora continued her experimental research, making substantial fundamental contributions in neuromuscular and cardiovascular pharmacology. Her experimental procedures were models of design and planning, and it was a joy to observe her full participation at the bench. Her work had a strong physiological flavour, always reaching out to vivid illustration (many will remember her striking demonstration with GAH Buttle of the spastic paralysis induced by decamethonium in the chick) and to broader implications. Her arrival at Hampstead coincided with the interest which had been aroused in two members of what is now called the methonium series, synthesized by Harold King. Her degree in chemistry equipped her to synthesize the remaining members, allowing us to identify peak activity in decamethonium and hexamethonium (originally coded Z4 and Z7). After working with William Paton on the methonium compounds, she continued to work on neuromuscular and ganglionic block, and explored many lines important for hypertension and migraine. This in turn led her to be one of the first to emphasize the importance of studying the chronic effects of low doses of drugs, as well as acute effects. Her interest in experimental work never weakened and her writing was cogent and distinguished. She was particularly influential in developing interest in the Levi-Montalcini nerve growth factor, in the face of considerable initial scepticism.

She was born in Galatz, Romania. Her father John Cristides was in shipping, and her mother Helen Hanoutsos was the daughter of a landowner. She adopted British nationality in 1954. She married twice; first in 1938, and again in 1943 to John Zaimis, a politician of note, but they separated some years later. She was a lively, lovely, generous, and fascinating person whose love for the country of her adoption and its people did not in any way detract from her essential 'Greekness'. She was shrewd, highly intelligent, tough, and a leader by nature. For some, perhaps, her finer qualities were occasionally obscured by the determination with which she practised the high standards she demanded of herself and others, in both academic and private concerns. She was always exciting and interesting, but her dominating personality sometimes caused problems, and her later years were clouded by ill health; but her work and that of her pupils (especially WC Bowman) carried forward the distinctive physiological influence which the Hampstead school exerted on British pharmacology.

Nora Zaimis contributed a great deal to the life and culture of this country and she will be remembered by her friends and colleagues for the warmth, energy, and scientific insight which characterized her in her prime. WP/GW/VL

[*Brit. med. J.,* 1982, **285**, 1280; *Lancet,* 1982, **2**, 1940; *Times,* 16 Oct 1982; *Notes and Records of Roy. Soc.,* **30**, pp.245-249 (HH Dale); Photo]

ZORAB, Phillip Arthur *b.*18 Dec 1915 *d.*8 Feb 1983
MRCS LRCP (1951) MB BS Lond (1952) MRCP (1956) MD (1960) FRCP (1972)

Phillip Zorab was born in Southampton, one of five brothers who, like their father, all qualified in medicine at Guy's.

After schooling at Cheltenham College, he went into the City until he joined the Royal Artillery at the outbreak of war. He had a distinguished war record, serving on several fronts in Europe and Greece and being mentioned in despatches. Like many of his generation he came late to medicine, qualifying at the age of thirty-seven in 1952. He took the MRCP in 1956 and was elected FRCP in 1972. After junior posts at Guy's and Brompton Hospitals, he was appointed consultant physician to St Charles's Hospital and the Paddington and Kensington Chest Clinic and subsequently to St Mary's Hospital, Paddington, and to the Brompton Hospital. He was part-time senior lecturer at the Institute for Diseases of the Chest (later the Cardiothoracic Institute) and was assistant director of the paediatric department there.

Zorab evinced an early interest in diseases of the spine when writing his MD thesis in 1960 on ankylosing spondylitis, and he devoted the rest of his life to the investigation and care of children and adults with various forms of scoliosis. With his colleagues at Brompton he led the field in the recognition and management of disorders of respiratory and cardiac function associated with spinal deformity.

His own research established normal growth data for various factors – hydroxyproline, creatinine, luteinising hormone, follicle stimulating hormone and testosterone – in a five year longitudinal study of adolescent boys and girls for comparison with scoliotic children. However, he will best be remembered for the breadth of vision which led him to organize a series of international, multi-disciplinary symposia held at the Cardiothoracic Institute to study every facet of causation and management of scoliosis and, not least, the emotional, social and economic consequences of the disease to the patients themselves. At an 8th symposium after his death, a Phillip

Zorab Scoliosis Trust was established to ensure the continuation of his work at Brompton and of these much valued meetings.

He had many other interests including a love of music, but all who knew him were impressed by his devotion to his family and his Christian faith which coloured much of his work. For many years he was church warden of Holy Trinity Church, Brompton. While at Guy's he met his wife Jane, who was a ward sister, and there can be few of his colleagues and friends who did not enjoy the hospitality of their home. He was survived by his wife and four children. EEFK

[*Brit. med. J.*, 1983, **286**, 655; *Lancet*, 1983, **1**, 603; *Times*, 12 Feb 1983; *Guy's Hosp. Gazette*, March 1983, **97**]

COLLEGE OFFICERS

The following lists are continued from Vol.VI, p.493.
* indicates that a life of the officer is included in this volume.
Civil honours, where indicated, are those to which the College officer was entitled at the time of holding the appointment. By tradition, only university degrees in medicine are included.

PRESIDENTS

91	1972	Sir Cyril Astley Clarke KBE MD Cantab
92	1977	Sir Douglas Andrew Kilgour Black MD St And
93	1983	Raymond Hoffenberg MD Cape Town

VICE-PRESIDENTS

35	1975	John Badenoch DM Oxon
36		Denis John Williams CBE MD Manch
37	1976	Sheila Patricia Violet Sherlock MD Edin
38		Sir Douglas Andrew Kilgour Black MD St And
39	1977	John David Nunes Nabarro MD Lond
40		John Peter Mills Tizard BM Oxon
41	1978	George Stephen Clive Sowry MD Lond
42		Sir Graham MacGregor Bull MD Cape Town
43	1979	Malcolm Davenport Milne MD Manch
44		John Forrest Goodwin MD Lond
45	1980	John Charles Batten MD Lond
46		Arnold Bloom MD Lond
47	1981	Raymond Hoffenberg MD Cape Town
48		John Bishop Harman MD Cantab
49	1982	Christopher John Dickinson DM Oxon
50		William Whittaker MD Leeds
51	1983	Thomas Ernest Oppé MB Lond
52		Sir Richard Ian Samuel Bayliss MD Cantab

TREASURER

57	1970	Nigel Dean Compston CBE MD Cantab

REGISTRARS

40	1975	David Alan Pyke MD Cantab

ASSISTANT REGISTRARS

15	1975	James Spencer Malpas MB Lond
16	1981	David Gwyn Williams MD Wales

HARVEIAN LIBRARIANS

11	1979	Sir Gordon Ethelbert Ward Wolstenholme OBE MB Cantab

LINACRE FELLOW

1	1965	Charles Edward Newman CBE MD Cantab
2	1967	Dame Albertine Louise Winner MD Lond
3	1978	John Melville Malins MD Birm

LECTURES AND LECTURERS

The following lists are continued from Vol.VI p.494ff.
*indicates that a life of the lecturer is included in this volume.
†indicates that the manuscript is in the College library.
**indicates that the lecture has not been published.

Complete information about the publication of lectures and their subjects is in the College library. Subjects are also given in the College list.

Civil honours, where indicated, are those to which the lecturer was entitled at the date of the lecture.

By tradition, only university degrees in medicine are included.

LUMLEIAN LECTURES

1976	Malcolm Davenport Milne MD
1977	John Badenoch DM
1978	Dame Sheila Patricia Violet Sherlock MD
† 1979	Sir John Walton MD
† 1980	John Forrest Goodwin MD
† 1981	Sidney William Stanbury MD
1982	Hugh Edward de Wardener MD
1983	David Nicol Sharp Kerr MB

GOULSTONIAN LECTURES

** 1976	David Keith Peters MB
† 1977	Simon Godfrey MD
† 1978	Anne Glen Ferguson MB
† 1979	Stephen Robert Bloom MB
† 1980	Lesley Howard Rees MD
† 1981	Richard Anthony Cranmer Hughes MD
1982	Mark Brian Pepys MD
1983	Paul Vincent Langham Curry MD

HARVEIAN ORATIONS

* 1976	Sir Ronald Bodley Scott DM
1977	Sir Douglas Andrew Kilgour Black MD
1978	Sir John Richardson Bt MD
1979	Sir Cyril Astley Clarke MD
1980	Sir Francis Avery Jones MD
1981	John Fisher Stokes MD
1982	Sir William Richard Shaboe Doll MD
1983	Sir Richard Ian Samuel Bayliss MD

CROONIAN LECTURES

† 1976	John David Nunes Nabarro MD
† 1977	Ivor Henry Mills MD
1978	John Peter Mills Tizard BM
1979	William Stanley Peart MD
1980	Anthony Fairclough Lever MB
† 1981	John Herbert Humphrey MD
1982	Leonard Birnie Strang MD
† 1983	John Charles Batten MD

BRADSHAW LECTURES

† 1976	William Walter Gooddy MD
1977	Robert Frederick Mahler MB
1978	Patrick Loudon Mollison MD
1979	Desmond Gareth Julian MD
† 1980	Kurt George Matthew Mayer Alberti DM
† 1981	Robert Donald Cohen MD
† 1982	Eric John Holborow MD
† 1983	Celia Mary Oakley MD

MILROY LECTURES

1976	John Pemberton MD
† 1977	John Peel Sparks MD
† 1978	Bertram Tullis Mann MD
† 1979	Frederic Stanley William Brimblecombe MD
† 1980	David Henry Morgan Woollam MD
† 1981	Robert Vernon Holmes Jones MB
1982	[No lecture]
† 1983	Arthur John Buller MB

FITZPATRICK LECTURES

† 1976	Gweneth Whitteridge
† 1977	Edwin Sisterton Clarke MD
1978	[No lecture]
† 1979	Christopher Charles Booth MD
† 1980	Alick John Robertson MD
† 1981	Peter Alec James Ball MD
† 1982	Arthur Hollman MD
1983	Robert Manoah Kark

OLIVER-SHARPEY LECTURE OR PRIZE

1976	John Vallance-Owen MD
1977	Abraham Guz MD
† 1978	Sylvia Dorothy Lawler MD
1979	Walter Fred Bodmer
1980	John Hughes
1981	[No lecture or prize]
† 1982	Richard Darwin Keynes
† 1983	Timothy John Biscoe MB

MITCHELL LECTURES

1979	Denis Anthony Mitchison MD
1982	Wallace Fox MD

LLOYD-ROBERTS LECTURES

Lectures given at the College

† 1977	Rt Hon Jo Grimond
1980	David Frederick Attenborough
† 1983	Rt Hon Edward Heath

BERTRAM LOUIS ABRAHAMS LECTURE IN PHYSIOLOGY

1976 John Guy Widdicombe DM
1978 James Whyte Black MB
1980 Roger Valentine Short
1982 Sidney Brenner MB

CHARLES WEST LECTURES

1976 Leonard Birnie Strang MD
1979 Charles Eric Stroud MB
1982 Alexander Parker Mowat MB

HUMPHRY DAVY ROLLESTON LECTURES

† 1977 John Edward Lennard-Jones MD
† 1980 Barbara Billing
1983 Philip John Randle MD

FE WILLIAMS LECTURES

† 1978 John Grimley Evans MB

ERNESTINE HENRY LECTURES

1976 Edward Philip George Houssemayne Du Boulay MB
1979 Peter Cardwell Elmes BM
1983 Kenneth William Donald MD

LANGDON-BROWN LECTURES

† 1977 Ronald Alfred Henson MD
1980 James Learmonth Gowans MD

TUDOR EDWARDS LECTURES

Lectures given at the College

† 1977 David Caton Flenley MB
† 1979 Stephen John Greenhill Semple MD
1981 Lynne McArthur Reid MD
† 1983 David Geraint James MD

WATSON SMITH LECTURES

1976	David Alan Price MD
1977	Samuel Shuster MB
** 1978	Reginald Hall MD
1979	Richard Humphrey Tudor Edwards MB
†* 1980	Patrick James Hare MD
1981	Charles David Marsden MB
† 1982	Attilio Maseri MD
1983	Donald Sinclair Munro MD

MARC DANIELS LECTURES

1976	Donald Darnley Reid MD
† 1977	David Alan Warrell DM
1980	Ian Sutherland

PARKES WEBER TRUST

1976	Peter Derrick Samman MD
† 1979	Robert Harold Meara MB
1982	Ian Bruce Sneddon MD

PHILIP ELLMAN LECTURES

† 1977	Harry Lloyd Fairbridge Currey MB
1980	Margaret Elizabeth Harvey Turner-Warwick DM

TEALE LECTURES

1977	Harold Philip Lambert MD
1979	John Allen Davis MB
† 1981	Charlotte Morrison Anderson MD
† 1983	Robert David George Milner MD

SAMUEL GEE LECTURES

1977	John Frederick Wilkinson MD
† 1981	Cecil Symons MD
1982	Edward Sydney Williams MD
	Jonathan Wolfe Miller MB
† 1983	Sir Charles Cyril Astley Clarke MB

LILLY LECTURES

1976	Victor Almon McKusick MD
1977	Edward Donnall Thomas MD
† 1978	Robert George Petersdorf MD
1979	Eugene Braunwald MD
1980	Sir Gustav Joseph Victor Nossal MB
† 1981	Julien Ivor Ellis Hoffman MD
1982	Donald Sharp Frederickson MD
1983	Daniel Carleton Gajdusek MD

OSLER ORATIONS

† 1978	William Drummond Macdonald Paton DM
† 1981	Walter Bryan Matthews DM

JOHN THORNTON INGRAM LECTURE

1977	Robert Stuart Wells MD
† 1979	William James Cunliffe MD
1982	Malcolm Watson Greaves MD

LOCKYER SCHOLARSHIP AND LECTURE

† 1978	James Spencer Malpas MB
1979	[No lecture]
† 1980	John Tomlinson

WILLIAM WITHERING PRIZE

In 1981 the College received the sum of £20,000 from the World Conference on Clinical Pharmacology and Therapeutics to endow a prize to be called the William Withering Prize of the Royal College of Physicians.

The prize shall be awarded triennially, or at such times as the Royal College of Physicians shall decide, to recognize distinguished contributions to the science and practice of clinical pharmacology and therapeutics.

The prizewinner shall be selected by the Council of the College on the advice of a committee to be appointed for the purpose by the President. The committee may make their recommendation after meeting or by correspondence. The President may invite any body or bodies of British clinical pharmacologists to nominate a representative or representatives on the selection committee.

The prizewinner shall be invited to deliver a lecture but the delivery of a lecture is not a condition of receiving the prize. The prizewinner shall receive a medal to commemorate the prize.

The value of the prize and other financial matters related to it shall be decided by the Council of the College on the advice of the Treasurer.

Prizeman

1983 Sir James Whyte Black MB

KEY TO CONTRIBUTORS' INITIALS

A	Lord Amulree
AB	A Bloom
ABD	Aileen B Donnison
ABH	Sir Austin Bradford Hill
ABS	A Batty Shaw
ACCH	ACC Hughes
ACK	AC Kendall
ACL	AC Lendrum
ACT	AC Tait
ADMJ	ADM Jackson
AFL	AF Lever
AG(1)	Sir Abraham Goldberg
AG(2)	A Guz
AGWW	AGW Whitfield
AH	A Hollman
AHC	AH Crisp
AHTR-S	AHT Robb-Smith
AHW	Agnes H Wilkinson
AJT	AJ Thomas
ALW	Dame Albertine Winner
AMC	AM Cooke
AMcQ	A McQueen
AMCM	A Margaret C Macpherson
AMN	AM Nussey
AN	A Neuberger
APD	AP Dick
ARC	Sir Alastair Currie
AS	A Sakula
ASM	A Stuart Mason
ATC	Maj.Gen.AT Cook
ATH	AT Howarth
AW	A Walk
AWB	AW Beard
AWW	AW Woodruff
BA	B Ashworth
BH	B Hudson
BMcC	B McConkey
BWL	BW Lewis
CAC	Sir Cyril Clarke
CBP	CB Prowse
CD	C Davidson
CES	CE Stroud
CFR	CF Rolland
CGP	CG Parsons
CGR	CG Riley
CHG	CH Gray
CJD	CJ Dickinson

CJH	CJ Hackett
CKS	CK Simpson
CKW	CK Warwick
CLB	CL Bray
CMD	Constance M Duddle
CP	C Pallis
CS-H	Sir Charles Stuart-Harris
CT	C Tetlow
CW	C Wilson
CWLJ	CWL Jeanes
DAKB	Sir Douglas Black
DAPE	DA Price Evans
DASB	DAS Blair
DAW	DA Williams
DBC	DB Carron
DCB	DC Bowie
DCFM	DCF Muir
DD	Dewi Davies
DDG	DD Gibbs
DEM	DE Meredith
DE-S	D Emslie-Smith
DGJ	D Geraint James
DHC	DH Croft
DHT	DH Teasdale
DJW	DJ Williams
DMM	DM Mitchell
DMTG	DMT Gairdner
DNC	DN Croft
DRH	DR Hay
DT	D Taverner
DTDH	DTD Hughes
DW	D Whitteridge
DWP	DW Pugh
EAD	EA Danino
EBR	Elizabeth B Robson
ECH	EC Hutchinson
EDRC	EDR Campbell
EEFK	EEF Keal
EEJ	EE Jones
EEP	Sir Edward Pochin
EFMcK	E Florence McKeown
EGW	EG Wade
EKC	EK Cruickshank
EMD	EM Darmady
EMMcG	EM McGirr
ERD	ER Davies
ERR	ER Rue
EJMC	EJM Campbell
FAJ	Sir Francis Avery Jones
FFH	FF Hellier

FHL	FH Lowy
FN	Sir Fraser Noble
FRB	FR Bettley
FS	F Stratton
FVF	FV Flynn
GAH	GA Harrison
GB	Sir Graham Bull
GBS	GB Shaw
GEB	GE Baur
GEG	Sir George Godber
GHF	GH Findlay
GIMS	GIM Swyer
GJ	G Jarratt
GJG	GJ Goldberg
GMC	GM Cochrane
GMD	GM Davies
GPB	GP Baker
GRS	GR Steed
GS	Sir George Smart
GSCS	GSC Sowry
GT	G Thomas
GW	Sir Gordon Wolstenholme
HA	Sir Hedley Atkins
HH	Sir Harold Himsworth
HJW(1)	HJ Wallace
HJW(2)	HJ Walton
HMR	HM Rennie
HPL	HP Lambert
HRR	HR Rollin
HTH	HT Howat
HWB	HW Balme
IAP	IA Porter
IABC	IAB Cathie
IBS	IB Sneddon
IHK	IH Kerr
IMH	IM Hilliard
IW	Sir Ian Wood
IWD	IW Delamore
JAD	JA Davis
JAAH	JAA Hunter
JB	J Bamforth
JBH	J Bishop Harman
JBR	JB Rennie
JC	J Carson
JCB	JC Batten
JCL	JC Laidlaw
JCR	JC Richardson
JDH	JD Hay
JDJ	JD Judah
JDHS	JDH Slater

JDS	JD Sutherland
JEC	JE Cotes
JEL-J	JE Lennard-Jones
JET	JE Talbot
JFB	JF Brock
JFG	JF Goodwin
JFS	JF Stokes
JGB	JG Bonnin
JGE	J Griffith Edwards
JGS	JG Scadding
JH	J Hampson
JHDM	JHD Millar
JJB	JJ Billings
JKGW	JKG Webb
JL	Jean Lawrie
JLN	JL Newman
JMJ	JM Jefferson
JMKS	JMK Spalding
JML	JM Lipscomb
JMM	JM Macfie
JMS	JM Swithinbank
JMT	JM Tweed
JNW	Sir John Walton
JPB	Sir James Baird
JPDM	JPD Mounsey
JPM	JP Martin
JRA	JR Anderson
JRBT	JRB Turner
JRE	Sir John Ellis
JRHT	JRH Towers
JSL	JS Lyon
JSM(1)	JS Malpas
JSM(2)	JS Mitchell
JSM(3)	JS Moos
JSR	JS Robertson
JW	J Wedgwood
JWLD	JW Lovett Doust
KCS	KC Simpkins
KDK	KD Keele
KEH	KE Heaton
KGL	KG Lowe
KLD	KL Dodd
KPB	KP Ball
KR	Sir Kenneth Robson
KWGGH	KWGG Heathfield
LGG	LG Goodwin
LJB-C	LJ Bruce-Chwatt
LJR	LJ Rubenstein
LJW	LJ Witts
LMP	LM Payne

LPEL	LPE Laurent
LPLeQ	LP Le Quesne
LW	Lyal Watson
MDM	MD Milne
MER	Margaret E Rowbottom
MFO	MF Oliver
MG	M Gelfand
MHL	MH Lessof
MHPS	Maj.Gen.MHP Sayers
MIAH	MIA Hunter
MIPW	MIP Wilkinson
MJ	M Johnstone
MK	M Kremer
MMacG	M MacGregor
MR	Sir Martin Roth
MRJ	MR Joseph
MWWW	MWW Wood
NB-J	N Bennett-Jones
NDC	ND Compston
NFM	NF Maclagan
NLR	NL Rusby
NSS	NS Scrimshaw
OHW	OH Wolff
OPG	OP Gray
P	Lord Platt
PB	P Beeson
PBSF	PBS Fowler
PC	P Cochrane
PCR	PC Reynell
PDS	PD Samman
PEM	Patricia E Mortimer
PJDS	PJD Snow
PJWM	PJW Mills
PKR	PK Robinson
PLM	PL Mollison
PLeQ	Pamela Le Quesne
PMSG	PMS Gillam
PRE	PR Evans
PRF	PR Fleming
PT	Sir Peter Tizard
PW	P Wildy
RAG	RA Gregory
RAH(1)	RA Henson
RAH(2)	RA Hickling
RAP	RA Parkins
RAS	RA Shooter
RAW	RA Womersley
RB	Rosemary Biggs
RBK	RB Khambatta
RBS	Sir Ronald Bodley Scott

RCC	RC Curran
RCK	RC King
RDC	RD Currie
RdeM	R de Mowbray
REH	RE Haist
REL	RE Lane
RES	RE Steiner
RET	Sir Ronald Tunbridge
REW-StC	RE Wright-St Clair
RFJ	RF Jarrett
RH(1)	RH Harris
RH(2)	R Hecker
RH(3)	R Hinchcliffe
RH(4)	R Hoffenberg
RHA	RH Andrews
RHE	RH Ellis
RHG	RH Girdwood
RHV	RH Vasey
RHST	RHS Thompson
RIMcC	RI McCallum
RING	RIN Greaves
RJP	RJ Pugh
RM(1)	R Mahler
RM(2)	R Murrey
RRB	RR Bomford
RSM	RS Mibashan
RVS	RV Sathe
SB	S Banerjea
SC	Sir Stanley Clayton
SCS	SC Shanks
SDMC	SDM Court
SDVW	SDV Weller
SFT	SF Taylor
SGB	SG Browne
SJDO'K	SJD O'Keefe
SJMG	SJM Goulston
SMT	SM Tucker
SO	S Oram
SP	S Padmavati
SPL	SP Lock
TC	Sir Theodore Crawford
TCH	TC Hunt
TCNG	TCN Gibbens
TFF	Sir Theodore Fox
TGF	TG Fox
TJBG	TJB Geffen
TJW	TJ Wilmot
TKL	TK Lyle
TL	Sir Thomas Lodge
TP	T Pilkington

VHS	VH Springett
VL	Valérie Luniewska
VW	V Wynn
WCG	WC Gibson
Wd'AM	Sir William Maycock
WE	W Evans
WGH	WG Harding
WHRC	WHR Cook
WHT	Sir William Trethowen
WIMacD	WI MacDonald
WMcIR	WMcI Rose
WO'B	W O'Brien
WP	Sir William Paton
WPUJ	WPU Jackson
WS	W Somerville
WSP	WS Peart
WSS	WS Suffern
WT	W Turner
Z	Lord Zuckerman